Ray Riley

AF711320

General Accident Group
1835 N Meridian St
Indianapolis, Ind

Bus Phone 317-923-5411
Home Phone 317-293-1951

MARINE INSURANCE:
Ocean and Inland

WILLIAM H. RODDA, C.P.C.U.
President, Marine Insurance Handbook, Inc.

MARINE INSURANCE:
Ocean and Inland

Third Edition

PRENTICE-HALL, INC.
Englewood Cliffs, New Jersey

MARINE INSURANCE: Ocean and Inland
Third Edition

(Formerly *Inland Marine and Transportation Insurance*)

13–557017–4

Library of Congress Catalog Card No. 73–102100

Current Printing (last digit):
10 9 8

PRENTICE-HALL INTERNATIONAL, INC., *London*
PRENTICE-HALL OF AUSTRALIA, PTY., LTD., *Sydney*
PRENTICE-HALL OF CANADA, LTD., *Toronto*
PRENTICE-HALL OF INDIA PRIVATE LTD., *New Delhi*
PRENTICE-HALL OF JAPAN, INC., *Tokyo*

Printed in United States of America

Preface

Insurance on property in transit has been the primary purpose of marine insurance since its beginning centuries ago. Most transportation was over water until the development of the railroads. Thus marine insurance became almost synonymous with transportation insurance. Property in transit always has been and continues to be threatened by many hazards. It was natural that marine insurance should provide coverage against a wide range of perils. A large proportion of marine insurance protects against loss from "all risks of physical loss and damage," or "perils of the seas," or "the perils of transportation." It was also a natural development that marine insurance underwriters should expand their operations to cover property at fixed locations where the hazards were such that underwriters in other fields of insurance were reluctant to provide the protection. Marine insurance has become a conglomerate of broad coverages for many kinds of property under a variety of circumstances. It is primarily a coverage for property in transit but the relation to transportation becomes strained in some respects.

Marine underwriters continue to operate with less restraint than other insurance underwriters. Commerce today requires a freedom from the time-consuming procedures of rate filing and official approval of forms. Any restriction of marine insurance into the patterns that bridle fire insurance, automobile insurance, and other lines of coverage would inevitably force marine insurance into the freedom of the international market.

The emergence of inland marine as a division of marine insurance is unique to the United States. This separation resulted from the desire of American insurance companies to participate in coverage of property on land as contrasted to insurance of oceangoing vessels and cargoes. It was characteristic of American insurance companies that they set apart this division of insurance as another "line," as such separations were called. There never has been a clear-cut separation of ocean marine from inland marine. Even the definitions of marine insurance which were established by the National Association of Insurance Commissioners in 1933 and 1953 made no distinction between the two. Some states did apply some rate filing requirements to the inland marine portion of the marine business. A few states set up statutory definitions of inland marine insurance, but all of these attempts were in general terms.

The growth of transportation by airplane is tending to dissolve the nebulous separation that has existed between ocean and inland marine insurance. The airplane travels over land and water with equal ease. It is no longer possible to divide the land portion of transit from the sea portion as it is separated at the port of shipment with ocean cargo. The airplane is not limited to operation over the seas as are oceangoing vessels. It is logical and convenient, therefore, to consider all marine insurance in this single text. The inter-relationships of all marine insurance are tending to merge rather than to separate.

This book is intended for use by those who have a basic knowledge of insurance. It is not a primer. The discussions of ocean marine insurance practices cover the principles. No attempt is made to describe all of the many ramifications of international trade or the marine practices that differ from country to country. The reader who has occasion to delve further into world trade and the application of ocean marine insurance to cargoes and vessels on the high seas will find many books on these subjects. The English textbooks must not be overlooked. They are written primarily with attention to the English marine practices, but these practices are dominant in many parts of the world.

The discussions of inland marine insurance are presented in more detail because there is no other full presentation of this topic. The unique position of inland marine insurance in the United States apparently has made the writers from other nations reluctant to devote time to this peculiarly American phenomenon. Throughout this book there are frequent comparisons of marine practices with those of other insurance fields. The author feels that the best understanding of marine insurance can be had by an understanding of the similarities and differences between this field and other insurance.

The reader will need collateral material in order to meet his business or academic requirements. As much collateral material is easily available, appendices of explanatory material were omitted from this book. The student should acquire a kit of insurance policies such as those published by the Insurance Information Institute or the American Mutual Insurance Alliance. These kits contain sample policies in the marine field. A copy of the Nation-wide Marine Definition is a necessity and it would be helpful also to secure copies of bills of ladings from railroad and other transportation companies. The serious student of ocean marine insurance also needs copies of the English Marine Insurance Act, 1906, the Lloyd's insurance policy of 1779, the United States Carriage of Goods by Sea Act, the Harter Act, the York-Antwerp Rules, and the Warsaw Pact, all available at most public libraries, and of current American ocean marine insurance policies and forms, available from any of the American insurance companies that do an ocean marine insurance business.

The material for this book has been accumulated from many sources and with the assistance of many people. The staff members of the rating bureaus, such as the Inland Marine Insurance Bureau and the Transportation Insurance Rating Bureau, were particularly helpful. Much information was secured from underwriters and other officials in the companies that do a large amount of marine insurance business. So many people were helpful that it would be impractical to list them all, and it would be unfair to list only a few. The author gratefully acknowledges the assistance of all of his friends in supplying information and comment.

W. H. RODDA

Contents

MARINE INSURANCE:
Ocean and Inland

1

Marine Risks and Insurance

Marine insurance differs in many respects from other kinds of insurance. There continues to be a need for the marine insurance contract because it is peculiarly fitted to the risks of transportation. The need exists in spite of the trend toward the packaging of insurance into all-inclusive multiple line policies.

Insurance of all kinds has the same basic purpose. The function of insurance is to transfer a risk of financial loss from the individual to an insurer that assumes risks in return for a consideration. The intent is to indemnify the insured for any loss which is covered by the insurance contract.

Marine insurance, as defined in the English Marine Insurance Act of 1906, is "A contract whereby the insurer undertakes to indemnify the assured, in manner and to the extent thereby agreed, against marine losses, that is to say, the losses incident to marine adventure." It is recognized that a marine adventure may involve a mixture of sea and land perils. The English Marine Insurance Act of 1906 further provides: "A contract of marine insurance may, by its express terms, or by usage of trade, be extended so as to protect the assured against losses on inland waters or on any land risk which may be incidental to any sea voyage."

INLAND MARINE INSURANCE PECULIAR TO THE UNITED STATES

In England, and in fact generally throughout the world outside the United States, marine insurance tends to be the coverage of marine adventures and losses incidental to sea voyages. In the United States there was a development of "inland marine" insurance. This was to a large extent the result of the division of insurance into "lines," which was characteristic of American insurance until the multiple line era starting in the 1950s. Inland marine insurance in the United States became principally the insurance of risks of land transportation. There were many variations and extensions of this basic idea, as will be explained later, but this was the principal distinction between ocean marine insurance and inland marine insurance. The distinction is colloquially described as "wet" marine and "dry" marine. Authority of insurance companies to write marine insurance, both ocean and inland, under most state insurance laws coincides with authority to write fire insurance as distinct from casualty insurance. This division of marine insurance is not needed in England or other parts of the world. Marine insurance is written in connection with marine adventures. If a purely land risk is to be covered, there is freedom to write whatever policy is needed. There have never been restrictions by line of coverage such as existed in the United States. For example, the only way to write insurance against loss of property by theft in the United States was under a casualty policy, unless the coverage were included as part of a marine policy. Theft coverage could not be added to a fire policy. Thus the development of inland marine insurance as a broad form of insurance against loss of property in the United States was a peculiarity that resulted from the mono-line system of insurance.

In the insurance parlance of the United States the words "marine" and "transportation" have become almost synonymous. The protection of goods in transit has become "marine" insurance. It is interesting to note that while the word "marine" has acquired a broad meaning relating to many forms of transportation in relation to insurance, the term "maritime" still retains a more limited meaning. Perhaps this results partly from the stabilizing effect of the English Marine Insurance Act. It defines maritime perils as "the perils consequent on, or incidental to, the navigation of the sea, that is to say, perils of the seas, fire, war perils, pirates, rovers, thieves, captures, seizures, restraints and detainment of princes, and peoples, jettisons, barratry, and any other perils, either of like kind or which may be designated by the policy."

MARINE RISKS RELATED TO COMMERCE

Marine risks are principally the risks of commerce or trade. Oceans and waterways were the avenues of commerce for centuries when land transportation was slow and costly. Dependence upon water transportation was so great in the early days of the United States that numerous canals were built to provide waterways where nature had neglected to supply a sea or river. Cities were dependent upon commerce for their growth, and there were few cities of any consequence that were not located on waterways or harbor sites. Transportation by water still is the cheapest form for bulk commodities when speed of delivery is not vital to the value of the goods.

The marine or transit risk to property differs in many respects from risks to property at fixed locations. A "peril," as used in insurance terminology, generally is the cause of a loss. Fire is a peril. A "hazard" is something that exposes the property to a possibility of loss. A ship is exposed to the hazard of fire, and if a fire occurs, that is the peril which causes the loss. The words "risk," "peril," and "hazard" have a similar meaning in general usage, but they tend to have these specialized meanings in the insurance business.

The word "risk" has a somewhat more specialized meaning as used in ocean marine insurance. It refers to the obligation assumed by the insurer, but it may also include the duration of the obligation, the object which is the subject of the risk, and the nature of the exposure to loss. The basic idea back of all these uses of the word "risk" is that there is a chance of loss or damage. This chance of loss is the risk which is assumed by the insurer in return for the premium which is paid by the insured.

EARLY ORIGINS OF MARINE INSURANCE

Protection of ocean commerce from financial loss resulting from perils of the seas goes back many hundreds of years. Forerunners of insurance as we know it were the bottomry bond and the respondentia bond. The bottomry bond was a form of note given by the owner of a vessel to a moneylender who financed the voyage, using the ship as collateral. If the vessel completed the voyage safely, the owner paid back the loan, plus an interest charge. If the vessel was lost, the owner was discharged from his debt and he paid nothing. The interest charge, to the extent that it exceeded the amount which would be charged on an ordinary loan requiring repayment without qualification, constituted a form of insurance premium for possible loss of the ship. A respondentia bond was a similar arrangement whereby the money was lent on a cargo of merchandise.

Bottomry and respondentia bonds have survived to this day but not as insurance equivalents. Such an arrangement is used rarely but may be used by the master of a vessel in distress to raise funds when all other means of securing funds have failed. The vessel may be in a port of refuge and the master may have exhausted all other means of securing funds to make the repairs necessary to complete the venture. An interesting variation from ancient practices of bottomry and respondentia is the fact that today the lender acquires an insurable interest in the ship or cargo that is pledged as security under the bond, and he may buy insurance to protect this interest. Except under the emergency conditions just described, the pledging of a ship as security for a loan is usually arranged under a bond which is secured by a mortgage on the ship.

Insurance as we know it today is relatively modern. Some forerunners of insurance were practiced two or three thousand years ago, but only since the late 1600s has insurance in the modern sense been in use. During the thousand years of intellectual stagnation in Europe, known as the Dark Ages, many ruling church dignitaries frowned upon any arrangement in the nature of insurance. Interest charged upon a loan was considered usury and thought to be contrary to divine law. Bottomry and respondentia bonds were discouraged. Any disaster which happened to a person was supposed to be a visitation decreed by the Almighty. An arrangement to alleviate distress or misfortune was a violation of the ordinances of God and as such was considered sacrilegious.

Expanding commerce and a broadened viewpoint in the era following the discovery of America led to a changed attitude toward interest charges as well as toward actions which might prevent or alleviate disaster. The term "usury" came to mean an unreasonable rate of interest. It became accepted practice for businessmen to charge interest for the use of capital. During this same period the idea of transferring a risk to an insurer in exchange for a premium also became increasingly common.

SEPARATION OF INLAND FROM OCEAN MARINE INSURANCE

There are many similarities and also many differences between ocean marine insurance and inland marine insurance. Ocean marine insurance is the insuring of goods in transit by water, that is, on the oceans and also on rivers, lakes, and other inland waterways. Inland marine insurance is essentially the coverage of property which is shipped over land, that is, by rail and motor truck. Shipment by air is increasingly important. Insurance of air shipments tends to follow ocean or inland marine practices, depending upon whether shipment is domestic or overseas.

Prior to 1921 all insurance on property in transit was called marine insurance in the United States. There was no segregation of ocean marine as distinct from inland marine. When they were first separated in the reports for 1921, ocean marine premiums written in the United States amounted to slightly more than $48 million whereas inland marine premiums were about $16 million. By 1970 these were $400 million for ocean marine insurance and $700 million for inland marine insurance. This growth of inland marine insurance in relation to ocean marine is not quite a true picture. A large portion of the premium increase for inland marine business comes from coverage on dealers' property and other property for which a broad form of insurance is classified as inland marine as a matter of convenience.

Marine insurance in the United States is subject to a document known as the Nation-wide Marine Definition. It was recommended to the states by the National Association of Insurance Commissioners and was adopted by most of the states as a regulation of the insurance commissioner. It makes no distinction between ocean marine and inland marine insurance, but its principal effect is upon inland marine insurance. It will be considered fully in a later section of this text relating to inland marine insurance. Its effect as far as ocean marine insurance is concerned is limited to the length of time that coverage may be effective under an ocean marine policy both before and after shipment by water. In general, imports may continue to be covered by a marine insurance policy as long as they maintain their identity as imports and are not mixed with the general body of property in the United States. Exports may be covered by a marine policy as soon as they are set aside and are designated as property for export. This follows the ocean marine insurance practices that developed in the use of the warehouse to warehouse clause. The use and effect of this clause will be considered later in this text.

Ocean marine insurance is international in character. There are some differences between practices in the United States and those in England. American practices are described in this text. Ocean marine insurance is the most flexible of all kinds of insurance in America as well as in England and the rest of the world. A person with an insurable interest in a marine adventure can secure insurance under almost any condition that prevails. The forms, coverages, and conditions that are described here are those which prevail for average or usual situations. The student who delves further into the intricacies of ocean marine insurance will find an endless variety of endorsements and clauses to meet virtually any situation that can arise in shipping via the high seas.

QUESTIONS

1. Explain the function of marine insurance in relation to marine losses.
2. Why is inland marine insurance peculiar to the United States?
3. Discuss the usage of the words "marine" and "transportation" in their relation to insurance in the United States.
4. What is a bottomry bond and what is its relation to marine insurance? Distinguish between its original use and its use today.
5. In what way did religious beliefs retard the development of insurance during the period known as the Dark Ages in Europe?
6. Differentiate between the applications of the words "marine" and "maritime" as they affect insurance practices.
7. Discuss the relative size and importance of ocean marine insurance and inland marine insurance in today's commerce. Do you consider the relative premium volumes a valid indication of importance?
8. Why is ocean marine insurance dominated by international practices?

2

Ocean Marine Insurance Principles

The necessities and conveniences enjoyed by most people today probably would not be available to them without ocean commerce. Exports and imports between countries help to raise the standard of living for all people, and this kind of international trade is largely dependent upon water transportation.

THE RELATION OF INSURANCE TO OCEAN COMMERCE

Importance of Ocean Commerce. The principal reason for the importance of water transport is its convenience and low cost. It is an economic fact that the cost of transportation goes up as its speed increases. This means that water transportation, though slower than air or rail, is commonly used for the movement of staple goods that do not justify high shipping costs.

Hazards to Ocean Shipping. Accidents occur with loss or damage to ships and cargo in spite of modern safety devices. The fury of ocean storms is a threat even to the largest and most modern ocean liners. Waves the height of a four- or five-story building may engulf a ship and drop tons of water onto the decks with crushing force. Portions of the ship may be carried away by the onrushing water, or the decks may be smashed open, letting water into the interior of the ship. The pressure of the wind against the surface of the ship which rides above the water line is tremendous. An error in navigation or lack of sufficient power from the engines may cause the ship to run aground. Fogs and poor visibility result in collisions. Fires occur with surprising frequency. People have sought means of protecting themselves against the loss of a venture at sea because losses occur in spite of all precautions. Other people have been willing to risk a portion of their fortunes to insure the ship owner and the shipper of cargo against loss in return for fees collected from all those who wish indemnification for loss. Ocean marine insurance is of ancient origin, and more than any other type of insurance has been a matter of individual venture.

Insurance As a Guarantee for Loans or Credit. Most of today's ocean commerce, like commerce on land, depends upon borrowed money or credit. Ships may be mortgaged; corporations operate on money advanced by their stockholders; money is advanced to merchants on cargoes being shipped from one country to another. Ocean cargoes may be at sea for weeks or even months at a time. The merchant who has sold goods to a foreign purchaser does not want to wait for delivery of the goods to receive his money. The documents that represent the shipment may be sold to a bill broker in return for immediate payment. The bill broker receives payment through commercial banking channels upon delivery of the goods. All of these mortgages, loans, and commercial transactions are guaranteed financially by the insurance that is written to protect the interested persons against financial loss from perils that threaten the goods or ships.

The need for banking credit in connection with overseas commerce is greater than it is with domestic commerce. Lenders of money usually require that their loans be protected by insurance on the property as a guarantee for the loans. The result is that goods shipped in ocean commerce are almost always insured.

Commercial transactions are a simple matter of buying and selling at an agreed price if delivery is immediate and payment is by cash or on direct credit between the buyer and seller. There are many situations in both domestic and foreign commerce in which cash sales or direct credit between buyer and seller are impossible. The seller may wish cash on delivery, or perhaps the buyer does not have the money to pay for the goods until he receives delivery and can secure a loan on the goods in his own name. (The "order bill of lading" used to handle such situations in domestic commerce is discussed in connection with inland marine insurance later in this text.) The time that goods may be in transit, plus the remote location of the purchaser, makes it even more important for the foreign trader to receive payment when the goods are shipped. A system of bills of lading and commercial drafts has been developed under which the seller receives cash or credit through his bank or other commercial channels. Upon receipt of the goods, the buyer makes payment through a banking house in his own country. There is no exchange of currency directly between the buyer and seller.

Commercial Transactions in Overseas Trade. An understanding of the methods used in overseas commerce is necessary to appreciate the role that insurance plays in protecting businessmen against loss. There are three principal types of transactions in overseas commerce. They are (1) sales on a cost basis, (2) sales on a cost plus freight basis, and (3) sales on a cost plus insurance and freight basis. There are many variations of these basic types of sales.

A cost sale is one in which the seller's obligation ends with shipment of the goods from his place of business, or with delivery of the goods to a specified point in his country. The seller takes no part in the overseas transportation. The cost sale agreement may specify F.O.B. the seller's city, which means "free on board" freight cars or some other suitable transportation. The responsibility for the goods is that of the purchaser from the time the goods are loaded on the freight cars or trucks at the named point. The seller might agree in connection with a cost sale to put the goods "free alongside" (abbreviated as F.A.S.) the ship at the port from which the goods are to be shipped overseas. The seller may insure the goods during transportation on land, which is at his risk, if he desires. Such insurance probably would be under an inland transit form, which probably would be written as an inland marine coverage. The overseas freight charges may be shown on the invoice for a cost sale, but this is for information only and is not a part of the contract of sale. Payment of the overseas freight charges is the responsibility of the buyer.

Under a cost and freight sale (abbreviated as C.& F.) the seller agrees to deliver the goods onto the ship and to see that space is available for the shipment. The cost of the freight is included in the invoice of the seller to the buyer. However, the seller is not responsible for the safe delivery of the goods overseas. His responsibility for safe delivery may end at his own loading dock, on board freight cars in his own city, or on shipboard, depending upon the sales agreement. Arrangements may be made under which the seller agrees to put the goods on shipboard. Under a C.& F. sale, the goods are at the risk of the buyer during the overseas trip, and it is his responsibility to insure them. The important difference between a cost sale and a C.& F. sale is that under a C.& F. sale the seller agrees to see that space is available on shipboard. The seller also takes the responsibility for paying or guaranteeing payment of the freight charges. He then adds the amount of the freight charges to his invoice as part of the charges to be collected from the buyer.

Shipping companies do not like to accept shipments for which they must collect the freight charges at the destination. A shipment under a cost sale arrangement ordinarily will be accepted only if the shipping company has some guarantee of payment or is doing business regularly with the consignee. The C.& F. arrangement is preferable for the shipping company because it guarantees payment of shipping charges.

Under a cost, insurance, and freight sale (abbreviated C.I.F.) the seller is obligated to deliver the goods on shipboard, see that shipping space is available, and provide insurance to the destination in the foreign country. The contract of sale may provide for delivery to an interior city in the country of destination. The insurance may cover continuously from the location of the seller to the destination of the buyer, including land transportation at both ends of the journey and while on shipboard.

Contracts of sale vary greatly according to conditions and customs. The buyer may agree to pay the freight charges, duties or customs charges, and insurance, or these may be included in the selling price, depending upon the contract of sale. When freight, duties, or insurance charges are apt to fluctuate, the sales contract often specifies a sales price to which the actual charges will be added on the invoice.

The obligation of the seller to obtain shipping space under C.& F. and C.I.F. sales may be an important obligation. At times overseas shipping space is limited. The seller of goods to foreign buyers must be certain that he can obtain shipping space before obligating himself to sell under a C.& F. or C.I.F. arrangement.

With many overseas shipments, it is necessary for the shipper to arrange for clearance of the shipment at the destination. Most countries have regulations governing imports. The consul of the foreign country in the United States gives a certification that the shipment and the documents in connection with it are in proper form and that the regulations have been complied with. Export and import licenses may have to be secured for some kinds of shipments or to certain countries.

The operator of a ship that carries goods is known as a carrier. The carrier (operator of the ship) may or may not be the owner of the ship. There are many ship lines operating regularly between certain points that do own the vessels they operate. There are other carriers that operate ships to any port in the world to which they can get cargoes. They may own some vessels, and they may charter others. The word "charter" used in reference to ships means "to hire." A charter is in the nature of a lease. Carriers that have an unusually heavy load for a period may charter additional ships just as a motor truck line leases additional trucks to handle peak loads. A ship may be chartered fully equipped and with a crew paid by the owner, or it may be chartered with the agreement that the operator will provide crew and provisions. Many different arrangements between ship owners and operators are used. From the shipper's standpoint, the carrier is the one who issues the bill of lading, or contract to carry the goods. It does not matter to the shipper whether the carrier operates his own ships or whether he charters them from others. The shipper is interested only in the competency of the carrier as an operator to make sure that the shipment will be transported with due care.

Much of the world's ocean commerce is carried in tramp ships. A tramp ship is one that does not travel regularly between the same ports, but is available to carry cargo to any port. Exporters and importers are constantly making sales and purchases all over the world. Many of the world's important ports have no regular shipping service. Ships call whenever they have a cargo to pick up or discharge. This enormous volume of irregular commerce is handled by the tramp ships. Tramp ships may be large, and generally are as seaworthy as their more glamorous sisters of the regular ocean lines.

Bills of Lading and Drafts. The objective of the shipper in overseas commerce is to get his goods delivered to his foreign customer and to get money in return. Ordinarily, the contract to carry the goods, the arrangements for transfer of money or credit, and the insurance to protect the investment are intermingled. It is necessary to understand the methods used in overseas commerce in order to understand the procedures of ocean marine insurance.

A basic shipping document is the bill of lading. It serves two purposes. It is (1) a receipt given by the carrier to the shipper for the goods, and (2) it is the contract to carry the goods. The simplest form of a bill of lading is used if the financial arrangements are directly between the shipper and the consignee. In this case, the bill of lading is a contract for delivery of the goods to the consignee at the place named in the bill of lading. The carrier accepts the goods, carries them, delivers them, and gets a receipt. He is not concerned with payment for the goods.

In many cases, however, the shipper does not have a direct financial arrangement with the consignee. It has been pointed out that direct financial arrangements between shippers and consignees in widely separated countries of the world are difficult to establish. The financial transactions are handled by means of an "order" bill of lading and drafts or bills of exchange through banking channels. The order bill of lading is (1) a receipt for the goods, (2) a contract for carriage of the goods, and (3) an order for delivery of the goods. The goods are consigned in such a way that the order bill of lading can be endorsed to whoever is to receive the goods. Ordinarily the order bill of lading is made out so that the goods will be delivered to the shipper or whomever he endorses the bill of lading to. The shipper then endorses the bill of lading in blank and delivers it to his bank for forwarding to the country where the goods are going. This order bill of lading endorsed in blank is equivalent to title to the goods. It is handled with as much care as so much currency. The order bill of lading passes through banking channels and eventually arrives in the country to which the goods are shipped. The consignee arranges for payment or credit to the shipper through his bank, and the bank at the destination then fills in the name of the consignee in the blank space on the endorsement. The consignee now has title to the goods. He takes the order bill of lading to the carrier and is given the goods.

The bill of lading as a receipt for the merchandise indicates that the goods were received in good condition as far as can be determined by external examination. Ocean bills of lading are uniform in many of their provisions because they are based upon the Carriage of Goods by Sea Act, which has been enacted by several countries, including the United States. In case goods are received in bad order, that is, with apparent damage, a notation to that effect is put on the bill of lading. A bad order notation may interfere with acceptance of the goods and payment for them at destination. Carriers are reluctant to accept goods for overseas shipment if there is a possibility of their being refused by the consignee.

Other documents are sent with the order bill of lading so that the shipper can collect his money from the consignee. An invoice shows the amount due including the freight charges if they are shown separately and are to be paid by the consignee. A draft or bill of exchange is written by the shipper ordering the consignee to pay the amount due. This bill of exchange becomes an obligation of the consignee if he accepts it and agrees to pay the amount. Should the sale be on a cost plus insurance plus freight basis (C.I.F.), an ocean marine insurance policy also goes along with the other documents.

The ocean marine insurance policy may be written for that particular shipment by an insurance company or underwriter, or it may be a special policy issued by the insured under a master or open policy that he has received from his underwriters.[1] If the insured issues the insurance policy, it is a complete insurance policy showing that the goods are insured by the underwriter or underwriters named. This ocean marine insurance policy is an order document and may be endorsed by the insured to another party. This is different from the situation with other types of property insurance under which the insured ordinarily does not have the right to assign an insurance policy prior to loss. It is also different from the practice in connection with ocean marine insurance on hulls.

The order bill of lading and the insurance policy are either endorsed to the consignee or are endorsed in blank so that the consignee's name may be filled in by his bank upon acceptance of the bill of exchange and arrangements for payment for the goods.

The typical package of documents which passes through banks or other financial channels referring to an overseas shipment includes (1) an invoice showing the sales contract between the shipper and consignee and the amount due the shipper, (2) an order bill of lading which is the receipt of the carrier for the goods and the contract of carriage, (3) a bill of exchange which the consignee accepts and agrees to pay, and (4) an ocean marine insurance policy obligating the underwriters to pay for any loss due to perils insured against. Usually the shipper is credited with the amount due him when he presents the set of documents to his bank, and he has nothing more to do with the transaction.

In some cases the shipper may sell the package of documents representing the shipment to a dealer in commercial paper rather than handle the transaction through a bank. The dealer buys the

[1]In the chapters regarding ocean marine insurance, the term "underwriters" means the insurance companies or the underwriters at Lloyd's of London who may insure the venture or risk under discussion. In many cases a ship or cargo may be insured by several insurance companies and also by several underwriters who are members of Lloyd's of London.

documents at a discount from the full amount to be paid. He then proceeds to collect the amount due in exactly the same way the shipper would if he had not sold the obligation to the dealer. The dealer collects the full amount due, and his profit consists of the difference between what he paid the shipper and what he collects from the consignee. The transaction between the shipper and the dealer in commercial paper is much the same as that under which finance companies buy notes from automobile dealers who sell automobiles to their customers under installment sales plans.

Some merchants import goods regularly from a country. They often find it advantageous to maintain a bank account in the country from which they are receiving goods. For example, an English merchant may maintain a bank account in the United States in order to facilitate his trade with American exporters. When an English merchant buys goods in the United States, he can send a letter of credit to the shipper. The shipper handles this letter of credit much like a check and makes collection through his own bank, which in turn receives the money from the bank on which the letter of credit is drawn. The transaction has much the same effect as payment by check. In such cases the buyer of the goods is likely to provide his own insurance and cargo space because he has paid for the goods or established his credit in such a way that he can take title in the country of shipment.

In all of these varying transactions, the insurance is essential in order to guarantee reimbursement to the party holding title to the goods in case they are lost. The time involved in the shipment and in completing the transaction makes it advantageous for the insurance to be tied in with the transaction. In case the shipment is lost, the documents reveal the name of the underwriters. The shipper or the consignee can make claim, depending upon which one is entitled to the payment for the loss. There is no delay in contacting the shipper to see which underwriters carry the insurance. The documents referring to the shipment are complete in themselves so that the transaction can be completed immediately.

MARITIME LAW AND OCEAN MARINE INSURANCE

Effect of English Maritime Law. The development of ocean marine insurance is closely tied to the development of English ocean trade and English maritime law. This resulted from the needs of English traders as England became the most important maritime nation. Custom and usage are extremely important in ocean marine insurance, and this is to a large extent the result of English practices. England, unlike the United States, does not have a written constitution. The common law and the acts of Parliament form the full body of English law. Just as the English common law became the basis for much of American law, English maritime laws and practices have greatly influenced American maritime practices and ocean marine insurance.

Many of the rules that developed as a result of custom and early court decisions eventually were enacted into statute law. American practices will be followed in this text. In some respects they differ from those currently followed in English ocean marine insurance.

Lloyd's of London. Lloyd's of London consists of several hundred underwriters who are associated for the purpose of assuming insurance risks. A corporation which is a governing body establishes the rules of operation and decides who is qualified for membership. The corporation does not do any insurance business; this is done by the individual members, each of whom takes whatever portion he desires of an insurance risk that is offered.

Lloyd's of London is unique as an insurance organization. There are other insurance groups known as Lloyd's organized on somewhat the same principle, but they have neither the prestige nor influence enjoyed by Lloyd's of London.

Insurance business with the members of Lloyd's of London is done through brokers. These brokers are familiar with the types of business preferred by different members. There are many groups of underwriters within the Lloyd's organization. Several members who are interested in the same types of risks will put the acceptance of risks into the hands of a person or a small group of persons who are specialists in this class of business. The members of these syndicates, as they are called, agree to take a certain proportion of each risk that is accepted by the specialists or managers. A member of Lloyd's may be a member of several such syndicates. The members of Lloyd's of London are wealthy people. Financial standards for admission to the organization are high, and the chance of insolvency of a member is small.

The name "Lloyd's" comes from a man named Edward Lloyd who in the late 1600s ran a coffee house in London that was a gathering place for people interested in maritime ventures. Lloyd encouraged the patronage of these people, and starting in 1696 published a small sheet giving maritime news which he called "Lloyd's News." Such a paper continues today as "Lloyd's List."

The people who frequented Lloyd's coffee house were not only ship owners and shippers, but men who, according to the practices of that day, assumed insurance risks on maritime ventures. The coffee house became an important center in London for the selling of ships and cargo. The risks of loss were assumed by the individuals, because there were no insurance companies as there are today. It was in 1769 that the underwriters set up a formal organization and took over the publication of Lloyd's List. The organization has continued uninterrupted since that time, and now has its own building in London in which the business is carried on.

Lloyd's Insurance Policy–1779 The agreements entered into between the owners of ships and cargoes and the underwriters who assumed the risks of maritime ventures gradually developed into insurance policies. In 1779 the members of Lloyd's agreed to use an insurance policy which they had developed. The resolutions of the Lloyd's organization including the marine insurance policy were submitted to Parliament for approval as was customary with business developments at that time. This 1779 Lloyd's marine insurance policy has been the basis for ocean marine insurance ever since. The language of today's ocean marine insurance policies in many respects follows the antiquated wording of the 1779 policy. Insurance underwriters and purchasers of ocean marine insurance alike have hesitated to change the wording. People who are interested in maritime ventures and ocean marine insurance are familiar with the meanings and intent of the ocean marine insurance policies. Disputes regarding the intent of the wording of ocean marine insurance policy are few in number. A change of wording, no matter how carefully drawn, might result in a period of adjudication in the courts to determine its exact meaning.

During recent years there have been efforts by American marine underwriters to modernize the wording whenever it can be done without disturbing the marine insurance market. One of the purposes of the American Institute of Marine Underwriters, organized in 1898, has been to formulate and clarify ocean marine insurance policy clauses. Modern language is used in new policy clauses whenever it can be done without upsetting court interpretations upon which reliance must be placed.

Marine Insurance Act, 1906, of Great Britain. The modern basis for English ocean marine insurance is the Marine Insurance Act of 1906. This covers many of the principles of ocean marine insurance and sets out the wording of the ocean marine insurance policy. The policy is not materially different from the Lloyd's policy of 1779. It has become necessary to make changes in coverage to meet changing world conditions, and these changes are made by endorsement to the policy. American marine insurance underwriters have tended to incorporate the wording of the endorsements into the printed ocean marine insurance policies and thus make them more intelligible.

Liability of Carriers by Sea. The coverage provided by ocean marine insurance policies has been developed to fit the liability of ocean carriers. There is an important difference between the liability of carriers by sea and carriers by land.

A common carrier by land in the United States is responsible for the safe delivery of goods with the exception of loss from a few uncommon perils over which he has no control. If the land carrier does not deliver property in good condition, he must, with rare exception, make good the value of the property to its owner regardless of care or negligence on his part.

The liability of the carrier by sea is not nearly as extensive as the liability of the carrier by land. As a result of custom developed over many years, the carrier by sea is liable only for loss due to lack of diligence on his part. The liability is expressed in much more complicated language than this, but the effect is that if the carrier by sea exercises due diligence he is not liable for loss of goods in his custody.

The liability of carriers by sea is set forth in the Carriage of Goods by Sea Act which was enacted by the United States Congress in 1936. It is similar in its provisions to acts of similar titles in force in England and other countries. The Carriage of Goods by Sea Act sets forth requirements in connection with bills of lading; the duties, rights, and liabilities of carriers by sea; and other related matters. The basic responsibility of the carrier is given as follows:

Due diligence before beginning voyage

1. The carrier shall be bound, before and at the beginning of the voyage, to exercise due diligence to -
   a Make the ship seaworthy;
   b Properly man, equip, and supply the ship;
   c Make the holds, refrigeration and cooling chambers, and all other parts of the ship in which goods are carried, fit and safe for their reception, carriage, and preservation.

Carrier's duty to cargo

2. The carrier shall properly and carefully load, handle, stow, carry, keep, care for, and discharge the goods carried.

Seaworthiness. A vessel is considered to be seaworthy if its hull and machinery are sound and in proper working condition, its fuel and provisions are adequate for the voyage contemplated, its crew is qualified for the voyage, and the ship is of a type designed for operation in the seas at the time of year contemplated for the voyage. A ship that might be considered seaworthy for a summer trip in waters normally smooth might be entirely unseaworthy for a winter crossing of the north Atlantic in the storms to be expected at that time of year.

A vessel may be seaworthy at the beginning of a voyage and become unseaworthy due to some occurrence during the voyage. Since many maritime losses are the result of unseaworthiness, the Carriage of Goods by Sea Act defines with some care that neither the carrier nor the ship shall be liable for loss or damage resulting from unseaworthiness unless caused by want of due diligence on the part of the carrier to make the ship seaworthy. However, the burden of proving the exercise of due diligence rests upon the carrier or other person who seeks exemption from liability under that provision of the act. It is reasonable to place the burden of proof on the carrier or ship operator because he normally is the only one who knows what measures are taken to assure seaworthiness. The shipper whose goods are being carried would have no way of proving whether or not due diligence has been exercised.

The act further lists seventeen exemptions of the carrier from liability from designated causes. These causes for which the carrier is not liable include loss or damage resulting from any act, neglect, or default of the master, mariner, pilot, or the servants of the carrier in the navigation or management of the ship; fire unless caused by fault or privity of the carrier; perils, dangers, or accidents or the seas; act of God; act of war; act of public enemies; seizure under legal process; quarantine restrictions; act or omission of the shipper or owner of the goods; strikes or lockouts; riot or civil commotion; saving or attempting to save life or property at sea; inherent vice or quality of the goods; insufficiency of packing or marking; and latent defects. A general exemption applies to any other cause arising without the fault or privity of the carrier or his agents or servants. The burden of proof is upon the carrier to show that there was no fault or privity on his part.

The purpose of the Carriage of Goods by Sea Act is to spell out the legal relationship between the shipper and the carrier. If a ship is lost due to perils of the sea, fire, or one of the other hazards that may cause loss without fault of the carrier or ship owner, the shipper loses the value of his goods the same as the owner of the ship loses the value of his ship. The shipper and the shipowner are joint venturers, and each has to take his own loss if there has been due diligence in the operation of the ship.

The effect to the insurer of goods carried at sea is that there is little chance of subrogation against the carrier in case of loss. The shipper of goods by land has a good chance of collecting from the carrier for any loss, regardless of the carrier's negligence. Often the shipper by land does not consider it worthwhile to carry insurance because he does have this chance of collecting from the carrier. The shipper of goods by sea ordinarily cannot collect from the carrier by sea. Insurance is a necessity if his investment in goods is to be protected.

Insurable Interests and Exposures. Maritime law follows insurance practices in general that there must be an insurable interest if a policyholder is to collect in the event of an occurrence covered by the policy. The English Marine Insurance Act of 1906 provides that a gaming or wagering contract is void. Insurable interest must exist at the time of the loss although it need not exist at the time the insurance policy contract is made. In general, any person or entity that would suffer a financial loss from a marine loss has an insurable interest. The four principal exposures to loss are the loss of the ship or the *hull*, the loss of the *cargo,* the loss of *freight,* and the loss from *liability* because of injury or damage to the person or property of another. Owners, mortgagees, charterers, and operators are among those who would lose from the loss of a ship. Insurance on hulls will be discussed later in this text. Anyone having an interest in the cargo may carry insurance. Special cargo policy provisions will also be discussed later.

Freight is the compensation which is paid, or is agreed to be paid, for the carriage of goods or for the use of a ship or a part of a ship. (It does not include money received for carrying passengers. This is "passage money".) The term "freight" as commonly used in the United States refers to goods which are being shipped. The marine usage of the word refers to money received for the carriage of goods. If an accident prevents a shipowner or operator from collecting this money, he has a loss, and this establishes an insurable interest. The carrier ordinarily cannot collect his charges for carrying goods unless he delivers them as called for by his contract of carriage. Therefore, if he loses his ship, or is otherwise prevented from making delivery, the carrier stands to lose not only the value of the ship but also what he expected to collect as freight. In the case of a freight loss that is covered by insurance, it is customary to pay the full amount of the earnings which are lost without deducting for any expenses which have not been paid. In this respect the practices differ from those of business-interruption insurance.

A ship owner or charterer may secure insurance coverage against loss from his liability for loss of cargo, injury to persons, or damage to property of others. This liability insurance will also be discussed later.

Many of the principles in connection with ocean marine losses of all kinds are similar. Loss and coverage principles will be discussed first and the differences in hull, cargo, and other policies will be discussed later.

LOSS PRINCIPLES

Ocean marine insurance losses may be separated into four general groups: (1) partial losses or "particular average," (2) total loss of part of a shipment, (3) total or constructive total losses, and (4) general average.

In ocean marine parlance the word "average" means a loss less than a total loss, that is, a partial loss. When coupled with the word "general" it means the proportionate distribution of a charge among the interests[2] chargeable for the loss or expense. The origin of the word "average" as meaning "loss" is not entirely clear, but it may come from the French word "avarie," which means damage to ship or cargo, or port dues.

Particular Average. A particular average is a partial loss to the property of a particular interest. It is a loss to be borne entirely by the person owning the property or having the insurable interest, without contribution by any other parties. An example of a particular average would be a case in which perils of the sea such as a storm caused damage to ship or cargo. If there were no voluntary sacrifice of any portion of the ship or cargo, but merely direct damage from the storm, each cargo owner and the shipowner would look to his insurance underwriter for payment of his loss in accordance with the terms of his insurance policy as it applied to particular average.

Ocean marine insurance policies frequently are written with

[2]The word "interest" in the chapters on ocean marine insurance is used to mean the owner of property, or other person or firm with an insurable interest in the property that is the subject of the insurance. Such a person or firm is the beneficiary of insurance covering that interest.

restrictions applying to particular average. The insurance policy may provide that the coverage is written "free of particular average." This means that a partial loss will not be paid. Coverage also may be written "free of particular average of less than __%," with a percentage figure inserted in the blank space. This means that the underwriter will not pay any partial loss that amounts to less than the specified percentage.

A free-of-particular-average clause may provide that it applies except when a specified peril has caused the loss. A clause which may be used provides: "Free of particular average unless caused by stranding, sinking, burning or collision with another vessel." This clearly would allow payment of a particular average when it is *caused* by such an occurrence. A somewhat more liberal provision which may be used provides: "Warranted free from particular average unless the vessel or craft be stranded, sunk, burnt, or in collision." This clause does not tie payment for the loss to the specified occurrence but allows recovery when the ship has been involved in the occurrence regardless of whether the loss was caused by the occurrence specified.

A particular average generally is adjusted by determining the proportion by which the value of the property has been lessened by the loss. The method usually is to determine what the property would be worth in an undamaged condition, what it is worth in the damaged condition, and thus find the percentage of damage. This percentage is then applied to the value of the property as agreed to in the insurance policy.

Total Loss of Part of a Shipment. When a shipment consists of several parts or separate units, policies usually provide that a total loss of one or more units is not considered a particular average. The amount of insurance on the unit lost can be determined from the insurance policy, and this amount is paid to the insured as the loss.

Total Loss. An actual total loss is one in which the insured property is so damaged by an insured peril that there is no value left. Total losses are relatively simple to adjust because of the agreed value basis upon which ocean marine insurance policies are written. The fact that the loss has occurred must be verified, and the ownership and interest must be checked to see that they are in order for payment of the loss. With cargo losses, it is necessary to secure the invoices to prove the invoice value, and to make whatever additions of freight or percentages may be called for by the valuation clause of the insurance policy.

Constructive Total Loss. There may be a constructive total loss without there being an actual total loss. For example, a ship may be stranded on a reef, and the cost of refloating the ship may be greater than the value of the ship. A constructive total loss is considered to have occurred if the cost of salvaging the cargo or ship or of making repairs would be more than the salved value. The underwriters have the right to any salvage value that may be recovered from the venture if the underwriters agree that the venture is a constructive total loss and make payment.

Abandonment. The problem of abandonment ties in with that of constructive total loss. It is customary in connection with total loss payments for underwriters to take an assignment of the property in the hope that some salvage may be secured. It is the practice in ocean marine insurance to consider abandonment proper under certain circumstances. If the insured finds that the ship or cargo, or both, are damaged to an extent that salvage would cost more than could be saved, he can tender abandonment to the underwriters and ask for payment as a total loss. Underwriters pay the insured for a total loss if they accept abandonment. The underwriters do not have to accept ownership of the remaining property even if they do accept abandonment. They would not accept ownership if such ownership would subject them to liability for damage to other property or vessels that might come in contact with the wreck.

If the underwriter refuses to accept abandonment, the insured is still obligated to use all reasonable means to recover the property until he can demonstrate conclusively that a constructive total loss has occurred. Abandonment is optional with the insured and cannot be forced by the underwriters. The insured must tender abandonment promptly if he sees that his situation is such that abandonment is desirable. Like any other contract, once the tender of abandonment has been made by the owner and has been accepted by the underwriters, it cannot be changed except by mutual consent.

General Average. General average is the name of a practice in ocean commerce in effect many hundreds of years before any insurance was available. It became the practice that when property is jettisoned (voluntarily thrown overboard) in order to prevent the loss of the ship and cargo, the owners of the property that is saved contribute in proportion to the owners of the property that has been sacrificed. For example, suppose that a ship, its cargo, and freight charges are worth a total of $100,000. In order to save the ship from sinking during a storm, $10,000 worth of cargo is thrown overboard.

The owners of the ship, the owners of the balance of the cargo, and those interested in the freight would contribute $9,000 to the owners whose cargo was thrown overboard. The owners of the ship, cargo, and freight would each contribute one-tenth of the value inasmuch as one-tenth of the total value was sacrificed in order to save the venture.

Ocean marine insurance policies cover general average charges which may be made against the insured ship or cargo. The underwriter pays any such charges which are assessed against the property covered by the policy, even though that property itself is undamaged, provided the property is fully insured. In case of underinsurance, the insured must pay a proportion of the general average charges in relation to the proportion of underinsurance.

There are certain elements necessary before a general average claim from the owners of a ship or cargo will be accepted. There must be:

1. The existence of imminence of some risk that appears to threaten all interests, that is, both ship and cargo.
2. A voluntary sacrifice, or some extraordinary expense, with the purpose of avoiding loss or reducing it for the common interest of all owners.
3. Some practical effect of the effort, and at least a part of the value saved.
4. A freedom from any fault on the part of the interests claiming contribution from the rest of the venture. For example, if the owners of a ship are claiming general average contribution, they must show that they were not at fault in connection with the risk that threatened the ship and cargo.

General average originally was a method of contributing toward the value of property which was jettisoned. Today other expenses in addition to voluntary sacrifice of property may be considered general average expenses. If a ship is stranded, and the engines are damaged because of racing them or otherwise overworking them in order to pull the ship off the reef, such damage to the engines may be a general average sacrifice. In case of fire, any damage by water, steam, or other materials used to extinguish the fire is a general average sacrifice to prevent loss of the entire ship and cargo. However, damage by the fire itself would be a particular average or specific loss applying to the property damaged by the fire and not subject to general average contribution.

There must be an actual peril common to all of the interests for a general average claim to be recognized. The elements necessary for general average contribution are not present if the peril is imaginary and the sacrifice is made in the mistaken belief that a peril exists when in fact it does not.

Extraordinary expenses rest upon the interest incurring those expenses if no part of the venture is saved. This is fair enough if the sacrifice is a jettison. If property is jettisoned, and the entire venture subsequently lost, it makes no difference that the jettisoned property is lost sooner than the rest of the property. The practice also applies to any sacrifice or extraordinary expense even though this is perhaps not completely fair. The other portions of the ship and cargo do not contribute when nothing is saved.

The value to be used for general average purposes is the value of the property after the occurrence that required the general average sacrifice. If the ship is damaged due to the sacrifice, the general average value is determined by taking the value of the ship immediately prior to the sacrifice and deducting the amount of damage resulting from the sacrifice. Any other loss due to marine perils not related to the voluntary sacrifice is not deducted in establishing the value of the ship. In the same way, the value of the cargo for general average purposes is the value in existence after whatever sacrifice has been made. If the cargo has been damaged by steam or water in fire extinguishing operations, the value for general average purposes of that cargo is the value in its damaged condition.

The adjustment of general average losses can be an extremely complicated business. This is particularly true if the vessel is large and there is miscellaneous cargo owned by many different people. The ship and every lot of cargo must be valued, the amount of the general average sacrifice must be determined, and the loss due to the sacrifice must be apportioned over the entire venture, including the ship, the cargo, and the freight charges. A general average adjustment may require hundreds of pages of descriptions and figures, and may take many months to complete. Each interest must guarantee that it will pay its proportion of the general average before its property is released. Insurance on the property is considered a sufficient guarantee if the underwriter guarantees payment of the general average charges. The owner of an uninsured cargo or ship would have to put up a bond or cash to guarantee payment upon completion of the general average adjustment.

The obligation of the underwriter to pay general average charges depends upon whether the insurance policy covered the peril against which the sacrifice or expenditure was made. Most ocean marine insurance policies cover general average charges resulting from threat by perils insured against under the policy. If the sacrifice was made because of some peril not covered by the insurance policy, the underwriter would not pay the general average charges.

The application becomes extremely involved although the principle of general average is relatively simple. Laws and practices differ in different parts of the world. General average is applied according to the rules of the land where the voyage ends unless the bill of lading provides rules to be followed. Marine interests for the last hundred years have attempted to codify general average practices. The "York-Antwerp rules" were first set up at conferences in York, England, in 1864 and in Antwerp in 1877. They have been revised several times since, most recently in 1950. The York-Antwerp rules are the general statement of how general average shall be applied. In the absence of specific rules or laws to the contrary, the York-Antwerp rules are followed as far as possible in establishing general average contributions.

Salvage. The word "salvage" used with property insurance on land means the preserving or renovation of goods damaged by an insured casualty. The term is applied also to reclaimed goods, often called "salvage." "Salvage" also may mean merchandise which has been damaged at sea and has been brought ashore to be renovated and sold for the benefit of the underwriters, the insured, or both.

In marine commerce, the term "marine salvage" is intended to mean the rescue of ships and cargoes at sea. A person or organization engaging in salvage operations is known as a "salvor." Marine salvage has a long history and legal background independent of its relation to insurance. The obligation to save life at sea is imposed on all mariners. The saving of life without the saving of property does not entitle the mariner to a salvage award. The person who does save property of another from a maritime peril is entitled to an award for his effort. Maritime law imposes a liability upon the thing saved. This is a salvage award which is compensation for the services of the person who aided the distressed property. There are three elements which are essential if a salvage award is to be made. First, the property involved must be in peril from some hazard. Second, the salvage service must be voluntary. A person who is under a legal obligation to preserve the property ordinarily cannot claim a salvage award. The master and crewmen are under an obligation to preserve their ship, and they cannot claim a salvage award for their own ship. The third element is that there must be success, at least in some degree, to the effort. These rules and much other law in connection with salvage are in effect regardless of insurance. Salvage is important in marine insurance because most insurance policies cover salvage charges for rescue of a ship from a peril which is covered by the policy.

There are a few large and well-equipped organizations that specialize in the saving of vessels in distress. Immediate action in case a vessel is in distress at sea may mean an enormous saving to the insured and to the underwriters. Damage that disables a ship, even though the damage is small, leaves the ship subject to total destruction by perils of the sea unless immediate assistance is given. The underwriters cooperate with ship and cargo owners in seeing that prompt salvage measures are taken when a vessel is reported in distress.

There are several different ways in which a salvor may operate. In the days before rapid communication, salvage operations were informal, and were likely to be on a voluntary basis. A vessel abandoned by her crew is considered to be a derelict and subject to salvage by anyone able to save a portion of the value. An old rule for such salvage operations allowed half of the value saved to the salvors. Many times there was a race between persons or organizations in an effort to be first on board the vessel in distress, in order to receive the salvage award. Under admiralty law, the salvors have a lien on any value that may be saved. Under modern practice the award usually is made by an admiralty court in case the owners, underwriters, and salvors cannot reach an agreement.

Many salvage operations are conducted under contract between the owners of a vessel and the salvors. This is not true salvage or pure salvage, and the rules of salvage ordinarily would not apply. The charges or payment to the salvors in this case would depend upon the contract. If a ship loses a rudder or is without power, the owners may dispatch a seagoing tug to tow the vessel to port. The operation of the tug is usually on a per diem basis under a contract. The tug owners are paid for their efforts under the contract even if the vessel should be lost in spite of the salvage operation.

Salvage also may be attempted on a "no cure, no pay" basis. The owners of the vessel or cargo arrange with a salvage company to attempt salvage of the distressed ship or endangered cargo. The salvor may be reimbursed on the basis of a percentage of the goods salvaged, on the basis of his expenses plus a bonus dependent upon the goods salvaged, or according to some other arrangement satisfactory to the owners, the underwriters, and the salvor. The underwriters usually assist in such negotiations in order to make sure that the best methods are used. If no value is salvaged under these arrangements, the salvor receives no pay. Such arrangements are used in the event that it is reasonable to expect a material part of the value to be saved, but the actual proportion that can be saved is indefinite. The salvor takes his chances on a speculative operation, and his success depends largely on his knowledge of what can be done under the circumstances at hand.

Salvage charges are specifically covered in the ocean marine insurance policy. Marine insurance policies issued in the United States frequently provide for payment of salvage charges as called for in the contract of affreightment, or payment in accordance with the laws and usages of the port of New York. This means that if salvage operations should be contracted for and the vessel is a total loss in spite of the salvage operations, the underwriters would be liable for the loss of the vessel plus the salvage charges assessed against the owner under the salvage contract.

Many complicated situations arise. Expenses that are incurred in order to preserve a ship or its cargo may be salvage charges; if there is a voluntary sacrifice (jettison), there may be a general average situation; if the effort relates to a particular portion of the cargo or to the ship itself, there may be a particular average expense; or the expenses may be a sue and labor expense (this will be discussed later in this text). Contribution to the expenses by the various interests involved in the maritime venture, and payment by the insurance underwriters, would be affected by the circumstances and whether the insurance policies covered the property or freight for the type of expenses which was determined.

QUESTIONS

1. Discuss the kind of perils that threaten loss or damage to ships at sea. How do they differ from perils that threaten land shipments?
2. Why is insurance generally considered necessary when goods are shipped in ocean commerce?
3. What is the function of an order bill of lading?
4. Explain the meaning of the term "underwriter" as it is used in ocean marine insurance.
5. What is Lloyd's of London and what is its significance in ocean marine insurance?
6. Explain the importance of the Lloyd's insurance policy of 1779 as it relates to ocean marine insurance today.
7. Compare the liability of a carrier by sea with the liability of a carrier on land for goods in its custody.

8. What is meant if a vessel is said to be seaworthy?
9. What is the Carriage of Goods by Sea Act?
10. Name and define briefly the four principal exposures to loss which would establish an insurable interest in a marine venture.
11. Explain the difference between general average and particular average.
12. What elements are necessarily present before a general average claim will be accepted?
13. Distinguish between a total loss and a constructive total loss.
14. Explain the privileges and obligations of insured and underwriters in regard to abandonment.
15. Explain the difference between "marine salvage" and "salvage" as it is used in connection with property insurance on land.

3

The Ocean Marine Insurance Policy

The preceding material has discussed certain features of maritime law and customs which apply regardless of insurance. They affect insurance because it has become customary for insurers to cover any loss or obligation which may rest upon an insured because of his participation in a maritime venture. The following material discusses insurance coverages, policies, and practices, and mostly from the standpoint of American practices. Ocean marine insurance is essentially an international business, but there are many differences in the way details of the business are conducted in different countries.

There is no standard ocean marine insurance policy in the sense that there is a standard fire insurance policy in many states. The provisions of the Lloyd's policy of 1779, as expressed in the Marine Insurance Act, 1906, of Great Britain, constitute the basis for most ocean marine insurance policies, but the variations are extensive. The coverages and principles most frequently found in present-day policies are presented here by considering first the clauses that appear in the Lloyd's policy and then considering the additional clauses that have come into use. Many different combinations of these clauses are used to provide the exact coverages desired by ocean marine policyholders.

CLAUSES AFFECTING COVERAGE

Valued Policies in Ocean Marine Insurance. Insurance policies covering property on land usually are on an actual cash value basis. The insured under such a policy is required to prove the amount of his loss as of the time and place of the loss. Ocean marine insurance policies, on the contrary, usually state the agreed value of the property for insurance purposes or provide a method of arriving at the value.

There is a practical reason for having an agreed value in an ocean marine insurance policy. When a ship and cargo are lost at sea, there is no physical evidence that could be used to help establish the value at the time of loss.

It has been pointed out that insurance companies do not like to issue valued policies covering loss of property on land. The principal objection to valued policies arises from the moral hazard. The insured under a fire insurance policy usually has control of the property covered. If he could secure insurance on the basis of an agreed valuation, he might be induced to burn the property in order to collect the insurance. The actual cash value basis upon which fire insurance is written makes it difficult for an insured to better himself financially by burning his property. Ocean marine insurance generally covers property which is not in the immediate control of the insured. This is particularly true of cargoes. In the case of insurance on hulls, the valued policy can be a danger to underwriters. During periods of commercial depression when ship owners have trouble finding employment for their ships, underwriters are careful to fix valuations sufficiently low so that the owners are not tempted to conspire with the crews to have the vessels lost.

Ocean marine cargoes generally are insured on the basis of the expected market value at the destination of the voyage. Goods ordinarily are worth more at the destination than at the place of shipment; otherwise the shipment would not be made. The agreed value of an insured hull necessarily bears a relation to its market or replacement value, depending upon circumstances. The value agreed upon in the insurance policy forms the basis for loss adjustment regardless of fluctuations in market value.

Parties to the Ocean Marine Insurance Contract (Policy). The insurer is one party to the ocean marine insurance policy contract. In the United States this is likely to be a corporate insurance company. In the case of a marine insurance policy issued by Lloyd's of London, the insurer is a group of underwriters who are members of Lloyd's. The name of a corporate insurer (insurance company) appears on the policy the same as it does on other insurance policies, and the policy is signed by an authorized agent. On a Lloyd's policy, the contract is signed by authorized representatives of the participating underwriters.

The other party to the ocean marine insurance policy contract is the insured person or corporation. Under an ocean marine insurance policy, the insured named on the policy may be a person or corporation holding the principal interest in the property, or the named insured may be someone holding an interest in the property for the benefit of another party. The ocean marine insurance policy states that it "does insure" the party named, followed by the words "for the account of." It is important and is customary for the policy to name the persons or corporations whose interests are covered, or to describe the interested parties in such a way that they can be identified in case of loss. A policy issued to a corporation that is shipping goods to various people all over the world would indicate that it is written to cover the interest of the consignees to whom the named insured may ship goods, as well as for the benefit of the named insured.

Ocean marine insurance policies sometimes are made out "for the account of whom it may concern." These words do not carry the broad implication that they do in general business in the United States. They are intended to apply only to those parties intended to be included by the person who ordered the insurance. Persons not specifically intended by the purchaser of the insurance, or persons not within the class of persons intended by him, cannot claim the benefits of the policy. It is not intended, for example, to permit someone who later acquires an interest in the property, but who was not in the mind of the purchaser, to make a claim under the policy.

Lost or Not Lost. Under a fire insurance policy, if the property which is intended to become the subject of the insurance has been destroyed before the policy is effective, there is no contract, and the insured cannot collect the amount of the loss.

Under ocean marine insurance practices, however, property may be insured even if it has been lost, as long as neither party knows at the time it is insured that it has been lost.

The typical ocean marine insurance policy covers property "lost or not lost." This practice developed in the period when it was often months from the time a ship left port until it was heard from again. Communications were slow, and there might be reason to change the insurance arrangements during the time the ship was at sea. Even today there may be a lapse of several days during which a ship is not heard from. The risk that a ship has been lost between the time it was last heard from and the time of placing the insurance is a risk that is assumed by the underwriters.

This practice is particularly advantageous to those who are continuously engaged in overseas commerce. Open policies are written so that they cover all of the goods described while in transit. Many times a cargo is lost before the insured learns that it has been shipped, but the policy covers the loss.

The utmost good faith is required of the insured. If the insured has received any indication at all that the ship is in trouble or lost, even if this is merely in the nature of a rumor, he must reveal this to the underwriters. Otherwise he would be guilty of concealment, and the contract would be void.

At and From. An insurance policyy covering a voyage is effective "at and from" the port named. When the policy covers for a period of time, it covers "at and from" the date specified. A policy may be written to cover voyages anywhere in the world, or anywhere within certain geographical limits, such as points within the Western hemisphere. Variations of wording following the words "at and from" in the insurance policy are numerous, and are made to fit the requirements for the particular ship or cargo or the requirements of the insured.

The words "at and from" are significant because they indicate that the insurance policy is intended to cover while the ship is in port. Use of the word "from" by itself would indicate that the coverage would be effective only after the ship had sailed.

The Lloyd's policy provides that the coverage is effective on goods and merchandise "from the loading thereof aboard the said ship." Coverage on the ship continues "until she hath moored at anchor twenty-four hours in good safety." An insurance policy covering during calls at several ports covers continuously during such calls and until the ship has been moored safely for 24 hours at the destination named in the policy.

Goods and merchandise are covered "until the same be there discharged and safely landed." The 24-hour limitation of coverage after arrival in port does not apply to cargo. The cargo is protected until it is safely unloaded, which means it is protected during unloading. If the port is one where small boats (lighters) must be used for unloading, the coverage on cargo remains effective until it is deposited on shore.

"Touch and Stay"–Deviation. The Lloyd's policy provides that it shall be lawful for the said ship in the voyage to "proceed and sail to and touch and stay at any ports and places . . ." without prejudice to the insurance. Within the blank space words are inserted to indicate the ports or geographical area within which the underwriters wish to provide coverage. The words "touch and stay at any ports and places" are not intended to be taken literally. The ship may call only at ports which are customary to the voyage contemplated. The stay must be reasonable for the purpose of the voyage.

One of the implied warranties in connection with ocean marine insurance is that the vessel shall proceed from the port of origin to its destination by the most direct or the customary route. Any variation from this route is a deviation, and causes the insurance to become void. The reason for this implied warranty is the likelihood that a deviation from an expected route would increase the hazard or prolong the journey. If some deviation occurs that increases the hazard, the underwriters feel that they should not be liable for the added risk brought about by the deviation. A deviation might not be a change in the route but might be a delay in beginning the voyage. An involuntary act such as that resulting from a ship's being blown off course by a storm is not a deviation. A deviation for the purpose of saving life or property does not void the coverage. Originally a ship was permitted to deviate from its course only to save life, but modern custom permits deviation to save property as well as to save life.

Deviation affects not only the insurance coverage, but in many cases the chances of the insurance company's recovering from the carrier under subrogation. It is customary for the ocean marine insurance policy to cover the innocent cargo owner who has no way of controlling whether or not there is a deviation from the normal route. In case a loss occurs and there has been a deviation, the insurer may be obligated to pay the cargo loss to the insured, but may then attempt to recover from the carrier because of the deviation.

A deviation may be considered reasonable and as not extending the liability of the carrier if the ship must go to a port of refuge in order to secure urgent repairs, to assist other vessels in distress if human life is in danger, or to land a sick crew man in urgent need of medical or surgical care, or if the recognized route between two ports includes the deviation in question. If most ships follow one route between two ports, a court is likely to take the position that there has been no deviation, even though the route is not the most direct.

PERILS INSURED AGAINST

The perils insured against by an ocean marine insurance policy generally are those listed in the Lloyd's policy. The wording is sufficiently interesting to be quoted:

> Touching the adventures and perils which we the assurers are contented to bear and take upon us in this voyage; they are of the seas, men of war, fire, enemies, pirates, rovers, thieves, jettisons, letters of mart and countermart, surprises, takings at sea, arrests, restraints, and detainments of all kings, princes, and people, of what nation, condition, or quality soever, barratry of the master and the mariners, and of all other perils, losses, and misfortunes, that have or shall come to the hurt, detriment, or damage of the said goods and merchandise, and ship, etc., or any part thereof.

Variations of this wording will be found in many policies. Shorter versions depend for their breadth of coverage on wording such as "and all other like perils, losses and misfortunes that have come or shall come to the hurt, detriment or damage of the said goods and merchandise." Each peril that is specified has been the subject of interpretation by the courts. Comments on some of these interpretations will be helpful in understanding the intent and practices in connection with such policies.

Perils of the Sea. Perils of the sea include the action of wind and waves; lightning; the collision of the ship with another ship or object; and the sinking, capsizing, or stranding of the ship. If any of these perils result in the ship's leaking so that sea water damages the cargo or the inside of the ship, such damage is also covered as resulting from a peril of the sea. It is not intended that the coverage protect against loss from ordinary wear and tear such as a ship would sustain from the normal stress of ocean voyages. There must be some unexpected and accidental occurrence.

Fire. Although lightning is considered to be a peril of the sea, fire is not so considered. Fire may occur on the sea, but it is not considered an accident related to the activity of the oceans or the weather. Fire is mentioned specifically in order that it may be covered by the ocean marine insurance policy.

Pirates. The danger of loss by pirates was a real one a few generations ago, but the danger from pirates and rovers was so lessened that they are not mentioned specifically in many of the newer policies. Piracy is robbery or an act of violence at sea. The hijacking of an airplane might be considered an act of piracy, particularly if it involved a flight over the sea or resulted in flying over the sea.

Assailing Thieves. The Lloyd's policy mentions as a peril the word "thieves," and the more recent policies specify "assailing thieves." The intention under all ocean marine insurance policies is that the theft coverage be against what on land would be known as burglary or robbery. That is, the intention is to cover theft by violence or with threat of violence. It is not intended that the coverage extend to pilferage or theft by stealth. If pilferage or theft by stealth is intended to be covered, it is specifically named by endorsement.

Jettisons. Property is jettisoned if it is voluntarily sacrificed in order to preserve the remainder of the property involved. For example, a portion of a cargo may be thrown overboard in order to lighten the ship, and thus preserve it and the remainder of the cargo. Since this is a voluntary act, it is considered necessary to mention it as a peril to be covered in order that there may be no misinterpretation regarding loss as a result of jettison. For the effect of general average practices upon jettison losses, see a consideration of general average in the preceding chapter.

Barratry. Barratry is a fraudulent, dishonest, or illegal act on the part of the master of the ship or the crew without the knowledge of the owners that results in injury to the ship or cargo. It would include such acts as running away with the ship, sinking the ship, or abandoning it for some illegal or dishonest purpose. Such an act must be without the knowledge of the owner if it is to be considered barratry.

Other Perils—*Ejusdem Generis.* The phrase "all other perils, losses and misfortunes" seems to be extremely broad, but it is more accurately expressed in some modern policies which state, "all other *like* perils, losses and misfortunes." Even without the word "like" this phrase has been interpreted by the courts to mean only perils similar to those specifically enumerated. A principle of law which is called *ejusdem generis* has been established relating to such coverage. This is a Latin phrase meaning "of like kind." The courts have held that other perils are not covered unless they are similar to those enumerated in the clause. It is not a phrase providing an "all risks" type of coverage.

Older marine insurance policies included the perils of war in the basic policy coverage, but the war perils are either specifically excluded or included in policies written today. War risk insurance will be discussed later in this text.

Sue and Labor. The "sue and labor" clause appears in the Lloyd's policy and in modern ocean marine insurance policies. A current version reads:

> Sue and Labor Clause. In case of any loss or misfortune, it shall be lawful and necessary to and for the Assured, his or their factors, servants, and assigns, to sue, labor and travel for, in and about the defense, safeguard and recovery of the said goods and merchandise, or any part thereof, without prejudice to this insurance; nor shall the acts of the Assured or Assurers, in recovering, saving, and preserving the property insured, in case of disaster, be considered a waiver or an acceptance of an abandonment; to the charges whereof, the said Assurers will contribute according to the rate and quantity of the sum hereby insured.

The primary object of the clause is to obligate the insured to save the property from further loss in case some loss or damage insured against should occur. The clause permits the insured to take any necessary action to save the property without waiving his right to offer abandonment of the property to the underwriters. The clause also permits the underwriters to recover, save, or preserve the property without their action being considered as a waiver of their rights, or as an acceptance of abandonment tendered by the insured. The final agreement in the clause is that the underwriters will pay their proportion of such expense in the ratio of the amount of insurance to the value of the property. The insured has no claim against the underwriters under the "sue and labor" clause if the peril threatening the property is not covered by the policy.

It is necessary to draw a distinction between "sue and labor" expenses and general average expenses. Expenses for which the underwriters are liable under the "sue and labor" clause are those that help directly to reduce the loss to the underwriters on the specific property insured. Court costs are allowable, and also the costs of reconditioning merchandise, unloading it, and forwarding it by other means.

General average expenses, on the other hand, relate to the prorating of a loss over an entire cargo and ship and freight. The distinction between "sue and labor" and general average may be whether the expenses are for the sole benefit of a particular interest in reducing loss, or whether they are of benefit to the entire venture. Expenses reducing damage to the vessel if the cargo is in no danger would be "sue and labor" expenses applicable to the vessel, because only that particular interest is in danger.

Salvage expenses are not considered "sue and labor" expenses. Salvage operations are specifically undertaken to rescue a ship in distress or danger. Usually a vessel is in distress when salvage operations are undertaken, whereas "sue and labor" expenses are intended to lessen the effects of a disaster which has overtaken the venture.

It has been held that "sue and labor" expenses may be paid to prevent a loss even though the property was not actually damaged. There are cases in which "sue and labor" expenses have been allowed to an insured in addition to payment for a total loss.

Proximate Cause—Direct Loss. A policy may state that coverage is provided for "direct loss" from the perils mentioned. The English Marine Insurance Act of 1906 uses wording that the insurer is liable for "any loss proximately caused by a peril insured against." It is permissible for an insurer to cover consequential loss, but such loss is not covered unless the policy so provides. A direct loss is one for which the proximate cause is the peril insured against. The proximate cause is the immediate, near, or direct cause. There must be a direct and unbroken link between the act or peril and the injury or damage. There cannot have been any intervening or independent cause between. The proximate cause is the act or peril without which the result could not have occurred. The result must have been one that would naturally follow and could have been anticipated under the circumstances.

CONDITIONS OF THE OCEAN MARINE INSURANCE POLICY

The Lloyd's policy is a bare skeleton of the insurance coverages needed in connection with modern marine activities. Many other clauses have been developed and attached to the Lloyd's policy, or are printed as part of the ocean marine insurance policies issued by American insurance companies. Different clauses may be used or not, depending upon the needs and desires of the insured and the requirements of the underwriters. Some important clauses are considered here with a discussion of their purposes and limitations.

Limitation to Fortuitous Losses. The coverage clause of an ocean marine insurance policy specifies perils of an accidental nature, but many policies strengthen this principle by excluding certain types of losses which may not be fortuitous. They exclude loss from dampness, change of flavor, or decay, or from being spotted, discolored, musty or moldy, unless caused by actual contact of sea water with the articles damaged, or unless occasioned by sea perils. Such clauses may also exclude loss or damage resulting from wear and tear, inherent vice, or other possible causes of loss not the result of an accidental occurrence. Leakage of liquids ordinarily is not covered, nor is breakage of merchandise unless caused by stranding or collision with another vessel.

Memorandum Clause. Commodities vary in their susceptibility to loss. Many ocean marine insurance policies contain a "memorandum" clause intended to eliminate the payment of small losses on goods particularly susceptible to damage. This is called a "memorandum" clause because it was added as a memorandum or note to the Lloyd's policy. Its use dates from about 1749. A typical memorandum clause lists thirty or forty articles such as certain types of ironware, food, and furniture for which particular average is not paid, and particular average to certain other enumerated commodities is paid only if it exceeds specified percentages.

Under this clause, the insurance company pays nothing if the loss is less than the percentage specified, but pays the full loss if the damage exceeds the specified percentage. This is known also as a "franchise" clause and differs from a deductible clause under which an amount is deducted from any loss. The franchise clauses usually read essentially as follows: "Warranted by the assured free from average under . . . per cent unless general."

Free of Particular Average. Some policies are written to exclude partial losses entirely and such policies are said to be written "free of particular average." Some of the "free of particular average" clauses provide for payment of partial losses if caused by the ship's being stranded, sunk, burned, or in collision.

Deductibles on Hull Coverage. Insurance on the ships themselves usually is written with a deductible or a franchise clause. Such clauses may provide that there is no loss payable by the underwriters unless the loss exceeds some percentage, such as 3 percent or 5 percent. Provision may be made for payment of losses above a specified amount rather than by using a percentage.

"Inchmaree" and Negligence Clauses. Following the introduction of steam power for ships, there was a question as to whether damage to machinery or damage from breakage of machinery was covered by ocean marine insurance policies. The question was decided by the English House of Lords (acting as a supreme court) in connection with a steamer named the "Inchmaree." There had been damage to the ship's machinery, apparently as a result of negligence of the crew. The House of Lords decided that the loss was not the result of another like peril to the perils covered by the policy and that the underwriters were not liable for the damage.[1]

It was evident that expensive damage to machinery, or to the ship as a result of a machinery breakdown, could occur and that operators of marine ventures needed insurance against such losses. The underwriters were willing to provide the coverage. The result was the development of the clause which specifically extends the coverage of the insurance policy to this type of loss. The clause became known as the "Inchmaree Clause," and it is commonly attached to marine insurance policies today.

The "Inchmaree" or negligence clause is intended to extend the coverage of the policy to loss resulting from the bursting of boilers, breakage of shafts, or from any latent defect in the machinery, hull or appurtenances, or from faults or errors in the navigation or management of the vessel by the master, mariners, mates, engineers, or pilots.

Insurance policies covering ships usually exclude "the cost and expense of replacing or repairing the defective parts." This is a recent insertion in order to make it clear that the underwriters are not obligated to pay the cost of replacing the defective part that is the cause of the loss.

Assignment. It has been pointed out that policies covering cargo are generally written so that the coverage may be assigned to other parties having an interest in the cargo. This is necessary in order to carry out the functions of ocean marine insurance on cargo in relation to commercial transactions.

[1]Insurance Co. v. Hamilton, 12 App. Cas. 484 (1887).

The situation is different with insurance on ships. The transfer of a ship to a new owner may result in a different and less desirable situation. Even though a ship may be insured in the name of an owner "for the account of whom it may concern," the policy usually provides that change of ownership or management cancels the coverage unless the underwriters agree to the change in writing.

In order to take care of special situations, there is a provision that in case of an involuntary temporary transfer by requisition or otherwise without the prior execution of a written agreement by the insured, the cancellation shall take place 15 days after the transfer. It is further provided that if the vessel has cargo on board and has already sailed from her loading port or is at sea in ballast, such cancellation shall be suspended until arrival at final port of discharge if with cargo or at port of destination if in ballast. A further provision is that the insurance shall not inure to the benefit of any such charterer or transferee, and if a loss becomes payable under a delayed cancellation, the underwriters are subrogated to all rights of the insured against the transferee.

WAR RISKS

War risks insurance is written on ships and on cargo aboard ships. This is feasible because the concentration of marine values, even those exposed to aerial bombardment in a port, is not nearly as high as the values of properties at locations in a large city.

The Lloyd's policy in its printed terms includes coverage against loss from "enemies, pirates, letters of mart and countermart, surprisals, takings at sea, arrests, restraints, and detainments of all kings, princes, and peoples of what nation, condition, or quality soever." More recently it has become customary to provide war risks insurance under a separate insurance policy from the regular ocean marine insurance policy on a ship or cargo. Therefore, it is customary to void the coverage just quoted by means of a "free of capture and seizure" clause (abbreviated F.C.&S. clause), which excludes loss from capture, seizure, arrest, restraint, detainment, or the taking of a vessel by requisition or otherwise, whether in time of peace or war and whether lawful or otherwise, and also from all losses resulting from hostilities or warlike actions.

The war risk insurance policy frequently is written in conjunction with the regular ocean marine insurance policy. The war risk policy on cargo usually refers to the marine policy, and includes by reference the terms regarding reports of shipments to be made to the underwriters.

The war risk policy provides that reports of shipments made under the marine policy mentioned are deemed to be reports under the war risk policy also. However, the war risk policy is specifically stated to be a separate contract. It is desirable wherever possible for the ocean marine policy and the war risk policy to be written through the same underwriters. Occasionally the exact cause of loss is doubtful. It may be difficult to determine whether the loss resulted from perils of the sea or from a war risk. If the ocean marine policy and war risk policy are written through the same underwriters, the loss will be paid to the insured without dispute as to whether war risks or perils of the sea caused the loss.

One of the reasons for developing a separate war risk insurance policy was the desire of marine insurance underwriters to avoid losses that might occur on land as a result of war risks. Recent wars have proved to be especially destructive to property on land, and especially to property at ports.

The war risk insurance policy provides coverage on cargo only if the property is loaded onto an overseas vessel, except that it covers against risks of floating or stationary mines and stray or derelict torpedoes when the property is loaded on a lighter, craft, or vessel. It would not apply to property on a wharf awaiting shipment. The goods are not covered after being discharged overside from an overseas vessel at the final port of discharge. The property is not covered beyond 15 days from arrival of the vessel at the final port of discharge even though the goods are still on board.

If the property is to be transferred to another vessel at some intermediate port, the war risk coverage expires after the original ship has been in the port for 15 days if the goods are still on board. The coverage attaches again as soon as the goods are loaded onto the on-carrying overseas vessel. During the 15 day period in which the coverage remains effective, it also applies to the goods while they are being transshipped to the on-carrying vessel.

Frustration. There may be many cargoes afloat at the outbreak of a war. Vessels may be unable to proceed to their ports of destination because of wartime conditions. Courts held that at the beginning of World War I the inability of a ship to make its intended port amounted to a frustration because of the war. The loss resulting from this frustration was covered if war risk insurance was provided by the policy. Ocean marine underwriters felt that this was not a loss intended to be covered. particularly when there was no actual damage to the cargo. As a result, the war risk insurance policy now contains a provision that the coverage is "warranted free from any claim based upon loss of, or frustration of, the insured voyage or adventure caused by arrests, restraints or detainments."

Frustration of a venture may result from perils other than war. There may be a closure of a canal such as has occurred with the Suez Canal. If the voyage is frustrated by perils insured against, there may be a claim against the insurers. Many complications can arise. The loss of the venture may result in a constructive total loss of the cargo even though the cargo may not be physically damaged.

Confiscation. It is not intended that the war risks insurance cover confiscation by a supposedly friendly government, but the coverage is limited to loss resulting from belligerent governments. In order to make this point clear, the war risk insurance policy may also contain a provision that the policy does not cover loss resulting from "commandeering, requisition or nationalization by the government (de facto or otherwise) of a country to or from which the goods are insured, or from seizure or destruction under quarantine or customs regulations."

Government Assistance in Providing War Risk Insurance. Some of the war risks insurance on hulls was provided by governments rather than by commercial underwriters during actual hostilities of World War II. The amount of war risk insurance available through underwriters often was not enough to cover the values at risk in one locality or on a particular group of ships. The United States government through the United States Maritime Administration supplemented the capacity of the private insurers in connection with war risk insurance.

Cancellation on Short Notice. It is customary for underwriters to retain the privilege of canceling war risks insurance on short notice. War risks insurance policies usually provide for cancellation which may be on 48 hours, 7 days, or 14 days notice, depending on circumstances and the desires of underwriters. Many ocean marine insurance policies contain an automatic termination clause under which war risks insurance is automatically cancelled within 48 hours if war breaks out between certain countries specified in the policies. Such cancellation notices or automatic termination provisions ordinarily do not affect property already at sea. Property at sea may be covered until it reaches the next port of call, or until it reaches its final destination, depending upon the exact provisions of the ocean marine insurance policy.

War risks insurance on ships ordinarily is written for short terms. War risks insurance policies covering cargo may be written to cover the cargo while waterborne for the same period as the ocean marine insurance policy with which the war risks policy is associated. Ocean marine insurance underwriters do not like to be committed to carry war risks coverage for long periods. International conditions change rapidly. Development of nuclear weapons of war affects the chances of widespread destruction. War risks insurance rates fluctuate widely as conditions change. Short-term policies and the privilege of cancellation on short notice are considered necessary so that underwriters may secure rates commensurate with the war risk if the risk is insurable.

STRIKE, RIOT, AND CIVIL COMMOTION INSURANCE

Marine underwriters have not been greatly concerned about damage to hulls from strikes, riot, and civil commotion. The chances of loss from these perils are mostly from fire while the ship is in port. The marine insurance policy does not specifically mention the perils of strike, riot, and civil commotion, but fire damage resulting from these perils would be covered under the fire insurance of the policy. Loss by fire to ships in port from strikes, riot, or civil commotion has been considered as insurable.

The situation is very different in regard to ships under construction or in dry dock or otherwise in port for an extended period of time. A marine port risk policy or a policy on ships under construction will exclude damage by strikes, riot, or civil commotion unless a substantial additional premium is paid. Insurance on yachts may exclude damage by strike, riot, or civil commotion because yachts usually spend a larger portion of their time in port and are more likely to be subject to these hazards.

Cargo insurance policies generally are warranted free of loss or damage caused by or resulting from strikes, lockouts, labor disturbances, riots, civil commotion, or the acts of any person or persons taking part in any such occurrence or disorder. Cargo may be exposed to such losses while in port, or while in transit to or from the port under the warehouse to warehouse coverage. Strike, riot, and civil commotion coverage may be written on cargo but at an additional premium. This coverage as usually written applies to physical damage to the cargo only, and does not cover delay, loss of market, or extra expense which may be necessary to unload or transship cargo because of the situation. Such consequential loss coverage might be written at an appropriate additional premium if an underwriter is willing to write it. Sometimes there is a question as to whether a particular loss is from riot or from rebellion. Rebellion is covered under a war risk policy but not under the strike, riot, and civil commotion coverage.

Marine insurance policies covering riot, strike, and civil commotion damage in the United States and some other parts of the Western hemisphere also may cover loss due to theft, pilferage, breakage, or destruction caused by vandalism, sabotage, and malicious mischief. This includes such losses directly caused by acts committed by an agent of a government engaged in war or hostilities if the agent is acting secretly and not in connection with a recognized military or naval operation.

Cancellation provisions are similar to the coverage on war risks. The coverage against loss from strike, riot, and civil commotion usually may be canceled upon notice to the insured.

CANCELLATION

There is no standard cancellation clause in ocean marine insurance except that in connection with war risks and riot insurance just described. In open cargo policies that do not have a termination date, or in time policies that run for a specified term, it is customary to provide for cancellation by either party upon 30 days notice to the other party. Cancellation clauses usually provide that the cancellation shall not affect any risk on which the insurance has attached prior to the effective date of the cancellation notice. This means that if a cargo is already at sea, or otherwise under the policy's protection, such cargo is covered until it is delivered to the point where the insurance would otherwise terminate.

A policy that covers a specific voyage may be written without provision for cancellation.

Marine underwriters feel that privilege for immediate cancellation is not important in connection with perils of the sea because they do not change materially from year to year. This is in contrast to the danger of war risks, or strike, riot, and civil commotion risks, which may increase tremendously within a matter of days.

WARRANTIES EXPRESSED IN THE POLICY

The premium for an ocean marine insurance policy is based upon the hazards to which the ship or cargo is expected to be subject. Marine hazards vary greatly from one part of the world to another and at different seasons of the year. The type of cargo, the type of ship and its equipment, the crew, and the state of international affairs are all considered by the ocean marine insurance underwriter in deciding how much to charge for an ocean marine insurance policy. Underwriters must maintain as much control as possible over hazards that may be changed by acts of the insured. This control is exercised by warranties in the ocean marine insurance policy. These warranties constitute agreements between the insured and the underwriters regarding conditions affecting the ship and the insurance.

Cargo insurance policies do not contain warranties concerning matters over which the shipper would have no control. There may be a provision for the payment of an extra premium in case a ship carrying the insured cargo does something or proceeds by a route that increases the hazard of the cargo.

Trading warranties are important in the insuring of ships. A trading warranty specifies the geographical area within which a ship may operate. The trading warranty may vary from one limiting the ship to a named port, or coastal service, to broad limits permitting worldwide trade. Trading warranties on policies covering ships operating on the Great Lakes and in some other areas usually restrict operation to the open season of navigation. A trading warranty sometimes is written to permit operation beyond the specified limits, but with a requirement that extra premium be paid if the ship does go beyond the limits.

Another warranty found in ocean marine insurance policies on ships specifies the amount of insurance permitted. The ocean marine insurance policy on a ship usually is a valued policy. It is important that the amount of insurance be kept within the actual value of the ship so that the owners will not be tempted to have the ship destroyed in order to make a profit.

Warranties on ocean marine insurance policies must be complied with literally. The breach is considered to void the insurance even though the breach of warranty did not cause or aggravate the loss.

Sometimes an insured will find that it will be difficult or impossible to comply with a warranty. He can give notice to the underwriters, and they may be willing to give permission for the breach of warranty. This situation could develop if it becomes necessary for the ship to change course, or to take on a different cargo, or otherwise change its operations from those contemplated at the time the insurance policy was written.

Many of the exclusions in an ocean marine insurance policy are expressed as warranties. The expression "warranted free from" is used preceding a description of a hazard not intended to be covered by the policy. The war risks exclusion clause states: "This insurance is warranted free from any claim for loss . . . ," followed by a list of the war hazards which are not intended to be covered. The same effect can be obtained by an exclusion stating that the insurance policy does not cover loss from the hazards listed. The use of exclusions rather than warranties has become the practice with inland marine insurance in contrast to that with ocean marine.

IMPLIED WARRANTIES

There are implied warranties in addition to the warranties expressed as provisions of an ocean marine insurance policy. These implied warranties are recognized by the courts and are just as binding upon the insured and the underwriters as if they were expressed in the policy.

Seaworthiness. The insured under an ocean marine insurance policy warrants by implication that the ship is seaworthy at the beginning of the voyage. The implied warranty of seaworthiness is applied strictly, but sometimes it is difficult to verify compliance. A ship may leave port in apparently good condition, but something may develop to indicate that it was not seaworthy. It is then a question of fact to be determined from the available evidence whether or not the ship was seaworthy when it left port. The English Marine Insurance Act of 1906 states: "A ship is deemed to be seaworthy when she is reasonably fit in all respects to encounter the ordinary perils of the sea of the adventure insured."

The mere fact that a ship sinks is not prima facie evidence of unseaworthiness. The sinking may have been the result of some unusual action of the wind or the waves, or the result of some other insured peril. The overloading of a ship so that it settled below the load line mark painted on the side of the vessel might support a charge of unseaworthiness. It might also be proved that a ship went to sea with inadequate fuel or provisions, or with engines known to be in questionable condition.

Changing conditions are bringing about some modifications in the application of the implied warranty of seaworthiness. There has been a relaxation of the warranty in ocean marine insurance policies covering fleets of ships, and particularly with time policies written to cover from one date to another date. Vessels covered under a time policy are likely to be at sea when the insurance policy becomes effective. It may be impossible for the owner or operator to determine at that moment whether or not each vessel in the fleet is seaworthy.

There has also been a relaxation of the seaworthiness warranty in connection with marine insurance policies covering loss to cargo. Many shippers of cargo have no idea what ship will carry the cargo, and they have little or no opportunity to determine whether the ship is seaworthy. Insurance policies covering loss to cargo usually agree that seaworthiness is admitted between the shipper and the underwriters. This admission of seaworthiness is not used in the event that the cargo is being shipped by a vessel chartered to the shipper, or under other circumstances in which the shipper can determine whether the ship is seaworthy.

Legality. The legality of the venture is warranted by implication in connection with all ocean marine insurance policies. Insurance purchased to cover an illegal venture, such as smuggling, would be void. The venture must be legal in the country under whose laws the ship operates and under any international agreements or treaties made by that country. The implied warranty of legality does not contemplate that the venture must be legal under the laws of every country in the world.

It is considered to be against public policy for underwriters to protect a person against loss in some illegal enterprise. This is the only one of the implied warranties which cannot be waived by agreement between the underwriters and the insured.

Implied warranty of no delay. When the insurance applies to a particular voyage or venture, it is assumed that the voyage will start within a reasonable time. Underwriters base their premium and acceptance of risk on existing conditions. If the voyage is delayed, there may be a change in weather (a different season of the year), a change in international conditions, or some other change that would increase the hazard. Under these conditions the underwriters may contend that the coverage is void because the implied warranty of no delay has been breached. This warranty does not apply to time policies. Policies written for a specified period of time cover all operations of the insured during the term specified.

Implied warranty of no deviation. An ocean marine policy is issued upon the assumption that there will be no deviation from the most direct or the customary route for the voyage insured. Deviation was discussed previously in this text.

The warranty usually would have no effect on a time policy in which all operations of the insured during the term of the insurance policy are covered. Cargo insurance policies usually contain a deviation waiver clause which permits deviations because the shipper has no control over the course of the vessel. Usually the shipper is required to notify the underwriters if he learns of a deviation, and to pay any additional premium that may be required because of additional risk incurred as a result of the deviation.

SUBROGATION

The right of subrogation is important to ocean marine insurance underwriters. The insurance policy is a contract of indemnity. If the underwriters pay a loss, they acquire any right of recovery that the insured may have against a third person responsible for the loss. Underwriters may depend upon their common law right of subrogation as the party at interest in recovering the amount of the loss. Ocean marine insurance policies may contain an agreement under which the insured is obligated to assign all rights to the underwriters for the amount paid, and under which the insured agrees to cooperate in the recovery of any amount paid by the underwriters.

Recovery is most likely to be effective if there has been negligence on the part of a third party. Negligence on the part of the operators of another ship may result in a recovery from that ship owner or the underwriters insuring it.

Subrogation recoveries of cargo losses are most likely to be made from carriers. Ocean marine insurance policies frequently cover during land transportation under warehouse to warehouse clauses. Recovery is more likely from land carriers because land carriers generally have more extensive liability for goods in their custody than ocean carriers.

Cargo policies usually carry a warranty that the insurance shall not inure, directly or indirectly, to the benefit of any carrier or bailee. For a discussion of the reasons for this clause and its effect upon recovery from carriers, see the "no benefit to bailee" clause in connection with inland marine insurance later in this text.

OTHER INSURANCE–DOUBLE INSURANCE

Ocean marine insurance practices differ from those in connection with other types of property insurance when there is overinsurance. In the United States if there is double insurance, the ocean marine insurance policy with the earliest effective date is considered the primary insurance. Another policy with a subsequent effective date is liable for coverage only if the first policy is insufficient in amount to take care of the loss. The "other insurance" provisions read in part: "In case the interest hereby insured is covered by other insurance (except as hereinafter provided) the loss shall be collected from the several policies in the order of date of their attachment, insurance attaching on the same date to be deemed simultaneous and to contribute pro rata." The provision is further made that if certain types of insurance taken out by a carrier or bailee are available to the beneficiary, then the insurance of the policy in question shall not contribute to such a loss.

The English practice is different. In case of double insurance under English policies, each underwriter or group of underwriters is liable for the full amount of its policy. The insured may collect from any one of his insurers that he chooses, but he cannot collect more than his loss. The other insurers are then liable to the insurer that paid the loss for their pro rata share of the loss.

It should be noted that double insurance does not exist if there are policies covering the same property but for different interests. It is considered double insurance only if there is more than one policy on the same property and for the same interest. Double insurance does not happen frequently in ocean marine insurance. Policies usually are negotiated on a valued basis so that the amounts of insurance are carefully determined.

UNDERINSURANCE

It is a principle of ocean marine insurance that if the insured does not have sufficient insurance, he is considered to be carrying a portion of the risk himself and he will contribute his share toward any partial loss that occurs. Underinsurance may occur if the amount of insurance is not equal to the agreed value of the property as expressed in the insurance policy. The principle is expressed in the English Marine Insurance Act of 1906 as follows:

> Where the assured is insured for an amount less than the insurable value or, in the case of a valued policy, for an amount less than the policy valuation, he is deemed to be his own insurer in respect of the uninsured balance.

QUESTIONS

1. Why is it an acceptable practice to use valued policies in ocean marine insurance to a greater extent than in other types of property insurance?

2. Contrast the effect of insuring a vessel "lost or not lost" with fire insurance that is written to cover a property which has been destroyed without the knowledge of either the insured or the insurance company.
3. What would be considered a deviation in the voyage of a ship and what would be the effect of a deviation on the insurance?
4. What are perils of the sea?
5. Explain why fire is or is not considered to be a peril of the sea.
6. Is pilferage or theft by stealth covered by an ocean marine insurance policy which covers loss from thieves?
7. Distinguish between piracy and barratry.
8. Explain the principle of *ejusdem generis.*
9. Explain the purpose of the "sue and labor" clause, and distinguish between sue and labor expenses and general average expenses.
10. What is the "Inchmaree" clause? Describe its origin.
11. How is the insurance of war risks handled in ocean marine insurance?
12. Explain the importance of warranties, and the difference between express and implied warranties.
13. What implied warranty cannot be waived by agreement between the insured and the underwriters? Describe how you would determine whether this warranty had been breached in a particular case.
14. What are the differences between American and English practices in the adjustment of losses where there is double insurance?
15. Under what circumstances would ocean marine underwriters anticipate recoveries under their subrogation rights?

4

Ocean Marine Insurance Coverages

HULL INSURANCE POLICIES

The Hull of a Ship. Under a literal definition, the hull of a ship consists merely of the basic structure without equipment, machinery, or furnishings, but hull insurance is written to cover much more than the bare hull. A typical hull insurance policy wording lists the property insured as the "hull, tackle, apparel, passenger fittings, equipment, stores, ordnance, munitions, boats and other furniture." Donkey boilers, winches, cranes, windlasses, and steering gear are considered part of the hull for insurance purposes and not as machinery.

Machinery providing power for operating the vessel and for lighting, heating, and cooling usually is listed in the insurance policy separately from the hull. A typical listing is "Boilers, machinery, refrigerating machinery and insulation, motor generators and other electrical machinery, and everything connected therewith."

The hull item and the machinery item may be valued separately in the insurance policy, or there may be a single blanket valuation and amount of insurance covering both items. A hull policy does not cover cargo, nor the personal effects of the passengers, officers, or crew.

General Types of Hull Insurance Policies. Hull insurance policies written to cover during operation of the ships are called "navigation" policies. Those policies may be written to cover during voyages between ports specified in the policy or may be written to cover for a period of time specified in the policy.

"Port risk" policies may be written to cover ships laid up in port and not subject to navigation hazards. Hull insurance policies may also be written to cover vessels during construction; these are called "builders' risk" policies.

Hull insurance policies may be written to cover individual ships or to cover fleets of ships. The different ships in a fleet may be owned by different corporations in order to limit the liability of the owners in case of liability claims by third parties. All of the ships under the same operation may be insured under a fleet policy even though there is diverse ownership.

Builders' Risk Insurance. Builders' risk insurance is written to cover a ship from the time the keel is laid in the shipyard until the ship is accepted by its owners. The insurance covers land construction risks before launching and marine risks after launching.

The builders' risk policy covers marine perils similar to other ocean marine insurance policies. In addition, it covers:

> All risks, including fire, while under construction and/or fitting out, including materials in buildings, workshops, yards and docks of the insured, or on quays, pontoons, craft, etc., and all risks while in transit to and from the works and/or the vessel wherever she may be lying, also all risks of loss or damage through collapse of supports or ways from any cause whatsoever, and all risks of launching and breakage of the ways.

The insurance covers during trial trips while loaded or otherwise. Usually the insurance policy includes a warranty that trials will be conducted within 100 nautical miles of the place of construction. If the trial trips must be conducted beyond a distance of 100 miles, the ship is still insured, but an additional rate is charged. Policies covering vessels of war give permission to fire guns and torpedoes, but there is no coverage for damage due to the firing of guns or torpedoes unless the accident results in the total loss of the vessel.

The builders' risk insurance policy covers loss that may result from settling of the land upon which the ship is being built, or from collapse of supports. It also covers damage resulting from launching or from failure to launch. The launching of a ship is a ticklish proposition, and an accident during launching may damage the ship seriously. Should the ship fail to launch, the additional cost of getting her into the water may be substantial.

The ocean marine builders' risk insurance policy does more than insure against loss from accidental occurrence. It is in the nature of a guarantee of the materials used in the construction. If latent defects in materials appear during trial runs, this policy covers the cost of replacing the defective parts unless the loss results from lack of due diligence on the part of the builder or owner. The insuring of warships may be particularly hazardous. For example, should a submarine fail to rise after submersion, the underwriters would be responsible for raising the submarine and putting it in satisfactory operating condition.

It is customary for builders' risk insurance policies to contain an F.C.&S. clause and to exclude damage by strikers and locked-out workmen. These risks may be covered at additional premium if the underwriters are willing to assume the risk. The policy ordinarily contains a negligence clause and a protection and indemnity clause. Builders' risk policies do not provide workmen's compensation or employers' liability coverage, nor do they cover earthquake damage, consequential loss, or loss from delay.

The premium for a builders' risk insurance policy is calculated upon the total value at risk upon completion of the vessel. Usually there is a time limit in the policy during which the insurance is effective. If the vessel is completed within that time, there may be a refund of a portion of the premium.

After launching and prior to acceptance of the completed vessel by the owners, the builders' risk underwriters would pay their proportion of any loss according to the amount of insurance and the completed value of the ship. There may be other insurance for a portion of the value, or a portion of the value may be uninsured.

Port Risks. Vessels may be idle for considerable periods of time or may be in port for repairs. It is customary under these circumstances to arrange insurance on a port risk basis. Inasmuch as there is little navigation hazard, the rates are lower than if the ship were operating at sea.

Usually the port risk insurance policy specifies the port in which the vessel is located, but privilege may be given for the vessel to change docks or to go into dry dock. Coverage during the lay-up period in port usually is broad, and may approach the builders' risk policy in the extent of coverage. The premium may be based upon a monthly rate, or on an annual rate, depending upon the expected length of lay-up. If a policy is written on an annual basis, and the port risk is canceled before the expiration, the earned premium is calculated according to a short rate table. If ships are moored in an open roadstead subject to collision from other vessels, the insurance premium may be as high as for a ship in navigation.

Navigation Policies. Most hull insurance policies are of the navigation type and cover the vessel during operation. Current practice is to write such policies on a time basis, usually for a period of one year. Ocean marine time policies continue to cover at expiration any vessel still at sea, in distress, or at a port of refuge or call. The vessel is covered at a pro rata monthly premium to her port of destination, provided notice has been given to the underwriters. This is a reasonable provision because new underwriters who may be taking over the insurance would not care to assume liability for a vessel at sea, in distress, or otherwise in questionable circumstances. Continuing the coverage until the vessel reaches port permits new underwriters to assume the coverage under known circumstances.

Ocean marine insurance policies may be written to cover during a specified voyage. The voyage policy is used mostly to cover ships during ventures that are specially hazardous, or if a ship is operating irregularly and without established routes. Insurance on a voyage basis gives the underwriters an opportunity to calculate the premium in accordance with the hazards of the particular venture.

Valuation. Two valuations of a ship may be used for insurance purposes. One valuation is the amount which the insured could recover in case the vessel is lost, and a second valuation is for the purpose of distributing partial losses. In many cases the insurance policy shows two valuations for the vessel, one for a total loss and the other for partial loss.

Factors taken into account in determining the value of a ship are the replacement cost of the vessel, its age and condition, the market value if the ship were sold, the amount of net freight that it could earn during its remaining lifetime, and the scrap value when it is broken up at the end of its useful life. In the case of new vessels for which there is an active market, the valuation for insurance purposes may be close to the replacement cost. In the case of ships for which there is little demand, the valuation for total loss purposes may be the market value of the vessel without regard to its replacement cost. It is important that the valuation for total loss purposes be set at a figure that will not encourage the owner to seek the destruction of the vessel.

Repair costs for partial losses may be high in relation to the market value of the ship. It is customary with older vessels to set a higher value for partial loss purposes than for total loss. An example will show the application of such a case. It is assumed that the replacement cost of a ship is $500,000. Its market value may be only $400,000, which is the amount underwriters would be willing to pay in case of a total loss. However, the cost of repairs would be in relation to the $500,000 replacement cost of the vessel. Therefore, the valuation for total loss purposes may be set at $400,000, whereas the valuation for partial losses would be set at a figure close to $500,000. Underwriters would then take a percentage of the $400,000 for total loss purposes and a percentage of the $500,000 for partial loss purposes. For example, if a particular group of underwriters took 25 percent of the insurance, they would issue an insurance policy for $100,000 for total loss purposes and for $125,000 for partial loss purposes. They would pay 25 percent of a total loss in case the ship were lost, and would pay 25 percent of the insurance contribution toward a partial loss. The balance of the valuation might be covered by other insurance, or might remain uninsured. If a portion of the valuation were uninsured, then the owner of the vessel would have to stand that part of any total or partial loss.

General average, salvage, or sue and labor charges are assessed according to the actual value of the ship. The insurer is obliged to pay the full amount of any such charges for which it is liable if the ship is insured for its actual value. The insured would have to contribute to these charges in proportion to the underinsurance if the ship is underinsured.

Franchise and Deductible Clauses. Most hull insurance policies include a franchise or a deductible clause applying to particular average (partial loss). A 3 percent or 5 percent franchise is commonly used on hull policies, usually subject to a maximum dollar limitation beyond which the underwriters pay, even though the loss has not reached the percentage specified. Deductibles may be in percentages, or they may be in amounts of from $500 to many thousands of dollars, depending upon the size of the ship and the willingness of the underwriters to pay partial losses.

"Thirds-off"–New for Old. The principle of "thirds-off" is a depreciation principle. Originally it was an arbitrary method of deducting from the loss an amount the insured was to stand due to depreciation. Replacement of new wood for old in a sailing vessel was supposed to improve the condition of the vessel. The insured was expected to stand a third of the cost in making the repair. Much hull insurance is written today without the deduction of "thirds," which is a way of saying that new material is used to replace old in the repair of damage to a vessel without any deduction for depreciation.

Total Loss Only. Occasionally an older ship or one that is engaged in a hazardous undertaking will be insured against total loss only. The insured is responsible for the repair of any partial losses to his ship regardless of extent, and can collect from the insurance company or underwriters only if there is a total loss or a constructive total loss.

Disbursements Warranty–Increased Value Insurance. The disbursements warranty is a clause relating to other insurance. It specifies the percentages of other insurance that may be purchased to cover intangible risks in addition to the coverage on the hull. A typical disbursements warranty permits not more than 25 percent of the insured value of the ship as additional insurance on disbursements, manager's commissions, profits, excess or increased value of hull or machinery, similar interests, and freight insured for time. Freight for hire, charter hire, insurance premiums, and similar amounts at risk may be covered under other insurance only for the percentages specified in the disbursements warranty.

The principal use of an Increased Value policy is where the ship is insured for less than its actual value. This would cover general average, salvage, or sue and labor expenses that might be assessed against the insured because of underinsurance. Excess collision liabilities may be covered for those rare cases where the actual collision liabilities are in excess of the insured value in the hull policy.

Fleet Policies. Fleets of ships usually are insured under policies that cover the entire fleet. Underwriters are more willing to insure older and less desirable ships when they form part of a fleet containing newer and better ships. A large fleet may be insured by several different insurance companies and groups of underwriters. All the insurance policies are identical and they all list the ships in the fleet. The different policies assume percentages of the insurance, and the underwriters receive proportionate shares of the premium and pay their proportionate shares of any losses.

Collision Liability. Ocean marine insurance is primarily a property loss coverage protecting the parties interested in a vessel against loss of the property. It is customary to include a limited third-party liability coverage in the same policy. Most hull insurance policies include a collision clause or "running down" clause which provides a measure of third-party property damage liability insurance.

If a ship is operated negligently and the property of others is damaged as a result, the owner or operator of the ship may be held liable for the damage. The collision or running down clause protects the ship operator or owner against loss resulting from his liability for damage to another vessel, for damage to cargo in another vessel, for loss of freight charges, or for loss to the owner of another vessel due to losing the use of his ship. Insurance under the running down clause usually does not cover liability for damage to piers, wharves, or other structures, or for loss of life or personal injury, nor does it cover any loss to the insured ship or its cargo.

The liability of a ship owner or operator for damage to property as a result of collision is limited in varying degrees by the size or value of the ship upon which the negligence rests. Under United States maritime laws, the liability for personal injury or loss of life ordinarily is limited to $60 per gross ton weight of the offending vessel. This is in marked contrast to the unlimited liability which may be applicable in case of personal injury, death, or property damage claims on land.

The insurance under the collision clause is in addition to the amount of insurance on the ship. It provides collision coverage up to the amount of insurance on the vessel and in addition to that insurance. Thus in the case of a total loss to the insured ship and its liability to another ship following a collision, the underwriters could be liable for twice the amount of coverage on the insured ship.

There are many complications that can arise in the settling of claims under the collision clause. If both ships are to blame for the collision, there are provisions for a proration of the damages to the two ships. Basically in such cases the ship with the greater liability will pay the difference between the respective liabilities of the two ships.

It is customary in covering collision liability on a fleet policy to add a "sister ship" clause. This provides that if two ships of the same fleet or belonging to the same owner are involved in a collision, the damages shall be assessed the same as if the two vessels were separately owned and separately insured. This differs from liability insurance coverage on land vehicles. If two land vehicles of the same owner are in collision, the owner cannot collect from his insurance company under his liability insurance coverage because he was negligent to himself.

Protection and Indemnity Insurance. It has been pointed out that the collision or running down clause provides only a measure of property damage liability coverage. Further liability coverage is provided by Protection and Indemnity Insurance, colloquially called "P. and I." coverage. This is a third-party personal injury and property damage liability insurance. The collision or running down clause forms a part of many ocean marine insurance policies. The protection and indemnity coverage in contrast usually is provided under a separate insurance policy. The only common exception to this is in yacht policies. Yacht policies as usually issued in the United States include the protection and indemnity coverage.

The P. and I. coverage protects against a wide range of possible liabilities which might be costly to the insured. This includes damage to property such as a ship other than what would be covered by the collision clause; property on another ship; property other than on a ship, such as goods on a wharf or in a harbor, a dock, cable, bridge, or other fixed or moveable object. Also covered is liability for the cost of raising, destroying, or removing the wreck if the ship is sunk and has to be removed. Liability for loss of life or personal injury is covered howsoever and to whomever the same may be caused as well as any liability for salvage. Also covered is liability for fines of any state or country for violation of its laws. This usually is subject to a deductible. Liability for disinfecting the ship and for quarantine expenses are covered, also usually subject to a deductible. Provision is also made for the payment of certain costs in resisting claims. The liability coverage is very broad and is comparable to the third-party liability coverage which a businessman would secure for operations on land. Liabilities to passengers and crewman for personal injuries or death are covered. Liability for damage to cargo on board the ship is covered.

The amount of coverage usually is the same as the insurance on the ship. This is adequate in those cases where the ship owner is permitted to limit his liability to the value of the ship. Such limitation of liability, however, is dependent upon a lack of privity, or knowledge, on the part of the owner. In the case of a yacht owner who may be on board or actually operating the yacht himself, he could not claim an absence of privity in case of accident. He may be liable for much more than the value of his ship. Even in the case of a yacht owner who is not on board and where his ship is being operated by a hired master and crew, there may be privity on his part. The yacht owner may need protection for much higher limits than the value of his ship. This can be provided by Excess Protection and Indemnity insurance. The yacht policy may provide this as separate and higher limits of liability in much the same way that an automobile liability policy may show specified liability limits. In the case of a commercial vessel these higher limits may be provided by a separate insurance policy.

Protection and Indemnity Insurance and Seaworthiness. The P. & I. coverage, as already pointed out, indemnifies the insured for his liability for loss of life or personal injury howsoever and to whomsoever caused. This is generally considered to be a negligence liability coverage. As to many persons who might be on board a ship, the ship owner would be liable for personal injury or death only in the event that the ship owner was negligent. However, the doctrine of warranty of seaworthiness states that the ship owner is under an absolute duty to provide a seaman with a seaworthy ship. If a seaman is injured on board a ship because of an unseaworthy condition, the ship owner is liable for the injury. In recent years this has been expanded to others who may be performing duties that traditionally have been performed by seamen. Its greatest impact has been in connection with longshoremen. The loading and unloading of a ship is traditionally the work of the crew even though this is rarely done by the crew under modern conditions in the United States. The warranty of seaworthiness to the crew extends to the longshoremen who load and unload the cargo. Therefore, if a longshoreman is injured because of some unseaworthy condition of the ship, even though there is no negligence on the part of the ship owner, the longshoreman can collect damages for his injury. It has even been held by a court that it constitutes unseaworthiness if the ship owner provides too few men to do a particular job and the longshoreman is injured in an accident that can be attributed to the fact that too few men were supplied for the job.

Longshoremen's and Harbor Workers' Compensation Act. An act of the United States Congress known as the Longshoremen's and Harbor Workers' Act requires workmen's compensation coverage for all employees in maritime employment on the navigable waters of the United States including drydocks, with the exception of the master or crew of any vessel, and persons unloading or repairing vessels of less than 18 tons. This coverage is normally written under a workmen's compensation policy. It is mentioned here because it is permissible to write this coverage as part of an ocean marine policy. The only case where this ordinarily is done is on a yacht policy. The owner of a yacht may not have any other reason for a workmen's compensation policy, and particularly no other reason to provide coverage under the Longshoremen's and Harbor Workers' Compensation Act. It is a convenience for the yacht owner who may have no other exposure to a claim under this act to have the coverage on his yacht policy. Among the miscellaneous employments which have been ruled as being employed in maritime employment are a machinist repairing a launch, a rigger making ready a vessel for a voyage, and the scraping and painting of a ship while tied up at a wharf. It can be seen that the yacht owner may be exposed to this liability. As long as he may hire someone to work on his boat even when tied up, he may have an exposure. This coverage on the yacht policy is desirable.

CARGO INSURANCE

Ocean marine insurance on cargo is now written separately from insurance on hulls. Many years ago the owner of a ship often traded in goods and carried his own property to foreign ports. Insurance on ship and cargo might have been written under the same policy. Today the owners and operators of ships are mostly carriers who carry the goods of other people. Even in the case of those who own and operate their own fleets of ships, such as petroleum companies, the hull and cargo insurance are written separately under policies specially designed to provide exactly the insurance desired.

It has already been pointed out that the liability of a ship owner or operator for loss of cargo is limited in comparison to the liability of a carrier of goods by land. The shipper of cargo by sea has a compelling reason to carry insurance to protect himself from loss or damage because his chances of collecting from the carrier for a cargo loss are limited.

Cargoes may be insured for a particular voyage or they may be insured under open policies which are in the nature of reporting form policies. The choice of an open policy or a voyage policy depends upon the volume and regularity with which a shipper has occasion to use ocean transit. Coverage under either form of policy can be arranged to meet the needs of the insured.

Coverage of a cargo policy may be provided in the quaint language of "Touching the adventures and perils which the said company is contented to bear and does take upon itself," or, in more modern wording, "against all risks of physical loss of or damage to the property insured from any external cause." Further provisions and exceptions are intended to grant essentially the same coverage in either case. A Free of Capture and Seizure clause excludes war risk. War risks may be covered separately at an extra premium. War risk policies usually are subject to cancellation on 48 hours notice except that such cancellation does not apply to property to which risk has already attached. If a cargo has been shipped and has left port, the coverage continues on that cargo until it reaches its destination.

Loss from strikes, riots, and civil commotion usually are excluded but may be added by endorsement. A 48-hour cancellation provision usually applies to this coverage similarly to the war risk coverage. Losses from delay, loss of market, and inherent vice, and losses from such causes as dampness, change of flavor, or becoming moldy, are excluded.

Additional perils which may be covered are theft and pilferage, or contamination from other cargo. The coverage of the marine policy against loss from thieves was intended to mean "assailing thieves," which in today's language would be equivalent to robbery or burglary. Underwriters have not liked to provide coverage against theft and pilferage, but modern demands of commerce have forced them to provide this coverage in many cases.

Most cargo policies are subject to a Free of Particular Average (franchise or deductible) clause. This may provide that the insurance is free of particular average except loss from stranding, sinking, or burning, or it may provide free of particular average above a specified percentage or dollar amount.

Provision is made for contribution to general average, sue and labor charges, and salvage awards. There may be circumstances in case of a collision when both ships are to blame where cargo would be subject to a contribution charge. This usually is covered under the cargo insurance.

Extended Cover or Marine Extension Clauses. The insurance also covers during deviation, delay, forced discharge, or reshipment because the voyage is terminated. This does not cover any loss which results from the deviation or delay but merely continues coverage during the extra time or other method of shipment to the destination. These marine extension clauses are intended to protect the insured from loss when there is some interference with the normal transit which is beyond his control. An additional premium may or may not be required for such delay or transshipment, depending upon the terms of the policy. These extensions of coverage usually are included in the transit provisions of the warehouse to warehouse clause.

An interesting form of loss which is paid in connection with cotton shipments is called "country damage." This damage is not really the result of marine perils but is damage that occurs while the cotton is still on land and often in unprotected locations. Cotton often is not baled properly, and the weather may cause deterioration of the cotton. Marine insurance underwriters have paid such losses, originally perhaps because it was impossible to determine just where the loss occurred, and it is now customary for "country damage" to be covered under ocean marine insurance policies.

On-deck Cargo. It seems obvious that cargo on deck is subject to greater damage than cargo stowed in a protected location beneath deck. Originally cargo on deck was not considered a proper risk, and many cargo insurance underwriters refused to insure it. Under modern conditions it is not always possible for the insured to know whether his cargo is safely stowed beneath deck or whether it is on deck. A customary clause in open cargo insurance policies provides that particular average will not be paid on cargo above deck unless loss is caused by the vessel being stranded, sunk, burnt, on fire, in collision or by jettison or washing overboard. However, if the cargo is shipped on deck without the knowledge and consent of the shipper, it shall then be treated as under-deck cargo as far as the insured is concerned. This is a considerable liberalization over earlier ocean marine insurance policy terms. The carrier should be held responsible for loss of the goods if he does carry them on deck without the consent of the shipper.

Valuation. Cargo insurance policies usually provide a method of determining the value of the cargo for insurance purposes. If the coverage is upon a specific cargo, the policy may set an agreed valuation, which will be paid if the cargo is lost in transit. In connection with open cargo insurance policies, it is customary to provide for valuation based upon the amount of invoice. A typical valuation clause provides that "the value of shipment insured under this policy shall be the amount of invoice, including all charges therein plus any prepaid or advances or guaranteed freight not included in the invoice, plus" a percentage to be inserted, usually about 10 percent. The added amount above the invoice cost is intended to take care of the additional value of the cargo to the insured at the destination. The percentage inserted in the valuation clause depends upon the circumstances of the shipment, the type of merchandise, and the anticipated value at the destination.

The shipping of goods in containers or loaded onto pallets has raised questions as to valuations and losses on property in such containers. The Carriage of Goods by Sea Act provides for a limitation of $500 per package or customary freight unit unless a higher value has been declared by the shipper. There is a question as to whether this limitation should apply to the large container in which many boxes or packages are placed, or on the individual box or package within the container. The problem can be resolved as to a particular shipment by a declaration of the value by the shipper which shows its actual value when it is more than $500 for the entire container. The insurance implications of this situation relate largely to cases where the insurer has a chance of subrogation from a carrier after a loss occurs. The carrier's insurer would be benefited by the limitation whereas the shipper's insurer would find itself restricted as to the amount that could be recovered from the carrier.

Warehouse to Warehouse Clause. A large proportion of ocean cargoes originate at points away from the ports of shipment and are destined for places many miles from ports where they are discharged from the ships. It has become customary for ocean marine underwriters to endorse their policies to cover cargo from the point of origin to the destination. This provides coverage during the land portion of the transportation as well as during the overseas transportation. The endorsement used for this purpose is called the "warehouse to warehouse" clause, and it is in practically every ocean marine policy covering cargo shipped in packages. A typical warehouse to warehouse clause, with related transit clauses, reads as follows:

A. This insurance attaches from the time the goods leave the warehouse or place of storage at the place named in the certificate, declaration or special policy for the commencement of the transit and continues until:

1. the goods are delivered to the Consignee's or other final warehouse or place of storage at the destination named in the certificate, declaration or special policy, or

2. the goods are delivered to any other warehouse or place of storage, whether prior to or at the destination named in the certificate, declaration or special policy, which the Assured elects to use either

(a) for storage other than in the ordinary course of transit, or
(b) for allocation or distribution, or

3. the expiry of 60 days (30 days on air shipments) after completion of discharge from the overseas vessel or aircraft, whichever shall first occur.

In the event of delay in excess of the limits specified in (3) above arising from circumstances beyond the control of the Assured, held covered at a premium to be named for an additional 30 days provided the Assured give notice thereof to these Assurers as promptly as possible but in any event prior to the expiry of the said 30 days period.

B. This insurance specially to cover the goods during deviation, delay, forced discharge, re-shipment, transshipment and any other variation of the adventure arising from the exercise of a liberty granted to the shipowner or charterer under the contract of affreightment.

C. In the event of the exercise of any liberty granted to the shipowner or charterer under the contract of affreightment whereby such contract is terminated at a port or place other than the original insured destination, the insurance continues until the goods are sold and delivered at such port or place; or, if the goods be not sold but are forwarded to the original insured destination or to any other destination this insurance continues until the goods have been delivered to the warehouse or place of storage as provided in paragraph 1.A.

D. If while this insurance is still in force and before the expiry of 15 days from midnight of the day on which the discharge overside of the goods hereby insured from the overseas vessel at the final port of discharge is completed, the goods are re-sold (not being a sale within the terms of paragraph 1.C) and are to be forwarded to a destination other than that covered by this insurance, the goods are covered hereunder while deposited at such port of discharge until again in transit or until the expiry of the aforementioned 15 days whichever shall first occur. If a sale is effected after the expiry of the aforementioned 15 days while this insurance is still in force the protection afforded hereunder shall cease as from the time of the sale.

E. Held covered at a premium to be named in case of change of voyage or of any omission or error in the description of the interest, vessel or voyage.

F. It is a condition of this insurance that there shall be no interruption or suspension of transit unless due to circumstances beyond the control of the Assured and that the Assured shall act with reasonable dispatch in all circumstances within their control.

The warehouse to warehouse clause may refer to discharge overseas from the vessel at the final port. The port includes not only the docks and wharves where ships unload but the entire geographical area of the harbor and the city or cities surrounding the harbor. Other provisions in the clauses quoted above are intended to protect the insured from loss due to special circumstances which could not be anticipated. Additional premium may or may not be due from the insured, depending upon the terms under which the goods are covered.

Open Policies. The open policy as already mentioned is essentially a reporting form policy. It is designed for the shipper who is continually sending goods by ship. Coverage is arranged to suit the type of goods shipped and the nature of the insured's business. The "open" nature of the policy refers to its arrangement and not to coverage. The coverage is effective as to all goods shipped by the insured during the term of the policy without any further notice to the insurer. The policy usually covers from the insured's place of business by whatever means shipped, railroad, trucks, airplane or harborcraft, if needed to reach the overseas vessel. At the other end of the transit the coverage continues until delivery to the consignee even if the destination is inland. It is also possible to write such a policy to cover only between named ports, or from the shipper's port to other named places, all depending upon the nature of the insured's business and his needs for coverage.

The open policy is usually continuous. Premium is payable periodically according to reports from the insured regarding the shipments made. This is comparable to reporting form policies in connection with insurance of goods on land. The usual provision is for cancellation upon 30 days notice from either party.

The typical open policy provides for issuance of special policies or certificates by the insured. The essentials of ocean commerce have been described previously under which an insurance policy or certificate forms part of the package of commercial papers which are sent to the consignee. This insurance is assignable or is effective for anyone having an insurable interest in the goods. The insurance policy or certificate shows what coverage is effective on the property and who the insurer is. Thus a claim can be made promptly for any damage that may appear upon delivery.

A special policy is a complete insurance policy in itself. This is customarily used where the full terms of the coverage must go with the package of commercial papers. If the full terms are not required by the transaction between the shipper and the consignee, a certificate form, somewhat abbreviated, may be used. The special policies which are issued by the insured under the authority of his open policy are often referred to as certificates. Actually a certificate is the shorter form which is used where it suffices. In either case, the insured issues as many copies of the special policy or certificate as may be needed for the transaction. These are reported to the insurer as part of the regular report of goods shipped and upon which premium payments are based.

FREIGHT COVERAGE

The word "freight" in ocean marine insurance terminology means the money paid for the transportation of goods. This amount of money represents a financial interest, and it may be insured. A ship owner can insure the anticipated freight in addition to insuring the value of his ship. When a ship is insured for a particular voyage, it is customary to add the freight charges which will be received from the voyage to the value of the ship.

If a ship is loaded with a miscellaneous cargo for delivery at various ports on the route of the ship, the freight to be insured is the total amount of the freight charges for all of the bills of lading relating to the goods on board. In the case of a charter, the amount of the freight may be the charge to be paid in a lump sum by the one chartering the vessel.

There may be circumstances in which future freight would be insured. This is proper if the ship has a definite contract which would bring in a certain amount of freight in the future. Anticipated freight sometimes is insured even if there is no actual contract for use of the ship if the underwriters are satisfied that the anticipation is real. Such coverage usually is on a total loss or constructive total loss basis only.

Freight may be specifically insured in connection with cargo, but ordinarily the freight charges are included as a part of the valuation of the goods. According to the practices in some trades the freight is payable on the cargo "lost or not lost." The freight is at the risk of the cargo owner in such cases and may be insured for the cargo owner.

Passage Money. Passage money paid by passengers on a ship is not freight and is not insurable as freight. A passenger who has paid a substantial amount of money for his passage on a trip could insure against the loss of that value if he wishes. A ship owner is not obligated at common law to provide continuing passage for passengers in case a ship is lost but the passengers saved. However, it is customary today for a ship owner in such a case either to arrange for the passengers to be forwarded to their destination or to be returned to the port of embarkation. This is an expense against which the ship owner can buy insurance. He can also buy insurance to pay the entire amount of passage money in case he decides to refund the passage money to the passengers because of some casualty.

Insurance on Duties. Some countries exact an export duty on goods leaving the country. Such a duty becomes a part of the value of the goods. It may be insured as part of the insurable value or insured separately. Import duties ordinarily would not be insured because they are not collected until the goods actually enter the country. According to United States tariff laws, duties are assessed against merchandise regardless of the condition in which they may be received. If goods are received in a damaged condition and the full duty has to be paid on them, there is a loss of a part of the duty which has to be paid. It is possible to insure against such loss as a result of accident during transit. Inasmuch as import duties are paid when the goods enter this country, the import duty becomes a part of the cost of the goods at that point. If loss occurs during transit within the country of destination while the goods are still covered under the warehouse to warehouse clause, the amount of the loss would include the amount of the import duties.

OFFICERS' PROTECTIVE POLICY

Cargo insurance does not cover the personal effects of passengers and crew members. Neither is the value of such personal effects considered in the application of general average. Passengers and crew must carry their own insurance if they wish to have coverage. Officers' protective policies are used to insure against loss of personal effects and equipment due to loss of the vessel. Such policies also may include coverage of a ship officer's loss if his license should be suspended or revoked because of his action in connection with some casualty at sea. This is somewhat in the nature of a personal use and occupancy policy because a ship officer's income depends to a large extent upon the maintenance of his license. An error which results in loss of a ship can mean the suspension or revocation of the license.

MISCELLANEOUS CRAFT

Any type of watercraft and many structures and equipment that are related to ocean transport may be insured under ocean marine policies. Ships designed for specific purposes, such as fishing boats and oil tankers, are insured for their owners or operators according to the peculiar needs and practices of those operations.

Tugboats. The tugboat is a working boat that assists other ships with its power. It does not carry cargo but assists with the docking of bigger ships, handles the towing of ships in distress, tows barges, and otherwise assists any vessel that needs extra power. Insurance on tugboats is much the same as insurance on other marine risks with the exception of the liability coverage. This coverage is written to protect the tugboat owner if his negligence results in damage to the property he is towing. An important underwriting consideration is the experience of the tugboat operator. Many tugboat operations are conducted in narrow waterways and through locks where expert handling is necessary. An error in judgment that might be held to be negligence would be expensive to the underwriters in case damage is done to the object being towed, or to locks, bridges, or other property along the waterway.

If the tugboat operator wishes to protect himself against loss due to his legal liability for personal injury or loss of life, he must secure protection and indemnity coverage. This is not covered under the running down clause normally written for tugboat operators.

Miscellaneous Properties. There are many other types of craft and structures insurable under ocean marine insurance policies. Barges, fishing boats, shrimp boats, car floats, ferryboats, and off-shore oil drilling rigs and dredges are but a few of the waterborne vessels used for special purposes. Dry docks may be insured under ocean marine insurance policies. Insurance on all of these properties is placed according to the needs of the owners and the willingness of the underwriters to cover the risks affecting the property. In insuring the regular waterborne properties such as barges and special purpose boats, ocean marine insurance practices are followed. If dredges and dry docks are to be insured, the coverage may be specially arranged with particular attention to the hazards of collision from other vessels and the hazards of fire. If such properties as dredges and dry docks are to be moved, they may be moved under the supervision of the insurance underwriters in order to make sure that all necessary precautions are taken to avoid damage. If such properties are moved at frequent intervals, one insurance policy may be written to cover fire, storm hazards, and collision with vessels while the property is stationary, and a special trip insurance policy may be written to cover while the property is being moved. The special trip policy covers the full marine hazards similar to the coverage of a ship at sea. Ships under construction are insured under marine builders' risk policies. These are comparable to builders' risk policies covering structures on land, but coverage follows marine practices.

RATES

Ocean marine insurance rates are calculated by the underwriters for each policy or risk to be insured. Such rates are not subject to filing with any insurance department in the United States, and ocean marine insurance is exempted from the rate regulatory laws of all states. Ocean marine insurance is subject to a world market. Foreign underwriters are not subject to rate regulation of the sort with which we are familiar in the United States for other types of property insurance. It is felt that American underwriters must be free to quote rates on a competitive basis without the filing and regulation of those rates.

Freedom from filing and regulation is also justified because of the constant variation in the hazards affecting ocean marine coverages. There is a constant variation in world trade conditions and innumerable variations in ships, voyages, and cargoes. Weather conditions vary from season to season, and the underwriter must take into account the route of the ship, the season of the year, and in connection with fleet coverages, the routes over which the fleets normally operate. It has not proved feasible to establish schedules by which such widely varying conditions can be measured. The underwriter establishes his rates according to all of the factors he believes will affect the chance of success or failure. The factors considered by the underwriter in determining rates are (1) the ship or ships and their ability to withstand the perils of the sea, (2) the route over which the ships operate, (3) the safety or dangers of the harbors into which calls are made, (4) the type of cargo and its inherent hazards, (5) the coverage of the policy, (6) the experience of the ship owner in relation to his ships and the routes over which he is operating, and (7) the competitive situation in the world insurance market at the time the policy is written.

Marine underwriters maintain careful records of the experience of insureds whose property they cover. The loss record of a fleet operator has an important influence on the rate for the fleet. The success or failure of an ocean marine underwriter is dependent upon his ability to judge the seriousness of the exposures to loss of the properties he accepts.

THE OCEAN MARINE INSURANCE MARKET

Ocean marine insurance in the United States is placed largely in American insurance companies or in American branches of alien insurance companies. A large portion of marine insurance written in England is written by members of Lloyd's of London. Lloyd's members also participate in the insurance written in the American market to a certain extent. Insurance on large ships or fleets may exhaust almost the entire world insurance market. It may be necessary for interested governments to participate in order to get sufficient coverage for hazardous operations such as war risks.

Groups or syndicates of insurance companies have banded together in order to provide sufficient coverage and some uniformity of underwriting for certain types of ships and cargoes. There are also groups of companies that develop uniform policy forms and clauses. The marine activities of some insurance companies are placed in the hands of marine managers who operate for several companies in a group. This has the advantage of placing the underwriting and insuring of marine risks under a single organization instead of spreading it among the marine departments of the companies. A considerable saving of expense results.

A large portion of ocean marine insurance business is placed through brokers especially qualified to handle ocean marine insurance. These brokers are familiar with the needs of their clients and are also familiar with the underwriters who will accept different classes of business. The marine insurance broker performs more functions than the mere selling and servicing of the insurance. He may handle the details in the application of general average and in the collection of losses.

PLEASURE BOATS

Pleasure boating is increasingly popular in the United States. An affluent society, more leisure time, and the building of many artificial lakes in connection with power and reclamation dams have all helped to make boating a major sport. Insurance on pleasure boats is not standardized. Much insurance and particularly that on larger boats with inboard motor power is written as ocean marine insurance. Smaller boats and most of those with outboard motors are covered under inland marine insurance. The Nation-wide Marine Definition (which will be discussed in connection with inland marine insurance) makes no distinction between ocean marine and inland marine insurance. The laws of the states do not separate ocean from inland marine as far as coverage on boats is concerned. In some states there is a regulation of the Insurance Commissioner that insurance on boats with outboard motor power which are 16 feet or less in length shall be classified as inland marine insurance. Except for this regulation, it is entirely up to the insurance company whether insurance of any kind of boat is classified as ocean marine or inland marine.

Traditionally, boats with inboard motor power and sailboats have been insured according to ocean marine forms and practices. These policies are generally termed "yacht policies." Although ocean marine coverages and practices are followed, there are differences from policies on commercial risks in order to meet the needs of yacht owners and operators. These differences and the special conditions of yacht policies will be discussed in the following pages.

Outboard motor boats are more likely to be insured under inland marine policies. The insurance of outboard motor boats will be covered in this chapter in order that pleasure boat insurance may be presented in a logical manner. Differences between the ocean marine and the inland marine approach to boat insurance will be pointed out.

A comparatively recent development in the boat field is known as an "inboard-outboard" motor boat. The motor in such a boat is inboard, but the thrust of the power is against the stern of the boat. In this respect it resembles the outboard motor, which is actually mounted on the stern. The conventional inboard motor boat has a shaft going forward from the propeller to the motor so that the thrust is against the forward part of the boat. One of the dangers in an inboard motor boat is the fact that the fuel is inboard. There is a greater likelihood of an accumulation of flammable vapors in the boat than is the case with an outboard motor boat. This additional fire hazard is present in the inboard-outboard type of boat. While there is no requirement as far as an insurance regulation is concerned, there is a tendency for underwriters to treat the inboard-outboard type of boat as an inboard motor boat.

YACHT INSURANCE

The yachtsman differs from the commercial ship operator in several respects. The yachtsman typically operates his own boat. He is likely to be on board and in command even if he does have a small hired crew. The yacht does not carry cargo; it is used for pleasure and not for hire. A yacht that is used for hire is a commercial operation for passenger carrying and does not come within the scope of this discussion. The yachtsman needs full ocean marine coverage, but the exposure from some features of yacht operation is relatively minor as compared with a commercial ship operation. This permits the insurer to include protection and indemnity coverage, Longshoremen and Harbor Workers' coverage, and medical payments coverage in the same policy. This is contrary to the practices in connection with commercial ship insurance. The yacht is likely to be out of service for several months each year. This may increase the risk from hazards at the point of lay-up as well as lessening hazards from perils of the sea.

Yacht Insurance Coverage. Coverage on the hull is comparable to that under other ocean marine policies. Perils covered are those listed in the Lloyd's policy. War damage usually is excluded by a Free of Capture and Seizure clause. Loss from strikes, riots, and civil commotion are excluded unless specifically assumed.

There are some extensions of coverage which are especially designed to protect the yachtsman from hull losses. Coverage is extended to hull or machinery damage from accidents in loading, discharging, or handling stores and fittings or in taking on fuel, or in hauling or launching or moving in shipyards. This latter coverage is important because many yachts are laid up in shipyards during a part of the year. Damage which occurs during preparation for lay-up or in preparing the boat for use in the spring might be expensive for the insured.

The boat is also covered while in shipyards or elsewhere on shore for damage by windstorm, tornado, hurricane, earthquake, floods, and collapse of building including collapse of shoring, blocking, or staging. Coverage also applies for loss from contact with aircraft or parts falling therefrom and contact with motor vehicles; for loss by explosions on shipboard or elsewhere; and for bursting of boilers, breakage of shafts, or other latent defect, except the cost of repairing the defective part. Loss resulting from negligence of master, mariners, engineers, or pilots is covered.

These extensions of coverage are not effective, however, if they are the result of want of due diligence by the owner, the manager, or the insured.

There is an extension of coverage to equipment of the yacht which is separated from the yacht and laid up on shore. This is limited to 20 percent of the amount of insurance on the yacht. The amount of insurance on the yacht itself is reduced by this 20 percent when there is property so covered.

The coverage is warranted free of loss to spars and sails during racing. There is also an exclusion of wages and provisions in respect to average (loss) whether particular or general.

Boats and launches of the yacht are insured while afloat. There is no "thirds off" (depreciation charge) deduction in case repairs are made, new for old.

Each individual policy is written to show the period of navigation and the period during which the yacht will be laid up for the winter, if any. The navigation limits are set forth. Premiums vary according to the area within which the yacht will be used.

The yacht policy, in line with ocean marine insurance generally, is a valued policy. The agreed value of the vessel is shown, and the amount of insurance is separately shown. If the amount of insurance is less than the agreed value, then the insurer is liable for hull damage only in the proportion that the insurance bears to the agreed value.

Running down (collision) coverage is provided as part of the hull insurance. The insurer agrees to pay damages that the insured is liable to pay and does pay for collision to another ship or vessel. The payment is limited to the value of the yacht and also by the amount of insurance. If the insured contests the liability with the consent of the insurer, the insurer agrees to pay the expenses incurred. If both vessels are to blame, the damages are to be settled according to the principle of cross liabilities under which each vessel is liable for a certain proportion of the other vessel's damage. There is a further provision amounting to a "sister ship" provision which allows for such payment even if both vessels are owned by the same insured. There is a specific exclusion of liability under this section for removal of obstruction under statutory requirements, and for injury to harbors, wharves, piers, stages and similar structures, cargo, or loss of life or personal injury. These running down clause exclusions follow the coverage generally appearing in ocean marine policies.

Section "B" of the policy provides Protection and Indemnity coverage. The face of the policy provides space to fill in the premium and rate for this coverage if the policy is to cover it. In addition, there are limits for loss of life and personal injury for any one person and for any one accident. This limitation per person and per accident for loss of life or personal injury is similar to such provisions in automobile and other liability insurance policies in the United States. Customary ocean marine practices for protection and indemnity insurance are to provide coverage for any insured situation up to the value of the ship. The yacht policy in contrast provides limits for loss of life and personal injury which may be substantially higher than the value of the vessel if the insured feels that he needs high limits. He might carry limits comparable to those which he would carry in his automobile or other liability policy. Coverage for property damage liability under this clause is limited to the amount of insurance on the hull under that section of the policy or the limit of liability per person under this section, whichever is greater. There is a further provision that where the amount of insurance on the hull is less than the agreed value, the insurer is liable only for that portion of the payment that the amount of insurance bears to the agreed value. This proration of a liability claim is different from practices in connection with liability claims in connection with automobile and other liability coverages on land.

There is an important difference between the probable liability of the yacht owner and that of the commercial ship operator. It has been explained that under maritime law the ship owner or operator generally is limited in his liability to the amount of value of his interest in the vessel. This limitation of liability applies if the act or the damage occurred without his "privity or knowledge." The practical effect of this is that the owner or operator is insulated from liability above his interest in the vessel unless he personally participated in the fault which caused the loss or damage. Even negligence of the master or crew does not result in "privity or knowledge" of the owner or operator as long as he did not actually participate himself. The yacht owner or operator in most cases either operates the vessel himself or is likely to be on board even if he had a hired crew. Thus he is very likely to have actual knowledge or be personally involved in any occurrence which results in injury or damage. It is important, therefore, that the yacht owner or operator have liability insurance coverage beyond the value of the vessel. That is the reason for liability limits in the yacht policy similar to those provided in automobile and other liability insurance policies covering risks on shore.

Longshoremen's and Harbor Workers' Compensation coverage is provided as a companion to the protection and indemnity coverage. Usually there is a single premium for these two coverages and the same limits apply to loss of life and personal injury. The yachtsman normally would not buy a longshoremen's and harbor workers' compensation policy because he does not have a regular exposure to such losses which a cargo carrying vessel would have in the loading and unloading of cargo in American ports. The yachtsman's exposure is casual and incidental. Therefore, he needs this coverage as an adjunct to his other insurance. This coverage is a workmen's compensation coverage for dockworkers and similar persons who may service the ship. It does not apply to any crew which the insured may have for the vessel.

It may be noted here that workmen's compensation insurance is not commonly written to cover crews of ships. The protection and indemnity coverage applies to any liability which the ship owner or operator may have to crew members. There is a rule of admiralty law that the vessel and owner are liable to indemnify a seaman for an injury resulting from unseaworthiness of the vessel. The Jones Act enacted by the United States Congress added a new cause of action for bodily injuries to a seaman or for his death because of negligence of any of the officers, agents, or employees of the ship. Any such liability on the part of the insured is covered under the P. and I. clause.

There is an interesting difference between the protection and indemnity coverage and the longshoremen's and harbor workers' coverage. The P. and I. section provides for indemnification of the insured if he shall become liable to pay *and does pay* the sums covered. It has been contended that if the insured does not pay (as might occur in case of bankruptcy of the insured) the insurer is not obligated to pay. In the case of the longshoremen's and harbor workers' coverage the bankruptcy of the insurer does not relieve the insurer of liability. This follows the law in connection with other workmen's compensation insurance and the practice under automobile liability insurance.

Medical payments insurance normally is provided under the yacht policy. This is another departure from usual ocean marine insurance practices. It is a concession to the fact that the yacht owner frequently has guests aboard and feels the same obligation to them that he feels toward guests in his automobile. The limit per person and per accident is specified in the yacht policy. An endorsement usually is attached which follows the medical payments coverage commonly written for liability coverages on land.

Port Risks. A yacht owner may consider the cancellation of the marine coverage during the lay-up period and the limitation of coverage to fire insurance during that time. Some saving in premium might be realized but there is a continuation of marine risks even during a lay-up. From the insurer's standpoint, there may be a serious conflagration exposure at a marina which would make the fire insurance an undesirable risk. The preferable arrangement in most cases is to continue the marine coverage during lay-up, subject to any reduction in premium that the insurer might be willing to grant because there is an absence of navigation hazards during that time.

Occasionally a yachtsman desires to use his yacht for entertaining during the lay-up period. This may be a serious additional exposure. There would be liability and medical payments exposures because of persons being on board and there would be an additional fire hazard. Inactivity of the vessel might increase the fire hazard because of accumulation of flammable vapors. Festivities on board might result in fire and serious accident. Underwriters often are reluctant to cover a yacht if it is to be used for entertaining during a lay-up period.

The variations which are possible in covering yachts under ocean marine insurance policies are innumerable. Almost any condition that exposes the insured to loss can be covered if the underwriters are willing and the insured is agreeable to paying a premium commensurate with the hazard. Restrictions may apply to coverage in order to bring the exposures to loss within those which underwriters are willing to assume. The definition of the insured may include others who may borrow the vessel. This is comparable to the omnibus coverage clause of automobile insurance policies which extends coverage to anyone operating the automobile with the consent of the insured. Restrictions may apply to breakage of propellers, shafts, or machinery in the case of high-speed vessels where such damage is likely from operating in waters that may have underwater obstructions. Ocean marine insurance is very flexible. Virtually the only limits on the possible variations are the desire of the insured for coverage, his willingness to pay a commensurate premium, and the willingness of the underwriters to accept the risks involved.

OUTBOARD MOTOR BOATS

The outboard motor boat has become a tremendously popular recreational vehicle. Motors and boats of this type are available in many sizes. The expense of operating an outboard motor boat can be much less than that of an inboard boat or yacht. The availability of trailers on which outboard motor boats can be hauled to different boating areas makes for flexibility and popularity. Many of the outboard boating enthusiasts have had no previous contact with insurance for marine risks. The tendency has been for insurance companies in the United States to provide insurance for outboard motor boats along the lines of insurance for land risks rather than according to ocean marine insurance practices.

Physical damage insurance for outboard motor boats tends to be written as inland marine coverage. Some of these policies also include the equivalent of the running down clause with a limited amount of physical damage liability coverage. Personal injury and medical payments liability coverage generally is not included under an inland marine policy. Such insurance usually is available to the outboard motor boat operator under a Homeowners policy or comprehensive personal liability policy.

Neither the insurance laws of the states nor the Nation-wide Marine Definition makes any distinction between ocean marine and inland marine insurance as far as boats of any kind are concerned. However, several state insurance commissioners have issued regulations which provide that insurance on outboard motor boats of 16 feet in length or less shall be classified as inland marine insurance. This tends to strengthen the insurance industry practice of covering small boats and particularly outboard motor boats under inland marine policies and covering inboard motor boats under ocean marine policies. Such insurance department rulings affect only the classification of such insurance. Rates, rules, and forms are subject entirely to insurance company determination, with one exception. A few states have ruled that rates, rules, and forms shall be filed for these outboard motor boats of 16 feet or less. The rating bureaus have filed the required material in those states, but not in all states.

COVERAGE UNDER OUTBOARD BOAT POLICIES

The coverage under policies for outboard motor boats tends to be for "all risks of direct physical loss and damage" except as excluded or restricted. The language follows that typical of inland marine policies on valuable articles, as will be discussed later in this text. Some insurance companies also issue policies with coverage limited to certain specified perils, usually at a lower premium.

The basic principle of "all risks" coverage is very broad. It is even broader in its concept than the "perils of the seas" coverage of the ocean marine policy because the coverage applies to any risk which may cause damage to the property. It must be emphasized that coverage applies only to a "risk," which is an accidental or unforeseeable occurrence. It does not apply to an event which is natural and foreseeable even though such an event may cause damage. Thus wear and tear losses are not covered because they are not the result of a risk.

The actual coverage of the outboard motor boat policy is determined by the exclusions and restrictions which apply to the "all risks" coverage. There is usually an exclusion of wear and tear type of losses such as deterioration, rust, corrosion, or mechanical or electrical breakdown. This is intended to reinforce and extend to understandable limits the basic coverage which applies only to risks or accidental occurrences.

Loss due to infidelity of persons to whom the craft is entrusted is excluded. The insured is expected to use reasonable care so that persons who use the boat are trustworthy. Coverage is suspended while the craft is being used for hire or while being operated in any official race or speed contest. These are considered to be extra hazards. They might be insurable hazards, but the company would want to know of such exposures to loss so that an extra premium could be charged.

There is a nuclear damage exclusion similar to that used on other policies covering property on land. The war damage exclusion is the same as that used for many inland marine policies. This will be discussed more fully later in this text. There is one provision which has an important application to boat insurance. This is the exclusion of loss from "seizure or destruction under quarantine or customs regulations, confiscation by order of any government or public authority, or risks of contraband or illegal transportation or trade." Smuggling or similar illegal use might subject the craft to confiscation. It is also possible that a boat owner operating in or near waters of other nations (such as near Mexico or Canada) might unintentionally violate some regulations which would subject his boat to confiscation. These risks are considered to be extra-hazardous. The average boat owner is not expected to be subject to this exposure, and the coverage and premium are designed to meet the needs of the average boat owner.

Loss resulting from work being done on the property is excluded unless fire or explosion ensues and then only for the damage resulting from the ensuing fire or explosion. The insured is considered to have an obligation to pick reliable repairmen for the servicing of his boat. However, if there is a loss from fire or explosion, that is covered.

Deductibles appear in many boat policies. These provisions usually are spelled out as deductibles rather than in the terms of "particular average" such as are used in ocean marine policies. Some policies have deductibles applying to all perils, while others limit the application of the deductible to collision, theft, or perhaps some combination of perils. Pilferage of parts is an important cause of loss to boats that are moored in marinas or harbors. Collision damage is comparable to automobile collision hazards. Increasing congestion as more boats come into use make the collision hazard a severe one.

The habits and practices of outboard motor boat owners make it advisable to insure the boat, motor, accessories, and carrier under separate policy items. The detachable motor makes it desirable to insure boat and motor separately. An insured may buy a new boat or a new motor without replacing the other. A third and separate item of insurance on many boat policies is one covering equipment. An owner may or may not have much extra equipment such as covers, anchors, life preservers, and other detachable or mobile equipment. The fourth item covered under many boat policies is a boat carrier. Boats of considerable size can be pulled on trailers behind the insured's automobile and launched at the lake or river of his choice. The great variety in nature and value of the boat, motor, equipment, and boat carrier make it desirable to specify amounts of insurance separately on these four types of property. Items such as the motor, boat, and carrier usually are listed on the policy by manufacturer, model, serial number, year of manufacture, and perhaps other identifying information. Such information can be helpful in effecting recovery in case of theft or other loss.

Liability coverage under an outboard motor boat policy usually is limited to property damage liability. This is a version of the running down clause of the ocean marine policy. This property damage liability coverage in many policies differs in an important respect from the running down clause. The ocean marine insurance running down coverage applies only to collision damage to another vessel. The property damage liability coverage of the outboard motor policy typically covers sums which the insured shall be legally obligated to pay for damage to or destruction of property caused by accidental collision of the boat or motor while afloat. Thus the coverage applies to all property damaged by such a collision and not merely to another vessel. This includes some of the coverage (that applying to property other than a vessel) which in ocean marine insurance is part of the protection and indemnity insurance. This property damage liability coverage for outboard motor boats usually is limited to $500 for any one accidental collision.

Outboard motor boat insurance policies seldom include any coverage which is comparable to protection and indemnity insurance. It is anticipated that the outboard motor boat owner will have liability coverage under a Homeowners policy or a comprehensive personal liability policy.

Some insurance companies also issue specified perils policies covering outboard motors and boats. The perils covered may be some combination of fire, explosion, lightning, windstorm (which may be limited to coverage while the boat is on land), collision, theft, and loss of the motor from marine perils including loss overboard. The term "marine perils," which is used in some policies, does not have any wholly satisfactory definition. It is probably intended to have somewhat the same meaning as "perils of the seas," which is used in ocean marine policies.

The equivalent of a 100 percent coinsurance clause is a part of most policies on outboard motors and boats. This follows ocean marine insurance practice. Coverage is on an actual cash value basis and seldom is on an agreed value basis. Policies may be written to cover a limited navigation period, but more common practice is to cover for the full year. This is preferable from the standpoint of the insured, particularly if there is a likelihood that he can use the boat early in the spring. Limited navigation periods for recreational boats pose a hazard for the insured. He may forget to notify the insurance company if he decides to take advantage of good weather before the policy coverage is effective.

Rates and premiums for boat insurance are determined by the company in accordance with local conditions and individual company experience, except in the case of the few states where the rating bureaus have made filings for certain small boats. Rates vary from 2 percent to 5 percent of the value, depending upon length of navigation season where the boat will be used, size of the boat and power of the motor, whether a deductible applies, and whether operation of the boat is in inland or coastal waters.

QUESTIONS

1. Compare the hull of a ship under a literal definition and what is generally covered under an ocean marine hull insurance policy.
2. Explain the coverage of a builders' risk ocean marine insurance policy. Compare the coverage with a builders' risk fire insurance policy.
3. What is the difference between a port risk insurance policy and a navigation policy?
4. Under what circumstances might an ocean marine insurance policy show different valuations for the same vessel?
5. Explain the difference between the coverage of the collision or "running down" clause and the Protection and Indemnity clause.

6. Compare the liability of an automobile operator on land with the limitations on the liability of a ship operator who is responsible for property damage, personal injury, or loss of life.
7. Discuss the effect of the "sister ship" clause and compare this effect with collision insurance on a fleet of automobiles.
8. How do the limitations on the liability of carriers by sea encourage cargo owners to carry insurance?
9. How does the "warehouse to warehouse" clause extend the coverage of an ocean marine policy?
10. What is "freight" in ocean marine insurance terminology?
11. Explain the relationship of the marine insurance market to the method of determining ocean marine insurance rates.
12. Discuss the liability to which a yacht owner may be subject because of his "privity or knowledge" as compared to the liability of a commercial ship operator.
13. Explain why ocean marine rates are exempt from rate filing requirements under the laws of the states.

5

Development of Inland Marine Insurance

Inland marine insurance is largely an outgrowth of ocean marine insurance, but it differs in many respects. It applies many marine insurance principles to the insurance of property on land. A better description might be "transportation insurance," but this would not be wholly accurate because inland marine policies do in many cases cover property which is not in the course of transportation. It is generally true that inland marine coverages are related to property in transit or to property which is moveable in character.

DEVELOPMENT FROM OCEAN MARINE INSURANCE

Many years ago, most commerce was over the seas or inland waterways. Land transportation was slow and laborious. Cities were built near harbors and on waterways where ships could dock and discharge their cargoes. It was customary for the recipients of merchandise to receive goods as they were discharged at the shipside. Marine insurance covered the goods against loss while on shipboard, and the consignee took responsibility after the goods were unloaded.

Warehouse to Warehouse Coverage. Land transportation improved as railroads were built inland from the waterways and oceans. Merchants no longer met the ships at the wharves; the goods were reshipped to them by means of railroads. Consignees did not want to bother about securing insurance for each shipment that they expected from overseas, so they asked that the ocean marine insurance be extended to cover until the goods were delivered to the ultimate destination.

Ocean marine insurance was extended to cover the hazards of transportation over land to the consignee's location by means of the "warehouse to warehouse" clause. It was included as part of the coverage of the ocean marine insurance policy, but it was a distinct and new form of coverage because it insured goods being carried on land as well as on the sea. It became customary for the warehouse to warehouse clause to cover from the original point of shipment until the goods arrived at the final destination, no matter how far inland it might be.

A division gradually developed between ocean marine and inland marine insurance. Inland marine insurance covers property being transported over land, and it also may cover goods being carried on coastwise vessels or on inland waters or held in temporary storage in the course of transportation. Inland marine underwriters also insure instrumentalities of transportation such as bridges, tunnels, wharves, docks, transmission lines for water and electricity, and also telegraph and telephone lines.

Broad Nature of Inland Marine Insurance. An important similarity between the insurance policies issued by ocean marine and inland marine underwriters is the tendency toward broad coverage. The ocean marine coverage of "all risks of transportation and navigation" is a direct ancestor of the "all risks" types of insurance so frequently provided by inland marine policies. This is in contrast to the policies on property at fixed locations on land, which for many years were phrased to cover loss from specific perils such as fire, lightning, windstorm, and burglary.

The broad coverage insurance policies in both the ocean marine and inland marine fields are worded to exclude wear and tear losses. Only fortuitous losses are considered insurable.

COMPARISONS BETWEEN INLAND MARINE AND OCEAN MARINE INSURANCE

The archaic language found in many ocean marine insurance policies has been largely discarded by inland marine underwriters. People shipping goods by railroad and motor truck are not likely to understand the traditional language of ocean marine insurance. Courts have been critical of special meanings hidden in the old language, and ambiguities often have been resolved in favor of policyholders.[1]

"General average" is of only minor importance in inland marine insurance. General average losses usually are covered under an inland marine insurance policy if the goods insured are ferried or are aboard a coastwise ship for part of the journey. It is desirable to include general average coverage in connection with air cargo because cargo or parts of an airplane may have to be jettisoned in order to save the plane and the balance of its contents.

"Particular average" is not often referred to in inland marine insurance policies. If partial losses up to a certain size are to be excluded, the policy contains a deductible clause. Franchise clauses seldom are used in inland marine insurance policies.

The principle that the amount of insurance should approximate the value of the goods has been continued from ocean marine practices. This principle is now expressed in the form of coinsurance, which is used extensively in insurance policies covering business properties. It has been found difficult to apply coinsurance to household goods and personal effects, but an effort is made to have inland marine insurance policies written in amounts approximating the full values. Rates for most inland marine insurance policies are calculated on the assumption that the amount of insurance will be close to the actual value.

Warranties. Implied warranties are not a factor in inland marine insurance. As long as the insured is not guilty of fraud, concealment, or misrepresentation, there are no implications as to the condition of the risk on the part of the insured.

[1]Gaunt v. John Hancock Mutual Life Ins. Co., 160 F. (2d) 599 (1947); cert den., 331 U.S. 849 (1947). Hoffman v. Illinois National Casualty Co., 159 F. (2d) 564 (1947).

The tendency of courts and legislatures in the United States to soften the effects of insurance policy warranties has discouraged underwriters from using them. Courts frequently have taken the position that a breach of warranty must have increased the risk of loss if payment of the loss is to be avoided by the insurance company. A legislative enactment affecting warranties is found in the Insurance Laws of New York, section 150, paragraph 2, which reads:

> No breach of warranty shall avoid an insurance contract or defeat recovery thereunder unless such breach materially increased the risk of loss, damage, or injury within the coverage of the contract.

Abandonment. The insured under an inland marine insurance policy ordinarily does not have the privilege of offering abandonment to the insurance company. Some inland marine insurance policies state that there shall be no abandonment to the company, and others are silent on the point. Should an inland marine policyholder make an offer of abandonment under a policy which does not prohibit it, insurance companies consider it advisable to act on the offer quickly to prevent being placed in the position of accepting abandonment by default.

PRINCIPLES BORROWED FROM FIRE AND CASUALTY INSURANCE

Inland marine insurance policies in many cases cover property at fixed locations. The practice of insuring property at fixed locations under inland marine insurance policies developed largely because of the inadequacy of coverage provided under fire and casualty insurance policies. Jewelers wanted an insurance policy that would provide fire and theft insurance in the same policy; owners of bridges needed coverage against loss due to collapse, ice jams, and flood, as well as against fire and wind; chain store operators wanted insurance to cover their property against loss at any location as well as while in transit between locations. The laws and rulings in effect in many states prohibited a fire or casualty insurance company from combining fire and casualty insurance coverages in one policy. The underwriting powers of marine insurance companies were very broad, and marine underwriters started to write inland marine insurance policies to provide the broad coverages desired.

Inland marine underwriters borrowed language from fire and casualty insurance policies to fit the needs for coverage on property at fixed locations. For example, coverage against burglary losses was provided in terms borrowed from burglary insurance policies, and the insurance policies covering theft often were extended to cover theft by stealth as well as theft by violence. Policyholders had become so accustomed to the coverage of the fire insurance policy that inland marine underwriters found it advantageous to follow fire insurance practices rather than ocean marine insurance practices in providing fire loss coverage.

Assignment of an inland marine policy usually is prohibited without the consent of the insurance company. Inland marine underwriters agree with fire underwriters that introduction of a new party to the insurance policy contract by assignment might create a moral hazard.

Cancellation provisions of inland marine insurance policies follow closely those of fire and casualty policies rather than those of ocean marine policies. Cancellation provisions of inland marine· policies are similar to those of a fire policy.

Inland marine insurance policies follow fire policies in requirements for reporting of losses, submission of proofs of loss, appraisal in case of disagreement between the company and the insured as to the value of the insured property, payment of loss, and waiver of policy provisions. Other insurance is contributing insurance regardless of the the date upon which it was effective.

DEPENDENCE ON CASUALTY INSURANCE DECISIONS

The theft coverage provided by inland marine policies follows the practice of the casualty companies rather than that of the ocean marine underwriters. The word "thieves" in ocean marine policies was intended to refer to theft by force and not by stealth. In the United States the word "theft" has come to mean the wrongful taking of property belonging to another, and this is the way the coverage is interpreted under inland marine coverages.[2]

"Burglary" is another term which inland marine underwriters have come to interpret according to casualty practices. By definition "burglary" is a term applying only to land coverages and not to ocean marine. Burglary is defined by statute in some states, but the definitions are not uniform, nor are they in agreement with the

[2]See Aetna Ins. Co. v. English, 204 S.W. (2d) 850 (Tex. Civ. App. 1947) for a case where proof of theft was entirely circumstantial and there was no threat of violence; nor was the custodian aware of the theft at the time it took place.

common law interpretation. The intention of inland marine underwriters is expressed in the following definition, which is inserted in many inland marine policies: " 'Burglary' as used herein means the felonious abstraction of insured property from within a building or room by any person or persons making felonious entry therein by actual force and violence of which there shall be visible marks made upon the exterior of such premises at the place of such entry by tools, explosives, electricity or chemicals."

The determination of what constitutes collision and overturn must depend largely upon decisions that have been made in the automobile portion of the fire and casualty insurance business. The actual coverage provided under these terms will be discussed in connection with transportation coverages.

Court decisions regarding automobile insurance have been helpful in determining what is meant by such expressions as "member of the insured's family," which are used in inland marine policies issued to protect personal property.

DEPENDENCE ON FIRE INSURANCE DECISIONS

Although the answer may seem commonplace today, there have been questions whether fire insurance covers damage by smoke from a fire and loss from the water used to extinguish a fire. The courts have followed the principle that the loss is covered by the fire insurance if the fire was the proximate cause of the loss. That is, the fire must be the direct occurrence causing the loss without which there would have been no loss. If there had been no fire, there would have been no smoke, nor would there have been any water used to extinguish the fire. Therefore, the fire has been ruled to be the direct cause of loss when the actual damage was by smoke from a fire or water used to extinguish the fire. The cases in support of this doctrine are fire insurance cases[3] and are used to apply equally to inland marine losses.

Fire and inland marine policies require that the insured shall use all reasonable means to save and preserve property endangered by fire in neighboring premises. It has been held that fire insurance covers property lost or damaged as a result of its being moved in an effort to preserve it from loss by a threatening fire.[4] This is a reasonable rule because the insured would be encouraged to leave his

[3]Whitehurst v. Fayetteville Mutual Ins. Co., 51 N.C. 352 (1859); Boak Fish Co. v. Manchester Fire Assurance Co., 84 Minn. 419, 87 N.W. 932 (1901).

[4]Case v. Hartford Fire Ins. Co., 13 Ill. 676 (1852); White v. Republic Fire Ins. Co., 57 Me. 91 (1869).

property in the path of the flames if damage occasioned by the moving were not covered by the fire insurance.

There must have been an actual fire if the loss is to be paid under a fire policy. The presence of heat and flame usually are considered necessary for an occurrence to be classed as a fire. Certain articles, such as hay, grain, and bituminous coal, may heat spontaneously, but damage from such heating is not considered to be from fire unless the heat is sufficient to ignite the material and result in flame. Damage caused by heat from steam is not considered a fire loss when there is no actual ignition.[5]

The cause of the fire is immaterial as long as it was not set deliberately by the insured. Carelessness on the part of the insured is not a bar to recovery if the carelessness does not come within the clause described above concerning perservation of property during and after a loss or threatened loss.[6]

Lightning is not fire. Most fire and inland marine policies cover lightning damage specifically, in addition to damage by fire. If, as in rare cases, fire insurance is provided without lightning coverage, the policy would cover damage done by a fire started by lightning but not damage by the lightning itself.

Closely allied to the question of lightning damage is that of damage by electricity artifically generated. At times it is difficult to distinguish between lightning (natural electricity) and artificially generated electricity, because a lightning storm may cause surges of current in wires carrying electricity for light and power. Inland marine policies frequently carry an "electrical apparatus" clause borrowed directly from fire policies. A typical version of this clause excludes "loss or damage to electrical apparatus caused by electricity other than lightning unless fire ensues and then only for loss or damage by such ensuing fire." The intention is to exclude losses for burned out motors, light bulbs, radio or television tubes, transformers, and other electrical equipment when the occurrence is a breakdown of the insulation or a short circuit and not really a fire. These losses are considered to be wear and tear losses that age or overloading causes to occur eventually in all electrical equipment; they are not regarded as fortuitous losses of a kind that can be insured.

Windstorm, cyclone, and tornado form another group of

[5]Gibbons v. German Ins. and Svgs. Inst., 30 Ill. App. 263 (1889).

[6]In the case of Karow v. Continental Ins. Co., 57 Wis. 56 (1883) the court stated: "In the absence of fraud or design, there can be no question but that a fire insurance company is not relieved from liability on its policy by reason of loss by fire through the negligence of the assured or his servants."

specified perils covered by many inland marine policies. Wording and practices are borrowed directly from the fire insurance field.

A cyclone is an area of low barometric pressure with an attendant system of winds revolving about the center. It covers an area of many hundreds of miles and characteristically brings in a succession of clear and rainy spells. A hurricane is a tropical cyclone and frequently is more violent than other cyclones experienced in the North Temperate Zone. A tornado is a small circular area of wind revolving at an extremely high speed. It may be described as a violent vortex in the atmosphere and is attended by a pendulous, more or less funnel-shaped cloud. It is local in area and seldom covers more than a few miles, but can be the most violent of all windstorms. Frequently it will cut a path only a few hundred feet wide over a distance of 10 to 100 miles.

Insurance companies and the courts have tended to ignore the technical definitions of the various types of windstorm, and commonly have paid for any damage occurring as a result of the wind.[7] Inland marine carriers have followed the lead of the fire underwriters in this respect.

A restriction common to windstorm coverages is that there must be an opening made by the wind before any loss is covered. Frequently the wind will drive rain, snow, or dust into a building through cracks in the structure, around windows, or between shingles on a roof. Insurance companies maintain that the damage is not payable under windstorm coverage unless there is an opening made by the wind through which the rain, snow, or dust has been able to enter the building. Most policies contain a specific provision clarifying this interpretation. Inland marine policies contain provisions limiting the windstorm coverage in a similar way. An example is the motor truck cargo policy, which often provides windstorm coverage in the following words: "cyclone, tornado and windstorm (excluding loss or damage caused by rain, hail, sleet, snow, sand or dust, whether driven by wind or not)." It is customary for inland marine insurance companies to pay a claim if rain, hail, sleet, snow, sand, or dust enters the vehicle through an opening made by the wind.

Inland marine policies often provide coverage against riot and civil commotion, vandalism, malicious mischief, and damage caused

[7]See Metropolitan Ice Cream Co. v. Union Mutual Fire Ins. Co., 210 S.W. (2d) 700 (Mo. App. 1948), in which the court stated: "Windstorms, like any other kind of storms, vary in violence and policies must be construed to cover a windstorm of any force and turbulence. If an insurer wishes to limit its liability to damage caused by storms of certain measured velocity or duration, the policy should so state."

by strikers and locked-out workmen. These are hazards affecting fixed locations in most cases, and the definitions of coverage follow that of policies issued in connection with fire insurance.

SIMILARITIES BETWEEN FIRE AND INLAND MARINE COVERAGES

As inland marine underwriters moved into the field of insurance on property at fixed locations, they adopted more and more of the restrictive practices of the fire insurance and burglary insurance companies that had been insuring such properties for many years. In addition to the "all risks" type of policy, inland marine underwriters began to issue policies covering against specified perils. There were few rules or court decisions in marine law and practice to cover specified perils coverage. Inland marine underwriters found themselves dependent upon decisions in fire and casualty cases to determine what their policies actually covered.

The hazard of fire is not considered to be a peril of the sea, and protection against loss by fire is found as a specified peril coverage in ocean marine as well as in fixed location policies. It is one of the few perils specifically mentioned in ocean marine policies. However, the situations in which fires damage property insured by inland marine policies approximate more nearly the circumstances covered by fire insurance policies than those covered by ocean marine policies. Therefore, whenever a question arises about the exact nature of the fire coverage under an inland marine policy, there has been a tendency to depend upon fire policy interpretations to determine the coverage.

FIRE AND CASUALTY PRACTICES IN INLAND MARINE UNDERWRITING

Many of the restricting conditions placed in inland marine policies are patterned after conditions of fire and casualty policies. Inland marine policies, for example, often provide that there can be no assignment of the policy prior to a loss without the written consent of the insurance company. This is in direct accord with the fire policy and is contrary to the accepted ocean marine practice of assignment prior to a loss in connection with cargo insurance. Assignment of a policy has the effect of making a new party to the contract. Fire and inland marine underwriters feel that they must have the right to consent to any change of party to the contract, since it is a personal contract and the moral hazard of the policyholder is an important factor in underwriting. This is especially true in the case of inland marine policies because the insured property is at risk while in the hands of the insured, whereas in the case of ocean marine insurance the insured property ordinarily is not under the control of the insured.

Cancellation provisions of inland marine policies follow closely those of fire and casualty policies and are different from those of ocean marine policies. Inland marine contracts usually provide for 5-day or 10-day notice of cancellation by the insurance company. Ocean marine policies usually provide for a 48-hour cancellation of war risks coverage, but there is no standard cancellation clause or practice as to other ocean marine coverages. Even when cancellation is made of an ocean marine policy, the coverage continues on a ship and cargo at sea until the destination is reached. In this respect the needs of land transportation insurance are much different from those of ocean marine insurance. It might be difficult to arrange for insurance on a sea voyage already under way, whereas most land transit is completed within the cancellation period provided by the inland marine policy.

The provisions of most inland marine policies concerning the reporting of losses, submission of proofs of loss, appraisal in case of disagreement between the policyholder and company regarding amount of a loss, and the payment of loss are all closely related to the provisions of fire policies. These will be discussed in detail in the chapter on adjustment of losses, but it is emphasized that practices as well as policy provisions follow closely those in the fire field.

Insurance companies have taken elaborate precautions to prevent the waiver of policy provisions by their representatives unless the waiver is expressed in the policy contract. The nonwaiver provisions of the fire policy that have been adopted in substance in almost all inland marine policies read:

> No permission affecting this insurance shall exist, or waiver of any provision be valid, unless granted herein or expressed in writing added hereto. No provision, stipulation or forfeiture shall be held to be waived by any requirement or proceeding on the part of this company relating to an appraisal or to any examination provided for herein.

The problem of what constitutes a waiver of policy provisions in the settlement of a loss is extremely important. The problems of waiver of policy conditions with inland marine coverages are resolved in accordance with practices and court decisions in the fire insurance field.

It was the established practice for many years in fire insurance that each partial loss under a policy reduced the amount of insurance and a total loss canceled the policy. This has changed, and much property insurance, including fire insurance, now is written so that losses do not reduce the amount of insurance. The insurance company might pay more than the policy amount if several losses occurred during the term of the policy. Inland marine underwriters tend to follow fire insurance practices in this respect, and most inland marine policies are not reduced in amount by payment of a loss.

This has been peculiarly a problem of insuring property at a fixed location. Property in transit usually is insured according to the whole value of all the property shipped, and there is no actual replacement of destroyed property. For example, under a transit policy the premium is based upon the total value of all the property shipped during the policy period. If some goods are lost, they may be replaced by other goods shipped at a later date, but the value of the replacing goods is included automatically in subsequent reports of property insured. In the case of property at a fixed location, the insurance is based upon a limit of liability, and the policy may provide for reinstatement of the insurance used up in any loss payment.

The English Marine Insurance Act of 1906 provides in section 77, paragraph (1), in regard to ocean marine:

> Unless the policy otherwise provides, and subject to the provisions of this Act, the insurer is liable for successive losses, even though the total amount of such losses may exceed the sum insured.

It is further provided in this Marine Insurance Act that in case of a total loss following a partial loss that has not been repaired, the insured can recover only the total loss.

Inland marine insurance follows fire practices rather than American ocean marine practices in the handling of "other insurance." According to the provisions of American ocean marine policies, the first policy to be written is the primary insurance. Policies with subsequent dates contribute only after the first policy is used up. In other words, the policy purchased first is the primary insurance and pays the loss in full if it is sufficiently large in amount. This is contrary to the practice in the inland marine field, which follows the fire practice. All inland marine policies in effect at the time of a loss are considered to be contributing insurance, depending upon their provisions as to other insurance. The dates on which the policies became effective have no effect on their contribution to the loss. Ocean marine policies are considered contributing insurance only if they bear the same date.

Most inland marine policies contain an "actual cash value" clause, and losses are payable according to the actual cash value of the property at the time of the loss. This is in accordance with fire insurance practice and is in contrast to the practice in ocean marine, where policies frequently are written on a valued basis. Inland marine policies are written on a valued basis only when the value of the individual items can be determined in advance of a loss and when such valuation would be difficult or impossible following a loss. Examples of such policies are those covering fine arts and occasionally jewelry.

It has been explained that ocean marine policies frequently do not provide for payment of small partial losses; in fact, some ocean marine policies cover only in case of total loss. This is in contrast to the practice in inland marine of paying most losses in full and of using deductible and franchise clauses in only a limited way. This follows the practice in fire insurance of paying all losses regardless of size, subject to the provisions of any coinsurance clause that may be attached to the policy.

The fire insurance field also has seen a breakdown in the rigid principle of requiring full insurance to value if the insured is to recover the full amount of any loss. Many fire and inland marine policies are written without any coinsurance, particularly in the personal coverages. Coinsurance provisions are difficult to apply on household effects because it is hard to determine the fair value of furniture and clothing in use. Inland marine underwriters have followed the lead of the fire insurance departments in abandoning the use of coinsurance on household property.

RATE MAKING PRINCIPLES FOR INLAND MARINE COVERAGES

The inland marine business has come to depend largely upon fire insurance practices in making rates. This development came about as inland marine insurance covered more and more property at fixed locations. The principal threat of large loss at a fixed location usually is by fire. Fire insurance rating bureaus have developed reasonably scientific methods of measuring the danger of fire loss. Their rates are the best that can be obtained and are used as a base for inland marine rates on such coverages as the jewelers' block, dealers' policies, furriers' customers, personal property floater, and fine arts policies. In many cases the fire insurance rate makes up most of the total rate for coverage at a location. In sections of the country where windstorm is a severe hazard, the windstorm or extended coverage rates of the fire rating bureaus are used as a part of the rate for the personal property floater.

It would be entirely possible for inland marine insurers to provide their own rates for location fire coverage, but they would have to duplicate work that is already being done by the fire insurance rating bureaus. Rates that vary according to the class or type of property can be used in territories and on classes of property where the hazard is reasonably uniform.

A class or flat rate system would not be satisfactory for jewelers' block coverage because the individual fire hazards of one jewelry store would be far different from those of others. A single rate for all jewelry stores, based on the loss experience of the entire class, would be too high for the well-protected store and too low for a store that is subject to a high hazard. Use of the rate promulgated by the fire insurance rating bureau avoids a duplication of work and saves the inland marine rating bureau the expense of inspecting and computing the fire portion of the rate. This saving of expense is important to the policyholder, because the expense of making rates eventually must be passed on to him as part of his insurance premium.

In computing the portion of an inland marine rate covering other than fire hazards, the companies and bureaus follow methods similar to those used by fire insurance rating bureaus. The jewelers' block and furriers' customers' rating schedules follow the same principles as those used in fire insurance rating schedules. Charges for deficiencies are added to a basic rate and credits for desirable features are subtracted.

There has been some dependence upon casualty insurance rates when there is a theft or burglary hazard at fixed locations. When the loadings for the personal property floater were first set up, they followed rather closely the burglary rates for various cities and sections of the country. After a credible experience had been developed for the personal property floater, it was no longer necessary to depend upon the casualty rates.

The tendency in the inland marine business is toward manual rating of more and more classes. A manual rate is one set out in a book or pamphlet called a "rate manual." Such rates are usually fixed according to classes of property. An example is the rates for insurance on cameras, which are the same for a large part of the United States. By the time insurance was declared to be commerce by the Supreme Court of the United States.,[8] half of the premium from inland marine business was from classes upon which the rates are fixed by manuals or are computed according to schedules prepared by rating bureaus. Inland marine insurance on property at fixed locations as well as on property in transit frequently can be rated according to manual and class rates. It is more efficient to rate it in that manner because the business is being produced by agents all over the country. An agent in Topeka, Kansas, for example, could not wait for an underwriter in a home office in New York or Hartford to quote him a rate for a personal jewelry floater. He wants something in a manual that will enable him to quote the rate and premium when he first calls on the prospect. The situation is quite different from that in the ocean marine field, in which most of the business is written in a few ports and the underwriters are in close contact with the sources of the business.

QUESTIONS

1. Explain the importance of the warehouse to warehouse clause in the development of inland marine insurance.
2. Name three important respects in which inland marine insurance practices differ from ocean marine insurance practices.
3. Explain the reasons for similarities in inland marine practices with many fire and casualty insurance practices.
4. Under what circumstances are valued policies issued in providing inland marine coverages?
5. Discuss the meaning of "thieves" in an ocean marine insurance policy and compare it with the interpretation of "theft" under an inland marine policy.
6. Name important points concerning which the interpretation of inland marine coverages depends upon court decisions of fire and casualty insurance policies.
7. Why do inland marine policies often exclude from coverage any damage to electrical apparatus caused by artificially generated electrical current?

[8]Prior to 1944, insurance was not considered to be commerce, and consequently was not believed subject to federal laws regulating interstate commerce. However, in 1944 the Supreme Court of the United States held that insurance is commerce. United States v. South-Eastern Underwriters Association et al., 322 U.S. 533, 80 L. ed. 1440 (1944).

8. Compare the cancellation provisions of inland marine insurance policies with those of ocean marine and fire and casualty insurance policies.
9. Discuss the reasons for using the fire insurance rates of the fire insurance rating bureaus as the basis for some inland marine rates.
10. Do inland marine practices follow ocean marine or fire insurance practices in respect to other insurance?
11. Why do inland marine underwriters feel that they must reserve the right to consent to any assignment of the policy prior to a loss?
12. Under what circumstances do you feel that existing rates for portions of a policy coverage (such as for fire insurance) should be used in establishing a new coverage, and when can the rate be set by judgment without a specific charge for segments of the coverage?

6

Principles of Inland Marine Protection

HISTORICAL BACKGROUND

Development of Land Transportation. Land transportation began to supplement water transportation in the early days of the railroads, and by the end of the nineteenth century the railroads were carrying the bulk of commercial traffic within the United States. The building of the railroads brought about the greatest change in transportation methods the world had ever seen. It was the first time in human history that men could ship large quantities of goods across dry land with reasonable speed and at low cost.

One of the most important effects of railroad expansion was the development of inland cities. No longer was it necessary for commerce to depend on waterways. Industry could be located close to raw materials and natural resources. Coal from the great inland deposits in West Virginia and Pennsylvania was shipped by railroad direct to the steel and iron centers. Finished products were sent in all directions to consumers in every city and town. Cities arose in the interior and factories sprang up all over the country. In less than a hundred years this completely new method of transportation had outstripped all the older methods, and it dominated American industry.

It is a tribute to the early vision and responsibility of the railroads that there was little demand for insurance on inland transportation. Soon after the railroads were established as freight carriers, they assumed the responsibility of delivering goods safely. By the time commerce was dependent for its existence upon the safe delivery of raw materials and finished goods, the liability of the railroads as common carriers was defined so clearly that shippers gave little thought to insuring property in transit.

Shipments were lost or destroyed occasionally, but a claim could be made against the railroad. It was easy for the shipper or consignee to make a claim, because a freight agent was located at the railroad office in every town. The railroads were wise in accepting the responsibility, and their settlements were sufficiently prompt and fair for industry not to feel the necessity for any other protection.

Effect of Conditions During World War I. The situation began to change during World War I. The additional burden of carrying war munitions and supplies overloaded the railroads, and it became difficult for them to keep their claim adjustments up to date. With the entry of the United States into the war, the federal government took over the railroads. It was not clear at the time whether the responsibility for lost or damaged property rested with the railroad corporations or with the government. The overloading of the railroads plus the presence of governmental red tape made the collection of freight claims a difficult task. Claims were many months or even years in being processed. The apparent division of responsibility between the government and the railroads caused many claimants to doubt the value of legal suits.

An increasing number of industries found it advantageous to buy insurance on their property in transit, so that they could collect for lost goods without delay and let the insurance companies worry about collecting from the railroads and the government. The cost of the insurance was unimportant to many policyholders, because war supplies were being produced on a cost-plus basis and the insurance premium was passed on to the government.

During this period, transportation insurance was provided by ocean marine insurers, largely under their ocean marine policies. No separation of inland from ocean marine coverages was made, and all the premium was reported as ocean marine. There was a direct continuity from the ocean marine coverage to this inland coverage. Problems were similar in the two types of transportation, and only minor adjustments were necessary to fit the insuring of land transportation.

Shipment by Motor Truck. Another factor that hastened the development of land transportation insurance was the use of the motor truck. The truck was not used for cross-country hauling until the transportation shortages of the war and postwar years made it economical. During the 1920s the motor truck became an established part of the transportation picture. Its ability to make overnight delivery between cities was in sharp contrast to the several days required for railroad handling of less-than-carload lots of freight. If the running time between cities was only a few hours for a motor truck, there might be a saving of several days over the time required for shipment by rail.

It soon became evident to shippers that motor truck transportation had its disadvantages. Claims for lost or damaged articles were uncertain of payment. Many of the truck lines were operating on extremely limited capital, and a large claim for damages would throw such lines into insolvency. Sometimes the trucker could not be found when a claim was to be made. Trucks could be driven to another part of the country to start a new business if the claims became too numerous. Merchants and manufacturers felt that they needed the facilities of the new mode of transportation but they also needed insurance protection against loss of goods being hauled by truck. The answer was provided by the insurance companies; the marine underwriters found an increasing number of prospects for transportation insurance.

The insuring of property in transit by land conveyance posed many new problems for insurance companies. Fire insurance departments had learned to appraise accurately the hazards to property located in a building, and casualty companies were accustomed to estimating the chances of loss by burglary. Neither of them was in a position to judge the probabilities of loss when the goods were being carried over rail or highway at speeds of fifty miles or more an hour. The coverages then being written in specific policies to cover loss by fire, windstorm, or theft were entirely inadequate, because the merchandise might be stolen, smashed in a collision, or dumped into a river as the result of a wreck. Marine underwriters, on the other hand, were accustomed to insuring goods against loss by "perils of the sea," and they already had accumulated some experience with land hazards under the "warehouse to warehouse" clauses of ocean marine policies. It was a natural development that the new forms of land transportation should be insured through marine departments of insurance companies. In order to distinguish this new type of coverage from the ocean marine policies, it became customary in the 1920s to designate these as "inland marine" policies.

Postwar Conditions. Other developments following World War I brought about a demand for another type of inland marine insurance coverage. There was a dispersal of wealth at the same time that a postwar crime wave was engulfing the country. More people had diamond rings and fur coats, and more people were interested in stealing them.

Fixed location insurance covered against relatively few hazards, whereas inland marine underwriters were able to write floater policies giving "all risks" coverage on personal effects. Fur coats and jewelry had to be worn to be useful, and they were frequently subject to transit hazards. The personal effects floater policy soon became a popular coverage for people of means who traveled for business or pleasure.

Broad coverage under a single policy began to appear desirable to many property owners. They wanted to know whether a similar full coverage policy could be issued on property at fixcd locations. The fire insurance departments and casualty companies were handicapped by the limitations on their underwriting powers. Many states prohibited a fire insurance company from writing what was designated as a casualty coverage, and the casualty companies could not write a fire coverage. Thus it was impossible in many states for either the fire insurance department of a company or a casualty company to write a full coverage policy.

The marine departments of the companies did not suffer under any such prohibitions. Their underwriting powers were practically unlimited. There was no definition of what constituted a transportation risk, and the imaginations of ambitious inland marine underwriters led to some ingenious interpretations.

Jewelers had long been subject to a greater theft hazard than other merchants, and London insurers had provided jewelers with a broad insurance policy that incorporated both fire and casualty protection. The marine departments of American companies saw an opportunity to fill this need in the American market. Owners of bridges needed protection not only from fire and windstorm but also from ice jams, from ships' running too close and colliding with the bridge, and from a host of unpredictable hazards. Marine underwriters came to the conclusion that such an "all risks" policy could be written, especially since a bridge has something to do with transportation—that is, it allows transporting vehicles to cross it. Neither the fire nor the casualty insurance companies objected strenuously to marine underwriters' insuring bridges or jewelers, because they believed that broad insurance coverage on bridges and jewelry stores was a hazardous business.

The 1920s saw another development in business that was to affect the insurance of transportation risks. Ambitious store owners saw the savings to be made by quantity purchases, and they branched out. This process spread throughout the country, and the great chain store systems developed.

Encroachment of Inland Marine Into Fire and Casualty Fields. Chain store proprietors became familiar with broad transportation insurance policies because they insured their goods in transit from warehouse to store and from one city to another. The idea of a single policy instead of dozens or hundreds of policies had a practical appeal. Inland marine underwriters were willing, and soon some of the big chains had their entire stocks insured under marine policies. Inland marine underwriters reasoned that this was a transit risk, inasmuch as the goods were insured during transportation from warehouse to store as well as in the store, where they remained only a short time before being sold.

The fire insurance departments of the companies began to see huge amounts of premium going to the inland marine departments. Much of the property covered by inland marine policies was at fixed locations and was subject to little or no transportation hazard. For example, factory and warehouse stocks were insured under inland marine policies when they were at fixed locations for many months at a time, the only transportation hazard being a brief exposure when the goods finally were moved a few feet to be loaded onto a purchaser's truck.

Fire underwriters felt that they were being deprived of premiums rightly theirs, and casualty underwriters similarly felt the loss of burglary premiums. In many cases it was charged that broad inland marine policies protecting against loss by fire, burglary, windstorm, and transportation hazards (or perhaps against "all risks" of loss or damage) were written at rates less than the fire companies were permitted to charge for the fire coverage alone. Fire underwriters were not able to compete on price or forms, because they were required by law or by the rules of fire rating bureaus to use only approved rates and forms.

The standard policy laws relating to fire insurance and the strict regulation of fire rates prevented the fire companies from giving the policyholders the protection they needed. Inland marine underwriters, being unhampered by restriction and rate regulation, could prepare a policy to fit the insured's needs.

An intense controversy arose within the insurance business. The fire insurance departments of the companies saw that they would have to provide some way of covering the stocks of chain stores and other multiple location risks. The answer to the fire departments was the organization of the Interstate Underwriters Board in 1929. This Board established rates and forms for interstate multiple location properties; the resulting coverages replaced the inland marine floaters insofar as the coverage of chain store property at fixed locations was concerned.

The establishing of the Interstate Underwriters Board helped the fire companies to give the chain stores blanket coverage on a fluctuating basis over an entire chain. However, this relieved only one part of the controversy between marine underwriters on the one hand and fire and casualty underwriters on the other. Inland marine underwriters were insuring many properties that the fire and casualty underwriters felt should be insured under fixed location coverages.

LIMITATIONS ON INLAND MARINE UNDERWRITING

It became evident to all sections of the insurance industry, as well as to state regulatory officials, that some line of demarcation should be drawn between the inland marine business and other sections of the insurance industry. The laws regulating the insuring powers of companies were drawn in general terms and it did not seem wise to redraft them. No matter how carefully or rigidly such laws were drawn, they would always be subject to interpretation, and it would be difficult to establish an accurate division between inland marine and other coverages.

The insurance companies were aware of the necessity for resolving the controversy, and numerous discussions were held between the marine, casualty, and fire insurance underwriters. The first actual agreement between different segments of the business was the Casualty-Marine-Merchandise Agreement between casualty and marine underwriters, which became effective July 1, 1930. This agreement established some principles between casualty and marine underwriters.

During this same year marine underwriters recognized the need for more uniformity in their own practices. Not only was there intense competition with other portions of the insurance business, but there was severe competition among themselves as well. Competitive rates were inducing the companies to write business at rate levels allegedly below the cost of doing business.

More than 100 insurance companies writing inland marine lines joined together in the formation of the Inland Marine Underwriters Association, which came into official existence on January 1, 1931. The purposes of the I.M.U.A. were to develop intelligent underwriting, to promote simpler and more nearly accurate rating methods, and to investigate hazards as well as promote means of reducing them. The Association adopted policy forms and clauses and established rating methods for the different types of business that underwriters believed could be rated on a schedule or according to the class of property. This was an ambitious program for the Association, in view of the confusion and sharp competition existing in the inland marine business at that time.

The Inland Marine Underwriters Association was an important step toward stabilizing the inland marine business, but there were other factors that could not be controlled by an organization within the inland marine segment of the business. For one thing, some companies writing inland marine business were not members of the I.M.U.A. and were not controlled by its efforts at stabilization.

Intense competition between inland marine and fire and casualty underwriters continued to result in conflicting policy provisions and inadequate rate levels. The former made it difficult for the public to determine whether policies were properly worded; the latter were a threat to company solvency.

Many conferences were held in 1931 and early 1932 among fire, casualty, and marine underwriters to establish a clear definition of what could be insured under an inland marine policy. These were urged and sponsored by officials of the New York State Insurance Department. It seemed evident that the companies were not in a position to agree on a definition and to bind all companies without some official action. In order to make the majority ideas of the industry effective, New York State Insurance Superintendent Van Schaick, on July 25, 1932, issued a tentative ruling on marine and transportation underwriting powers. He issued a final ruling on September 30, 1932, that defined the circumstances under which property could be insured under a marine or inland marine policy.

It was apparent that there would be many borderline cases under any general definition of marine insurance, and some authority would be necessary to make rulings and interpretations. At the request of Superintendent Van Schaick, on November 3, 1932, the American Institute of Marine Underwriters set up its special marine committee as a committee on interpretation and complaint. The ruling of the New York State Superintendent and the work of this committee were effective for New York State only, but they did tend to stabilize further the practices in the inland marine field, building upon the work of the Inland Marine Underwriters Association.

THE DEFINITIONS OF MARINE INSURANCE

There was a strong feeling in the insurance industry and among state insurance superintendents that some action should be taken on a nationwide basis to define the underwriting powers of marine underwriters. A proposed nationwide definition of marine insurance was submitted at a meeting of the National Association of Insurance Commissioners in December, 1932.[1] This was referred to a committee of the Commissioners' Association for a report at the next meeting. Extensive discussions followed during the first half of 1933, and the commissioners' convention on June 2, 1933, adopted the Nation-Wide Definition and Interpretation of the Insuring Powers of Marine and Transportation Underwriters. This document was commonly known as the Nation-Wide Definition. Adoption by the commissioners' convention did not make it effective in any state, but it served as a recommendation to the individual states that it be adopted officially and be given the force of state law or insurance department ruling. This was done by a majority of the state insurance departments and the Nation-Wide Definition became effective in thirty-four states.

It is important to note that this document was a definition and interpretation of the *underwriting powers* of marine and transportation underwriters. It specified what the insurance companies could write as marine or inland marine insurance. It made no distinction between ocean and inland marine. All insurance companies writing marine insurance were asked to become signatories to the Definition and a majority of them did. The adoption of the Definition by a state insurance commissioner made it applicable to all companies regardless of whether they had become signatories.

A Joint Committee on Interpretation and Complaint was set up

[1] The provisions of this proposed definition were based largely upon the ruling made effective in New York State on September 30, 1932.

to interpret the Definition and to assess penalties when companies violated the terms of their agreement to abide by the Definition. The Joint Committee could assess penalties only against signatory companies, but state authorities could take action against nonsignatory companies that violated the terms of the Definition.

During the twenty years following the adoption of the Nation-Wide Definition in 1933, there were two important changes in the insurance business that made a new definition desirable. First, there had been a gradual expansion of what was considered to be eligible for marine insurance. The Nation-Wide Definition had been amended in every state that had adopted it, and in many states the amendments were extensive. It was felt that a new definition should be adopted to include the generally accepted amendments. Second, the traditional lines of demarcation separating fire, casualty, and marine insurance had broken down, and many insurance companies had authority to write all kinds of property loss insurance. It was felt that a definition of a type of insurance no longer could be a definition of underwriting powers.

At its June, 1953, meeting, the National Association of Insurance Commissioners adopted a revised Nation-wide Marine Definition. The general terms of this new definition followed the pattern of the 1933 Nation-Wide Definition, but there were two important differences. (1) The conditions under which it was considered proper to issue marine or inland marine policies were expanded greatly. (2) The document specified that it was intended for classification purposes, and that "this instrument shall not be construed to restrict or limit in any way the exercise of any insuring powers granted under charters and license whether used separately, in combination, or otherwise." Thus this new document is a definition for classification purposes only and is not a definition of what a company can write.

Experience had proved that some machinery was necessary for the interpretation of borderline cases. Provision was made in the Nation-wide Marine Definition for a Committee on Interpretation to consist of fifteen persons, five to be marine and inland marine representatives, five to be fire insurance representatives, and five to be casualty and surety representatives. The Committee on Interpretation considers questions submitted by insurance companies and state insurance departments when there is doubt as to whether insurance in a particular situation should be classified as marine insurance. Decisions of the Committee are submitted to the states for adoption, and become effective or not, depending upon the action of each state insurance department.

Like the 1933 Nation-Wide Definition, the 1953 Nation-wide Definition was adopted by most of the states, and the interpretations of the Committee are adopted by most of the states. A couple of states have their own definitions which differ in some details from the Nation-wide Marine Definition, and there are a half dozen states that have not adopted any definition of marine insurance.

Throughout the Nation-wide Marine Definition there runs the principle that property must be in transit, or bear some relation to transportation, in order to qualify for coverage under a marine or inland marine policy. It was regarded as necessary to make many compromises between the various insurance interests involved, and it also was held necessary to recognize certain long-established practices in the transportation field.

Among the five types of property set out by the Nation-wide Marine Definition as classifiable for coverage under marine or inland marine policies, the first two tie in closely with practices in ocean marine commerce. Imports and exports both are permitted to be covered under marine or transportation policies just as long as they retain their peculiar characteristics. Whenever an import reaches its destination, it ceases to be a proper subject for marine or transportation insurance. Similarly, an export becomes a proper subject just as soon as it is designated as an export or is being prepared for export. An exception is made concerning established methods of insuring certain commodities, such as cotton. Cotton in bales had been insured under marine policies for many years, regardless of whether the particular bales of cotton had been designated specifically for export.

Domestic shipments form the third type of property that may be insured under a marine or transportation insurance policy. It was believed necessary to specify a length of time after which a domestic shipment would no longer be considered "in course of transportation." This was a compromise and was based largely on the provisions found in many ocean marine policies that coverage does not extend beyond a limited period from the time goods are unloaded from an oceangoing vessel.

The fourth classification of property held to be a proper subject for marine or transportation policies is a class known as "instrumentalities of transportation and communication." These consist of bridges, tunnels, and, with some restrictions, piers, wharves, docks, and slips. Also included within this classification are transmission lines for electrical power, pipe lines, radio and television communication equipment, and outdoor cranes. The decision to classify the insurance of such instrumentalities of transportation and communication as marine insurance was a recognition of a long-standing practice in the business. Such insurance had been written by marine underwriters for many years, largely because fire underwriters did not care to give broad protection on this type of property. Buildings used in connection with bridges and other instrumentalities of transportation and communication may not be classified as insurable under a marine or transportation policy, according to the Nation-wide Marine Definition. It is interesting to note that neither ships nor boats are mentioned specifically in the Definition. Long tradition made it obvious that they are eligible for marine coverage and are instrumentalities of transportation.

The fifth type of property eligible for a marine or transportation policy is designated as "personal property floater risks." This must be distinguished from what is known as the "personal property floater" policy. "Personal property floater risks" in the Nation-wide Marine Definition refers to personal property as distinct from real property. Not all personal property may be insured under a marine or inland marine policy. The Nation-wide Marine Definition contains a long list of individual marine insurance forms that may be issued to cover property of individuals, business property, and property in the hands of a bailee. Most of these policy forms are intended to cover property of such a nature that it can be used in many different locations. Some of the designations were the result of practices that had stood for many years in the marine insurance field. Fine arts floaters are specifically permitted, even though the objects may not move from a fixed location from one year to another. Jewelers' block policies are permitted specifically, although they are intended primarily to cover stocks of jewelry at a fixed location. For many years jewelers' block insurance had been written by London underwriters on a broad coverage basis. Several years prior to the establishment of the 1933 Nation-Wide Definition, this type of coverage had been defined by law in many states as a permissible marine coverage. (Many state laws also permit jewelers' block insurance to be classified as a casualty coverage.)

A final section of the Nation-wide Marine Definition specifies several types of property that may not be classified as insurable under a marine or transportation policy. This section serves largely to clarify the intent that the insured's property on his own premises is not generally considered a proper subject for marine or inland marine insurance.

Certain principles are present throughout the Nation-wide Marine Definition:

> First, an element of transportation must be present if property is to be eligible for insurance under an inland marine policy. This

> may seem a bit farfetched in such cases as those involving bridges and tunnels, but they are held to be insurable under an inland marine policy because they are instrumentalities of transportation.
>
> Second, property which is located on the premises of an owner is not in transit. Therefore, most policies must exclude coverage on the premises of the insured. Here again, as it has been pointed out, custom and compromise resulted in the permission of marine protection for some location coverages, as in the case of jewelers' block policies, fine arts policies, certain dealers' policies, and policies covering electric and mechanical signs.

There are provisions for many specific floaters in which these two principles seem to be violated. In most cases these inconsistencies result from the recognition of customs in the business. There is also a recognition that owners of many types of property need "all risks" protection. The policyholder is believed to be entitled to buy broad coverage in a single policy, and inland marine underwriters are willing to write such coverage.

Modification of the Nation-wide Marine Definition. The Nation-wide Marine Definition is subject to modification in two ways. It may be modified by action of the National Association of Insurance Commissioners, with subsequent adoption by the individual states of the change. This was done, for example, in 1954 when the provisions relating to the Physicians and Surgeons floater were expanded to include furniture and fixtures under certain conditions. It may also be modified by each state individually. Such modifications are made by rulings of the state insurance departments, and they become effective only in the states in which such action is taken.

General Effects of the Definitions. After adoption of the 1933 Nation-Wide Definition, the acrimonious disputes of the 1920s abated, but there remained a strong competition between the different sections of the insurance business. A large amount of premium was diverted from the inland marine departments of the companies immediately after the adoption of the 1933 Nation-Wide Definition. In 1931 inland marine premiums amounted to 5.64 percent of the total fire insurance company premiums written in the United States. It was in 1931 that the first effective restriction on inland marine underwriters was felt, and in 1932 inland marine premiums amounted to only 4.64 percent of the total fire company premiums. It appears that the demarcation set up by the 1933 Nation-Wide Definition and the arrangement that preceded it resulted in a loss to the inland marine underwriters of $6 or $7 million of premiums a year. There has been a healthy growth of the business since that time, and the loss was regained in a few years. Inland marine coverages were established and the industry found itself in good condition to stand the impact of the rate regulatory legislation that followed the United States Supreme Court decision declaring insurance to be commerce.

The stabilization brought about by the definitions enabled policyholders to determine more easily the adequacy of their protection under inland marine policies. Standardization of coverages, where possible, helps companies and state authorities to determine that rates are adequate but not excessive.

Although the definitions served to smooth out some of the difficulties between fire, marine, and casualty companies in the writing of insurance, it did not prevent these branches of the business from issuing overlapping coverages. Adjusters and the loss departments of the companies had great difficulty in determining which was the primary insurance when each of several policies covering a property had "excess insurance" clauses that attempted to make the other policy the primary coverage. Many times a policyholder would be left waiting for his claim settlement while the insurance companies argued to decide which one would pay the loss. Eventually the fire, casualty, and marine underwriters decided upon several "agreements of guiding principles," which set out rules by which such overlapping coverage questions would be decided. These agreements will be discussed in connection with the handling of inland marine claims.

EFFECT OF MULTIPLE LINE DEVELOPMENTS

During the late 1940s and the early 1950s the state insurance laws were modified so that in all states an insurance company with adequate financial resources could write both fire and casualty insurance. This resulted in what is called "multiple line" underwriting. Such multiple line insurance companies can write all forms of insurance except life insurance. Another result of these multiple line laws was the development of insurance policies that combined many coverages that previously had been divided between fire and casualty or between inland marine and casualty insurance. Inland marine coverages were expanded to include complete property loss insurance for certain types of retail merchants or dealers. A description of these "dealers' policies" is given in Chapter 15.

Multiple line underwriting resulted in some loss of business by inland marine underwriters. Package policies which were classified as multiple line insurance rather than as inland marine insurance in many cases include floater coverage of a type previously issued only as inland marine insurance.

Some of the multiple line package policies are made up of divisible sections according to the traditional fire, casualty, and inland marine lines of insurance. Filings of rates and forms for such packages in many instances are made cooperatively by several rating bureaus. A typical arrangement is for the fire insurance rating bureau in a state to file the fire and allied portions of the package, a casualty rating bureau files the casualty portion, and an inland marine rating bureau files the inland marine or in some cases an "all risks" portion. This cooperation among rating bureaus is a result of the tendency toward providing as broad a coverage as possible in a package of insurance.

QUESTIONS

1. Why was there little demand for insurance on goods being shipped by railroad prior to World War I?
2. What situations during and following World War I brought about an increased need for insurance on goods in transit by land carrier?
3. What restrictions on the underwriting powers of fire and casualty insurance companies helped inland marine underwriters to expand their activities?
4. How was the organization of the Interstate Underwriters Board intended to restrict the activities of inland marine underwriters?
5. What were the purposes of the Inland Marine Underwriters Association?
6. What was the purpose of the 1933 Nation-Wide Definition?
7. Describe the functions of the Committee on Interpretation of the Nation-wide Marine Definition.
8. What types of property are set out in the Nation-wide Marine Definition as properly classifiable for marine insurance coverage?
9. What principles are present throughout the Nation-wide Marine Definition?
10. Name several important compromises that were made in drafting the definitions in order to recognize established customs of the inland marine insurance business.
11. Have the effects of the definitions been desirable?
12. What combinations of fire, casualty or marine insurance coverages are available under multiple line policies in your state?

13. What in your opinion brought about the change in insurance laws which permitted the writing of multiple line policies?
14. Do you feel that package policies or policies providing individual coverages are better for the policyholder and why?

7

Basic Inland Marine Coverage

THE INLAND MARINE POLICY CONTRACT

Elements of an Insurance Contract. An insurance policy is always a contract between two persons. This fact is not understood by most policyholders, and the misunderstanding results in confusion concerning the obligations of the insurance company and the policyholder. The persons who are party to an insurance contract may be either actual persons or corporations. The contract is always personal and is not a contract attaching to the property covered. The property that is the subject of insurance may change many times during the term of the insurance contract, as in the case of mercantile stocks or property being carried by a motor truck operator.

The insurance protects the policyholder just so long as the policy description fits the property he has at the time of the loss. The only exception to this rule occurs when the insurance covers scheduled property, such as a specifically described piece of jewelry. Even in this case the policy is a contract between persons and does not follow the property. If the property is sold to another person not named in the policy, that particular property is no longer covered by the insurance.

Certain elements must be present to make any contract legal and binding upon the parties thereto.

Both parties must be legally competent to enter into the contract. Ordinarily a person who is not of age or a person of unsound mind is legally incompetent to be party to a contract.

A consideration must pass for a contract to be valid. In the case of an insurance policy, the consideration is the premium paid by the policyholder in return for the obligations assumed by the insurance company. The express or implied promise to pay the premium is a valid consideration even if the premium has not actually been paid. Frequently insurance policies provide that the contract is issued "in consideration of representations made by the insured" as well as in consideration of the premium paid.

There must be a meeting of the minds of the parties to the contract. That is, the parties to the contract must understand each other, and the contract must express what both of them have in mind when the agreement is made. If one party willfully conceals essential facts that the other party should know or if there is fraud on the part of either party, there is not a meeting of the minds, and the contract will be void. An important purpose of the warranties previously discussed is to make certain that each party understands the intentions of the other.

An insurance contract (policy) must be executed by the insurance company and accepted by the policyholder; this action is comparable to the signing of a contract by the parties in other legal contracts. The signatures of the principal officers of the company are by facsimile or printed signature, and the actual execution of the document ordinarily is by an authorized agent who is given power by the company to countersign.

The fact that an insurance policy is signed by only one party to the contract may be responsible for the fact that it is not generally thought of in the same way as other contracts in which both parties sign the agreement. However, the fact that the policyholder is not required to sign the policy does not make it any less binding upon him, because this obligation is ratified by the insured's acceptance of the insurance contract.

The insured must have an insurable interest in the property covered. Inasmuch as this is a contract to pay money in certain eventualities, the insurable interest must be a financial one. An insurance company cannot issue a policy to an individual agreeing to pay an amount of money upon the occurrence of an event if that event would not cost the insured any money. The lack of a financial insurable interest would make such an insurance policy a gambling contract and legally unenforceable.

One of the best definitions of insurable interest is that appearing in the insurance laws of New York State: "The term 'insurable interest,' as used in this section, shall be deemed to include any lawful and substantial economic interest in the safety or preservation of property from loss, destruction or pecuniary damage."[1]

It will be seen that this is an extremely broad definition and that an insurable interest can be any financial interest or risk of loss from the occurrence of a certain event.

Binders. Legal contracts may be either oral or written. An oral contract may be difficult to prove, especially if there are no witnesses other than the parties executing the contract.

There is a period of oral contractual relationship with many insurance contracts. The agent or salesman persuades the prospect that he needs certain coverage, and the prospect agrees. From this point until the policy is written and accepted by the policyholder, the contract is oral. This is known in the insurance industry as an "oral binder." Because it is difficult to prove what two people may have discussed, it is extremely important that the binder be confirmed in writing at the time the agreement is made or as soon thereafter as possible. It is even more important in the case of inland marine insurance than in the case of some other coverages because standardization is lacking. If a standard policy contract is required by state law, as in the case of fire insurance, the provisions of the standard contract would be presumed to apply to any oral agreement. If there is no standard policy contract, this presumption is not present and it probably would be more difficult to resolve any misunderstanding regarding the terms of an oral contract.

Reformation of a Policy. Once the policy contract has been placed in writing, it is presumed to be the entire agreement between the parties unless there is strong evidence to the contrary. In order to emphasize this point, most insurance policies contain a statement to the effect that no agent has authority to modify the contract except in writing. When disputes arise in connection with the coverage under a policy, it sometimes is asserted by the policyholder that the agent

[1] Section 148.

told him the policy provided certain coverage not specified in writing in the contract itself. In the absence of clear evidence to the effect that the agent had made an agreement to have the policy extended, the contention of the policyholder probably would not hold, because the written contract generally is presumed to be the entire agreement.

A reformation of the policy contract occasionally may be secured by one party to the contract. It is necessary to show that the contract does not express the intentions of the parties. If it can be proved to the satisfaction of a court that the intentions of both parties at the time the contract was drawn were different from what the contract actually states, the court might rule that the contract be reformed and made to express what the parties had in mind. This is difficult to prove and ordinarily the written contract is the entire agreement. Most insurance court cases revolve around a difference of opinion concerning the meaning of the written contract rather than an attempt to secure reformation. In securing reformation of a contract, it is not sufficient to show that it does not express the intention of one party; it is necessary to show that both parties intended something other than what is written in the contract.

Generally a court will construe any ambiguity in an insurance policy against the insurance company. This is based on the idea that the company prepared the wording of the policy and would have used a more restrictive wording had it intended to specify the meaning unfavorable to the policyholder.

Makeup of An Insurance Policy. The physical form of an inland marine insurance contract does not differ greatly from that of other insurance policies covering damage to property. There is usually a printed piece of paper called the "policy," which is the document containing most of the conditions and clauses common to inland marine contracts. This policy (1) includes the insuring clause (which states the consideration for the contract), (2) names the parties, (3) states the term of the insurance, (4) contains the facsimile signatures of the principal officers of the insurance company, and (5) contains the actual countersignature of the issuing or countersigning agent.

No state requires by law a standard form of inland marine insurance policy contract. This is in contrast to the fire insurance business, in which a special policy contract is required by state law or administrative ruling in most states. The inland marine rating bureaus have filed a basic policy for those types of inland marine coverage for which the clauses can be standardized, but this contract is used for only about half of the inland marine policies.

A sheet of paper or document called the "form" is usually attached to the policy. The form (1) includes a description of the property insured, (2) delineates the hazards insured against, (3) contains the exclusions or modifications, and (4) specifies any territorial limits which may be applicable to the coverage. This form, as well as the policy, is usually countersigned by an authorized agent of the company. In most states the agent must be a resident of the state in which the subject of the insurance is located.

Other endorsements may further extend or modify the coverage. These are attached to the policy and form, and each of them is usually countersigned by an authorized agent.

Some inland marine contracts are printed wholly on single pieces of papers, with no distinction between policy and form. This is usual when the contract is short.

There is great flexibility in the policies, forms, and endorsements that may be used in inland marine insurance as contrasted with fire insurance. This is necessary because of the great variations in the nature of property that may be covered under an inland marine policy and because of the many different circumstances under which the property may be insured. Uniformity in coverage has not been feasible for property in transit between different parts of the world.

Preparing an Inland Marine Policy. The names of the parties to an insurance contract must be stated correctly and fully. For example, a transportation company may have one corporate name and may be operating under another name insofar as the public is concerned. It is good practice to follow the corporate or individual name of the insured by the words "doing business as" and the name by which the organization is known. This becomes extremely important in connection with motor truck operations when a truck line has purchased more than one franchise and may be operating under different names in different territories.

When it is necessary to cover more than one interest under a policy, the full names of all parties having an interest should be stated correctly. If names are stated incorrectly or incompletely, the insured may not have the coverage he needs and desires, or the insurance company may be exposed to liability it does not contemplate in the rate and in its underwriting.

The coverage intended for a policy may be printed in the form attached to the policy, but frequently additional information concerning the coverage must be inserted specifically by the policy writer.

Territorial limits are important in many policies, particularly transportation policies, and a certain location may be specified for a portion of the coverage. Such conditions must be inserted correctly because the rates often are dependent upon the territorial limits and the location of the property.

The wording referring to the term of the policy, which is stated in the contract, is extremely important when a loss occurs near the time of inception or expiration of the contract. When the policy states a day upon which the coverage commences and another day upon which the coverage ends but does not specify the time of day, it is understood that the policy term starts at the beginning (immediately after midnight) of the day stated as the inception date of the policy and expires at the end (midnight) of the day stated as the ending date for the coverage.

Many policies state that coverage begins and ends at noon. Unless the time of day is further explained in the policy, there is a possibility of controversy as to whether it refers to sun time, standard time, or daylight saving time, and also whether it refers to the time at the place of the loss or at the place of issuance of the policy. This is particularly important with inland marine policies because they cover property in course of transportation. There may be several hours' difference in time between the place of issuance and the place at which any loss occurs. A satisfactory wording to cover this situation is "at noon, standard time at place of issuance." The place of issuance is the location where the agent countersigns the policy.[2]

A description of the property or interest insured is another important piece of information to be filled in by the policy writer. It is necessary to make a clear distinction between a policy that provides coverage relating to physical goods and insurance to protect a certain interest, such as legal liability for loss of or damage to property. A policy issued to an owner of property is intended to indemnify the owner for loss of or damage to the property. If the property is destroyed by a peril named in the policy, the loss is payable to the insured. However, an inland marine policy may be issued to a person who does not own the property but who has it in his custody; in this case the policy may be issued to cover his legal liability for loss or damage. In some cases, as in a bailees' customers

[2]As long as the agent is authorized to countersign at the location named in the policy as the place of issuance, and it is the intention of both parties that the contract be effective at that place, it would not affect the application of the contract if the agent actually affixed his signature at some other location. Wooten Hotel Corporation v. Northern Assur. Co., 155 F. (2d) 988 (1946).

policy, the legal liability of the bailee is insured and the value of the goods also is insured as to the owner. This is a dual interest policy. The rates vary according to the property or interest covered, and it is extremely important that the description of the property or interest insured be accurate in order that the rate contemplated may be in conformity.

The description of the property or interest covered may be in general terms; a policy issued to a motor truck operator, for example, may describe the cargo as "general merchandise." With specifically described property, such as furs and jewelry, the description may be in considerable detail and apply only to a specific piece of jewelry or fur garment.

When the business or nature of property belonging to the insured may vary, it is necessary to use a wording that could be extended to property other than that specifically described, provided the insurer intends to grant that coverage. For example, a policy that covers a stock of "dry goods" might be interpreted as not covering items of hardware if they are a part of the stock. In order to take care of this contingency, it is customary to use such words as "all kinds of lawful goods and merchandise consisting principally of dry goods."

The policy ordinarily states a limit of liability. In addition to being careful that the amount stated is that contemplated by both the policyholder and the company, it is important to have the wording show clearly whether this limit of liability includes salvage and other charges or whether such charges would be payable in addition to the limit of liability applying to the property loss.

Inland marine policies may contain warranties. As already explained, warranties are looked upon with disfavor by many legislatures and many courts. Most, if not all, warranties can be rephrased as conditions of coverage that are just as strong as the warranty and at the same time acceptable under insurance laws and rulings. For example, a typical warranty found occasionally in inland marine policies is: "Warranted free of loss or damage caused by or resulting from strikes, lockouts, or labor disturbances." This can be reworded to state: "It is understood and agreed that this policy does not cover loss or damage resulting from strikes, lockouts, or labor disturbances."

CONTRACT PROVISIONS AFFECTING COVERAGE

Coinsurance. Coinsurance is not universal in inland marine insurance, but it appears sufficiently often to require an examination of its application and use. The principle of coinsurance is that the policyholder must carry insurance in an amount equal to a prescribed percentage of the value of the property covered if he is to collect his loss in full. If the policyholder fails to maintain insurance up to the required percentage of the total value, he is penalized in proportion to this deficiency in the settlement of any loss under the policy. For example, when insurance equal to the full value is required (100 percent coinsurance) and the policyholder carries insurance equal to only half of the value of the property he would collect only half of the amount of any loss. He is required to stand the rest of the loss himself and in that respect becomes a "coinsurer" with the insurance company; hence the word "coinsurance" is used.

Inland marine policies frequently do not title the coinsurance clause by that name, as fire insurance policies do. The wording of an inland marine clause frequently used is:

> In no event shall this company be liable for a greater proportion of any loss than the limit of liability under this policy bears to the total value of the property insured under this policy at the time such loss occurs.

It is obvious that the purpose of the coinsurance clause is to influence the policyholder to carry insurance equal to the value of the property or, in the case of a lower percentage clause, equal to the amount specified in the clause. This is necessary in order that all policyholders will pay an equitable share of the premiums needed to pay the claims resulting from that class of business.

Inland marine rates are based upon the assumption that policyholders will carry approximately full insurance to value. However, a policyholder may feel that he can gamble on the possibility that he will never suffer a total loss, and he may decide to carry insurance equal to only a part of the value he owns. His motive would be to save a portion of the premium he would have to pay for full insurance. If a large number of policyholders did this, the insurance company's premium income would be reduced proportionately. The losses to be paid by the insurance company would not be reduced in the same proportion as the reduction in premium, because most losses are partial. The rates for insurance would have to be higher if a large proportion of policyholders carried only partial insurance than if all policyholders carried full insurance to value. The coinsurance clause makes it advantageous for all policyholders to carry approximately the same proportion of insurance on their property; the rates will be based on that proportion and will be fair to all policyholders.

The coinsurance principle is used with inland marine policies on commercial property. Commercial property has a sales value or a cost value that can be determined within close limits. However, coinsurance seldom is used with insurance on household furnishings, clothing, and personal belongings because of the difficulty of arriving at a fair value for such property.

The presence of coinsurance always complicates a loss settlement. It is necessary to determine not only the amount of the loss but also the cash value of all property covered under the policy, since the amount to be paid depends on the ratio of the insurance carried to the value of the property.

Coinsurance is particularly troublesome when the values insured are not under control of the policyholder. This occurs with bailee coverages and other legal liability coverages, such as motor truck cargo insurance. Coinsurance clauses on these policies penalize the insured if the value in his custody at the time of a loss is greater than the limit of liability on the policy. This is a difficult problem for a policyholder when, as in the case of motor truck cargo insurance, he does not know the value of the property he is carrying. It is necessary for the policyholder to get some idea of the values from his customers and discuss this with the insurance company so that the limit of liability will be sufficiently high to take care of any loss that may occur.

Coinsurance is not necessary when the nature of the policy requires the insured to carry full insurance to value. Policies covering property in the course of transportation usually require that the insured report all shipments covered by the policy, and the premium is based upon the total value shipped. Reporting less than the actual value is a violation of the policy terms. The insured is penalized if there is a loss and it is found that the values reported are less than those actually shipped.

Many motor truck cargo policies are rated on the basis of the insured's gross receipts, so that the amount of premium varies in relation to the exposure as indicated in the gross receipts of the business.

When the amount of premium does not fluctuate in relation to the amount of exposure, about the only way to secure an adequate premium is to put in the policy a coinsurance clause whereby the insured participates in the loss if he has inadequate coverage.

Concealment, Misrepresentation, and Fraud. Inland marine insurance policies contain a clause concerning concealment, misrepresentation, and fraud by the insured. A clause frequently used reads as follows:

> This policy shall be void if the insured has concealed or misrepresented any material fact or circumstance concerning this insurance or the subject thereof or in the case of any fraud, attempted fraud or false swearing by the insured touching any matter relating to this insurance or the subject thereof, whether before or after a loss.

The use of the word "material" in the concealment and misrepresentation clause is a practical acknowledgment of the situation under the insurance laws of many states. The insurance laws of New York State provide that "no misrepresentation shall avoid any contract of insurance or defeat recovery thereunder unless such misrepresentation was material. No misrepresentation shall be deemed material unless knowledge by the insurer of the facts misrepresented would have led to a refusal by the insurer to make such a contract."[3]

The thinking of the courts regarding concealment and misrepresentation under an inland marine policy is different from that in connection with an ocean marine policy. It has been stated that the historical basis for the writing of inland and ocean marine insurance by the same company does not warrant or necessitate the same treatment for both types of policies. The ocean marine rule calling for all facts material to the insurance is seen to have a logical basis when it is considered that the insurer may have no opportunity to inspect a vessel, particularly when it is in a foreign port. The same consideration does not exist with an inland marine policy, because the inland marine underwriter has a better opportunity to inquire into the hazards that might result in a loss.

The "ordinary rule" applying to fire insurance coverage is that "concealment" is the intentional withholding of any fact material to the insurance which the insured in honesty and good faith ought to communicate to the underwriter. If there is no intent to conceal material facts, the insured may remain silent in respect to many matters concerning which the underwriter fails to question him. The "ordinary rule" has been upheld as applying to inland marine insurance rather than the "marine rule," which requires full disclosure of the facts whether or not the underwriter asks for the information.[4]

Misrepresentation differs from concealment in that there must

[3]Section 149, paragraph 2.

[4]Stecker v. American Home Fire Assurance Co., 299 N.Y.1, 84 N.E. (2nd) 797 (1949).

be an incorrect statement made with intent to deceive the insurer. Misrepresentation that would invalidate a policy also must be material to the risk. It is seldom that an insurance company can avoid payment of a loss on the plea of misrepresentation unless the misrepresentation is such that, had the true facts been disclosed, the company would not have issued the policy. The New York law further provides that it is permissible to introduce in evidence in such cases the regular practice and procedure of the insurance company in the underwriting of its business in order to show the type of information that would have caused it to reject the risk.

When fraud is proved, the courts seem favorable to the insurance companies and have held that an attempt to defraud the insurance company will invalidate the policy. Fraud is extremely difficult to prove and the proof must be conclusive. The mere making of a false statement is not proof of fraud. A false statement might be made unintentionally or without intent to defraud; in such a case there is a serious question whether it would be considered a fraud by the courts.

Actions that have been interpreted by the courts as constituting fraud or attempted fraud have included the making of a false statement of loss[5] and attempts to show that certain merchandise was on location and destroyed in a fire, when as a matter of fact it was not present and was not destroyed.[6]

The distinction between misrepresentation and fraud sometimes is a rather fine line. In general, a fraud is a misrepresentation known to be false by the person making it and made with an intent to defraud the other party, in this case the insurance company.

Territorial Limits. The territorial limits specified in inland marine transportation policies differ from the fixed locations specified in other property insurance policies. The coverage is not limited to a single location but applies anywhere within the territorial limits described. Many of the personal inland marine policies, such as the personal property floater and personal articles floater, cover the property anywhere in the world.

Another common territorial designation is "within the continental United States and Canada." The question has arisen whether the term "continental United States" includes Alaska. In order to make the policy absolutely clear, many underwriters use such wording as "including Alaska" or "excluding Alaska." In the absence

5Columbian Ins. Co. v. Modern Laundry, Inc., 277 F. 355 (1921).

6Virginia Fire and Marine Ins. Co. v. Vaughan, 88 Va. 832, 14 S.E. 754 (1892).

of any such statement, Alaska would be regarded as a part of the continental United States.

Alaska, even before it became a state, was a part of the United States by virtue of the treaty concluded with Russia in 1867, which provided that the inhabitants of Alaska should be admitted to the enjoyment of all the rights, advantages, and immunities of the citizens of the United States and should be maintained and protected in the free enjoyment of their liberty, property, and religion. In an early case, Mr. Chief Justice Marshall, speaking for the United States Supreme Court, said that "United States is the name given to our great Republic, which is composed of states and territories. The District of Columbia, or the territory West of Missouri, is not less within the United States than Maryland or Pennsylvania."[7] Alaska is on the same continent and therefore is a part of the continental United States.

The use of the word "continental" would seem to limit the area so that, for example, Hawaii would not be covered by such wording. If a policy provided coverage "within the United States," the coverage would be broader and would cover Hawaii, which is a part of the United States but not part of the continental United States.

Some inland marine policies, such as motor truck cargo policies, may cover within a radius of a specified number of miles of a fixed location. The question has arisen whether the radius of operation is intended to mean a geometric radius or the distance by highway. Inasmuch as the geometric radius ordinarily would give a broader radius of operation and would be more favorable to the policyholder, it may be assumed that the simple words "radius of operation" or "within a radius of" so many miles would be interpreted to be a straight geometric radius and not the distance by highway. This seems reasonable because the distance by highway could vary from year to year as highways were changed.

Some companies have inserted in their motor truck cargo policies a further statement to the effect that the radius is to be measured by the shortest highway distance from the point of operation. The use of the radius by airline measurement is simpler and offers fewer complications to both the insured and the company.

Valuation of Insured Property. The valuation clause in the policy should be coordinated with any clause regarding valuation that may appear in the form. A commonly used clause in inland marine policies reads:

[7]Loughborough v. Blake, 5 Wheat. 317, 5 L. ed. 98 (1820).

> The said goods and merchandise shall be valued at actual invoice cost, including prepaid or advanced freight, if any, together with such costs and charges (including the commission of the Insured as selling agent, but excluding duty) as may have accrued and become legally due thereon. In the event of there being no invoice, the valuation of the merchandise insured hereunder shall be the actual cash market value of the property insured at point of destination on the date of disaster.

The presence of this clause without any modifying endorsement means that the insured has to prove the value of any property damaged or destroyed before he can recover the amount of the loss. This means that he must prove two things: first, the fact that the property is lost or damaged; and second, the amount of the loss.

Two types of valuation endorsements may be used to modify the valuation clause in the policy. The first of these is a statement that sets a dollars-and-cents value on a specifically described article. For example, the value of a painting described in a fine arts floater may be set at $500. If the painting is destroyed, the company is obligated to pay the amount of $500. This type of endorsement makes the policy a "valued policy."

The second type of modification of the valuation clause prescribes a method by which the value of the property is to be determined for loss adjustment purposes. For example, a clause used on motor truck cargo policies reads:

> The company shall not be liable beyond the actual cash value of the property at the time any loss or damage occurs and the loss or damage shall be ascertained or estimated according to such actual cash value with proper deduction for depreciation, however caused, and shall in no event exceed what it would then cost to repair or replace the same with material of like kind and quality.

A policy writer may inadvertently make a policy on a valued basis. Many inland marine policies specifically list the articles covered. The heading at the top of a column listing an amount of money opposite each article may determine whether the policy is on a valued basis. If the word at the top is "value" or a similar designation, the amount set opposite each item becomes the agreed value of the item.

There might be some question concerning the value of the items if the words at the top of this column are "amount of insurance." It may be presumed that the amount of insurance is not necessarily the value of the articles, but many underwriters feel that the preferred wording is "limit of liability." This makes it clear that there is no agreement concerning the value of the item.

There should be an understanding between the policyholder and the company as to whether the policy is on a valued basis. The terms of the policy should state clearly whether the amounts are limits of liability or are agreed upon as the value of the items to be paid in case of loss.

Limitation of Recovery for Partial Loss. Three clauses frequently found in inland marine policies are designed to limit the recovery if the damage occurs to only a portion of the property insured.

The first of these is the "pairs and sets" clause. A frequently used version of this clause provides:

> In event of loss of or damage to any article or articles which are a part of a set, the measure of loss of or damage to such article or articles shall be a reasonable and fair proportion of the total value of the set, giving consideration to the importance of said article or articles, but in no event shall such loss or damage be construed to mean total loss of set.

A similar clause with a slightly different application is the machinery clause, which reads:

> In case of loss or injury to any part of the insured property consisting, when complete for sale or use, of several parts, this company shall only be liable for the insured value of the part lost or damaged.

The adjustment of losses under these two clauses presents a difficult problem for the adjuster. He must arrive at a fair proportionate value of the part or parts lost or damaged in their relation to the entire machine or set. These provisions are necessary in order to make it clear that the insured is not entitled to receive payment for a total loss under the policy when only a part of a set or of a machine is lost or damaged.

A third clause with a similar intent is the labels clause, which reads:

> In case of loss or damage affecting labels, capsules or wrappers, the loss shall be adjusted on the basis of an amount sufficient to pay the cost of new labels, capsules or wrappers, and the cost of reconditioning the goods.

This clause is useful in the handling of claims involving canned goods in which the only damage may be soiling or destruction of the labels. It is simpler to adjust losses under this clause than under the "pairs and sets" or machinery clauses, inasmuch as the exact method of determining the loss is set out.

Insured's Obligation to Protect Threatened Property. One of the clauses found in almost all inland marine policies, and at the same time one of the most misunderstood clauses, is the "sue and labor" clause. It is borrowed directly from ocean marine policies and is couched in the language of American colonial days. It reads:

> In case of loss or damage, it shall be lawful and necessary for the Insured, his or their factors, servants and assigns, to sue, labor, and travel for, in and about the defense, safeguard and recovery of the property insured hereunder or any part thereof without prejudice to this insurance; nor shall the acts of the Insured or this Company, in recovering, saving and preserving the property insured in case of loss or damage, be considered a waiver or an acceptance of abandonment, to the charge whereof this Company will contribute according to the rate and quantity of the sum herein insured.

The clause is intended to do several things. Its primary objective is to obligate the insured to save the property from further loss, in case some loss or damage occurs. In addition to placing this obligation on the insured, it also permits him to take action or spend money toward the saving of the property without waiving any of his rights to offer abandonment of the property to the insurance company. This clause also permits the company to recover, save, or preserve the property without its action being considered as a waiver or as an acceptance of abandonment tendered by the insured. The final agreement is that the company will pay its proportion of such expense in relation to the amount of insurance and the value of the property.

The clause originated at a time when cargoes might be at locations remote from the representatives of the insurance company and when representatives of the insured frequently traveled with their cargoes to remote parts of the world. In case of loss, this representative of the insured was obliged to do everything he could to preserve the property from further damage. It also has been held that "sue and labor" expenses may be paid to prevent a loss even though the property was not actually damaged.

The insured has no claim under the "sue and labor" clause if the peril threatening the property is not insured against by the policy. For example, if the policy did not cover against loss by fire, the insured could not collect from the insurance company any expenses incurred to prevent a fire loss.

"Sue and labor" expenses also may be collected when the efforts were not successful in preventing a total loss. There are ocean marine cases in which "sue and labor" expenses have been allowed to an insured in addition to payment for a total loss. It appears that this interpretation would be carried over to inland marine cases, inasmuch as this would be favorable to the insured. The wording is sufficiently obscure so that the courts are likely to give any benefit of doubt to the insured.

Many underwriters have felt that the archaic language of the "sue and labor" clause should be discarded for modern language that would express its intent in terms the policyholder would be able to understand without reference to ocean marine court decisions. There is some improvement in the wording of the "protection of property" clause in the Scheduled Property Floater policy promulgated by the Inland Marine Insurance Bureau, but there still is no clear statement about whether it is intended to pay "sue and labor" expenses in addition to a total loss. This clause reads:

> In case of loss it shall be lawful and necessary for the Insured, his or their factors, servants and assigns, to sue, labor, and travel for, in and about the defense, safeguard and recovery of the property insured hereunder, or any part thereof, without prejudice to this insurance, nor shall the acts of the Insured or the Company, in recovering, saving and preserving the property insured in case of loss be considered a waiver or an acceptance of abandonment. The expenses so incurred shall be borne by the Insured and the Company proportionately to the extent of their respective interests.

A distinction should be made between "sue and labor" expenses and general average expenses. Expenses for which the company is liable under the "sue and labor" clause are those that help directly to reduce the loss to the insurance company on the specific property insured. Court costs are allowable, as are the costs of reconditioning merchandise, unloading it, and forwarding it by other means.

General average expenses, on the other hand, relate to the prorating of a loss over an entire cargo and ship and freight. Sometimes there may be a close question whether the costs are "sue and labor" expenses or expenses to prevent loss of an entire venture. Inasmuch as general average expenses are not common in inland marine insurance, this question has not caused much difficulty, although it could arise in connection with shipments of air freight.

Subrogation. The right of subrogation is important to insurance companies. It is recognized under the common law that a person who is responsible for a loss ultimately should make good the amount of the loss. The insurance contract is one of indemnity; when the insurance company pays a loss, it acquires any right of recovery which the insured may have against a third person responsible for the loss. This right does not rest upon the insurance contract itself but is a matter of equity in that the insurance company is the one ultimately wronged by the person causing the loss.

Inasmuch as the insurance company is acquiring from the insured a right of collection, the amount the company can collect is limited to the amount the insured could have collected if there were no insurance. The insured must not do anything that would impair this right of recovery; otherwise he may impair his right to indemnity from the insurance company.

Although the insurance company has a right of subrogation under common law and equity, companies usually insert in their inland marine policies a clause outlining the exact obligations and procedure in connection with subrogation rights. One of the clauses relating to this right reads:

> If in the event of loss or damage the Insured shall acquire any right of action against any individual, firm or corporation for loss of, or damage to, property covered hereunder, the Insured will, if requested by the Company, assign and transfer such claim or right of action to the Company, or, at the Company's option, execute and deliver to the Company the customary form of loan receipt upon receiving an advance of funds in respect of the loss or damage; and will subrogate the Company to, or will hold in trust for the Company, all such rights of action to the extent of the amount paid or advanced, and will permit suit to be brought in the Insured's name under the direction of and at the expense of the Company.

This requires the assignment of any right of recovery to the insurance company. It also requires the insured to provide a loan receipt for payment of a loss. In some cases the outright payment of a loss by the insurance company may be construed as eliminating the insured's right to recover from the person who caused the loss. In such cases the loss payment is treated as a loan to the insured, which he is obligated to pay back to the insurance company if the amount of the loss is recovered from the person responsible for the loss. This clause also gives the insurance company the right to bring suit in the insured's name if it is felt that a court or jury would be more likely to allow recovery to the insured than to the insurance company.

Carrier or Bailee Not to Benefit From Insurance. Closely tied to the right of subrogation is a clause in the inland marine policy providing that the insurance shall "in no wise inure directly or indirectly to the benefit of any carrier or other bailee." Carriers and bailees frequently insert in their contracts or bills of lading a provision that any insurance carried by the insured will be for the benefit of the carrier or bailee. If it were not for the policy provision quoted in this paragraph, payment by the company to the insured might relieve the carrier or bailee from his obligation to make good the amount of a loss for which he may be liable.

Inland marine policies sometimes include a further provision regarding the liability of a carrier or bailee to the effect that, if the insured has agreed to release or lessen the liability of any carrier or bailee, the policy will be void. The use of such a clause on the policy would make the policy voidable by the acceptance of an ordinary bill of lading, such as is used by railroads. A further discussion of this subject will be found in the chapters covering transportation policies; mention of it is made here in order to associate it with the provision in the policy that the insurance shall not inure to the benefit of a carrier or bailee. Insurance companies use every means to protect their rights of subrogation, inasmuch as rates and coverages are based upon the right to recover portions of the losses they pay. Any release of these rights of subrogation would require higher rates for the coverage.

Other Insurance. Almost all inland marine policies contain some reference to other insurance. A clause commonly used on inland marine policies reads that the insurance "shall not cover to the extent of any other insurance whether prior or subsequent hereto in date, and by whomsoever effected, directly or indirectly, covering the same property and this company shall be liable for loss or damage only for the excess value beyond the amount of such other insurance."

A discussion of the problems in connection with "other insurance" clauses appears in the chapter concerning adjustment of losses.

QUESTIONS

1. What elements are necessary in a contract to make it binding?
2. In what important respect does an insurance policy differ from other contracts?
3. What is insurable interest?

4. Describe the use of coinsurance on inland marine policies with particular attention to the effect of coinsurance on insurance rates.
5. What precautions are needed in describing the insured, his insurable interest, property covered, and territorial limits in a policy which provides transit coverage as compared with a policy covering at a fixed location?
6. Explain the difference between the ordinary rule and the marine rule as it affects misrepresentation and fraud in connection with an inland marine policy.
7. How do the territorial limits specified in an inland marine policy differ from those given in a policy covering at a fixed location?
8. Under what circumstances would you consider it proper to issue a valued policy for inland marine coverage?
9. What is the purpose of the "pairs and sets" clause?
10. What obligation is placed upon the insured by the "sue and labor" clause?
11. Describe circumstances under which you would expect general average to be applied in connection with an inland marine loss.
12. Why is it reasonable to expect the insured to protect property which is threatened by loss?
13. What is the right of subrogation?
14. What effect does the enforcement of subrogation rights have upon insurance rates? Would your answer be the same if you assumed that all persons against whom subrogation rights were pressed also carried insurance against such claims?

8

"All Risks" Insurance

THE DEVELOPMENT OF "ALL RISKS" INSURANCE

Need for Broad Insurance Coverage. The insuring of property on land for "all risks" of loss or damage is a development of the present century. Previously "all risks" coverage was available only to property being transported by sea, and there was little demand for broad coverage on property at fixed locations on land. Land transportation was not sufficiently general to justify broad insurance coverage. Fifty years ago property occasionally burned or was blown away, but people did not consider that their property was subject to many other hazards. Travelers carried a small amount of luggage of which the dollar value was seldom sufficient to justify insurance.

Insurance protection always has been developed to meet specific needs of the public. Fire insurance was an early form of protection because the threat of fire was recognized generally. The great fire of London in 1666 gave an early impetus to plans for insuring not only against conflagration losses but also against individual losses from smaller fires. In this country the New York City conflagration of 1835 made many people realize the need for insurance protection.

Later in the nineteenth century the people of the United States saw tornadoes on the western plains and coastal winds along the Atlantic Ocean wipe out their belongings. There grew up a demand for protection against destruction by the wind.

In this century there has been a greatly increased amount of travel, and people carry with them things of much greater value than formerly.

Property in the home is now subject to a great variety of hazards. In addition to the risks of fire and windstorm, the installation of modern plumbing threatens extensive destruction from leakage when the owner happens to be away for a few hours or a few days. Modern heating equipment occasionally goes wrong and smokes up an entire house. Airplanes and motor vehicles offer other threats to property. Higher standards of living have brought additional mechanical devices and have added new threats to the property man accumulates.

The present generation has seen an extensive revolution in travel and shipping methods. From 1905, when the Pennsylvania Railroad's Broadway Limited established a record speed for trains of 127 miles per hour, until the 1930s there had been no outstanding improvements in the equipment or running time of the railroads. At this time the railroads began to feel increasing competition from the motor truck in the hauling of freight and from airlines and buses in the carrying of passengers. The development of the Deisel locomotive permitted the speeding up of train schedules for both passengers and freight.

The handling of passenger baggage also has undergone a great change. It was customary for many years for railroad porters to carry a traveler's bags to the train and then return for another customer. At no time was the baggage out of sight of the owner. A shortage of porters during the war years made it necessary for them to check baggage and to deliver it to the passenger on the train. Air lines and bus lines also set up checking routines for the handling of baggage. Current baggage handling in all forms of travel requires that the traveler hand over his baggage to the carrier. At many terminals there is little, if any, surveillance to make certain that travelers get their own bags. The result is a much larger proportion of lost baggage than was the case when more leisurely procedures were possible. The value of the lost baggage may far exceed the liability of the carrier. The public has found it advantageous to purchase travel baggage insurance or to carry a broad form of personal property insurance which includes protection for baggage lost in transit.

A specified perils policy cannot cover all the possible chances of loss, no matter how extensive the list of perils may be. An example of a loss due to modern transportation was the breakage of a bottle of perfume in a woman's luggage at high altitude. Even with a pressurized cabin and baggage compartment there is a change in pressure. The perfume bottle burst and soaked with perfume all the clothes in a suitcase. The cost of cleaning the garments was paid as a loss under an "all risks" policy.

The "all risks" policy has been developed because of a realization that the insured needs indemnification for any loss large enough to hurt him financially, regardless of the cause. It is just as much a misfortune for the policyholder to have a $2,000 loss from leakage of plumbing as it is for him to have a $2,000 fire loss. This principle was recognized at an early date in the handling of cargo and ships at sea, but it is relatively new in its application to property on land.

"All Risks" Not Synonymous With "Inland Marine." The fact that marine and inland marine underwriters developed "all risks" coverage for property on land has resulted in a misunderstanding concerning the nature of inland marine protection. A great many people, including many in the insurance business, believe that the terms "inland marine" and "all risks" are synonymous. This is not the case. Many inland marine policies cover against loss from specified perils; in such cases the coverage is the same as would be given under other specified perils policies naming the same hazards.

As pointed out in previous chapters, the term "inland marine" refers to the insurance of property that is in transit or related to transportation. "All risks" is only one type of coverage that happens to be common under inland marine policies. More recently "all risks" types of insurance have been written to cover property at fixed locations on land. While some of these policies are classified as inland marine, many of them are considered to be multiple line policies.

NATURE OF "ALL RISKS" PROTECTION

A further misunderstanding regarding the nature of "all risks" protection is the belief that an "all risks" policy covers against any loss or damage that can happen to the property. The "all risks" policy is not an "all loss" coverage, because a "risk" is merely a chance of loss.[1] Things that occur or may be expected to occur in the normal course of events are not the result of risks and are not covered by "all risks" insurance. For example, a pair of shoes will wear out in the normal course of their use by the owner. There is no chance involved, for this is an expected result of wear and tear. The loss is not from a risk and is not covered by an "all risks" policy.

A loss resulting from a deliberate act of the insured is not the result of a risk, even though the consequences are unexpected. Claims have been received under the "all risks" personal property floater for damage done to dresses by deodorants. This damage is not the result of a risk because it came from a deliberate act of the insured in applying the deodorant. Had the deodorant been spilled onto the dress, the loss would be covered by an "all risk" policy. The shrinking of wool in hot water is not a loss due to a risk, because wool shrinks naturally when placed in hot water and damage is the result of a deliberate act.

Another type of loss not covered by an "all risks" policy, because it is an expected occurrence and does not result from chance, is deterioration from natural causes. The spoilage of food is not the result of a risk. An exception to this rule would be food under refrigeration that spoiled when some accident caused the refrigeration to break down.

The "all risks" form of coverage is the broadest insurance protection generally available. It indemnifies for a great many miscellaneous losses not covered by any other type of policy. In addition to the losses covered by the many different specified perils policies, "all risks" protection insures against unexpected losses from causes too numerous to list in an insurance policy. For example, the loss of property without any other cause except that the property was misplaced or is unaccountably missing is covered under the "all risks" policy. Mysterious disappearance causes a large portion of the claims under the "all risks" type of coverage and is a difficult problem in underwriting. Truly mysterious disappearance is insurable, because the loss may result from theft or another peril under circumstances that make it impossible to determine the cause accurately. In order to maintain a satisfactory loss ratio, the companies must underwrite their policies in such a way that they do

[1]One court stated: ". . . I have followed the English authorities, because I think them right in holding that, even in an 'all risk' policy, there must be a fortuitous event—a casualty—to give rise to any liability for insurance." Mellon v. Federal Ins. Co., 14 F. (2d) 997 (1926).

not insure a person who is habitually careless and loses things constantly.

The odd losses paid under "all risks" policies involve several cases in which squirrels have been trapped in houses and have done considerable damage during the absence of the owners. Ink or paint accidentally spilled on carpets or furniture also has resulted in many insured losses, and water damage from burst pipes or a leaky roof is covered.

An "all risks" policy covers damage by flood in the absence of any exclusion to the contrary. It has proved feasible to insure property in transit against loss by flood because it is only by chance that such property would be in a flood area. Flood coverage is provided also by policies covering jewelry, furs, fine arts, and similar property. This can be done without incurring unreasonably high losses because the homes of most people who own valuable property are located outside of flood areas. Flood insurance has not been provided generally for property at fixed locations because of the extreme catastrophe hazard. Many "all risks" policies covering such property exclude loss from flood.

Fire As a Risk. In connection with losses by fire, there is an important distinction between an "all risks" policy and the coverage under a fire policy. The ordinary fire insurance policy does not define the word "fire," but by general custom of the business, supported by a long line of court decisions, the word has come to mean a "hostile" fire. A "hostile" fire is one that has gone beyond the place where it is intended to be. A fire in a stove or furnace or fireplace is considered a "friendly" fire just as long as the flames do not extend beyond the bounds of the place where the fire is intended to be. Any damage done by a fire that remains within its proper bounds is considered the result of a "friendly" fire and is not intended to be covered by the fire insurance policy.

There have been cases in which property has been thrown into a stove unintentionally, but courts have held that the loss is not covered by the fire insurance policy. Neither is the fire policy intended to cover damage resulting from smoke if the fire itself is confined to the furnace and the smoke is the result of faulty operation of the furnace. If damage by smoke from a furnace is to be covered under a specified perils policy, a special provision must be added to the policy giving smoke damage coverage.[2]

[2]For a discussion of "friendly" and "hostile" fires, see the following cases: Reliance Ins. Co. v. Naman, 6 S.W. (2d) 743 (Tex. 1928); Weimer v. St. Paul Fire & Marine Ins. Co., 207 N.Y.S. 279 (1924); Youse v. Employers Fire Ins. Co., 238 P. (2d) 472 (Kans. 1951).

The "all risks" policy does not specifically mention loss by fire, but it covers against "all risks" of loss or damage. A loss resulting from the accidental throwing of property into a fire is the result of a risk and as such is covered.

Exclusions Under an "All Risks" Policy. The discussion of "all risks" insurance up to this point has been based upon an interpretation of the coverage provided by the words "all risks of loss or damage." All such policies contain exclusions, and the actual limitation of coverage under an "all risks" policy is determined by the exclusions. The exclusions are intended (1) to clarify the basic coverage, (2) to eliminate risks that cannot be insured at reasonable rates, and (3) to exclude coverage that might encourage the policyholder to be careless.

Five general types of exclusions appear in "all risks" policies.

The first is an exclusion relating to property subject to an *excessive hazard.* An example of this type of exclusion is one relating to property on exhibition, such as that in museums. Experience has shown that property on exhibition frequently is damaged as a result of vandalism or accidental mishandling by the public. Coverage that protects easily damaged articles while on exhibition requires an extremely high rate, and the average policyholder does not need the protection. For that reason such property is excluded from coverage except when there is a specific need for it and an additional charge is made.

A second type of exclusion similar to the first relates to *unusual or catastrophic losses.* War damage is excluded under most policies because it is held that modern war causes such widespread destruction that it is not an insurable hazard. Present thought is that war damage can be compensated for only by a governmental arrangement such as the War Damage Corporation put into effect during World War II.

A third general type of exclusion relates to *property normally covered by other insurance.* It has become customary for automobiles, motorcycles, aircraft, boats, and other vehicles or conveyances to be insured under policies especially designed to give them the protection they need. This type of property must be excluded under an inland marine "all risks" policy both to prevent double coverage and to avoid covering a type of property for which the hazard requires rating on a different basis from that contemplated in an inland marine "all risks" policy.

A fourth type of exclusion relates to *losses that are partially or wholly under the control of the insured.* These are the losses to fragile articles and losses resulting from marring or scratching property. A careful policyholder takes extreme precaution to see that easily damaged articles are protected from loss. The covering of losses caused by carelessness would result in an excessive number of claims and would necessitate higher rates.

Similar to this group of exclusions is the provision excluding damage to property while being worked upon in the course of a refinishing, renovating, or repair process. This exclusion in the policy is intended to influence the insured to select a careful cleaner or repair man and also places the responsibility for such damage on the person doing the processing. The contention is that the processor should be responsible for any damage done as a result of his work on the property.

The fifth type of exclusion, and one that covers an extremely wide range of losses, is that relating to damage of a *wear* and *tear* nature. There are cases in which the dividing line between an actual risk and wear and tear is so fine that a specific exclusion helps to mark the limitation between an insured loss and one that is a matter of wear and tear. These exclusions usually mention wear and tear and also such losses as those growing out of mechanical and electrical breakdown. It is considered that any machine will wear out in the course of time, and the burning out of an electric motor or the eventual breakdown of mechanical apparatus should not be considered an insurable loss because it is a result to be expected after the machine has seen normal use for a considerable period. It is worthy of note that lightning damage to electrical apparatus may be covered because lightning is a fortuitous occurrence and resulting damage is properly insurable.

Loss or damage resulting from inherent vice usually is excluded. This may not be necessary, inasmuch as inherent vice is not a risk but is a quality normal to the property. It is customary to exclude inherent vice specifically in order that the intent of the policy may be entirely clear. The term "inherent vice" has come down to us from ocean marine insurance and the meaning may not be entirely clear from the words themselves. "Inherent vice" may be defined as a quality within an object that results in the object's tending to destroy itself. A frequently used example is the fact that rubber automobiles tires deteriorate whether or not they are in use and eventually become worthless even though they have never been put on an automobile. This results from an inherent quality of the rubber that tends to cause deterioration and eventual destruction of the tires.

In a case decided in the Texas courts, some cattle had been

frightened by a locomotive whistle and were injured in a stampede. The owner of the cattle sued the railroad but was denied damages. It was the decision of the court that cattle have a natural tendency to become frightened and stampede, and that the damage resulted from something inherent in the nature of cattle that might be expected to manifest itself in the vicinity of the railroad.[3]

"All risks" policies contain other exclusions designed to handle problems peculiar to the type of property being insured.

Personal policies frequently exclude business property, in order to avoid payment for losses on property that is subject to hazards greater than those contemplated in the rates charged for personal policies. This and other specific exclusions will be discussed in the sections concerning the individual policies.

Reasons for Deductible Clauses in "All Risks" Policies. In spite of the fact that carefully worded exclusions are included in "all risks" policies, there remains a wide section of coverage in which it is difficult to determine whether the loss is from ordinary wear and tear or from an insurable risk. For example, a small slit in the skin of a fur coat probably would be considered normal wear and tear resulting from deterioration of the skin. If the tear extended for several inches and was caused by the coat's being caught on a nail, the cost of repairs might be sufficiently high to be considered an insurable risk under the "all risks" type of policy. It is difficult to determine just where to draw the line between such damages as rips and tears, or cigarette burns, and more serious losses that are a burden to the insured. The dry cleaning of wearing apparel and the laundering of other household property are considered normal expenses of living, but an unusual amount of smoke from the faulty operation of heating or cooking equipment can produce an expensive loss and one that is properly insurable. The upsetting of a bottle of ink on a rug or suit is clearly a risk, and the cleaning bill would be a proper charge to be paid by the insurance company. There could easily be a controversy over the cleaning of wearing apparel or draperies on the question of whether damage resulted from wear and tear or was the result of a risk contemplated by the policy.

The basic function of insurance is to indemnify the insured for an unexpected loss that is beyond his normal running expenses. The specified perils type of policy covers losses from fire, windstorm,

[3]On appeal, the lower court's charge to the jury was upheld. In it "inherent vice" was defined as follows: " 'Inherent vice' in an animal is some quality or characteristic of the animal that brings about its own injury or destruction without fault on the part of any other supervening cause." Texas & P. Rwy. Co. v. Prunty, 233 S.W. 625 (Tex. Civ. App. 1921).

lightning, and a list of other hazards that ordinarily occur in such proportions that the results are catastrophic to the individual. Under such policies there is little likelihood of numerous claims resulting from normal wear and tear.

Under the broad coverage of the "all risks" policies, the underwriters have found it desirable to use deductible clauses in order to mark the dividing line between ordinary wear and tear losses and an insurable loss. For example, a $25 deductible clause effectively eliminates claims for small rips in suits and for ordinary cleaning bills, or the loss of hats and fountain pens that the insured would expect to replace at his own expense if there was no insurance on the property. The deductible clause eliminates payments for the numerous small losses that are relatively costly to adjust and that would make the rate for "all risks" coverage much higher than is necessary for a broad insurance coverage on catastrophic losses.

Full coverage "all risks" insurance is likely to encourage carelessness, because the insured may feel that any loss will be covered by insurance. The use of the deductible clause lessens the hazard of carelessness and helps the company select careful policyholders. A policyholder who is willing to accept a deductible clause in his policy is more likely to be the careful type of individual. The use of the deductible is regarded as the most effective means of handling the problem of numerous small claims under the "all risks" type of coverage.

QUESTIONS

1. How have changes in travel methods caused a need for broad insurance protection?
2. Do all inland marine policies provide "all risks" coverage?
3. How does an "all risks" coverage differ from an "all loss" coverage?
4. Is mysterious disappearance an insurable risk?
5. Why can flood coverage be written successfully as part of an "all risks" coverage but not separately?
6. Discuss the feasibility of providing flood coverage on property in transit as compared to flood coverage on property at fixed locations.
7. Distinguish between a "friendly" and a "hostile" fire, and explain why an "all risks" coverage may insure against certain losses from a "friendly" fire whereas a fire insurance policy does not.
8. Why are exclusions put in "all risks" insurance policies?

9. What types of exclusions usually appear in an "all risks" insurance policy?
10. What is "inherent vice"?
11. Discuss the difference between a wear and tear loss and an inherent vice loss.
12. Explain why deductible clauses are commonly used in "all risks" policies.

9

Common Carrier Liability

LEGAL DEFINITIONS

It is the general rule that a common carrier in the United States is responsible for the safe delivery of goods that it has undertaken to transport from one place to another. The liability of the common carrier always has been subject to some exceptions. It is also true that there are some hazards which the common carrier must bear and from which it cannot relieve itself in any way. A "common carrier" is one that holds itself out to the public as being able and willing to transport passengers or cargo between certain points. The common carrier is obliged to serve anyone who requests the services as long as the carrier has the facilities and is able to perform the service.

Shippers by railroad in the United States did not feel any great need for insurance on goods in the custody of the railroads until World War I. The railroads had accepted their obligation as common carriers and often went beyond their legal liability in making restitution for lost and damaged property.

It became difficult, however, for shippers and consignees to recover damage claims during World War I when the railroads were being operated by the government. It was during this same decade that the Supreme Court of the United States decided that common carriers can limit their liability under certain conditions.[1] It was also between 1910 and 1920 that shipping contracts and bills of lading were being made more nearly uniform, partly as a result of new laws and partly through efforts of these common carriers toward standardization. This classification of the obligations imposed on common carriers made it evident that there were many circumstances under which a common carrier would not be held liable for the full amount of damages occurring to property in its custody. The railroads began to take advantage of these new limitations on their liability, and shippers and consignees found themselves unable to collect damages that might have been paid in full in previous years.

It has been a principle of the common law[2] for several hundred years that a person or firm that makes a business of carrying property for a consideration is responsible for the safe delivery of the property. If a common carrier could relieve itself of liability for safe delivery, it might be encouraged to connive with thieves or others for the loss of the property in order to make a dishonest profit. Therefore the common carrier is held responsible for any loss that might in any way be preventable by the exercise of caution or diligence on its part.

It came to be recognized that certain calamities are beyond the control of a common carrier, and it is held not responsible for loss resulting directly from

1. Acts of God.
2. Acts of the public enemy.
3. Exercise of public authority.
4. Fault or neglect on the part of the shipper.
5. Inherent vice or the nature of the property.

An *act of God* is an occurrence of nature that cannot be

[1] Adams Express Company v. Croninger, 226 U.S. 491, 57 L. ed. 314 (1913).

[2] The common law of England was developed over a long period of time. Its principles were built up in decisions that drew inspiration from a variety of sources. There never was any pressure in England for codification and enactment of statutes embodying the legal principles. The English common law became the basic law of the United States. With few exceptions the common law applies throughout the United States in all circumstances in which no statute has been enacted to cover the point involved.

foreseen or prevented. Examples are storms, lightning, and earthquakes.

The *public enemy* refers to a nation or government at war with the nation in which the carrier is domiciled. (It must not be confused with the designation "Public Enemy Number 1," which occasionally is attached to individual criminals. A common carrier is responsible for losses due to the depredations of criminals.)

A typical *act of public authority* would be action taken to stop the spread of a conflagration or the building of a dike to halt rising flood waters.

Losses due to the negligence of the shipper or to an inherent quality of the property are obviously not under the control of a common carrier and it should not be held responsible for them.

There are circumstances in which a common carrier may be held liable for loss even though the cause is one of the five enumerated above. It may be that the loss could have been anticipated and that the carrier did not take proper precautions. An example might be a case in which a carrier could have moved cars from the path of rising flood waters but neglected to do so.

Relatively few circumstances relieve a common carrier of liability. It was natural that such carriers would want to limit their extreme liability. Contracts for shipments or bills of lading[3] were drawn that limited the liability to specified amounts of money or that listed perils for which the carrier held itself not responsible. These contracts generally were binding when accepted by the shipper. There was a great deal of confusion because of the many different types of contracts used, and shippers claimed that they were abused in the application of them. Frequently the shipper had no choice but to accept the contract if he wanted to have his goods transported.

The need for some regulation resulted in the passage of the Interstate Commerce Act by Congress in 1887.[4] This act set up the Interstate Commerce Commission and gave it authority to regulate common carriers by railroad operating in interstate commerce.

The Interstate Commerce Act applies to common carriers operating between two or more states, and a 1915 amendment makes

[3]A "bill of lading" is a written document given by the carrier to the shipper. It acknowledges receipt of the goods by the carrier and sets forth the terms of the contract for carrying the property. When it specifies a maximum amount for which the carrier will be liable in case of loss or damage, it is called a "released bill of lading."

[4]Act of Feb. 4, 1887-C. 104; 24 Stat. 379; U.S.C.A. Title 49, Secs. 1-22, 25-27.

it apply also to shipments between any state and one of the adjoining countries.[5] The Interstate Commerce Act makes it obligatory for a common carrier to serve any one who makes a request for the services, as long as the carrier has the facilities and is able to perform the service.

An important deficiency in the Interstate Commerce Act as originally passed was that a common carrier receiving goods for shipment was not required to be responsible beyond its own lines. The contract for shipment (bill of lading) could provide that the carrier was discharged from obligation when it had passed the goods safely into the hands of another carrier.

Cross-country shipments might pass through the hands of a dozen common carriers before reaching their destinations. In order to collect for a lost or damaged shipment, the shipper would have to ascertain which carrier was responsible for the loss. Frequently this was difficult or impossible for the shipper to prove. Even if he could determine the location and cause of the loss, he might find it necessary to press a suit against a carrier many hundreds of miles away. If the loss were small or proof doubtful, the expense of the suit might not be justified and the shipper might not be able to recover.

In 1906 Congress passed the Carmack Amendment to the Interstate Commerce Act,[6] which requires the originating common carrier to issue a receipt or bill of lading for a shipment and makes the initial carrier responsible to the holder of the receipt for damages occurring while the goods are in its custody or the custody of any succeeding carrier. The shipper makes his claim on the original carrier and does not have to deal with any succeeding carrier. (The original carrier can attempt to recover from a succeeding carrier if the loss did not occur on the lines of the originating carrier.) The shipper merely has to prove damage in transit; the only way in which the original carrier can avoid payment is to prove that the loss was occasioned by one of the few causes for which common carriers are not liable.

Before passage of the Carmack Amendment, there had been no clear definition of the liability of a common carrier in connection with interstate shipments. Some states had statutes on the subject, and the common law controlled where there was no superseding statute. Decisions in the courts followed the local rule, with the result that no shipper could know for a certainty what his rights

[5]First Cummins Amendment, Act of March 4, 1915-C. 176; 38 Stat. 1196; U.S.C.A. Title 49, Sec. 20 (11).

[6]Act of June 29, 1906-C.3591; 34 Stat. 584; U.S.C.A. Title 49, Sec. 20 (11).

might be for recovery of damages. The right of recovery in one state might not be parallel to the right to recover in another. With the passage of the Carmack Amendment the liability for loss was set out in the receipt and was placed on the originating carrier; all succeeding carriers were subject to the same liability; and the shipper usually could determine from his bill of lading what his rights of recovery might be. This amendment superseded any local rules or statutes that might be in effect at the place where a loss occurred.

Although the Carmack Amendment to the Interstate Commerce Act made a common carrier "liable to the lawful holder thereof [bill of lading] for any loss, damage, or injury to such property caused by it," there was no prohibition against a common carrier's inserting a provision in a bill of lading limiting the amount to be paid in the event of loss.

Limiting clauses in bills of lading became increasingly frequent. Up to the beginning of World War I, many common carriers tended to ignore the limiting provisions and settled claims on the basis of the full value. In 1913 the Supreme Court of the United States decided that the provisions of such limiting clauses were binding upon both shippers and carriers.[7] This gave common carriers authority to enforce the provisions of these limiting clauses.

The terms of the First Cummins Amendment to the Interstate Commerce Act seem to have resulted from a reaction to the limitations placed in bills of lading by common carriers. Passed by Congress in 1915, it made common carriers liable for the full loss or damage regardless of the terms of any receipt or bill of lading. The only exception was in the case of packaged goods of which the carrier had not been notified of the character. On this type of shipment the carrier could limit its liability by requiring a written statement from the shipper setting forth the value of the goods.

The First Cummins Amendment was of tremendous importance to carriers and shippers because it set out the principle that

> . . . any such common carrier, railroad, or transportation company so receiving property for transportation . . . shall be liable to the lawful holder of said receipt or bill of lading or to any party entitled to recover thereon, whether such receipt or bill of lading has been issued or not, for the full actual loss, damage, or injury to such

[7]Adams Express Co. v. Croninger, 226 U.S. 491, 57 L. ed. 314 (1913). In a case decided before the passage of the Interstate Commerce Act, Hart v. Pennsylvania R.R. Co., 112 U.S. 331, 28 L. ed. 717 (1884), the Supreme Court had held that a valuation and limitation of liability in a bill of lading were just and reasonable and binding on the shipper, but the Adams Express Co. v. Croninger case is frequently cited as the basic case after passage of the Interstate Commerce Act.

> property caused by it or by any such common carrier, railroad, or transportation company to which such property may be delivered or over whose lines such property may pass within the United States or within an adjacent foreign country when transported on a through bill of lading, notwithstanding any limitation of liability or limitation of the amount of recovery or representation or agreement as to the value in any such receipt or bill of lading, or in any contract, rule, regulation or in any tariff filed with the Interstate Commerce Commission; and any such limitation, without respect to the manner or form in which it is sought to be made is hereby declared to be unlawful and void . . .

This principle of recovery for loss caused by a common carrier is still in effect and is the basis for the subrogation rights insurance companies enjoy in connection with policies issued to cover goods in transit.

It did appear, however, that the terms of this First Cummins Amendment might be too rigid in their prohibition of any agreements limiting value. The Second Cummins Amendment,[8] passed in 1916, gave the Interstate Commerce Commission power to authorize or order the establishing of "rates dependent upon the value declared in writing by the shipper or agreed upon in writing as the released value of the property, in which case such declaration or agreement shall have no other effect than to limit liability and recovery to an amount not exceeding the value so declared or released. . . ." An exception was made of ordinary livestock, which must be shipped subject to full recovery. "Ordinary livestock" is defined to "include cattle, swine, sheep, goats, horses, and mules, except such as are chiefly valuable for breeding, racing, show purposes, or other special uses."

The passage of the Carmack and Cummins Amendments and the issuing of rulings of the Interstate Commerce Commission served to evolve a standard or "Uniform" set of bills of lading. It is not necessary to review here the various hearings and disputes that occurred, but it may be noted that the present bills of lading of rail carriers are based upon the provisions of the Bills of Lading Act[9] passed by Congress in 1916, and the wording has not been changed substantially since 1922.

[8]Act of Aug. 9, 1916-C. 301; 39 Stat. 441; U.S.C.A. Title 49, Sec. 20 (11).

[9]Act of Aug. 29, 1916-C. 415; 39 Stat. 538; U.S.C.A., Title 49, Secs. 81-124.

BILLS OF LADING

Functions of a Bill of Lading. It is important for the inland marine underwriter to know the functions of the bill of lading and what it requires on the part of the shipper or consignee in order to collect for damaged goods. Unless its provisions are carried out, the insurance company may be unable to collect a loss under its subrogation rights.

The underwriter also should know what are the chances of recovery and what part of a loss a common carrier is obligated to pay under released bills of lading. The desirability of insuring a prospect and the insurance rate are largely dependent upon the shipper's methods of handling shipments and upon the extent of liability of the carriers. It is not always possible or economical for the policyholder to contract for full recovery from the carrier on all types of merchandise. The transportation charges on goods shipped under a released bill of lading may be much lower than the rates charged for full valuation. Owing to this fact, a shipper may find it economically desirable to accept a released bill of lading.

On its face, the bill of lading shows where the property was received and from whom, and the date of receipt. It includes a description of the goods showing the number of packages, the weight, any special marks, and other description that would serve to identify them. There is also on the same page a statement to this effect: "The agreed or declared value of the property is hereby specifically stated by the shipper to be not exceeding . . . per . . ." On a released bill of lading this space is filled in with an amount, usually per 100 pounds, depending upon the tariff filed by the carrier for the particular commodity being shipped.

The contract portion of the bill of lading provides for filling in the name of the consignee, the destination, and the route over which the shipment is to travel; specifies who is to pay the freight charges (the consignor or the consignee); and indicates the rate for freight charges. On the back of the bill of lading are ten sections of conditions reading much like an insurance policy, in very fine print. The use of fine print is not so subject to criticism as might appear, because the terms of all railroad bills of lading are identical and they have not been changed for many years. The terms are available in larger print for easy reading if the shipper or consignee has need to study them.

Straight Bill of Lading. In the *straight* bill of lading, the carrier is instructed to deliver the goods to the consignee, who is presumed to have title or at least the right to possession of the property. Goods are shipped under a straight bill of lading when the shipper wants the carrier to make delivery directly to the consignee named in the bill of lading. If a straight bill of lading should fall into the hands of someone other than the consignor or the consignee, it would not give him any right to the goods; the goods would be delivered to the consignee named in the bill of lading. The straight bill of lading is a contract between shipper and carrier for the shipment of the goods. It is nonnegotiable, which means that it cannot be endorsed to convey to a third party the right to receive the goods.

Order Bill of Lading. The *order* bill of lading also is a contract for shipment of goods, but it serves an additional function. The use of the order bill of lading can best be explained by examining first the needs of commerce that give rise to its use. A manufacturer, for example, may wish to ship a large quantity of goods to a dealer but not to extend credit for the shipment. The dealer may not want to pay for the goods in advance of receipt; perhaps he does not know the exact amount of the invoice, or he may not know just when the manufacturer can ship the goods, or perhaps he is working on a close margin of cash and will need to borrow money from his bank in order to pay for the goods. The banks perhaps would not lend the money until the goods were actually in the hands of the dealer. The situation requires some sort of cash-on-delivery arrangement whereby the manufacturer can ship the goods and be assured of payment upon their delivery to the dealer.

The cash-on-delivery arrangement is made with the help of an order bill of lading. The principal difference between the order bill of lading and the straight bill of lading is that the consignee named in the order bill of lading may endorse it to another party. This endorsement conveys to the party named (the endorsee) the right to receive the goods described in the order bill of lading. The order bill of lading is somewhat in the nature of a check, which may be endorsed to another party or parties. It is known as a negotiable instrument.

The steps in the use of an order bill of lading are usually as follows:

1. The manufacturer (or other shipper) delivers goods into the custody of a common carrier.
2. The shipper receives from the carrier an order bill of lading naming the

shipper not only as the shipper but also as the consignee. The shipper has himself named as the consignee so that he has the right to endorse the bill of lading to whomever he pleases (since the consignee has the right to endorse the order bill of lading).

3. The shipper then notifies the purchaser that the goods have been shipped and that the railroad (or other carrier) will notify the purchaser when the goods arrive at the freight station at the destination.
4. The shipper takes the order bill of lading he has received from the carrier and endorses it in blank. That is, in the space provided for endorsement he signs his name, but he does not fill in the name of the party who is authorized to receive the goods. This is equivalent to making out a check without putting in the name of the payee; it could be cashed by anyone in possession of it.
5. The shipper also draws a sight draft on the purchaser. This is a written order in which the shipper directs the purchaser to pay a specified sum of money (in this case the selling price of the goods). This sight draft usually names the shipper as the person to whom the money is paid.
6. The shipper takes the order bill of lading and the sight draft to his bank and endorses it either to the bank or in blank, as he did the order bill of lading.
7. The bank sends the order bill of lading and the sight draft to a bank in the city where the goods are to be delivered. (Sometimes this transaction passes through several banks if the shipper's bank does not have a regular correspondent bank in the city where delivery is to be made.) The order bill of lading and the sight draft are handled with extreme care, especially when they are endorsed in blank. As in the case of any negotiable instrument, a thief might fill in his own name and present them at a bank in order to secure the value in cash, or he might present the order bill of lading to the railroad and receive the goods. Such documents usually are sent by registered mail in order to prevent loss in transit.
8. The bank in the city where delivery is to be made receives the order bill of lading and the sight draft. The bank notifies the purchaser that it has them and that the order bill of lading will be endorsed to the purchaser upon payment of the amount named in the sight draft.
9. The railroad meanwhile has carried the goods to its destination. At about the same time that the bank receives the sight draft and the bill of lading, the railroad will notify the purchaser that it has the goods, which it will deliver to him upon presentation of the order bill of lading.
10. The purchaser pays the sight draft at the bank and receives the order bill of lading endorsed to him. He can now go to the railroad office and receive the goods upon presentation of the order bill of lading.

This sounds like an involved way of arranging for cash-on-delivery, but it is being carried out with thousands of shipments every day and works smoothly. Common carriers do not want to handle the millions of dollars involved in these transactions, as they would have to do if they handled cash-on-delivery shipments the way the Post Office does for relatively small amounts on parcel post shipments. The same effect is secured by this method, and the money is handled through regular banking channels.

Shipper's Weight, Load, and Count. When shippers have their own loading facilities, it is customary for the shipper to load and seal the railroad car without the carrier's having any opportunity to check the nature, quality, weight, or quantity of the load. In such cases the carrier stamps the bill of lading with the words "Shipper's weight, load, and count" or words of similar intent. This means that the common carrier assumes no liability for loss resulting from short load or count unless it can be shown that the car was entered and goods removed before delivery.

It is railroad practice to keep a record of the car seals at the point of shipment, at junction points where a car is turned over to another carrier, and at destination. When the shipper loads and seals the car and the seal record is clear, it is extremely difficult to place responsibility for shortage on the carrier. It is possible to break into a car and to reseal, but such occurrences are rare, and strong proof would have to be secured. For all practical purposes, the shipper is held responsible when there is a shortage in a car and the bill of lading contains a "shipper's load" notation. This means also that the loss did not occur as a result of a transit risk and would not be covered under a transportation insurance policy.

It always is possible that the description of the goods in the bill of lading is in error, either through mistake or because of misrepresentation by the shipper. If the carrier can prove that it did not receive the goods as indicated by the bill of lading, it may be able to limit its liability to the shipper to the value of the goods actually received. As to an innocent third party, such as a consignee, however, the carrier under an order bill of lading is responsible for delivery of the goods listed in the bill of lading, even though it never received them. This liability may be lightened if the carrier inserts a statement in the bill of lading to the effect that it does not know the nature of the contents.

Most property is shipped under one or the other of the two classes of bills of lading described. Other types of bills of lading are used for export shipments. It will be recalled that ordinary livestock cannot be shipped under a "released" bill of lading but that the carrier is liable for the full value. Ordinary livestock is shipped by railroad under the Uniform Livestock Contract Bill of Lading, which is similar to those already described except that there is no limitation upon the amount of recovery when the carrier is liable for a loss.

TARIFFS

The contractual terms and conditions of the bills of lading make reference to the tariffs filed by the carrier. A tariff is a set of rules and rates for the shipment of freight. Interstate tariffs are filed with, and approved by, the Interstate Commerce Commission for use with interstate shipments. A tariff is public information and is available for examination by anyone who desires to see it. Because it is public information, its terms are presumed to be known by all who ship goods by the carrier involved and are binding on shipper and carrier alike, even though the actual terms of the tariff may not be included in the contract of shipment. It becomes necessary, therefore, for the inland marine underwriter to have a knowledge of the provisions in the tariffs and of how their terms affect the liability of common carriers.

Railroad freight tariffs in use in the United States contain a freight classification list naming all the articles that may be shipped by freight. If an article is not listed, it may not be shipped by freight, but the railroads will refer the would-be shipper to the express companies. Notable among the articles not listed as permissible for freight shipment are valuable commodities such as money, negotiable securities, jewelry, gold, silver, and precious stones.

The tariff specifies a class for each commodity, and the class determines the rate to be paid. It also specifies the rules for limitation of value and the changes for value declared in excess of the standard value. The valuations are in cents or dollars per pound, and certain items will not be accepted for shipment at values in excess of certain specified amounts per pound. The tariff specifies a value per pound and the bill of lading is filled in with a value per hundred pounds. The settlement of railroad freight claims is on the basis of the value per pound, and any partial loss is prorated.

DELIVERY AND ACCEPTANCE OF GOODS

Delivery to the Carrier. Less-than-carload lots[10] of freight ordinarily are delivered by the shipper to the carrier's freight depot and a

10A less-than-carload lot of freight is a quantity smaller than is necessary to fill an entire freight car. It usually is abbreviated as "L.C.L."

bill of lading is issued by the carrier to the shipper. The actual receipt of the goods by the carrier and its acknowledgement by the bill of lading constitute delivery to the carrier. If pickup and delivery service is maintained for freight shipments, the trucker carrying merchandise usually acts for the railroad company, and the picking up constitutes delivery to the carrier.

The question of what constitutes delivery to the carrier may not have a simple answer when the shipper himself loads the car on a siding. The issuance of the bill of lading by the carrier after notification by the shipper that the car is ready will acknowledge receipt of the car, even though the railroad has not actually moved the car. Sometimes a bill of lading may be issued before the loading is actually completed. This might occur when the shipper intends to have a car loaded by late afternoon, ready for night or early morning movement, and the shipper asks the freight agent to make out the bill of lading during the afternoon before the shipper closes his office for the day. If it could be proved that the loading never was finished and that the railroad never received the goods, the carrier might be able to avoid liability.

Delivery by the Carrier. There have been many disputes over the question of whether the carrier had made delivery. Less-than-carload lots of freight are delivered through the carrier's freight station or warehouse, or by means of a pickup and delivery service. In either case the goods ordinarily are turned over to the consignee and a receipt is taken by the carrier. If the consignee is expected to pick up the goods, the carrier must mail a notice of arrival. The carrier's liability as a carrier continues for 48 hours from 7:00 A.M. after written notice of arrival has been sent or given to the consignee. After the expiration of the 48 hours, the liability of the carrier becomes that of a warehouseman, and it is then liable only in case of negligence. It is extremely important for the consignee to take the goods before the expiration of the 48-hour limit, because the burden of proof of negligence is on the consignee after the liability of the carrier becomes that of a warehouseman. For a further discussion of the liability of warehousemen, see Chapters 16 and 18.

Delivery also may be made on public team tracks,[11] in the case of full carloads. Notice is given to the consignee, and it is his obligation to remove the goods within the 48-hour period. The

[11]A "public team track" is a railroad sidetrack with a driveway alongside that enables consignees to park their trucks at the freight car door and unload goods. Public team tracks are used by consignees who receive carloads of freight but who do not have private sidetracks.

carrier remains liable as a common carrier during this period until all the goods have been removed.[12] After the 48-hour period, the carrier's liability becomes that of a warehouseman.

Sidetrack Agreements. In the case of cars delivered to a private or semiprivate sidetrack, delivery is made by placing the car upon the sidetrack at a reasonable hour for unloading. There may be a sidetrack agreement between the carrier and the consignee, and its terms may have to be consulted to determine when delivery has been made. There is no 48-hour notice requirement in connection with sidetrack deliveries. The question of delivery is important to the inland marine underwriter, because transportation policies ordinarily cover property only while it is in the hands of a common carrier in due course of transit. If the property has been delivered, it is no longer in transit or in the custody of the common carrier, and the policy no longer covers it.

The terms of sidetrack agreements signed by a policyholder should be examined by the inland marine underwriter. The agreement may contain some provision to the effect that the railroad may place carload freight on the siding at its convenience (without restriction as to hour of the day or night) and that such placing constitutes delivery. This waives the right of the policyholder to any notice and would allow the railroad to deliver at a time when the consignee might not be in a position to protect the car from damage or theft.

The terms of the sidetrack agreement also might relieve the consignee's insurance company of liability, because the placing of the car would constitute delivery and remove it from the custody of the common carrier. A loss after such a delivery would be likely to result in a dissatisfied policyholder if the consignee's insurance company denied liability. The insured should be informed in advance exactly what coverage is provided by the policy under the conditions brought about by the terms of the sidetrack agreement.

Carloading Companies or Freight Forwarders. It will be noted from an examination of the freight tariffs that the rates are relatively higher for small shipments than for large shipments. A carloading company or freight forwarder is one that makes a business of collecting thousands of small shipments from shippers and consolidating them into carload lots. The carloads are handled by the

[12] Michigan Central Railroad Co. v. Owen & Co., 256 U.S. 427, 65 L. ed. 1032 (1921).

railroads at carload rates, and the carloading company usually charges its clients a rate somewhere between the individual package rate and the carload rate. The carloading company usually arranges for pickup and delivery of the freight, either by means of its own trucks or by arrangement with public truckmen. The carloading company is able to operate at a profit on the difference between the single package rate and the carload rate, and the shipper gets the convenience of the pickup and delivery service, usually plus a part of the saving made by the carloading company.

The carloading company that handles interstate shipments is a common carrier operating in interstate commerce, and usually it issues a bill of lading identical with that issued by the railroads. If delivery is made to the carloading company, the shipper's rights of recovery are the same as they are against any other common carrier.

There is the possibility that a pickup may be made by a public truckman under circumstances that make him not an interstate common carrier but merely a local truckman or contract carrier. This is possible if it can be shown that the contract for hauling to the carloading company is strictly a local contract between the shipper and the truckman. In such cases, loss while the property is in the hands of the truckman might not be protected to the same extent as it is protected in the hands of a common carrier. The method of delivery to the carloading company or railroad is important to the inland marine underwriter.

It is also important to determine whether the carloading company is forwarding the goods by railroad. Shipments may be forwarded by motor truck, and in this case the tariffs and bills of lading of the trucker may make the rights of recovery different from those against a railroad.

MAKING CLAIM AGAINST CARRIERS

The contractual terms and conditions of the uniform bill of lading include provisions for the filing of claims for lost or damaged goods. The paragraph concerning the filing of claims reads:

> Sec. 2 (b) As a condition precedent to recovery, claims must be filed in writing with the receiving or delivering carrier, or carrier issuing this bill of lading, or carrier on whose line the loss, damage, injury or delay occurred, within nine months after delivery of the property (or, in the case of export traffic, within nine months after delivery at port of export) or, in case of failure to make delivery,

> then within nine months after a reasonable time for delivery has elapsed; and suits shall be instituted against any carrier only within two years and one day from the day when notice in writing is given by the carrier to the claimant that the carrier has disallowed the claim or any part or parts thereof specified in the notice. Where claims are not filed or suits are not instituted thereon in accordance with the foregoing provisions, no carrier hereunder shall be liable, and such claims will not be paid.

Some features of these provisions deserve attention. When goods are signed for by the consignee, it is customary for him to note on the receipt any damage or shortage. This is called a *bad order* notation and indicates to the carrier that there was damage or shortage. In case of concealed damage discovered after the receipt has been given to the carrier, the carrier is notified so that a representative can inspect the damage. A bad order notation or a request for inspection of concealed damages does not qualify as a notice of claim. The claimant must file with the carrier a written claim for the damage or shortage. The insurance company's subrogation rights against the carrier will be impaired or lost if the notice of claim is not filed as stipulated. Therefore, it is important to both claimant and insurance company that a claim be filed promptly upon the discovery of a loss.

Concerning the form of notice, it was stated by a court that, "while the notice need not be in any particular form, it must possess the characteristics of a demand for compensation or amount to a notice of intention to claim compensation for loss suffered."[13]

The claim must be for an amount of damages. There have been many disputes over what constitutes the actual loss of the claimant. It has been held by the Supreme Court of the United States that the amount of damage in the loss of a carload of grain was the value at the destination at the time the car should have been delivered. A provision in the bill of lading limiting recovery to the value at time and place of shipment was held invalid as contrary to the provisions of the Interstate Commerce Act as amended by the Cummins Amendments.[14]

This case was determined on the basis of a market value that could be ascertained accurately at the time and place of delivery. The determination of the actual value is more difficult when the claim involves commodities for which there is no open market comparable to the grain market.

13Browning, King & Co. v. Davis, 120 Misc. 520, 199 N.Y.S. 775 (1923).

14Chicago, Milwaukee & St. Paul Railway Co. v. McCaull-Dinsmore Co., 253 U.S. 97, 64 L. ed. 801 (1920).

There is no general rule applying to all cases, but the principle followed is to measure the loss to the claimant. If a sale of goods is involved, the value may be the cost of replacing the lost or damaged articles at the time they should have been delivered. Common carriers tend to take advantage of any trade discounts available to the claimant and would seem to be justified in doing so, because these affect the actual loss. Carriers would not seem to be justified in taking advantage of cash discounts unless the settlement is handled in such a way that the cash discount actually is available to the claimant.

The shipper or consignee can collect damages for unreasonable delay when such delay results in a loss. An example would be a case in which a shipment of seasonable merchandise was sent in plenty of time to reach its destination for sale but delivery was delayed until after the season had passed. The claimant could collect the difference between the market value at the time the goods should have been delivered and the market value at the time they were delivered.

The carrier is not permitted to promise a definite delivery date unless it has filed a tariff providing for such expedited service. The Interstate Commerce Act is based upon the principle that all clients of common carriers must be given equal service and that there can be no discrimination. Carriers might be tempted to promise special delivery service to favorite customers if the law did not provide that any special services must be available to all shippers.

The consignee ordinarily should accept goods even though they are damaged. Under many circumstances, bills of lading authorize carriers to sell goods that are refused, and this would jeopardize the consignee's rights to collect damages. The usual procedure is to accept the goods, making an appropriate notation of any damage or shortage, and then make every effort to salvage the goods and sell or use them to the best advantage.

When claims have been denied or are unpaid, it is important that suit be filed against the common carrier within the time limit specified in the bill of lading. Under the terms of the Interstate Commerce Act, the time limit for filing suit cannot be less than two years and one day after the carrier has given notice in writing that the claim is disallowed. Negotiations by the carrier for settlement after the notice has been received cannot be relied upon as a waiver of the time limit for filing suit.

COMMON CARRIER SHIPMENTS OTHER THAN RAILROAD FREIGHT

Common Carrier Liability in Handling Baggage. All the discussion of common carrier liability up to this point has referred to that of the railroads in hauling freight shipments between states, that is, in interstate commerce. This liability is basic to all common carrier liability in the United States, and other forms of such liability will be discussed as variations from it.

One important variation relates to passenger baggage. The railroads have filed baggage tariffs with the Interstate Commerce Commission providing for the handling of a certain amount of personal baggage in connection with a passenger's travel on the railroad. The baggage tariffs define personal baggage to include wearing apparel and personal effects of such a nature that a traveler would use them for his own purposes during a trip, but excluding any articles for sale and also certain prohibited articles of such a nature that the railroad could not handle them conveniently or safely in its baggage cars. Sample baggage is defined to include samples of merchandise and catalogs such as a salesman would use in selling his ware.

Valuation is limited by the tariffs to a nominal amount per piece or per passenger unless a higher value is declared and an extra charge paid. Other rules in the tariffs deal with the methods of making claims, charges for excess value and weight, and rules for the handling of baggage. One important rule that may affect merchandise is an emergency provision for the carrying of merchandise other than personal or sample baggage. This has been used at times to permit the carrying of goods normally sent by express that the express companies were not able to handle by reason of strike or other emergency. The value to be allowed in such cases usually is not in excess of $25. If an insurance company should cover such a shipment, it would be able to recover only $25 from the common carrier in case of loss or damage.

Special baggage car service is provided when a group of people need an entire car. A typical example of such a group would be a theatrical troupe. This baggage car is carried by the railroad under a special contract, and a provision usually included in such contracts limits the liability of the railroad to that of a bailee.

The shipper of baggage is presumed to know the contents of the tariffs filed by the carriers and is bound by them even though the provisions are not printed on the baggage receipt. The tariff as well as the baggage receipt must be examined in order to determine what the carrier's liability is in connection with lost or damaged articles.

Railway Express Shipments. Shipments by express are handled more rapidly than freight shipments, and this service usually includes pickup and delivery. The best known express organization is the Railway Express Agency, an organization which operates an expedited service. The liability of the express companies is basically the same as that of other interstate common carriers. The uniform express receipt serves the same purpose as the uniform bill of lading. There is a special receipt for livestock and another special receipt for fine arts. The insuring of fine arts during shipment by express will be considered in the chapter on fine arts insurance.

The value limitation in the uniform express receipt is $50 for each shipment or 50 cents per pound for shipments in excess of 100 pounds. The valuation may be increased by the payment of an extra charge. The receipt includes a space in which the declared value of the shipment is to be inserted.

There is a long line of court decisions supporting the right of carriers to limit the recovery of shippers according to a declared value and according to the relative charges paid. The basic case is that of Adams Express Co. v. Croninger, decided in 1913 and referred to previously. This case established the principle that charges for carrying goods should bear a relation to the amount for which the carrier would be liable in case of loss or damage.

In a more recent case (1947) the United States Circuit Court of Appeals for the Seventh Circuit upheld a $50 limitation on a $4,880 mink coat, even though the valuation was placed upon it by a hotel employee who delivered the coat to the express company for the owner. Apparently the owner did not read the receipt until after the loss had been discovered and did not call the attention of the express company to the grossly inadequate valuation. The court decided that the hotel employee was the agent of the owner, that the express company's receipt was binding upon it in regard to the charge it could make, and that it was equally binding upon the owner for the amount she could collect.[15]

There is an important difference between the settling of claims for partial loss under the express receipt and under the bills of lading used for freight shipments. It will be recalled that the bills of lading provide for a valuation per pound, whereas the express receipt puts a value upon the entire shipment. Freight claims are settled pro rata according to the limit per pound. Express claims, however, are settled in full up to the limit in the receipt. For example, suppose a 100-pound shipment is valued at 50 cents per pound for freight purposes and at a maximum of $50 for express. Further, suppose that 40 pounds of the shipment are lost with an actual loss to the owner of $75. The freight claimant would receive $20 (at fifty cents

[15]Feinberg v. Railway Express Agency, 163 F. (2d) 998 (1947); cert. den., 332 U.S. 847, 92 L. ed. 230 (1948).

per pound), whereas the express claimant would receive $50 (the maximum amount declared on the receipt).

There are package consolidating companies in the express field similar to carloading companies in the freight field. The relative cost of shipping by express becomes less as the weight of the shipment increases. A considerable saving in express charges is secured when numerous shipments can be combined into one. For example, a large Chicago department store may receive packages every day from a dozen different sources in New York City. It will instruct its New York shippers to send all their express packages to a package consolidating company, which will combine into a single express shipment all of the packages consigned to that department store. The saving in express charges is split between the store and the package consolidating company. This is important to the inland marine underwriter, because the packages often are received at the loading platform of the consolidating company amid a rush of afternoon deliveries, and the chances for theft are considerable. It is important to determine whether the consolidating company is a common carrier or is acting for the shipper or consigness, and under what terms.

Intrastate Shipments. Most shipments move under uniform bills of lading or uniform express receipts, but the liability of carriers may be different for shipments within a single state. This is most likely to occur in connection with the change from carrier's liability to warehouseman's liability when the goods have reached their destination. In the absence of a contractual provision to the contrary, it is the rule in some states for the liability of a common carrier on an intrastate shipment to become that of a warehouseman when the goods reach its warehouse at the destination. A notice of arrival to the consignee may not be required.

Tariffs filed with state railroad or transportation commissions should be consulted for the provisions applying to shipments within a particular state. This may be especially important in case of loss by fire. Common carriers are liable for loss by fire to goods in their custody, but a warehouseman is liable for a fire loss only if he is negligent. If the carrier's liability becomes that of a warehouseman upon arrival of the goods in its warehouse at destination, there is much less chance of recovery from the carrier in case of loss at that point. This should be determined in advance by the underwriter if a policy has a considerable number of intrastate shipments subject to fire loss in a carrier's warehouse.

Waterborne Shipments. Occasionally shipments insured under inland marine policies are carried by water carriers. This carriage may include lighterage across bays or rivers, or it may involve coastwise steamers. The uniform freight bills of lading contain a provision that "the term 'water carriage' in this section shall not be construed as including lighterage in or across rivers, harbors or lakes, when performed by or on behalf of rail carriers." That is, lighterage in connection with a rail journey is considered part of the rail journey and not carriage by water. The effect of this is that any loss or damage occurring during such lighterage is subject to the same rules and liability that would apply if the loss or damage occurred during some part of the actual rail journey.

The situation is entirely different in connection with waterborne losses occurring otherwise, even though the goods are shipped on a through bill of lading issued by a rail carrier. The bills of lading provide for the handling of waterborne losses according to the general rules applying to such losses.

Ocean marine liability is much different from common carrier liability of the railroads. If the coastwise ships are in direct competition with railroads, they may assume a liability similar to that of the railroads or they may arrange automatically for marine insurance on the cargo. In other cases, if there is no direct rail competition, the water carriers may make no provision for marine insurance. The situation is likely to be different between East Coast ports and ports on the Gulf of Mexico. It also may be different in the case of Pacific Coast ports. The underwriter who has a prospect using water carriers should investigate carefully the liability of the carriers and the insurance that may be provided automatically. It may also be advisable to examine the tariffs that have been filed, including the joint rail and water tariffs that may have been filed to cover the particular segment of route involved in the shipments to be insured.

Motor and Air Carriers. Since 1920 the motor truck has taken over an ever-increasing amount of freight hauling. Operators of motor trucks in interstate commerce are subject to the Motor Carrier Act of 1935 under the supervision of the Interstate Commerce Commission. Airplanes carrying cargo are subject to the economic regulations of the Civil Aeronautics Board. These two types of carriers are so different from the railroads in their operations, regulation, and liability that special chapters will be devoted to each, as well as to the insuring of the carrier's liability and of the cargo carried by them.

QUESTIONS

1. What is the liability of a common carrier?
2. What is the purpose of the Interstate Commerce Act?
3. What changes in common carrier liability were brought about by the amendments to the Interstate Commerce Act in 1906 and 1915?
4. What principle of recovery stated in the First Cummins Amendment to the Interstate Commerce Act forms the basis for the subrogation rights insurance companies enjoy against common carriers?
5. What is a bill of lading?
6. What is the essential difference between a straight bill of lading and an order bill of lading?
7. What is the significance of the words "shipper's weight, load, and count" on a bill of lading?
8. What is a tariff?
9. Why is it important for an inland marine underwriter to understand what constitutes delivery to or by a common carrier in connection with insured shipments?
10. How do sidetrack agreements affect the liability of a railroad for goods in its custody?
11. What is the function of a carloading company?
12. Name the principal requirements for filing notice of claim against a common carrier?
13. What is the difference between the settling of partial loss claims under the uniform bill of lading and under the uniform express receipt?
14. In what important respect may the liability of a common carrier for an intrastate shipment be different from its liability on an interstate shipment?
15. What differences are there in the liability of common carriers for intrastate shipments under the laws and regulations in your state from that applying to interstate shipments?

10

Transit Insurance Coverage

Transit insurance generally includes those coverages that indemnify the owner of property for loss that may occur while his property is being carried from one point to another. Transit insurance policies usually cover property while it is in the hands of others and not under the control of the owner, although such policies may be written to cover property being carried on vehicles belonging to the owner of the property.

The transit policy serves three purposes for the benefit of the policyholder.

The first purpose is to guarantee immediate payment of a loss even though a carrier may eventually be held liable. Transit insurance first became popular on a wide scale when businessmen found it difficult to collect freight claims from the railroads during World War I. The carrying of insurance permitted them to collect immediately for lost or damaged merchandise and relieved them of the burden of collecting from the carrier. Freight claims are handled by the railroads in a fairly prompt manner but businessmen find it convenient to pass the collection problem along to insurance companies by purchasing insurance coverage.

A second function of the transit policy is to indemnify the insured for any loss in excess of the liability of the carrier. The carrier may have filed a tariff that provides for a maximum valuation insufficient to cover the full value of the property. This is especially likely to happen during periods of rising prices, because the maximum valuations specified in the tariffs may remain fixed for many years without revision. The policyholder frequently finds it to his advantage to declare a nominal value to the carrier and to arrange with the insurance company to cover the excess. The excess valuation charges of the carriers usually are higher than are the insurance premiums for the same amount of protection.

The third purpose of the transit policy is to protect the insured against losses for which the carrier is not liable. The carrier is not liable for "acts of God," which may include such insurable hazards as windstorm, tornado, and earthquake.

The liability of a common carrier is extensive, and the insurance company expects to recover most of the losses it pays on goods lost or damaged while in the custody of a common carrier. The rates for transportation insurance are low because the insurance companies do have excellent chances of recovering their losses under their subrogation rights against common carriers. The rates would be many times higher if the insurance companies had to assume the full obligation of paying for goods lost or damaged in transit.

Transit insurance policies are tailored to fit the circumstances of individual policyholders. There is no standard form or policy. No matter what a prospect's business, the inland marine underwriter usually can design a coverage to fit the requirements. It may truly be said that there are as many different forms of transit policies as there are businesses in the United States.

Standardization has not been feasible because every business has its own way of shipping merchandise. No two merchants receive their goods from the same set of shippers or over the same routes. One merchant may receive the bulk of his goods from manufacturers in New York City and it may be shipped mostly by railroad. Another merchant in the same business and seemingly subject to the same hazards may buy his goods from wholesalers and manufacturers in Cleveland, Pittsburgh, and Birmingham, and may receive most of his merchandise by motor truck. The variations are endless, and the insurance policy and rate must be adjusted to the needs of the insured and to the chances of loss.

ANNUAL TRANSIT POLICIES

The annual transit policy is written to insure the incoming (and sometimes outgoing) shipments of the policyholder during the policy term, usually one year. The provisions common to many transit policies will be described, but any particular policy may vary from the usual provisions.

Annual transit policies usually enumerate specified perils, and loss or damage to the property described is covered when resulting from those perils. Land hazards usually covered include fire, lightning, windstorm, flood (meaning rising waters), earthquake, landslide, theft, and the perils of transportation. Sometimes the phrase "perils of transportation" is broken down into specific hazards such as collision, derailment, or overturn of the transporting vehicle and collapse of bridges. Flood coverage, when provided, may be limited to the rising of navigable waters. Theft coverage often is limited to the theft of entire shipping packages and excludes pilferage from packages. Strike, riot, and civil commotion coverage may be included.

Collision frequently is restricted in such a way that the coming together of cars during coupling operations is not deemed to be a collision. This is an important limitation because switching operations on railroads may result in violent bumps as the cars are coupled.

The annual transit policy usually includes coverage on waterborne goods while in course of transit by regular coastwise lines of ships between inland, Atlantic Coast, and the United States Gulf Coast ports, but excluding the Pacific Coast. Policies may be written to exclude coverage upon the Mississippi and Ohio rivers and on the Great Lakes, or upon any waters where the underwriter feels that there is a hazard not contemplated by the rates acceptable to the prospective policyholder. Coverage while waterborne customarily includes fire, perils of the sea, general average and salvage charges, and particular average (partial loss) if such partial loss exceeds 3 per cent of the value of each shipping package. Theft also may be covered. The waterborne coverage is extended to apply while the property is in depots and stations and on wharves, platforms, or piers while in due course of transit.

Waterborne coverage of transit policies does not apply to exports or imports. The land coverage would not become effective on such imports until the ocean marine coverage had ceased to be effective and on exports would cease at the point where the ocean marine coverage becomes effective. Many policies exclude coverage on exports and imports entirely unless there is a special endorsement extending protection to them.

Transit policies cover "while the insured property is in the custody of" any railroad or railroad express company; regular coastwise line of ships navigating United States inland, Atlantic, and Gulf waters not south of the Gulf of Mexico; and public truckmen, land transfer, and land transportation companies, provided these carriers are used in connection with railroad, railroad express, and the described waterborne shipments.

All the carriers mentioned are common carriers, and they are liable to the shippers under the rigid law of common carrier liability as previously described. The insurance companies' function in connection with shipments by such carriers is primarily that of serving the shipper by paying claims immediately and making collection from the carrier.

The phrase "while the insured property is in the custody of" deserves some comment. A question frequently arises concerning what constitutes delivery to the carrier and when the carrier effects delivery to the consignee. A misunderstanding may occur if it is customary for the policyholder to send the goods to the railroad or express station by his own trucks. A policy does not cover while the property is on the policyholder's own trucks unless there is a provision in the policy to that effect. Coverage on property in the custody of public truckmen may be limited to shipments being handled in connection with shipment by railroad, express, or ship.

Mistaken delivery to an impostor has been held as not constituting delivery to the carrier. In one case in which the policy covered property while in the custody of a truckman and also while in the hands of the policyholder's messenger, a court ruled that an employee of the insured who helped load goods onto an impostor's truck was not a messenger. It was held that the goods never were in the custody of a truckman and never were covered by the policy.[1]

In another case in which the policy covered only while in the custody of a common carrier, the court held that delivery was never effected.[2] The facts were that the shipper's employee delivered the goods to a man who was standing alongside an express company

[1] Starlight Fabrics, Inc. v. Glens Falls Ins. Co. 297 N.Y. 426, 79 N.E. (2d) 812 (1948).

[2] Hindus v. Scottish Union & National Ins. Co., 76 N.Y. Supp. (2d) 335 (1947).

truck and who was presumed to be an express company employee. It developed that the man was an impostor, and the express company never actually had possession of the goods. Since the property never came into its custody, the express company was not liable for the loss and neither was the insurance company.

A clause in a transit policy extends the coverage to property while it is on wharves, piers, and bulkheads, in depots and stations, or on platforms if it is in the custody of a common carrier incidental to transportation.

Another clause that seeks to make the coverage continuous has been adopted from the ocean marine "warehouse to warehouse" clause. It reads:

> This insurance attaches from the time the goods leave the factory, store or warehouse at initial point of shipment, and covers thereafter continuously, in due course of transportation, until same are delivered at store or warehouse at destination.

The intent of this clause would be clearer if it repeated the phrase "only while in the custody of a common carrier." In the second case just mentioned, it was contended by the plaintiff that this clause gave coverage from the time the goods left the shipper's premises, or at least that there was enough ambiguity to permit the policy to be read that way. However, the court did not feel that the policy was ambiguous and held that it covered only while the property was in the custody of a common carrier. The intent of the clause is to prevent lapse of the coverage if the goods are placed temporarily in a storage location while in the course of transit. It is not intended to extend coverage to an actual storage situation when the goods are no longer in a state of transit.[3]

Transit policies may be written to cover goods while in the hands of truckmen who are common carriers or while in the hands of any truckmen. (Truckmen who are not common carriers would be contract carriers, and their liability will be discussed in the chapter on motor truck cargo insurance.) Many underwriters believe that there is greater hazard of loss to property in the hands of truckmen than in the hands of the railroads. Rates for policies covering property in the hands of truckmen generally are higher than for policies covering property only while in the custody of railroads and express companies.

[3]In the case of Exchange Lemon Products Co. v. Home Ins. Co., 235 F. (2d) 558 (1956), the property had been in storage for more than a year although the storage was incidental to transportation. The court decided there was no coverage under a policy provision: "This policy also covers while . . . in depots, warehouses . . . but only while in due course of transit and not if such property is in storage."

Occasionally transit policies are extended to cover goods on a policyholder's own trucks. This introduces an entirely new factor into the underwriting because the insurance company must pay losses occurring to property on the insured's trucks with no chance of recovery from a carrier. If the exposure of goods to loss on the insured's trucks is of short duration or if the values exposed are low, the coverage may be added to a transit policy at a nominal cost. However, if the major part of the shipping is done on the insured's trucks, the hazards are primarily those of a motor truck operation, and must be underwritten as such. Sometimes it is desirable to write two policies, one on the transit hazard in the custody of common carriers and another to cover the motor truck cargo operation.

It should be noted that shipments by mail ordinarily are not covered by policies that insure property in the custody of common carriers. Shipments by mail usually are covered separately under a parcel post policy.

Accounts, bills, currency, deeds, evidences of debt, money, notes, and securities usually are not covered under an annual transit policy. Goods that have been refused or returned by the consignee usually are excluded also. It is considered that such property offers a hazard not contemplated in the rates for transit policies and must be insured under specific policies at adequate rates.

An annual transit policy excludes loss by leakage, breakage, marring, or scratching unless caused by fire, lightning, cyclone, tornado, or flood; or by collision, derailment, or overturning of the transporting vehicle while on land; or, if the shipment is waterborne, by the transporting vessel, craft, or lighter being stranded, sunk, burned, or in collision. This is intended to exclude the mysterious and unaccountable losses likely to occur in any transportation, especially if the shipper is careless about packing.

Another exclusion eliminates claims for damage due to delay, wet or dampness, and causes that make the goods become spotted, discolored, molded, rusted, frosted, rotted, soured, steamed, or changed in flavor, unless they are made so by one of the specific perils named in the policy.

Damage from strike, riot, and civil commotion is excluded in many transit policies, but coverage against such losses may be included for an extra premium. War damage and nuclear damage are excluded and seldom are added. Any damage resulting from neglect of the insured is excluded, as is damage to merchandise shipped on the decks of oceangoing ships.

Valuation Under Transit Policies. Policies may or may not include a clause defining the amount of loss. If there is no such valuation clause, the insurance company would be liable for the actual amount of any loss at the time and place of its occurrence. It is the duty of the insured to present a proof of loss setting out the value and supporting data.

Occasionally a policy specifies that the value is the invoice cost at the time and place of shipment. As pointed out in the chapter on common carrier liability, this type of valuation could result in a difference between the liability of the insurance company to the insured and the liability of the common carrier, because the common carrier is liable for the actual loss and cannot specify a method of valuation.

A valuation clause may specify that the goods are to be valued at invoice cost plus prepaid freight charges and any other charges that may be due on the shipment plus an allowance of 5 to 10 per cent to cover the expense of replacing the goods. This latter allowance is not included if the policyholder would not be put to expense in replacing the goods ordinarily covered under the policy.

Limits of Liability. Transit policies ordinarily show two limits of liability. The first is a limit of liability in any one place. This should be set high enough to protect the largest value that could accumulate at any place of shipment or anywhere along the route over which shipments travel. The largest amount shipped or received in any one day is a good figure. Routes should be examined to determine whether holidays or delayed shipments could result in an accumulation of two or three days' shipments.

The second limit of liability applies to any one disaster. A conflagration or forest fire might involve several locations within a community. A hurricane or flood might involve several communities and could destroy a number of shipments spread over a large area. The insurance company must know the maximum amount it could pay as a result of such an occurrence. The determination of this limit depends upon the total amount of goods in transit within the same geographical area over a period of several days or perhaps of several weeks.

The limitation on liability must be worded carefully to include not only the loss and damage itself but also any salvage charges or other expenses. A commonly used clause reads:

> This company shall not be liable for more than   dollars in any one casualty, either in case of partial or total loss, or salvage charges or other expenses or charges, or all combined.

Recoveries from Common Carriers. The history of transit insurance reveals efforts by common carriers to secure the benefit of any insurance carried by the owner of the property. There were equally strong moves by insurance companies to hold the carrier liable for all losses for which the carrier is responsible. The uniform bill of lading provides that the carrier shall have full benefit of any insurance that may have been effected on the property, so far as this shall not avoid the policies or contracts of insurance. If this clause were permitted to have effect, the insurance company would have to pay the loss without any hope of recovery from the carrier.

In order to protect their interests and be able to recover from the carriers, the insurance companies have inserted in transit policies a provision to the effect that the insurance "shall in no wise inure directly or indirectly to the benefit of any carrier or other bailee." The wording aims directly at the clause in the bill of lading that attempts to secure the benefit of insurance for the carrier.

Many policies have been written with an additional clause strengthening the position of the insurance company. It provides that any act of the insured, whether prior or subsequent to the date of the policy, that impairs the right of the insured to collect the full value of any loss or damage from a carrier or bailee shall invalidate the policy. Impairment of the insured's right to collect would in turn impair the insurance company's right to collect under a subrogation agreement.

The presence of these two clauses in unmodified form presents a serious problem to shippers. It is customary to ship goods under released bills of lading in which a specified value or limit of liability is stipulated. As a matter of fact, it is impossible under railroad tariffs to ship some types of merchandise without specifying a limit of liability. Under a strict interpretation of the clauses described, it would be impossible for a shipper of goods to collect from his insurance company.

This problem has been met in many cases by placing in the policy permission for the insured to release carriers to a valuation of not less than a specified amount. If the shipments are largely by railway express, the endorsement may give permission to release the carrier for not less than $50 per package. If the shipments are largely by freight or by carrier, the endorsement may be worded to give permission for the insured to accept the bills of lading ordinarily issued by carriers.

If the policy includes permission for the insured to accept ordinary bills of lading or to release the carrier to a stipulated value, the policy may contain another provision to the effect that the insured will not enter into any special agreement with a carrier without the written permission of the insurance company.

Emphasis is placed on the word "special." Ordinary bills of

lading may be accepted, but if the insured enters into any agreement that is special or not customary to that type of shipment, the coverage is void. Insurance rates and underwriting are based upon the recoveries to be expected under the ordinary bills of lading or express receipts, and the insurance company needs to know the circumstances of any special agreement so that the rates may be adjusted to fit the hazard.

Courts are likely to take into consideration the customs of a business in determining what may be considered a special agreement. A preceding chapter described the arrangements under which the effects of a troupe of actors may be carried as baggage in a special car. The agreement customarily used calls for a release of the carrier's liability except for negligence, and as a bailee rather than as a carrier. In a case involving a fire loss for which the carrier would have been liable as a carrier but for which it was not liable under the special baggage agreement, the court decided that this was not a special agreement within the meaning of the insurance policy because it was customary for show troupes to travel in that way and the underwriter is presumed to be acquainted with the practices of the trade he insures.[4]

Passage of Title to Goods in Transit. The sales contract between shipper and consignee usually specifies that the goods are shipped F.O.B. a designated point, either the point of shipment or the destination. As previously noted, the abbreviation "F.O.B." means "free on board" and originated in the shipping of goods by water carrier. The usual arrangement is for goods to be shipped F.O.B. the point where the carrier's liability begins. That is, the shipper delivers the goods to the railroad company or puts them in the custody of the express company.

The terms of the sales contract in this respect are important, because the title to the goods ordinarily passes from shipper to consignee at the point where they are F.O.B. If they are sent F.O.B. point of shipment, they usually belong to the consignee from then on, and any claim to be made against a carrier for loss or damage must be made by the consignee. If they are shipped F.O.B. the consignee's location, the title remains in the shipper until they are delivered, and the shipper would make claim against the carrier for any loss.

There may be circumstances in which a shipper is responsible for delivery of goods to the consignee even though technically he has

[4]Globe & Rutgers Fire Ins. Co. v. Winter Garden Co. 9 F. (2d) 227 (1925).

made delivery when the goods are placed in the hands of the carrier under an F.O.B. point of shipment arrangement. The shipper may wish to assume this responsibility for business reasons. In such cases the shipper's transit policy should include coverage on shipments until they are delivered to the consignee, regardless of the terms of the sales contract in respect to the F.O.B. provisions. This extension may be granted by a simple clause reading substantially as follows:

> This policy is hereby extended to cover shipments sold F.O.B. point of shipment or otherwise, and the interest of the insured in such shipments is admitted.

Annual transit policies covering incoming goods ordinarily cover the property from the time it is placed in the hands of the carrier at point of shipment. In writing such a policy, inquiry should be made regarding the customs of a particular business, in order to avoid overlapping insurance coverage between shipper and consignee.

There is a possibility of questionable title if the shipper is negligent and does not declare a sufficiently high value when he delivers goods to the carrier. A circumstance might arise in which the goods are shipped F.O.B. point of shipment, but the shipper is negligent and releases the carrier at an amount far below the actual value. This would prevent the consignee's collecting full value from the carrier in case of loss, and the consignee might be able to collect from the shipper for the difference. The rights of the consignee's insurance company to collect from the carrier would be impaired, and the insurance company might well proceed against the shipper.

Rates. The range of rates for annual transit coverage when property is insured while in the custody of railroads or in connection with railroad shipment is from about 2 cents to 10 cents per $100 of value shipped. The exact rate depends on the distance goods are shipped, whether there is any trucking of the property at the terminal points, and the susceptibility of the property to damage or theft. Occasionally policies are written at rates as low as one-half cent per $100 of value when the underwriter believes there is only a remote chance of his company's sustaining a loss not collectible from the carrier. Rates for property shipped by coastwise vessel or by motor truck may be twice as high as rates for rail shipments.

Some policies show different rates for different methods of shipment. In such cases, the insured is required to report the value of the goods shipped by each method of transportation, so that the premium can be calculated separately for the values carried by each type of carrier.

Basis of Premium Computation. The premium for an annual transit policy is based upon the total value of all the goods covered during the term of the policy. In this respect the policy differs from most other insurance policies, for which the premium is based upon a limit of liability. In the case of an annual transit policy, the premium is figured by applying the rate to the value of the goods insured (that is, the value of all the goods shipped that come within the definition of coverage in the policy).

It is impossible for a merchant to determine accurately in advance what his annual sales and merchandise receipts and shipments will be. Consequently it is customary for annual transit policies to be written on a reporting basis. If the annual premium is small, the policy may be written on an annual reporting basis. The policyholder estimates his receipts or shipments as closely as possible and pays an estimated annual premium. At the expiration of the policy, he makes a report to the insurance company of the actual values covered by the policy. An adjustment is then made in the premium, and he pays an extra premium due or receives a refund of any overpayment.

Many transit policies produce sufficient premium to justify a monthly reporting of values and monthly premium payment. Company practices differ in regard to what constitutes a premium large enough for monthly reporting. Some companies feel that monthly reporting is not justified unless the premium averages at least $50 per month, whereas others will write such a policy for a monthly premium as low as $10. The factor to be considered is the expense to both policyholder and insurance company of handling the reports and payments.

It is customary for a policy to provide for a deposit premium that may be a quarter or a third of the estimated annual premium. In many cases the monthly premiums for the first few months are charged against the deposit premium, and the policyholder starts making actual payments only when the deposit is exhausted. Sometimes the policy provides that the premium payments start immediately, and the company holds the deposit until expiration, upon which a final adjustment is made. This latter arrangement may be used if the company has doubts as to the policyholder's ability or willingness to pay all the premium.

The policy contains a clause governing the reporting of values. This clause constitutes a warranty or an agreement on the part of the policyholder that he will report to the insurance company the actual values shipped that are covered by the policy. The same clause usually contains the rate and the provisions for payment of the premium. The premiums are due when the report is made, and it is customary for the premium payment to be sent with the report.

The policy usually requires that the policyholder keep a record of all values shipped that are covered by the policy. That is, he must not only report them to the company but also keep an accurate record that the company may check at a later date. Many companies make it a practice to have an auditor check the books of the policyholder before final settlement is made at the expiration of the policy. The knowledge that such a check will be made is a deterrent to the policyholder who might be tempted to omit part of the values, and it reveals honest mistakes, which may be in favor of either the insured or the company.

It is possible to write transit policies on a continuous reporting basis. These differ from the policies just described only in that the policy has no expiration date and continues in effect until canceled by either party. Monthly reporting is required just as in a policy that expires annually, and the company makes its audits periodically to see that the reports are made correctly.

Occasionally policies are written for a flat annual premium with no provision for adjustment. This can be done in the case of a small, steady business, which is not likely to fluctuate from year to year. Companies require prospects to submit reports of previous shipments and insurance experience. Many underwriters consider at least three years' reports to be necessary for a satisfactory estimate. At expiration and before the next year's policy is issued, a careful underwriter will again examine the record to see whether any change in rate or premium is justified.

VARIATIONS IN ANNUAL TRANSIT POLICIES

Railway Express Transit Form. A variation of the annual transit form is the "Railway Express transit form." This usually is written for policyholders whose shipments are exclusively by Railway Express, and it provides a broader coverage than is feasible if several types of carriers are used regularly. In addition to the coverages provided under other annual transit policies, it protects against pilferage and nondelivery.

Railway Express companies are not liable for more than $50 per shipment (or 50 cents per pound for shipments in excess of 100 pounds), unless a greater value is declared and an extra charge paid. The extra charge usually amounts to 10 cents for each $100 of value or fraction thereof. The Railway Express transit insurance coverage permits a policyholder to accept the minimum valuation allowed by the express company, and the insurance company pays for any loss in excess of the amount for which the express company is liable. The rates for this coverage are less than the 10 cents per $100 charged by the express company and may be as little as 3 cents per $100 of value reported.

The policyholder saves the difference between the express company charge and the insurance rate, and in addition is saved the trouble of declaring the exact value when it exceeds the $50 minimum express company liability. The policy contemplates that the insured will collect from the express company up to the amount of its liability. When incoming shipments are covered by a Railway Express transit form, the shippers should be instructed by the insured not to declare any excess value to the express company.

Shipments by air express are not covered by the usual policy, but coverage may be endorsed on the policy. The rate may be higher than for railroad shipments. If both rail and air shipments are covered, there may be a separate rate for each, and in this case the policyholder must report rail and air shipments separately.

Department Store Transit Policy. The insurance needs of department stores are different from those of other mercantile and manufacturing risks, and a special transit policy is used to meet their requirements. The coverage is at least as broad as the annual transit policy generally used, and in many cases it covers against loss "from any external hazard." This is broader coverage than is provided by a specified perils policy, as explained in the chapter on "all risks" coverage.

The property covered includes goods being delivered to customers, but it excludes property of customers that is intended for storage or repair. That is, it covers property that is being delivered to a customer who has purchased it, but it does not cover property already belonging to the customer that the store is picking up or returning. This exclusion is necessary to avoid overlapping coverage with such bailee insurance policies as the furriers' customers policy, which will be discussed in another chapter.

The department store transit policy covers property while it is in the hands of common carriers, including railroads, express companies, air carriers, and truckmen, and also while on the insured's own trucks and in the hands of its messengers. Losses are settled on the basis of the invoice cost plus a percentage (frequently 10 per cent) to cover handling, and in the case of goods being delivered to customers the policy may provide for loss payment on the basis of the retail sales price. There is usually an actual cash value clause to cover those cases in which there is no invoice upon which to base the value.

The premium is based upon the insured's gross sales. This has practically the same effect as basing it upon the value of the merchandise shipped and is a much easier figure for the store to secure. The premium may be payable annually and adjusted at expiration or may be payable monthly depending upon the size of the premium.

Contingent Transit Coverage. There are some policyholders who wish to make their own collections from the carriers and who desire insurance coverage only for losses they cannot collect from the carriers. They have their own traffic departments and are in daily contact with their carriers.

These policyholders may desire a contingent policy that covers a loss only after the policyholder has exhausted every effort to make collection from the carrier. The rates are low because the insurance company does not have to bother with numerous claims and does not have the trouble of collecting them under subrogation. This form is desirable only for the policyholder who is well able to make his own collections and who needs coverage only for those catastrophes for which the common carrier is not liable. The coverage under these policies is the same as that under other transit forms, but loss payment is contingent upon the insured's making the primary effort to collect.

TRIP TRANSIT POLICIES

The trip transit policy serves the same purpose as the annual transit policy, but it is issued to cover a specified lot of goods on a particular trip. It is issued to insureds who ship only occasionally and do not have sufficient shipments to justify an annual policy. It is used, for example, to cover shipments of household furniture, heavy machinery, and merchandise or livestock en route to and from exhibitions.

The policy issued to provide trip transit coverage is sometimes called a certificate, because it is an abbreviated form and does not look as bulky as the typical insurance policy. However, it contains the usual conditions of a transit policy. The certificate contains a description of the property being shipped, the place of shipment and the destination, the mode of transportation, and the name of the carrier if it is going by motor truck. A limit of liability is specified, and if the property is commercial goods, there is a clause that will determine the value in case of loss.

The coverage is usually the same as that described for the annual transit form. Variations are possible, depending on the needs of the policyholder. In case the goods consist of a valuable machine, the policy may include coverage during loading and unloading. The insurance company should know who is the carrier, as well as his qualifications for taking care of the type of equipment to be handled. The moving of machinery is a highly specialized business, and insurance companies ordinarily do not insure machinery under a trip transit policy unless the carrier is known to be competent.

Household goods may be insured under a trip transit form for the owner, particularly when they are being shipped by railway freight. There is also a form of trip transit certificate issued for motor truck operations.

A trip transit certificate may be issued to cover during temporary storage while in transit as well as during the actual movement. Sometimes household furniture is stored temporarily before it is sent on to its final destination. The trip transit coverage can be written to cover from the time the property leaves its original location, during transit to the temporary location, while in temporary storage, and while in transit to its final destination. The coverage during temporary storage should be limited according to the provisions of the Nationwide Marine Definition applying to domestic shipments.

The policy also can cover a shipment while it is being sent to a temporary location for exhibit and while it is on exhibit, as well as on the return trip. This type of policy is commonly used to cover livestock when shipped for exhibition purposes. It may be used also when goods are shipped to a factory or other plant for processing, repair, or renovation.

The rates for trip transit coverage vary all the way from one cent to $1.00 or more per $100 of value. The principal variables are the type of carrier, the length of the trip, and the susceptibility of the property to damage. The lowest rates are given to merchandise shipped by railroad freight under a uniform bill of lading. The rates are higher when the goods are shipped under a released bill of lading, because the insurance company is more likely to have to pay a portion of any loss. Rates usually are higher for motor truck shipments than for comparable railroad shipments.

Shipments of purebred livestock may cost much more than other goods to insure; these rates may be 2 to 4 percent of the value for a long shipment by motor truck. Easily damageable articles, such as fine arts and antiques, also take high rates, depending on the carrier and on the knowledge of the shipper and the carrier regarding the handling of such special types of property.

It is important that the premium for a trip transit policy be collected when the order for it is taken. It is a unique policy in that the period of possible loss usually has passed by the time the policy is delivered. The prospective policyholder frequently calls his insurance agent when the goods are ready to leave and asks for immediate coverage.

INSURANCE ON PARCEL POST SHIPMENTS

Since the parcel post service was established in 1912, a large part of the commerce of the country has been carried on through the Post Office. The federal government is not a common carrier, and it does not incur any liability for the property it carries in the postal service unless the property is insured by the Post Office. Annual transit and trip transit policies exclude coverage on parcel post shipments. This exclusion is used because the Post Office does not have the liability of a common carrier.

Insurance company coverage of parcel post shipments is underwritten on an entirely different basis from that on which coverage for shipments by common carrier is provided. It is customary to issue separate policies specifically covering parcel post shipments. Coverage on property sent by unregistered mail or by ordinary parcel post is primary insurance, and the insurance company is obligated to pay the loss with no chance of subrogation against the carrier. The only chance of subrogation is in the rare instances when collection could be made from a third party who was responsible for a loss while the property was in the custody of the Post Office.

Parcel post is used commercially by thousands of firms. In addition to the nationally known mail order houses, many other concerns sell entirely or largely by mail. Some of them handle specialty items not generally available in stores, some ship such articles as cigarettes from states with low taxes into states with higher taxes; and others cater to the people who like to purchase from catalogs rather than from store counters. Parcel post is used also by city stores for delivery to their suburban customers. The cost may be less than that of a parcel delivery service, and next-day service by parcel post is available in some metropolitan areas. Almost every merchant has occasion to send some packages by parcel post, and many use this method of shipment to the exclusion of all others.

Coverage Under Parcel Post Policies. Parcel post forms and rates are not filed by the rating bureaus. The policy conditions and rates which are described here are those generally used, but there is considerable variation in the practices of different insurers. There are two forms of parcel post insurance. The coupon or certificate form is sold to concerns having relatively few shipments a year, whereas the open form is better adapted to the shipper of a large number of packages. The coverage is identical, the principal difference being in the mechanics of recording and paying for the insurance. The coverage is almost "all risks," for the policy insures the safe arrival of the property and covers it against loss or damage from any external cause, including nondelivery, subject to exclusions peculiar to this policy. The type of property must be described specifically in the policy and must be property usual to the business of the policyholder.

The policy covers while the property is actually in the custody of the Post Office Department. Domestic policies limit the coverage to the continental United States and Canada, but foreign coverage can be written. The policy does not cover while the property is in the hands of the insured's employee or other messenger on its way to the Post Office.

There may be a question as to when a package is "actually in the custody of the Post Office Department." Frequently parcels are placed in collection boxes, and sometimes they are placed alongside or on top of them. The collection service is maintained for the convenience of the public and is not required by the postal laws. The postal regulations do not require that the postal employees pick up other than first-class mail. They are not required to pick up mail deposited outside a mail box, although it is a federal offense to steal mail so deposited. Here is a peculiar situation; for a person who steals such mail, which the postal employees are not required to pick up, is nevertheless subject to prosecution for stealing from the United States mail. A concern that makes it a practice to deposit packages outside collection boxes is taking a chance that its parcel post insurance will not cover such packages.

The exclusions are important in defining the actual coverage. Perishable merchandise is covered only against the perils of fire, theft, pilferage, and nonarrival. The Post Office assumes no responsibility for speedy delivery, and insurance companies cannot afford to insure perishable merchandise against spoiling.

The policy does not cover accounts, bills, currency, deeds, evidences of debt, money, notes, or securities. This type of property is subject to an extreme theft hazard, and the values can be so tremendous that the parcel post insurance rates are not adequate for the hazard. They may be insured under registered mail policies, which will be discussed later.

Another exclusion refers to merchandise shipped on consignment, memorandum, or approval. Such property is not covered unless it is shipped in fulfillment of an order or request, or is consigned to parties to whom the policyholder previously has sold goods. Some firms have made it a practice to ship goods to people without orders, upon the theory that most people will pay for goods rather than go to the trouble of sending them back. Of course, the recipient is under no obligation to pay for something he did not order, but many people do not realize that. There is a natural tendency for the recipient to be careless about such a package and to deny that he ever received it. In addition to the obvious hazards of insuring such merchandise, there is the likelihood that a firm engaged in this type of business would not bc a desirable policyholder.

It is important that all packages be addressed correctly and fully, that they be wrapped securely, and that the postage be prepaid in full. There is a provision in the insurance policy excluding coverage on packages that do not meet these requirements.

Another exclusion relates to shipments to transients at hotels unless they are sent by registered mail or government-insured parcel post. This is necessary because it is difficult to trace the delivery of packages in hotels unless there is a signed receipt for the delivery. This exclusion does not apply to packages mailed to salesmen of the insured destined to hotels. It is believed that there is less chance of loss if the package is addressed to an employee of the insured than if the package is consigned to a person who does not have a direct personal interest in the goods.

The parcel post policy does not cover packages that bear labels on the outside tending to describe the nature of the contents. Theft or pilferage is much more likely when the contents are described and the thief knows in advance what is inside. This exclusion does not apply when the goods shipped are of such a nature that the postal regulations require disclosure of the contents. An example would be the shipping of books, on which a special postage rate is allowed when they are so marked.

Packages must bear the notation "Return Postage Guaranteed." Only first-class mail is forwarded or returned without additional charge. All other classes, including parcel post, are disposed of by the

Post Office if forwarding or return postage is not provided or guaranteed.

The policy also contains a war exclusion clause similar to that found in other transit policies, but special significance may be attached to the portion of this clause referring to "seizure or destruction under quarantine or customs regulations, confiscation by order of any government, public authority, or risks of contraband or illegal transportation or trade." It would be contrary to public policy[5] to insure illegal operations involving the risks of contraband or illegal trade, and it would be extremely hazardous to the insurance company.

It is agreed in the policy that all packages will be mailed in accordance with the General Parcel Post Act of the United States, Act of August 24, 1912, and amendments thereto, and shall comply with the regulations of the parcel post system as prescribed by the Postmaster General. The obvious reason for this provision is to prevent loss or damage as a result of packages being improperly mailed. Merchandise of a hazardous nature, such as flammable materials, may not be shipped through the mails, and an insurance company could not afford to insure such shipments.

The limits of liability are specially designed to fit the needs of parcel post coverage. For ordinary parcel post or unregistered mail, the limit of liability is $100 per package. For registered mail or government-insured parcel post, the limit of liability is $500 per package. The limits of liability may be increased under the open form. In connection with government-insured parcel post, it is required by the policy that each package valued at $100 or less be insured by the Post Office for at least 50 percent of its actual value and that packages valued at more than $100 be government-insured for at least $50. There also is an "actual cash value" clause limiting the recovery to the actual value of the property lost or damaged, and the insurance company has the option of replacing the lost or damaged articles.

There is an "other insurance" clause providing that the company shall not be liable for loss or damage to property covered by other insurance, but this is worded so that government insurance is not considered to be other insurance.

Proof of loss is required to be made within four months of the date of mailing, and notice of loss must be given to the insurance company immediately after the loss has become known. The original

[5]"Public policy," a common legal term, is defined as the policy recognized or established by the state in determining what acts are unlawful as being injurious to the public or contrary to the public good.

wrapper must be secured and submitted to the insurance company if it is available, and the receipt for government insurance must accompany the proof of loss papers. Loss is payable within 30 days after receipt of the proof of loss. The insurance company receives by subrogation any rights of the insured to recover the loss from others, but, as pointed out above, this right is of little value except when there is government insurance or when the loss was caused by a third party and not by the Post Office Department.

The postal regulations provide for C.O.D. (cash on delivery) shipments. The charge for such shipments includes government insurance up to the amount to be collected from the consignee. Therefore, there is no reason to insure such packages under a parcel post insurance policy unless the actual value of the package is greater than the C.O.D. amount. In such cases the excess above the C.O.D. amount may be insured. Otherwise C.O.D. shipments should be excluded from coverage under the policy.

Foreign Shipments. Policies may be endorsed to cover foreign shipments (those outside the continental United States and Canada), or a separate policy may be issued. The general provisions of such a policy are the same as for domestic shipments, but there are a few important restrictions. Packages to be insured must be addressed to a country to which United States parcel post service is maintained. The parcel post service to foreign countries changes from time to time according to international conditions.

A second restriction of foreign shipments relates to the insuring of parcels. Insured or registered mail service is maintained to some foreign countries, but ordinary parcel post service is the only kind available to others. Wherever registered or insured parcel post service is available, the parcels should be registered or partially insured by government insurance and a return receipt requested. If the only service available is ordinary parcel post, the shipper should obtain a certificate of mailing from the Post Office when the package is mailed.

Occasionally there will be a request for a trip parcel post policy to cover the shipment of a single package or group of packages. The premiums on domestic shipments are so small that this is seldom justified in this country, but there are occasions when a trip policy is justified on a foreign shipment. The conditions would be the same for any other parcel post policy except that the individual shipment would be described in the policy in much the same manner as a shipment would be described under a trip transit policy.

Coupon Form. The coupon form of parcel post policy is sold to policyholders whose parcel post shipments are modest in amount. Many insurance companies make the break between the coupon and open types of policies at $25,000 worth of merchandise shipped in a year, approximately the amount that would produce an annual premium of $50.

The coupon form of parcel post policy consists of a master policy and a book of certificates (coupons). The master policy contains the coverage provisions and usually specifies a term of one year. The book of certificates is numbered to correspond to the master policy and contains 100, 200, 500, or 1,000 certificates. Each certificate is worth 5 cents; and the amount paid for the policy and book depends on the number of certificates (that is, $5 for a book of 100, $10 for a book of 200, and so on).

The coupon form of parcel post policy is expensive to handle. Only a few companies continue to use it. The open form of parcel post policy is preferred where there is a sufficient volume of shipments to justify the purchase of such a policy.

Open Form. The open form is used when shipments are extensive. It is less cumbersome than the coupon form and allows the insurance company to give credit for a good experience and expert handling of shipments. The policy refers to a record book in which all shipments are entered and to the payment of premium as it is earned.

The record book is furnished with the policy. The information must be entered for each package before it leaves the insured's premises for the Post Office. At the end of each month, the total value of the shipments is added up and reported to the insurance company. There is usually a minimum premium of $50 paid at the inception of the policy, and the monthly premiums are charged against this minimum premium. When the minimum premium is used up, the policyholder is required to send the additional premium with the report of values each month. Payment of premium may be required monthly, quarterly, or annually, depending on the volume of business expected under the policy.

The rate for an open form parcel post policy is calculated by the insurance company according to the type of merchandise shipped, the average distance packages are sent, the loss record, and the experience of the insured in mailing merchandise. The rates may be from 15 to 35 cents per $100 of value shipped.

Incoming and returned shipments may be covered under the open form by adding a special endorsement to the policy. Under the endorsement, shipments made by the insured are covered from the time they are placed in the custody of the Post Office until delivered or returned. It also covers incoming shipments which the insured owns or has purchased or in which he has an insurable interest. The insured is required to keep a record of the shipments received, with information similar to that required for outgoing shipments. The rate for incoming shipments may be the same as that for outgoing shipments or it may be different, depending upon the type of merchandise received, how it is shipped, and the distance over which it has to travel.

Insurance companies usually require that an additional minimum premium be charged whenever the incoming shipments endorsement is added to the policy. This is one of the few cases in which there is provision for two minimum premiums on the same policy.

The open form may be endorsed to cover only shipments that are insured by government insurance or sent by registered mail. This is done frequently in connection with valuable merchandise when there is need for the receipt given on all government-insured mail. The government insurance in such cases would be an agreed amount (less than the actual value) or perhaps a proportion of the actual value.

Loss Prevention Service on Parcel Post Policies. A parcel post policy usually needs servicing by the insurance company or agent. Large accounts may have expertly managed traffic departments that know how to ship packages properly. The smaller accounts are likely to be plagued by frequent losses, the causes of which may be improper wrapping and addressing. Parcel post is necessarily subject to rough handling at times, and all packages must be securely tied and wrapped. Large stacks of mail subject the packages underneath to tremendous pressure.

Labels should be typed, not written by hand. State names should be spelled out in full because many of the abbreviations are similar. Labels must not indicate the nature of the merchandise, even by indirection. Sometimes it is advisable to show a return address by some name other than the full name of the shipper if the name discloses the nature of the contents.

Many times the source of dishonest losses will be found within the insured's own organization and not within the Post Office. The parcels may never have been mailed. When this is suspected, it may be required that a receipt for mailing be obtained from the Post Office in connection with packages sent by ordinary parcel post. A test check by this method for a period of time may indicate whether losses are occurring in the Post Office or before the parcels reach it.

When losses are frequent, the loss records should be examined to see whether the losses form any pattern. It may be that many losses will show up on packages from a certain branch of the insured's business. This may indicate carelessness or dishonesty on the part of the insured's personnel, or it may show trouble in the Post Office in that city. In other cases there may be losses over a certain postal route. The Post Office inspectors will be helpful whenever there is any indication that the fault may lie within the Post Office.

REGISTERED MAIL AND EXPRESS

Registered mail insurance is designed to indemnify for loss of property with a relatively high value. Financial institutions such as banks and investment houses must settle their accounts by sending large amounts of money and securities from city to city. These are sent by registered mail, express, or air express, but the maximum amount recoverable from the Post Office is $1,000 per package. Express shipments of valuable articles may be declared for their full value, but the cost of the extra valuation is higher than the rates usually charged by insurance companies. The $1,000 limit of recovery on registered mail shipments and the charges of the express companies make it desirable for financial institutions to insure their valuable shipments under insurance policies.

It is permissible under the rating bureau filings to endorse the policy to cover shipments of negotiable securities under air bills of airline carriers which are approved by the bureau. This extension is permitted where the security precautions of the airline are considered to be the equivalent of express operations.

The types of property eligible for registered mail and express coverage are:

1. Bonds, coupons, stock certificates, and other securities; postage and revenue stamps; postal, express, and other money orders; certificates of deposit, checks, drafts, notes, bills of lading, warehouse receipts, and other commercial papers, and other documents and papers of value;
2. Bullion, platinum, and other precious metals;
3. Currency (whether coin or paper), jewelry, watches, necklaces, bracelets, gems, and precious and semiprecious stones; and other valuables of like kind.

Policies are issued only to persons, firms, or corporations of a fiduciary character, such as banks, trust companies, insurance companies, security brokers, and investment houses. The property covered may be that owned by the insured or it may be the property of others. Valuable articles shipped for customers may be insured under the policy of the bank or investment house. Incoming as well as outgoing shipments may be covered. Shipments must be declared to the insurance company or be entered on the record prior to shipment.

A peculiarity of registered mail insurance is the extremely high values that may be covered. Many insurance companies have arrangements for automatic protection up to $5 million, and amounts in excess of that may be covered on special notice to the company prior to shipment. The chances of catastrophic loss are obvious, especially when it is realized that shipments may be sent by registered air mail or by air express. Such shipments are a great temptation to thieves, who may lay elaborate plans to steal a million dollars' worth of currency or securities. Policies frequently provide for limits of $5 million to any one addressee in any one day, and $250,000 in one package in the case of currency and jewelry.

The coverage is among the broadest found in any inland marine policy. Policies may cover within the continental United States, or they may cover within the continent of North America and between places on the continent of North America and any place in the world. Coverage to and from Alaska and Puerto Rico may be added by endorsement. Rates and rules are filed by the rating bureaus for domestic shipments. Foreign shipments are subject to special rates and rules according to the risk. Coverage is effective from the time the property leaves the premises of the insured until it is delivered to the addressee or, if returned, until the property reaches the insured's premises again. The policy covers not only while the property is in the custody of the Post Office or the express company but also while in the hands of a messenger or on a conveyance on the way to and from the Post Office or express company at the place of shipment and delivery. This differs from the parcel post policy, which covers only while the property is in the custody of the Post Office.

The registered mail and express policies insure against "all risks" of physical loss or damage or destruction of the property, subject to only two exclusions. These exclusions relate to war damage and to loss or damage resulting from civil war or the risks of piracy, contraband, or illegal transportation or trade and seizure or destruction under quarantine or customs regulations. It is interesting to note that the nuclear damage exclusion does not appear in this policy.

An excess insurance clause applies to theft by employees of the sender or addressee. If the theft is covered by other insurance, the registered mail policy becomes excess insurance as far as such loss or damage is concerned. However, if the loss is paid under a blanket or fidelity bond, the registered mail policy obligates the insurance company to pay the amount of premium experience credit that would have been earned under the bond if the loss had not been paid by the bond.

Another peculiarity of registered mail policies is that they may be issued for an amount in excess of the value of the property at the time the coverage becomes effective. This is done so that the policyholder will be reimbursed for any increase in value between the time the property is lost and payment of the claim. Such an increase in value might occur in connection with a loss of stocks if the price of the stocks rose in the interim. This additional value usually is limited to a percentage of the value at the time the coverage becomes effective.

Policies provide that the insured shall endeavor to have the contents of each package verified by two people. Losses are payable within 7 days after receipt of proof of loss. This is an unusually short period of time compared to that provided for in other insurance policies. The 30 or 60 days provided for payment of loss under other insurance policies would result in a heavy loss of interest in the case of security losses.

Registered mail policies usually are continuous, and reports of business are made to the insurance company on a daily, monthly, or annual basis, depending upon the amount of value shipped during the year. The recording of shipments and the payment of premium are handled in much the same way as those for parcel post shipments. Individual trip policies can be written, but individuals who have valuables to be shipped often find it more convenient to have a bank or security house ship them and insure them under its open policy.

Negotiable securities, currency, and other negotiable property are insured for their full value. Nonnegotiable property may be insured for an amount sufficient to secure the reissue of the securities or the replacement of other property. The posting of a bond is usually required for the reissuing of securities, and the policy covers payment for this bond and any other expenses. Nonnegotiable securities usually are insured for from 10 to 30 percent of their value, depending upon anticipated cost of replacement and on possible increases in value. Bonds usually are insured for 10 percent of their value. The rates are reduced materially if nonnegotiable securities are insured for their full value.

Rates for registered mail insurance vary from 4 to 40 cents per $1,000 of value, depending on the distance property is shipped, whether it is shipped by surface carrier or by air, and whether reports are made daily, monthly, or annually. These low rates for shipments of such tremendous value are a tribute to the efficient methods of the Post Office and the express companies in protecting shipments of valuable property.

FIRST-CLASS MAIL

Many organizations wish to avoid the trouble involved when property is shipped by registered mail. This is particularly true if the property consists of nonnegotiable securities or some other property which is not subject to a severe hazard of loss. Ordinary first-class mail is a reasonably safe method of shipping such property. The first-class mail insurance policy covers bonds, coupons, stock certificates, postage and revenue stamps, postal, express and other money orders, certificates of deposit, drafts and other securities and papers of value, but excludes checks and currency. It does not cover such property as bullion and precious metals, gems, jewelry, or watches.

The coverage and terms of the first-class mail policy are similar to those of the registered mail and express policy. Shipments by ordinary first-class mail and first-class air mail are covered. The policy is issued to fiduciary organizations of the same types for which registered mail policies are issued. The rates are higher than for registered mail policies. The rates range from 2 cents to 48 cents per $1,000 of value shipped, depending upon the nature of the property covered, whether it is negotiable, whether it is shipped by ordinary or certified mail, and whether it is shipped between offices of the insured and fiduciary organizations, or to other persons or organizations. First-class mail insurance provides a convenient way of covering valuable papers and similar property that are not subject to a severe theft hazard.

ARMORED CAR AND MESSENGER INSURANCE

Armored cars are used extensively for the delivery of money and securities. There are also occasions when banks and investment houses transfer valuable property by messenger, either armed or unarmed, depending on the value of the property. These are similar to the situations covered under registered mail policies, but armored car and messenger service may be more convenient for short hauls. Such service is used for the transfer of funds within a city and for the delivery of payrolls to large industrial concerns. A factor that encourages the use of armored car and messenger service is the addition or surcharges to the registered mail rates of the Post Office when the declared value of the property exceeds that for which a registry charge is paid.

The coverage under an armored car or messenger insurance policy is similar to that under a registered mail policy, but there are different limits of liability to fit the circumstances of such shipments. The top limit without special notice to the company may be as high as $5 million on securities other than coin and paper money when the property is carried by armored motor cars or in the custody of messengers under the protection of armed guards. If similar property (not coin or paper money) is transferred by messenger not under the protection of armed guards, the limit is likely to be $250,000.

The usual limits on coin and paper money are $1 million when carried by armored motor car, $250,000 when carried by messenger under the protection of more than one armed guard, and $100,000 when carried by messenger under the protection of an armed guard. The policy usually excludes any loss on a shipment which exceeds the limit in the policy unless the company is notified in advance. This provision of the policy is considered necessary because the larger a shipment is, the greater is the temptation to a thief. The policyholder must be careful to keep his shipments within the policy limits or notify the company of any excess before the shipment is made.

Rates are based on the hazard of the insured's operations and apply to each $100 of value shipped. When paper money is shipped by aircraft in the custody of a messenger, it is customary to charge an extra rate. Shipments must be reported to the insurance company just as in the case of registered mail policies, and premium must be paid thereon.

It is possible to issue a trip policy either to cover an unusual shipment or for a person or firm that infrequently ships valuables by armored car or messenger. This sort of policy is used at times to cover securities and money when a financial institution is moving to a new location.

Frequently a financial institution has a banker's blanket bond that gives protection on shipments by armored car or messenger. However, the institution may need protection for armored car and messenger shipments in excess of the limits provided by the blanket bond. An armored car and messenger policy may be written on a deductible basis, the deductible being the amount of the blanket bond. The deductible would ordinarily be something in excess of $100,000. The same thing may be done if the primary insurance is a messenger robbery policy. The premium for such a policy usually is on a flat basis and depends upon the hazards of the operation, the amount of the primary coverage, and the amount of property shipped during the year.

Armored car and messenger policies are tailored to fit the individual needs of the policyholders, and seldom will two policies read exactly alike. For example, when a bank has a contract to deliver payrolls to its clients, it needs protection to the plant of the consignee. In other cases, the armored car company may take the responsibility for delivery and carry insurance on the shipments, and the bank's policy may cover only to the point at which the armored car company's responsibility begins. Banks with branches need protection for funds being transferred between the branches and the main bank. Security houses use messengers to deliver securities to their clients. The variations are endless, and the inland marine underwriter must know the intricacies of his prospect's business in order to prepare a policy giving complete protection. No filings of either rates or forms are made by the rating bureaus for armored car and messenger insurance. The rates are calculated by the company according to the hazards affecting each insured's operations.

TRANSIT COVERAGE OF THE SMP POLICY

Property in transit may be covered under the Special Multi-Peril (SMP) policy. This is an inland marine coverage even though it is included in this broad package of insurance. The SMP policy also may include other inland marine coverages. These are covered later in this text. Attention is given here to the transit coverage which is comparable to that described in this chapter.

The transit coverage of the SMP Commercial Property form applies to the personal property that is covered by the policy. This is the business personal property of the insured, including stock of merchandise, furniture and fixtures, and other personal property which is usual to the insured's business. Three divisions of transit exposure are listed. The first is property in transit on the insured's own vehicles other than property in the custody of a salesman. Second is property in the custody of a salesman. Third is property in the custody of carriers for hire, or otherwise in transit. Each of these three is made subject to a limit of liability for that situation.

The coverage is the same as that which is provided to property at the locations named in the policy. This is customarily against "all risks" of physical loss, subject to limitations and exclusions. There are dollar limitations applying to such property as jewelry and furs. There are exclusions applying to such property as currency, bullion, securities and other documents, and to property shipped by mail. Some of these limitations and exclusions are written with the transit exposure in mind, but they apply equally to personal property at the locations specified in the policy and to personal property in transit. The effect is an integration of the transit coverage with the premises coverage of the policy. The "all risks" type of coverage which the policy provides does result in a broad form of transit insurance under the policy. The coverage does take the place of a regular transit policy except for such special exposures as property being sent by mail.

Other forms of the SMP policy provide degrees of transit coverage which are commensurate with the needs of average insureds. The SMP Special Office Personal Property form permits the insured to apply up to 10 percent of the amount of insurance, but not more than $10,000, to loss of property while temporarily away from the premises named in the policy. This extension of coverage also applies to losses in transit. The coverage applies only for property which is temporarily away from the premises for not more than 30 consecutive days, but this would be adequate transportation coverage for most office property. The property covered and the perils insured against are the same as those described in the policy for coverage on the named premises.

The SMP Physicians' and Surgeons' Equipment Floater form also provides an off-premises coverage which is a transit coverage. This form is comparable in its use and coverage to the inland marine form known as the Physicians' and Surgeons' Equipment Floater. This form will be described later in this text. Medical, surgical, and dental equipment and instruments are covered both while at the premises of the insured and while away from the premises. This coverage recognizes that such equipment may be customarily used away from the premises in the pursuit of the insured's profession and thus must have constant coverage. The insured may also apply up to $1,000 of the coverage on furniture and fixtures while temporarily away from the premises. This coverage is similar to that under the office form. The off-premises coverage for furniture and fixtures does not need to be continuous because such property would be away from the premises only under unusual circumstances.

The charges for transit and off-premises coverage are included in the rates for such property as physicians' and surgeons' equipment and for office equipment. The exposure to loss during transit either is moderate as in the case of furniture and fixtures, or is reasonably uniform in the case of physicians' and surgeons' equipment. It is not necessary to establish any separate rating factor.

The exposure to transit loss of commercial property does vary substantially from one situation to another. The rates and premiums for an SMP policy are developed from the rates for the various types of coverage which are provided by the policy. The final rate is considered as indivisible as far as the insured is concerned, but it is developed in segments. There is a segment for the transit exposure in all cases except those where the transit exposure is negligible. This segment of the rate for the transit exposure is developed by the company underwriter in much the same way that a rate is developed for a separate transit policy.

The presence or absence of a specific rating factor for the transit coverage of an SMP or other multiple line policy depends upon the nature of the transit exposure to loss. The transit exposure can be ignored in the rate makeup if the transit exposure is infrequent and negligible. A nominal factor can be included in the overall rate for properties where the transit exposure is relatively uniform. A specific factor for the transit exposure is put into the rate where the property is subject to a considerable exposure and where the exposure may vary from the property of one insured to another. This follows the general practice in the rating of multiple line policies. Homogeneous and uniform exposures to loss are measured in the general rates, and any unusual exposures to loss are the subject of specific rate factors.

QUESTIONS

1. What are the three purposes served by a transit insurance policy?
2. Why has it not been feasible to standardize transit insurance coverage and rates?
3. What important difference is there between the underwriting of a transit policy covering goods shipped by common carrier and one covering goods shipped on the insured's trucks?

4. What two limits of liability frequently appear in transit policies?
5. Explain the significance of the provision that the insurance "shall not inure directly or indirectly to the benefit of any carrier or other bailee."
6. Upon what are the premiums for annual transit insurance policies usually based?
7. Name some important variations of the annual transit form of coverage.
8. Under what circumstances is it to the policyholder's advantage to buy a contingent transit policy?
9. Under what circumstances is a trip transit policy issued to an insured?
10. What is the difference between the liability of a common carrier and the liability of the Post Office department for goods in their custody?
11. Explain the differences between the coupon form and the open form of parcel post insurance.
12. What types of insurance coverage are available to protect valuable shipments of currency, securities, and jewelry?
13. Describe the inland marine coverages that you would recommend for an investment firm that ships negotiable and nonnegotiable securities, money, and at times valuable property belonging to customers, between its own offices and to customers.
14. Outline the inland marine insurance program that you would recommend for a department store that receives merchandise by railroad and motor truck freight and express, that does a substantial mail order business, and also delivers locally by its own trucks.
15. Discuss the relative merits of covering an insured's transit exposure to loss under an inland marine transit policy and under the transit section of a Special Multi-Peril (SMP) policy.

11

Motor Truck Cargo Insurance

MOTOR COMMON CARRIERS

Early Motor Carrier Operations. Following World War I and in the 1920s, the motor truck was used increasingly for hauling merchandise. The building of good cross-country highways permitted the motor truck to extend its operations between cities.

The motor truck has certain advantages over the railroads in the carrying of less-than-carload lots of freight between nearby cities. The shipper by railroad has to arrange for delivery of his goods to the railroad freight house, and the consignee has to pick up the shipment at the freight house on his end of the trip. A 50- or 100-mile trip may take three or four days by railroad. The motor truck can pick up the goods at the shipper's place of business and deliver it the next morning at the consignee's location.

At first the railroads seemed to make little effort to keep freight business from going over to the motor truck. Many railroad representatives believe that the railroads lose money on short haul, less-than-carload lots of freight. They contend that the handling costs on short haul freight traffic are greater than the revenue. Consequently some railroad representatives considered it a small loss when trucks began to carry intercity freight between nearby cities. This viewpoint changed, however, when the development of highways permitted trucks to make overnight and door-to-door deliveries between cities several hundred miles apart. Railroad spokesmen began to contend that truck freight rates should be regulated and that motor truck operation should be subject to the same sort of regulation as that to which the railroads were subject.

Motor truck operation prior to 1935 was largely unregulated and in places was a haphazard business. Anyone could set himself up in business as a trucker by the purchase of a secondhand truck. In many cities it became the custom for these truckers to park at a stand in the industrial or commercial neighborhoods and for businessmen to send their messengers or handy men over to the stand when they had goods to be transported. In other cases, the trucker would arrange for his garagekeeper or his landlady to receive telephone calls for him. The financial responsibility of truckers oftentimes was questionable, and only a small proportion carried insurance to indemnify themselves and their clients for loss of cargoes.

Motor Carrier Liability. A truckman, the nature of whose operations put him into the classification of a common carrier, was subject to the same broad liability under the common law as that applying to other common carriers. He was responsible for the safe conduct of his cargo except for damages resulting from the rare occurrences for which common carriers are not liable.

Three difficulties arose in the application of common carrier liability to motor carrier operations.

First was the irresponsible nature of some truckers' operations. They refused or were unable to pay for lost or damaged cargo. If the pressure for payment became too great, it always was possible for them to move their truck or trucks to another city and to start in business anew. If a shipper's claim for damage was small, it would not be worthwhile for him to pursue the trucker to enforce the claim. The trucker's assets frequently were insufficient to pay a large claim.

A second problem arose because many truckers put clauses limiting their liability into their bills of lading or receipts for cargo.

They followed the example set by the railroads in the days before railroad common carrier liability was defined by law, and they attempted to limit their liability to nominal amounts. Shipping receipts and bills of lading would contain statements to the effect that liability was limited to $50 per shipment, or to some other nominal figure. There was no uniformity in the shipping receipts used; in many cases the only receipt a shipper received was the truckman's signature on the shipper's memorandum of shipment. Neither party had a clear definition of the truckman's liability.

The third difficulty was the uncertainty whether a particular truckman was a common carrier or a private carrier. Under the situation existing before the passage by Congress of the Motor Carrier Act of 1935, a private carrier usually was considered to be any truckman who hauled goods under a private contract with a shipper, as contrasted to one who held himself open to employment by the general public. Under the definitions in the Motor Carrier Act of 1935, however, the trucker who hauls under contract is called a "contract carrier," whereas a "private carrier" is defined as one who carries his own goods or goods for which he is the lessee or bailee. The definitions of the contract carrier and private carrier as contained in the Motor Carrier Act of 1935 will be followed in this discussion.

The liability of a contract carrier ordinarily is less than the liability of a common carrier. It is limited to the liability agreed to in the contract and to any loss resulting from negligence on the part of the carrier. The early contracts with motor carriers seldom imposed any liability upon the carrier, with the result that most contract carriers considered themselves liable only for negligence. This would not have been so difficult a situation had all shippers understood clearly the responsibility of their truckers. Unfortunately, a trucker might operate as a common carrier and then claim that, in regard to a particular shipment, he was a contract carrier and liable only for negligence.[1]

Federal Regulation of Interstate Motor Carriers. It became increasingly clear that interstate motor truck carrier operations

[1]An example of such a case is Stevenson & Co. v. Hartman, 231 N.Y. 378, 132 N.E. 121 (1921), in which a truckman licensed as a public cartman under a New York City ordinance attempted to avoid liability by claiming he was a contract carrier. In that case the court decided that he held his services out to the general public and that he was a common carrier. See also S. Naitove & Co. v. Davis, 273 App. Div. 368, 77 N.Y.S. (2d) 330 (1948), for a more recent case in which a carrier contended he ceased to be a common carrier because he had made arrangements to handle all the shipper's deliveries on a flat fee basis. The court held otherwise and ruled he was still liable as a common carrier.

should be regulated. Several states passed laws relating to motor truck carrier operation within their borders. In 1935 Congress passed the Motor Carrier Act as an amendment to the Interstate Commerce Act. Its provisions affect all interstate commerce by motor carrier and have a profound influence on the insurance of motor truck cargo risks.

Similar laws relating to intrastate motor truck operations are in effect in most of the states. The discussion here will be limited to the effect of the federal act. The state laws regulate intrastate commerce to a similar extent. The specific provisions of a particular state law should be consulted by the underwriter when he has occasion to insure a trucker with intrastate operations.

Administration of the Motor Carrier Act is by the Bureau of Motor Carriers of the Interstate Commerce Commission. The act applies to the carrying of passengers for hire as well as to cargo hauling, but attention is given here only to those sections that affect the insuring of motor truck cargo. Exempt from the act are farm vehicles, vehicles operated by certain agricultural cooperative associations, haulers of livestock and agricultural commodities (not including manufactured products thereof, and provided the vehicles are not used to carry other products for hire), and vehicles used exclusively for the distribution of newspapers. Provision also is made for the exemption of local interstate hauling where a municipality or commercial zone is cut by state lines.

The act gives authority to the Interstate Commerce Commission to grant a certificate for interstate hauling to an applicant "if it is found that the applicant is fit, willing, and able properly to perform the service proposed and to conform to the provisions of this part and the requirements, rules, and regulations of the Commission thereunder, and that the proposed service, to the extent to be authorized by the certificate, is or will be required by the present or future public convenience and necessity . . ." This provision prevents a trucker's starting a new service at will. It requires that he establish the need for the service and that he demonstrate his ability to perform the service before a certificate is granted.

The act contains a "grandfather" clause which provides that any carrier in bona fide operation when the act became effective would be issued a certificate, upon application, without further proof of public convenience and necessity. This permitted established carriers to continue operating without the necessity of going through the formality of proving that their service was needed. They are protected from competition from new carriers in their territories unless the public convenience and necessity require additional service. This limiting of new carriers has had a stabilizing influence upon the motor carrier industry.

Another provision of the act requires that motor carriers set up tariffs and that all charges be made according to the filed tariffs.[2] This ended the highly competitive rates prevalent before passage of the act and permitted the carriers to establish rates on a basis of cost and service.

An important section of the act, from the standpoint of the insurance companies, is that relating to safety of operation and hours of driving. The Interstate Commerce Commission is given authority to establish reasonable requirements to promote safety of operation and to prescribe qualifications of employees, maximum hours of service of employees, and standards of equipment. The Bureau of Motor Carriers of the Interstate Commerce Commission has worked in cooperation with the motor carrier industry and with the insurance companies in setting up standards of safety and has done an excellent job of promoting safety.

The act made applicable to motor common carriers the provision of the Interstate Commerce Act in regard to liability of common carriers. Motor common carriers have the same responsibility as the railroads for safe delivery of their cargoes. Under the act, motor carriers are permitted to limit their liability for loss or damage if a lower rate is charged for hauling goods upon which the liability is limited. The motor carriers have not availed themselves of this right to so great an extent as the railroads. As a result, much of the cargo hauled by truckers must be paid for in full if it is lost or damaged. This is desirable from the standpoint of the insurance company insuring the owner of goods being hauled by a motor common carrier, but it increases the potential liability of the insurance company insuring the trucker.

Provisions Regarding Insurance in the Motor Carrier Act. One of the most important provisions of the Motor Carrier Act from the standpoint of the insurance companies is the section relating to "security for the protection of the public." This provides that the Commission may require insurance policies or other evidence of security to make certain that a trucker will meet his obligations to the public. Under this authority, the Commission requires that each trucker provide insurance of $2,500 for loss or damage to the contents of any one vehicle and $5,000 for aggregate losses or

[2]Motor truck cargo tariffs are filed with and approved by the Interstate Commerce Commission.

damages at any one time and place. (Self-insurance may be permitted if the financial stability of the carrier warrants such permission.)

Insurance policies issued to interstate motor common carriers must contain an endorsement prescribed by the Commission. The effect of this endorsement will be discussed later. The Commission must be provided with a certificate of insurance indicating that a policy has been issued, and the insurance company must be licensed to operate in all states in which the motor carrier has authority to operate.

If an insurance company wishes to insure a motor carrier that operates in a state in which the insurance company is not licensed, the insurance company may arrange with another insurance company to cover the operations in that state. The other insurance company then issues an insurance certificate to the Commission covering operations of the insured in that state. Under such an arrangement, the original insurance company usually takes care of all losses. The only charge made by the second company is a policywriting fee, because the arrangement does not make it actually liable for any losses.

Thirty days' notice must be given to the Commission when an insurance company wishes to cancel a policy covering a motor carrier for which it has filed an insurance certificate with the Commission. This does not prevent the company's canceling the coverage to the policyholder within the usual 5 days provided for by insurance contracts, but the Commission endorsement would remain in effect until the end of 30 days after notice has been given to the Commission. If a policy is canceled and the insurance is rewritten in another insurance company, it is customary for the succeeding insurance company to assume all liability for the motor carrier from the effective date of the new policy, even though the old Interstate Commerce Commission endorsement liability still has several days to run.

The endorsement that the Commission requires to be attached to all insurance policies covering regulated motor truck common carriers has resulted in the insurance companies' paying large sums in losses for which they would not have been liable under the terms of the policy as issued to the motor carriers. This clause must not be taken lightly, and it is imperative that the underwriter examine with great care the operating methods and the financial stability of every prospective motor carrier policyholder.

Effect of the I.C.C. Endorsement. The endorsement which the Interstate Commerce Commission requires makes the insurance company responsible for payment of any claim for which the policyholder is liable, up to limits of $2,500 per truck and $5,000 per accident. This responsibility is not limited to the coverage written into the policy but covers the full common carrier liability. This makes the insurance policy an extremely broad "all risks" policy. The insurance company by the terms of the endorsement guarantees payment for every lost package, for every breakage due to carelessness of the carrier's employees, and for infidelity losses resulting from theft by the carrier's employees.

The endorsement includes a reimbursement clause which provides that the insured shall reimburse the insurance company for any loss paid by the insurance company for which the insurance company is not liable to the insured under the terms of the policy. The insurance policy thus is a double contract. It agrees:

1. To indemnify the insured for financial loss as a result of his liability for damage to cargo from the hazards specified in the policy, up to the limit specified in the policy.
2. To pay the carrier's customers for any loss for which the carrier is liable, up to the $2,500 and $5,000 limits. (The insurance company is to be reimbursed by the carrier for this latter payment if the loss is due to a hazard not covered by the policy or if the loss is in excess of the policy's coverage.)

In actual practice, the trucker reports losses to the insurance company only when the loss is covered by the policy itself. The carrier pays his customers directly for other losses. It is seldom that the insurance company pays a loss to a trucker's customer (under the liability imposed by the I.C.C. endorsement) and then secures reimbursement from the policyholder.

The danger to the insurance company in the I.C.C. endorsement arises when the trucker is unable to pay these claims for which he is liable but which are not covered by the insurance policy. The insurance policy may cover for limits within the company's underwriting practices, and the loss experience of the trucker may appear to be satisfactory. However, the trucker-insured may get into financial difficulty. He may defer payment of customer's claims that are not covered by the insurance policy. The insurance company would have to pay every claim up to the limits of $2,500 per truck and $5,000 per accident if financial troubles continue to a point where the trucker becomes insolvent. Such an accumulation of losses can reach staggering figures.

It is important that the insurance company maintain a check upon the financial condition of any motor carrier for which it has issued a policy containing the I.C.C. endorsement. If any financial troubles are reported, the insurance company should immediately investigate to see whether the carrier is allowing claims to pile up, and whether these claims are of such a nature that the insurance company would have to pay them under the I.C.C. endorsement if the carrier should become insolvent.

It is important to send a company representative to the headquarters of the trucking company at once when a carrier becomes insolvent. The insured's terminal may contain hundreds or thousands of packages that are part of the overages and shortages of customers' shipments. Packages may have been simply piled in a corner when labels became displaced and identification was difficult.

In case of one insolvent trucker, such packages were sold by the receiver for a small fraction of their original value and the proceeds of the sale were used to help pay the general creditors. The insurance company representative arrived on the scene a few days later and found that many of the customers' claims could have been satisfied by identification of the packages. As a result, the insurance company had to pay the claims and received only a small portion in return as one of the general creditors.

It may seem strange at first glance that motor carriers should be required to carry insurance when railroads are not. This situation seems to have developed out of the early history of the two types of carriers. The railroads assumed the responsibility for safe delivery of goods entrusted to their care. It is true that they attempted to limit their liability before it was defined by law, but when liability was proved, the railroads had a record of paying the claims against them. The early record of the trucking industry contained cases of truckers' who disappeared without paying claims.

A railroad must have extensive physical properties in order to operate. Some truckers in the early days operated without large investments in physical assets. Shippers (and Congress) did not feel the same assurance that truckers would have sufficient resources to pay all claims. As a matter of fact, there are sufficient cases of insolvency to indicate that it is a reasonable requirement for motor common carriers to carry insurance or otherwise show evidence of financial responsibility as required by the Motor Carrier Act.

COVERAGE UNDER MOTOR TRUCK CARGO POLICIES

Inland marine insurance for motor carriers differs from the transportation insurance coverages previously discussed. A "truckmen's form" of motor truck cargo insurance policy indemnifies the policyholder (the trucker) for loss or damage resulting from his legal liability as a carrier. It does not insure against loss of the property unless the insured is legally liable for such loss.

For example, suppose a trucker had an insurance policy that insured (among other things) his legal liability for loss of property by flood, but that it is determined that the circumstances under which the flood caused the loss constituted an "act of God." If it is determined that the trucker is not liable for such a loss resulting from an "act of God," the insurance company would not be liable under its policy.

The motor truck cargo policy is issued to cover the single interest of the truckman. It does not cover the interest of the shipper, owner, or consignee of the cargo. (The only exceptions to this are in connection with household furniture warehousemen and armored car carriers; both of these cases will be discussed specifically later.) Such policies are not written to cover more than one truckman under a single policy and seldom cover the interest of a railroad or other carrier in connection with the operations of the motor carrier.

Since motor truck cargo policies insure against loss from the legal liability of the truckman, it would seem logical for such policies to cover all the losses for which the truckman is liable. However, this is seldom the case. Most policies carried by truckmen cover their legal liability for certain specified perils only and do not give complete protection.

This is not so illogical as it appears at first glance. The specified perils enumerated in the policies include most of the accidental hazards that can cause large losses, but the policies do not cover mysterious disappearance, unexplained shortage, or damage to packages because of careless handling. Such losses are primarily the result of poor operating practices on the part of the policyholder. If these losses were insured, it would remove much of the incentive the trucker has for careful operation. Consequently, insurance companies ordinarily insure only against those losses that are not likely to result from carelessness of the insured. When an insurance company occasionally does write an "all risks" policy, there usually is a large deductible clause applying to all losses, and this serves to give the necessary incentive for careful operation. In addition, it is more economical for the trucker to pay the smaller losses as a business expense than to have them handled through an insurance company and pay the insurance company's costs of adjustment.

Trucking companies differ widely in their methods of operation, in the commodities hauled, in the territories served, and in the length of hauls. Insurance policies are designed individually to meet the needs and desires of each trucker. There is no standardization either of rates or of coverage, and the following descriptions are necessarily general in nature.

It is customary to insert in the policy a description of the goods hauled. In the case of a common carrier hauling all kinds of goods, the description would be "general merchandise." The coverage applies to goods for which the carrier is legally liable as carrier, bailee, or warehouseman under tariff, or bill of lading or shipping receipt issued by the insured. The broad phraseology is used in order to include circumstances in which the trucker would be in the position of a bailee or warehouseman in regard to some particular shipment.

The policy is written to cover only "lawful goods and merchandise," because it is against public policy to insure unlawful goods, and it also is considered poor underwriting practice to insure illegal operations. Illegal operations would be subject to loss by racketeering or to confiscation by legal authority.

Among the specified perils covered by almost all motor truck cargo policies are the hazards of fire and lightning (including self-ignition or internal explosion of the conveyance), windstorm, and flood. The windstorm coverage frequently is limited by the exclusion of loss or damage caused by rain, hail, sleet, snow, or dust, whether driven by wind or not. This exclusion is customary because rain, snow, and dust damage may be caused or contributed to by carelessness on the part of the insured in not keeping the cargo covered.

In spite of the fact that lightning, windstorm, and flood may be considered "acts of God," the carrier still may be held liable for damage therefrom. It is necessary for the carrier to show that he has done everything possible and that the loss was entirely due to the "act of God" if he is to avoid liability for the loss. As a practical matter, insurance companies pay for such losses without much question.

Policies ordinarily cover losses resulting from the stranding, sinking, burning, or collision of a regular ferry, including general average and salvage charges for which the insured is legally liable in respect to the cargo carried. This is one of the few situations in which jettison and resulting general average charges might be applicable under an inland marine policy.

Collision and Overturn Losses. Collision of the motor vehicle with any other automobile, vehicle, or object is covered. Policies do not always define collision, but differences of opinion concerning just what it means have made it advisable to insert a definition to clarify the underwriter's intentions. A commonly used definition of collision provides that "the striking of curbing or any portion of the roadbed or the striking of rails or ties of street, steam or electric railroads, or contact with any stationary object in backing for loading or unloading purposes, or the coming together of trucks and trailers during coupling and uncoupling shall not be deemed a collision."

It is believed by many underwriters that such losses are likely to occur only when the trucker is careless in the operation of his vehicles, and that such carelessness is not properly insurable.

Another difficult problem with collision coverage arises when the cargo extends above or to the side of the transporting vehicle. If the load is in collision with a culvert, overhead bridge, or other object but the vehicle itself does not strike the object, there may be a question whether there is a collision within the meaning of the policy. If the word "collision" were used alone, it would seem that any doubt would be resolved in favor of the insured and the loss would be covered. If the coverage clause refers to "collision of the motor vehicle," it might be contended that the vehicle is not in collision when only the load comes in contact with another object, but it has been held otherwise.[3]

It is the intent of many underwriters to have the collision coverage apply only when the vehicle itself is in collision. Some underwriters insert in their motor truck cargo policies a further exclusion of "collision of the insured property with another object unless the transporting vehicle is in collision within the meaning of the policy."

Overturning of the motor truck or trailer is another risk that is covered, and like collision it has been interpreted in many ways. Underwriters usually intend "overturning" to mean the upsetting of the vehicle to such an extent that it comes to rest on its side or top. It has been held, however, that when a truck partially tipped over, spilled the contents, but righted itself when the load was removed, there was overturning of the truck within the meaning of a

[3]See Bucks County Construction Co. v. Alliance Ins. Co., 162 Pa. Super. 153, 56 A. (2d) 338 (1948), for discussion of case in which a piece of equipment extending beyond the transporting vehicle was damaged by striking a concrete pillar. In another case in which the cargo collided with an object but the conveyance was not in collision, the court held that there was no collision within the meaning of a policy which insured against loss from collision of land conveyance while the insured property was being transported thereon. Old Colony Ins. Co. v. W. R. Anderson, 246 F. (2d) 102 (1957).

transportation insurance policy on the material, since anything was "overturned" when it was sufficiently tipped over to spill the contents.[4]

In another case the wheels on the right side of a truck loaded with fruit sank down to the axle in the earthen shoulder of the highway, causing the load to shift its weight and break the sideboards of the truck. Part of the fruit fell to the ground and was damaged. An insurance policy covered the insured's liability as a private or common carrier for loss or damage to goods caused by "Overturning of the motor truck and/or trailer." A court held that the loss was covered, saying: "A slight overturning is as much an overturning as a complete overturning."[5]

A different decision was given in a case in which flaps had been added to a platform trailer in order to increase the width of the platform. The flap on one side broke, allowing the cargo (a large power shovel) to slip to the ground. The majority of the court held that there was no overturning and said:

> It is our view that there was no overturning of the conveyance (the trailer) merely because the flap or added width of the platform broke off on one side, even assuming that the flap was part of the platform and the material of which this flap was constructed did overturn as it fell to the ground. The equilibrium of the conveyance (the trailer) was not disturbed in any way so that it could not be said to have overturned, the accident being due solely to the collapse or breakdown of the flap on the edge of the trailer platform.[6]

There was a dissenting opinion in this case, one justice feeling that there was overturning within the meaning of the policy. It seems clear that any upsetting of the equilibrium of a vehicle to an extent that causes the cargo to be injured would be considered an "overturning" if the word is not defined in the policy. Some underwriters have added to their policies this statement: "Overturning as used herein shall mean the upsetting of the vehicle to such an extent that it comes to rest on its side or top." The intent is to exclude the type of loss that might occur as a result of careless loading of the cargo or from the driver's attempting to negotiate roads not in condition for safe travel.

Damage from the collapse of bridges or culverts usually is insured against. Many underwriters feel that they should not be liable

[4]Carl Ingalls, Inc. v. Hartford Fire Ins. Co., 31 P. (2d) 414 (Cal. App. 1934).

[5]Moore v. Western Assurance Co. of Toronto, 186 S.C. 260, 195 S.E. 558 (1938).

[6]Orlando v. Manhattan Fire & Marine Ins. Co. 266 App. Div. 319, 42 N.Y.S. (2d) 228 (1943).

for loss when the truckman takes a heavily loaded truck onto a bridge or culvert marked to indicate that the carrying capacity is less than the weight of the truck and its load. These underwriters limit the coverage to "where the total load is not in excess of the indicated carrying capacity of the bridge or culvert." This makes it advisable for the truckman to use care not to load a truck beyond the capacity of bridges on his route.

Theft Coverage On Motor Truck Cargoes. Theft insurance in motor truck cargo coverage presents a paradox. It is one of the most frequent and most costly causes of loss, yet it is omitted from the basic coverage of many policies. Frequently it is added by endorsement.

It has long been the belief of ocean marine underwriters that theft by stealth is a peril within the control of the insured, although ocean marine policies have covered theft by violence, or by "holdup" as it has become known in this country. Much of this thinking has carried over into the insuring of cargo on land.

Mysterious disappearance of cargo is a frequent reason for loss at motor truck terminals, and it is responsible for some losses on the road. Some mysterious disappearance losses are due to misdelivery. Many people will accept packages delivered to them in error and not make any effort to return them. The driver or dispatcher has little chance to trace the misdelivery once it is out of his hands.

Occasionally packages are lost off the back end of trucks and are picked up and kept by the finders. Sometimes the identifying labels are lost from shipments, and they may be in the terminal but are not identifiable. These make up the O.,S., and D.'s (overages, shortages, and damages) that every trucker attempts to locate and identify. Many inland marine underwriters believe that such losses should not be insured against because they can be kept to a minimum by careful operating methods on the part of the trucker.

Theft by employees of the insured, or by outsiders with the collusion of employees, is responsible for many shortages. It is extremely difficult to prove the cause of such shortages; the packages disappear and there is no evidence to show where they went. This, too, is a hazard the insured can control by means of a rigid checking system, and many underwriters do not consider theft by employees as a proper hazard to be covered by a cargo policy. A provision usually appears in the theft endorsement excluding loss caused by infidelity of the insured's employees.

The theft endorsement usually specifies that it covers the theft of entire shipping packages only and does not cover pilferage.

"Pilferage" is intended to mean the theft of a part of the contents of a shipping package as distinct from theft of the entire package.

In spite of what appears to be a clearly worded coverage concerning theft, the insurance companies have had numerous claims under the theft coverage in which there was no evidence of what happened to the vanished merchandise. One truckman claimed that any lost package must have been stolen and therefore was a proper theft claim. It was pointed out to him that the package might have been lost off a truck, or misdelivered, or stolen by employees. He then contended that anything lost was eventually stolen if the finder did not return it and that the same thing was true in the case of misdelivered goods. He ignored the fact that, in the case of misdelivery and loss by falling off the truck, the direct cause of the loss was not theft but misdelivery or loss off the truck. Theft may have occurred subsequently, but the policy insured only direct causes of loss, which in the case of misdelivery and mysterious disappearance are not insured hazards.[7]

The insured wishes to have his claim paid regardless of whether it was caused by employee theft or by outsiders. It has been proposed that the bonding company and the cargo insurance company decide between them which one is liable. This argument ignores the fact that each insurance policy is a separate contract under which the insured is obligated to prove that he has a loss under that contract. In addition, the insured is in the best position to determine how the loss was caused.

Some underwriters insert an additional clause to help prevent misunderstanding on the part of a policyholder. This additional clause reads: "It is agreed that this policy does not cover misdelivery, mysterious disappearance, or shortage unless there is reasonable evidence that a theft has occurred."

An incentive to install theft prevention methods is supplied by a deductible clause applying to theft losses. The amount of the deductible depends on the nature of the goods carried and the likelihood of package thefts. The minimum is usually $50, but the deductible may be as high as $500 if the insured is interested primarily in protection from a catastrophe and feels that he can afford to pay the smaller losses himself.

Miscellaneous Coverages On Motor Truck Cargoes. Other hazards that may be covered are those caused by flood, riot, and civil

[7]See Savin Express Co. v. Hanover Fire Ins. Co., 132 Conn. 181, 43 A. (2d) 69 (1945); for discussion of a case in which packages were lost and the insured could not prove that a theft had occurred.

commotion; strikers and locked-out workmen; and explosion. A few insurance companies provide a broad coverage of the "all risks" type. A wording used occasionally covers losses caused by "external hazards." Some underwriters use wording similar to that in ocean marine policies and grant protection against "the perils of transportation."

Such policies cover mysterious disappearance and nondelivery unless they are excluded. A method of controlling this hazard under a broad coverage policy is to include a deductible of $500 or more. Whenever a high deductible is used, it is advisable for the insurance company to keep a close check on the insured's handling of the losses for which he is liable to his customers. If he allows losses to remain unpaid, it may indicate that the trucker is in financial difficulties. Under the I.C.C. endorsement the insurance company would be responsible for unpaid losses in case the insured became insolvent.

Terminal Coverage. The insuring clause of the motor truck cargo form usually covers the legal liability of the insured for loss or damage to goods "when loaded for shipment on and in transit in or on the vehicles owned, operated or hired for or by the named insured. . . ." In the early days of motor truck operations, this was a satisfactory coverage because the trucker picked up the goods at the shipper's door and delivered them to the consignee's place of business without any transfer from one truck to another.

The trucking industry became more and more complicated, and truckers established terminals at which goods are sorted by routes and trans-shipped. A motor common carrier ordinarily is responsible for the safety of goods while they are in a terminal in course of transit to the same extent as when they are in the trucks. Most policies now contain an extension of coverage to terminals while the goods are in the custody of the insured and while they are in due course of transit. These extensions of insurance coverage to terminals sometimes limit the coverage to 24, 48, or 72 hours, depending upon the needs of the insured and the length of time the goods are likely to be in a terminal during transfer.

From the insurance company's standpoint, this extension of coverage to terminals is a serious additional hazard. The largest insured motor truck cargo losses have been in terminal fires. The highest value regularly carried in a single motor truck may be somewhere between $30,000 and $50,000, but the concentration of value in a terminal may reach hundreds of thousands of dollars. The fire hazard of each terminal is underwritten with caution, and the insurance company is entitled to a considerable additional premium when the terminal hazard is covered. The published fire insurance rate for contents of the terminal customarily is used as a basis for the additional premium charge.

Limitations on the Coverage. Policies almost always show a radius of operations. Experience has shown that the hazard of a motor truck operation increases with the distance traveled by the trucks. Rates are determined upon the basis of the radius of operations from the insured's headquarters as stated in the policy; losses occurring beyond that radius are not intended to be covered.

A local hauler is one that operates within a radius of approximately 50 miles. The hazard presented by this class of trucker usually is considered to be less than that presented by a long-haul trucker.

An intermediate hauler may operate over a radius of 200 miles; his operations are characterized by the fact that the drivers are out and back the same day. It is not necessary for them to drive on night runs or to be away from home overnight. On the longer hauls of several hundred miles, the drivers may operate at night, and driver fatigue seems to be an important cause of loss. Long-distance operations must carry high value loads to be profitable, and the losses that do occur on these runs are likely to involve large amounts.

A policy may or may not list the trucks covered. On smaller policies it is customary to list the trucks, with a complete identification by motor and serial number. Cargo is covered only while on the described trucks. On larger operations the trucks are not listed, and all operations of the insured are covered, including any with hired trucks used temporarily.

Policies include a limit of liability per truck and a catastrophe limit of liability when more than one truck is involved or when terminal liability is covered. If the trucks are listed specifically in the policy, an amount of liability for each truck is shown.

An important factor in the chance of loss by theft is the type of commodities hauled. Companies often insert a limitation in the policy providing that limited amounts apply to commodities that are especially susceptible to theft. This limitation may be by percentage. For example, a policy may provide that not more than 20 percent of the limit of liability shall apply on the special commodities. The limitation may also be expressed in dollars.

The specially hazardous commodities listed in many policies include butter, oleomargarine, furs, liquors, silks, rayons, woolens, tires, tubes, tobacco products, radios, televisions, clothing, and textiles. The rating and the underwriting of motor carriers depend largely upon the type and quantity of merchandise hauled. The desirability of insuring a motor carrier can change materially if it starts to haul larger quantities of the hazardous materials. The limitation is intended to require the insured to notify the insurance company if his operations change.

Limitations also apply to articles that are especially susceptible to breakage. Coverage on eggs is limited by percentage or by a specified amount. Frequently there is no loss payable on eggs unless there is at least 50 percent breakage in each package for which a loss is claimed. This limitation can be modified when the principal cargo consists of eggs and the rate is commensurate with the hazard.

Losses to paintings and other works of art usually are paid only in case of total loss from a peril insured against. Some policies contain a dollar or percentage limitation on the amount that will be paid on fine arts losses. Losses payable on livestock are limited to those caused by death from a peril insured against or from destruction made necessary by such a peril. Death from natural causes is not covered.

Exclusions. Many of the exclusions in a motor truck cargo policy are similar to those appearing in other transportation policies. There are exclusions of loss to accounts, bills, currency, evidences of debt, money, securities, and jewelry, and an exclusion of loss resulting from war, hostilities, or nuclear hazards.

Several exclusions are intended to avoid loss due to carelessness on the part of the insured or his employees. One refers specifically to loss or damage caused by neglect of the insured to use all reasonable means to save and preserve the property at and after any disaster insured against. This provision reinforces the terms of the "sue and labor" clause, which forms a part of the basic policy to which the motor truck cargo form frequently is attached.

Other exclusions relate to damage caused by poor packing or rough handling and contact with oil or grease or with another commodity, and to loss due to inherent vice or delay, loss of profit, loss of use, or loss of market.

Specially designed for the motor truck cargo policy are exclusions of loss or damage to the contents of any vehicle owned by the insured and rented to others, and loss or damage to any goods that the insured is carrying gratuitously or as an accommodation.

Freight charges on the goods being hauled usually are excluded except charges which are earned prior to the acceptance of the merchandise and for which the insured is legally liable. Under special circumstances, freight charges earned by the insured up to the time of the accident may be covered.

Special Conditions. Policies usually contain a valuation clause similar to that appearing in other transportation policies. It is customary to include a coinsurance clause requiring full insurance to value. The insured cannot collect a greater proportion of any loss than the amount of insurance on the vehicle involved bears to the amount of property involved in the loss. (For information on the application of a coinsurance clause, see the discussion elsewhere in this text.)

An "other insurance" clause usually is included in the policy in order to make cargo policy excess over any other coverage.

If individual trucks are listed and specific amounts of insurance are made to apply to each, the amount of insurance may be reduced by any loss that occurs and the amount subject to reinstatement following payment of the loss. This is not true of the blanket policies in which there is no specific amount of insurance applying to each truck.

TYPES OF MOTOR TRUCK CARGO POLICIES

Reference already has been made to policies that list the trucks specifically and to those that cover all operations of the insured. In the first type of policy, a specific amount of liability is listed for each truck. The amount of the policy is the total of all the amounts of liability applying to the different trucks.

The rate for the policy is multiplied by the policy amount to compute the premium, and the premium for this type of policy usually is paid annually in advance. For example, suppose there were eight trucks listed on the policy, with $1,000 coverage on four of them and $2,000 coverage on the other four. The policy amount would be $12,000. If the rate were $3 per $100, the premium would be $360.

The limit of liability payable as a result of any one loss is not necessarily the same as the policy amount. A lesser limit of liability may be specified. In the example used in the previous paragraph, a limit of liability in any one loss might be set, for example at $7,500.

The other type of policy is known as a "gross receipts form," because the premium payments are based on the gross receipts of the motor carrier. This form usually covers all the operations of the insured as a trucker, and the individual trucks are not listed.

Frequently it is used in insuring the larger truck operations. There would be a great deal of additional work involved in endorsing the insurance policy if it were necessary to issue an endorsement every time a large trucker secured a new truck. The rate is expressed as an amount per $100 of gross receipts. The insured agrees to keep an accurate record of his gross receipts from the trucking business and to pay the premium at the rate given in the policy. Usually the premium payments are made monthly.

The calculation of a rate for a gross receipts method of premium payment is largely a matter of knowing the experience of the motor carrier. The underwriter calculates what premium he needs to cover the expected losses, adds a factor for catastrophe losses, and applies the total to the expected gross receipts to get the rate.

For example, suppose the trucker had been averaging losses of $10,000 for each of the past three or four years. The underwriter might estimate that this average loss would be likely to continue. He may also consider that every three or four years even a good operator will have at least one total loss from some accidental cause. The underwriter may add about a third of the maximum liability per truck, which may amount to another $10,000. This would make a total loss expectancy of $20,000 per year. For purposes of the illustration, a permissible loss ratio[8] may be taken as 50 percent. Accordingly, the insurance company would need to receive a total premium of about $40,000 a year. The motor carrier might have $2,000,000 of gross receipts annually. Since $40,000 is 2 percent of $2,000,000, 2 percent of the gross receipts would be the rate to be quoted for the policy.

Other factors used in calculating a gross receipts rate include the limits of liability, the nature of the commodities hauled, and the degree of cooperation by the insured. There is no uniformity in method or in the rates that result, because each underwriter has his own experience and judgment to use as a basis for his quotations.

The gross receipts method of paying motor truck cargo insurance premiums represents one of the few cases in which the premium payment may bear little relation to the insurance company's liability. An insurance premium usually is calculated by applying a rate to a measure of the insurance company's liability. For example, a transportation policy premium is based on the total values shipped during the year.

The gross receipts of a motor carrier bear almost no relation to

[8]"Permissible loss ratio" is a term used to indicate the proportion of the premium which is estimated as the amount necessary to pay losses.

the liability of the insurance company. The trucker's gross receipts depend primarily on the weight and volume of the goods he hauls. Value has only a minor effect. The result is that during a period of rising prices the losses of insurance companies increase at an astounding rate. The value of an average load of merchandise doubles in a few years' time, and the losses are the dollar values of these loads. The gross receipts of motor carriers do not increase so rapidly as the values of the loads they haul, and the insurance companies are faced with sharply increased loss ratios.

Many inland marine underwriters feel that the gross receipts method of premium payment should be regarded merely as a method of distributing premium payments by the month and that it is not truly a method of rating. These underwriters add up the total liability represented by all the trucks insured for a trucker and then calculate the hazards of the operation, applying a rate for the hazards to the amount of liability. This calculation produces an annual premium on much the same basis as that used for the small trucker whose trucks are listed on the policy. The annual premium is divided by the estimated annual gross receipts to get a rate of premium payment. A recalculation of the premium each year in accordance with price trends and the changing hazards of the operation will keep the premium in line with the insurance company's actual exposure to loss.

MOTOR TRUCK CARGO INSURANCE EXPERIENCE

Insurance company experience with motor truck cargo insurance shows a need for loss prevention measures and the selection of desirable insureds. Among the principal reasons for the unsatisfactory experience are the following:

1. Stabilization of the insurance rate level has not been achieved because of a continuing rapid growth of the trucking industry.
2. Larger motor carriers each pay insurance premiums of several thousands of dollars each year. Insurance agents and companies compete with each other for these premiums, sometimes tending to ignore the hazards involved.
3. Insuring motor carriers is essentially the necessity for paying a few large losses. It takes several years' experience to determine the loss level of an individual motor carrier operation. One or two good years have led truckers to ask for rate reductions. Insurance companies have tended to grant these requests for lower rates, when a longer period of experience might have indicated that the reductions were not justified.

The importance of the insurance problem to the trucking industry can be appraised by considering that almost 5 percent of the trucking industry's gross income goes to pay insurance premiums and that almost half of this amount (about 2 percent of the gross income) is used to pay for cargo insurance. Losses grow principally out of collision, fire (both on the road and in terminals), and theft (including loss of valuable loads by robbery and theft of individual shipments by stealth).

Collision losses are preventable (1) through safety programs encouraging better driving, (2) through excellent maintenance to prevent mechanical failure of brakes and other equipment, and (3) through relieving drivers of long runs, so that they do not go to sleep while driving and do not take chances to make a schedule.

Fire following collision frequently is aggravated by burst gasoline tanks. It is a standard recommendation of insurance engineers that all trucks be equipped with "safety" gasoline tanks. These tanks are specially built for truck operation and are made of extra-heavy steel. They also are constructed in such a way that gasoline cannot spill out even if the tank is turned upside down. It is further recommended that all trucks be equipped with overturn switches that automatically cut off the electrical current from the battery if the truck becomes involved in a collision or is overturned.

Many trucks are lost each year as a result of fires that start when truck tires become overheated. Underinflation is the principal cause of tire fires, which are extremely difficult to extinguish. All trucks should carry fire extinguishers. They should also carry flags and flares to be set out to warn other vehicles when it is necessary for a truck to stop on the road.

Terminal fires result in tremendous losses. Preventive measures depend principally upon good housekeeping in terminals and upon the installation of automatic sprinklers and other fire protection devices. Recommended good practice pamphlets which are published by the National Fire Protection Association give the accepted methods of fire prevention in truck and terminal operation.

Prevention of theft in the terminals is mainly a matter of having a system of checking goods in and out. If an employee knows that a theft will not be discovered until the consignee reports a shortage in a shipment, he knows that he has several days in which to secrete and dispose of stolen goods. If the packages are checked in and out of each terminal so that a shortage will be discovered immediately, there is much less chance of successful theft. Watchman service should be maintained whenever a terminal is not operating.

The best precaution against loss of valuable loads by robbery is the installation upon each truck of an automatic alarm system. These alarms, which are not under the control of the driver, are so installed that a loud siren begins to sound if the truck is opened. Robbers do not like to take chances with an automatic alarm and they tend to operate against unprotected trucks.

Robbers are most likely to pick out loads consisting of a single type of merchandise, although mixed loads are not immune. Road patrols by highway police, having the drivers check in with the highway patrol, and the use of more than one driver per truck are other deterrents to robbery. Some state police departments suggest preferred routes for truck operations, along which continuous patrols are maintained.

Progressive truck company management is glad to cooperate with its insurance advisers in the prevention of losses. Such management realizes that any industry must stand on its own record of insurance losses and that eventually it makes its own insurance rate level. Some truckers have been able to cut their losses to such a point that their cargo insurance cost is less than 1 percent of their operating costs, whereas others are paying 3 percent or more for cargo insurance. The difference between these figures could mean the difference between success or failure for a trucker.

SPECIAL MOTOR TRUCK CARGO CARRIERS

Household Furniture Movers. Movers of household goods are subject to regulations of the Interstate Commerce Commission that apply specially to such movers. This is necessary because household goods cannot be moved according to regular routes but must be moved from the owner's old home to his new location. The common carrier of household goods has a liability to his customer which is comparable to the liability of other motor common carriers. They file tariffs which give their rates for their services, and they operate under bills of lading which spell out their responsibilities.

The Uniform Household Goods Bill of Lading and Freight Bill provides for three valuations. The shipper is required to indicate which valuation is to be used in case of loss or damage. The shipment may be released (1) to a value of 60 cents per pound per article, (2) at a lump sum value to be declared by the shipper, or (3) for an amount equal to $1.25 for each pound of weight in the shipment. Most household goods shipments are worth considerably more than $1.25 per pound. The shipper would have to declare a lump sum value in order to have full protection of his value. This would still leave the shipper unprotected for his value if there were a loss from one of the rare causes for which a common carrier is not liable.

The carrier usually carries motor truck cargo insurance to protect him from loss because of his liability to his customers. Such a policy would be similar to those which are issued to other truckers. The shipper can buy a trip transit policy which would give him complete protection in case of loss in transit. Usually the charge for this insurance would be less than the charge of the carrier for a higher valuation. The shipper would buy this insurance from an insurance agent or company because the trucker is prohibited by the Interstate Commerce Commission regulations from selling or acting as agent for such insurance.

Armored Car Operator's Coverage. A trucker that is providing an armored car service may want to protect the interest of his clients as well as his own liability. An armored car company frequently makes a contract with a bank or other financial institution to deliver money or securities. The shipper or consignee may not carry its own armored car insurance policy and the trucker may desire to protect its customer for any loss that may occur. These policies cover in much the same manner as the armored car policy and give almost full protection.

Consolidation of Motor Truck Shipments. Freight brokers and consolidators perform much the same service in the motor truck field that the carloading company performs in the railroad freight field. Some of these concerns qualify as common carriers, and their legal liability may be covered in the same way as that of a trucker. Each case would be rated individually. The policy would be arranged to fit (1) the terminal hazards of the insured's operation, (2) whether any actual trucking is done, and (3) the contracts with other truckers. Many of these consolidating operations are really local truckers and would be treated in the same way as other local trucking risks.

Contract Carriers. The discussion up to this point has been confined to those truckers defined under the Motor Carrier Act as common carriers. The act defines a "contract carrier by motor vehicle" as a person not defined as a common carrier who "under special and individual contracts or agreements, and whether directly or by lease or by any other arrangement, transports passengers or property in interstate or foreign commerce by motor vehicle for compensation."

The contract carrier effects agreements or contracts with people who have hauling to be done. He deals with a limited number of people and operates under the terms of his agreements with them. He does not hold himself out to the general public as being in a position to haul for them.

The contract carrier has certain operating advantages over the common carrier. He can arrange for full loads and can set up his schedules on an economical basis. The common carrier, on the contrary, must maintain a regularity of service even though this forces him to operate at times with partial loads. Many truckers try to operate as contract carriers so that they can pick and choose the more profitable contracts and not be obligated to take the general hauling required of a common carrier.

The Interstate Commerce Commission has spent much time in deciding whether individual motor carriers are common or contract carriers under the Motor Carrier Act. From the standpoint of the insurance company in underwriting a trucking risk, the intricacies of why a trucker is a common or contract carrier are mainly of academic interest. It is important, however, to know what class of carrier the Interstate Commerce Commission has determined a trucker to be and what effect this has on his liability to his clients.

The liability of the common carrier has been discussed fully. The essential difference between the liability of the common carrier and that of a contract carrier is that the contract carrier is liable only for the obligations assumed under his contract and for losses due to his negligence. He does not have the responsibility of the common carrier unless he has agreed by contract to accept such liability. Therefore, an insurance policy covering the legal liability of a contract carrier may involve a much more restricted liability than one covering a common carrier. The liability is similar to bailee liability, which will be discussed later in this text.

There are some variations of this rule that must be investigated in connection with each trucker insured. The contract carrier can assume extra liability under his contract. He may assume the liability of a common carrier or he may agree to keep the cargo insured. In fact, there is almost no limit to the liability a contract carrier can assume. It is important for an insurance company to determine the terms of the hauling contracts entered into by any insured who claims to be a contract carrier and eligible for preferential rate treatment on that ground. Contracts are required to be filed with the Interstate Commerce Commission and may be examined in its offices if it should become necessary to examine a contract without the cooperation of an insured or prospect.

The mere existence of a contract between the trucker and the shipper does not make the trucker a contract carrier. Many common carriers have contracts with people for whom they do a considerable amount of hauling in addition to their work for the general public.

These contracts may be a part of their common carrier arrangements and may not change their status at all. The status as determined by the I.C.C. must be established in each case where there is a question.

Owner's Goods On Owner's Trucks (Private Carriers). The third type of carrier defined in the Motor Carrier Act is the "private carrier of property by motor vehicle," which means a person who is not defined as a common or contract carrier and who transports property of which he is the owner, lessee, or bailee, when such transportation is for the purpose of sale, lease, rent, or bailment, or in the furtherance of any commercial enterprise. Private carriers are subject to the safety regulations of the Interstate Commerce Commission. These specify the qualifications and maximum hours of service for employees and standards of equipment. These private carriers are known in the insurance business as truckers carrying owner's goods on owner's trucks.

The insurance policy on property being carried by the owner is a direct damage policy and is not a legal liability policy. If the property is damaged or lost as a result of one of the perils insured against, the loss must be paid by the insurance company. There is no possibility of avoiding loss payment on the ground that the trucker is not liable for the loss. There is not even the remote possibility of the loss being considered the result of an "act of God" and not payable on that ground. The policy must be underwritten on the basis of the commodity hauled and the hazards covered by the policy.

It might be expected that experience with private carriers would be worse because of the insurance company's more extensive liability. This is not the case. The average experience with private carriers is better than that with common and contract carriers. There appear to be several reasons for this. Many private carriers operate over shorter routes than common or contract carriers; their operations are more likely to be short and medium hauls. It is also probable that an owner tends to take better care of his own property than he would of property belonging to others.

Another favorable factor undoubtedly is the absence of the terminal hazard that results when the goods of many shippers are mixed together and sorted for distribution over various routes. The owner's truck goes from point of shipment directly to its destination. The cargo is not reshuffled at terminals en route where it may be lost and mis-shipped. The owner's policy covers no terminal hazard, because inland marine policies ordinarily do not cover owner's goods on his own premises. Therefore, there are no large terminal fires to be charged against the loss record of the private carrier.

Many owners can afford to maintain their trucks in the best

condition. They may not be under pressure to make runs to keep customers, since the trucking is a minor part of their operations.

Another factor probably is the rating method. The private carrier customarily is rated on the basis of the amount of liability provided in the insurance policy. The exposure to loss is directly proportional to the premium, whereas the large motor common carriers are rated on the basis of gross receipts, which often bear no real relationship to the chances the insurance company runs of paying a large loss.

The operating hazards of private and contract carriers are the same as those of common carriers. Underwriting of the physical hazard is on about the same basis.

Policies covering both the trucker's own property and that of persons for whom he hauls also are written. In such cases the hazard is primarily that of the common or contract carrier.

QUESTIONS

1. What conditions in connection with the operation of motor carriers brought a demand for federal regulation of interstate motor carriers?
2. Describe the more important provisions in the Motor Carrier Act regarding insurance on motor truck cargo.
3. Explain the effect of the I.C.C. endorsement to motor truck cargo insurance policies.
4. Why did Congress feel that motor carriers should be required to carry insurance on cargo although railroads are not subject to a similar requirement?
5. Explain the statement that "a motor truck cargo policy indemnifies the truckman for loss or damage resulting from his legal liability as a carrier."
6. What is an "overturn"?
7. How broad is the theft coverage usually provided in a motor truck cargo policy?
8. Why is the extension of coverage to goods in terminals considered by insurance companies to be a serious additional exposure?
9. What are the more important exclusions usually found in a motor truck cargo policy?
10. Why is the gross receipts method of paying motor truck cargo insurance premiums likely to result in an inadequate premium to the insurance company during a period of rising prices?

11. Describe some important measures to prevent motor truck cargo losses.
12. What is the difference between the liability of a common carrier and that of a contract carrier?
13. Discuss the relative merits to a large trucker of
    (a) a specified perils policy giving full coverage for loss covered by the policy, and
    (b) an "all risks" type of policy with a large deductible.
14. What are the principal differences between the I.C.C. regulations applying to interstate truckers and those applying to intrastate truckers in your state?

12

Air Cargo

The use of the large jet transport planes which started in the 1950s was the most important step in the economic transportation of property by airplane. Scheduled air transportation began in the 1920s, but shipment of cargo by air was mostly an emergency measure until after World War II. Transit insurance policies excluded transportation by airplane except in those unusual cases where the nature of the insured's business required that he make use of emergency transportation. Air express charges were high as compared to surface transportation costs. Air express cost about 80 cents per ton-mile, whereas bulk shipments of such freight as coal by railroad were carried for slightly less than 1 cent per ton-mile.[1] The average charge for Class 1 rail freight is between 2½ and 3 cents per ton-mile;

[1]The term "ton-mile" is a unit for the measurement of freight hauling. It is equivalent to the hauling of one ton of freight for a distance of one mile.

the charge for truck transportation near 6 cents per ton-mile; and the charge for surface express about 15 cents per ton-mile. Current charges for bulk shipment of air freight are competitive with the charges for surface express. There are many situations in which it is more economical to ship by air than by rail or truck.

ECONOMIC FACTORS AFFECTING AIR FREIGHT

The economics of whether property is shipped by railroad, truck, or airplane depend upon several factors in addition to the transportation charges. It is helpful to the underwriter to understand these factors so that he can judge the relative exposure to loss of property in the various situations.

The principal advantage of air transportation is speed. This greater speed makes it desirable to ship perishable commodities by air. Large quantities of cut flowers are shipped by plane because they can be cut, packed, shipped, and received in saleable condition many hundreds of miles away. These flowers and many other perishable products could not be marketed at long distances except by air shipment. The economic question is whether the air freight charges are sufficiently low so that the commodities will sell at their destinations.

Fast transportation has advantages for many commodities that are not perishable in themselves but for which the market may be perishable. A retailer of ladies' clothing, for example, can secure a few samples of a particular style in order to test the market, and then can order additional supplies for almost next-morning delivery. His market might be gone if he had to wait several days for delivery by rail or truck. His alternative in the absence of air transportation would be to order a larger stock of clothing and take a chance on his judgment as to saleability. This would require a higher inventory investment and might result in losses if his judgment was wrong. Similar savings can be achieved by manufacturers and distributors of goods by filling orders from a fewer number of warehouses at more distant points than would be possible if ground transportation is relied upon. The economics of using air transportation depends upon the relationship of sales value to time. The determining factors in most cases are the perishability of the goods themselves or the perishability of the market. Possible reduction in size of inventories or reduction in the number of distribution points all are affected by the speed with which goods may be transported from one place to another.

The increased use of air transportation also increases the need for insurance of the goods in transit. This results from the fact that the goods are in a state of transportation for a larger proportion of their life prior to final sale to the consumer. It is true that ground transportation is longer in time of transit for a specific journey, but the use of ground transportation requires that the goods be kept in storage at many points so as to be available for quick delivery. Present merchandising methods enable the manufacturer to meet the needs of his customers within hours of the time that a need develops. The goods are shipped and can be provided to the consumer within a short time. The result is that the property is subject to a transit hazard during a higher proportion of the total time between the factory and the consumer. This effect is multiplied millions of times by the items that are shipped in commerce throughout the world so that more goods are in transit. A further multiplying effect results from the fact that the goods which are shipped by air are the more valuable merchandise.

Risks of Loss to Air Cargo. The hazards to cargo in air transportation differ in many respects from the hazards during rail or truck transportation. These must be evaluated by the underwriter in determining what rates to charge for transit policies covering air cargo, what limits of liability can be granted in the policies, and what exclusions or limitations must be provided. The earlier air transit hazards of turbulent flights, rarefied air during flight, and even the dangers of crashes have been reduced to minor considerations by modern safety devices, by better packing of goods and improved containers, and by the pressurization of cargo as well as passenger space. Most air cargo losses are related to cargo handling on the ground or in the transfer from air to ground or ground to air, rather than from the hazards of actual flight.

Insurance on air cargo is complicated by the necessity for surface handling and usually surface transportation of the property. This is in contrast to insurance of surface transportation where only one or at most two methods of transportation must be evaluated. Many surface shipments are made by rail or truck alone without any combination of the two. The hazards to cargo are similar even where a combination of rail and truck transportation is used.

Most air shipments are handled by two means of transportation which are very different. Cargo must be picked up by truck and carried many miles to an airport that is located on the outskirts or beyond the limits of the city. There is the exposure to loss during the truck haul on the highway as well as the exposure during pickup or delivery in the city. The most vulnerable point for air cargo losses has proved to be the cargo terminal in the airport. There are huge concentrations of valuable merchandise. Security is difficult because of the haste which is inherent in the handling of high-speed shipments. One marine underwriter stated that theft claims on air cargo in a recent year were 70 percent of all claims. It is unquestionable that the most important hazard which must be evaluated by the air cargo underwriter is that of theft from airport terminals.

Governmental regulation of air carriers and the liability of such carriers for property in their custody differ from the regulation and the liabilities of surface carriers. The underwriter must have a knowledge of air carrier regulation and responsibilities in order to determine the potential losses under an air cargo insurance policy and the chances of recovery from the carrier.

AIR CARRIER REGULATION

Economic regulation of air carriers is under the Civil Aeronautics Board (hereinafter referred to as the CAB). Thc CAB was first established under the Civil Aeronautics Act of 1938 and was continued under the Federal Aviation Act of 1958. It performs a function similar to that of the Interstate Commerce Commission in the field of surface transportation. An air carrier must have a certificate of convenience and necessity from the CAB before it can act as a common carrier in interstate air transportation. There are also some intrastate air carriers which are subject to the appropriate state authority. The CAB regulations recognize as a direct air carrier one that is engaged in the operation of aircraft. This would include the scheduled airlines and also other carriers that operate airplanes as carriers in interstate commerce. The regulations also specify that an indirect air carrier is one that does not engage directly in the operation of aircraft in air transportation. An indirect air carrier may be an organization such as the REA (Railway Express Agency, Inc.), which collects and delivers air express in connection with the airlines, or it may be an air freight forwarder. Air freight forwarders perform a function similar to that of other freight forwarders in the collection and consolidation of shipments. They use direct air carriers for the actual transportation by air.

The liabilities of the direct air carrier and of the indirect air carrier are substantially the same. Air common carriers are subject to the common law liability of the common carrier, and also to such statutes as may apply to them as air carriers and to common carriers generally.

The liability of a common carrier is different from that of a contract carrier, and there may be occasion for the underwriter to determine whether goods are shipped by an air common carrier or by an air contract carrier. In its investigations and orders, the CAB has followed surface carrier precedent in ruling that the status of a carrier as a contract or common carrier is determined by what it does rather than by its declared purpose.[2] In one case, the CAB ruled that the making of individual contracts with each passenger did not remove the carrier from its status as a common carrier, nor did it make any difference whether the transportation was solicited by the carrier or by the passenger.[3]

DOMESTIC REGULATIONS

The liability of the air carrier may differ depending upon whether the shipment is in domestic or in international commerce. Air carriers are required to file and publish tariffs which include a statement of the carrier's liability for cargo in its custody. The contract between the shipper and the carrier is called an air waybill, and this is comparable to the bill of lading used in connection with surface shipments. The air waybill and the tariff filed by the carrier determine the liability for loss or damage to cargo. The shipper is charged with knowledge of the tariff filing even though he may never have seen it. This is comparable to the situation with surface shipments. It is important for the shipper to know the contents of the tariff, and it is also desirable for the underwriter to know the provisions of the tariff in cases where substantial values are at risk.

Air carriers have more freedom in setting their liability than do surface carriers. The air waybill which is used by most air carriers is not prescribed but is adopted voluntarily. The tariffs and waybills of most air carriers limit their liability to $50 per shipment or 50 cents per pound if the shipment weighs more than 100 pounds, unless the shipper declares a higher value.

There is an interesting and important variation from surface valuation procedures in the handling of air cargo. The shipper may declare a higher valuation to the carrier, or he may purchase insurance on the cargo from the carrier. There may be a difference in the desirability of these two possibilities. A declaration of higher

[2]See United States v. California, 297 U.S. 175, 80 L. ed. 567, 571 (1936), for language of the Supreme Court of the United States on this question.

[3]Page Airways, Inc., Investigation, May 17, 1946, Docket No. 1896, 6 C.A.B. 1061.

value increases the liability of the carrier to the declared value or to the actual value, whichever is less. The recovery is limited to the actual value. The purchase of insurance, in contrast, permits the shipper to recover the actual value at the destination, plus a percentage. The recovery from the insurer in many cases is actual cash value plus 10 percent. This is in accord with marine insurance practices, which often allow a recovery in excess of actual cash value in order to compensate the shipper for intangible increases in cost because of the loss or damage.

The air carrier is not required to take the responsibility for loss while the property is in the custody of a connecting carrier. This is contrary to requirements in connection with surface transportation under Interstate Commerce Commission rules and applicable laws. There could be difficulty in recovering a loss if there were a question as to where the loss occurred. The air waybill in general use specifies a time within which notice must be given of concealed damage. This is usually 15 days. It is important that the consignee realize the need for immediate inspection for concealed damage because the air carriers are likely to invoke this exclusion of any claim after the time limit has expired.

Air carriers also have the benefit of the common carrier exemption from liability where the damage is caused by an act of God, and act of the public enemy, inherent vice, improper packing, and fault of the shipper.

Air Carrier Insurance. An air carrier is likely to have an insurance policy which is similar to a motor truck cargo policy. This protects him against loss because of his liability for loss or damage to cargo in his custody. This policy is likely to cover any loss for which the carrier is liable, in contrast to many motor truck cargo policies which cover the insured's liability for only certain specified perils.

The air carrier's insurance policy usually provides for the purchase of insurance by the shipper to cover his interest. This is the method previously mentioned, of providing insurance coverage for the shipper at an additional cost. The air carrier issues a certificate to the shipper, or makes the proper notation on the shipping papers, and collects the premium from the shipper. This premium is then passed to the insurer. The shipper thus becomes an insured of the air carrier's insurer.

Ground Transportation of Air Cargo. Some direct air carriers maintain their own pickup and delivery service for air freight, or they contract with a trucker under circumstances that make the trucker an agent of the air carrier. The direct air carrier in such cases is the sole carrier involved and would be responsible for any loss for which it is liable. There may be other circumstances in which the trucker who handles the ground transportation would be considered the agent of the shipper. A significant factor which has affected some cases is whether the pickup and delivery charges were included in the charges shown on the air waybill. It has been held that direct billing to the shipper by the truckman for the ground transportation removed the liability from the air carrier. An important question in such cases is whether the limitation in the air waybill as to value would be available to the truckman. Subrogation rights of the shipper's insurer would be affected by the limitations which would apply to the shipment.

INTERNATIONAL SHIPMENTS

There may be a difference in the liability of the carrier for cargo if it is carried in international commerce as compared to domestic commerce. A treaty called the "Warsaw Convention" has determined to a large extent the liability of international air carriers. The agreements in this treaty were established at a convention in Warsaw, Poland, in 1929. The treaty was signed by many countries, and commerce between any two "Warsaw countries" has been limited by its terms. In addition, air waybills of most international carriers have followed the conditions of the Warsaw Convention. The Hague Protocol provided for interpretations of some problems that arose from the Warsaw Convention, but this is not yet in effect even in all of the "Warsaw countries." There continues to be dissatisfaction with the provisions of the Warsaw Convention and the Hague Protocol, particularly with the low limits of liability of the carriers. It is likely that the general conditions of the Warsaw Convention will continue to affect the liability of the international carriers of cargo. The principal change that might occur from time to time would be an amendment in the limits of liability of the carriers. Familiarity with the provisions of the Warsaw Convention is helpful to the underwriter of international air cargo shipments.

Article 18 of the Warsaw Convention provides, in brief, (1) that the air carrier shall be liable for damage sustained during the transportation by air, (2) that transportation by air shall include the time during which the goods are in the custody of the carrier on board an airliner or in an airport, but (3) that the transportation by air shall not include any transportation by land, by sea, or by river performed outside an airport.[4]

Article 19 provides that the carrier shall be liable for damage occasioned by delay in the transportation of passengers, baggage, or goods.

Article 20 provides that the carrier shall not be liable if it proves that it or its agents have taken all necessary measures to avoid the damage or that it was impossible to take such measures. The practical effect is similar to that of the common law, which does not hold common carriers liable for "acts of God." The burden of proof is on the carrier to show that everything was done that could be done to avoid the accident. This may be difficult for a carrier to prove.

Article 20 also states that in the transportation of goods and baggage the carrier shall not be liable if it proves that the damage was occasioned by an error in piloting, in the handling of the aircraft, or in navigation and that, in all other respects, the carrier and its agents have taken all necessary measures to avoid the damage. It is evident that this is an important limitation on the liability of the carrier.

This easing of the carrier's liability because of pilot error is not as much of a help in avoiding claims as might appear at first glance. It applies to cargo only and not to liability for injury or death to passengers. Liability for injury or death of passengers is likely to amount to a greater sum than cargo liabilities, so the tendency of a carrier is to avoid any admission of pilot error. To do so might prejudice the case against the air carrier in connection with its liability to passengers.

Article 21 provides that contributory negligence on the part of the injured party may exonerate the carrier wholly or in part from his liability, depending on the circumstances.

The second portion of Article 22 provides for the limitation of liability to a specified amount unless a higher valuation is declared. This is similar in its effect to the released liability provisions of the Interstate Commerce Act. It reads:

> In the transportation of checked baggage and of goods, the liability of the carrier shall be limited to the sum of 250 francs per kilogram, unless the consignor has made, at the time when the package was handed over to the carrier, a special declaration of the value at delivery and has paid a supplementary sum if the case so requires. In that case the carrier will be liable to pay a sum not exceeding the

[4]This clause has a different effect from that of the definition of an air carrier quoted above applying to domestic air carriers in the United States.

declared sum, unless he proves that the sum is greater than the actual value to the consignor at delivery.

The figure of 250 francs per kilogram is defined as a gold franc of specified fineness and is equivalent to approximately $7.48 per pound in United States currency. There is no limit on the value that can be declared.

It is customary for international air carriers to arrange for insurance on behalf of their customers when they so request. This insurance is charged for at rates in addition to the extra valuation charge.

TYPES OF AIR CARRIERS

Air Express. There are several different types of air carriers, which perform various functions. The Railway Express Agency is the principal organization handling air express. An express company performs the same function for air express that it does for railway express. It picks up the package at the shipper's door, hands it over to the direct air carrier for air transportation, accepts the package from the airline at the airport nearest the destination, and delivers it to the consignee.

The charge for the entire trip is specified in a tariff filed by the express company. The total rate is based upon the charge made by the airline to the express company, to which the express company has added its own charges for pickup and delivery. Neither the shipper nor the consignee needs any contact with the airline, nor does either have to consult airline tariffs to determine the cost of the shipment. That is all a part of the express company service.

Many shipments are made by air to locations that are remote from an airport. In such cases, the package may be shipped by railroad (in the custody of the express company) from the nearest airport city to the destination. For example, such a shipment might be handled (1) by an express company truck from shipper's plant to the airport, (2) by airplane to the airport nearest destination, (3) by express company truck from the airport to a railway station, (4) by train to the city of destination, and (5) by express company truck to the address of the consignee. The carrier throughout the entire trip is the express company, insofar as any claim for damages is concerned, and the terms of the express company's bill of lading and tariffs would determine the liability for damages.

Consolidation of Air Shipments. Another type of air carrier is the consolidator or forwarder. He performs the same function as the consolidator of surface shipments, and he may operate for air freight or air express shipments or for both. The express or freight charges for shipping a single shipment of ten packages, for example, are much less than the charges for handling the same ten packages as ten separate shipments. The consolidator may operate his own trucks for pickup and delivery purposes, or his operation may consist entirely of consolidating the shipments. In either case, he is the originating air carrier, and his liability is that of a common carrier as limited by the bill of lading he gives.

Air Freight. Some of the airlines have arrangements for pickup and delivery of air freight. Air freight differs from air express in that it consists of bulk shipments and is directly comparable to railroad freight. Pickup and delivery of air freight is handled on much the same basis as the pickup and delivery of less-than-carload lots of rail freight. The pickup and delivery usually is done by a trucker who operates under a contract for the airline. The charge for pickup and delivery may or may not be a part of the tariff filed by the airline.

There are several possible arrangements, and the air waybill may or may not cover the pickup and delivery service. Underwriters inquire whether the airline takes the responsibility for the pickup at the shipper's place of business and for delivery to the consignee's place or whether the trucker is responsible. An indication could be secured by determining whether the shipper calls the airline and reports a shipment to be picked up or calls a trucker and arranges for him to deliver the shipment to the airline at the airport.

Scheduled Airlines. The most important air carriers are the airlines. There are several different classes of airlines, but most of them are common carriers insofar as their relations with the public are concerned. There are many differences in their methods of operation that affect the chances of safe delivery.

First to be considered are the scheduled airlines. These lines operate according to regular timetables filed with the CAB and advertised to the public. No airline can operate on a regular schedule for the carrying of passengers or cargo for hire, or advertise to the public such regularity of operation, without securing a certificate of convenience and necessity from the CAB. The scheduled airlines are common carriers.

Scheduled airline operation has reached a high standard of safety, and crashes are rare. When a crash does occur, it is likely to result in total loss of the cargo, owing to a shattering of the load in case of a high-speed crash or to the fire that occurs frequently when fuel tanks are ruptured. In order to avoid catastrophe losses, it is advisable for a shipper to arrange for extremely high value loads to be divided between two or more planes. The chances of loss from air accident on the scheduled airlines are not much different from those in rail shipments. The chief differences between underwriting air and surface shipments arise from the differences in type of merchandise shipped by air, which will be discussed later.

Nonscheduled Airlines. Nonscheduled airlines may be carriers of passengers or cargo or both, but they do not operate on regular schedules. They are extensive haulers of freight and may participate in the hauling of mail or express.

Strong competition between the scheduled and the nonscheduled lines was a factor in bringing the rates for air freight to low points. In 1948 the CAB put a floor under air freight rates to avoid what might have developed into ruinous rate cutting. The floor set by the CAB at that time was 16 cents per ton-mile for the first 1,000 ton-miles of a freight shipment and 13 cents per ton-mile above that.

INSURANCE ON AIR CARGO

Airlines are not required to carry insurance on the cargo they haul. In case an air carrier goes out of business without having insurance to cover loss of cargo, shippers may be unable to collect for lost or damaged cargo.

Insurance companies may be called upon to insure cargo to be hauled by a local airplane operator who does not make a business of carrying cargo. There may be an emergency in which the insured charters an airplane to handle a special shipment. Such an airplane operator may not be a common carrier but is likely to be a contract carrier. The liability of a contract carrier usually is limited to damage resulting from his negligence unless he has assumed a greater liability by his contract.

There also is the possibility that such a local operator may not be equipped to handle cross-country flights with the degree of safety attained by the airlines. Most airlines, both scheduled and nonscheduled, use multi-engined planes with more than one pilot aboard. Smaller operators who are called in for emergency flights may fly in single-engine ships with a single pilot.

There may be occasion when a policyholder will ask for insurance on the contents of his own plane. Many corporations and individual businessmen use aircraft for the transportation of employees and occasionally to carry cargo. Insurance on such cargo is comparable to insurance on the contents of an insured's trucks. Underwriters inquire carefully into the safety of such air operations. Some business airplanes are operated with the same care as airline operations and with skilled pilots, but this may not be true of others.

There is no opportunity to recover the amount of a loss from a carrier when the cargo is shipped in the insured's plane. This situation justifies a higher rate for the insurance than is required for cargo shipped by common carrier.

Insurance companies are likely to have requests for trip transit insurance on air cargo. It has been customary for insurance companies to exclude coverage under ordinary trip transit policies for shipments by air. An increasing volume of freight is being flown to its destination, and many trip transit policies are endorsed to cover air shipments. It is likely that the exclusion of air coverage eventually will be eliminated from transit policies. Whenever air freight is covered, the underwriter has an additional factor to evaluate in considering the desirability of the insurancc prospect.

The liability of an air carrier depends primarily upon its common law liability, which is almost an absolute liability, as explained in a previous chapter. The important thing to be investigated is the limitation that may be placed on the amount of liability by the terms of the air waybill or applicable tariffs. Domestic waybills issued by the airlines are not required to be uniform, but many airlines do use waybills containing identical provisions. A typical air waybill contains a space in which to insert a declared value, following which are the words:

> Declared Value agreed and understood to be not more than the value stated in the governing tariffs for each pound on which charges are assessed, unless a higher value is declared and applicable charges paid thereon.

The conditions applying to many air shipments are similar to those covering express shipments in that the value is limited to $50 for shipments of less than 100 pounds and to 50 cents per pound for shipments in excess of 100 pounds. Inasmuch as air freight consists largely of high-value merchandise, the average shipment is likely to be worth more than 50 cents per pound. Underwriters may insert in the policy a provision regarding the value to be declared by the insured on his shipments. This provision should be called to the attention of the insured so that he will make the proper declarations when shipping goods.

When shipments are made on other than scheduled airlines, it is customary for the underwriter to determine whether the goods are shipped under circumstances that make the carrier a contract carrier and hence liable only for negligence losses. Many of the nonscheduled airlines are common carriers and issue air waybills similar to those used by the scheduled airlines, but this cannot be taken for granted.

The underwriter may be asked to furnish coverage against loss of market due to delay. There are occasions when airplanes are grounded for a day or more by bad weather. The perishability of the goods or of the market must be examined with great care when coverage for delay is to be provided. Insurance to cover loss due to delay may be provided when the policyholder requires it to fill a special need.

Insurance for the Shipper. Insurance on air cargo usually is against "all risks" of external loss or damage. This is in contrast to specified perils insurance policies usually written to cover goods sent by surface carrier. The broad coverage on air cargo is justified by the valuable nature of most air cargo. It is characteristic of transportation insurance that broad coverage is given on property that has a concentration of value within a small space. Such property is much more susceptible to pilferage than less valuable cargo. The owner of such property feels that he needs and is willing to pay for insurance against mysterious disappearance and other unaccountable loss ordinarily not covered under a specified perils policy.

It has been brought out that most air transportation includes transportation for part of the way by surface carrier, frequently by motor truck. Insurance company experience has indicated that "all risks" coverage on motor truck operations can be provided only on the highest type of motor truck carrier. The checking of packages must be handled carefully at all transfer points. There may be times when the underwriter would be willing to provide "all risks" coverage for the air portion of the transportation, but he may believe that only a specified perils coverage can be written on the surface transit. When this situation occurs, the break between air and ground coverage should be specified in language similar to that used in the Warsaw Convention, in which air carriage is limited to the custody of the airline while in an airplane or on an airport.

Air cargo insurance coverage ordinarily excludes war risks, and this may be the only exclusion of consequence. Loss by strike, riot, and civil commotion may be excluded if there is reason to believe that the hazard is out of proportion to the rate for the policy.

An air cargo policy should be so written that it covers general average charges. It has been explained previously that there is seldom an occasion to apply the principles of general average to inland marine losses when the property is being carried by surface carrier or when it is insured at a fixed location. However, an airplane is similar to an oceangoing ship in that jettison of cargo or of a portion of the plane might be necessary to save the rest of the ship and cargo. It is likely that marine law would be applied to such a case, and the owner of cargo might be liable for general average charges. His insurance should cover such a possibility.

Transportation policies covering loss of air cargo usually specify a limit of liability per plane, as well as a limit of liability in any one catastrophe. Underwriters make inquiries regarding the value of a policyholder's shipments in order to set the limit per plane high enough to cover the usual shipments. The catastrophe limit is intended primarily to cover a concentration of goods in a terminal. There is also the possibility of a mid-air collision involving two planes on which an insured's cargo is being carried. The limit should be at least as high as the total values the insured might ship or receive through a single terminal in one day.

Many of the airlines have arrangements whereby they can procure insurance for their customers on shipments of goods. A typical insurance arrangement excludes coverage on livestock, on perishables, and on radio, X-ray, and electronic tubes. This form of trip transit policy covers against all risks of physical loss or damage from any external cause except loss directly or indirectly due to legal seizure, war risks, or hostilities. The amount of insurance the shipper may obtain is the same as the valuation he declares for the purpose of carriage under the air waybill. However, recovery also is limited to the actual value of the goods at destination at time of loss, plus 10 percent. The rates for such coverage are in addition to the valuation charge the carrier receives to compensate him for carrying valuable goods.

There may be occasions when a policyholder wishes to secure insurance through the air carrier for a part of his value and to insure the remaining value otherwise. In such cases, underwriters check to see that there is no conflict with the airline coverage and also that the coverage is excess insurance above that arranged by the airline.

Insurance for the Carrier. An insurance policy written for the air carrier covers primarily its legal liability for loss of, or damage to, property in its custody. The air carrier that is a common carrier has a heavy liability amounting almost to that of an absolute insurer of goods in his custody. Many insurance policies purchased by airlines provide for the insuring of the shipper's interest, as described above.

Most policies issued to air carriers differ from legal liability policies for surface carriers in that they insure against loss from the complete legal liability of the air carriers. Policies issued to truckmen usually are limited to cover certain specified perils; seldom is a policy issued to a truckman to provide "all risks" coverage of his legal liability. The air carrier policy usually covers loss from physical damage only and does not cover his liability for loss due to delay. This liability for delay could be covered if an insurance company wished to grant the coverage and could secure a rate commensurate with the hazard.

There are some typical restrictions on policies written for air carriers. These policies may provide that war risks are not covered, and exclude legal seizure. It is provided that the shipper is required to declare a value on each shipment and that the insurance company is not liable above the value declared by him. Certain extremely high value goods are excluded from coverage in the usual policy; such items include currency, watches, jewelry, precious stones, negotiable paper, and uncancelled stamps. Such property can be covered under special forms at rates commensurate with the hazard. As a matter of fact, much of such property is carried as mail and is insured under registered mail policies. The carrier would have no reason to insure his legal liability for such mail shipments under his cargo policy, because the Post Office Department is responsible to the shipper for registered mail shipments.

Premiums for air carrier cargo liability policies are paid to the insurance company upon the basis of the total values declared by the shippers. This method of calculating premiums makes certain that the company receives premiums in proportion to the risk assumed. This is one reason why a broad coverage can be granted on air cargo whereas it has not been feasible on motor truck cargo policies. If all shippers by truck were required to declare the value of their shipments and all truckers paid their insurance premiums upon the basis of the value shipped, an equally broad coverage might be feasible for motor truck cargo insurance.

An air carrier's responsibility may be different from that of a surface carrier in respect to damage done on the lines of a connecting carrier. The originating carrier is not responsible for damages beyond its own line. This responsibility, insofar as the shipper is concerned, is a matter of contract between him and the originating carrier.

There is no governmental requirement for the carrying of insurance by airlines to protect shippers. Thus if an airline should go out of business, there would be a possibility of loss to shippers who had claims against it. In the absence of an insurance provision such as the Interstate Commerce Commission endorsement on the motor truck cargo policy, the airline's insurance policy protects the shipper only to the extent of the policy coverage and is not intended to guarantee the payment of any loss not covered by the policy.

The underwriting of an air cargo risk must take into account many factors that are peculiar to this mode of transportation. The combination of air and ground transportation provides a complication that is not present in other transportation fields. The nearest comparable situation is that in ocean ports where goods are transferred from sea transit to land transit. It is true in both situations that much of the insured losses occurs from theft during the transfer from plane to truck and from ship to truck. The use of containers to hold large numbers of packages has been helpful in reducing pilferage, but it is more difficult for the consignee to detect concealed damage to a containerized shipment. Any concealed damage must be reported to the air carrier within a limited time, otherwise the damage will probably be disallowed. The insurance underwriter should determine the practices of his shipper-insured and of the shipper's customers in the handling of incoming shipments in order to determine whether subrogation rights against the carrier are being preserved.

Some of the larger air terminals have experienced a tremendous increase in losses by theft. The underwriter should determine whether his insured shipments are going through those particular terminals. The underwriting of a carrier's liability insurance also requires a great deal of information regarding the operations of the insured airline as well as a survey of the terminals through which the line operates. Deductible coverages often are desirable so that the insured airline can handle its small claims directly with its customers, and also to lower the cost of the insurance.

QUESTIONS

1. What factors in addition to cost of transit are considered by a shipper in determining whether to use air or ground transportation?
2. Does the use of air transportation increase or decrease the need for insurance on goods in transit?

3. What hazards other than an air crash affect the probabilities that an air shipment will reach its destination in good condition?
4. Discuss the similarities and differences in the regulation of air carriers as compared with the regulation of surface carriers.
5. What is the "Warsaw Convention"?
6. Discuss the effects of the Warsaw Convention on the liability of air carriers operating in international trade.
7. What is an air carrier as defined by the laws and regulations applying to domestic air carriers in the United States?
8. Describe the information that you would require in order to underwrite insurance for a policyholder who ships a large amount of property by air.
9. Compare the liability of a common carrier by air with the liability of a surface common carrier in domestic commerce in the United States.
10. Compare the coverage which is customary on air cargo with the insurance which is generally provided on surface shipments.
11. What are the principal differences between motor truck cargo policies and the policies which are issued to cover the liability of air carriers for property in their custody?
12. Discuss the probabilities of loss by theft of cargo in the airports in your part of the country as revealed by newspaper accounts of such occurrences.

13

Miscellaneous Business Floaters

The discussion of inland marine insurance in the preceding chapters has covered three types of property or general situations in which inland marine policies may be used. These are:

1. Property in a state of transit or in temporary storage incidental to transit from one place to another.
2. Instrumentalities of transportation which may be insured under an inland marine policy because of their relation to transportation or because marine underwriters traditionally were the only underwriters who were willing to provide broad coverage.
3. Stocks of merchandise in the hands of dealers for sale which could be insured under inland marine policies because of the special nature of the property and the willingness of marine underwriters to provide broad coverage.

Another type of property that may be insured under an inland marine form of policy is that which has become known as floating property and the insurance on which has come to be known as floater coverage. This does not mean that the property floats on a body of water, but rather that it is of such a nature that its location is not fixed. Such property may rest at one location for a long time, but the location is not permanent, and the property may be moved at anytime.

There are circumstances under which it is difficult or impossible for an owner to foretell when he will need to move such property. It is essential that the insurance coverage be continuous, whether the property is in transit or resting temporarily in one place. The Nation-wide Marine Definition lays down conditions under which movable property can or cannot be insured under floater policies.

Several principles are used to establish the eligibility of property for inland marine floater coverage:

First, the property must be movable in nature.

Second, it must not be at any location where it is expected to remain permanently.

Third, floater policies must include transportation coverage to and from any temporary location where the property may be covered. Otherwise the policy would be providing a storage, not a floater, coverage.

Typical property eligible for floater protection includes (1) exports and imports (which may be insured indefinitely at a fixed location as long as they retain their identity as exports or imports), (2) domestic shipments (but they are not considered to be in transit after having been more than 90 days at any place of storage or deposit), and (3) property that by its nature must be used at different locations and is in storage only incidental to such use. Examples of this latter group would be contractors' equipment and road building machinery.

Insurance policies covering business and commercial property that is eligible for floater protection (in addition to exports, imports, and domestic shipments of goods) may be divided roughly into the following groups:

1. Equipment floaters covering equipment, instruments, and supplies used for work, demonstration, or sales.
2. Contents or stock floaters covering property in temporary storage and property undergoing processing outside the owner's premises.
3. Consignment or sales floaters covering property that is held for sale under consignment, or that is being installed, or that has been sold under an installment payment plan.

Floater policies contain basic provisions similar to the inland marine policies previously discussed. Added to these are special clauses to fit the needs for covering the particular type of property to be insured. This chapter discusses various business floaters individually and comments upon the peculiarities of the property and of the insurance protection. Few of these policies are standardized or subject to rate filing requirements, and insurance companies write the policies individually to fit the needs of the insured. Rates are based largely upon the experience and judgment of the underwriter. The past loss experience of the policyholder may influence the rate if the individual premium is large enough for this experience to have statistical credibility.

I. EQUIPMENT FLOATERS

Equipment floater policies cover movable property that is not on sale or consignment or in course of manufacture and that is in the hands of the insured to be used for the purpose for which it was made. Such policies do not cover property in storage at premises controlled or leased by the insured except when the storage is purely incidental to the regular and frequent use of the property for its intended purpose.

Contractors' Equipment. The contractors' equipment floater is designed to cover machinery of the type used by road builders, mining contractors, builders of dams and tunnels, bridges, building contractors, and others who use heavy and expensive equipment. Typical equipment to be insured under such policies are cranes, vehicles such as earth movers that are not designed or licensed for highway use, power shovels, air compressors, concrete mixers, pumps, boilers, stone crushers, pile drivers, tractors, bulldozers, portable tool houses, and scaffolding. Snow removal and road building equipment used by municipalities may be insured under this form. Any portable equipment used by a contractor may be covered, provided that it is regularly used out on a job and storage on the premises of the policyholder is purely incidental to regular use away from such premises. Automobiles, trucks, and concrete mixing units that are permanently attached to highway trucks are exceptions because they are insurable under automobile policies.

Policies are written on a schedule basis, with each piece of equipment listed and an amount of insurance specified for each. Small items such as wheelbarrows and shovels may be included in a blanket item, but it is customary to have a 100 percent coinsurance clause apply to any blanket items. Very large groups of equipment may be written on a blanket basis subject to 100 percent coinsurance. It would be difficult for both the insured and the insurance company to maintain schedules for an insured who has dozens or sometimes even several hundred pieces of equipment. Territorial limits may be restricted to a particular state or county, or the policy may cover anywhere in the United States and Canada, depending upon where the insured works.

Coverages are set out in each policy according to the needs and desires of the insured. The usual coverages are for direct loss and damage by fire, lightning, explosion (except explosion originating within steam boilers or internal combustion engines), windstorm, earthquake, collapse of bridges and culverts, flood, and collision or overturning of a conveyance upon which the equipment is being transported. Riot, civil commotion, and strike coverage may be added at an extra premium.

For theft coverage, which is desired by some contractors, it is customary to include a deductible of at least $25. This eliminates small, troublesome losses and encourages the insured to provide watchmen and keep easily pilfered equipment under lock and key. It makes possible a lower rate than for a full coverage policy.

Damage resulting from collision of the insured equipment, landslide, overturning, and cave-ins may be covered at an extra premium, and usually a substantial deductible is required. There is an obvious collision hazard to equipment being used in mountainous country and in conjunction with other heavy machines. The upsetting and cave-in hazards also may be severe in mountainous country or near rivers and lakes.

Some of the equipment used in strip mining operations may weigh 100 tons or more. This weight may be sufficient to overload ground surfaces, particularly where there have been underground mining operations. Even if damage to the equipment is slight in such a cave-in, the expense of righting and pulling out a sixty- or seventy-ton machine is considerable and may run to many thousands of dollars. Gold dredges and other kinds of equipment that work in water or mud are subject to an overturning hazard. The loss may consist chiefly of the expense of salvaging the equipment, but this expense can be high.

Fire hazard may be severe to equipment used in cross-country operations. A forest fire could ruin an entire group of machines. Although the machines are usually made of steel and will not burn, it does not require much fire to take the temper out of the metal. Gasoline fires from fuel in the equipment itself constitute another hazard, especially when the work is being done out in the country and at a distance from municipal fire-fighting apparatus. Self-propelled equipment may be put out of commission by a seemingly minor fire, and it then becomes necessary to send flat-bed trucks to bring out the damaged equipment for repair.

The values involved in a contracting operation may run to high figures. Single pieces of equipment may cost from $20,000 to $100,000. At the site where a dam was under construction a few years ago, the value of the equipment was reported to exceed a million dollars. One insurance company is reported to have paid a loss in excess of a half million dollars for equipment that was lost in California landslides following heavy rain and mud slides.

The loss experience on contractors' equipment tends to vary considerably between different insurance companies. Rates are computed by the company underwriter on the basis of his judgment and experience. The rate may be as low as 1/2 percent of the value annually for a large line which is subject to competition. The average rate for such equipment is around 1 percent of the value per year. Additional rates for specific coverages are included as needed. Deductible theft coverage may cost from 1/10 to 1/2 percent. Strike and riot coverage costs about the same amount, depending upon the locality, the type of work being done, and any past history of strike trouble. Rates for collision coverage may range from ½ to 2 percent depending upon the type of machinery, its weight, and the work being done.

Occasionally the contractors' equipment insurance is written at a "competitive" rate in order to obtain other parts of a large contractor's line of insurance. The result may be an inadequate rate for the inland marine portion of the line. This practice appears to have been partly responsible for the high loss ratio on this type of coverage.

Business interruption insurance may be written on contractors' equipment if it appears that the contractor would have to rent equipment as a replacement for his own in order to finish a contract on time.

Some contractors rent their equipment to other contractors from time to time. It is possible to write an inland marine rental value policy to cover the loss of rent if the equipment were destroyed or put out of commission for a time.

Most of the exclusions contained in the policy are those common to other inland marine policies. A specific exclusion designed for this type of policy excludes any loss resulting from an attempt to lift a weight heavier than the registered lifting capacity of the machine. Sometimes a policy also excludes any loss resulting from an attempt to go over a bridge or culvert if the total weight of the machine is more than the indicated carrying capacity of the bridge or culvert. These are intended to encourage the insured to use proper care in handling this equipment.

Most policies exclude such property as plans and specifications. They also exclude equipment used underground unless a tunnel job is intended to be covered and the policy is so written.

Agricultural Equipment Floater. The inland marine rating bureaus have filed coverages and rates for farm equipment under the names of "mobile agricultural equipment floater" and "farm equipment floater." This form often is combined with a "livestock floater" in order to provide a complete coverage for the farmer's equipment and stock. Livestock insurance will be discussed subsequently.

Coverage. The coverage applies to mobile agricultural equipment and machinery, including harness, saddlery, liveries, blankets, and similar equipment. Property may be insured on a blanket basis or on a scheduled basis. Excluded are motor vehicles, aircraft, watercraft, and feed, hay, grain, or crops of any nature. While the form is designed to cover farm property, it may also be used in conjunction with the livestock floater to cover property of riding stables.

The coverage is against "all risks of physical loss or damage from any external cause," except as excluded. Exclusions are few and are principally those of wear and tear, mechanical or electrical breakdown, infidelity of persons to whom the property is trusted, damage to tires and tubes unless coincidental with other loss, war damage, and nuclear damage. A $50 deductible applies to losses except from certain enumerated causes. An 80 percent coinsurance clause applies.

Rates. The annual rate varies from considerably less than one dollar on ordinary farm machinery to considerably more than a dollar for cotton pickers and harvester–thresher combines. These rates in some areas may be less than the fire insurance rate for farm buildings in which equipment may be stored when not in use. The rating bureaus justify this on the ground that the equipment is away from the buildings during much of its life, and is not subject to the building fire hazards.

Underwriting. The rules and rates filed by the rating bureaus do not apply to self-propelled harvester-thresher combines and self-propelled mechanical cotton pickers used for custom work, that is, for hire. Neither do they apply to equipment used in logging or forestry work, nor to portable saw mills. Such property is insurable under inland marine policies, but the bureaus feel that such property is subject to extra hazard, and the filed rates are not adequate. Companies wishing to insure such property can do so at whatever rates they consider proper for the risk.

It is considered preferable for each of the larger items of equipment to be scheduled with an amount of insurance applying to it. Modern farm machinery may cost many thousands of dollars per unit, and there is a likelihood of underinsurance if expensive items are not scheduled.

Livestock. The coverage filed by the rating bureaus for livestock is intended to apply to farm animals, horses used for riding, and related activities. Excluded from the rules are horses or mules used exclusively for racing, show, or delivery work, including breeding therefor, livestock while being transported to or while at stockyards, livestock at public sales, circus or theatrical animals, mortality policies, and policies covering veterinarians or humane societies. These latter types of property and policies are classifiable within the inland marine class, but rates for them have not been filed.

Coverage. The policies cover loss due to death, or destruction made necessary, by fire, lightning, windstorm, riot, strike, aircraft, hail, earthquake, flood, collapse of bridges or culverts, collision or derailment of a conveyance on which the property is being carried, collision of the animal with other vehicles except those owned or operated by the insured or a tenant of the insured, and the sinking or burning of a vessel on which the property is being carried. An optional coverage at an extra rate protects against loss from accidental shooting, drowning, artificial electricity, attack by dogs or wild animals, and collapse of building. It is to be noted that this does not provide any coverage against death from natural causes.

Monthly reporting policies may be written. Somewhat different rules apply to livestock that is out on the range during the winter. Such policies also cover loss from blizzard and freezing.

Rates. The filed rates for livestock are similar to those for farm machinery. The rates for optional coverage are extra. The rates for winter range livestock are more than three times the rates for ordinary livestock. The rates for the optional coverage are higher for sheep than for other livestock because of the susceptibility of sheep to attack by dogs and wild animals.

Miscellaneous Coverages on Animals. Coverage for dealers in animals is not subject to filed rates and rules but is written according to the needs of the insured. Most policies are on a specified perils basis similar in coverage to the livestock form, but full mortality (life insurance) coverage can be written if the insured will pay a rate commensurate with the hazard.

Few companies write full mortality coverage. There are certain livestock insurance companies that specialize in that form of coverage. Full mortality coverage ordinarily is written under inland marine policies only when it is incidental to transportation insurance.

Property in the hands of stockyards may be covered. This coverage may take effect at a point away from the stockyard where the animals are purchased, or it may take effect when the animals are delivered to the yard. Not only horses and mules but cattle as well are covered for stockyards.

It is also possible to cover breeding animals, as well as fancy animals in the hands of circuses, carnivals, or theatrical producers, covering whatever hazards may be agreed upon between the insured and the insurance company.

Occasionally policies are written to cover the legal liability of veterinarians, humane societies, and others who may have animals in their custody for treatment or other professional purposes. Rates are on an individual basis, depending largely upon the fire rate where the animals are customarily located. Dealers who handle large numbers of animals may pay their premiums at so much per head (five or ten cents, perhaps). In the case of stockyards, the rate may be at so much per carload. These rates must be determined by the company on the basis of the hazards covered in transportation and at the location after delivery, as well as upon the concentration of value at any one time and place.

Theatrical Floaters. The theatrical floater is designed to insure the scenery, costumes, and other theatrical properties used in the production of individual plays, and each policy names the play for which the property is insured. The form covers such property if it is owned, if it is held in trust, on consignment, or on commission, if the insured has made advances on it, or if it has been sold but not delivered. The form does not cover buildings, their improvements or betterments, or furniture and fixtures not shipped from place to place with theatrical troupes. It does not cover animals.

The hazards covered by the filed form include fire, lightning, explosion, collapse of bridges or culverts, flood, windstorm, aircraft, smoke, theft, burglary and holdup, collision or derailment of a transporting conveyance, and the stranding, sinking, burning or collision of vessels. Coverage applies anywhere in the United States and Canada.

The form excludes coverage on jewelry, accounts, bills, currency, deeds, evidences of debt, documents, money, notes, securities, and railroad or other tickets. Costume jewelry is covered, but this coverage does not extend to jewelry containing precious or semiprecious stones or made of gold or platinum. Also excluded is any loss caused by war and nuclear hazards. Loss caused by riot, civil commotion, strikes, or labor disturbance is excluded unless the coverage is provided in a special endorsement.

The form also includes a full contribution or 100 percent coinsurance clause, making it necessary for the insured to carry full insurance to value if he is to recover the full amount of a loss.

The coverage may be broadened to insure against loss from water damage, earthquake, sprinkler leakage, riot and civil commotion, and breakage. Rates vary according to the amount of insurance. The additional charges for the optional coverages vary from 5 cents to 25 cents per $100 of coverage, except that breakage coverage costs $4 per $100.

The standard form and rules do not apply to circuses, carnivals, costume rental agencies, or theatrical supply houses. Many such properties qualify for inland marine coverage, but the hazards vary to such an extent that standard forms and rates are not feasible for them. Such properties are insured under forms specially drafted to fit the circumstances of the individual case.

Morticians' Equipment. A mortician's activities require that portions of his equipment be used outside his place of business. Such property is subject to transportation hazards while being carried from place to place, and it also is subject to fire and other hazards while in use. The principal items usually are scheduled on the policy, but a miscellaneous item may be inserted to cover small pieces of equipment. The form excludes (1) automobiles and their equipment, (2) furniture and fixtures intended for use at the premises of the insured (except perhaps folding chairs that may be used outside the premises), and (3) caskets and other stock for sale.

The coverage usually included in a morticians' equipment policy protects against loss by fire and lightning, windstorm, earthquake, transportation, and theft. Frequently a $25 deductible clause applies to theft coverage. The exclusions refer to gradual deterioration, moth, vermin, inherent vice, electrical distrubances, infidelity of insured's employees, and war damage. Some companies exclude loss of anything shipped by mail.

This form is not standardized, and the coverage varies considerably between companies. Rates are calculated according to the underwriter's experience and may be from 1½ to 2 percent of the value.

Morticians' Liability. Occasionally companies insure the legal liability of a mortician for damage to corpses. This covers the legal liability for damage resulting from the perils specified in the policy. Sometimes this is written as a separate policy, and sometimes it is added by endorsement to the morticians' equipment policy. The coverage is of questionable status because of the uncertainty regarding property rights in a corpse.[1] Many underwriters consider this a casualty coverage rather than an inland marine coverage.

Physicians' and Surgeons' Equipment. Physicians and surgeons may carry several hundred dollars' worth of instruments with them. Their instrument bags are stolen not only for the value of the instruments but also for the narcotics that may be contained therein. Dentists also have occasion to treat patients at home or in hospitals and occasionally must carry instruments with them. The equipment used by physicians and dentists in their offices is expensive, and susceptible to loss from many causes in addition to fire and the extended coverage hazards. There is need for a broad coverage on such property.

The 1953 Nation-wide Marine Definition classifies as inland marine a policy which covers not only the physician's equipment that he takes with him, but also furniture and fixtures located in that portion of the premises used by the insured in the practice of his profession. This is another of the departures from the theory that property insurable under an inland marine policy should be of a mobile nature. For example, only the mobile equipment belonging to a farmer is considered insurable under an inland marine policy, but the physician can so insure all of his equipment whether it is mobile or not. These inconsistencies are brought about by competitive pressures within the insurance industry more than by any logical development.

Coverage. Almost anything used by the physician, surgeon, or dentist can be insured under this policy. Radium is excluded, but this is for underwriting reasons. A special policy is provided for radium. Furniture and fixtures are specifically included when it is intended to

[1]For a discussion of such property rights, see Percival E. Jackson, *The Law of Cadavers,* 2d ed. (Englewood Cliffs, N. J.: Prentice-Hall, Inc., 1950).

cover them. The policy may be written to cover only the types of property which the insured would normally carry with him. A higher rate is charged in this case because the property carried with a physician is more susceptible to loss than the equipment in his office. The territorial limits are the continental United States and Canada. Policies may be written to cover in Hawaii or Puerto Rico.

An optional extension of coverage endorsement may be added to the policy for a nominal premium. This extends coverage to furniture and fixtures temporarily away from the premises; it provides a limited amount of extra expense insurance; it covers up to $250 of money and stamps; it adds a limited amount of coverage on personal effects of the insured and others while on the premises if such property is not otherwise insured; and it covers up to $500 on account books, manuscripts, and records. This endorsement is intended to make the policy a complete coverage for the property of the doctor.

The coverage is against "all risks of loss of or damage" except as excluded. Exclusions apply to loss from wear and tear, breakage of glass other than scientific lenses except from certain specified hazards, loss due to the property's being worked upon, electrical damage, nuclear damage, and war damage. If equipment on the insured's premises is covered, an 80 percent coinsurance clause applies.

Rates. When the only property covered is that which is carried by the doctor, the rates range from 2 percent downward, depending upon the amount of insurance. If the coverage also applies to equipment in the office, the fire contents rate is used as a basis, with a loading to cover the additional hazards which are insured against.

The filed rules and rates do not apply to dealers, clinics, hospitals, medical schools, and the like. However, an explanatory note in the rules states that "clinics" and "the like" are not intended to mean doctors who share offices and equipment but maintain their own individual practices.

Radium. The radium floater is a specialized version of the scientific instruments form. Radium is extremely expensive. Because it is used in small quantities and in tiny containers, it is lost easily. Radium is used extensively by doctors and hospitals for the treatment of cancer and skin diseases. The standard form of radium floater is intended for the protection of radium used for medical treatment purposes only. Radium used for other purposes may be covered, but it is subject to special rates and rules depending upon the hazards attendant upon the expected use.

Radium is used in small containers such as tubes or needles that may be placed on or in the body of the patient. It is standard practice to have some person constantly in attendance when a patient is being treated with radium. This is to make certain that the dosage is properly timed and also to see that the radium container is not misplaced.

This practice is taken into account in the rating of a radium floater, and the standard form contains a provision that the insured will use due diligence in the maintenance of special care and supervision of each patient under radium treatment, by a doctor, nurse, or other person specially designated to exercise such care and supervision. The person specially designated may be a member of the patient's family if the doctor in charge feels that the circumstances are such as to justify such a designation. An extra rate is charged when the insured wishes to have this special supervision clause deleted.

The coverage is against "all risks" of loss or damage, and there are only three exclusions. The first excludes loss or damage resulting from gradual deterioration and damage sustained, owing to, and resulting from any repairing and restoration process. The second is a war damage exclusion, and the third excludes loss of shipments by mail unless shipped by first-class registered mail.

In addition to the special care clause mentioned above, the radium floater has another clause peculiar to this form. It requires that immediate notice of loss be given to the insurance company by telephone or telegraph. The recovery of a lost radium container is like looking for the proverbial needle in a haystack. Unless the search is started at once and makes use of proper methods, the container is likely to be swept out with the trash or washed down a drain and lost forever. A radium expert can use scientific detecting devices such as a Geiger counter to locate the radium. It is essential that an expert be secured at once; most insurance companies send one to the scene of a loss immediately upon receiving the notice that a loss has occurred.

The form contains a full contribution clause and the insured must maintain full insurance to value in order to recover losses in full. The territorial limits are within the continental United States and Canada. Policies may be endorsed to cover in Hawaii or Puerto Rico. The form is attached to the scheduled property floater policy, which contains the usual clauses found in other inland marine policies. A deductible of 10 percent or 25 percent of each loss may be used to secure lower rates.

It is required that each tube, needle, plaque, or cell be listed specifically, showing the number of milligrams of radium, the character of the container, the Bureau of Standards Certificate Test Number, and the amount of insurance. Rates for the standard form are $1.75 for the first $5,000 of coverage, $1.50 for the next $5,000, and $1.00 for the excess above $10,000. Deletion of the supervision clause calls for an increase of 75 cents in the rates, and the use of a deductible allows a credit.

Radium in solution or in a bomb is rated specially, depending upon the nature of the container and the method of use. When radium containers are rented, an extra hazard is involved and the property may be specially rated.

Signs. It has long been customary to insure neon signs and automatic or mechanical electric signs and street clocks under inland marine policies. Such property seldom is subject to a transportation hazard after it has been installed, nor can it be considered an instrumentality of transportation.

Signs are of such a nature that their owners need a broad insurance protection, which marine and inland marine underwriters have been willing to provide. (Ordinary billboards or signs lighted by reflected light from electric lights are not customarily insured under inland marine forms.) Many neon or mechanical signs are expensive and are sold on the installment plan. This makes it desirable for the seller to protect his interest from the many hazards to which the signs are subject. Street clocks are considered to be mechanical signs.

The coverage has been filed by the rating bureaus. The form is attached to the scheduled property floater policy and provides coverage against "all risks" of loss or damage. It contains the usual exclusions of loss due to wear and tear, gradual deterioration, neglect of the insured, dampness of atmosphere or extremes of temperature, mechanical breakdown, electrical loss other than by lightning, war damage, and nuclear damage.

Two special exclusions are designed to take care of peculiarities of sign coverage. The first excludes loss or damage caused by faulty manufacture or installation, or loss occasioned by the inherent character of the insured property. The second excludes loss caused by breakage during installation, repairing, or dismantling, and also excludes breakage during transportation unless caused by fire, lightning, collision, derailment, or overturning of vehicle. The form does not limit coverage to where the sign is installed but covers wherever the sign may be. In this respect the policy does provide a floater coverage. This is important because occasionally the signs have to be taken to the shop for repairs.

Full insurance to value is contemplated and a full contribution clause is included in the form. Deductibles are used in many cases in order to eliminate the numerous small losses due to broken tubes and bulbs. Each sign insured must be listed specifically, showing the type of sign, the lettering, where it is installed, and the amount of insurance.

The form provides for a deductible of 5 percent of the amount of insurance on the item damaged, but not less than $10 nor more than $100 on any one item. The deductible may be eliminated at an increased rate and higher minimum premium.

Rates vary from 3½ percent to 16½ percent of the amount of insurance, depending upon the location of the sign and whether there is a deductible. Rates are higher along the southeastern coast of the United States than for inland locations because of the hurricane possibilities along the coast. Signs that are entirely within buildings are insured at half the rates for outdoor signs.

Underwriters customarily secure reports on the locations of signs in order to avoid those that might be damaged by snow and ice falling from roofs and those that are so close to the street that they might be damaged by persons carrying ladders or poles, or by trucks passing in the street or backing into loading docks.

Dealers' policies covering signs which they have installed and for which they have not been paid in full may be issued on a schedule basis, with new signs reported at periodic intervals. Policies may be issued to manufacturers or dealers to cover signs sold under a maintenance contract.

Salesmen's Samples–Commercial Travelers. Many salesmen must carry expensive samples of their wares. Manufacturers, jobbers, and wholesalers need insurance protection for the goods in the hands of their salesmen.

The use of the automobile by the salesmen brought about a great change in the desirability of salesmen's sample floaters. Prior to 1920 salesmen's travel was mostly by railroad, and their goods were in the custody of the railroad or in their own hands. The chances of loss were remote if the salesmen were careful individuals. Today it is necessary at times for the salesman to leave his car and samples unattended. The principal hazard in connection with salesmen's sample floater insurance is that of theft from his automobile. Consequently, this hazard is covered only under restricted conditions.

A salesman's sample floater may be issued as a specified perils policy or on an "all risks" basis. The specified perils policy issued by many companies covers loss by fire, lightning, and transportation while the property is in the hands of the insured's salesmen within the continental limits of the United States and Canada. The policy also covers the property while it is being shipped to or from the salesman by common carrier. The coverage remains effective while the property is located in a hotel checkroom or while checked with a common carrier.

Theft coverage may be granted, but usually under restrictions. Theft from a checkroom or while in the hands of a common carrier may be limited to theft of the entire package. Many companies will not issue a policy covering theft from an unattended vehicle except when the property is in the hands of a common carrier. (When the property is stolen from an unattended vehicle while in the custody of a common carrier, the insurance company has a good chance of recovering a part or all of the loss from the carrier.) If property is stolen from a vehicle owned and operated by the insured or his salesman, there usually is little chance of recovery.

When theft from an unattended vehicle is covered, it is customary to limit coverage to theft from a fully enclosed and locked body. Installation of burglar alarms or other theft preventive devices may be required on a vehicle used to carry expensive goods. The hazard of theft from automobiles is so great that the coverage requires the addition of considerable extra premium.

An "all risks" form is issued by some companies. The theft coverage is restricted in much the same manner as it is under a specified perils form. The principal difference between the two forms is in the coverage of the unusual loss by the "all risks" form.

Specified perils and "all risks" forms exclude coverage while the property is on the premises of the insured. They also exclude loss from breakage, marring, or scratching unless caused by fire and other specified perils, and they exclude loss from the perils of war. The policies contain the usual exclusions of loss from wear and tear, infidelity of persons to whom the property is entrusted, and inherent vice. There are no filings, and rates are calculated by the companies according to the coverage and hazards.

Patterns and Dies. Many industrial firms have large sums of money invested in patterns and dies used in the manufacture of their products. When a portion of their work is subcontracted, it may be necessary for them to send their dies or patterns to the subcontractor. They may be insured under an inland marine policy while they are off the premises of the insured. (Dies and patterns on the premises of the insured are not eligible for inland marine coverage.)

Coverage and rates on patterns and dies are not filed but are determined according to the hazards and the needs of the insured. Most policies protect against fire, lightning, windstorm, explosion, smoke damage, and falling aircraft, and also against the perils of transportation while being shipped to and from the subcontractor's premises. Occasionally theft insurance may be desired if the property has a commercial value. It is seldom that an "all risks" policy is written.

Prospective insureds are investigated to determine the chances of a large loss and the susceptibility of the property to loss. If the insured uses only a few subcontractors and the patterns and dies are concentrated at a few locations, the hazards can be evaluated with some degree of accuracy, and the rate can be based upon the fire and extended coverage rates at the subcontractors' locations. If the property is sent out to many different places and at irregular intervals, the problem of underwriting is more complex, and the underwriter secures all the information available and uses his best judgment.

The difficulty and cost of duplicating patterns and dies are important factors. Coverage should be for the full value, and the policy usually contains a full insurance to value clause. The amount at risk would be the value of all the patterns or dies that might be away from the insured's premises at any one time.

Paraphernalia. Lodges and fraternal organizations frequently have several thousand dollars' worth of paraphernalia. This may be used in the lodge hall much of the time, but it also is taken out for ceremonies at other places. It is subject to transportation hazards and may be insured under an inland marine form of policy as property that is stored at a fixed location only incidentally to use outside the premises.

The hazards usually covered are fire, lightning, windstorm, explosion, smoke, falling aircraft, theft, flood, collision, and overturn of transporting vehicles. Policies take into account the individual needs of the insured; there is no standard form. Exclusions, which are much the same as in other floater policies, eliminate coverage from loss by wear and tear; infidelity of persons in whose custody the property is placed; war risks; electrical distrubances other than lightning; and moth, vermin, inherent vice, and nuclear damage.

The property usually is scheduled in the policy, although the insured may be permitted to blanket the small miscellaneous properties in a single item. The property is required to be kept in a locked room when it is not in use, according to the terms of most policies.

Full insurance to value usually is required, and a 100 percent coinsurance clause is attached to the policy. Rates depend largely upon the fire and extended coverage rates at the location where the property ordinarily is stored, plus a loading to take care of the other hazards that may be covered by the policy. In the absence of an unusually high fire rate, many such policies are issued at rates of 1½ to 2 percent of the value.

Coin-operated Machines–Mechanical Sales Devices. Recent years have seen a tremendous increase in the use of coin-operated vending machines. Amusement devices, coin changing machines, hot and cold drink, candy and food vending machines, and stamp machines are located in airports, in bus stations, in railroad stations, and in industrial plants to dispense anything from a bar of candy to a steaming cup of coffee. Weighing machines tell fortunes along with the amount of a person's avoirdupois. Millions of dollars are invested in this equipment and much of it is insured under inland marine policies. (Insurance companies do not insure gambling machines or machines operated in defiance of the law.)

There is not a great deal of difference between machines in susceptibility to the kinds of damage covered under an insurance policy. The heavier machines, such as the drink and food dispensers, are difficult to handle and there is likelihood of damage in transportation. The transportation coverage usually includes protection against loss from collision or overturn of a transporting vehicle.

The policy should be specific regarding coverage during loading and unloading of the equipment. If it is not the intent of the insurance company to cover the loading and unloading hazard, the policy should so state in a carefully worded exclusion. On the other hand, if it is the intent to cover the hazard, it should be included as one of the specified perils. When loading and unloading damage is covered, it is a good idea to apply a deductible of $15 or $25 to this hazard in order to eliminate claims for minor scratches and dents that are in the nature of wear and tear.

Coverage at the location where the machine is in use usually includes protection against fire, lightning, windstorm, explosion, smoke, vehicles, and falling aircraft. Other hazards such as flood, water damage, and earthquake may be covered when the circumstances justify and if the insured is willing to pay a premium commensurate with the hazards.

Riot, civil commotion, strike, vandalism, and malicious mischief are not covered in most policies because of the extreme susceptibility of individual machines to such damage. Drink machines occasionally spill a cup onto the floor; some of the machines may jam; and an irate customer may damage the machine in retaliation. If the insured desires principally a catastrophe coverage, the policy may include a deductible approximately equal to the value of one machine.

Owners of smaller machines may desire theft coverage. This may be granted on the entire machine, but it is seldom feasible to grant pilferage coverage. Neither is it desirable to insure money. There may be frequent attempts to steal money from the machines, and such coverage may result in a large number of small claims. Policies usually exclude damage to the machine resulting from attempts to steal the money. The coverage could be granted if the insured is willing to pay a sufficient premium to cover a multitude of small losses. Most operators of these machines have their own repair shops and they are in a position to take care of such damage as an operating expense. These small losses may be eliminated by the use of a deductible on the theft coverage. The deductible may be 5 or 10 percent of the value of the machines, but not less than $25, if it is desired to keep the loss frequency at a reasonable level.

The rates for coverage on coin-operated machines are not filed and the company underwriter calculates the rate according to the hazard. The basic rate would be the fire and extended coverage rates for the type of property in which the machines are located. This requires the determining of an average rate if the machines are scattered throughout a community. A loading is then added to take care of the other hazards covered by the policy. Ordinarily there would not be a catastrophe hazard except where the machines are stored or repaired. The coverage may be continuous and may include the storage and repair locations as long as the storage is purely incidental to the regular and frequent use of the machines in other locations.

The underwriter needs to determine the maximum amount that might be exposed at any one location. If the amount is large, the fire rate at that location would have an important bearing on the final rate for the policy.

Office Machine Floaters. A floater policy may be issued to cover typewriters, adding machines, and other office equipment that is rented or loaned to others. There are no standard forms or rates for such a floater. The policy and rates would be developed by the underwriter to fit the needs of the owner.

Office equipment in use on the premises of the owner is not eligible for inland marine coverage. There is a multiple-line office contents policy which is part of the Special Multi-Peril policy program. The inland marine type of exposure to loss under that policy will be discussed in connection with multiple-line package policies.

II. CONTENTS OR STOCK FLOATERS

Floater policies on stocks of goods cover property that is not under the control of the owner or that may be at one or more of many different locations. The stock may be intended for sale ultimately when it reaches its destination or when certain processing steps are completed, but it is not ordinarily for sale at the time of coverage. It may have been sold and be on its way to delivery; it may be undergoing processing or for other reasons be in the hands of a bailee; or it may be property in a technical state of transportation, although in temporary storage during much of the policy term. Several of the important stock floaters are considered in this chapter.

Processing Risk Policies. Under the general heading of "processing risks" there are two types of insurable interest. The first is that of the owner of property in the hands of a contractor or subcontractor for the performance of some work or process. The second interest is the legal liability of the contractor or subcontractor as bailee for loss or damage to the goods. The latter type is more accurately called "processor's liability" insurance and is a form of bailee liability coverage. It will be discussed in the chapter on bailee liability and bailees' customers policies. The actual property covered by a processing risk policy and a processor's liability policy may be the same, but the insurable interest of the bailee is much different from that of the owner and will be discussed separately along with other bailee coverages.

The function of a processing risk policy is to cover the goods against loss or damage when they are sent out by the owner to the premises of others for processing. The owner's fire insurance policies may not cover the property when it leaves the premises described in the fire policy, and the owner frequently cannot depend on the processor's having insurance to cover it. The owner's need is for a policy that will cover him for loss during the transportation of the goods to and from the processor's premises and that will also cover the goods while they are on the premises of the processor. The fact that such property is subject to a transportation hazard makes it eligible for inland marine insurance.

The type of property intended to be classified for inland marine insurance is indicated by Section E. 2. (n) of the Nation-wide Marine Definition, which reads:

> Property in transit to or from and in the custody of
>
> 1 bleacheries, throwsters, fumigatories, dyers, cleaners, laundries and similar bailees;
>
> 2 needleworkers;
>
> 3 other bailees (not owned, controlled or operated by the bailor) for the purpose of performing work thereon (as distinguished from the making of a complete article) including the treatment of, or assemblage of property on the premises of bailees.
>
> Such policies shall not cover bailee's property at his premises.

Typical processes considered to come within the intent of the processor's risk definition are the annealing of metals and plastics, chroming of metal, degreasing of wool or leather, heat treating of metals, lithographing of paper, recapping of tires, sponging of cloth, and tanning of leather.

Garment contractors. Typical of such policies is the garment contractors floater. The name may be misleading because it is a policy issued to the owner of the property as well as to the garment contractor. The garment contractors floater has been standardized, and the coverage and procedures are typical for the insuring of garments in the hands of processors. Policies are adjusted by means of optional coverages to fit the needs of the insured. Coverages and rates vary widely with the nature of the property to be insured, the location and number of the processors, and the fire hazards at the processors' plants.

The garment contractors floater may be issued to the clothing manufacturer who lets out some of his work to others, or it may be issued to a contractor or subcontractor to cover his liability for loss while the property is in his custody. Originally a garment contractors policy was permitted to cover only while the property was away from the premises of the owner, either in transit or at the premises of a contractor or subcontractor. A majority of the states have now approved an extension of coverage to the premises of the owner of the property. This is a convenience to the owner because it permits him to cover all of his work in process under a single policy. In the states where this extension is not permitted, it is necessary for the manufacturer to have two policies, one covering on his premises and another to cover the property while it is in transit and on the premises of the contractor or subcontractor.

It is customary in the clothing business for a manufacturer to send the goods out to other plants for much of the work. Embroidery, buttonholes, pleating, putting on trimmings, inserting shoulder pads, and in some cases cutting and stitching material are all processes that may be done by specialists and not by the manufacturer himself.

The policy basically is a transportation floater, and the coverage while the goods are in transit is similar to that available under an annual transit form. The form filed by the rating bureaus covers property in transit against "all risks" of direct physical loss or damage from any external cause, subject to certain exclusions.

Property on the premises of contractors or subcontractors is covered against physical loss or damage caused by fire, lightning, sprinkler leakage, water damage (meaning actual contact with water), burglary, holdup, windstorm, hail, smoke, vehicle, aircraft, and boiler explosion.

Burglary is limited to felonious entry by force and violence when the premises are not open for business, and there has to be visible evidence of the forcible entry. Holdup includes the forcible taking of property by violence or threat of violence, or by an overt felonious act which is committed in the presence of the custodian and of which he is aware at the time it occurs. For example, if someone came in and grabbed the property and ran, getting away with it from the presence of the people in whose care it was located, the loss would be covered. If it were stolen or disappeared without there being any actual knowledge of the theft at the time it happened, it would not be covered. Mysterious disappearance is not covered.

Optional coverages that may be added for the payment of an extra premium include protection against loss from strikes, riots, malicious mischief, explosion, theft, and consequential loss.

Protection against loss by theft covers theft that could not be construed as burglary or holdup. The definition of "theft" specifically excludes loss resulting from conversion or dishonesty of the insured, contractors, subcontractors, or their employees, and from mysterious disappearance or shortage when there is no evidence that the loss was caused by theft.

In addition to the exclusions commonly found in inland marine insurance policies relating to war damage, loss resulting from infidelity of persons to whom the goods are entrusted, and loss due to the neglect of the insured, there are exclusions designed particularly for this policy. Loss resulting from delay or loss of market is excluded. The exclusion concerning gradual deterioration, insect, vermin, and inherent vice is expanded to exclude loss from chafing and rubbing.

There is provision for expanding the coverage to "all risks of direct physical loss of or damage to the property covered." The exclusions are essentially the same as those just described. The only additional exclusion of consequence refers to loss from any process or treatment or while the property is being worked upon unless there is fire or explosion. In this case the fire or explosion loss is covered. Mysterious disappearance, unexplained loss, and shortage disclosed on taking inventory are specifically excluded.

Damage as the result of a consequential loss may be severe in the garment trades. For example, a manufacturer of men's suits may send the coats out to have the buttonholes put in. Since there are few buttonholes in the trousers, the trousers may not be sent out from the manufacturer's place of business or perhaps may be sent to a different contractor for other work. If the coats are destroyed, the trousers lose much of their value, because it may not be possible to sell them for as much independently as they are worth as parts of suits.

The garment contractors floater can be extended to cover this consequential loss to portions of garments resulting from the damage or destruction of other portions of the garments. Under this coverage, the company pays the difference between its liability for loss of the entire garments and the realizable value of the undamaged portions. The insured is obligated to try for at least 21 days to replace the lost or damaged portions before the company is obligated to pay the loss. The company has the option of taking the undamaged portions in case it pays a consequential loss. An extra premium is charged for this coverage.

Garment contractors business is divided into the following four divisions for rating purposes:

1. Women's wear consisting of cloaks, suits, jackets, skirts and dresses, made of one or more parts, including fur and fur-trimmed garments when insured under this form of policy.
2. Men's and boys' wear except types of property not subject to these rules (as described below).
3. Other women's wear, except types of property not subject to these rules.
4. All policies covering liability to property insurable under a garment contractors floater.

Certain articles that are considered clothing in a practical sense are excluded from the garment contractors rules because the hazards and customs of manufacturing them are different from those of the garment trades. Leggings, spats, cartridge belts, knapsacks, canteen covers, leather or canvas containers, bags, purses, bedding, hosiery, footwear, headwear, umbrellas, walking sticks, and jewelry including costume jewelry, when being processed, are not subject to the garment contractors rules and rates. (If eligible for insurance under an inland marine form, such articles may be insured according to the judgment of the underwriter.)

Rates for garment contractors policies are quoted by the inland marine rating bureaus upon submission of a completed application by a member or subscriber company. Independent companies use much the same schedule for rating as that used by the bureaus. The rates are based upon the average fire insurance rate of all the contractors used by the insured for more than a period of 30 days during the year preceding the application for rate. If the insured has been in business less than 30 days, the rate is based on the average fire insurance rate of the contractors whom the insured intends to use. The rates are set up in brackets according to the average fire insurance rate, the amount of insurance, and the types of garments being made. The highest rated group is women's wear, on which the rate can be as high as 6 percent of the value. From this figure the rates vary downward to less than one dollar per $100 for the top bracket of a large policy amount on men's wear. All rates contemplate 100 percent insurance to value, and the policy contains a full contribution clause applying to all goods in the hands of contractors at the time any loss occurs.

Film Floaters–Video Tape. Two types of property are insured under motion picture film floaters. The first type consists of motion picture positive films, which are used for projection. Many organizations that rent out motion picture films for educational or promotional purposes carry transportation insurance policies to cover the films when they are outside their own premises. The policies cover the films from the time they are put in the custody of the Post Office Department or in the hands of a common carrier, while they are being exhibited, and until they are returned to the insured. Television or "video" tapes that are rented and shipped may also be insured. This form of floater policy covering films or tapes is a transportation floater, which has been discussed. There are no bureau filings and the companies develop their forms and rates as they do for other transportation floaters.

A person or firm which has films or tapes in its custody for the purpose of exhibiting them may insure them. This is a form of bailee coverage and will be discussed later in this text.

The second type of motion picture film insurance covers negatives and is more complicated. It is the insuring of the original negative during and after a motion picture production is being made. A full-length motion picture production may cost anywhere from a few hundred thousand to several million dollars. From the time the production starts until it is completed and the positive prints for projection are made, the entire cost of the production is wrapped up in the negatives that have been made. Should they be destroyed, it would be necessary to make the whole production over again and almost the entire cost would be duplicated.

Insurance on the negatives is not for the mere value of the film or tape itself but for the cost of the production up to the time of the loss. The insurance may run into millions of dollars by the time the production is finished. The policy may require that weekly reports of values be given to the insurance company so that adequate reinsurance may be arranged.

The coverage under this type of policy is broad and usually is against "all risks of physical loss or damage from any external cause," subject to a few exclusions. The usual war damage exclusion appears, and this is important in its provisions relating to seizure or destruction under quarantine or customs regulations, confiscation by order of any government or public authority, or risks of contraband or illegal trade. Another exclusion is designed for insurance on this type of property. It excludes loss or damage caused by or resulting from exposure of negative film to light, the use of developing chemicals, or the developing, cutting, or printing of film or other laboratory work, deterioration, atmospheric dampness, or changes of temperature. This exclusion is amplified when magnetic or video tape is insured to exclude loss or damage resulting from electrical or magnetic injury, disturbance, or erasure, except by lightning.

There is also the usual exclusion which appears in inland marine policies applying to loss by nuclear reaction, nuclear radiation, or radioactive contamination.

Sound tracks and records are insured if they are part of the production. The policy may cover the property of the insured and also property for which he is legally liable. No coverage is provided for cut-out film, unused footage, or library stock.

In determining the amount of any loss, the cost of the story, scenario, music rights, continuity, permanent sets, owned wardrobe, and props are deducted because these items would not have to be reproduced in order to remake the film.

Each policy covers a specifically named production. The insured must give full information to the insurance company regarding the studios, laboratories, vaults, and cutting rooms used in connection with the production, the estimated cost (or periodical reports of value for a reporting form), and full information regarding ownership and any mortgagee interest.

Rules and forms for the coverage have been filed by the Inland Marine Insurance Bureau. It is required that all proposals be submitted to the Bureau for rating when IMIB members and subscribers wish to write the coverage. The fire insurance and extended coverage rates are important factors in the calculation of the rate applying to such property. Loadings must be added when coverage extends beyond studios, laboratories, vaults, and cutting rooms.

Wool Growers. The growers of wool need a continuous insurance coverage from the time the sheep are sheared until the wool reaches the purchaser. This may take several months, during which the wool may be in several warehouses. The time of layover in any location is likely to be indefinite, and it would be difficult for the owner to keep track of the exact location of the wool at all times and to arrange for specific location coverage each time the wool is moved. The wool growers' floater is basically a transportation policy and covers during transportation and while in warehouses incidental thereto.

The coverage starts at the shearing barn or corral where the wool is removed from the sheep, or where the pelt is removed from the carcass. It is continuous from that point as long as it is at the risk of the insured and until delivery to the premises of a buyer, or the warehouse designated by a buyer.

The coverage at the shearing barn, corral, or warehouse is against loss or damage directly caused by fire, lightning, cloudburst, flood, and explosion.

While on land conveyances, the wool is insured against loss or damage directly caused by fire, lightning, cloudburst, flood, collision, upset or overturn of the conveying vehicle, or collapse of bridges. Flood is defined as the rising of navigable waters, but under special circumstances the bureau may permit extending this to include overflow or breaking of boundaries of ponds, lakes, streams, or arroyos.

While waterborne, the wool is insured against loss or damage directly caused by fire, lightning, stranding, sinking, burning, or collision of vessel or craft with any external substance (ice included) other than water. However, all ocean or coastwise shipments are excluded.

Other coverages that may be added for the payment of an extra premium are tornado and windstorm, theft (either in transit or while at a shearing plant or warehouse), strike, riot, and civil commotion.

Policies may be written for auctioneers and warehousemen and for growers' associations as well as for growers. There must be a transportation hazard in order for it to qualify as an inland marine risk.

Rates and forms have been filed applicable to the coverage in the principal wool growing states. The rates vary according to territory, and according to the coverage granted. They range from $1.30 to more than $2.00 per $100 of value, and contemplate full insurance to value.

Cotton. The insuring of baled cotton is similar in many respects to the insuring of wool. Policies cover from the time the cotton is weighed at the gin in the town adjacent to the plantation until the cotton is delivered to the purchaser. This delivery may take place many months later, and the delivery may be in a foreign country.

The insuring of cotton provided one of the early cases of ocean marine insurance coverage being extended to a land hazard. Much of the cotton insurance is ocean marine insurance because the cotton is shipped by water to overseas ports. As a matter of fact, insurance on baled cotton usually is under a marine form of policy, without any designation of whether it is inland or ocean marine. Part of the cotton insured may be destined finally for a foreign country and part may be shipped to a mill in the United States.

The baling of American cotton long has been considered inferior to that done in other parts of the world. The result is that bales are more often damaged to a considerable extent in transit, and insurance companies have paid for this as a transit loss. It is called "country damage," although it may be damage largely resulting from poor baling. The fact that the insurers have paid for such damage has retarded efforts to improve baling methods.

Cotton buyers' transit insurance. One form of cotton insurance that has been standardized and for which the Inland Marine Insurance Bureau has made filings is cotton buyers' transit insurance. Cotton may be owned by several persons between the time it is harvested and the time it is processed. Much cotton is purchased by professional buyers who hold the cotton for resale to manufacturers or exporters. These cotton buyers need insurance coverage to protect them from loss in case the cotton is destroyed by some accident or catastrophe.

The buyers' transit form provides continuous coverage until canceled. It covers cotton in bales of United States or Mexican growth while in the United States and Canada, and while owned by the insured or legally at his risk under contract of purchase or sale. It does not cover cotton held by the insured as bailee. Such cotton can be insured under a marine or inland marine policy, but the buyers' transit filings do not apply to such cotton.

The coverage is against "all risks" of physical loss or damage from any external cause except:

1. Country damage.
2. Influx of rising waters occasioned by rains on cotton stored in the open.
3. War damage (The exclusion is in the terms usual to inland marine policies).
4. Cotton while waterborne.
5. Cotton not yet delivered to the insured and not identified in a specified manner as intended for him.
6. Cotton for which bailees are liable under certain conditions.
7. Cotton linters or hull fibres.
8. Cotton in course of delivery to purchasers by land carriers if delivery is stopped or delayed by the insured or the purchaser except under certain conditions.
9. Nuclear damage.

The insured is covered for loss of cotton which he owns or for which he is legally responsible under contract of purchase or sale. As to cotton that the insured has contracted to sell, he usually has the privilege of issuing certificates of insurance as soon as the cotton has been delivered to the land carrier that is to transport it.

The policy contains detailed provisions for determining the amount to be paid in case of loss. The amount of loss is based on market values as determined by quotations in the cotton markets. The insurance company has the right to replace the cotton if it desires to do so.

Variations of coverage and in the methods of valuing the property are provided for in the filings. The rates are developed from schedules which are filed. The rates vary according to the location of the cotton, the optional coverages which may be included, and the fire protection available.

Cotton buyers' transit insurance and other forms of inland marine coverage on cotton are handled mostly by syndicates that specialize in this type of coverage. Because company inland marine underwriters do not often have occasion to handle the details of such coverage, this discussion has been confined to a brief summary of the needs of the insured and the means of meeting these needs.

Accounts Receivable Insurance. A large part of the assets of commercial establishments may consist of accounts receivable. The destruction of the records might make it difficult or impossible to collect these accounts, because the firm could not determine who owed them money. Fire insurance companies offer insurance against destruction of such records by fire, windstorm, and the other hazards usually insured against by fire insurance companies. Casualty insurance companies sell insurance against the loss of such records by theft or burglary.

Some policyholders feel that they need a broader protection than that available through the fire and casualty departments of the insurance companies, and they also prefer to have the coverage provided in a single policy. Inland marine underwriters have been willing to provide a broad coverage on such records. In most cases this is not a transportation coverage because the records remain at one location and are not subject to transit hazards. The 1953 Nation-wide Marine Definition recognizes accounts receivable insurance as an inland marine coverage. Filings of rules, rates, and forms have been made by the inland marine rating bureaus. The coverage is also recognized as a casualty coverage, and similar filings have been made by the casualty rating bureaus.

Accounts receivable insurance is really a consequential loss coverage. It is intended to cover, not the physical value of the records themselves, but the amount of money the insured would be unable to collect because the records were destroyed.

The coverage applies to sums due the insured from customers, interest charges on any loan necessary to offset slow collections resulting from an insured loss, any collection expenses above normal collection expense, and other expenses incurred in re-establishing records of accounts receivable. The perils insured against are "all risks of loss of or damage to the insured's records of accounts receivable," except as excluded.

The policy contains a war damage and a nuclear exclusion similar to those which appear in other inland marine policies. There are also exclusions referring to dishonest or criminal acts of the insured or an official of the insured; to falsification of records; to accounting errors; to loss depending upon an audit or inventory for proof that a loss occurred; and to loss from electrical or magnetic injury of electronic records, except by lightning.

Loss settlements are a problem if the records are destroyed to such an extent that the insured cannot determine accurately what his uncollectible accounts are. The policy provides a method of estimating the accounts receivable based upon the experience of the previous year. The insured is obligated to make collection efforts to the best of his knowledge and ability. The insurance company pays any unusual collection expenses that may be incurred in reducing the amount of the loss. The insurance company pays any extra expenses incurred in conditioning the records so that they can be read and used for collection purposes.

The rates for the coverage vary according to the safe in which the records are kept, whether duplicate records are kept at another location, the construction of the building, the fire protection, and the coverage provided by the policy. The rate frequently is about one-half of what it would be for similar coverage on actual goods. That is, if the rate on the contents of the building is $1.00, the rate on the accounts receivable might be about 50 cents. This rate is applied to the amount of outstanding accounts receivable. Policies usually are written on a reporting basis. The insured reports at the end of each month the amount of his outstanding accounts receivable and pays a premium on that amount.

Valuable Papers and Records. Many types of records and other valuable papers resemble fine arts in that they have a value beyond the physical worth. Blueprints, architectural plans, manuscripts, deeds, maps, and historical documents either are irreplaceable or cannot be replaced without the expenditure of large sums of money. This value represents an insurable interest which may be covered by the valuable papers and records policy.

The Nation-wide Marine Definition recognizes this as an inland marine coverage, and the rating bureaus have made filings of rates, rules, and forms. It is also considered to be a casualty coverage, and the casualty rating bureaus also have made similar filings.

The property covered by the policy is divided into two groups. Property that cannot be replaced with other property of like kind and quality must be specifically listed with a value assigned to each item. This follows the practice in connection with the insuring of fine arts (which will be described later in this text). It is intended that this method be followed in covering historical documents and other papers or records that cannot be replaced and for which the value must be determined in advance of any loss. The second section provides a blanket coverage for papers and records that can be replaced. A blanket coverage is feasible for such property because it has a commercial value that can be determined even after the property has been destroyed.

The coverage is against "all risks of direct physical loss of or damage to the property covered," with the following exceptions:

Wear and tear, deterioration, vermin and inherent vice.

War damage, in terms of the customary inland marine exclusion.

Dishonest or fraudulent loss due to the act of any insured, partner, officer, director or trustee.

Property held as samples or for sale or for delivery after sale.

Nuclear reaction, nuclear radiation or radioactive contamination.

Errors or omissions in processing or copying unless fire or explosion ensues and then only for the loss caused by the fire or explosion.

Electrical or magnetic injury to electronic recordings, except by lightning.

Rates are based primarily on the fire insurance rate at the location where the property is kept. A loading is added for the hazards covered in addition to fire. Credits are allowed for the use of safes or vaults as storage places.

Underwriting must take into account the fire hazard to the premises, and the protection afforded to the property by safes or vaults. If the property would be attractive to burglars, the protection against theft must also be considered. A limited amount of coverage applies while the property is away from the premises named in the policy. If portions of the property are transferred frequently to other locations, this may involve a transit exposure which affects the desirability of the risk.

Miscellaneous Floater Policies. An important and desirable feature of inland marine insurance is its facility for insuring any type of property that may be subject to a transit hazard. Modern transportation is so flexible that huge structures can be carried from their place of manufacture to any part of the country. The requirements of commerce and trade are such that these objects must be insured, and the inland marine underwriter is able to fill the need. It is impossible to make a rate schedule to fit the many objects that must be insured; indeed, it would be impossible to list them. A few examples will serve to illustrate the need and the methods used by underwriters to fill it.

Huge electrical transformers for power stations are built at the factory and are transported by motor truck or by special railroad flatcar to the place of installation. The transportation may take a week or two and the value may amount to many thousands of dollars. Individual pieces of machinery, which are shipped frequently, may cost $20,000 to $50,000 each.

Machinery frequently is loaned or rented, and the insurance may cover from the time it leaves the owner's premises, while on location, and during return to the owner's premises. Exhibits of various kinds, such as expensive advertising pieces, are insured during transit to and from the place of exhibition, and also while at the exhibition. The hazards and length of each trip are different, and the exposures at various temporary locations are seldom precisely the same. The susceptibility of the property to damage is calculated by the underwriter.

With the growth of television, there is a need for insurance on television cameras which may cost many thousands of dollars. Many of them are not portable cameras in the sense that they can be carried easily from place to place, but they are demountable and are moved about and set up as the need arises.

The underwriter of an unusual transit risk determines his chances of a total loss from an examination of all factors involved in movement of the property. The chances of numerous partial losses are taken into account. From the combination of the two, he can arrive at what he believes is an adequate premium for the risk to be taken. If there is to be a location hazard at any point (as in the case of a television camera installed at a football or baseball stadium for the season), the fire and windstorm hazards are taken into account.

It is in the handling of insurance for these unusual properties that the inland marine underwriter finds the greatest interest of the business, and it is here that his experience and judgment mean profit or loss to his company. There are no formulas or schedules for making rates for such policies, and a good underwriter is the company's hope of securing a satisfactory experience on them.

Radioactive Contamination Insurance. Most inland marine policies exclude loss from nuclear hazards and radioactive contamination. This exclusion is considered necessary because (1) the nuclear and radioactive hazards are so new that underwriters have difficulty in evaluating the chances of loss, and (2) the exposure to such losses varies widely from one situation to another. Most property insured under inland marine policies does not ordinarily have any nuclear or radioactive contamination exposure. Therefore, the simplest way to reduce inland marine risks to a common base for underwriting and rating is to exclude these hazards.

Inland marine underwriters recognize that the property of some policyholders does have a radioactive contamination exposure. It is considered good practice to cover this possibility of loss, but under a special policy. This allows a proper control of underwriting and of rating this hazard.

The rating bureau filings contain rules, rates, and forms to provide radioactive contamination insurance on property which is also covered by an inland marine policy in the same company. The bureau filing is restricted by its terms to use in conjunction with an inland marine policy covering the same property against other perils. The filing also provides that radioactive contamination insurance must follow the bureau filings when written on property for which the bureau has other filings in effect.

A company may write radioactive contamination insurance according to its own desires for an inland marine class if there are no bureau filings applicable. For example, a company could add this coverage to a motor truck cargo policy or to a transit policy if it wishes to do so.

The bureau filing permits a policy to cover only within a named building or part thereof, and only in the building or part which is occupied by the insured or a bailee to whom the property is entrusted. The purpose of the policy is to provide radioactive contamination coverage for property that is being processed in a building where radioactive materials are present. The radioactive exposure which is intended to be covered by this insurance is from radioisotopes. These are used to an increasing extent in manufacturing and processing. Their presence in a building creates a possibility of accidental radioactive contamination to other property in the building. The policy covers only loss or damage to property which is within a building designated in the policy and only on the floor and within a section of such building designated in the policy. The coverage is against sudden and accidental radioactive contamination except as excluded.

The entire policy is void if at the time of loss or damage there is on the premises either a nuclear reactor capable of sustaining nuclear fission in a self-supporting chain reaction or any new or used nuclear fuel which is intended for or which has been used in such a nuclear reaction. This is a serious type of nuclear exposure which is not contemplated in this coverage. The insurance of the more serious nuclear exposures is handled by special groups of insurance companies with facilities for evaluation of nuclear risks.

The exclusions include several provisions that are common to inland marine policies, such as the war risk exclusion; the exclusion of loss due to delay, loss of use, loss of market, or interruption of business; and exclusion of loss due to neglect of the insured to save and preserve the property at and after a loss. There is a specific exclusion of loss from seizure, destruction, or confiscation by order of any public authority. This is in addition to the similar provision in the war risk exclusion. There is also an exclusion of loss from gradual accumulation of radioactive contamination.

Coinsurance is required in the same percentage as in the inland marine policy which covers the property for other perils, but in any case not less than 80 percent.

The proposal which must be completed by the prospective insured is in considerable detail and is several pages long. The information is required for both rating and underwriting purposes. A signed copy of the proposal is attached to and is made a part of the policy. This is comparable to the similar requirement for jewelers' block policies. These representations by the insured are very important, and any misrepresentation is intended to void the policy.

The calculation of the rate is a complicated procedure. The company calculates the rate according to a schedule which is part of the bureau filing. Factors which affect the rate include the kinds and strengths of the radioisotopes, the proportions of sealed and unsealed radioisotopes, and the presence in the property covered of certain occupancies which are considered highly susceptible.

III. CONSIGNMENT AND SALES FLOATERS

A variation of the stock or contents floaters is the group of policies that insure goods in connection with sales of merchandise or equipment. They insure property from the time it leaves the premises of the insured until his interest ceases. The goods may be (1) on consignment, (2) under a conditional bill of sale, or (3) encumbered by a loan. The insured may be the seller or a lending agency.

Inland marine insurance is desirable because there is a transit hazard during shipment and it may be difficult for the insured to determine his values at individual locations as he would have to do for a fire and extended coverage policy. Some of these policies are basically transportation floaters and others are specially designed for the risk to be insured. They will be discussed with particular attention to the peculiarities of each.

Consignment Floaters. The Nation-wide Marine Definition states that a shipment "on consignment" shall mean "property consigned and intrusted to a factor or agent to be held in his care, or under his control for sale for account of another, or for exhibit or trial or approval or auction, and if not disposed of, to be returned."

Imports on consignment may be covered by an inland marine policy without restriction of time and place just so long as the insurance coverage includes the hazards of transportation. Domestic shipments on consignment for sale or distribution may be insured under an inland marine policy, according to the Definition, while in transit and for not more than 120 days after arrival at the consignee's premises or other place of storage or deposit. Goods on consignment for exhibit, trial, auction, or approval may be covered without limitation of time so long as they are in the custody of someone other than the owner or are being returned.

The coverage on goods on consignment would be the same as that under transportation policies previously discussed. These policies go beyond the scope of transportation policies in that they also cover the property while it is temporarily at a fixed location. In that respect they are stock or contents policies.

The interest of the consignee is that of a bailee. The insurance of the bailee interests will be considered later in this text.

Installment or Conditional Sales–Deferred Payment. A large proportion of merchandise and equipment sales are on a time payment basis. Everything from a watch to a million-dollar railroad train can be purchased on installments. In many cases the transaction is by means of a conditional bill of sale under which the purchaser does not acquire title to the property until the last installment has been paid. The seller has the right to repossess the property if the payments are not met.

The ultimate safety of the seller's money is dependent upon his being able to get the property back in case of default. Destruction of the property from any cause means that the seller can no longer take it back. In many cases the purchaser would be unwilling to continue payments if the property were destroyed. Therefore, the seller needs to insure the property so that he can collect from the insurance company in case the property is destroyed.

Inland marine policies may cover property sold under conditional contract of sale, partial payment contract, or installment sales contract. Leased property that is mobile in character may be insured under an inland marine policy if title remains in the lessor.

Inland marine policies covering such installment sales, partial payment, or leased property must cover the property while it is in transit and they may not cover beyond the termination of the insured's interest. Policies may be issued to a retailer or manufacturer who sells or leases the property, and they also may be issued to banks or finance companies that finance the sales.

The property must be under sale or lease contract. Property that is sold on open account without a written contract is not considered eligible for deferred payment floater coverage.

There are three types of installment sales insurance coverage. Under the first type, the interest of the merchant or bank which is the insured is covered against loss by certain specified perils. If a loss that is covered by this policy occurs, the unpaid balance is paid by the insurance company and the purchaser's debt is canceled, but the purchaser's interest above the unpaid balance is not covered.

Under the second type, the insured's interest is covered, but the insured agrees not to release the purchaser from his obligation and agrees to make all reasonable efforts to collect the money even though the property is destroyed. The purchaser receives no benefit from this policy. It is sometimes called the "contingent" form of installment sales floater. These two types of installment sales floaters are single interest forms. They cover only the single interest of the seller or the financial institution.

The third type of coverage is a double interest form and not only covers the unpaid balance but also covers the purchaser's interest and pays him for his loss. In many states it is permissible for the insurance company to arrange with the seller to issue certificates of coverage to the purchaser when the purchaser's interest is insured. In all cases, however, the coverage expires with the final payment and the cessation of the seller's interest.

Most installment sales policies insure against loss by fire and lightning while the property is on the premises of the purchaser. Windstorm, explosion, riot, civil commotion, vehicle, smoke, and falling aircraft damage may be covered. While the property is in transit, it is protected against the perils usually covered under a transit policy, such as collision or overturn of the transporting vehicle, collapse of bridges, windstorm, flood, and fire and lightning.

Theft insurance may be provided during transit, particularly if the transit is partly or wholly by common carrier, but theft coverage is not often provided for property on the insured's own trucks. Burglary coverage on the premises of the purchaser may be provided, but the policy usually is worded to exclude loss by concealment or conversion on the part of the purchaser. The granting of conversion coverage might enable the insured to relax his care in the selection of customers.

When the merchandise consists of musical instruments, breakage coverage may be included applying to losses in excess of a deductible figure of $25. When the policy is issued to a jeweler, a broader form may be written to include loss of stones from settings. Burglary and theft may be included in such a policy, but seldom does it insure against loss by mysterious disappearance.

The installment sales floater fits in well with a jewelers' block policy, because the jewelers' block policy does not cover property sold on the installment plan. The jeweler needs the installment sales policy to complete his protection.

Exclusions are those common to transit policies and usually also exclude loss occurring on any premises owned or controlled by the merchant or the financial organization, which is the insured. The clause excluding damage from artificially generated electrical currents is important in the case of television sets and other electrical equipment.

Rates are based primarily on the average contents fire rates for the type of buildings in which the insured property is located. If the property being sold by the merchant consists of television and household appliances, the average dwelling contents rate in the sales territory would be the basis of the rate. To this would be added a sufficient loading to take care of the transit hazards and of the other perils covered.

Rates for the "contingent" form under which the insured agrees not to release the purchaser from his obligation to pay in case of loss, are usually from one-half to two-thirds of the rates for other types of policies. This is justifiable because the insurance company does not anticipate many losses under this type of policy. Losses would be paid only when the purchaser had disappeared following loss or when the seller was unable to collect from him.

Installment sales policies are written on an open basis with the insured making periodical reports, usually monthly, to the insurance company. If the policy covers the insured's interest only, the monthly report states the amount of the unpaid balances. If the policy is a double interest form and covers the interest of the purchaser as well as that of the insured, the amount reported must be the total value of all the property covered by the policy. The rate stated in the policy is applied to the value reported, and the insured pays premium monthly according to the amount reported.

Underwriting of installment sales floaters takes into account the possibility of catastrophe losses. A tornado or conflagration could wipe out a large part of a community where the insured has sold quantities of merchandise. Policies usually contain a catastrophe limit, and they may also contain a limit per sale or per customer. The standing of the insured in his business is examined by the underwriter, because his customers probably are no better prospects for insurance than the dealer himself. The probabilities of loss depend largely upon the integrity of the insured and his care in selecting the customers with whom he will execute conditional sales contracts or leases.

Installation Floater. Like the installment sales floater, the installation floater involves property sold by the policyholder. The installation floater, however, covers only during a period of installation. The purpose is to insure the work and materials put in by the insured before the work is completed and accepted by the purchaser. The property covered usually is a large installation that takes weeks or months to complete. Typical properties are electrical generators and power stations, elevators in skyscraper buildings, newspaper printing equipment, and air conditioning equipment in industrial or theatre buildings.

Building materials such as structural steel, lumber, bricks and mortar may be insured under an inland marine policy while in transit to a place of installation and after arrival. However, such materials are not considered to be eligible for inland marine coverage after they have been installed and are a physical part of the realty. The machinery and equipment that are insurable under an inland marine installation floater may also become a part of the realty, but a distinction is drawn between such property and ordinary building materials.

Smaller installations may be covered also when the insured is engaged in making many installations of a similar character in widely scattered areas. Typical of these insureds is a company that installs grain driers in grain elevators. The installation is not a lengthy job, but there is considerable exposure of materials and equipment from the time they leave the insured's factory until each unit is installed completely and tested.

The coverage under an installation floater policy is suited to the needs of the insured. Fire, windstorm, hail, explosion, riot, and civil commotion coverage frequently are needed. The installation may also require protection against loss by earthquake and perhaps flood. Conditions of the policy follow those of the transportation policy, to which the installation form usually is attached.

A 100 percent coinsurance clause generally is included so that the insured will report full values and not take a chance that he will suffer only a partial loss. Exclusions are so worded that the company is not liable for careless work on the part of the contractor.

When many identical properties are insured for a contractor, a reporting form of policy may be written. The insured reports each installation and the values as they are accumulated. The premium can be based on the total value of all the installations made during the policy term. As each installation is accepted by the purchaser, its value is deducted from the amount at risk.

In the case of larger installations, it is customary to write a specific policy on each installation, for large values are sufficient to justify separate policies. The values are reported weekly or monthly as the work progresses. The insured's total investment in labor and materials is to be reported even though he believes that only a part of his investment could be destroyed by a catastrophe. The rates are based upon full insurance to value.

The rates are computed from two factors: the transportation hazard and the hazard at the location. The transportation hazard depends upon the susceptibility of the materials to damage during transit, the method of transportation, and the length of the haul. The rate for this is calculated in much the same way as for other transit policies.

The rate at the location is based upon the rates for similar coverages at the building where the installation is being made, plus a loading for any hazards for which location rates are not available. A great deal of judgment is necessary in fixing the rate on a large installation for which there is no precedent. The hazard of loading and unloading is particularly troublesome, and many underwriters hesitate to give such coverage unless they know that the contractor is an expert in handling the type of equipment and materials that are going into the job.

Many installations have provisions for a test period of from 30 to 90 days before the purchaser is obligated to make payment. The coverage continues in effect during this period but must cease when the insured's interest ceases.

It is possible for such an installation to be paid for on an installment payment plan. In such cases, there might be a need for a combination installation and installment sales policy. It is likely, however, that expensive installations would be financed through some financial institution and not by direct payment to the contractor. An installment sales policy may be written for the financing institution after the installation is complete and ready for acceptance by the purchaser.

Dealers' Floaters. It is customary for dealers in many types of equipment to demonstrate equipment and occasionally to permit trial use by a prospective purchaser. The values of such equipment may run to several thousand dollars per unit. The dealer needs a floater type insurance coverage on this property. He may have many thousands of dollars' worth of equipment off his premises, and his premises insurance coverage might not take care of a loss to such property.

An inland marine policy can be written to cover the property that the dealer may have away from his premises and subject to loss. The form covers not only property owned and held for sale by the dealer but also equipment held in trust or on commission or consignment. The form usually is written to include property that the insured may have in his possession for alteration or repairs. In this respect the policy provides bailee coverage, although the principal amount at risk ordinarily is the property owned and held for sale.

The hazards normally covered by such policies are those of fire, lightning, windstorm, explosion, vehicle, falling aircraft, riot, civil commotion, and transportation. Collision, overturn, and collapse of bridges or culverts constitute the principal transportation coverages. Theft of an entire machine or shipping package frequently is covered, but most forms exclude loss by pilferage as well as by embezzlement or conversion.

The territorial limits usually are those of the continental United States and Canada, and they may exclude Alaska and the Yukon Territory. The exclusions provide that the policy does not cover in any place of business owned, leased, or controlled by the insured. This exclusion is necessary to make the form acceptable according to the Nation-wide Definition. The exclusion also may provide that the coverage does not apply at any place of sale, display, or storage at which the insured property has been situated for more than 30 consecutive days. This provides an off-premises and transit coverage, in contrast to the equipment dealers' policy which covers both on and off the insured's premises.

The form may be extended to include coverage on home appliances. This is not intended to cover ordinary hardware, but rather the heavier type of home appliances, such as refrigerators and stoves.

Rates for the coverage vary somewhat according to the property to be covered. The rate is somewhat higher for home appliances because of their greater susceptibility to damage. A small dent or scratch acquired during delivery would not affect the sale of a plow or tractor, but the same injury to a refrigerator or stove might require repair of the damage and a resultant claim.

One bureau has a filing of a Hardware and Implement Dealers' Floater which is used to provide floater coverage for dealers in implements and household appliances. However, most of these dealers' floaters are written according to rates and forms which are devised by the companies.

It is important that the insured understand thoroughly the nature of the coverage and the fact that it covers only outside his own premises. Many companies write the form only if the fire and extended coverage policy on the stock of merchandise is in the same company. This eliminates any difficulty as to which company pays a loss if it occurs during the transition period from storage to a transit condition.

When the amount of repair business is large, companies sometimes issue a separate policy covering the bailee liability so that an accurate report can be kept on the exposure under the bailee hazard. The amount of insurance under the dealers' form is the estimated largest amount that will be needed at any time during the year.

QUESTIONS

1. What principles are followed in the Nation-wide Marine Definition in the conditions under which floater policies may cover property?
2. What are some of the hazards to which contractors' equipment may be subject?
3. Discuss whether a farmer needs broad coverage insurance on his equipment and livestock.
4. Tell what underwriting safeguards you would establish for the writing of insurance on signs.
5. How would you establish the rate for a group of vending machines?
6. Why does the radium floater policy require that notice of loss be given by telephone or telegraph?
7. What is a major cause of loss under salesmen's sample floater policies?
8. Outline the procedure used by inland marine underwriters in arriving at the rate to be charged for a floater coverage for which there are no manual rates.
9. What is meant by a "consequential loss" under a garment contractor's policy?
10. Why are the insurable values so high under a motion picture negative insurance policy?

11. Discuss the cotton buyers' and the wool growers' need for continuous insurance coverage from the time the cotton or wool is prepared for market until its arrival at destination.
12. Why do inland marine underwriters feel it is unwise to provide conversion coverage in an installment sales floater?
13. Distinguish between an installment sales floater and an installation floater.
14. Describe the coverage of an accounts receivable policy and tell how it differs from the property coverage of most inland marine policies.
15. Tell what inland marine policies you think a dealer in hardware and farm implements should have, and explain why you picked that particular group of policies.
16. Discuss the logic of providing a broad coverage inland marine policy for the entire equipment of a physician's or surgeon's office and not doing it for other professional men.

14

Instrumentalities of Transportation

The Nation-wide Marine Definition provides that a policy covering the following kinds of property may be classified as marine or inland marine:

> Bridges, tunnels and other instrumentalities of transportation and communication (excluding buildings, their furniture and furnishings, fixed contents and supplies held in storage) unless fire, tornado, sprinkler leakage, hail, explosion, earthquake, riot and/or civil commotion are the only hazards to be covered. Piers, wharves, docks and slips, excluding the risks of fire, tornado, sprinkler leakage, hail, explosion, earthquake, riot and/or civil commotion. Other aids to navigation and transportation, including dry docks and marine railways, against all risks.

The Definition goes on to explain that the foregoing includes such property as bridges and tunnels, piers, wharves, docks and slips, pipelines, power transmission and telephone and telegraph lines, radio and television equipment, and outdoor cranes. It is evident that most of these "instrumentalities of transportation and communication" are structures that do not move in the performance of their intended functions.

Other instrumentalities of transportation which actually are movable may also be insured under inland marine policies. These include such property as railway cars and equipment, horses and wagons, and boats. The Nation-wide Marine Definition includes such property in the general classification of "mobile articles . . . property of a mobile or floating nature, not on sale or consignment, or in course of manufacture, which has come into the custody or the control of parties who intend to use such property for the purpose for which it was manufactured or created."

The consideration of instrumentalities of transportation may be divided into three sections. The first section considers those properties defined by the Nation-wide Marine Definition as instrumentalities of transportation and includes those structures that may be insured under an inland marine policy. The second section considers what may be termed "land hulls" and includes property that acts as a carrier of other property. The third section would be those marine hulls and vessels for which ocean marine or inland marine insurance may be provided, as already described.

I. STRUCTURES

Bridges, tunnels, and like structures are similar to buildings in their nature and logically would be insured in the same manner as other fixed structures. Bridges and tunnels are insured under inland marine policies because the fire departments of insurance companies did not meet the needs of bridge and tunnel owners. Bridges and tunnels are subject to many hazards that do not threaten ordinary buildings, and only an "all risks" type of insurance policy affords adequate protection.

Fire and windstorm losses to such structures have occurred frequently. Bridges have suffered serious damage from ice jams that form upstream of a bridge and exert tremendous pressure on the structure. Floods are likely to cause damage when the waters carry debris, or the waters may undermine the footing and piers. Bridges across navigable streams are subject to collision damage from passing ships. Earthquake is a serious threat in some parts of the country and is a possibility in any part of the United States. The severest earthquake ever to strike the United States occurred in the lower Missouri River valley a little over 100 years ago. Structural damage was slight only because there were few structures in the area at that time.

The fire insurance departments of the companies were not familiar with "all risks" insurance and were not favorable toward writing such coverage on bridges. Marine underwriters approached the question of insuring bridges in much the same way they looked at the insuring of vessels or property in transit. They were familiar with "all risks" insurance and were willing to extend the coverage to a new type of property. Lloyd's of London was among the first to write insurance on bridges under an "all risks" form, and this encouraged the American marine market to follow suit. By the time state insurance authorities found it advisable to define marine insurance, the insuring of bridges and tunnels under a marine form of "all risks" policy was so well established that the definition followed the custom.

There are two other justifications for the allocation of bridge and tunnel insurance to the marine classification. First, marine dry docks had been insured under ocean marine policies for many years. Second, bridges over navigable streams are subject to a marine hazard in so far as collision with ships is concerned. If the classification of instrumentalities of transportation as marine risks seems a bit far-fetched, it should be remembered that it is a historical development from the fact that marine underwriters were the first to recognize and fill the needs of the owners of such property.

Bridges. Many early bridges were wooden structures and were subject to destruction by fire or windstorm. Seldom were they built over navigable streams because they could not be made long enough to stretch across a large river. There were some stone-arch bridges even in ancient times, but these were difficult to construct over a deep river because a supporting structure had to be built to hold the sections of the arch until it was completed. The successful construction of long bridges awaited the invention of steel and the development of strong steel wire. About 100 years ago, John Roebling proposed the suspension of bridges from steel cables.

The completion of the Brooklyn Bridge in 1883 marked the beginning of modern bridge building. It is a suspension bridge with a clear span of 1,595 feet and still serves. A few suspension bridges had been built prior to the Brooklyn Bridge, but the success of that venture assured the acceptance of the principle. Cantilever, steel arch, and truss bridges are also dependent upon steel for their construction. More long bridges are of the suspension type than of any other construction. However, there is one cantilever bridge 3,500 feet in clear span, and there are steel arch bridges more than 1,600 feet in length.

The construction of a bridge is a highly technical job and requires the most careful engineering planning. The weight of the structure and its traffic load must be computed and foundations built that will be sufficient to carry the load without settling. The pressure of flood waters, ice jams, and the wind must be anticipated and planned for in the strength of the structure. Occasionally, when the forces of nature are more powerful than the engineers anticipate, the insurance companies have an unexpected loss to pay. Windstorms, ice jams, flood waters, and collisions with ships account for many of the partial losses.

One of the most serious bridge losses was that of the Tacoma Narrows Bridge on November 7, 1940, in the state of Washington. The bridge was only about four months old and was of a modern suspension type. Shortly after it was put into service, it was noticed that the bridge swayed and began to weave when the wind was from a certain direction. In fact, the people living in the vicinity nicknamed the bridge "Galloping Gertie." During a particularly strong wind (although not severe enough to be considered of hurricane force) the bridge collapsed. A loss of $4,000,000 was paid on the bridge out of a total insurance of $5,200,000, in addition to a use and occupancy loss of $240,000. The supporting girders on the sides of the bridge were solid and presented a broad surface against which the wind could exert its force. In the reconstruction of the bridge, the roadway consists of four lanes instead of two and therefore has more lateral strength; and the side supports are of open trusswork so that the wind pressure will be reduced.

The hazard of fire was severe on the older bridges, which had roadways of wood planking, but the newer bridges have incombustible roadways. This adds to the weight of the bridge but is considered necessary to eliminate the danger of losing the plank flooring in a fire. A severe fire in the wood planking can cause collapse of the steelwork.

Another severe threat to even the most modern bridges is the transportation of gasoline and explosives by motor truck. There have been several cases in which gasoline transports have caught fire on a bridge and have severely damaged or destroyed the structure. Fortunately this has not happened to any of the largest bridges. It is possible that the burning of a load of several thousand gallons of gasoline on a bridge would create sufficient heat to weaken the suspension cables and cause the entire bridge to fall in the river. Factors considered by underwriters are (1) whether a bridge is used regularly by trucks carrying flammable liquids or explosives, (2) the width of the bridge, (3) whether there is sufficient room for passing without danger of sideswiping, and (4) whether the approaches are straight so that there is little danger of a truck's skidding into the end of the bridge in slippery weather.

A major problem in connection with bridge insurance is that of insurance capacity. Some of the larger bridges are insured for many millions of dollars. Experience is such that underwriters must anticipate a possible total loss to insurance in case of a disaster. The Verrazano-Narrows Bridge between Brooklyn and Staten Island, New York, is reported to have cost $325 million. Insurance coverage is said to be considerably less than the total value, even with participation by all of the insurers in the world that are willing to grant coverage.

Coverage under bridge insurance policies. The insurance coverage on bridges is against "direct physical loss or damage however caused except as hereinafter provided." This is broader basically than an "all risks" coverage because the loss does not have to result from a risk. The exclusions determine the actual coverage, and there are only four sets of exclusions.

First, the war damage exclusion is similar to that in other inland marine policies. It specifies and describes in some detail warlike action, any weapon of war employing atomic fission, insurrection, rebellion, civil war, and seizure or destruction under quarantine or customs regulation, or confiscation by order of any government or public authority. The only difference from other inland marine war exclusions is that damage done by an agent of a hostile government is covered if the agent is acting in secret and not in connection with any operation of armed forces.

A second set of exclusions refers to loss from inherent defect, wear and tear, gradual deterioration, or expansion or contraction due to changes in temperature, unless resulting in collapse of the property or a material part thereof. Collapse of the bridge is considered to be from an insurable hazard even when it is from inherent defects, wear and tear, or gradual deterioration, unless it is the result of the insured's failure to keep the bridge in repair.

The third exclusion refers to loss caused by neglect of the insured to use reasonable means to save and preserve the property at the time and after any loss or damage.

The fourth exclusion is similar to the nuclear exclusion found in many inland marine policies. The clause does, however, provide for coverage of a direct loss by fire resulting from a nuclear incident.

The extremely broad coverage described above is the accepted form of bridge insurance, but there are times when specified perils policies are issued. Such policies list the perils to be covered and usually include fire, windstorm, flood, ice, collision, earthquake, and explosion; and they may also include collapse, riot, and civil commotion.

The policy is voidable if there is any material change in the interest, title, or possession, or if the policy is assigned or transferred.

The usual fraud and misrepresentation clause is included to void the policy if the insured has been guilty of fraud or misrepresentation.

The coverage is subject to an 80 percent coinsurance clause.

Most bridge policies include a substantial deductible in order to eliminate claims for small losses. The amount of the deductible is set according to the rate and the total amount of insurance on the bridge. The deductible clause is one peculiar to the bridge policy in that it provides that the deductible shall not apply if the cost of repairing the damage amounts to or exceeds 80 percent of the actual cash value of the property immediately prior to the loss.

Replacement cost coverage may be written on steel and concrete structures, subject to 80 percent coinsurance relating to the replacement cost of the structure. An additional premium usually is charged for this coverage.

The computation of insurance rates for bridges must be largely a matter of judgment, because no two bridges are alike. Companies that are members of or subscribers to a rating bureau secure their bridge rates from the bureau after submission of all pertinent information. This includes plans and specifications used in the construction of the bridge and a bridge inspection report. This report is a lengthy document that can be completed properly only by an engineer familiar with bridge construction.

Use and occupancy insurance on bridges. As every motorist knows, many of the bridges in the United States are toll bridges. Any accident that closes the bridge to traffic results in a loss of revenue, in addition to the loss from physical damage to the bridge. Business interruption, or use and occupancy, insurance may be written to cover this loss of revenue. Most other types of inland marine policies exclude loss resulting from delay or loss of use. Bridge insurance is one of the few inland marine coverages that make provision regularly for a use and occupancy coverage.

The use and occupancy policy follows closely the bridge property damage form. It provides the same broad protection with a few special provisions adapting it to the use and occupancy coverage. Three additional exclusions are:

1. Failure or breakdown of machinery or accessories unless it results from an external cause not otherwise excluded.
2. Suspension of use by a governmental authority unless such suspension results from damage by an external cause not otherwise excluded.
3. Suspension of use or prolongation of suspension due to an ordinance, law, or governmental order regulating the repair or rebuilding of the bridge, or by cancellation of or delay in the issuing of a license or permit.

The use and occupancy policy usually contains a seven-day deductible clause. The insured also is required to put the property back in complete or partial operation as soon as practicable after loss or damage, and the company is not liable for loss of revenue after the time when the property could have been restored to use with ordinary diligence.

Coverage may be on a daily basis, with a limit of recovery per day, or the limit per day may be varied according to the seasonal fluctuation in revenue. It also is possible to write a reporting form with a provisional amount of insurance so that the recovery will be the actual amount lost, as closely as it can be calculated on the basis of the past experience. These use and occupancy forms in other respects follow the similar forms written in connection with fire insurance policies.

Builders' risk bridge insurance. Protection may be afforded bridge builders by a builders' risk form to cover during construction of a bridge. The coverage is much more restricted than that under the property damage form. It covers against fire, lightning, flood, rising waters, ice, explosion, windstorm, earthquake, and collision, but excludes loss or damage caused by collision with construction material or contractors' or construction equipment. It includes coverage on the materials and structures the contractor must use in building the bridge. Loss or expense is excluded if caused by strike, riot, civil commotion, vandalism, or malicious mischief. Coverage for these hazards, if added to the policy, would be underwritten with care and usually at an additional premium. A deductible clause usually is a part of the conditions. The exclusions and general conditions are almost identical with those of the property damage form. The values are reported monthly by the contractor, and the amount of insurance increases with the construction of the bridge.

An "all risks" form similar in its coverage to the bridge insurance policy also is provided. Both builders' risk forms provide that the policy shall become void if the general design or method of construction be materially altered during the policy term.

A "full reporting" clause similar to that used on fire reporting policies provides that the company shall not be liable "for more than this company's percentage of that proportion of the actual loss sustained which the last reported value of the property covered herein bears to the actual value of said property as of the date for which such values were reported." In case of underreporting of values, this clause penalizes the insured on any loss to the extent of such underreporting.

Tunnels. The preceding discussion has used only the word "bridges," but in general the same facts and observations are true of insurance on tunnels. Any tunnel that qualifies as an instrumentality of transportation or communication may be insured under the same conditions as a bridge. There are far fewer tunnels to be insured than bridges, and each is an individual problem. The value of a tunnel always is high because of the great construction problems, and the insurance must be spread among many companies.

Wooden supports sometimes are used in the construction of tunnels, and these present special fire hazards. A relatively small fire in the wooden supports may fill the tunnel with smoke and gases so that it is impossible for fire fighters to reach the seat of the blaze. A construction project that uses large amounts of wood is underwritten with caution, and a tunnel with permanent supports of wood usually is considered of questionable desirability.

The burning of a trailer-truck loaded with carbon disulfide in the Holland Tunnel under the Hudson River in 1949 illustrates the extreme difficulty of fighting a fire in the confined space of a tunnel. In spite of immediate and well-organized fire department and emergency action, the damage to the interior of the tunnel amounted to $600,000, and there was damage to trucks, cargoes, and telephone cables, bringing the total damage to a million dollars or more. Had the fire resulted in the breaching of the tunnel wall so as to permit the entry of water, the damage might have been many millions of dollars.

The earthquake hazard must be considered with special care in connection with a tunnel that extends under water. A crack in the tunnel wall might allow water to enter and flood it.

Other Instrumentalities of Transportation and Communication. The instrumentalities of transportation and communication that may be classified as insurable under inland marine policies have become more numerous as additional property owners wished to secure the broad type of insurance which is written to cover bridges. The listing in the Nation-wide Marine Definition attempts to draw a line between properties which perform a transportation or communication function and those which are not an integral part of such a system. For example, buildings and building equipment ordinarily are not considered part of such systems, and are not considered to be insurable under inland marine policies. Thus an oil refinery is not eligible for inland marine coverage, but the pumping station which forms part of a pipe line is so insurable. The Committee on Interpretation in deciding borderline cases considers whether the purpose of the property in question is that of transportation or communication, or storage or manufacture.

Radio and television transmitting equipment. Radio and television transmitting towers and equipment are costly, and are subject to a wide variety of hazards. No matter what hazard causes the collapse of the tower, the expense of repairing or replacing it is high. The towers are carefully designed, but there are occasions when unusual weather conditions result in serious damage or collapse. In the vicinity of Chicago on New Year's Day, 1948, several radio towers were partially destroyed as a result of ice accumulations from a sleet storm. The ice built up over a period of several hours until the towers were holding many tons. The ice also increased the width of each structural member and gave the wind more surface against which to exert pressure. The extreme load plus the high wind pressure was more than the towers could stand, and upper portions went down. Many losses to radio and television towers have occurred from tornadoes, strong winds, or a combination of wind and freezing rain in the central latitudes of the United States.

Forest and brush fires are another serious threat to towers located in remote areas. Underwriters inquire whether a tower is in a wooded area and whether there is a clear space of several hundred feet on all sides. The typical construction for radio towers is a steel truss, and the open steelwork would soften and collapse under forest fire conditions.

Rates and forms for radio towers and equipment are not filed by the rating bureaus; the underwriter must determine the needs of the insured and the coverage the company is willing to write. Each policy is made to fit individual conditions. The basic hazard is that of windstorm, but the windstorm rate may have to be adjusted according to the danger of ice accumulations. When underwriters are offered a tower of high value, or several towers in the same locality, they secure information from the United States Weather Bureau regarding the frequency and severity of ice storms in that region.

Use and occupancy and consequential loss insurance may be

written in addition to the property damage coverage. Under the Nation-wide Marine Definition it is not permissible to insure buildings, their furniture and furnishings and supplies under an inland marine form of policy. Such property may be insured separately under fire and extended coverage policies.

Transmission lines. Electric power transmission lines may be insured under much the same conditions as radio towers. The owner of a transmission line is interested primarily in protecting himself against a catastrophe loss such as might be caused by a widespread sleet storm or by a forest fire. Many transmission lines pass through heavily forested areas where there is a clear space of only 50 to 100 feet through which the line passes. A forest fire could destroy many miles of line, and complete reconstruction would be necessary.

Sleet storms and freezing rain cause the wires to break, but usually there is much salvage of materials. The towers may be intact and the wires can be restrung, but the labor of restringing the wires can be tremendous if the storm extends over a wide area. The rates for windstorm insurance are not of much help in determining an adequate rate for storm damage to transmission lines. Usually, it is the ice accumulation and not the wind that pulls down the wires. It is necessary to find out the frequency and severity of sleet storms in the area and calculate the probable time interval between storms of sufficient severity to pull down the wires.

It is desirable to have a deductible clause on policies insuring transmission lines in order to avoid small losses that might result from occasional vandalism or from strictly local freak weather conditions. These losses are much in the nature of ordinary business losses to a power company and the insurance contract should not be burdened with them.

Use and occupancy or consequential loss coverage is underwritten with caution because of the high losses that may occur. The restringing of wires that are down from a storm probably could be accomplished within a few days or a few weeks at most, but the rebuilding of a line destroyed by a forest fire could take months. The steel towers are built to individual specifications. It may take a long time to replace towers that are damaged beyond repair.

Pipe lines. Pipe lines carrying water, gas, or oil may be insured under inland marine policies. This is done when the insured feels that there is sufficient danger of loss to justify the protection. Occasionally the pipes are laid on top of the ground or partially exposed. In other cases they may be exposed where they are carried across rivers or canyons. Each pipe line must be considered individually and underwritten according to the chances of loss from the causes that the underwriter can foresee. Pumping stations may be covered if they form an integral part of the transmission system.

Traffic lights. Traffic lights may be insured under an inland marine policy inasmuch as they are instrumentalities of transportation. The underwriting depends on whether the municipality desires a catastrophe coverage or is interested in a policy that would provide reimbursement for damage to individual sets of lights. A catastrophe coverage could be written with a deductible approximately equal to the cost of replacing one set of lights. This could be written at a favorable rate because the chances of several sets being involved in a single loss would not be large. If coverage for individual accidents such as might result from traffic collisions were desired, the rate would have to be considerably higher and probably would be comparable to collision rates for automobile coverage.

Piers, Wharves, Docks, and Slips. The Nation-wide Marine Definition provides that marine and inland marine policies may be written to cover piers, wharves, docks, and slips when the policies exclude the risks of fire, lightning, windstorm, sprinkler leakage, hail, explosion, earthquake, riot, and civil commotion. Piers, wharves, docks, and slips are aids to marine transportation. It is customary to insure the hazards of fire and the other risks enumerated above under fire policies. There are occasions when the owners of such property desire insurance against loss or damage from collision by vessels, high waves, and other miscellaneous hazards that may be covered under an "all risks" policy. This is one of the few cases in which an inland marine policy would be written to cover these miscellaneous hazards but exclude the hazards of fire, lightning, windstorm, sprinkler leakage, hail, explosion, earthquake, riot, and civil commotion.

There is no uniform method of establishing rates and coverage for such property. Each one is considered individually in much the same manner as a bridge or tunnel. Elements to be considered would be the amount of marine traffic to which the property is subject, the exposure to collision, the protection from wave wash that might be afforded by breakwaters, and the construction and condition of the structures.

Dry Docks, Marine Railways, and Cranes. According to the Nation-wide Marine Definition, dry docks, marine railways, outdoor cranes, and loading bridges may be insured under marine and inland marine policies against "all risks." The policy may include coverage against fire and the other hazards that must be excluded from a policy covering piers, wharves, docks, and slips.

A dry dock is a dock into which a vessel may be placed and

from which the water may then be pumped out, exposing the sides and bottom of the vessel. It is used to facilitate repairs to vessels and for examination and cleaning of the hulls.

A marine railway serves a purpose similar to that of a dry dock, but it generally is intended for smaller vessels. The marine railway consists of inclined ways that extend from a sloping shore into deep water. A cradle on the way is let down into the water far enough so that a ship can be placed above it. The ship and the cradle are pulled toward shore at the same time until the ship rests in the cradle. The cradle and ship are then pulled onto shore, where the ship may be examined, cleaned, and repaired in the same manner as if it were in a dry dock.

Outdoor cranes and loading bridges are large structures, usually similar to a bridge in appearance, upon which a movable crane travels for the purpose of loading and unloading material from ships, barges, railway cars, and trucks. They are subject to damage from collision with ships, switching engines and trucks, and also may be subject to flood and marine hazards.

The entire structures of dry docks, marine railways, cranes, and loading bridges, including the movable and stationary parts, may be insured. The hazards are much the same as those to which piers, wharves, docks, and slips are subject. There is danger of total loss by fire in many cases because the structures are likely to be of wood or open steelwork. Windstorm and wave wash are other threats. There is also the possibility that a vessel may upset if it is not secured properly before the water is pumped from a dry dock or before the vessel is pulled from the water on a marine railway. Collision is a possible hazard if there is marine traffic in the vicinity.

Rates and coverage are developed to fit each individual structure. Judgment necessarily plays a large part in the calculation of these rates, because no two structures are alike.

II. "LAND HULLS"

The term "land hulls" is convenient to designate the type of rolling stock or vehicles that are used to transport goods and that may be insured under inland marine policies. This includes almost any transporting vehicle on wheels except automobiles and motor trucks. Although the laws of many states define inland marine or marine insurance in such a way that automobiles may be insured under inland marine policies, the practice is to insure automobiles under policies specifically designed to insure motor vehicles. The Nationwide Marine Definition provides that policies covering motor vehicles designed for highway use are not classifiable as marine or inland marine policies. Included in the "land hulls" insurable under inland marine policies are railroad rolling stock, mine rolling stock, and horses and wagons.

Railroad Rolling Stock. Railroad rolling stock includes locomotives and cars, both freight and passenger. The larger railroads do not insure their rolling stock. Their equipment is spread over such a wide area that only a small portion of their total value would be involved in a single accident. There are hundreds of short-line railroads in the United States that operate only a few miles of right of way. The shortest line listed in the *Official Guide of the Railways* is the Virginia Central Railway, which has one mile of track between Fredericksburg and West Fredericksburg, Virginia. From this small size they range upward to the gigantic systems with thousands of miles of track.

Many of the short railway lines operate for freight service only. They may provide trackage rights to other railroads and may not operate any equipment of their own. Other short lines do operate their own equipment and handle all traffic themselves. The short line that operates its own equipment needs insurance to cover any loss. This has been particularly true since the development of the Diesel locomotive. A single Diesel locomotive of the type used by small railroads for freight switching service may cost $100,000 or more. In fact, the locomotive may constitute more than 50 percent of the value of the entire rolling stock of a small line.

It is customary for a railroad to assume liability for damage to the equipment of other railroads when the damage occurs on its tracks. This is comparable to a bailee liability, but it may be partly or wholly a contractual liability. The short railway line needs insurance to protect it from financial loss due to accidents to the equipment of other railroads. This may be written as an inland marine coverage.

Inland marine policies for a small railroad are written with two or more items.

One item lists its own equipment which is covered, because the railroad probably would not want to insure miscellaneous small items such as handcars and small work cars. Any new equipment acquired during the term of the policy can be covered automatically for a short period to give the road a chance to report it.

A second item may cover the liability of the railroad for damage to the rolling stock of other railroads for which it is responsible. This is shown with a maximum amount per loss and also a maximum amount per unit. A small railroad might desire a maximum coverage per unit of $25,000 or $30,000, depending upon the type of cars usually handled over its tracks. The amount named might be adequate for a railroad handling freight cars only, but some passenger cars far exceed those values. If the line regularly handles one of the streamlined trains over its tracks, it might need much higher limits.

The maximum limit per accident would depend upon the number of cars and type of equipment regularly handled over its tracks. The value of a streamlined train may exceed $1,000,000, whereas $100,000 may be a sufficiently high limit per accident if the equipment handled per day consists of only a few freight cars.

A third item sometimes included covers the liability of the railroad for damage to goods in its possession. A common carrier has a heavy responsibility for goods in its custody. A small railroad might find it advantageous to insure against loss from this liability, the same as a truckman does. The desirability of insuring this liability from the standpoint of the railroad depends upon the spread of value. If the road is operating only a few trains, a single trainload might contain a value entirely too high for the road to assume the risk. There may be valuable concentrations of goods in a freight warehouse or in a yard where many loaded freight cars would be subject to a fire or other catastrophe.

Many railroad cars are owned by private corporations or persons other than railroads, and these also may be insured. Many commodities need special-type freight cars that may be furnished by the companies dealing in those commodities. Examples are acids, pickles, certain types of ores, cement, oil, liquified petroleum gases, and refrigerated products. Other examples of costly railroad equipment owned by private corporations are the test cars used by manufacturers of railroad equipment.

If an owner has only a few cars, it is worth his while to insure them, even if his arrangements with the railroads are such that they assume responsibility for their safety or repair. The insurance would make certain of immediate payment in case of loss, and the insurance company could take the responsibility of collecting from whatever railroad company was responsible for the loss.

Industrial railroad rolling stock used in a manufacturing plant may be insured, and so may mine rolling stock used in connection with mining operations. Some of this equipment may be similar to contractor's equipment and present similar insurance problems. The advantage of insuring such property under an inland marine policy is that the property is insured against loss from the many perils to which movable property is subject. The owner is relieved of worry concerning chance concentrations of value that may occur during periods when the equipment is brought in off the road for repair or during seasons when work is slack.

Railroad equipment trusts. One of the largest fields for insurance on railroad rolling stock is in connection with new equipment. Much of the new equipment, such as Diesel locomotives and streamlined trains, is not owned by the railroads but is leased by them from equipment trusts. The purpose of the equipment trust is to secure a loan by using specific equipment as security rather than to use the general property of the railroad. This method is used particularly to finance the purchase of new equipment.

The equipment trust method of financing is used generally throughout the railroad industry, and it is particularly advantageous for railroads in the hands of receivers. If a railroad in the hands of a receiver desires to borrow money to make equipment purchases, the lenders of the money would have no security other than the general assets of a corporation already in financial difficulty. The purchase of new equipment is essential to the continued operation of a railroad and a help in bringing it back to a state of financial stability. Financial institutions are eager to lend the money if they can safeguard their investment.

The equipment trust arrangement solves the problem of financing equipment purchases for solvent railroads and for those in financial difficulty. The title to the equipment is held by the trust or by the financial institution lending the money, and the railroad leases the equipment under an installment purchase agreement. If all the payments are made on the lease agreement, eventually the railroad acquires title to the equipment. In case of default, and if the lender feels that there is no chance of that particular railroad's being able to make good on its commitments, the lender can take the equipment and lease it to another railroad.

The situation is similar to that under which individuals purchase automobiles or household equipment on the installment plan and under which the purchaser gets a conditional title but the true title rests in the seller until all the payments have been made. The person holding the true title has the right to repossess the equipment any time the installments are not paid. Each car or locomotive is titled specifically, and a plate is attached to the car or locomotive stating that it is owned by the person or corporation that holds the title. The name of the railroad operating the equipment may be painted all over the sides of it in big letters, but the true state of ownership is indicated by the small plate on the side of the car or locomotive.

The holder of the title to equipment financed under an equipment trust needs insurance on it. Inasmuch as the equipment may be in the hands of a railroad in financial difficulty, the lender could not afford to depend on the railroad to make good the loss of the equipment in a wreck or other catastrophe. The amount of the loan to build a streamlined train is sufficient to justify insurance because of the concentration of value. A Diesel-powered streamlined train may cost more than a million dollars. A major portion of this investment could be destroyed in a single wreck. Fires in Diesel locomotives occur frequently enough to be important hazards to the investment. Diesel locomotive fire losses have been reported in excess of $100,000 each.

Rates. Railroad rolling stock rates must be largely a matter of judgment, because each railroad operation is entirely different from any other. The hazard to a high-speed Diesel-powered streamlined train making a run from Chicago to Los Angeles over the Rocky Mountains is entirely different from the hazard to equipment of a small midwestern railroad that operates slow-speed freight trains in level country. Between these two extremes there are hundreds of variations in road conditions and geographical hazards.

The spread of value is important, and the rate must also take into account the loss experience of the railroad, whether the roadbed and trackage are kept in the best condition, and the financial standing of the railroad. When liability for loss of goods is insured against, the railroad's police organization must be examined to see how well it protects freight cars and terminal areas from loss by theft.

The rates on much of the railroad rolling stock are made by rating bureaus, and each proposal for insurance must be submitted to the bureau for specific rating. A few independent companies specializing in this type of insurance make their own rates.

Horse and Wagon Floater. Horses and wagons are still used to some extent for delivery purposes in cities where the speed of the motor truck loses its advantage. The rating bureaus provide rates and forms to cover horses and mules used for delivery purposes and for wagons, harness, and other equipment used with them.

The insurance on horses and mules is against death or destruction resulting from or made necessary by the specified perils listed in the form. An animal may be injured to such an extent that it cannot recover or that destruction of the animal may be necessary to prevent intense suffering on its part.

The perils specified in the form are (1) fire and lightning, (2) collapse of bridges or culverts, (3) flood (meaning rising waters), (4) collision, derailment, or overturning of land conveyance while the insured property is in transit thereon, and (5) the stranding, sinking, burning, or collision of vessels, including general average and salvage charges. This collision coverage is not coverage for collision of the animals or vehicles insured, but is limited to collision of a vehicle on which the insured property is being transported.

The form is so arranged that additional optional coverages may be given by filling in appropriate spaces and amounts. The optional coverages include windstorm, hail, riot, riot attending a strike, civil commotion, explosion, aircraft, and objects falling from aircraft. The windstorm and hail coverage does not include loss or damage caused by frost or freezing weather or by snow, sand, dust, or rain, whether driven by wind or not. Horses and mules are not covered while in any aircraft.

Theft coverage may be added as one of these optional coverages, but this does not include conversion or dishonesty on the part of persons to whom the property may be loaned or rented.

Losses from collision of the animals or vehicles insured may be granted, either as full collision of the property insured with any land conveyance other than a conveyance upon which the property is being transported.

It is optional to extend the collision of land conveyance coverage to include any accident to a land conveyance upon which the property is being transported except damage from coupling operations on railroad cars. This extension would cover, for example, damage resulting from collapse of the conveyance, which would not bc covered under the basic provisions of the form.

Earthquake coverage is available as one of the optional extensions. Coverage may also be added against loss from accidental shooting, drowning, artificial electricity, attacks by dogs or wild animals, and collapse of building.

There is a 100 percent coinsurance clause. This clause may be deleted insofar as it applies to any scheduled item when a specific amount of insurance is provided for that time. It is customary to schedule valuable items and animals because it might be difficult to prove the value after they have been lost or destroyed.

The rates for the horse and wagon floater are based primarily upon the fire insurance rates for the premises where the animals and equipment are housed. The "in and out" rate is used if one is published by the fire insurance rating bureau; otherwise a fraction of the contents fire rate is the basis. Loadings are added for the additional coverages according to a table of rates which is filed by the rating bureaus. The rate for theft coverage on harness, saddlery, and other equipment is substantially higher than for animals, which reflects the greater likelihood of equipment theft.

QUESTIONS

1. How did it come about that bridges and tunnels are insured under inland marine policies?

2. Discuss the bridge owner's need for a broad insurance coverage.
3. Describe the factors which you would take into account in determining the rate for insurance on a tunnel.
4. What are the most likely causes of severe damage to electric power transmission lines?
5. Explain why the full fire insurance rate on contents of a building is used in calculating some inland marine rates, whereas only a portion of the fire rate is used for horse and wagon policies.
6. In what respect does the coverage on piers, wharves, docks, and slips differ from that usually provided for dry docks and marine railways?
7. Why does a small railroad need insurance coverage on its rolling stock whereas a large railroad may feel justified in carrying its own risk on rolling stock?
8. What is a railroad equipment trust?
9. Distinguish between the coverage under the usual horse and wagon policy and full mortality coverage on animals.
10. Compare the effect of the "all risks" type of coverage that might be written to cover such properties as dry docks and marine railways with coverage against "perils of the seas," which might apply to ships in dry docks or on marine railways.
11. Discuss the logic of classifying as inland marine insurance the coverage on a radio tower, but deciding that insurance on the building to which the tower is attached cannot be so classified.

15

Dealers Insurance

DEVELOPMENT OF DEALERS POLICIES

An early demand for a broad type of insurance coverage for stocks of merchandise came from jewelers. Jewelry stocks are subject to loss not only from fire, windstorm, and other hazards commonly insured against, but also from burglary, theft, and many miscellaneous hazards. Burglary and theft insurance often was difficult to secure during the early years of this century. Jewelers wanted an "all risks" type of insurance coverage that would indemnify them against all insurable losses under a single policy.

American insurance companies in most states were not able to write a single policy covering both fire and casualty risks because of the statutory separation of underwriting powers. This separation of underwriting powers is not characteristic of English insurance, and underwriters at Lloyd's of London began to write a broad form jewelry policy about 1900. It was called a jewelers' block policy, taking its name from the French words en bloc, meaning "all together."

For about twenty years the underwriters at Lloyd's were the principal writers of jewelers' block insurance. During the 1920s the loss experience became poor. Increased crime in the period following World War I was largely responsible for the higher losses, and this also increased the demand for this coverage. Lloyd's restricted their writings just at the time when more jewelers wanted the coverage. In order to permit American companies to write the coverage, laws were changed in many states so that jewelers' block insurance could be written either by marine or inland marine companies, or by casualty companies. Although empowered to write the coverage, casualty companies never took advantage of the change in statutes, and most of the jewelers' block insurance has been written as inland marine coverage.

The established practice of writing jewelers' block insurance as an inland marine coverage was recognized in the 1933 Nation-Wide Definition. With this exception, the Definition effectively blocked any general writing of "all risks" types of coverage on other kinds of merchandise. It was not until the late 1940s when multiple line insurance became permissible in most states that there was a trend toward the furnishing of "all risks" or "block" types of policies for storekeepers other than jewelers.

The 1953 Nation-wide Marine Definition recognized that policies covering the following types of dealers may be classified as inland marine:

Musical instrument dealers
Camera dealers
Fur dealers
Equipment dealers selling agricultural and contractors' equipment
Fine arts dealers
Dealers in stamps and coin collections

Several states amended the 1953 Nation-wide Marine Definition to include some or all dealers handling the following additional types of merchandise: household appliances, office machinery and supplies, heating and air conditioning equipment, sporting goods, industrial machinery and tools, professional and scientific instruments, and marine supplies.

The inland marine rating bureaus filed rates and forms applicable to these additional kinds of "block" insurance. All of these dealers handle kinds of merchandise that are susceptible to theft or damage by a variety of hazards. Their need for broad coverage brought a demand from policyholders for the coverage already available to jewelers. These amendments to the 1953 Nation-wide Marine Definition were rescinded by most of these states after broad coverage insurance for dealers became available as multiple line insurance under the commercial property policies.

For a time during the middle 1950s it appeared that inland marine insurance might be expanded to include insurance of an "all risks" type on all kinds of merchandise in the hands of dealers. However, this expansion of inland marine insurance into the dealers' field was checked, and coverage for practically all kinds of mercantile and manufacturing risks came to be filed on a joint basis by several different rating bureaus. The fire insurance rating bureau in each state filed the fire and allied lines portion of the coverage, a casualty bureau filed the theft portion, and an inland marine bureau filed the transportation portion. This came to be known as the "hand-in-hand" method of filing. This was later supplanted by the Special Multi-Peril policies.

The principal forms of inland marine dealers insurance policies are discussed here.

THE JEWELERS' BLOCK POLICY

The jewelers' block policy was the earliest of the dealers policies, and its format and coverage have exerted considerable influence on more recently developed policies. Inasmuch as it was developed largely independently of other policies, its terms differ in many respects from those of other inland marine coverages.

The insured property is covered "while within or in transit between the states of the United States, District of Columbia, Puerto Rico and Canada," subject to limitations, exclusions, and conditions. While this wording indicates a floater coverage, the limitations restrict the transit coverage and make the principal coverage apply at the business premises of the insured.

There are five limitations of liability applying to property in different situations. When a policy is written, dollar limitations are inserted in the blank spaces provided for each of the five limitations. The first applies to property at the insured's premises described in the policy. The amount of insurance desired by the insured on his stock is the amount inserted in this space.

The second limit of liability applies to property in transit by first-class registered mail, railway express, or armored car service; to property deposited in the safe or vault of a bank or safe deposit company; and property in the custody of another jeweler.

The third limit applies to property in transit by first-class registered mail or air express.

The fourth limit applies to shipments by customer parcel delivery service, and the parcel transportation service of certain common carriers.

The fifth limit applies to all other property. This group includes property in the hands of salesmen, property deposited for safe keeping with other jewelers, property on loan or demonstration with customers, and any other situation not described in the first four groups.

The limits of liability which are inserted in a policy depend upon the insured's methods of doing business, how much property he might have in transit, how much would be in the hands of salesmen, or in other places. Underwriters examine with care any prospect who has large amounts of property outside of his premises, particularly if salesmen carry expensive samples. The past history of each salesman is an important part of the information necessary for proper underwriting.

The property insured is described in general terms to include that which is usual to a jewelry establishment and includes pearls, precious and semiprecious stones, jewels, jewelry, watches and watch movements, gold, silver, platinum, other precious metals, and alloys and other stock usual to the conduct of the insured's business.

This type of property is insured by the policy in three situations specified in the policy.

The first occurs when such property is owned by the insured.

A second situation occurs when it has been delivered or entrusted to the insured but belongs to others who are not dealers in such property and not otherwise engaged in the jewelry trade. This refers to customers' property in the custody of the jeweler. The coverage indemnifies the jeweler for loss due to his legal liability as a bailee and also insures the property for the customer. It is known as bailees' customers insurance. The principles of this type of coverage and the liability of a bailee will be discussed later inasmuch as this coverage is largely incidental to the jewelers' block policy.

A third situation occurs when the property is "delivered or entrusted to the insured by others who are dealers in such property or otherwise engaged in the jewelry trade, but only to the extent of the insured's own actual interest therein, because of money actually advanced thereon, or legal liability for loss or damage thereto." This is a more limited coverage than the bailees' customers protection granted for customers' property because it covers only to the extent of the insured's interest or liability.

The policy presumes that other members of the jewelry trade will have insurance of their own, and they should look to their own insurers for protection of their interests. Customers, on the other hand, are not presumed to have insurance against all the hazards covered by the jewelers' block policy. The jeweler should give his customers as broad a protection as he gives his own property.

The basic coverage of the jewelers' block policy is extremely broad. The coverage clause reads, "This policy insured against all risks of loss of or damage to the above described property arising from any cause whatsoever except," followed by the exclusions of the policy. It is doubtful whether the words "Arising from any cause whatsoever," add anything to the coverage. It is still limited by the preceding words, "All risks."[1]

Exclusions. The true coverage of the jewelers' block policy, however, must be determined from an examination of the exclusions. This is the case with any broad policy of the "all risks" type. The exclusions of the jewelers' block policy are peculiar to the needs and conditions of the jewelry trade and will be examined in detail.

The first exclusion relates to infidelity and excludes:

> Loss, damage or expense caused by or resulting from sabotage, theft, conversion or other act or omission of a dishonest character (1) on the part of the Insured or his or their employees, or (2) on the part of any person to whom the property hereby insured may be delivered or entrusted by whomsoever for any purpose whatsoever, unless such loss arises while the goods are deposited for safe custody by the insured, officer of the corporation, member of the firm or salesman while traveling, or while the goods are in the custody of (a) the Post Office Department as first class registered mail, or (b) a carrier mentioned in Section 2, or (c) a person serving as a mere porter or helper not on the payroll of the insured.

The principle of this exclusion is that loss is not covered when it results from infidelity of any person under the control of the insured. It is recognized that the insured cannot control the actions of (1) employees of common carriers, (2) employees of the Post Office Department, or (3) employees of a hotel or other place where the goods may be deposited for safekeeping.

The last phrase of this exclusion is a recognition of the fact that salesmen frequently make use of porters or helpers to carry their sample cases. Obviously it is impossible to investigate the background

[1]In an ocean marine case the court interpreted "other causes of whatsoever nature" and "all risks" as meaning the same thing: Mellon v. Federal Ins. Co., 14 F. (2d) 997 (1926).

and possible criminal record of casual employees. The insurance company assumes the risk of loss by infidelity on the part of these helpers.

The second exclusion relates to delay, loss of market, gradual deterioration, moth, vermin, inherent vice or insufficient or defective packing; or damage sustained while the property is being worked upon and directly resulting therefrom. Such losses either are not direct property losses, are not the result of insurable risks, or are considered to be within the control of the insured.

The war damage exclusion is in the same terms as found in other inland marine policies. The exclusion of loss from "seizure or destruction under quarantine or Customs regulations, confiscation by order of any government or public authority, or risks of contraband or illegal transportation or trade" could be important to a jeweler who is doing an import or export business. It is difficult even for the honest businessman to know all of the regulations of all foreign countries.

Losses from flood and earthquake on the insured's premises are excluded, but provision is made for eliminating these exclusions if the insurance company is willing to assume the risk.

A rather lengthy exclusion refers to shipments of insured property. Mail shipments are covered only when sent by registered first class. (Registered air mail is the same as registered first class for this purpose.) Railway express and air express shipments must be declared to the carrier for at least 25 percent of their value; packages worth $1,000 or more must be sealed with lead or wax or by other method prescribed by the carrier and shipped by the carrier's money classification. Other restrictions apply to transit by railroad, ship or air, or by motor carriers or truckmen. These provisions of the policy are intended to exclude the property from coverage in transit unless the insured takes the special precautions that are available for the handling of valuable merchandise.

The breakage of articles of a brittle nature is not covered unless the breakage is caused by burglars, thieves, fire, or certain other perils listed.

There is no coverage on goods sold on the installment plan after the property leaves the custody of the insured.

There is an exclusion that takes cognizance of the temptation for jewelers and their families to wear jewelry in their possession for sales purposes. It excludes loss or damage while the property is being worn by the insured or by any officer, director, agent, employee, servant, or messenger of the insured, or by any dealer or other person, firm, or corporation engaged in the jewelry trade or by any of their officers, directors, agents, employees, servants, or messengers, or by any member of the family, relative, or friend of any of the aforesaid, or while in their custody for such purpose. The wearing of jewelry adds to the chances of loss, and the added hazard is not contemplated in the premium for the jewelers' block coverage.

This clause is so worded that it excludes coverage on jewelry displayed by models. This too presents an extra hazard that the insurance company cannot afford to assume unless there is an added premium for it and unless the company has an opportunity to specify the protection to be given the jewelry so displayed. When jewelry of considerable value is to be displayed by modeling, it is regular practice to arrange for special police protection. If the insurance company is satisfied that the protection is adequate, it can provide coverage.

Another exclusion refers to loss or damage to property while at any public exhibition promoted or financially assisted by any public authority or by any trade association. Such concentrations of jewelry are a temptation to thieves. The insurance company must have an opportunity to examine the protection of the exhibit before it is committed to coverage. Exhibitions may be insured, but the conditions surrounding each exhibit must be appraised by the insurance company and a special premium commensurate with the hazard must be paid.

This exclusion refers specifically to exhibitions promoted or financially assisted by a public authority or trade association. It is worded in such a way as to allow coverage on a private exhibition arranged by the insured for sales purposes. It is regular practice for jewelry salesmen to exhibit their samples to prospective buyers. There is no intention of excluding coverage on such displays, even if the circumstances of the exhibit might bring it within the definition of a "public exhibition."

An unattended vehicle exclusion excludes coverage when the property insured is in or upon any automobile, motorcycle, or other vehicle unless, at the time the loss occurs, there is actually in or upon such vehicle the insured or a permanent employee of the insured, or a person whose sole duty it is to attend the vehicle. There is no coverage if the insured, or his employee, leaves the vehicle unattended, even if it is locked. This exclusion does make allowance for the insured to hire someone specially to look after the vehicle during his absence, but the person so hired must stay in or upon the vehicle. This would seem to exclude any loss while the vehicle is in a garage or parking lot in the sole custody of the garage or lot-keeper but is so located that it is not under the constant surveillance of an attendant.[2]

The unattended vehicle exclusion does not apply to property in the custody of a common carrier or to property in the custody of the Post Office Department as first-class registered mail.

Another clause provides that there is no coverage for mysterious disappearance, unexplained loss, or shortage disclosed upon taking inventory. Even with such valuable property as jewelry, there are losses from carelessness, from shoplifters, and from pilferage by employees. Underwriters believe that jewelers can reduce their unexplained losses by good supervision and by rigid control of their premises. It would be an invitation to the insured to abandon loss prevention procedures if insurance were provided against losses from carelessness.

It is not the intention of the unexplained shortage exclusion to eliminate losses by sneak thievery when there is reasonable evidence of theft. Jewelry stores frequently are the victims of confidence men and women who operate in pairs, one of whom will divert the attention of a clerk while the other secretes a valuable piece of jewelry and makes off with it. Seldom is the theft actually seen, but the circumstances make it virtually certain that the theft was accomplished in this manner. Such losses are paid when the insured or his employee is certain that the jewelry was taken at a definite time and place and that the jewelry was in its proper spot just previous to the occurrence.

The policy does not cover any reported shortage of goods from a package that was shipped by the insured and was received by the consignee in apparent good order and with the seals unbroken. Neither does it cover loss or damage to goods sent C.O.D. with the privilege of inspection by the consignee before delivery to him.

Losses resulting from theft accomplished by window smashing or cutting are excluded unless an additional premium is paid and the policy endorsed to cover such losses.

Special Conditions Several special conditions appear in the

[2]See William Kinscherf Co. v. St. Paul Fire and Marine Ins. Co., 234 App. Div. 385, 254 N.Y.S. 382 (1931). In this case the insured's salesman had left a car locked with jewelry inside, and the car was broken into and the jewelry stolen. The court granted the defendant insurance company a judgment and said: "Such language can only be interpreted to mean that if the permanent employee of the plaintiff is not actually within or on the automobile, or so near as to be able to observe a theft of the contents, he shall not be deemed to be in attendance at the time the loss occurs."

policy as precedent to any recovery under the policy. The actual cash value clause is similar to such clauses in other inland marine policies. It states specifically that the loss shall not exceed the lowest figure put upon such property in the insured's inventories, stock books, stock papers, or lists existing at the time the loss occurs. It also provides that any antiquarian or historical value shall be excluded.

Claims for loss or damage of pledged articles (on which loans have been made) are limited to the amount actually loaned and unpaid plus the accrued interest at the legal rate.

The clause referring to coverage on the property of others reserves to the insurance company the right to adjust such losses with the owners. The insurance company also reserves the right to conduct and control the defense of the insured in any court proceeding in respect to any claim from others. The expenses connected with such defense are paid by the insurance company.

There is a provision that the insured shall keep a detailed and itemized inventory of all property, including salesmen's stocks, in such a manner that the exact amount of any loss can be determined accurately therefrom. The clause does not specify that the inventory must be kept in duplicate or in an iron safe (as does the iron safe clause used on some fire insurance policies), but the loss or destruction of the inventory would make it difficult for the insured to prove that he had kept an inventory in such a manner that the company could determine the loss therefrom.

The insured is obliged in case of loss to produce all accounts, books, papers, and invoices, to submit to examination and to cause all other persons to submit to examination, as far as the insured can control the actions of the other parties. This clause is similar to provisions in other inland marine and fire policies.

The "other insurance" clause is similar to those in other inland marine policies. It is intended to make the jewelers' block policy excess coverage over other policies.

The policy contains the usual inland marine provision that the insurance will not inure directly or indirectly to the benefit of any carrier or other bailee.

It is required that the insured will maintain, insofar as it is within his control, the watchman or other protective devices described in the proposal. This provision is not common in inland marine policies, but it is found in many fire insurance policies.

There is a provision that the policy shall be reduced by the amount of any loss payment, but the amount is reinstated automatically unless the policy is endorsed to the contrary. An extra premium is payable to the company on a pro-rata basis from the date of the loss to the expiration of the policy. This is similar to the provisions of many inland marine policies. It is distinguished by an additional statement that any rewards paid by the insurance company for the recovery of insured property shall reduce the amount of insurance the same as a loss payment. (Rewards are not considered part of the loss payment insofar as the policy limits are concerned.) This recognizes an established practice in the jewelry insurance business of paying substantial rewards for the return of stolen jewelry.

The following additional clauses appear in the policy and are either identical or similar in their effect to the parallel provisions in other inland marine policies as discussed elsewhere in this book:

Concealment and misrepresentation.
Notice and proof of loss.
No abandonment to the company.
Payment of loss sixty days after receipt of satisfactory proof of loss.
Subrogation rights of the company.
Sue and labor clause.
Suit clause.
No assignment of interest or change or waiver of conditions without written consent of the company endorsed on the policy.
Cancellation.

Procedure in Writing Jewelers' Block Insurance. There are important differences between procedures for handling jewelers' block insurance and the practice in handling other inland marine business. The proposal for jewelers' block insurance is much more important than the application for other inland marine policies. With most inland marine lines, the application is at best a representation on the part of the insured. Occasionally the application is omitted entirely, and in many cases the agent fills out the application to the best of his knowledge without the prospective insured's ever seeing it. Few companies require new applications for renewal policies.

The procedure is entirely different in connection with a jewelers' block policy. The proposal must be filled out in detail and signed by the prospective insured, because it reveals information that is vital to the proper rating and underwriting of the policy. It is standard practice for the proposal to be attached to the policy and made a part of it. (This practice has been standard for many years in connection with life insurance but has never been adopted to any extent in other insurance fields.) The jewelers' block proposal, by its terms, is made a warranty by the insured in regard to the facts stated. The fact that it is attached to the policy and forms a part of it tends to give this warranty more effect than if it were not so attached.

The proposal is a four-page document inquiring into every detail of the insured's business and the protection of the premises from the hazards insured against. Full information must be given concerning all losses sustained by the insured during the five years previous to the submission of the proposal. This includes both insured and non-insured losses.

The proposal also indicates the coverage desired; whether insurance is desired to the full value of the stock; whether patterns, money, or furniture and fixtures are to be covered; and whether fire and extended coverage protection is desired in the policy.

There is no coinsurance clause in the jewelers' block policy, nor is there any requirement that the insured carry full insurance to value. However, the proposal discloses the full value of the insured goods, and the premium is calculated according to the relationship between the amount of insurance and the full value.

Rates and Premiums for Jewelers' Block Policies. Jewelers' block insurance is one of a half-dozen inland marine lines on which a specific rate for each insured customarily is computed by a rating bureau. There are only a few classes of inland marine business on which specific rates are so promulgated. The procedure differs from the fire insurance practice in that the rating bureau does not make any inspection of the insured property. The insurance company desiring the rate quotation is required to furnish the rating bureau with all the information necessary for the rate calculation. The completed and signed proposal furnishes the necessary information for the rate-making purposes.

The rating schedules used by the rating bureaus for computation of the jewelers' block rates follow the same principles as fire insurance rating schedules. The basic rate depends upon the nature of the insured's business, whether it is retail or wholesale, how large the values are, the protection afforded the premises, and the protection of the safes in which the property is kept when the premises are closed to business.

Charges are added according to the size of the community in which the property is located and other hazards to which the premises are subject. Credits are applied for special features of protection. The final quotation made by the rating bureau is a quotation of premium rather than a rate quotation. The premium varies with the amount of insurance that the insured desires to carry, but not in direct proportion. Most losses are partial. The premium for insurance equal to 50 percent of the value, for example, must be higher in relation to the amount of insurance than if full insurance to value is carried.

The rules of the Inland Marine Insurance Bureau make provision for special rating of properties when circumstances justify variation from the rating schedule. Circumstances justifying such treatment are an exceptionally good loss record, the size of the policy, and the nature of the insured's business if it differs from the average contemplated in the rating schedule. Diamond merchants handling large stocks (having average inventories of more than a million dollars) or diamond dealers having small travel limits (less than $25,000) are examples of the types of business that may deserve special treatment.

Companies that are not members of or subscribers to a rating bureau compute their premiums on the basis of their own schedules, many of them using schedules similar to those of the rating bureaus.

Protection Against Loss. Values in the jewelry trade are so large that they are a constant temptation to the criminal. Exceptional precautions must be taken to avoid loss. Special devices and procedures have been developed that can make larceny extremely dangerous for the criminal.

The most effective means of preventing losses by theft is the use of central station burglar and holdup alarm service. The protected jewelry store is equipped with electrical devices connected to a central station by special electrical circuits. The central station is manned twenty-four hours a day and has direct telephone or signal circuits to the police department of the city. Upon receipt of an alarm from a protected premises, the central station immediately relays the alarm to the police and also sends its own guard to the premises.

Show windows often present a severe theft hazard. It is relatively simple for a thief to break a show window, grab the most valuable items, and disappear from a deserted street before anyone notices him. It is highly desirable that the values in windows be kept as low as possible when the premises are closed.

Central station alarm service is an effective method of protecting show windows. Narrow strips of metal foil glued near the edges of the windows are broken if the window is broken or cracked. In case the window is smashed, an alarm is given immediately. Window smashers tend to avoid windows that are equipped with the foil of a burglar alarm service.

Another method of protecting show windows is by means of a double, swinging window. The second pane of glass is behind the regular show window and is arranged to swing inward. When the regular show window is smashed with a rock or club, the second pane of glass swings back with the blow, but it seldom breaks. It then swings forward into position again and is an effective barrier to the thief in his efforts to scoop up valuable jewelry. Gates that can be pulled across inside of the show windows when the store is closed are also used, but some jewelers object to the gates because they interfere with a view of the merchandise in the show window. New types of shatter–resistant glass are used in many stores as a deterrent to show window breakage.

Large jewelry stores and factories maintain other protective systems and procedures. Watchmen are employed as guards when the premises are not open for business. Watchmen should be required to register on a clock to insure the regularity of their rounds through the building. The burglar alarm central stations have arrangements whereby the watchman reports to the central station as he makes his rounds.

The jewelry industry is keenly aware of the hazards of the trade and of the necessity of keeping losses at a minimum if insurance premiums are to remain reasonable. The industry maintains the Jewelers' Security Alliance, which has as its purpose the prevention of theft, the apprehension of jewel theives, and the recovery of stolen property. Its work is so effective that a substantial credit is given in the rating schedule for membership in the Alliance.

Underwriting Problems. Jewelers' block insurance is tied in so closely with the jewelry trade that it has many underwriting problems peculiar to this type of insurance and quite different from those of other inland marine lines. The coverage is so broad that extreme care is exercised in accepting policyholders.

Although it is intended that the jewelers' block policy should provide insurance protection for all the insured's merchandise, there are circumstances in which exceptions are made. A department store that operates a jewelry department would not want to insure the entire stock of the store at the relatively high rates of the jewelers' block policy. In such cases the covering clause is amended to include the described jewelry and "other stock usual to the conduct of the insured's jewelry department" instead of all other stock usual to the insured's business.

It is permissible to exclude the risk of fire. In the many cases when the insured desires to carry a separate fire and extended coverage policy, the fire coverage is excluded from the jewelers' block policy. This exclusion refers only to fire loss on the insured's premises, since the fire insurance policy might not provide the needed coverage outside the premises.

Patterns, money in a safe, and furniture and fixtures may be covered if desired by the insured. Other restrictions and extensions may be made to fit peculiar needs of an insured's business.

The location of the property is an important factor in underwriting. A large city lends itself more readily to window smashings and holdups than do smaller communities. It is difficult for strangers to "case" a jewelry store in a small city without being detected, because the people who frequent the locality are known. In larger cities strangers are common and no one notices them. The store's customers are not always known to the clerks or the proprietors, whereas the smaller town store has a regular clientele.

Some large cities maintain special police details whose job it is to protect jewelry stores and salesmen. Specially picked detectives know the jewelry salesmen, and they also know many jewel thieves and their methods of operating.

Police convoy protection may be provided when a salesman or jeweler is carrying a specially valuable collection of jewelry. The salesman may not actually carry the jewelry on his person while traveling but may arrange to pick up the property at an express or baggage office. A police convoy or private guard when provided would stay with the salesman as long as the property is in his possession and until it is put into a vault for safekeeping at night or until it is shipped to the salesman's next stop.

The police detail often attends exhibits and social functions where large displays of jewels are likely, and they watch for thieves and confidence men. The value of the jewels under the protection of a police detail may be tremendous. Millions of dollars' worth of jewels may be contained in a single shipment to an exhibit, and department store or convention exhibits may have total values up to $10,000,000.

FINE ARTS DEALERS

The 1933 Nation-Wide Definition and the 1953 Nation-wide Marine Definition recognize that fine arts and antiques may be insured under inland marine policies whether they are in the possession of individuals, dealers, museums or others. Rates and forms for fine arts dealers are not filed by the rating bureaus but are established by individual companies in accordance with each dealer's needs and the exposure to loss.

Coverage. The coverage usually is of an "all risks" nature, with exclusions applying to wear and tear, damage resulting from any repairing or retouching process, breakage, and war and nuclear damage. All of the dealer's stock is covered, and it is not customary for the policy to list individual articles.

One of the principal reasons for individual scheduling of fine arts in private collections is the difficulty of determining their value after the works of art have been destroyed. This situation should not be true to the same extent in connection with dealers' property. Dealers should have complete records of cost on all articles, and such detailed inventories enable them to prove losses to the satisfaction of insurance companies. A dealer is expected to be an expert in his knowledge of fine arts, and the amounts paid for his stock should represent reasonable values.

There are two ways in which fine arts dealers' coverage may be written. A blanket form is satisfactory if the dealer's stock is constant and without any important fluctuations in value throughout the year. The form covers antiques and works of art of every description owned by the insured. It also covers property of others held on consignment or in trust, and sold but not removed, as well as any other property which the insured holds and for which he would be liable in case of loss. It is similar to the jewelers' block policy in that it gives an extremely broad coverage, including the property of others that may be in the custody of the insured for sale, repair, or other purposes. It is customary in the fine arts business for dealers to hold property on joint account (similar to a consignment arrangement), and such property also is covered by the policy. The exact wording is prepared in accordance with the needs and the business practices of the insured and varies in different policies.

The blanket policy almost always contains a 100 percent coinsurance clause. The dealer must be certain that his insurance is adequate to cover his values if any loss is to be paid in full. If there is little transit hazard, the policy may cover at the business location of the insured without any outside coverage.

Most fine arts dealers deliver property to their customers, and they may do an extensive business outside their home cities. The policy can provide transit coverage in addition to the location coverage. This usually is so arranged that the dealer periodically reports all his shipments to the insurance company. The transit coverage is written along the lines already discussed for annual transit policies. The transit coverage, for which there is an additional premium, may be different from the location coverage.

For dealers whose values fluctuate widely, the blanket policy is not satisfactory and a reporting form of policy is used. They are required to report their total values, usually at the end of each month. The reporting form contains a clause which provides that in the event the values reported are less than the actual values, any loss shall be adjusted in the proportion that the last reported values bear to the actual values. Thus, if a dealer reported only 75 percent of his values (by mistake or in an effort to save on his premium costs), he would collect only 75 percent of any loss which occurred. This is the so-called "honesty" clause, which appears in almost all reporting form policies written by fire and marine insurance companies.

Transit coverage may be included in a reporting form policy. As a part of his monthly reports, the dealer is required to report all the property shipped, its value, and the points to which it was shipped. The underwriting and rating of the transit risk is similar to that for any annual transit policy.

Special Conditions. Dealers' fine arts policies contain a few special clauses not found in policies covering private fine arts collections. Three of them are exclusions.

The first of these is an exclusion of any fixtures or equipment used by the insured in the conduct of his business. The broad coverage of the fine arts policy is not needed for such furniture and fixtures.

The second exclusion relates to any losses resulting from the infidelity of employees of the insured or of persons to whom the insured property is entrusted. Underwriters feel that the insured should use special diligence to check the honesty of his employees and persons to whom he entrusts fine arts property. It would encourage carelessness to cover the infidelity hazard, and in addition the coverage would overlap that of a fidelity bond.

The third exclusion applies to property that disappears mysteriously or to a loss revealed by the taking of an inventory. Inventory shortages are most likely to result from infidelity of employees or carelessness on the part of the insured in handling or watching his property. Underwriters consider such losses uninsurable in the field of fine arts, because to cover them would be to encourage carelessness.

Inasmuch as the values of the pieces are not agreed upon in advance (as they are in the private fine arts policy), it is necessary to include some provision for establishing the value in case of loss. The value may be set at the cost to the insured, or it may be the replacement cost of items that have an established value in the open market. It is necessary for the insured to keep detailed records, and the policy usually requires that the insured's books be open to inspection by the insurance company both before and after a loss. If the insured's books are destroyed in a catastrophe, he will find it difficult to collect in case of loss, because he must prove his value and loss under a dealer's fine arts policy.

Policies may contain an excess clause which provides that the coverage of the fine arts policy shall be excess above any other insurance applying to the loss. As pointed out above, it is customary to include a 100 percent coinsurance or other clause which provides that the insurance company will be liable for no greater proportion of any loss than the amount of insurance under the policy bears to the total value. This coinsurance clause seems to give the insurance company adequate protection without the excess insurance clause, and the presence of both clauses in the policy might complicate the settling of a loss if there were other insurance.

Rates. The companies determine the rates in relation to the hazards which threaten the property. The hazards at the fixed location are principally fire, lightning, theft and burglary, windstorm and explosion. The rates for these hazards are taken into account, and a loading is added to take care of the miscellaneous hazards covered by the policy. The 100 percent coinsurance fire and extended coverage rates of the fire rating bureaus are often used as the base rates. Loadings are added to cover the exposure from vandalism burglary and theft, and the transit hazards. These may be established by judgment, although any published bureau rates would be considered.

It is customary for a dealer's fine arts policy to show two rates: one for the location coverage, which applies to the amounts reported each month at the fixed location; and a second for the transit coverage to be applied to the values shipped each month.

STAMP AND COIN DEALERS

Although the 1933 Nation-Wide Definition did not specifically recognize that inland marine policies could be written to cover stamps and coins, it has been customary for many years to cover both dealers and private collectors of stamps and coins under inland marine policies. The 1953 Nation-wide Marine Definition specifically lists such policies as classifiable in the inland marine category.

Policies issued to stamp and coin dealers provide a broad coverage of the "all risks" type. Exclusions relate to fading, creasing, and similar kinds of wear and tear loss that are likely to affect stamps and coins. Mysterious disappearance, theft from an unattended automobile, or unaccountable loss may be excluded, depending upon the needs of the insured and the premium that he is willing to pay.

Many stamp and coin dealers maintain stores at street level and cater to the general public. The stock of such dealers is likely to be largely of low value articles, and they may deal largely in packets of stamps. They may also carry souvenirs and general merchandise. This type of store has many customers coming in and out, and a broad coverage insurance policy may result in many losses to the insurance company.

Another type of stamp and coin dealer sells from an office on the upper floor of an office building, or from his home, and caters to a restricted clientele. His stock usually consists of more valuable items than that of the store proprietor, and he is more likely to have a good inventory of his stock. The preparation, underwriting, and rating of such a policy would follow the same lines as that for a fine arts dealer's policy. The integrity of the insured is an important underwriting consideration.

Coin collections as well as coin dealers have been subject to increasing burglary hazards. A good safe is an important protection for the more valuable items. Underwriters generally avoid insuring coins that may be carried from place to place in automobiles or exposed to theft away from the insured's premises.

Auctioneers occasionally need coverage for stamp and coin collections. Such policies may be written for short periods if the auctioneer deals only occasionally in stamps or coins. Policies may be written to cover according to the needs of the insured and the hazards affecting the property. There are no filings of rates or forms by the rating bureaus.

"FLOOR PLAN"

During the middle 1940s there arose considerable interest in the insuring of merchandise in the hands of dealers under a "floor plan." This is an arrangement by which merchandise or equipment is placed in the hands of a dealer by the manufacturer or wholesaler. Money to pay for the goods is loaned to the dealer by a financial institution, such as a bank. The property is specifically encumbered by the loan. This arrangement had been in use for a number of years in connection with the distribution and sale of automobiles, and the practice spread to the merchandising of such other equipment as household appliances.

It was ruled by the Joint Committee on Interpretation and Complaint that this type of coverage was not contemplated by the 1933 Nation-Wide Definition. However, many states amended the Definition to permit its being written as an inland marine coverage. Subsequently it was included in the 1953 Nation-wide Marine Definition as an inland marine coverage. The inland marine rating bureaus have filed rates, rules, and forms for "floor plan" insurance.

The merchandise while in the possession of the dealer must be subject to a "floor plan" or similar arrangement under which the dealer borrows money from a bank or other lending institution with which to pay for the merchandise, and also subject to the following restrictions:

1. The property must be identifiable specifically as encumbered to the bank or lending institution.
2. The dealer's right to sell or otherwise dispose of such merchandise is conditioned upon its being released from encumbrance by the bank or lending institution.
3. The policy must cover in transit and not extend beyond the termination of the dealer's interest.

These limitations prevent an insurance company's issuing an inland marine policy to cover on a general stock of merchandise, even though it may be encumbered by a chattel mortgage or loan. The property to be insured must be identifiable specifically as that which is encumbered and upon which the money is loaned.

The inland marine rating bureaus specify that their rules do not apply to motor vehicles, water craft, aircraft, livestock, jewelry, or furs. The Nation-wide Marine Definition excludes motor vehicles and the merchandise for which the dealer's collateral is stock or inventory as distinguished from merchandise specifically identifiable as encumbered to the lending institution. Therefore, a "floor plan" policy could be issued as an inland marine policy on water craft, aircraft, livestock, jewelry, or furs as long as the conditions of the Definition were met, but such a policy would not be subject to the rating bureau filings.

A dealer under a "floor plan" policy may not include an individual, firm, or corporation engaged in manufacturing, blending, aging, rectifying, or any other form of processing for the trade. The policy must name the type or class of merchandise to be insured; the phrase "general merchandise" or any other similar term is not permitted.

Policies may be issued to cover either the single interest of the dealer, the single interest of the lending institution, or the two interests together under one policy. When the interest to be insured is that of a dealer or when both the dealer's and the lender's interests are covered, the policy provides that the insurance company shall not be liable for a greater proportion of any loss than the amount of the insured's interest in the merchandise bears to the value of the merchandise.

Lending institutions may secure a form which provides that the insurance company shall not be liable for any loss unless the interest of the insured in the lost or damaged merchandise has been impaired, and then only to an amount not exceeding the extent of such impairment or the amount of outstanding balance on the merchandise lost or damaged, whichever amount is less.

Coverage. The coverage granted under the "floor plan" policy is interesting because it was the first instance in which "all risks" coverage was made available on mercantile stocks (other than for such valuable items as jewelry, fine arts, stamps, and coins).

The exclusions follow to a large extent those found in other "all risks" types of policies, but some of them are specially designed for this policy. War damage is excluded, as well as damage to electrical appliances or devices from artificially generated current unless fire ensues, and then only for direct loss or damage caused by such ensuing fire. There is an exclusion referring to mechanical breakdown, inherent vice or defect, wear and tear, and gradual deterioration.

A specific exclusion designed for this type of policy refers to loss or damage resulting from delay, loss or market, bankruptcy, foreclosure, or similar proceedings.

The exclusion relating to conversion is detailed, and refers to misappropriation, secretion, infidelity, and any dishonest act on the part of the insured or other party at interest as well as to conversion. This exclusion does not apply to loss or damage resulting from infidelity and similar dishonest acts of a carrier for hire.

Breakage of glass or similar fragile merchandise is excluded unless caused by fire, lightning, explosion, cyclone, thieves, or the overturning, derailment, or collision of a conveyance in which the merchandise is being transported.

Loss or damage resulting from rain, hail, sleet, snow, or freezing while the merchandise is in the open is excluded, except while the property is in transit. Nuclear damage is excluded, except that direct loss by fire from nuclear causes is covered.

There is an exclusion of loss or damage caused by or resulting from flood, which is defined as meaning rising waters, except while in transit. This exclusion may be deleted at an additional charge to be determined by the rating bureau in each specific case.

Rates. The rates are based primarily on the average fire insurance rate at the location covered. The windstorm or extended coverage rate, whichever is lower, is added to the average fire rate, and a monthly loading of less than 2 cents per $100 is added for the other hazards. When locations are not specified, the rates are less than 10 cents per $100 per month for the entire coverage.

The policies are written on a reporting basis. Under the single interest form, the insured must report the total amount of outstanding balance. For the double interest form, the insured must report the total value of all property covered as of the last business day of the preceding month. Failure on the part of the insured to render such reports within a month renders the policy null and void insofar as it concerns any amount in excess of the last report. There is provision for correcting an error or omission, if prompt notice is given to the company as soon as the error or omission is discovered. The company has the right to audit the books of the insured to determine the accuracy of the reports.

The clause regarding valuation in case of loss provides that merchandise that has not been sold by the dealer shall not be valued in excess of the purchase price plus transportation charges. In regard to merchandise that has been sold by the dealer but has not been delivered, the value is the net selling price of the dealer after all allowances and discounts. These valuation clauses are both subject to a restriction that the value shall not exceed the cost to repair or replace the merchandise with material of like kind and quality.

EQUIPMENT DEALERS

The 1953 Nation-wide Marine Definition recognized the inland marine classification of policies covering dealers' stocks of mobile argicultural equipment and equipment for construction work. This was the result of pressure for such coverage from insurance companies that wanted to provide a broad type of coverage for such dealers. Credibility was given by the mobility of the equipment and the fact that such stocks often are away from the insured's premises for temporary storage or demonstration, or are in transit.

Coverage. The equipment dealers policy is designed to cover mobile agricultural and construction equipment, and this is listed in the inland marine bureau manuals as consisting principally of binders, reapers, harvesters, plows, harrows and tedders, and bulldozers, road scrapers, tractors, pneumatic tools and compressors, including accessories therefor, attached or otherwise, all of which is the property of the insured or the property of others in the custody or control of the insured, for sale, display, demonstration, storage, service, or repair.

While the policy is designed to cover the type of mobile equipment listed, other stock belonging to the insured may be covered in some states, and subject to certain limitations. In many states, all stock of the insured may be covered as long as the insured is a dealer in the types of equipment listed. This has the effect of making the coverage available to hardware stores, home appliance stores, and others, just so long as they are dealers in agricultural or construction equipment. In some states the proportion of other stock is limited to 15 percent.

Excluded from coverage are motor vehicles, aircraft and watercraft, property sold on an installment sales plan after it leaves the custody of the insured, and property in the course of manufacture.

The perils insured against by the policy are "all risks of direct physical loss of or damage to the insured property from any external cause" except as excluded. The exclusions apply to loss from delay, loss of market, consequential loss, wear and tear, mechanical breakdown, and similar causes not really risks of loss. Loss to tires and tubes is covered only if it results from fire, windstorm or theft, or is coincidental with other loss. Loss disclosed upon taking inventory is excluded. Electrical damage is excluded unless fire ensues, and then only the fire loss is payable. Conversion and infidelity losses are excluded, and so are war damage and nuclear damage. Flood losses are excluded except flood loss in transit. The flood exclusion may be eliminated at an extra charge. Other provisions as to valuation of property and special conditions are similar to those of the "floor plan" policy which has been described.

Rates. Provision is made for monthly reporting policies and rates, and also for flat annual rates. Rates are calculated in two parts, according to the average amounts of property inside and outside of buildings. The base rate for mobile agricultural and construction equipment inside of buildings is 50 percent of the fire rate. This is one of the few cases in which the fire rate is discounted in the calculation of the rate for a broader form of coverage. This appears to be justified because such mobile equipment is in and out of the buildings, and is not constantly subject to the building fire hazards. It is comparable to the "in and out" rate used in calculating the rate for the horse and wagon floater. The base rate for accessories and other stock is the full fire rate, inasmuch as such stock is expected to be subject to the building fire hazard at all times. To the base fire rate is added a loading to compensate for the other hazards covered by the policy.

For property located outside of buildings, the base rate is the rate established for such property by the fire insurance rating bureau, or a flat 20 cents if there is no established fire rate. A loading is likewise added to this base rate to cover the other hazards.

The loadings for both inside and outside property vary from 20 cents for the first bracket of values to 5 cents, depending upon the amount of insurance. The result of this rating formula is that some policyholders can secure the broad coverage of this policy at premiums less than they would have to pay for fire and extended coverage. Experience shows that such treatment is justified, which probably is due to the fact that much of the value is located outside of buildings, and in transit, and is not subject to the building hazards.

Underwriting. An important consideration in underwriting an equipment dealer's line is the theft hazard. There is no deductible applying to losses. While there is little likelihood that entire machines will be stolen, there is a chance of frequent pilferage of parts, or theft of other stock. Such possibilities must be examined with care. The fire hazard may be severe at temporary storage locations, or at county or state fairs where property may be on exhibit. The rating schedule does not include any provision for extra fire hazard at such temporary locations. The company would have to consider it in determining the desirability of the line.

The collision hazard during deliveries is potentially severe. Deliveries from metropolitan areas may subject the equipment to more serious hazard than would be the case for dealers located in smaller communities.

CAMERA AND MUSICAL INSTRUMENT DEALERS

Photographic equipment and musical instruments are somewhat comparable to jewelry in their susceptibility to loss from theft and hazards other than fire and windstorm. It was natural that among the merchants for whom a broad coverage insurance was considered desirable were dealers in cameras and musical instruments. As was the case in an earlier day with jewelers, no one but the inland marine underwriters was willing to provide the broad coverage desired by these dealers. The 1953 Nation-wide Marine Definition recognized the need for the coverage and the willingness of the inland marine people to provide the coverage, and listed policies covering camera and musical instrument dealers as among those to be classified as inland marine.

Coverage. The property insurable under a camera dealers policy includes "Cameras and accessories pertaining thereto." This is given a broad interpretation in the writing of such policies, and includes almost everything that a camera store would be expected to handle. In addition to cameras and photographic equipment and supplies, it may include all kinds of optical equipment such as telescopes and binoculars. The form uses the words "stock in trade consisting principally of," thus giving leeway for the coverage of any other stock so long as the camera business is the insured's principal business.

The property insurable under a musical instruments policy includes "Musical instruments and accessories pertaining thereto," but there is a further provision that "Radios, television, record players and combinations thereof are not deemed musical instruments." The effect of this provision seems to be that the value of the radio and television stocks would not be considered in determining whether the principal business of the insured is that of a musical instrument dealer. There is no exclusion of coverage on such radio and television stocks. They are covered if they are incidental to the operation of a musical instrument store.

The Committee on Interpretation has ruled that the proportion of other stock should not exceed 25 percent if the stock is to be insured under the camera or musical instruments dealers form.

The coverage is against "all risks of direct physical loss of or damage," subject to appropriate exclusions. These provide a coverage similar to that of the jewelers' block policy. There are a few exclusions specially designed for these types of stock. Unexplained loss, mysterious disappearance, and loss disclosed upon taking inventory are excluded. Wear and tear types of loss and infidelity losses are excluded. Also excluded are losses from short circuit, blow-out or other electrical disturbance, and breakage of tubes, bulbs, lamps, or other articles of glass (except photographic lenses). Earthquake and flood losses on the premises of the insured are excluded, but these exclusions may be deleted for an extra premium. Theft from an unlocked, unattended vehicle is excluded. This is broader than the jewelers' block policy in that coverage is provided for theft from an unattended, locked vehicle when there are visible marks of forcible entry.

There is a \$25 deductible applying to all losses except those from fire, lightning, the extended coverage hazards, burglary and hold-up.

Coverage is extended to the property of others in the custody of the insured. Policies may be written on an annual adjustment basis. In other respects the form follows the provisions of other inland marine policies.

Rates. The rates are based upon the contents fire insurance rate for the insured's location, with appropriate loadings to cover the other hazards covered by the policy. The loadings are higher for cameras than for musical instruments. Credits are given for watchman service and burglar alarm systems. Rates also vary according to the size of the community in which the store is located.

Underwriting. The proportion of secondhand goods may be an important factor in underwriting. There is active market in secondhand cameras and equipment, and to a somewhat lesser extent in the musical instruments business. If a dealer gets overloaded with such merchandise, he might be tempted to stage a loss in order to dispose of unsaleable merchandise. Theft is an important hazard, and the susceptibility of the premises to burglary, robbery, or sneak thievery should be examined in considering the desirability of a prospective insured. Another factor to be checked is the amount of deliveries. There is no specific charge in the rate for delivery exposure. A store with a high proportion of delivery business might not be as desirable as one doing a cash and carry business.

FURRIERS' BLOCK

Another of the dealers' policies classified as inland marine by the 1953 Nation-wide Marine Definition is the furriers' dealers policy. This is called a "furriers' block" policy in the filings of the rating bureaus. Furriers had been able for many years to secure an "all risks" type of insurance for their customers' property. The value of their stocks made the same type of coverage desirable for their own merchandise.

The coverage of the furriers' block policy follows closely that of the jewelers' block policy. It provides an "all risks" type of insurance but with exclusions and limitations that are considered necessary in covering this type of merchandise, which is especially susceptible to loss. Limitations on property in transit are much the same as the jewelers' block provisions. Deductibles from \$500 to \$5,000 are provided. These are often necessary in order to make the risk insurable or to secure a reasonable rate. Annual or reporting forms may be written. Property of others which the insured accepts for storage may not be insured under this policy. The furriers' customers policy is available for this purpose and will be described later in this text.

Each risk is specifically rated by an inland marine rating bureau for its members and subscribers. Rates are based upon the fire rates at the insured's location, the type of vaults or safes in which the furs are kept, the amount of show window exposure, and the protection against burglary and robbery. An elaborate proposal form similar to that used for jewelers' block insurance must be completed for rating purposes.

"DEALERS INSURANCE"

During the middle 1950s when it was uncertain how "all risks" insurance would be provided for mercantile operations, several states amended the 1953 Nation-wide Marine Definition to classify as inland marine the policies which cover several additional kinds of dealers. These included subject to some variations and restrictions, dealers in household appliances, office machinery and supplies, heating and air conditioning equipment, sporting goods, industrial machinery and tools, professional and scientific instruments, and marine supplies. The inland marine rating bureaus filed rules, rates, and forms applicable to these dealers in the states where the coverage was approved. This modification of the Nation-wide Marine Definition was withdrawn later in most of these states when the commercial property coverage became available.

Coverage. The coverage of the dealers form is similar to that of the camera and musical instruments dealers form. The property covered is personal property usual to the business of the insured, consisting principally of the named type of property and accessories pertaining thereto. Thus unrelated stock incidental to the insured's business is covered. As in connection with the camera and musical instruments dealers form, it is intended that unrelated stock be covered only when it does not exceed 25 percent of the insured's stock. Specifically excluded are money, securities and accounts, property in the course of manufacture, motor vehicles, boats or marine equipment while afloat, aircraft, animals, property rented or sold to others on an installment payment plan after it leaves the custody of the insured, improvements and betterments of buildings, and furniture and fixtures used by the insured in the conduct of his business.

Limits of liability apply to each location of the insured, and to property in transit and otherwise away from the insured's premises.

The coverage and exclusions are practically identical to those of the camera and musical instruments dealers form. There is a $50 deductible applying to all losses except those from fire and lightning.

Rates. Rates for the dealers form are based upon a schedule almost identical to that used for the camera and musical instruments dealers except that different loadings apply for some classes of dealers. Provision is made for individual rating of wholesalers and distributors in accordance with the hazards affecting each risk. The large amount of transit exposure to a wholesaler or distributor makes it impossible to tie such risks to definite rating schedules.

PACKAGE INSURANCE FOR DEALERS

The development of multiple line insurance made it possible for insurance companies to provide policies which not only include full protection for the dealer's merchandise but also cover his liabilities to customers and others whom his business activities might affect. The result was an increasing popularity of such programs as the Special Multi-Peril policy program. This is comparable to the Homeowners policies in the housing field. These broad form package policies all contain some form of transit and off-premises coverage for property of the insured while it is away from his dwelling or business premises. Some of these off-premises coverages retain their identity as inland marine protection. The transit and off-premises coverage in any case must be underwritten in the same way that an inland marine coverage would be handled. A subsequent chapter in this text will consider the inland marine exposures under the package policies.

QUESTIONS

1. Discuss the conditions in the jewelry trade that brought about legislation to permit American marine insurance companies to write jewelers' block insurance.
2. How much transit insurance coverage is granted in the usual inland marine policy covering a dealer's stock?
3. What property other than that owned by the insured is covered by the jewelers' block policy?
4. What principles are recognized in the exclusion in the jewelers' block policy relating to infidelity?
5. Why does the jewelers' block policy exclude loss or damage to property being worn by the insured?
6. Of what importance is the proposal form in connection with a jewelers' block policy?
7. Explain why the rates for several of the dealers' policies are specifically calculated by the rating bureaus in contrast to the usual method of permitting the companies to calculate rates from filed schedules or tables.
8. Describe special devices used to detect burglars and robbers in stores containing valuable merchandise.
9. Discuss the reasons for excluding from dealers' coverages those losses which result from mysterious disappearance or that are disclosed by taking inventory.

10. Explain why flood losses can be insured against for property in transit but not ordinarily for property at a fixed location.
11. What characteristic is there in common among the types of dealers' property that can be covered under an inland marine policy?
12. What is a "floor plan" arrangement and why does it justify a broad insurance coverage?
13. Discuss the justification for using only a portion of the fire rate as the basis for certain dealers' coverages, whereas the full fire rate is used as the basis for others.
14. Compare the exposures to loss in camera stores, fur stores, and jewelry stores.

16

Bailees' Customers Insurance

BAILMENT–LIABILITY OF A BAILEE

Bailment is the delivery of property by one person to another to be held by him for some special purpose. The purpose may be the safekeeping of the property, or it may be the performance of some work upon the property. In bailment, title to the property does not change, and there is no intention that the title will change in the future. The parties to the act of bailment are the "bailor," who is the owner or a person in rightful possession before the bailment, and the "bailee," who receives the property and is to perform the service.

Bailment ordinarily is distinguished from two other similar situations in which property is turned over to someone other than the person holding legal title.

The first is a conditional sales contract in which the property is turned over to another party, but in this case it is intended that the title will pass to the other party upon the completion of certain conditions, such as the payment of the balance due.

The second situation to be distinguished from bailment is one in which the owner retains some control over the property, as in a master and servant relationship. In a bailment, the owner relinquishes control of the property, and the bailee has entire control of what is done with the property while it is in his custody. For example, a laundress working under the direction of her mistress is not a bailee, because the mistress is in a position to direct the washing of the clothes. If the laundress takes the clothes with her to her home to do the work according to her own wishes, she becomes a bailee.

There are three kinds of bailment.

The first is a gratuitous bailment for the benefit of the bailor, such as would exist when a housewife agrees to keep her neighbor's cat or plants while the neighbor is away. There is no compensation involved and the benefit is entirely to the bailor—the owner of the property.

The second kind of bailment is gratuitous for the benefit of the bailee. An example of this would be a friend's borrowing a lawn mower. Again there is no payment, but the benefit is entirely to the bailee.

The third type of bailment is a bailment for hire and for the mutual benefit of both bailee and bailor. Typical examples are the laundering of clothes, the storage of furs, and the repairing of jewelry. In such cases the bailor receives the benefit of the service performed and the bailee receives the benefit of the charge he makes for the service.

The bailee has certain responsibilities to the bailor for the safety of the property. This responsibility is not clear-cut, and it may vary according to the circumstances. The responsibility of a bailee was described by one court in these words: ". . . the bailee thereunder was bound to exercise ordinary care of the subject matter of the bailment, and is liable for ordinary negligence. Ordinary care means such care as ordinarily prudent men, as a class, would exercise in caring for their own property under like circumstances. . . ."[1]

Ordinary care varies according to the circumstances and the nature of the property. A bailee who is storing property or performing a service gratuitously would not be required to exercise so high a degree of care as a bailee for hire. A greater degree of care would be required in the storage or handling of expensive jewelry than would be required in the care of ordinary laundry. The bailee must antici-

[1]Fraam v. Grand Rapids & Indiana Rwy. Co., 161 Mich. 556, 126 N.W. 851 (1910).

pate the hazards to which the property is subject, and exercise care commensurate with the risk. For example, he must take precautions against theft when the nature of the property is such that it is a temptation to thieves.[2]

The care required of a bailee is less than that required of a common carrier. As explained previously, the responsibility of a common carrier is so great and he must exercise such extraordinary care that he becomes virtually an insurer of property in his possession. The bailee, in contrast, is required only to use the care an ordinarily prudent man would exercise under the circumstances in the handling of his own property.

The common carrier is liable for loss by fire (except in the rare instance when he can prove that it was an "act of God" or act of the public enemy), whereas the bailee is responsible for loss by fire only if he has been guilty of negligence. If the bailee can prove that he took all reasonable precautions, that his fire protection equipment was in good order, and that he was in no way responsible for the loss by fire, he is not liable for the loss. On the other hand, it has been held that it was negligence for a dry cleaner to leave his truck unguarded during the time garments were stolen from the truck.[3]

Although the bailee must be guilty of negligence for the bailor to collect the value of lost or damaged property, the courts generally have taken the view that the bailor can make a prima facie case of negligence by showing that the property was not returned or that it was returned in damaged condition. This appears reasonable, because the bailor would have little chance of learning what happened to missing property that disappeared while in the hands of a bailee. The bailee is the only one who has a reasonable opportunity to determine the cause of the loss, and ordinarily he must show that he exercised due care. The rule has been stated that "Where property is in the exclusive possession of a bailee for hire and is damaged in a way that ordinarily does not occur without negligence, the burden of proof is upon the bailee to show that the injury was not occasioned by his negligence."[4]

The liability of a bailee can be extended in several ways. He may agree in an oral or written contract to assume certain additional liabilities. For example, a dry cleaner may assume responsibility for loss by fire and windstorm by so stating in the receipt he gives the bailor when the clothing is received. There is almost no limit to how far the bailee can extend his liability by contract with the bailor.

[2]See Peet v. Roth Hotel Co., 191 Minn. 151, 253 N.W. 546 (1934).

[3]See More v. Fisher, 245 Ill. App. 567 (1927).

[4]Braman-Johnson Flying Service, Inc. v. Thomson, 167 Misc. 167, 3 N.Y.S. (2) 602 (1938).

The bailee may extend his liability by advertisement. It is common practice for laundries and dry cleaners to advertise that they purchase insurance for the benefit of their customers. They also may advertise that they assume certain responsibilities for the safe return of property entrusted to them. The writing of a letter to the bailor concerning the care to be given the property might result in the assumption of additional liability.

In addition to the deliberate extensions of liability just described, the bailee may inadvertently extend his liability by doing something outside or beyond the bailment contract. If the bailment contract provides for the storage of the property in a specific building or location and the bailee stores it in another place, from which it is lost, the bailee may be held absolutely liable for the loss, even though the circumstances are such that a bailee ordinarily would not be held liable.

In a case involving loss of a fur coat, the owner had asked the bailee to make certain repairs, and the bailee sent the coat to a subcontractor to make them. The coat was lost while in the hands of the subcontractor. The court held that the sending of the coat to the subcontractor without the knowledge of the bailor terminated the bailment contract, and the bailee was held liable for the value of the coat.[5]

It is considered to be against public policy to permit a person to contract away his entire liability for negligence. The courts will not sustain a contract in which the bailor agrees to waive all his rights against the bailee for negligence.

Many garages attempt to limit their liability by posting signs to the effect that the proprietor is not liable for loss by fire or theft. Such signs are not effective in relieving the proprietor of his liability for loss by fire or theft when he is guilty of negligence. Even a contract that is assented to by the bailor is of questionable effect when it attempts to relieve the bailee of his entire liability for negligence.

It is possible for the bailee to limit the amount of his liability. The one type of restriction that has stood up reasonably well is a limitation on the value of the property. It is common practice in certain types of bailment contracts for the bailor to agree that for the purposes of the contract the value of the property is limited to a specified figure. A higher charge is made when the bailor wishes to have a higher value inserted in the contract. This type of limitation has been held binding on the bailor except in some cases where gross negligence has been proved on the part of the bailee or where the

[5]Aetna Cas. & Surety Co. v. Higbee Co., 80 Oh. App. 437 (1947).

bailment contract has been terminated by some act of the bailee (see the third preceding paragraph). The effect is similar to that of the released bills of lading used by common carriers to limit the amount of their liability in case of loss. The limitation of value as it applies to fur garments and furriers' customers policies will be given more detailed consideration in a later chapter.

INSURANCE BY BAILOR OF PROPERTY IN THE HANDS OF A BAILEE

The bailor may insure his property under all circumstances, including while it is in the custody of a bailee. The most common form of such insurance is that in connection with household goods and clothing. The household goods fire insurance policy covers to the extent of 10 percent of its amount on property away from the location named in the policy, including while in the hands of a bailee.

The personal property floater (an inland marine form to be discussed subsequently) covers all the property of the insured in all locations, including while it is in the hands of a bailee. This coverage by the bailor is incidental and is not intended primarily to cover property in the hands of a bailee.

The garment contractors floater policy discussed in a preceding chapter is an example of a policy which may be purchased by a bailor specially to cover his property while it is in the hands of a bailee. Persons who have property in storage in a furniture warehouse frequently buy an insurance policy to cover the property while in the hands of the warehouseman, who is a bailee. Commercial and industrial concerns ordinarily carry insurance on property stored in a warehouse, even though the warehouseman, as a bailee, has some responsibility for the safety of the goods. The bailor considers such insurance to be necessary because the values are large and the bailee is liable for the loss only if there is negligence on his part. It is not customary for warehousemen to insure property for the benefit of the bailor. Therefore, the bailor must carry his own insurance if he desires protection.

BAILEE LIABILITY INSURANCE

The bailee may purchase insurance to protect him against his legal liability for loss of bailed goods. This is similar in its nature to the motor truck cargo insurance purchased by a truckman to protect him from loss as a result of his liability as a carrier for damage to the property of others in his possession. The legal liability of a bailee for property in his custody may not be insured under an inland marine policy unless the bailed property itself is eligible for inland marine coverage. For example, a warehouseman may wish to protect himself against his liability for damage to a stock of paper stored in his warehouse. Because there is no transit hazard, it is not proper to issue an inland marine policy to cover the warehouseman's liability. This is a subject for casualty insurance.

A furniture warehouseman may move some furniture from a customer's house to his own warehouse for a period of a few days, after which the furniture is to be moved on to a new location. This storage is incidental to the transit exposure, and an inland marine policy may be issued to cover the liability of the furniture warehouseman during the entire period, including the storage period. (The Nation-wide Marine Definition provides that an inland marine policy may not cover such storage beyond a limited period because storage for an indefinite length of time is not incidental to transportation.)

BAILEES' CUSTOMERS INSURANCE

Customers of retail establishments, such as laundries, dry cleaning plants, and fur shops, expect their property to be returned in good condition regardless of liability. A merchant who refuses to reimburse customers for loss of their property because he is not liable for its loss would soon find himself without customers. Processors who deal with the public have found it necessary to make good all legitimate claims. They have turned to the insurance companies for protection against the larger losses, which they cannot assume as part of their operating costs. The spoiling of a coat due to some error in processing or the misdelivery of a bundle of laundry is considered a business loss that the processor can stand out of his operating expenses. He needs insurance, however, to protect him if his plant is burned down or if an entire truckload of goods is stolen.

The hazard in connection with a laundry or cleaning establishment is primarily a transit hazard. The property is picked up by the bailee's driver and is carried to the plant at the risk of the bailee. It is at a fixed location for only a limited period of time, after which it is again placed on the truck for delivery to the owner. The only practical way to insure the bailee's liability and the customer's interest is to issue a single policy covering the property while it is in the hands of the bailee and at his risk.

The Nation-wide Marine Definition recognizes this and provides for insurance under bailees' customers policies, subject to the exclusion that they must not cover the bailee's property at his own premises. The furriers' customers policy goes a little further and insures during a period of actual storage, but the theory is the same and is based on the fact that the bailee is insuring what is essentially a transit hazard, with storage incidental to the transportation and for an indeterminate period.

Laundry and Dry Cleaning Insurance. The bailees' customers insurance policy provides direct coverage against loss or damage from the perils specified in the policy to property that the insured has accepted for the type of processing described in the policy. Payment of a loss is not dependent on the legal liability of the insured, but any loss from the perils insured against is paid up to the limit in the policy.

Bailees' customers insurance is not standardized, and no rate filings are made. Insurance companies issue many variations of this coverage. Policies are tailored to fit the needs of individual laundry and dry cleaning plants, but the basic provisions of most policies are similar. The property covered by such a policy is that accepted by the insured from his customers for cleaning, renovating, pressing, dyeing, repairing, or laundering. Processing charges that the insured is unable to collect because of a loss may be insured also. Many companies have separate insurance policy forms for dry cleaning plants and exclude dry cleaning from their laundry forms. The fire hazard in a dry cleaning plant may be much greater than in a laundry. Underwriters feel that they must have an opportunity to appraise the hazards of dry cleaning on its own merits.

The insured property is covered while in the custody of the insured (1) at his premises, (2) at the premises of his agents or branch stores, and (3) while in the course of transportation. The locations of the insured's premises are specified in most policies. Agents' premises usually are not specified if they are not under the control of the insured. Some policies give 72 hours' coverage at unnamed locations owned, rented, or controlled by the insured, in order to give the insured time to report any new locations he may establish.

Perhaps the greatest variation between bailees' customers policies is in the limits of liability. Some policies specify (1) limits of liability for each location named in the policy, (2) a limit for any unnamed location that may be covered under the 72-hour automatic provision, (3) limits for any locations occupied by agents, and (4) limits on any one vehicle or in the hands of any one messenger. Policies may contain limitations on the amount that will be paid for any one bundle of laundry or any one suit or article of dry cleaning.

In sharp contrast, some companies issue policies containing no limits whatever except that the amount paid will not exceed the actual cash value of the property. This is one of the few inland marine policies (and in fact one of the few insurance policies of any kind) in which insurance companies may write coverage without specifying in the policy a limit of liability.

A policy without a limit of liability obviously is desirable from the standpoint of the insured because he cannot control the total value he may have in his custody. A temporary breakdown in his plant may cause goods to pile up and may increase his liability several times over the normal amount. On the other hand such an increase in liability is a problem to the insurance company and might result in a loss far beyond what the company anticipated. Many insurance companies try to compromise between the two extremes of (1) no limit of liability and (2) rigid limits on all parts of the coverage. They set a catastrophe limit high enough to cover any loss that can be foreseen and at the same time within the limits of what the company can afford, considering its reinsurance and its own capacity.

The perils covered in the usual bailees' customers policy are much the same as in transportation policies and include fire, lightning, explosion, collision or overturn of transporting conveyance, theft, burglary, robbery, tornado, cyclone, windstorm, flood, sprinkler leakage, transportation risks by common carrier or mail, earthquake, strike, riot or civil commotion, and confusion of goods resulting from any of the above perils.

The explosion coverage differs from that of some inland marine policies in that it is not restricted and includes steam boiler explosion. The windstorm coverage is broad, covering damage from hail, rain, sleet, and snow whether driven by wind or not. The "confusion of goods" provision is intended to cover losses that might result from inability to identify property after it has been in the confusion attendant upon a fire or other loss. Flood coverage may be eliminated or restricted if the plant is subject to the hazard of frequent flooding.

The theft coverage almost always is restricted, either in the coverage clause or in the exclusions. Theft of individual pieces or articles is excluded from most laundry policies unless the theft is the result of burglary or robbery. This is to eliminate claims from loss of small pieces as a result of misplacing or from infidelity of employees. Most dry cleaning policies and some laundry policies exclude theft of goods left on a vehicle overnight unless the vehicle is locked in the insured's private garage or some other building occupied by the insured. Policies may contain deductible clauses applying to the theft hazard, or they may provide that theft from within a vehicle is covered only if the vehicle is locked at the time of the loss and there is visible evidence of forcible entry. This is considered necessary in some cities in order to encourage the insured to lock his trucks in neighborhoods where theft is frequent.

Several of the exclusions in the bailees' customers policies are specially designed for this type of coverage. Loss or damage that occurs while goods are in the custody of any other laundry or dry cleaner is excluded unless it is specifically assumed by endorsement. This is necessary in order to give the insurance company an opportunity to examine any other plants where the goods might be processed.

Goods held in storage usually are excluded. This exclusion is worded to apply to any goods on which the customer gives storage instructions or on which the insured makes a storage charge. Occasionally a bailees' customers policy is endorsed to provide storage coverage. If the insured has a large amount of garment storage, it may be desirable for him to buy a furriers' customers policy to cover the storage operation. In this case, he would have two policies, one a bailees' customers policy covering laundry or dry cleaning operations and the other a furriers' customers policy on the storage portion of his business.

It has been customary for insurance companies to put in an excess insurance clause, which attempts to make the policy excess insurance over any other insurance carried by the bailee and also over any other insurance carried by the bailor. This practice has been nullified largely by the "Agreements of Guiding Principles," which will be discussed later. Current practice is to make the excess value clause apply only to insurance purchased by the insured (the bailee) and to allow the bailees' customers policy to be primary insurance as far as insurance purchased by the customer (the bailor) is concerned.

Even though this is a specified perils policy, many companies put in an exclusion applying to loss resulting from misdelivery, or careless destruction of goods, or other unaccountable loss when there is no evidence that the loss resulted from one of the perils insured against. This exclusion does not change the terms of the coverage, but it does help to make clear to the insured the intent of the coverage, and it avoids many misunderstandings.

The insured is permitted to adjust small losses (usually less than $100 in the aggregate) with the customer in accordance with the policy terms and to collect from the company upon presentation of a claim and all the facts. The insurance company has the option to adjust losses with the customers or with the insured. In the case of large losses, the insurance company frequently takes over the task of adjusting with the customers and relieves the insured of this task.

Many dry cleaning policies and some laundry policies contain a provision that all thefts for which claims are made must be reported to the police department. Occasionally an insured is reluctant to report a theft to the police because he suspects an employee and does not want to embarrass him.

It is customary for bailees' customers policies to be written on a continuous basis, with the premium payable monthly. The premium is based upon the gross receipts of the insured, and the rate is expressed in cents or dollars per $100 of his gross receipts. The insured is obliged to keep an accurate record of his gross receipts and report them to the company. Uncollected gross receipts must be reported because the work they represent has been done and the gross receipts are intended to serve as a measure of the amount of processing the plant has done. Many companies include a "full reporting" clause in their policies similar to those used in fire reporting forms. A typical clause reads:

> Liability under this policy shall not in any case exceed that proportion of any loss hereunder, which the last reported gross receipts bear to the actual gross receipts for the period included in the said last report.

In the absence of such a clause the company would be liable for the full loss even though the insured was underreporting unless the company could prove fraud in the reporting by the insured.[6]

There are as many different methods of calculating a bailees' customers rate as there are inland marine underwriters. Each has his pet formula, but certain basic ideas prevail in all of them. The first problem is to determine the value of the customers' goods for which the insured may be liable. Fortunately there seems to be a fairly constant relationship between the value of the average laundry bundle or dry cleaning package and the charge made for it. This will vary among different sections of the country, and even among sections of a city, depending upon the wealth of the community, but the relationship stays reasonably constant within these limits. Many underwriters figure that laundry and dry cleaning bundles are worth from 20 to 30 times the processing charge. The value of a dry cleaning bundle may average a little higher than that of a laundry bundle in proportion to the processing charge.

The underwriter is able to calculate the total value of the goods

[6]See Automobile Ins. Co. v. Barnes-Manley Wet Wash Laundry Co., 168 F. (2d) 381 (1948); cert. den., 93 L. ed. 41 (1948), for a case in which the insurance company charged fraud in the reporting of gross receipts and the insured was forced to stand a substantial portion of the loss.

that go through an insured's plant in a year by multiplying the annual gross receipts by 20 or 30 (depending upon what figure he decides upon after consultation with laundrymen and dry cleaners in his part of the country). The next step is to determine how much of this value may be in the plant at any one time. Underwriters find out from each plant operator how long it takes him to process the average bundle. If the average time is five days, in 365 days the plant will have 73 complete turnovers of goods. The total value of the goods in a year's time should then be divided by 73 to get the average amount in the plant at any one time. The figure will fluctuate up and down with holidays and with the seasons. The longer the time for processing, the higher will be the average value in the plant at one time.

The basic factor in the rate is the fire insurance premium for the average value in the plant. To this is added a loading for burglary, theft, robbery, transportation, and any other hazards covered by the policy. The ultimate measure of proper rating is whether each laundry or dry cleaning plant is producing enough premium to take care of all its regular losses plus enough to help pay for the occasional large fire loss among such plants. The premium produced by the loading must take care of the recurring losses, and the fire portion of the premium must go toward the fire losses of all insured plants of this class.

A principal underwriting problem in connection with laundry and dry cleaning plants is the threat of large loss by fire. Inspection by a fire protection engineer is desirable, and the amount of liability accepted should be set at a figure no higher than would be accepted for a comparable fire policy. Automatic sprinklers, fire alarms, watchman service, and fire resistive buildings are all desirable features.

The fire insurance rate is intended to measure the fire hazard, but there are many features in the management of a property that cannot be measured on schedules. Dry cleaning plants using flammable solvents are particularly susceptible to fire losses. The most desirable plants are those using nonflammable solvents, of which there are several good ones on the market. A large proportion of dry cleaning plants use a so-called "safety solvent," which is a highly refined form of kerosene. It does not give off flammable vapors at temperatures below 100° Fahrenheit, but it will burn and does give off flammable vapors at higher temperatures.

Many policyholders have a tendency to carry too little insurance. In an effort to cut down on their costs, some insureds ask for low limits in the belief that they never will have a total loss. There have been several severe fire losses in which the amount of bailees' customers insurance was inadequate. In such cases the customers' losses are not fully covered.

The theft hazard is examined in regard to the probability of recurrent losses from delivery trucks. In the larger cities an unattended truck is likely to have the contents stolen unless it is securely locked whenever the driver is not present. Many companies recommend that their insureds equip their trucks with snap locks that lock automatically when the doors are closed. The drivers are provided with long key chains that make it easy for them to open the doors. It has been found that drivers will not use the locks on the trucks unless it is convenient for them to do so.

A comprehensive application form is desirable for the agent's use in submitting a bailees' customers proposal to the company. Inspection of the plant includes a check of the insured's gross receipts to make certain they are being reported correctly. Policies usually give the insurance company the right to audit the insured's books. Many insureds do not understand that all their receipts must be reported. It is much better to have an inspector or auditor point out the correct method in advance of a loss, rather than to have the deficiency interfere with a loss settlement.

Rug and Carpet Cleaning Form. A variation of the bailees' customers policy is written for rug and carpet cleaning plants. It is similar in most respects to the laundry and dry cleaning form except that it contains a special clause limiting the liability of the company according to the type of rugs or carpets. These special limits are on a unit basis rather than as a limit per location or per vehicle, although there may be limits per location or per vehicle in addition. A typical endorsement for a rug and carpet cleaning policy reads as follows (the limits may vary according to the average financial standing of the insured's customers):

> It is hereby understood and agreed that the following limits of liability shall apply to goods insured under this policy:
>
> a. On domestic rugs and roll carpets, not exceeding $2 per square foot,
>
> b. On oriental and foreign rugs, including semi-antique rugs, not exceeding $10 per square foot;
>
> c. On draperies, not exceeding $50 per set;
>
> d. On cushions, not exceeding $50 per cushion;
>
> e. On other articles, including furniture $100 per article.

Pressing or Tailor Shop Form. Many tailor shops do repairing and pressing and act as receiving stations for laundries and dry cleaning plants. The values and the nature of their operations do not justify the elaborate policy provisions and the monthly payment methods used in connection with the regular bailees' customers policy. Some companies write a simplified bailees' customers policy for such properties. The premium is on an annual basis and averages about 1 percent of the gross receipts. However, the premium usually is figured on the limit of liability, so that a tailor shop with $5,000 of gross receipts might have a limit of liability of $1,000. The premium of $50 a year (for example) would be 1 percent of the gross receipts but 5 percent of the limit of liability. The rate would vary according to the fire rate on the premises and might be considerably in excess of the figure used in the example.

It is not customary for insurance companies to permit insureds under tailor shop policies to adjust losses. Policies usually contain a provision that any loss payment will reduce the amount of insurance. This makes it necessary for any loss to be reinstated if the insured is to continue having full insurance.

In all other respects, the tailor shop form is similar to the bailees' customers form in its coverage and conditions. Many companies write a tailor shop policy for shops having less than $10,000 of gross receipts per year and a monthly reporting bailees' customers policy if the gross receipts exceed that amount. This depends largely upon how small a monthly premium the insurance company is willing to handle. Some companies are willing to insure on a monthly basis any plant developing $10 a month or more premium, whereas others feel that the minimum amount that can justify the extra bookkeeping of a monthly account is $50 per month.

Linen Supply Floater. Laundries may be interested in the purchase of a floater policy to cover towels, coats, and other supplies that may be rented out to customers. This is not a bailee form but a floater policy covering the owner of the goods. It may be written as a transportation floater. Usually the coverage is similar to that given in the bailees' customers policy, and the form is mentioned here for that reason. According to the Nation-wide Marine Definition, the coverage on the insured's premises must be limited to property that is there only incidentally to its regular and frequent use outside the premises. The principal hazards to linen supplies are those of transportation and those on the insured's premises. These are similar to the hazards under a bailees' customers policy. The hazards at the premises of linen supply customers are important only when a large supply is delivered to a single building. Usually the property is so spread out when it is in the hands of customers that only a small amount would be affected by a single loss.

QUESTIONS

1. What is a bailment?
2. What is the responsibility of a bailee for property that is in his custody?
3. Compare the liability of a common carrier with that of a bailee for the property in his custody.
4. What acts on the part of a bailee or his employee may result in an extension of the bailee's liability?
5. In what way may a bailee restrict his liability?
6. Under what circumstances may a bailor insure his property?
7. Under what circumstances may a bailee purchase an inland marine policy to protect himself against loss as a result of his legal liability for damage to bailed property in his custody?
8. What type of property ordinarily is covered under a bailees' customers policy?
9. Explain the advantages to the insured and the disadvantages to the insurance company of a bailees' customers insurance policy that has no limit of liability.
10. What is the usual basis for premium payment under a bailees' customers policy?
11. Discuss the usual methods of arriving at a rate for a bailees' customers policy on a laundry or dry cleaning plant.
12. What factors does an inland marine underwriter consider in judging the desirability of insuring a laundry or dry cleaning plant?
13. What are the usual differences between a bailees' customers policy and a tailor shop policy?
14. Describe the loss prevention program that you would recommend for a laundry and dry cleaner that operates its own plant, as well as several pickup stations and truck routes serving customers' homes.

17

Furriers' Customers Insurance

The furriers' customers policy provides a special form of bailees' customers coverage. The customs of the fur business and the coverage of the hazards are different from those of laundries and dry cleaning plants and require special treatment.

Years ago the ownership of a fur coat was an indication of wealth, and only members of wealthy families were able to sport such garments. This no longer is true, and the warmth and beauty of furs are enjoyed by women in all walks of life. Furs are extremely susceptible to moth damage, and it is difficult for the householder to protect them at home. Coincidentally with the increase in the sale of furs, there developed a large business in the storage of them during the months when they are not in use. Many storage warehouses are refrigerated to a temperature too low for moths to remain active, and other warehouses are fumigated so that all moth life is killed.

THE FURRIER'S LIABILITY AS A BAILEE

The furrier and the warehouse that store furs are bailees, and they are responsible for the safekeeping of the property in their possession to the same extent as any other bailee. As in the case of laundry and dry cleaning plant customers, the owners of fur garments have come to expect the furrier and warehouseman to make good any loss, regardless of liability. There is the same need for a bailees' customers insurance policy as in other cases of the bailee's servicing the personal property of his customers.

There are two important ways in which the insurance of the furrier's liability differs from the insurance of laundries and dry cleaning plants.

The first is in the breadth of the coverage. Owners of fur garments have come to expect a broad coverage. The furrier is forced by the competition of the coverage furnished under individual fur coat insurance policies to provide an equally broad coverage for his customers.

The second difference is brought about by the custom in the fur storage business of issuing for each garment a receipt in which the value of the garment is stated. As explained in the preceding chapter, the courts generally have given effect to agreements limiting the amount a bailor may recover from a bailee. Although it is considered to be against public policy to permit bailees to avoid completely the consequences of their own negligence, the courts have held that the parties to a bailment may relieve or limit by contract the amount of the bailee's liability. Such limitations on the amount of liability have been upheld most frequently when the bailor has been given a choice of protection to the full value at one price or protection to a lesser amount at a lower price.[1]

Whenever a furrier accepts a fur garment for storage, he ascertains the valuation the owner wishes to place upon the garment and issues a receipt for that amount. The most effective of the receipts are those stating that the garment is worth the amount specified and no more. Even if the furrier is liable for loss because of negligence, his liability is likely to be limited to the amount stated. However, the furrier may be held liable for the full value of the garment (even if it exceeds the amount stated in the receipt) if it can be proved that the bailee has violated the property rights of the owner by some act that is tantamount to conversion.[2]

[1]See Schoen v. Wallace, 334 Ill. App. 294 (1948).

[2]See the preceding chapter for a discussion of acts by a bailee that may be held equivalent to conversion.

FURRIERS' CUSTOMERS INSURANCE

The Nation-wide Marine Definition lists among the policies that may be classified as inland marine:

> Furriers or fur storer's customers policies (i.e., policies under which certificates or receipts are issued by furriers or fur storers) covering specified articles the property of customers.

This means that furriers' customers insurance may be issued only to furriers or other persons or organizations that store furs, but the articles that may be covered under such policies are not limited to furs. Any article that is stored by a person or organization qualifying for the coverage may be covered by the policy. In practice most of the articles that are covered are fur garments or garments trimmed with fur. However, cloth garments are covered also when the customer so desires. A fur storer may be a furrier, bank, store, laundry, cleaner, general or fur warehouseman, cold storage concern, or other bailee who would accept a fur garment for storage.

The Furriers' Customers Policy Coverage. The standard form of furriers' customers policy states:

> This policy covers only the following described property owned by or under contract of sale to customers of the named Insured or other bailee(s), and for which the named Insured issues a receipt which includes an agreement that the named Insured shall effect insurance and contains the provisions required by condition 1 of this Rider:
>
> a. Furs and garments trimmed with fur accepted by the named Insured for storage, alterations, repairing, cleaning or remodeling;
>
> b. Other garments, textile and similar articles customarily accepted for storage by garment stores, provided such property is accepted by the named Insured for storage.

The provision regarding the issuing of a receipt is important. There is no coverage under the policy on property taken in by the insured for any purpose (including storage) unless he issues a receipt for it in the proper form. If this provision is not called to the attention of the insured, he may be careless about issuing receipts for garments that are brought in for a small amount of work. The furrier may find himself liable for large uninsured losses if he fails to issue receipts for garments left in his possession.

Condition 1 of the rider mentioned in this extract specifies certain conditions that must appear in the receipt issued by the insured. Other provisions not in conflict with these may be added, but these are necessary in all receipts:

a. The customer accepts the receipt as correct in all respects unless the customer notifies the named Insured in writing within ten days after the date of issue thereof of any error or irregularity therein;

b. the named Insured will have effected for the benefit of the customer insurance on each article listed in the receipt which shall, in terms usual to such insurance, cover against loss by fire and theft for the value set opposite each item, which value shall also be stated to be the limit of the named Insured's liability for any loss or damage to said article;

c. the provisions of the receipt shall inure to the benefit of the Company to the same extent that they inure to the benefit of the named Insured;

d. the provisions of the receipt shall not extend in kind or amount the insurance provided by the policy;

e. it supersedes any temporary or interim receipt given by the named Insured.

The insured agrees in the receipt given to the customer to provide only fire and theft insurance, although the policy actually grants much broader coverage than that. It also is clear from an examination of the description of the property covered that only the property of customers is insured, and there is no coverage on the property of the insured. The stock of merchandise of the insured is not covered, and the furriers' customers policy cannot be extended to cover it. If the insured desires a similar coverage on his stock of furs, he can purchase a furriers' block policy.

The property is covered at locations within or in transit within and between the states of the United States, the District of Columbia, Puerto Rico and Canada, except that the policy does not insure property shipped via the Panama Canal, or to or from Alaska, Hawaii, or Puerto Rico. The property is covered within these territorial limits just as long as it is in the custody of the insured. This means that if the property has to be shipped to another location for storage, repair, cleaning, or delivery to the customer, it still is covered by the policy as long as the insured is responsible for it and it is within the territory specified.

The coverage is against "all risks" of loss or damage with a few exclusions. The insured's legal liability is specifically included.

Exclusions. Property belonging to the named insured and its subsidiaries or affiliates is excluded in order to clarify the intent of the policy as strictly a customers' goods coverage. There are war risk and nuclear exclusions similar to those in transportation policies. Only three other exclusions appear, and these are particularly designed for this policy.

The first excludes loss or damage "occasioned by gradual deterioration, insect, vermin or inherent vice, or by processing or by any work upon the property unless caused by fire or explosion."

The second excludes "liability assumed by the named Insured under any agreement, express or implied, (1) to guarantee the results of processing or any work to be performed upon the property, or (2) to effect insurance upon such property in any amount except as provided herein." As noted above, the policy covers the legal liability of the insured, and this includes contractual as well as common law or statute liability. However, underwriters do not consider it feasible to insure the liability that the insured might assume for the completion of some work or process. The other restriction in this clause is necessary because the premium for the policy is based upon the amounts declared in the receipts, and any agreement by the insured to effect insurance outside or above that amount would result in the insurance company's being liable for losses for which no premium is received.

The third exclusion refers to "any amount of loss or damage on account of which the named insured, in the absence of this insurance, would be entitled to indemnity under any applicable fidelity bond or similar undertaking." The policy does not exclude loss due to infidelity of the insured's employees, and in the absence of a fidelity bond the insured would be able to collect any such loss under the furriers' customers policy. If the insured carries a fidelity bond, however, this clause is intended to make it the primary insurance for an infidelity loss.

Limits of Liability. Limits of liability are set out carefully and clearly. The clause covering this point calls attention to the fact that premiums are to be paid on the basis of the aggregate amount of values set forth in all the receipts, but the clause also states that the limits of liability shall apply even if the aggregate of the values stored should exceed the limits of liability.

Specific dollar limitations of liability are set forth applying to (1) the aggregate amount for which the company shall be liable in any one casualty, (2) storage enclosures at specified premises, (3) locations outside storage enclosures at the storage premises, (4) other premises not used for storage purposes, (5) any other unnamed premises, and (6) property in transit.

The general clause on limitation of liability states that the company shall not be liable for more than the amount stipulated in the storage receipt, or the actual value, or the cost of repair with materials of like kind and quality, whichever is less. These limitations are all considered necessary because the values of fur garments are high. The total values can pyramid so rapidly that the company must be notified when the amount at risk goes beyond the point for which reinsurance has been arranged. No insurance company could afford to issue an unlimited policy covering furs as some companies do in connection with laundry bailee policies.

Special Conditions. The special conditions of the policy are designed for the peculiar situations affecting the fur insurance business. The insured is obligated to use due diligence in maintaining the protective devices described in the proposal for the insurance. This is important because many fur storage premises are protected by burglar alarms, sprinkler systems, or watchman service. Rates and underwriting are based upon the presence of these devices, and the insurance company must be notified if any of them are discontinued.

In case of loss, the insurance company has the option of adjusting losses with the insured or with the customer. The company also has the right to take any steps it deems necessary to protect, rehabilitate, or recondition the property, including the removal of the property from the place of loss and the employment of independent contractors to do the work. This is an important right in case the insured should not be cooperative in the reduction of the loss. Fur losses need immediate attention to prevent further damage. Extensive additional damage might occur while any controversy was being settled.

Cancellation may be made by the company in fifteen days instead of in the five days provided for by many inland marine policies. This is a concession to the insured, because it might take more than five days to arrange for insurance on such large values as may exist in a fur storage warehouse.

The insured is required to keep an accurate record of all the receipts he issues, together with the customer's name and address, description of the property, amount of value stipulated, and the location of the garment in storage. The company has the privilege of examining these records at any reasonable time during the policy period and for one year thereafter. The insured is required to report to the company by the fifteenth of each month the aggregate amount of values set forth in all outstanding receipts as of the last day of the preceding month and to pay premium on these aggregate values. If there is more than one storage location, the report must show the values at each location.

Certificates Issued by the Furrier. The policy also provides that the insured shall not issue certificates of insurance to customers on the insured property except in the company issuing the policy, and then only when permitted by endorsement to the policy.

Many furriers' customers policies are written with a provision for certificates to be issued by the named insured to cover outside the storage premises and while the garments are not in the custody of the insured. They are, in effect, insurance policies that cover for the benefit of the individual owner whenever the garment is out of storage. Thus the owner of a fur garment can go to the furrier and store his garment for the summer (during which time the garment is insured under the furriers' customers policy) and at the same time get a certificate insuring the garment for one year from the date it is put in storage regardless of how long it stays there. This saves the owner the trouble of buying an individual fur coat policy.

The certificate cannot be issued for any greater amount than the owner declares to the furrier for storage purposes. The owner cannot put a value of $100 on the fur coat for storage purposes and get a certificate of insurance for $500.

The exact form of the certificate differs according to the requirements of the state insurance departments. Some states require that the certificate show the exact amount of the storage and premium charges. In other states, it merely is necessary for the furrier to show the total amount of the charges, and under this arrangement the customer cannot see what he is charged for the insurance.

The rate for such a certificate generally is less than the rate for an individual fur coat policy. This lower rate is considered to be justified by the fact that the furrier already has paid a premium for insurance on the property while it is in storage. There is perhaps some additional saving to the insurance company in that a certificate is less expensive to issue than a full policy.

Most states require that the certificates be countersigned by an agent of the insurance company in accordance with the state countersignature laws. The countersignature requirements usually are taken care of by the agent who writes the furriers' customers policy. Copies of the certificates must be forwarded to the company. The insurance company has the privilege of cancelling any certificate on five days' notice, but the cancellation of the underlying furriers' customers policy does not cancel the certificates that have been issued. It is necessary for the company to cancel each certificate individually if it desires cancellation. (Cancellation of the underlying furriers' customers policy does cancel the coverage on furs for which storage receipts have been given, but not the coverage on furs on which individual certificates of insurance have been written.)

Excess Legal Liability. It has been explained that the furriers' customers policy covers the legal liability of the insured and the interest of the owner only up to the amount stipulated in the storage receipt given by the furrier to the owner. It also has been explained that the furrier may be liable for the full value of the garment (in spite of the limitation in the receipt) if the owner can prove that the furrier has performed some act that is tantamount to conversion. Even if the owner has other insurance to indemnify him for the loss, the other insurance company is likely to sue for its loss if it appears that the furrier can be proved liable. This potential liability of the furrier above the values stated in the receipts is called "excess legal liability," and it can be insured against by an endorsement to the furriers' customers policy.

There are two forms of this endorsement covering excess legal liability. The first is issued to cover the liability in connection with garments for which the insured has issued receipts to garment owners. The other endorsement is used to cover the bailee who stores garments for other bailees. For example, many cold storage warehouses, in addition to storing garments for individual fur owners, also rent out space to furriers and other storers who do not have storage facilities of their own. These bailees might be held liable for loss to the bailee, or to the owner of the garment, or to the owner's insurance company. Both endorsements might be attached to a policy that covers a storage warehouse doing both a retail and a wholesale fur storage business.

Other provisions of the two excess legal liability endorsements are the same. Both cover any loss that the insured is obligated to pay because of direct loss or damage in excess of the amount stated in the receipt to property covered by the policy. The exclusions are few and refer to liability assumed by the insured, war damage, nuclear damage, loss due to gradual deterioration, insect, vermin, inherent vice, or by processing, or by any work upon the property unless caused by fire or explosion. These exclusions are similar to those in the policy to which the endorsement is attached.

The insured is obligated to notify the company as soon as practicable when it appears that an excess legal liability claim may be presented, and he must cooperate with the company in settling or defending the claim. The company has the right to defend or compromise the claim at its sole option.

Two limits of liability appear on the excess legal liability endorsement. The first is a limit per article, and the second limits the amount the company shall be obliged to pay as a result of any one accident, casualty, or event.

An extra premium is charged for the excess legal liability endorsement. This premium is a percentage of the policy premium. The percentage varies with the relation between the limit in the excess legal liability endorsement and the aggregate of declared values in the storage premises of the insured.

It is important for the insured to carry excess legal liability coverage. Many customers declare their garments for less than the actual value, either to save on storage charges or because they have other insurance. In case the insured is liable for loss above the declared values, he would have to pay the excess amount himself unless the legal liability endorsement were attached to the policy.

Rating Procedure and Proposal Form. The rates for furriers' customers storage policies are computed by the rating bureaus for their members and subscribers. Independent companies use a method and schedule similar to those used by the rating bureaus. The information for the computation of the rate is furnished to the bureau by the insurance company on a lengthy proposal. In addition to the information requested in other inland marine proposal forms regarding the insured and the nature of his business, the furriers' customers proposal inquires regarding the peak values stored during the preceding 12 months, the details of any losses during the past five years, a list of the storage locations, the limits desired on the policy, and much detail regarding the construction and protection of the storage vaults. The insurance company must secure the fire insurance rates for general contents and for vault contents (if published) at the storage locations.

The basic rate is the 80 percent coinsurance fire rate for vault contents as published by the fire insurance rating bureau. If there is no rate published specifically for the contents of the vault, the schedule provides a method of computing a vault contents rate from the general contents fire rate. The vault contents rate can be as low as 50 percent of the fire contents rate for a small vault and graduates upward for larger-sized vaults. The annual fire rate for the vault contents (calculated according to the schedule or taken from the fire rating bureau) is divided by 12 to secure a monthly rate.

The loading for the other hazards covered by the policy graduates downward from 6 cents per $100 per month, depending upon the construction of the vault, the type of fire doors at the vault openings, and the burglar and fire protection provided. This loading can be as low as one-half cent per month for a well-constructed vault with good fire and burglar protection.

An additional charge is made when the insured's receiving location is different from the storage location. This is a flat charge and does not vary with the protection of the storage premises. There is a substantial hazard in the transfer of several fur coats from the insured's sales location to the storage location.

UNDERWRITING FUR STORAGE RISKS

The underwriting of fur storage operations is a difficult problem. An underwriter appraises the likelihood of theft of individual garments at the store or receiving station and investigates the possibility of a catastrophe loss from fire or burglary at the storage location. The total values at storage locations may run into many millions of dollars. In a community where a company has many personal fur policies in effect, a bad fire might result in the company's being liable not only for damage to garments insured under the furriers' customers policy but also for the value of garments insured under individual fur policies.

The premium received for a fur storage policy is not sufficient to carry a load of frequent losses of individual garments. A loss of one or two garments a year could offset the entire premium for a medium-sized fur storage policy.

An important possibility of loss occurs during pickup and delivery to the customer. Many garments are called for by the furrier at the customer's request, and many furriers advertise a pickup and delivery service as part of the inducement to store furs with them. The delivery truck may be held up while out on its route, or a sneak thief may pick up a coat and walk off with it when the driver is not watching. All trucks used for pickup and delivery of insured furs should be provided with good locks of the snap type that will lock automatically when the door of the truck is closed. It is not safe to rely on the memory of the driver to lock his vehicle when he leaves it. Automatic alarms are recommended for trucks used by furriers and have proved effective in preventing thefts.

Sneak thieves sometimes are responsible for losses from within the furrier's shop. The store and shop should be arranged so that no one except employees has access to the spot where customers' garments are received and stored. Counters should be continuous, so that an outsider cannot walk around them into the shop portion of the premises. Stocks of merchandise for sale should be kept separate from the customers' goods to avoid the chance of a customer's garment getting out onto the sales floor where it can be sold by mistake or picked up by someone in the store. Rear entrances should be kept locked except when actually in use, and some means should be provided for the person inside the store to see who is at a rear entrance before the door is opened.

Many furriers do not maintain their own vaults for storage but store their customers' goods in a large warehouse in rented space. The garments again are exposed to theft or other loss during the transfer from the furrier's place of business to the warehouse. Loading and unloading should be done under the supervision of a reliable employee. The driver must not be permitted to unload alone, for this procedure requires him to leave the truck unattended when he goes into the building with an armload of garments.

All employees who have access to the furs should be bonded. This arrangement has two advantages. First, any loss that can be proved to be the result of theft by a bonded employee is not covered under the furriers' customers policy, since the bonding company would be responsible for that as an infidelity loss. Second, the investigation bonded employees undergo is likely to show up any employee who has been involved in previous thefts. Honesty of all employees is an extremely important factor in a favorable experience on a fur storage line.

Sometimes garments are lost without any indication of how the loss occurred. The identification may have been lost from the garment so that it cannot be matched to the claim ticket. Identification tags must be attached securely, and the records should show a good enough description of the garment that there can be no question of identity if the tag does come off. The furrier should also keep a record of where the garment has been placed in the vault as a further means of locating it.

A careful insurance company inspector follows each step a garment takes as it goes through the furriers' hands to and from storage and to the customer. The procedure should be changed at any point where it could result in loss or theft of a garment. It is only by a strict control of the individual loss possibilities that the company can hope to retain enough premium to pay for the catastrophe losses inherent in this class of insurance.

FUR VAULT CONSTRUCTION AND PROTECTION

If the underwriter finds that the garments are protected satisfactorily on their journeys to and from the customer's premises and the storage location, he then must determine whether the chances of a catastrophe loss are serious at the storage location. The furrier who has a small vault and a few thousand dollars' worth of furs in storage does not offer the temptation to thieves that is offered by an accumulation of furs worth a million dollars. The greater the temptation to thieves, the more formidable must be the protection against them.

The vaults used for storage by some small fur stores are nothing more than cabinets in which the furs are fumigated to keep moths from eating the garments. Such cabinets offer little resistance to a clever burglar, but this does not mean that they need to be an open invitation to burglars. The most effective protection is a good burglar alarm system by which any attempt at burglary is reported immediately to a central station and thence to the police. This central station burglar alarm service is similar to that described for jewelry stores.

There are many medium-sized fur stores in which the vaults are large enough to accommodate from $100,000 to $500,000 worth of furs. This concentration of value justifies strong protection, not only from burglary but also from the danger of fire. The desirable features of construction and protection are described in the following paragraphs. The greater the value, the more nearly perfect should be the combination of protective features.

The vault should be constructed like an independent building within a building, so that if the entire surrounding building is destroyed by fire, the vault will remain intact. Walls of brick, tile, or concrete block in thicknesses of 12 inches or more offer a good degree of fire resistance. It is not difficult, however, for a burglar to breach such a wall if he can work on it for an hour or more inside a building. Reinforced concrete is a more nearly satisfactory protection, because the steel rods running through it make the work of burglars more difficult. Some vaults contain a lining of burglar-resistant steel plate, and this is desirable, especially for brick, tile, or cement block walls. Floors and ceilings should be equivalent in construction to the walls.

All doors, windows, and vents should be protected with fire doors that are capable of withstanding a severe fire for several hours. Openings large enough for a person to enter should be protected by burglar-resistant doors as well. The best-protected vaults have two doors at each opening, one labeled by the Underwriters' Laboratories for fire resistance and the other for burglar resistance. The double protection makes it unlikely that either burglars or fire can get through the opening.

It is generally recognized that there is no door or wall made that a clever burglar cannot get through if he has sufficient time and the proper tools. In addition to strong construction, there should be an alarm system to give warning when an attempt at burglary is made. The best burglar alarm systems are those that report to a central station maintained by a burglar alarm company and manned 24 hours a day. The electrical connections are monitored constantly, so that the wires cannot be cut or otherwise put out of commission without the central station's being notified.

The simplest of the burglar alarm devices consist of electrical contacts on the doors and windows that send in an alarm when the door or window is opened. Because burglars may go through the walls instead of the doors and windows, the walls may be wired in such a way that it is impossible to cut a hole large enough for a person to get through without sending an alarm. Another device for vault protection is a sound device that sends an alarm if there is an unusual noise. The breaching of a masonry wall is a noisy job, and a burglar could not get into a vault with a sound alarm without setting it off.

There are electronic protective devices that give an alarm if anyone enters the fur vault or the premises. These include electric eyes and beams of invisible light, ultrasonic devices which can detect unusual sound within the vault, and capacitative electronic equipment that signals the presence of a person if he enters an area where he should not be.

A watchman is desirable for patrol purposes when the premises are closed for business. The simplest device to check on his movements is the watchman's clock, on which he records his rounds. The standard requirement is that the watchman make a complete round of the building at least once an hour. The clock should be checked each morning to see that he actually has made the rounds and did not sleep part of the night. Insurance inspectors check the watchman's records to see that the service is not being neglected.

Unfortunately, the watchman's clock cannot give any indication during the night if the watchman neglects to make his rounds, has an accident, or is held up by burglars. This service is provided in a supervised watchman's service of the burglar alarm companies. The watchman is required to turn a key in devices set about the building. If he misses a round or is late, the central station sends a guard to investigate. The devices are so arranged that the watchman can signal for help if he is held up or becomes incapacitated. Even if the burglars are aware of the watchman's signaling system and force him to continue his rounds, there are devices by which the watchman can signal for help without the knowledge of the burglar who is accompanying the watchman.

Large concentrations of value require that fire protection be installed in the vault. Automatic sprinklers are considered an excellent all-round fire protection, both for the vault and for the premises outside it. If there is a sprinkler system, there is not likely to be nearly so severe an exposure fire to the vault as there is without such protection. It is desirable to have the sprinkler system connected to a central station burglar and fire alarm company, so that any fire at night will be detected as soon as the sprinkler system operates. Otherwise the sprinkler system might operate for several hours until the premises were opened in the morning, and enormous water damage would result.

Vaults may be equipped with apparatus that floods a vault with carbon dioxide in order to smother fire. Carbon dioxide does no harm to the garments, and many fur storage operators prefer such a system to automatic sprinklers.

In a cold storage vault, sprinklers may be slow to operate because (1) fur fires are likely to smolder for a long time before giving off enough heat to operate the sprinklers and (2) the refrigerating system tends to carry off the heat and slow down the operation of the sprinklers. A variation of the electric eye device used for burglary protection can be used to detect smoke that passes through the beam of light. Such a smoke detection system might give an alarm of fire much in advance of any other means of discovery.

A $3,000,000 fur vault fire at New Haven, Connecticut, a few years ago illustrates the way a combination of circumstances can result in an enormous loss to the contents of such a vault. The vault area was entirely without windows, and the time lock arrangement on the vault doors prevented the firemen from getting into the vault in the early stages of the fire. There were no automatic sprinklers, nor was there any carbon dioxide flooding system by which the fire could be controlled from the inside. The fact that the furs were packed in tightly resulted in a smoldering, extremely smoky fire.

Eventually it was necessary for the firemen to break through the walls with pneumatic drills and to flood the entire three floors of the vault. It was reported that the fire had been started by an electric light bulb that had been left turned on and in contact with a fur coat or some other combustible material. A ventilating duct that ran through three floors without cutoffs permitted the smoke to fill the entire building and prevented firemen from working inside the structure. The installation of automatic fire detection and control equipment in the building, as described in the preceding paragraphs, probably would have confined the fire to the area of its origin and might have kept the loss to a nominal figure.

QUESTIONS

1. How does furriers' customers insurance differ from the coverage under a bailees' customers policy for a laundry or dry cleaning plant?
2. What type of property may be insured under a furriers' customers policy?

3. Why does the furriers' customers policy cover only garments for which the insured gives a storage receipt?
4. What are the principal exclusions in the furriers' customers policy?
5. Why do inland marine underwriters consider it necessary to specify in detail the limits of liability under a furriers' customers policy?
6. Why does an insurance company consider it necessary to have the right to proceed with salvage operations in case of a loss under a furriers' customers policy?
7. What coverage is provided by a certificate issued by a furrier under a furriers' customers policy?
8. Discuss the furrier's need for excess legal liability insurance.
9. Outline the procedure used in calculating the rate for a furriers' customers policy.
10. Discuss procedures for preventing loss of fur garments as a result of theft.
11. Discuss the construction and protection recommended for fur storage vaults in order to prevent fire and burglary losses.
12. Outline a program of insurance that you would recommend to cover a furrier's stock of merchandise and also his liability for the property of customers in his custody.
13. Distinguish between the purpose of the furriers' customers insurance policy and that of the furriers' block policy.

18

Miscellaneous Bailee Coverages

Preceding chapters have discussed forms of bailees' customers insurance that have been written for many years and are firmly established as inland marine coverages. Other bailees' customers coverages have been developed more recently and are intended to fit the needs of specific industries. The hazards vary according to the operations covered. Underwriters find it desirable to become familiar with each industry because the coverages are not standardized and must be adapted to the needs of each policyholder.

COLD STORAGE LOCKER BAILEE FLOATER

The Nation-wide Marine Definition classifies as inland marine "cold storage locker plant policies, covering [customers'] merchandise . . . consisting principally of meats, game, fish, poultry, fruit, vegetables, and property of a similar nature." There is no restriction as to the type of customer, nor as to how the property is to be stored. Bulk storage, or storage for persons or firms that do a commercial business, would be eligible just as long as the property belongs to customers of the insured.

Most of the goods stored in a locker plant are brought to the plant by the patrons, although some plants maintain a pickup and delivery service. The locker owner is maintaining what is primarily a storage operation, and he is in the position of a bailee. The relative amount of transportation while in the custody of the locker operator is less than in the case of a launderer or furrier.

The liability of the cold storage locker plant operator is similar to that of any other bailee. He is dealing with the public, and not only is he interested in protecting himself from liability for loss, but he wants also to reimburse his patrons for any loss regardless of his liability. The insurance coverage available for this purpose is fundamentally the same as that used for launderers or furriers, although the coverage is adapted to the peculiar needs of food storage.

Coverage Under Cold Storage Locker Policy. There are several variations of the coverage in use. Specified perils policies issued by many companies protect against loss by fire, lightning, windstorm, hail, explosion (except boiler and machinery explosion), riot and civil commotion, falling aircraft, motor vehicle, earthquake, theft and burglary, and collision or overturning of vehicles on which the property is being transported at the risk of the insured. The definitions and limitations of these coverages are much the same as in other bailee policies.

Also included is a coverage similar to that in the laundry bailee policy which protects against loss due to confusion of property from any of the perils specifically covered.

A coverage peculiar to the cold storage locker bailee form is that insuring against consequential loss or damage caused by changes in temperature resulting from:

a. Total or partial destruction of refrigeration or cooling equipment connections, or supply pipes by the perils enumerated;

b. Electrical interruption caused by breakdown of the electric generating or transmission system preventing the insured from maintaining operation of the cooling system;

c. Mechanical breakdown of the refrigeration or cooling equipment, connections, or supply pipes.

An "all risks" form is written. The principal difference between the "all risks" and the specified perils form is in the coverage clause, the exclusions and special conditions being much the same. The "all risks" form is broader in its coverage and protects against some miscellaneous hazards not listed in the specified perils form. The "all risks" form covers losses resulting from general curtailment of electrical power.

The usual inland marine exclusions of loss due to gradual deterioration, spoilage, insect, or inherent vice are expanded to exclude loss due to any processing. This is intended to avoid loss by smoking processes. Many locker plants do smoking of meat, and the insurance does not cover loss due to a fault in the process. Most of the policies are so worded that damage resulting from a fire that breaks out as a result of the smoking operation would be covered.

Like the laundry bailee policy, the cold storage locker bailee policy excludes loss resulting from misdelivery or careless destruction of goods, losses due to the infidelity of the insured's employees or any person to whom the goods are entrusted, war damage, nuclear damage, and loss resulting from neglect of the insured to save and preserve the property at the time of a loss.

A special exclusion relates to leakage of refrigerant gases. Many policies exclude such damage unless it results from a bursting of the containing system. It is not clear where the line can be drawn between a gradual leak and a rapid leak that can be considered a bursting of the system. There have been some large losses from leakage of refrigerant gases and consequent contamination of all the food stored in the plant. Insurance companies can provide the coverage if the insured is willing to pay a rate that is adequate for the protection.

The property covered and the conditions of coverage usually include meat, fowl, game, fish, vegetables, fruits, and other edible goods held by the insured as bailee for the purposes of chilling, cutting, freezing, and storing, all while situated in the locker plant described in the policy and while being transported to or from the plant by the insured. Some policies also extend the coverage for five days to any other place where the property must be removed for preservation from a peril insured against. The property is covered anywhere in the locker plant and not merely within each locker rented by a patron.

There are two limits of liability in almost all policies. One is a limit per locker and the other is a limit per catastrophe. The limit per locker commonly is $50, but this may be changed when the lockers are odd sizes or when the nature of the goods is such as to justify a different figure.

The limit per catastrophe usually is the limit per locker multiplied by the number of lockers in the plant. Some policies also contain a further limitation that coverage on property outside lockers while on the premises and in the course of transportation shall be limited to 10 percent of the catastrophe limit. This is intended to prevent the company's being held liable for a large amount of bulk storage for which no premium is provided in the rate calculation.

Like other bailees' customers policies, this one contains a provision that the insurance company has the option of adjusting losses with the customers or with the insured. Some policies require that the insured report to the police department any thefts in excess of a nominal figure, usually $25.

Many variations of coverage are possible, depending upon the nature of the insured's operation. There may be storage rooms or lockers capable of containing hundreds of pounds of property. Policies can be arranged to fit the insured's needs and operations.

Rates. Rates are based primarily upon the fire and extended coverage rates on contents of the locker plant. A loading is added to cover the other perils insured against and also to cover the consequential loss coverage assumed by the policy. The loadings are small, in many cases not exceeding 20 cents per $100 of coverage, but the insurance company has some margin because the actual liability per locker frequently is less than the limit per locker specified in the policy. At the end of winter, when lockers are almost empty, the actual values may be far below the limits specified in the policy. This enables the insurance company to use what appears to be a low loading in the rate, since the rate is paid on the basis of the full limits.

Underwriting Cold Storage Locker Bailee Plants. The underwriting of cold storage locker bailee plants is primarily an appraisal of the total loss possibilities. The fire hazard must be examined with care because most of the large losses are the result of fire.

A specially constructed one-story plant usually is preferable to a remodeled building. There have been cases in which fire spread into concealed spaces around the locker installation in a remodeled building and considerable water damage resulted before firemen could control it.

Slaughtering, smoking of meats, and other processing may add a considerable fire hazard. It is preferable to have all processing done in a section of the building that is cut off by fire doors from the storage section.

Power interruption is a serious threat. Some plants have an auxiliary power plant, so that any interruption of the electric power will not cause a total loss of refrigeration. The temperature maintained in most plants is about zero degrees Fahrenheit. It takes about 24 hours after refrigeration is stopped for the temperature to rise to a point at which food will spoil, provided the storage section is kept closed. An electric power interruption from an electrical storm usually is corrected within 24 hours, but there may be widespread damage to transmission lines as a result of sleet storms.

Experience of the operator is an important factor, and the preferable plant is one with an operator who has been in the business for some time and knows all the hazards. The business prospects of the insured are important, because poor business is likely to result in poor maintenance. Many operators get almost their entire income within a few weeks at one period of the year. A careful budgeting of income is essential to efficient operation, and the newcomer or poor businessman may prove to be an inefficient operator.

PROCESSOR'S LIABILITY

As pointed out in connection with the garment contractors floater, there are many manufacturing processes in which a portion of the work is done by subcontractors. The plastics manufacturing industry is one in which this situation is prevalent. The forming of plastic parts of a product is likely to be done by specialty factories and not in the plant of the manufacturer. Makers of mechanical pencils, for example, may have the barrels of the pencils fabricated by a plastics shop before putting the pencils together with the metal parts made in their own machine shops.

In some cases the processor contracts for the delivery of a certain number of pieces and provides the material. In such cases there is no bailee-bailor relationship because the processor buys his own material and supplies a completed product (insofar as his work is concerned). In other cases the manufacturer supplies the material, and in these cases the processor is a bailee, with the same responsibility to the bailor as other bailees.

The processor who is a bailee may purchase a casualty insurance policy to protect himself against loss as a result of his liability to the bailor. Another way for him to secure protection is to buy a fire and extended coverage policy from a fire insurance company to cover his interest in the property while it is on his premises. These methods are deficient from the bailee's standpoint because the casualty company coverage does not afford any protection to the interest of the owner of the property and the fire policy does not give coverage against transportation hazards when the bailee transports the property at his risk. When there is a transportation hazard, inland marine coverage is available for the protection of both the insured (the bailee) and the owner (the bailor).

An inland marine policy that protects the bailee against loss as a result of his liability or that protects both the bailee's and the bailor's interests must cover in transit as well as at the premises of the bailee. Property does not qualify for inland marine coverage as a processing risk unless there is a transit exposure, even though the policy states that there is transit coverage.

There is a practical reason why the owner of merchandise has come to expect a processor to protect his interest. The owner may have goods out being processed in many different plants, and the arrangements may have to be made on short notice. It is difficult for the owner of goods to call his insurance agent or broker every time he needs coverage at a new location. Only in a few industries, such as the clothing industry, has the business become sufficiently stabilized that the owner of goods can go to his insurance company and get a blanket policy covering him on a blanket basis for all the goods he may have in the hands of processors during the year. In connection with many other industries, an insurance company wants to be kept informed regarding its liability at all times. The processor knows about how much goods he can process at one time, and an insurance company can issue a policy to him that will cover the value of goods he is likely to have at risk.

Insurance policies written for processors as bailees usually are on a specified perils basis. The basic coverage is that of a transportation policy, and the hazards covered are divided between those at the location of the processing and those during transportation. At the location of the processor, the policy covers against loss by fire, lightning, windstorm, explosion, riot, civil commotion, vehicle and falling aircraft damage, sprinkler leakage (if the plant is equipped with automatic sprinklers), and water damage.

In connection with valuable merchandise, such as furs, woolens, silks, and precision instruments, the hazards of burglary or perhaps both burglary and theft may be covered.

In the course of transportation, the policy protects against loss by fire, theft, collision, and overturn of the transporting vehicle, or, as the wording reads in some policies, "perils of transportation." The coverage for each property is written to fit the insured's needs, and no two policies are likely to read the same.

Rates are based primarily on the rates for fire and extended coverage at the location where the processing is done. If sprinkler leakage coverage and burglary coverage are added, the rates are increased according to the sprinkler leakage and burglary rates for the location. A loading also is added to take care of the transportation coverage, according to the territory where the hauling must be done and the length of the haul. The rate is applied to the amount at risk, or perhaps to the average amount at risk during the course of the year. Coverage and rate factors for the transit risk follow those described for annual transit policies.

In some cases the rate is quoted as a percentage of the gross receipts of the business. In these cases, the premium fluctuates monthly with the gross receipts. As explained in connection with gross receipts rates for motor truck cargo policies, the gross receipts method of paying premiums is satisfactory if the gross receipts fluctuate with the actual values at risk. This is the case in some processing plants, but underwriters try to make certain that a policy is producing a premium commensurate with the hazards covered.

PROPERTY ON CONSIGNMENT

There are occasions when property is held on consignment at the risk of the consignee. The consignee is a bailee in that he holds the property of others in his custody, and he is responsible for the use of ordinary care in the preservation of the property from loss or damage. The Nation-wide Marine Definition provides that goods on consignment may be insured under an inland marine policy under certain conditions. Merchandise on consignment for sale or distribution may be insured under an inland marine policy during actual transit and for a period of 120 days after arrival at the premises of the consignee. If the property remains at a fixed location for more than 120 days, the property must be insured under a location policy, such as a fire policy. The theory is that 120 days is sufficient time for the consignee to determine whether the property is to go back or to stay there until sold or otherwise used.

The Nation-wide Marine Definition is more liberal in connection with property that is intended to go back to its source or to be forwarded to another destination. Property shipped on consignment for exhibit, trial, approval, or auction may be insured while in transit, while in the custody of others, and while being returned. Such property is considered to be in a technical "state of transportation" (even though it is actually at rest during a part of the time) and is eligible for inland marine coverage. Either the bailee or the bailor may insure such property. When insured by the bailee, he has the privilege of insuring it against his legal liability only or of insuring the owner's interest as well. Policies covering such property are issued as transportation policies, and the coverage and rates are similar to those already discussed for that type of coverage. The interests of the various parties should be stated correctly in the policy if the interests of both the bailee and the bailor are covered.

BAILEE STORAGE OF MISCELLANEOUS ARTICLES

It happens frequently that a bailee has goods in storage at his risk, and he may desire an inland marine policy in order to secure the broad coverage inland marine policies provide. It is a principle of inland marine insurance that goods in storage and not subject to a transportation hazard are not proper subjects for inland marine coverage. This is true regardless of whether they are to be covered for the owner or for a bailee.

For example, there have been many attempts to write a policy covering warehousemen's legal liability as an inland marine form. The Committee on Interpretation ruled that an inland marine policy may be written if the goods that are to be the subject of the insurance qualify of themselves for inland marine coverage.

In some states that have not adopted the Nation-wide Marine Definition warehousemen's legal liability coverage may be written as an inland marine coverage, even though there is no transit hazard.

These policies are written as transportation policies in the same way as a policy covering property on consignment. The rates depend upon the established rates for the coverage at the location insured plus a loading for any hazards insured for which there are no established rates.

INNKEEPERS' LIABILITY AND CHECKROOM LIABILITY

Soon after the establishing of the 1933 Nation-Wide Definition the question arose whether the liability of an innkeeper (or hotel proprietor) could be insured under an inland marine policy. It was contended that the innkeeper was in the position of a bailee and that the situation was similar to that of bailees whose liability could be insured under inland marine policies.

The Joint Committee ruled that the innkeeper is not a bailee in regard to property of guests in the hotel but that he has an absolute liability to his guests for the safety of their property. This liability, which is not dependent upon the principle of bailee liability, is based upon the common law as it specifically applies to innkeepers and as it is modified by the statutes of many states. There is another distinction in that the owner is in partial control of the property in his custody. Since the innkeeper is not a bailee, there is no provision of the Definition under which such liability can be insured under an inland marine policy.

Although the innkeeper is not in the position of a bailee in regard to property of guests in the hotel, he is a bailee in regard to any property that is checked with him in a checkroom incidentally to its transportation. These circumstances include the checking of hats and coats in the hotel dining room and also may include the checking of baggage in a checkroom after the guest has checked out and is no longer registered as a guest. The exact liability of the innkeeper under varying circumstances of checking baggage varies according to the hotel and business laws of the states and will not be discussed here.

Property checked by a hotel or other establishment in a checkroom incidentally to its transportation can be insured under an inland marine policy by either the owner of the property or by the custodian. A hotel may not secure an inland marine policy to cover its liability for the property of guests in the hotel, but it may secure an inland marine policy on the property while it is checked in the hotel checkroom. The checkroom situation provides either a bailee-bailor relationship or something close enough to it to justify permitting the issuance of an inland marine policy.

An interesting case decided by the United States District Court for the Southern District of New York in 1948 illustrates both the limitation that hotel laws may place upon the recovery to be had from a hotel when it has checked property and the strict interpretation that may be placed on the limitation when the checking is not done by the hotel corporation itself.[1]

The subject of the dispute was a mink coat that had been checked with a concessionaire in the hotel. The coat was given to an impostor by the checkroom girl, who did not require the presentation of the check. The owner of the coat sued the concessionaire and the hotel for $4,500, the value of the coat. The court decided that the checkroom girl was "guilty of gross negligence in delivering the coat to an impostor without production of the check, and her employer, the concessionaire, is liable for the value thereof. Its obligation was that of a bailee—whether gratuitous or for hire is unimportant. Wrongful delivery was a breach of its contract and amounted to a conversion of the coat."

The opinion of the court goes on to discuss the concessionaire's attempt to limit its liability by reason of the New York General Business Law, which does restrict the liability of hotels under certain conditions. The applicable portion of the opinion reads:

[1] Jacobson v. Belplaza Corp. 80 F. Supp. 917 (1948).

> The Concessionaire contends that its liability is limited to $75 under Section 201 of the New York General Business Law. The material portion of this section reads as follows: "as to property deposited by guests or patrons in the parcel or check room of any hotel or restaurant, the delivery of which is evidenced by a check or receipt therefor and for which no fee or charge is exacted, the proprietor shall not be liable beyond seventy-five dollars, unless such value in excess of seventy-five dollars shall be stated upon delivery and a written receipt, stating such value, shall be issued, but he shall in no event be liable beyond one hundred dollars, unless such loss occurs through his fault or negligence."
>
> This section as originally enacted, Laws of 1855, Chapter 421, applied only to hotel keepers. The portion just quoted was added by the Laws of 1924, Chapter 506. It did nothing more than to create a limited liability for both hotel keepers and restaurant proprietors. There is no hint that the amendment was intended to apply to independent operators of check rooms, such as the present Concessionaire, and it should not be so extended by implication. . . .
>
> The Concessionaire did not operate the restaurant. Nor was plaintiff's coat "property deposited by guests or patrons" of the Concessionaire. Plaintiff was a guest or patron of the Hotel, not of the Concessionaire. Furthermore, the Concessionaire cannot be considered as an employee or agent of the Hotel and, therefore, protected by the limited liability accorded to the Hotel. It was an independent contractor operating, as it admits, the check room for profit.
>
> No New York authority has been cited, and I have found none, holding that an independent operator of a check room in a restaurant is entitled to the limited liability of $75 for property deposited there. I find nothing to that effect in Gardner v. Roosevelt Hotel, Inc., 263 App. Div. 268, 32 N.Y.S. 2d 208, relied upon by the Concessionaire.
>
> I hold, therefore, that the Concessionaire is liable for the full value of plaintiff's coat. With this disposition I think the complaint should be dismissed as against the Hotel.

It becomes evident from this decision that inland marine underwriters who issue checkroom policies need to determine the probable liability of the insured for loss of property. When the insured's liability may be limited by the hotel or general business laws of the state, a more favorable rate may be in order. On the other hand, if the position of the insured is such that he may be held liable for the full value of any property that is lost, the underwriter anticipates occasional losses of considerable size. Patrons of hotels, restaurants, and night clubs are likely to wear fur coats and other garments worth many thousands of dollars. Such property is spotted by criminals and they make an effort to steal the better garments that are checked.

Underwriters attempt to reach a complete understanding with the insured about whether the coverage includes only certain specified perils or all liability of the insured for loss of a checked garment. Carelessness on the part of the insured's employees in handing out garments is likely to result in liability on the part of the insured. The policy wording should be such that there can be no misunderstanding of its meaning. It is important to include or exclude carelessness and misdelivery in positive terms.

QUESTIONS

1. What situation brought about a rapid increase in the number of cold storage locker plants?
2. Why does the operator of a cold storage locker plant feel the need for a bailees' customers policy?
3. Describe the coverage generally available under a cold storage locker bailee policy.
4. Why do some underwriters believe it is not feasible to insure locker plants against such loss as might result from a prolonged power shortage?
5. Upon what basis are the rates calculated for cold storage locker bailee insurance?
6. Distinguish between the circumstances where a processor is merely a supplier to another manufacturer and the circumstances which establish a bailor-bailee relationship.
7. Under what circumstances may an inland marine policy be written to cover goods in the custody of a processor as a bailee?
8. Why do bailors usually prefer to have the processor arrange for insurance coverage on goods undergoing processing?
9. Upon what theory is it considered proper to issue an inland marine policy covering goods on consignment even though the goods may be actually in storage much of the time?
10. Why is it considered that warehousemen's legal liability insurance is not an inland marine coverage when the goods to be insured do not of themselves qualify for inland marine coverage?
11. What are some of the important factors in the underwriting of a checkroom policy for a hotel or concessionaire?

12. What limitations do the business laws of your state place upon the liability of hotel and restaurant proprietors for property checked with them?
13. Compare the liability of a hotel for loss to property of a guest from his hotel room and loss from a checkroom in which the property had been placed.

19

Limited Purpose Personal Policies

A large proportion of the inland marine insurance that is written in the United States covers personal property of individuals. The need for this coverage is partly the result of transit exposures to loss and partly because many people have articles of considerable value. Jewelry, fur garments, cameras, fine arts, musical instruments, and recreational equipment are types of property that may be away from home much of the time, and also that are sufficiently valuable so that a broad form of insurance coverage is desirable. Rates, rules, and forms for most of these inland marine coverages have been filed by the rating bureaus. The principal features of these policies are described in the following pages.

PERSONAL EFFECTS POLICIES

Fire insurance policies on household furnishings provide that a limited amount of the coverage may be applied to a loss that occurs off the premises named in the policy. This was not generally adopted throughout the United States until the early 1940s. Before that time fire insurance policies covered only at the premises named, and there was no off-premises coverage of any kind under such a policy covering at a fixed location. Persons who traveled wanted some form of insurance to cover any loss that might occur to property carried with them.

Masters and seamen on oceangoing vessels could secure a "master's effects" policy (or "slop chest" policy as it was sometimes called), and travelers also could secure ocean marine policies on their property while traveling by sea. Marine underwriters met the demands of travelers on land by issuing tourists' policies and travelers' effects policies to cover property while it was being carried by the tourist or was being shipped in connection with his travels.

The tremendous increase in travel and use of the automobile had a strong effect on the habits of the traveling public. It encouraged travel, and it also permitted travelers to carry more baggage than is convenient when traveling by train. It had been customary for travelers by train to ship their large pieces by express or by train baggage. In either case the carrier was responsible for most of the losses that occurred. When the baggage is carried by automobile and is lost in transit, the owner is responsible personally, and he came to feel the need for insurance protection.

Some of the early forms of personal effects insurance policies covered certain specified perils. Disputes with policyholders arose because it was difficult to determine whether a piece of baggage had been stolen and was thus covered by the theft provision or had been merely lost or mislaid. Eventually it became clear that an "all risks" type of policy was needed, subject to exclusions that would eliminate claims resulting from negligence of the insured. For a time the pendulum swung completely away from the restricted coverage idea, and an extremely broad form was written. There were few restrictions; the policy covered jewelry and furs in full and contained no restrictions on theft from automobiles. The loss experience was bad, with the result that the present form was settled upon.

Coverage Under the Personal Effects Policy. The policy covers "personal effects such as are usually carried by tourists and travelers, belonging to and used or worn by the insured and/or his wife and their unmarried children permanently residing together." The intent is to cover clothing, luggage, toilet articles,and the many miscellaneous items a person takes with him on a trip.

It is not intended that the policy cover property, such as furniture, that is not ordinarily carried by travelers. A portable typewriter or a portable radio customarily carried and used by the insured would come within the coverage. The problem of determining whether a questionable item is a personal effect such as is usually carried by travelers is similar to the problem of determining what is considered "baggage" under a common carrier's contract to transport baggage. The reader is referred to the previous discussion of this question for comparable information.

The personal effects policy contains an exclusion designed to eliminate most of the questions that arise concerning what are not considered to be personal effects. The policy does not cover:

> Automobiles, motors, motorcycles, bicycles, boats, or other conveyances or their appurtenances, accounts, bills, currency, deeds, evidences of debt, letters of credit, passports, documents, money, notes, securities, railroad or other tickets, household furniture, animals, automobile robes or other automobile equipment, salesmen's samples, physicians' and surgeons' instruments, contact lenses, artificial teeth or limbs, merchandise for sale or exhibition, theatrical property of any kind, nor any property specifically or otherwise insured.

The last phrase of the clause is intended to avoid payment for loss to property that may be insured under some other form of floater policy. For example, many people who carry personal effects policies also have floater policies covering their furs or jewelry. Policies applying specifically would cover the property named, and the personal effects policy is not intended to cover such articles.

The coverage clause provides that the policy insures against "all risks of loss of or damage to the insured property, except as hereinafter provided." The actual extent of the coverage is found in the exclusions.

There are nine paragraphs of exclusions, all of them placing important restrictions on the "all risks" coverage of the policy.

The first excludes loss "while on the premises of the domicile of the insured." The reason is to avoid overlapping of coverage between this policy and other policies covering household goods. In most states the exclusion may be deleted and the policy extended to cover in the domicile, subject to 100 percent coinsurance.

The word "domicile" is not defined in the personal effects policy, but the Inland Marine Insurance Bureau manual cites a New York Supreme Court case to the effect that "The domicile of a person is where he has his permanent home and principal establishment, to which, whenever he is absent, he intends to return."[1] This

[1] Plant v. Harrison, 36 Misc. 649, 74 N.Y.S. 411 (1902).

definition is accepted as a good description of what constitutes a domicile.

Whenever a personal effects policy is extended to cover within the domicile of the insured, the values should be determined and the policy amount adjusted accordingly. Otherwise the insured is likely to have insufficient insurance to meet the requirements of the 100 percent coinsurance clause and consequently will not receive full payment of any loss that may occur. An additional premium is charged for the extension of coverage to the domicile.

The second exclusion applies to property "while in storage, except at points and places en route during travel and incidental thereto." Property in storage is likely to be subject to many additional hazards. It may be without attention for long periods and there would be little opportunity for the insurance company to check pilferage or theft. Many warehouses present serious fire hazards. It also is true that inland marine policies are not intended to cover property in storage unless the storage is incidental to transportation.

The third exclusion, which is peculiar to the personal effects and tourist baggage type of policy, applies to "personal effects in the custody of students while in fraternity or sorority houses, dormitories or on the premises of schools or colleges, except against risk of fire only." Fraternity and sorority houses and dormitories may be left unattended during class hours, and they are seldom locked. Pilferage is relatively easy, whether it be by outsiders or by students. The fact that many students feel free to borrow the belongings of other students is likely to result in an exposure beyond that contemplated by the rates for the policy. The fire risk is not affected to the same extent by this casual way of living, and underwriters feel that they can allow fire coverage upon school premises. This student exclusion clause may be eliminated for the payment of an additional premium.

It is interesting to note that this exclusion would not apply to students who live in private homes or rooming houses not on the premises of a school or college. Although a rooming house presents a greater hazard than a private home, there is not the same tendency to leave doors unlocked and the house unattended that is common in many fraternities or sororities.

The fourth exclusion also is characteristic of this type of policy. It limits recovery on jewelry, watches, articles consisting in whole or in part of silver, gold, or platinum, and furs or articles trimmed with or consisting principally of furs to 10 percent of the total amount for which the policy is written and to $100 on any one such article. It is expected that expensive articles of jewelry, watches, and furs will be insured, specifically under fur and jewelry policies. The rates for the personal effects policy would have to be increased if more than a limited amount of coverage for such valuable articles were to be provided under it.

The fifth exclusion does two things. First, it eliminates coverage on any loss caused by theft or pilferage of the insured property while it is left unattended in or on any automobile unless the automobile is equipped with a fully enclosed body and has all windows and doors securely locked and the loss is the direct result of violent and forcible entry of which there is visible evidence. That is, theft from an open or unlocked vehicle is not covered. The clause allows for recovery if the theft is from within a locked compartment even if the doors and windows are not locked. Second, the clause provides that any one loss by theft from an automobile shall be limited to 10 percent of the total amount of the policy or to \$250. That is, theft or pilferage losses from within a locked and enclosed automobile would be paid up to 10 percent of the policy amount or \$250, whichever was less.

This entire clause is inapplicable to losses that occur while the property is in the custody of a common carrier. Such losses are payable upon the theory that the insured cannot be charged with the carelessness of the common carrier and that he needs the protection while the property is out of his own custody. In addition, the insurance company has an opportunity to recover the amount of any such losses from the common carrier. The unattended vehicle exclusion may be eliminated from the policy for the payment of an additional premium.

The four remaining exclusions are common to many inland marine policies. They refer to loss by gradual deterioration, insect, vermin, inherent vice, loss as the result of a process or work done on the article, loss due to breakage of brittle articles (unless caused by thieves, fire, or accident to conveyances), and loss as a result of war or nuclear hazards.

Special Conditions. The special conditions are typical of those found in many inland marine policies. It is provided that the amount of insurance shall be reduced by the amount of any loss, but, unless provision otherwise is made by endorsement, the insured agrees to immediate reinstatement, for which he shall be charged a pro rata additional premium from the date of the loss.

Other clauses are as follows:

No benefit to carrier or bailee.

Requirement for reporting loss and filing proof of loss.

No loss will be paid that has been recovered from others.

Actual cash value clause.

Payment within thirty days after acceptance of proof of loss.

Sue and labor clause.

Suit clause.

Cancellation clause.

Several variations in the coverage are written. A $25 deductible clause may be used and when used is applicable to all losses. A credit in the premium is allowed for this restriction. Additional persons who reside permanently with the insured may be covered if an additional premium is paid for each. Loss resulting from theft, larceny, burglary, robbery, mysterious disappearance, vandalism, and malicious mischief may be excluded for a substantial reduction in premium. This exclusion is worded so that it will fit in with the coverage under a residence theft policy without any overlapping of coverage.

The personal effects policy may be extended to cover furniture and furnishings belonging to and used by any person insured by the policy while the property is contained in an auto trailer or trailer-home owned or leased by the person insured. The endorsement excludes from such coverage equipment and accessories built into and forming a permanent part of the trailer and equipment usually attached to an automobile. It also excludes loss due to marring, scratching, dampness of atmosphere or extremes of temperature, mechanical breakdown, or damage to electrical apparatus caused by electricity unless fire ensues and then only for loss by such ensuing fire. An additional premium is charged for this extension to cover the contents of auto trailers.

It is permissible to issue blanket personal effects policies covering conventions and tours. Such policies must name each individual insured and shall show the amount of insurance applicable to each. Premium is computed the same as if each individual were issued a separate policy.

Rates. The rating system used for personal effects policies is somewhat different from that used for other inland marine policies. The rate is a flat charge plus a percentage of the policy amount. This method of rating is based upon the theory that insureds having "all risks" policies report some minor claims regardless of the policy amount. That is, the losses of hats, fountain pens, and similar small articles occur with about the same frequency for small policies as they do for large policies. A substantial minimum premium must be charged to take care of these losses. The percentage charge is intended to take care of the larger and less frequent claims. The credit for the deductible clause is applied only to the flat charge, inasmuch as the deductible eliminates the smaller claims but does not have much effect on the larger claims.

Underwriting Personal Effects Policies. An important problem in underwriting personal effects coverage is the short-term policy. Customary short rates are charged for policies issued for less than one year subject to a minimum earned premium of $15. The result is that an insurance company is likely to receive an inadequate premium for a period during which the exposure is high. For example, a policy in the amount of $1,000 may produce a premium of $25 for one year. The person who goes on a trip of three or four weeks may get a month's coverage for only $15 in spite of the fact that the property is exposed constantly during the entire policy term. Many companies discourage the issuing of short-term policies and try to persuade their policyholders to carry the coverage on a year-round basis. In this way the insurance company gets a spread of risk over the entire year, and there are some periods during which the exposure is less than when the insured is on a trip. The insurance companies point out to their policyholders that they need the coverage all the year round because they are likely to have losses outside their domiciles in their home cities. The policy covers anywhere away from the insured's domicile, and he may have losses while at his place of business, while commuting to his work, or while out for an evening's entertainment. The personal effects policy may also be used to provide a broad coverage on property away from the domicile for a person who has one of the more limited forms of the Homeowners policies.

Even though the premium may be small and the amount of the policy limited to a few hundred or a thousand dollars, underwriters keep in mind the fact that "all risks" coverage gives the insured an opportunity to make claims that cannot be checked or substantiated. The moral hazard is extremely important, and the personal integrity and claims record of each prospect are investigated carefully.

TOURIST BAGGAGE POLICIES

Similar in purpose to the personal effects policy, but more restricted in its coverage, is the tourist baggage policy. The personal effects covered by this policy are listed specifically as "wearing apparel, toilet articles, canes, parasols, umbrellas, printed books and music, photographs and their frames, musical instruments, portable typewriters, photographic apparatus and supplies, toys and games, sportsmen's implements, travelers' clocks, watches, jewelry, plate and plated wear, trunks, suit cases, bags, and other receptacles of travel." It is further specified that coverage applies only to property belonging to and used or worn by the insured and his wife and their unmarried children permanently residing together.

The policy clause describing property not covered is shorter and excludes specifically "pianos, conveyances of any type and their motors and their appurtenances, salesmen's samples, merchandise for sale or exhibition, and theatrical property of any kind." Also excluded are any property not described in the list of items insured and any property specifically or otherwise insured.

The specific listing of the property covered results in a much more limited group of insured items than is covered by the more general description of the personal effects policy. For example, a portable radio could be considered a personal effect such as usually is carried by tourists and travelers. As such it would be covered under the personal effects policy, but its status is questionable under the tourist baggage policy because it is not listed, and radios are not generally considered to be musical instruments.

The perils insured against by the tourist baggage policy are listed specifically. It is not an "all risks" policy, and the coverage is much more limited than that of the personal effects policy. Fire and lightning damage are covered under all circumstances except when the exclusions provide otherwise. The perils of transportation and navigation are covered while the property is in due course of transit on land or water in the custody of any railroad, express, transfer, transportation, steamship, or steamboat company or licensed public truckman, but the perils of transportation are not covered while it is in transit in the insured's custody.

The policy also covers loss due to the stranding, sinking, burning, or collision of a yacht on which the insured may be a guest. If he has hired the yacht or if he is the owner, there is no coverage for these hazards.

Damage due to collision is covered if the property is contained in an automobile at the time of the collision. Collision damage is not covered while the property is in a vehicle other than an automobile or if it is not in a vehicle at the time of any loss. Under the motor vehicle laws of many states the term "automobile" includes any self-propelled motor vehicle except a motorcycle. This interpretation would mean that collision damage occurring while the property is in a bus or truck would be covered. It is likely that the courts would resolve any doubt on this point in favor of the insured and allow payment of such a claim.

Theft of property that is in the custody of a common carrier is covered. There also is coverage for the theft of entire trunks, traveling bags, or other shipping packages, with their contents, from rooms occupied by the insured or when checked in any hotel, boarding house, or public parcel room, provided the local police authorities are notified immediately after discovery of the loss. This is a narrow theft coverage. It does not cover the theft of garments from checkrooms, nor does it cover the theft of a bag from the lobby of a hotel if it has not been checked. Neither would it cover the theft of property from a hotel room unless the trunk or traveling bag and its contents were taken.

It can be seen that a tourist may have many losses that are not covered by this policy. It does not cover articles that are lost but are not stolen under the special conditions described. Several exclusions further restrict the coverage. No coverage is provided within a permanent residence of the insured.

An exclusion peculiar to this policy provides that there is no coverage on property located in any place where the insured ordinarily keeps an automobile. The principal effect of this exclusion would be to eliminate the fire coverage in such a location.

There is no coverage in storage warehouses except at points and places en route during travel and incidental thereto. Furcoats in storage warehouses are not covered, and the bureau rules prohibit any extension of the policy to so cover.

Jewelry, watches, and furs are covered only to 25 percent of the policy amount and for not more than $100 on any one such article. A student property exclusion is similar to that of the personal effects policy and may be eliminated for the payment of an extra premium. Other exclusions and conditions are similar to those appearing in the personal effects policy. The policy may not be extended to cover physicians' instruments and kits.

The rate and minimum premium for the policy are low. The customary short-rate cancellation table applies for policies in effect for less than one year. The only difference in rate between this policy and the personal effects policy is that no flat charge applies to the tourist baggage policy. The percentage rate is the same.

Considerable space has been used to describe this policy because of the confusion existing between the tourist baggage and the personal effects policies. Often the two are sold interchangeably without a clear understanding of the wide difference in coverage. The tourist baggage policy provides extremely limited coverage, and its use is likely to result in policyholder dissatisfaction unless the nature of the policy is made clear to the purchaser. In all cases the policyholder should be given an opportunity to examine the two policies and to make his own choice upon the basis of the cost, so that he will not expect to receive the coverage of the personal effects policy for the price of the tourist baggage policy.

RAILROAD, STEAMSHIP, AND AIRLINE TOURIST BAGGAGE POLICIES

The rules of the Inland Marine Insurance Bureau contain a provision that the tourist baggage rules shall not apply to "policies sold through railroad, steamship, bus line or air line ticket agencies, or through vending machines located in transportation terminals." Several insurance companies have arrangements with ticket agencies for the sale of tourist baggage insurance policies. These are limited coverage policies similar in their effect to the tourist baggage policy described above. There is no underwriting involved because the policies are sold to anyone who applies at a ticket agency. The sale of these policies can be successful for an insurance company only if it has widespread connections with railroad and steamship companies or bus lines, so that the policies can be sold in large numbers and at minimum cost. The premium for each policy is small, amounting to only a dollar or two, and the coverage is so restricted that claims are relatively few.

DIPLOMATIC, MILITARY, AND GOVERNMENT SERVICE POLICIES

The tremendous increase in the number of federal government employees during the 1930s and the war years of the early 1940s brought a demand for an insurance policy that would cover more than personal effects of the type ordinarily carried by travelers. In the diplomatic and military services, there are many people who are assigned to various locations for periods of several weeks or several months at a time. They take their families with them whenever possible and carry much more in the way of personal belongings than an ordinary traveler carries. Because there is no standard form that fits the need, many insurance companies have developed special forms. The rules for personal effects policies exempt government service policies from their application.

Although there has not been any uniformity in the special service policies, they are similar to each other in their coverage. The policies are basically the personal effects policy. The description of property covered is expanded to include household furniture and professional equipment of the sort that might be carried by military or diplomatic personnel. Some of the service policies are of the "all risks" type, but many of them cover specified perils.

Specified perils policies seem to be the preferred type. Many underwriters do not consider it feasible to insure against mysterious disappearance for policyholders who are required to travel about at frequent intervals, taking with them all the insured property. The specified perils covered by these policies include burglary, theft from within locked vehicles, fire, lightning and windstorm, and loss from transportation hazards on land or water. The exclusions are similar to those of the personal effects policy and limit the amount that may be recovered for loss of such items as jewelry, watches, and furs.

The demand for government service policies fluctuates with changes in international conditions. Insurance companies are reluctant to issue broad coverage policies to insure property which will be subject to pilferage and careless handling in foreign areas where police protection is questionable and the site of a loss would be remote from the company's loss adjustment services. Insurance companies do feel an obligation to care for the needs of their customers and the personnel of government agencies. Sometimes it is necessary to work out a compromise to provide the best coverage that is practical.

TRAVEL BAGGAGE INSURANCE

A development which resulted from multiple line underwriting was a demand for a baggage insurance policy which could be used in conjunction with travel accident insurance. A person who is traveling and wants to buy personal accident insurance can also be interested in buying insurance to cover loss of his personal effects.

The travel baggage insurance as filed by the Inland Marine Insurance Bureau provides a broad coverage of the "all risks" type with only four sets of exclusions. The first is the usual inland marine exclusion of loss due to wear and tear, gradual deterioration, insects, vermin, inherent vice, and damage sustained due to any process or while being worked upon and resulting therefrom. There are also the usual war damage and nuclear damage exclusions. The fourth exclusion applies to property specifically or otherwise insured, except that declaration of value on checked baggage is not considered to be other insurance.

The property covered is personal effects owned by and for the personal use, adornment, or amusement of the insured or any member of his family traveling with him. Coverage is effective while in transit or while in any hotel or other building en route during any journey anywhere in the world on water, land, or in the air.

Excluded from coverage are animals, automobiles, automobile robes, automobile equipment, motorcycles, boats, motors, or other conveyances or their appurtenances (excepting bicycles while checked as baggage with a common carrier), household furniture, contact lenses, artificial teeth and limbs, money, securities, tickets, and documents. There are no limitations applying to special types of property such as jewelry and furs. This makes it an extremely favorable policy as compared to personal effects policies or tourist baggage policies.

Policies may be issued for amounts from $100 to $5,000. The policy may be effective for periods of one day to six months. Rates are shown on a table, and range from 60 cents for $100 coverage for one day to $67 for $1,000 coverage for six months. It can be seen that the average rate would be more than $6 per $100 of coverage on an annual basis, which is a high rate compared to other inland marine rates. The rate is cut in half for any portion of the insurance above $1,000.

The travel baggage policy usually is issued only in conjunction with an accident policy issued to the same insured. The filings do not permit the issuing of separate policies.

WEDDING PRESENTS FLOATER POLICY

The wedding presents floater policy is designed to cover the property of a bride during the temporary period in which she accumulates the presents and before she and her new husband are settled in their home. It is customary for presents to be sent to the bride-to-be as soon as the invitations are received. Such presents are considered to be the property of the bride, but there is a joint interest on the part of both the bride and the groom as soon as they are married. It is proper to make out the insurance policy in the names of the bride and the groom, as their interests may appear.

Inland marine rating bureau rules provide that no insurance shall be granted beyond 90 days after the date of the wedding. It is intended that a permanent policy of some form shall replace the wedding presents floater as soon as the bride and groom are settled.

The scheduled property floater policy is used as the basic policy, and a form is attached to give the exact coverage desired. The standard form covers against "all risks" of loss or damage subject to exclusions. The policy excludes loss from wear and tear; dampness of atmosphere or extremes of temperature unless caused by certain specified occurrences; deterioration, insect, vermin, inherent vice; and damage resulting from any repairing or renovating process. There are also the usual war damage and nuclear exclusions.

Breakage of certain fragile articles is excluded unless occurring from specified causes such as fire, theft, windstorm, flood, earthquake, and transportation hazards. This exclusion may be deleted for the payment of an extra premium. There is also an exclusion of marring and scratching losses applying to the same articles, and this may not be deleted.

The policy does not cover realty, animals, automobiles, motorcycles, aircraft, bicycles, boats or other conveyances or their appurtenances, money, notes, securities, stamps, accounts, bills, deeds, evidences of debt, letters of credit, passports, documents, railroad or other tickets.

There is an "other insurance" clause which makes this policy excess insurance over any other policy that would apply had this policy not been effected. There is also a coinsurance clause, which may be filled in for the percentage determined by the rate charged. The other insurance and coinsurance clauses may be waived if the articles to be insured are scheduled specifically on the policy. Scheduled articles may be insured on an agreed value basis.

Two sets of rates are provided. One set is used when a 50 percent coinsurance clause is attached to the policy. The second set of rates is somewhat lower and is used when an 80 percent coinsurance clause is attached.

Underwriting of wedding presents floaters follows the same principles as the underwriting of other broad form inland marine policies. The broad coverage of the policy makes it essential that it may be issued only to persons of unquestioned integrity. Many alert insurance agents use the policy to get leads to new policyholders. Most brides are proud of their wedding presents, and their fathers and grooms are good prospects for a wedding presents policy. Following the wedding, the agent has an opportunity to call on the bride and groom to arrange for permanent coverage.

SPORTING EQUIPMENT FLOATERS

An inland marine policy can be written to cover almost any kind of movable equipment. The terms "general property floater" or "scheduled property floater" are used to describe policies prepared to fit particular needs of a policyholder or the needs of a small class of policyholders.

Golfing equipment, guns, and fishing tackle are examples of the types of property people frequently desire to insure. Occasionally there are requests for insurance on contact lenses, dentures, ship models, trophies, rare books and manuscripts (which also may be insured as fine arts), portable radio and television equipment, mobile telephone equipment, and collections of odd sorts, such as dolls, matchbook covers, pitchers, and hotel soap wrappers.

With the exception of the golfer's equipment floater, the inland marine rating bureaus have not filed rules, rates, and forms for policies covering sporting equipment. However, the coverages and rates do fall into patterns. Coverage of golfers' equipment is provided under the Personal Articles Floater, which will be discussed later in this text. Typical coverages and rates for other types of equipment are described here.

Guns. Many sportsmen own and use expensive guns for hunting or trapshooting. Guns and equipment used with them are insurable, and the policy usually issued is of the "all risks" type. Rates are likely to be less than for comparable golf equipment because the guns are not subject to the same breakage hazards. An owner of an expensive gun usually gives it thc greatest of care. Unless the gun is stored in a building with a high fire rate, the rate for an "all risks" type of coverage may be as low as 1 percent of the value. It is customary to schedule all guns and valuable accessories at their full value on the policy and any miscellaneous item should be limited to 10 percent of the policy amount.

Exclusions in the gun floater policy are few, and are limited to a nuclear exclusion; a war damage exclusion; an infidelity exclusion; sometimes an exclusion of loss due to strikes, riots, and civil commotions; and a special exclusion designed to exclude loss due to improper care of the guns. The exclusion of strike and riot damage is needed because persons taking part in riots or labor disturbances might steal the gun for use in the riot or the insured might become involved in the riot and use the gun for defensive or offensive purposes. The risk of loss from such use is not considered to be insurable at the low rates charged to cover guns used for sport.

The wear and tear exclusion is specially designed for the gun floater. It excludes loss or damage caused by explosion, rust, fouling, marring, scratching, wear, tear, gradual depreciation, or loss caused by or during any process of repairing, refinishing, or renovation. Proper care of a gun will prevent loss from the causes specified in this exclusion.

The most desirable prospects for this coverage are collectors and those sportsmen who are interested in trapshooting and skeet. The hunter who takes his gun into the woods exposes it to more hazard than does the trapshooter and skeet enthusiast.

Recreational Vehicles–Snowmobiles. The Nation-wide Marine Definition provides for inland marine coverage of mobile articles, machinery, and equipment, excluding motor vehicles designed for highway use. There are several types of motor-driven recreational vehicles which can be insured under inland marine policies. Typical of these are golf carts or golfmobiles, snowmobiles, dune buggies which are used to travel over sand dunes and beaches, and similar equipment which is designed for use across country rather than on the highways. A few states require the licensing of snowmobiles, and these states may require that such vehicles be insured under automobile policies rather than inland marine policies. Golf carts may be insured under the golfers' equipment portion of the personal articles floater as well as under a recreational vehicle floater.

There are no filings by the rating bureaus for recreational vehicle policies. The inland marine policies that are used by many companies provide an "all risks" type of coverage with exclusions. Most such policies exclude wear and tear, deterioration, latent defect, mechanical breakdown, and freezing or extremes of temperature. Also excluded in many policies is damage by any repairing or service operation, unless fire ensues and then only for the resulting fire damage. Infidelity of employees or others to whom the property has been entrusted usually is excluded. War damage and nuclear damage are excluded in most policies.

There are also some exclusions which are specially aimed at abuses which might arise in the use of snowmobiles. These exclusions apply to racing, to use as a public livery or while the snowmobile is rented to others, and while the property is used in any illegal operation. A typical wording of the racing exclusion applies to participation in any prearranged or organized race or speed contest. This can be interpreted to exclude coverage even during an impromptu race if it is prearranged.

Deductibles are considered necessary by most underwriters in order to eliminate small claims for the numerous bumps and scratches that are inevitable from snowmobile operation.

Rates are determined by the companies because there are no bureau filings. The rates generally charged are comparable to automobile collision rates. They may be several dollars per $100 of coverage even with a deductible coverage. Coverage may be provided for racing vehicles or for equipment which is rented to others if an underwriter is willing to accept the risk, but the rates would be substantially higher for such equipment.

Amphibious Vehicles. An amphibious vehicle could be insured under an inland marine policy if it is not designed or licensed to operate on the highways. An amphibious automobile could be insured under a marine policy only while it is operating in the water. Coverage and rates for such equipment would have to be established according to the nature of the vehicle, the desires of the insured for coverage, and the willingness of the underwriter to insure the particular vehicle for its contemplated use.

Miscellaneous Equipment Floaters. Other sporting and personal equipment, such as archery and tennis equipment, for example, may be insured according to the needs of the owner and the hazards to the property. The loss experience has been better on policies that schedule each item individually than on those that provide blanket coverage. Apparently there are two reasons for this difference in experience. The first is that individual scheduling results in the policy's being written for almost the full value of the property. A blanket policy is likely to be for less than the full value, and in this case the insurance company does not receive a premium commensurate with the hazard. Second, scheduled articles are likely to be property the insured prizes highly, and better care is to be expected.

QUESTIONS

1. Trace the development of the personal effects floater insurance coverage.
2. What type of property is meant by the term "personal effects"?
3. Why is a 100 percent coinsurance clause added to a personal effects policy when it is extended to cover in the domicile of the insured?
4. Why does the personal effects policy provide only a limited amount of coverage on jewelry and furs?
5. Compare the coverage provided under a personal effects policy and that provided under a tourist baggage policy.
6. In what respects does the coverage under a military or government service policy differ from that under a personal effects policy?
7. Describe the different markets for insurance in which you think the various forms of personal effects, travel baggage, government service, and tourist baggage policies may be sold. Why do you think there is or is not a justification for the many different forms of coverage?
8. Describe the effects of the coverage descriptions and exclusions which are intended to limit the insurance to property which a traveler would carry with him.

9. What precautions in coverage must be taken to avoid excessive losses from policies which are sold by ticket agents and for which no underwriting is possible?
10. Compare the rates and coverage for the extremely favorable "travel baggage insurance" of the Inland Marine Insurance Bureau with other baggage policies. Why do you think this policy is filed only for use with a personal accident policy?
11. Describe the use of the Wedding Presents Floater as a leader to get other insurance business.
12. Describe some of the sporting equipment and recreational vehicles which are used in your state, and outline the coverage against property loss which you think should be provided.
13. Why do you think the loss experience would be better or worse on property which is scheduled on an insurance policy subject to a specified amount or which is insured on a blanket basis?

20

Personal Articles Floater

The personal articles floater form is a combination form which is designed to accommodate the coverages for several types of personal property. It had been the practice for many years to issue separate policies to cover such property as jewelry, fur garments, fine arts, cameras, and musical instruments. The basic coverage under each of these policies was similar, although there were special provisions to allow for peculiarities in each kind of property. The personal articles floater is a single form which combines the coverage provisions of the several policies. It may be issued as an inland marine policy, or it may be an endorsement to such package policies as the Homeowners policy. The coverage is the same in either case.

The form is arranged with a space to indicate the total amount of insurance on each of the following kinds of property: personal jewelry, personal furs, cameras, fine arts, golfers' equipment, musical instruments, silverware, stamps, and coins. There are also several blank lines on which additional kinds of property may be listed. These blank lines serve a twofold purpose. They permit the use of the form to cover additional kinds of property which the company may be willing to insure even though the bureaus do not have filings applicable to them. An example of such property would be outboard motors and boats. The company probably would add a boat form to provide the exact coverage desired for the outboard motor and boat because the provisions of the personal articles floater are not correctly applicable to an outboard motor and boat. The blank lines also make it possible for the bureaus to make the form applicable to other kinds of property if that should become desirable in the future.

The coverage under the personal articles floater is against "all risks of loss of or damage to the insured property except as hereinafter provided." There are only three paragraphs of exclusions applying to jewelry, furs, and cameras. The first is an exclusion of loss or damage caused by wear and tear, gradual deterioration, insects, vermin, or inherent vice. The other two sets of exclusions are the war damage and nuclear damage exclusions which are common to inland marine policies. There are additional exclusions and provisions applicable to fine arts, golfers' equipment, musical instruments, silverware, stamps, and coins. These special provisions as well as the underwriting of insurance for all of the properties which may be insured under the personal articles floater will be described for each kind of such property.

It is intended that valuable pieces of property be specifically scheduled with an amount of insurance applicable to each piece. This is required for some kinds of property such as jewelry and furs, and is desirable for other pieces of property where this is feasible. Specific provisions for each kind of property will be described.

Occasionally the property owner may pick out the items he believes are most subject to loss and insure only them. For example, a camera hobbyist may insure only the cameras, light meter, and carrying cases he takes with him and not the enlarger, printer, and developing equipment he leaves at home in a protected location. This may result in the company's receiving an inadequate premium for the exposure, because the rates contemplate that all hobby property will be insured, including that which is subject to a smaller degree of hazard.

There have been proposals that "master" insurance policies be issued to manufacturers or dealers under which they could issue certificate policies to purchasers of hobby equipment, but the practice violates one of the cardinal principles of good inland marine underwriting. An arrangement whereby a certificate of insurance can be issued to anyone who purchases equipment does not give the insurance company an opportunity to investigate the desirability of the insured.

CAMERAS

Cameras used for private and commercial purposes are considered together because of their similarity. The rules, rates, and forms for camera insurance have been standardized and are promulgated by the inland marine rating bureaus. The rating bureau filings are applicable to:

1. Cameras, projection machines, and articles of equipment pertaining thereto.
2. Movable sound equipment pertaining to the recording, projection, reproduction, and operation of motion pictures.

An explanatory note in the rules provides that miscellaneous property such as films, binoculars, telescopes, microscopes, and similar property used in connection with cameras or photographic equipment may be insured under a camera forms, rules, and rates.

The rules, rates, and forms promulgated by the rating bureaus are not applicable to:

1. Television cameras and equipment.
2. Coin- or token-operated devices.
3. Property of dealers or manufacturers.

The property just listed may be insured under a camera policy when it meets the requirements of the Nation-wide Marine Definition or other applicable regulation, but the forms and rates are not prescribed. The companies may use whatever forms and rates the underwriters believe are justified by the hazards to which such property is subject.

The rating bureau rules require that all items be scheduled individually and that either an amount of insurance be set opposite each item or an agreed value be made to apply to each.

It is permissible to include a blanket item not exceeding 10 percent of the total policy amount. This blanket item is intended to cover small articles such as sunshades, filters, and other small articles that would make the schedule unnecessarily long. The intent is that major items shall be scheduled and that they shall include at least 90 percent of the total value. The 10 percent miscellaneous item is intended to cover the few small articles with low individual value.

The Inland Marine Insurance Bureau rules provide that the Bureau may authorize a larger miscellaneous item than 10 percent on specifically submitted and approved cases. Such authorization might be given when there is an unusually large proportion of small items and it is considered impracticable to schedule them all.

Additional property acquired during the policy term is covered up to 25 percent of the amount of insurance, or $10,000, whichever is less. The insured is required to report the new acquisitions within 30 days and pay an additional premium.

Property of others that may be in the control or custody of the insured may be scheduled and covered under the policy.

Rates. The rates are uniform over most of the country. The principal chances of loss have proved to be those outside the premises of the insured, regardless of the location. There does not seem to be much difference in the habits of camera owners in different parts of the country; losses occur from about the same causes wherever the camera may be. Camera owners take many pictures while traveling on vacations. The insured who is a resident of New York, for example, may have a loss while traveling in Utah or Arizona.

The rates vary from about $1 per $100 of insurance to several dollars, depending upon whether the use is for amateur purposes, for commercial purposes, or by motion picture producers. The bureau filings provide that special conditions, charges, and credits may apply to policies covering in an amount larger than $50,000 when the circumstances justify special treatment. The minimum premium is $15 irrespective of term.

Underwriting Camera Policies. The losses under camera policies are much the same as those under other policies of the "all risks" type. Many losses are from theft. There are others from mysterious disappearance, forgetfulness, and accidental dropping of equipment. There is an occasional fire loss at the premises of the insured. The underwriting of a noncommercial policyholder is largely a matter of ascertaining that the person is careful with his property and that he can afford his hobby. An investigation of a policyholder's income may be advisable when the amount of the policy or frequent additions to it indicate that large sums of money are being spent on new equipment.

The underwriting of a commercial camera policy takes into account the hazard at the location of the property. The rates for camera policies are high enough to provide for the fire and burglary hazards in a residence. This may not be the case with a commercial policy. Many photographic studios are in mercantile buildings that have a fire rate as high as the entire camera rate. In such cases the insured would get the "all risks" protection of the camera policy for little or nothing above the fire rate. When the amount of the policy is in excess of $50,000, there is the possibility of securing special rating to take care of an excessive fire or burglary hazard. The underwriter may decline to write the policy if the hazards are excessive for the rate.

Commercial photographers who are covering news events may encounter such unusual hazards as riot and civil commotion. In some instances newsmen have had their cameras smashed while taking pictures of picket lines and labor disturbances, and there is the possibility of unintentional damage by unruly crowds at athletic contests and other assemblies. The nature of a commercial photographer's work should be ascertained to make certain no unusual hazards not contemplated by the rate are involved.

Expensive equipment used on expeditions to photograph animals may be subject to special hazards. The insured may be careful, but the use of cameras in remote locations and in the forests and jungles involves chances of loss that may be beyond those contemplated by the standard rates. Expeditions frequently find it necessary to travel by small boats or native canoes in their journeys through uninhabited territory, and there may be a total loss of equipment in case of accident.

Films and negatives may be insured under the camera policy. The amateur or professional who uses motion picture equipment may have a large investment in films. The policy should indicate the value of such films clearly. There may be a question whether the value is the cost of unexposed film of the same type or includes the cost of taking the pictures. In the case of amateur films, it is best to specify that the value is that of unexposed film or to specify an agreed value for each film. A large proportion of amateur pictures are taken at or near home, where the expense of taking the picture is little or nothing, or on vacation trips, to which the picture taking is incidental. A policyholder might feel that he is entitled to recover the entire cost of a vacation trip if his films of the trip are lost, unless the policy is entirely clear on this point.

The commercial photographer may have a real reason for wanting coverage to include the expenses of taking the pictures. Such a situation would be similar to that of a motion picture studio. If such coverage is desired, the same underwriting practices should be followed as those outlined for motion picture risks. The value of the property can be agreed upon in advance whenever it appears that difficulty would be encountered in establishing the value after a loss.

The insured should be encouraged to have duplicates made of films that would be expensive to replace. There may be occasions when the underwriter will decline to insure expensive films that would be impossible to replace, unless the insured does have duplicates made.

Camera Equipment Not Covered by Bureau Rules. Rates for television cameras and equipment are not filed by the inland marine rating bureaus. Underwriters feel that the conditions under which television cameras are used vary so greatly that manual rating is not justified. Portable television cameras may be transported in several parts because of their weight. Values may be many thousands of dollars. Rates depend upon the amount of transportation involved and would be higher for a unit that is moved frequently to cover spot news events than for heavier cameras, such as might be set up for a period of several weeks at a time. The rating of a policy for television cameras that remain for extended periods of time at fixed locations would take into account the fire and extended coverage rates for these locations.

There are no bureau rate filings applying to token- or coin-operated photographic devices. The most common common form of such equipment is that set up in bus stations and airline terminals in which people may take their own pictures. The hazard to such equipment is much the same as that to any coin-operated vending machine. The rating and underwriting of these machines should be handled the same as in the case of any other coin-operated device, as previously discussed.

The camera floater is not used to cover property held for sale by dealers or manufacturers. The camera dealers floater may be used where appropriate for this purpose. It is the intent that the camera floater be used to cover property in the custody or control of parties who intend to use it for the purpose for which it was manufactured. Thus, a dealer or manufacturer could secure a camera floater to cover property he intends to use for photographic purposes but not property he intends to sell. For example, he could insure experimental camera equipment that he is testing but will not sell.

Policies covering dealers' or manufacturers' camera equipment are specially rated and underwritten because of the peculiar problems involved. The values are likely to be high on special or experimental equipment, and the susceptibility to damage may be entirely different from that of standard equipment. Underwriters secure full information regarding the property and its damageability. Rates are based upon established rates for known hazards plus a judgment factor to cover hazards upon which there has been little or no experience.

INSURANCE ON PERSONAL FURS

The need for a broad insurance policy is obvious to most women who own fur coats. The cost of a fur coat represents a large investment, and such a coat is one of the average woman's most prized possessions. A fur coat does not stay in the relative security of the home but is worn to work or to social functions where it may be stolen or lost. It is difficult to identify a recovered fur garment because there are few distinguishing marks. This makes it easy for thieves to sell or to pawn stolen garments.

The fur coat floater policy was one of the earliest of the "all risks" types of inland marine insurance policies. It was written first for carefully selected policyholders, because insurance companies were afraid of the broad coverage provided by the policy. Apparently there was a feeling that only the wealthier people who could easily afford fur coats would be acceptable policyholders. Fur coats now are purchased because of their warmth and long-wearing qualities as well as for display. In spite of the package insurance policies now available, the demand for individual fur coat insurance continues, because many people who own fur coats do not have a large investment in other personal property.

The protection which is provided for fur garments under the personal articles floater is one of the broadest available on the property of an individual. It was customary at one time to exclude damage sustained as a result of any process or while the garment was being worked on. This has been eliminated, partly because of the generally favorable experience with fur coat insurance and partly because the insurance company would have a good chance of recovering such a loss under a subrogation against the processor.

The war damage exclusion deserves comment as it relates to fur coat insurance. A possible application of this exclusion in peacetime might be if a coat were confiscated by customs authorities because of an attempt to smuggle it into the country. It has been pointed out that the war damage exclusion goes beyond actual hostilities in its application to certain confiscation losses.

The property that may be covered by the fur floater policy consists of furs and garments trimmed with fur or consisting principally of fur that are the property of the insured and members of his or her family of the same domicile. There are several man-made fabrics which closely resemble fur, and often these are considered the same as furs by the public. However, fur by definition is the dressed pelt of certain animals, so that man-made fabrics are not furs even though they may appear similar.

All insured property must be scheduled specifically; there is no provision for miscellaneous or blanket items. Several pieces that constitute a set, such as a coat, muff, and hat, may be scheduled as a single item.

The basic inland marine policy, or scheduled property floater policy, to which the personal articles floater is attached contains an actual cash value clause. It is not customary for companies to write personal fur insurance on a valued basis. Fur garments generally depreciate in value as they are worn. The insured is obligated by the policy to prove the value of the garment at the time of any loss.

The insurance is effective wherever the property may be located, anywhere in the world.

Rates. The rates for fur garment insurance vary substantially from state to state, ranging from a low of about 30 cents to a high of about $1.50 per $100 of value. It seems that the principal hazard is that of the wearer, but the chances of theft losses vary greatly between different parts of the country.

Additional property acquired during the policy term is covered up to 25 percent of the amount of insurance on furs, or $10,000, whichever is less. The insured is required to report the new acquisitions within 30 days and pay an additional premium.

Underwriting Fur Floater Policies. Successful underwriting of fur floater policies depends largely upon three factors: (1) conditions in the fur garment trade, (2) accuracy of the value placed upon insured garments, and (3) the moral hazard in relation to individual insureds.

There is considerable fluctuation in prices as a result of conditions in the fur garment trade. During periods of rapidly rising prices there is little change in the value of a garment from the time a policy is written until expiration of the policy. The normal depreciation in value from wear and tear is largely offset by the price increase.

In a period of deflation there is a double depreciation in value. In addition to the normal depreciation from wear and tear, there may also be a considerable drop in value as a result of price decreases. Underwriters usually adjust the amounts of insurance to allow for depreciation when policies are renewed.

It was the practice in the fur industry for many years to develop odd and exotic names for the furs of common animals. This was thought to enhance customer appeal. Regulations of the Federal Trade Commission now require that the name of the actual animal be shown on the sales tag. However, there can be several grades of fur from the same kind of animal. A true indication of value is difficult unless the age, the purchase price, and the name of the fur merchant can be secured. In the case of new garments, the underwriter usually can get the information he needs for correct valuation. This may prove to be inaccurate if, for example, the insured says merely, "The coat was bought last summer for about $400." It is desirable to secure a copy of the invoice or bill of sale if possible. The cost price of a new coat may be accepted as the correct value at the time of purchase if the store is known to be reputable.

It is desirable for the underwriter to keep a list of the principal fur shops in the territory from which fur coat business is received in considerable volume. Whenever a high-valued coat is insured and the application shows that it was purchased from an unknown store, underwriters usually investigate to make certain that it is correctly valued.

The problem of determining value is more difficult when the garment has been in use. It is not desirable to accept the valuation put upon the garment in an insurance policy issued by another company, for the original underwriting may have been careless.

The first step is to try to determine the original purchase price and exact date of purchase, the same as for a new coat. If this is not possible, it may be desirable to require an appraisal, especially if the value is more than a few hundred dollars. It should be made clear to the furrier who makes the appraisal that the present value of the coat is the amount desired. There have been many cases in which the appraiser set the value at what he would charge for a new coat of similar quality.

Always to be kept in mind is the fact that if the garment is valued at too low a figure, the insurance company is not getting sufficient premium for the risk it is carrying. If the value is set too high, there may be difficulty in arriving at a fair settlement in case of a loss.

The moral hazard in connection with each policyholder is probably the most important single factor in successful fur floater underwriting. Many insurance companies feel that professional entertainers are more likely to have losses than average policyholders. This is not so much because professional entertainers are dishonest but because their business requires that they be seen in many places and they must wear their furs under circumstnaces that make them easy victims for thieves.

Property of students may be subject to extra hazards because of their habit of borrowing and lending clothing. Dormitories and sorority houses may not be so well supervised as the average private home. The property of persons who live in hotels may be subject to frequent losses because of the ease with which many hotel rooms can be entered by a sneak thief or burglar. Expensive furs offer the underwriter the possibility of a large loss, and they are more likely to be stolen because they offer a greater temptation to a thief than furs of low value.

Underwriters recommend to their insureds that some identification be sewed inside the lining or that several skins be marked on the inside with indelible ink. Many lost or stolen coats are recovered by the police, but the owners frequently cannot claim them because they are unable to make a positive identification.

PERSONAL JEWELRY COVERAGE

The growth of jewelry floater insurance for individual policyholders parallels the growth of fur floater coverage. Years ago, in grandmother's day, a married woman had a diamond engagement ring, a wedding ring, and perhaps a gold watch. The man of the family carried a watch and a few men wore rings. Values were comparatively small, and there was little hazard of loss by robbery or burglary. It was only the extremely wealthy who had much jewelry and felt any need for insurance protection. Today many women have several pieces of jewelry, and the total value of watches and jewelry in a moderately successful family will be several thousands of dollars. In no other respect has the spread of wealth during the past generation been so much in evidence as in the increased use of jewelry by people of modest means. This fact plus the increased hazard of loss from crime has brought about a need for broad insurance protection on personal jewelry.

The coverage of the personal articles floater for jewelry is the same as that for furs. However, the pair and set clause in the basic inland marine policy to which the personal articles floater form is attached is of particular importance to the jewelry coverage. This clause reads:

> In the event of loss of or damage to any article or articles which are a part of a set, the measure of loss of or damage to such article or articles shall be a reasonable and fair proportion of the total value of the pair or set, giving consideration to the importance of said article or articles, but in no event shall such loss or damage be construed to mean total loss of the pair or set.

If this clause were not a part of the policy, the insured might claim that the loss of a single item of a set destroyed the entire value of the set. The adjuster who is handling a loss under the pair and set clause may have a difficult task in determining what is a fair proportionate value for the lost item, but he has a contractual provision upon which to base his adjustment.

Each item must be individually scheduled, and no miscellaneous items are permitted. An amount of insurance is indicated for each item of the schedule. If the amount is shown as a limit of liability, the insured would be obligated to prove the value in case of loss.

Jewelry may be insured on a valued basis but this is unusual. Most policies show an amount of insurance for each item of the schedule and the coverage is subject to the actual cash value provisions of the basic inland marine policy to which the personal articles floater is attached. A valued policy may be issued to cover antique jewelry or other items for which the value would be difficult to determine after a loss. It is important in such cases that the value be established accurately by appraisal or by verification of the cost.

It is permissible to insure as jewelry such articles as cigarette cases, trophies, and other articles made of precious metals and similar in nature and value to jewelry. Silverware and plated ware are not insurable as jewelry but are insurable under the provisions for silverware coverage.

Rates. The rates for jewelry coverage vary considerably from state to state, depending upon the experience in different parts of the country. From a low of about $1 they range to a high of almost $3 per $100 of coverage.

There is no provision in the filings for a deductible. Most jewelry losses are total losses so that a deductible coverage would not have a material effect upon the loss ratio.

There is provision for a very low rate for jewelry that is kept in a bank vault. It is the practice of some people who have expensive jewelry to keep it in a bank vault except when it is actually in use. The policy does not cover such jewelry when it is outside the vault unless the company has been notified in advance and an additional premium paid at short rate of the regular jewelry rates.

Underwriting Jewelry Insurance. There is a considerable difference in the salvage possibilities with different types of gems. Diamonds have a high salvage value even when they have passed through a severe fire. The outside of a diamond will char, but frequently a large diamond can be cut down and a portion of the value salvaged. This is less true of the softer gems, which are likely to be ruined completely by intense heat.

It is important that all jewelry be described accurately in the insured's application for a jewelry policy. Occasionally an application for a jewelry policy may list "one diamond ring," without any qualifying description. Such an inadequate description makes it impossible to determine whether the ring is correctly valued and, in case of loss, makes it impossible for the adjuster to find out whether the claim is being made for the insured ring. A complete description of a piece of jewelry should include the following information:

1. The name of the stone or stones. If the stone is synthetic or reconstructed, this should be indicated.
2. The weight of the stone or stones. This weight usually is expressed in carats. There are approximately 151.5 carats in a troy ounce. An international carat is 200 milligrams.
3. The cut of the stone or stones. For example, the diamond may be "full cut," with 58 facets, including the top and bottom, or it may be "single cut," with only 18 facets.
4. An accurate description of the metal used for mounting or, in the case of items not containing stones, of the metal used to make up the piece. The gold used for jewelry making usually is an alloy, because pure gold is soft and wears away quickly. The fineness of a gold alloy is expressed in terms of how many twenty-fourth parts of the alloy are pure gold. The units are called "karats" or "k." Pure gold is 24 k. A 10 k. gold alloy is ten twenty-fourths pure gold and fourteen twenty-fourths alloy. (This use of the word "karat" means a twenty-fourth part and must not be confused with "carat" which is used to indicate the weight of a precious stone.)
5. A general description of the piece, including its intended use, shape and size, color decorations, and any peculiarities that would help to identify it in case of loss.
6. Photographs, when the value is such that extensive efforts would be justified to secure recovery in case of loss or when the items are such that descriptions are difficult.
7. In the case of watches, the name of the manufacturer, the number of jewels, the size, and a general description of the case and works, serial numbers, and any special identification such as pawnbrokers' marks.

The underwriter is on the alert for trade terms that are not indicative of the true nature of a material. For example, "German Silver" does not contain any silver whatever but is an alloy of nickel, copper and zinc. The term "full jeweled" sometimes used in connection with watches is an inaccurate term, and the description should give the actual number of jewels.

Sterling silver must have 925 parts of silver and 75 parts of copper. When the term "silverware" is used, as it frequently is, the description should indicate the exact proportion of silver, since there is no such standard for silverware as for sterling silver. Gold- or silver-plated ware has a coating of the precious metal, usually put on by an electrolytic process. A gold-filled article has a thicker coating of gold put on by soldering a sheet of gold to a base metal. The description should indicate the proportion of gold and the degree of fineness, such as "1/10 18 k. gold-filled."

The previous loss record of the insured is one of the most helpful pieces of underwriting information. The record of losses usually is required in detail, and underwriters do not accept such general statements as "negligible" or "few small losses." A series of small losses may indicate careless habits that are likely to culminate in one or more large losses. Credit reports are desirable in order to check the accuracy of statements on the application for a policy and to determine the insured's personal history.

When the insured is the possessor of valuable pieces of jewelry purchased abroad, it may be worth inquiring to see if the customs declaration agrees with the statements in the application for insurance. The prospective insured may be asked to furnish such information in connection with large and valuable items.

When gambling debts become extremely pressing, jewelry that is sold to pay them may be reported to the insurance company as lost. Sometimes the motive is to recoup the gambling losses from the insurance company; sometimes the real motive is to prevent husband or wife from learning what was done with the jewelry.

The recovery of stolen jewelry is a specialty of loss adjusting that will be discussed later. Careful underwriting often is of great help to the adjuster after a loss has occurred. Many times a loss can be kept at a minimum if the underwriter has secured in advance all the information the adjuster needs to identify and prove ownership of jewelry recovered from criminals.

Wedding and Engagement Ring Insurance. Jewelry floater policies are not written to cover jewelry or furs belonging to more than one person not related, even though they are residing together. An exception is made in the case of engagement rings, wedding rings, and guard rings, which may be insured prior to the wedding in the names of the two interested parties as their interests may appear.

The question of ownership of an engagement ring can prove troublesome to an insurance company (and to the interested parties) when an engagement is broken. When the policy is made out in both names, the insurance company can step out of a dispute by paying the proceeds of any loss into a court and letting the court decide who is entitled to them. A case decided in 1947 by the Texas Court of Civil Appeals gives an interesting view of an engagement ring dispute.[1]

The plaintiff had secured $1,500 insurance on an engagement ring, the policy being written in his name. He gave the ring to his fiancee as an engagement ring and procured a marriage license. While it was in the possession of his fiancee, the ring was stolen, and subsequent thereto the plaintiff refused to carry out his agreement to marry. He sued the insurance company for the loss of the ring. He contended that the ring was still his, or at least that he still had an interest in it because the gift of the ring was a conditional gift. The court held that the gift of the ring, even if conditional, conferred title to the donee. It was held that the plaintiff had no interest in the ring at the time of the loss, had not sustained any legal loss, and therefore could not recover from the insurance company.

Social usage holds that the engagement ring and other gifts of value should be returned in case the engagement is broken off. There are instances in which the gifts are not returned following the breaking of an engagement, and the insurance company may find itself in the middle of an acrimonious dispute if the policy is written in the name of only one of the interested parties.

FINE ARTS AND ANTIQUES

From the dawn of civilization, people have treasured certain articles far beyond any value that might be placed upon them because of their utility. The paintings and statuary of the old masters are venerated because of their beauty and grace. Objects of antiquity are revered, sometimes solely as a result of their age but more often because the ancient pieces that survive are those that have a lasting beauty. Insurance companies give practical recognition to the fact that antiques and works of art may have a cash value in excess of their utility value. This market value may properly be insured.

For many years after fine arts insurance first was written, the only persons interested in such coverage were collectors, museum officials, and dealers. During recent years, however, many people have purchased works of art. People of culture and taste like to be the possessors of art objects even though their "collections" are small. There are many people who take every opportunity to add to their collections of antique furniture. The result is that fine arts insurance today is written for a large number of people.

The Nation-wide Marine Definition recognizes the need for inland marine coverage in its statement that fine arts floaters can be written to cover "objects of art such as pictures, statuary, bronzes

[1] Ludeau v. Phoenix Ins. Co., 204 S.W. (2d) 1008 (Tex. Civ. App. 1947).

and antiques, rare manuscripts and books, articles of virtu, etc." Art glass windows of the character of fine arts are considered to be insurable under an inland marine policy even if they are permanently installed in a building.

The manual of the Inland Marine Insurance Bureau defines fine arts to include "paintings, etchings, pictures, tapestries, art glass windows, and other bona fide works of art (such as valuable rugs, statuary, marbles, bronzes, antique furniture, rare books, antique silver, manuscripts, porcelains, rare glass and bric-a-brac) of rarity, historical value or artistic merit." "Articles of virtu," mentioned in the Nation-wide Marine Definition may be defined as articles having artistic merit.

It often is difficult to determine whether objects have the qualities of fine arts or antiques, even with the elaborate definitions inserted in the Definition and the manual. How can an insurance underwriter or insurance agent know whether a specific object would qualify for fine arts coverage?

Several tests can be applied. First, does the object have any quality that makes it worth more than its utility value? This additional value must be something that would appeal to many people and may not be solely a sentimental value that would attach to an object belonging to the members of a single family. For example, a bedspread worked by the insured's mother would not qualify as a fine arts object solely because of the insured's sentimental attachment. There must be a quality that would make it appeal to other people who are not influenced by the sentimental attachment.

A second test to be applied is that of rarity or historical value. The personal letters of George Washington and of Abraham Lincoln are excellent examples of objects that are both rare and of historical value. Once their contents have been copied and recorded, these letters have no practical value, yet they do have a considerable monetary value.

Antique furniture has a practical value, but it has a commercial value in excess of the untility value. This is due largely to its age, and a puzzling problem for the underwriter is to determine how old a piece of furniture must be before he is justified in insuring it as an antique. An arbitrary rule used by many insurance adjusters is that an object must be approximately 100 years old before it can be considered antique. The rarity of the object also has an effect, as well as any artistic qualities that may be present.[2]

[2]The United States Tariff Act of 1930 provides that certain works of art and antiques may be brought into the United States free of duty. In order to qualify for such treatment, works of art and antiques must have been produced prior to 1830, violins and certain similar instruments prior to 1801, and rugs and carpets prior to 1701. Insurance adjusters and underwriters often are not as stringent as the Tariff Act in determining what may be classified as an antique.

It is often advisable to secure the opinion of an art appraiser in connection with paintings. Many contemporary paintings are now considered works of art, but it is difficult for an untrained person to tell which ones will survive as such. Styles and customs change from one generation to another, and the ultimate measure of the value of fine arts objects is the value the public puts upon them when they are in the market.

JUSTIFICATION FOR INLAND MARINE COVERAGE ON FINE ARTS

Many objects of art are more easily damaged than ordinary household furniture and appliances. The paint on some of the old paintings may peel if there is too much moisture in the air, and a cut or scratch may do irreparable damage. The value of many fine arts pieces makes them a constant temptation to the thief.

Art collectors were among the first to feel the need for a broad insurance protection that went beyond the coverage available in the fire, lightning, and windstorm insurance policies available fifty years ago. Fire insurance companies were restricted by law to narrow lines of coverage. Marine underwriters were relatively unhampered by such restrictions, and they had had much experience with an "all risks" type of insurance coverage in their ocean marine operations. Inland marine underwriters, therefore, were willing to write a broad coverage insurance policy for art collectors. Coverage on fine arts objects now is written as a regular inland marine line of insurance despite the fact that much of the property so insured is not subject to transportation hazards.

The property of some owners of fine arts is subject to a travel hazard. Art collectors are justifiably proud of their possessions and wish to exhibit them. Pictures and other collections of art objects are loaned by one collector or one museum to another in order that more people may have the pleasure of seeing them. The result is that art objects are shipped about the country more frequently than household furniture or other equipment. It is troublesome for the owner to arrange for insurance each time he wants to send some of his collection out for exhibition. The floater coverage of the inland marine policy fits the needs of the art collector more closely than would a fixed location policy.

PRIVATE FINE ARTS COLLECTIONS

Fine arts may be divided roughly into three groups. They are (1) private collections, (2) commercial or dealer property, and (3) museum or art gallery collections. Commercial and museum property is underwritten largely according to the individual needs of each insured. There is little standardization; the coverage varies with the needs of the insured and the rates vary with the hazards. Private fine arts collections, on the contrary, have many characteristics in common, and the rates, rules, and coverage are prescribed by the inland marine rating bureaus.

Private collections of fine arts are defined by the rating bureau rules to include the property owned by individuals, firms, corporations, and associations that are not (1) dealers or auction rooms, or (2) museums, art galleries, or art institutions ordinarily open to the public. The rules further specify that privately owned property in the custody of a dealer or museum insured may not be considered a private collection when insured in the name of the dealer or museum for the account of whom it may concern. Further explanations provide that property of hotels and schools or colleges shall be considered private collections, even though the school or college property may be insured in the name of a state or other political subdivision. Property of federal, state, county, or municipal authorities other than school property may not be considered private collections.

Coverage for Private Fine Arts Collections. The coverage of the personal articles floater which has already been described is modified as it applies to fine arts. There are three additional sets of exclusions and several special conditions that affect the fine arts coverage.

The first additional exclusion applies to damage sustained due to and resulting from any repairing, restoration, or retouching process. The words "repairing, restoration or retouching process" differ from the comparable wording in other inland marine policies, because they are designed to fit the type of work that may be done on fine arts. Age results in deterioration in many works of art, and it is customary among collectors to have experts retouch and repair the ravages of time. Underwriters believe that workmen should be responsible for the results of their work, and any damage resulting from such repairs is not considered an insurable hazard.

Another exclusion refers to "breakage of art glass windows, statuary, marbles, glassware, bric-a-brac, porcelains, and similar fragile articles, unless caused by fire, lightning, aircraft, theft and/or attempted theft, cyclone, tornado, windstorm, earthquake, flood, explosion, malicious damage or collision, derailment or overturn of conveyance, unless endorsed hereon."

The intent of this paragraph is to exclude loss from the ordinary dropping and breaking of fragile articles. It is the belief of underwriters that owners of such property should take special precautions to prevent breakage. There is provision, however, for endorsing the policy to cover breakage when the insured is willing to pay the extra charge and the underwriter feels that the circumstances are such that the company can extend the coverage.

The exclusion discussed in the preceding paragraph lists damage by aircraft as one of the perils for which breakage would be covered. This is a different wording from that used in many policies, which refer to "damage by falling aircraft and objects falling therefrom." The vibration from a low-flying aircraft, or the shock of a "sonic boom" when a jet aircraft exceeds the speed of sound, might be sufficient to shake small articles from a shelf. Such an occurrence might be construed as "aircraft damage" and as such would be covered, but it could not be considered damage by a falling aircraft unless the plane actually crashed.

There have been occasions when blasting in the neighborhood has caused sufficient vibration to upset fragile articles and to result in breakage. There can be no doubt that a blast is an explosion. The problem is to make certain that the particular damage for which any claim is made did result from the blast and not from vibration from some other cause not covered by the policy.

There is no coverage for property on the premises of fairgrounds or the premises of any national or international exposition unless specific permission is given for such exhibition.

There are two reasons for this exclusion. The first is that there is a severe fire and conflagration hazard at many fairgrounds and exposition grounds. Insurance underwriters feel that they cannot afford to be exposed to the extra fire hazard unless they have an opportunity to check the location and to collect an extra premium when it is warranted. The second reason for the exclusion is that such an exposition might have a concentration of insured works of art. It might happen that a dozen or more of the insureds who carry their insurance in the same company would send property to the same fair or exposition. The insurance company must have an opportunity to check the location of any possible accumulation of property to make sure it is not exposed to a greater amount of possible loss than its reinsurance will permit.

Schedule Requirements. It is required that fine arts be scheduled. When the schedule of items is not long and does not change frequently, it is customary to put the schedule on the policy in much the same way that fur coats and jewelry are scheduled.

Many art collectors have extensive lists that change as they have an opportunity to improve their collections. It is permissible to provide that the coverage shall apply to items listed on a schedule that is on file at a specified office of the insurance company, or according to a schedule on file at some other designated place if the schedule has been examined and signed by a representative of the insurance company.

Blanket items are permitted up to 10 percent of the amount of the policy, and a 100 percent coinsurance clause applies to the blanket item. Under special conditions, the Inland Marine Insurance Bureau will permit blanket items in excess of the usual 10 percent limit.

It is important that the listing be made in some detail. If the piece is a painting, the list should give the title, the artist, and other information that would make correct identification easy. The color, size, type, age, and such other designation as there may be for porcelains and glassware should be described. Similar pieces must be distinguished so that there can be no doubt regarding identity of the damaged or destroyed pieces in case of loss.

Valued Policy Provisions. It is customary to issue fine arts policies on a valued basis. The insurance company agrees to the value of each item on the schedule, and in case of loss the amount listed is paid. This is reasonable because often it is difficult to determine the value of a work of art after it has been destroyed or damaged. The situation is entirely different from that in connection with ordinary merchandise or household goods. Ordinary goods have been purchased within a sufficiently recent period that their market value can be determined by checking the value of like merchandise. In the case of a 500-year old painting, it is necessary to check in advance whether it is an old master or merely an old painting.

It is important that the underwriter have clear evidence of the value of the property covered by a fine arts policy. The cost price of a piece may be taken as good evidence of its value if it was bought in the open market. Many fine arts purchases are made privately, however, and it is possible that the insured has paid more than the piece is worth. On the other hand, there are occasions when pieces are acquired at forced sales, and the real value may be in excess of the cost price. Many underwriters establish contact with reliable art appraisers who advise them on the values of insured property. In case of doubt, an appraisal may be required.

There may be occasions when the underwriter does not feel that a valued policy should be issued. It is permissible to include an actual cash value clause. A policy containing an actual cash value clause should also include provision for appraisal after a loss, with wording similar to that used in other inland marine policies written on an actual cash value basis. This method of insuring fine arts would be satisfactory if the items could be compared with other property having an established market value. It would be of doubtful desirability when the property is unlike other property in the open market and when the value is dependent upon some peculiar characteristic of the piece itself.

Special Conditions. The personal articles floater contains a special pair and set clause that applies to fine arts. This clause reads as follows:

> In the event of the total loss of any article or articles which are a part of a set, the company agrees to pay the insured the full amount of the value of such set as specified in the schedule attached, and the insured agrees to surrender the remaining article or articles of the set to the company.

The use of this clause may eliminate a great deal of trouble in the adjustment of a claim. There could be a wide difference of opinion regarding the relative values of different parts of a set. The effect of this clause is considerably different from that of the "pair and set" clause appearing in the personal jewelry policy. The agreement by the company to pay the full amount of the value as set forth in the policy upon surrender of the remaining parts of the set provides a definite method of settling a claim. Nothing is left to judgment or negotiation.

Newly acquired property is covered automatically. The clause granting this extension provides for the insertion of a percentage figure limiting the amount of such automatic extension to a proportion of the original policy amount. The insured is required to report the new acquisitions within 90 days from the date acquired and pays a pro-rata additional premium from the date acquired. The policy ceases to cover such newly acquired items if they are not reported within the 90-day period. The maximum that may apply to new acquisitions is 25 percent of the insurance on fine arts under the policy.

One of the special conditions is an agreement that reads: "The insured represents and agrees that the property insured hereunder will be packed and unpacked by competent packers." This agreement is peculiar to fine arts insurance. The packing of fine arts property is extremely important and cannot be trusted to ordinary movers. It is necessary that many fine arts objects be packed in moisture-resistant coverings. A nail carelessly driven can ruin a canvas. The collector who makes a specialty of some particular type of art work is likely to know the dangers of improper packing and will see that only the best-qualified packers are used. This may not be the case with persons who have only a few pieces that have been bought at random or inherited.

The policy as ordinarily written covers anywhere within the continental United States and Canada. The policy includes a list of places at which the property is located at the time the policy becomes effective. The fire insurance rates at these locations are used in computing the premium for the policy.

Rates. Most fine arts remain at a fixed location during the policy term. The basic rate is the fire contents rate promulgated by the fire insurance rating bureau having jurisdiction. Because it is intended that fine arts shall be insured for their full value, the 100 percent coinsurance rates apply if such rates are published. The rules make provision for special rating when the property is kept in vaults and when the fire rating bureau has not published any vault contents rate.

Loadings are added to the base (fire) rate in order to secure the total rate. Loadings range from four cents per $100 of value for the first $10,000 of insurance down to two-tenths of a cent per $100 of value for the portion between $500,000 and $800,000, and are one-half cent per $100 of value for the entire amount when the policy amount exceeds $800,000. The rate so determined may then be modified by a percentage factor in order to arrivc at a final rate which is justified by the loss experience.

These loadings do not contemplate extensive or frequent windstorm exposure. Policies covering property located in states bordering on the Gulf of Mexico exclude the hazard of windstorm unless additional rates are charged.

If a comparison is made between the fine arts policy rates and the rates for extended coverage, it will be seen that a fine arts policy may be written in some locations for less than the cost of fire and extended coverage. This is most likely in the case of large policies when the loading above the fire rate for the fine arts policy may be as low as one-half cent per $100.

At first glance this seems to be improper because the fine arts policy gives much broader coverage than a fire and extended coverage policy. It must be remembered, however, that most household furniture fire and extended coverage policies are written for a small fraction of the total value of the insured's property. The fine arts policy is intended to be written for the full value of the property. The experience on fine arts policies has shown that the rates are adequate when full insurance to value is required. Another factor that justifies a low rate, as compared to the usual extended coverage rate, is the fact that fine arts usually are given better care and protection than ordinary household furniture.

The minimum premium is $15 irrespective of term. There are

no rates for trip transit policies. These charges are subject to company judgment, depending upon the hazards involved and the length of the trips. A trip may be covered either under a trip transit policy or by issuing a short-term floater policy. It is up to the underwriter to determine which would give the insured the better protection and the company an adequate premium.

The rules of the Inland Marine Insurance Bureau provide for special rates and rules for policies covering in excess of $100,000 if the Bureau feels that the circumstances justify special treatment. Many privately owned fine arts collections are housed and protected in a manner equal to that of the finest museums. The rates appearing in the manual must be based upon the conditions surrounding the average collections of fine arts and do not do justice to collections that have special protection. Such collections are relatively few in number, and it is not feasible to develop special rating schedules to cover them.

MUSEUMS

The property of museums may not be insured under the personal articles floater, but the museum in many respects is a large private collection. The principles of underwriting such a collection of fine arts are much the same as the underwriting of private collections. Museum risks are considered here for convenience. Museums acquire works of art for permanent display, and there is little more trading or selling of property than there is in connection with a private collection. Many large museums do not insure their permanent collections. They have superior protection in their fire-resistive buildings and in their guard systems, and they feel that the expense of complete insurance would not be warranted.

It is customary for museums to lend property to each other, and most museums carry insurance on the property of others in their custody. Where the lending is constant, the museum may have a reporting form policy on property acquired temporarily for exhibition purposes. The coverage is effective from the time the property leaves the premises of the owner, while it is on exhibition in the borrowing museum, and until it is returned safely to the owner. These policies are similar to the reporting form policies issued to dealers, and they must provide some method of arriving at the value of the property in case of loss. There is no standard form; each policy is written to fit the needs of the museum.

Rates are based upon the principles already discussed for private collections. In the case of borrowed and exhibition property, it is necessary to evaluate the proportion of location and the proportion of transit hazard. When the exhibitions are of short duration, the chief hazard may be that of transportation. Museums employ people who are experts in the handling and packing of fine arts, and it can be anticipated that proper care will be given the property.

UNDERWRITING OF FINE ARTS COLLECTIONS

Fine arts collections range from those of the wealthy collector whose property is equivalent to a museum to the person who has two or three good pictures or antiques that have been handed down as heirlooms. The integrity of the insured is an important point to consider, as is the case in underwriting any of the extremely broad inland marine policies.

The first step in underwriting is to investigate the insured's background and the origin of the property upon which he is requesting insurance. Credit reports are an excellent source of general information. Another subject to be investigated is the financial standing of the insured and the possibility of his being forced to liquidate some of his valuables in thc event of financial reverses. A true art lover hates to let go of his choice pieces. It is possible that financial difficulties might force a person to secure money from the sale of his art collection. There might be a temptation to fake a loss so that he could get the money without actually letting go of his treasures.

The number of frauds in the fine arts business is small, considering the millions of pieces insured, but there are enough that the art collector and his insurer must not overlook the possibility. There have been some clever imitations of the paintings of the great masters. Some of these were made many years ago and actually are almost as old as the works of the masters they imitate. Only an expert can tell the difference, and in some cases there have been differences of opinion among the experts concerning who was the painter. These frauds are usually unintentional as far as the dealer and the present owner are concerned. The chance of loss to the insurance company as a result of such a fraud lies in the possibility that the owner may discover the fraud and attempt to recover his investment from the insurance company by causing the destruction of the spurious work.

Occasionally a dealer or collector commits an active fraud by trying to sell an imitation. In many cases the consequences are not serious, if the owner believes he has a genuine work of art and has no inclination to destroy it. There is a legitimate business in the manufacture of "antiques," and many of the manufacturers are absolutely honest in making and marketing their products as imitations. It is not so certain that they will continue to be labeled as imitations once the articles reach trade channels. It is important for the purchaser of antiques to depend upon the opinion of an expert unless he has an opportunity to check upon the history of the piece. Underwriters try to determine the methods by which the insured acquires his property and whether he is careful in checking authenticity.

The determination of value is an important part of the underwriting. The ultimate test is the market value of the property when this test can be applied. For example, the Currier and Ives prints marketed so extensively during the middle of the last century have acquired a value far beyond their original sales prices. Many of them are in existence, and they have a well-established market value that can be determined and accepted as the value for insurance purposes.

The problem of valuation is much more difficult when each work of an artist is the only one of its kind. It is necessary for the appraiser to consider the general excellence of the artist's work and the individual merit of the painting in question. The only way for an underwriter to determine this with any degree of accuracy is to secure an appraisal by an expert in the particular field of art concerned. The insured may be required to present such an appraisal for any important schedule of art works.

Real difficulties arise with works of lesser-known and particularly of contemporary artists. It is difficult for the experts to agree which artists will become famous as the years go by. There are fads in art, and it may be that a "modern" painting of strange design will sell at a high price today under the pressure of the fad and that its value may decrease sharply in future years. Collections consisting largely of modern works should be reappraised every few years to bring the values into line with current conditions. Changes in economic conditions affect the value of collections. During periods of depression the values are lower because people do not have so much money to invest in their hobbies.

A catastrophe hazard may be present in connection with both large private collections and museum property. Institutions such as universities may borrow collections of art works for special exhibits. For example, a midwestern university borrowed a collection of valuable paintings in 1948 for a special exhibit. The total value of these paintings exceeded a million dollars. They were insured in the name of the lending museum, and the university paid the premium for the 30 days of the exhibit and the transit coverage to and from New York.

The exclusion of coverage at fairgrounds and expositions is put in the policy because the fire hazard at such locations may be severe. The exclusion may be waived, but the insurance company must have an opportunity to examine any such location before it is committed to liability on it. Large exhibits such as those at world's fairs from time to time involve liabilities of many millions of dollars. Special precautions are taken to protect the priceless works of art from fire and theft. These exhibits present a reinsurance problem, which will be discussed later in this text.

The breakage hazard is severe with certain types of statuary and with porcelains. Objects with protruding arms and other extensions are easily damaged. Porcelain and chinaware are fine grades of ware and are superior in translucence, whiteness, and hardness to ordinary pottery. They give a clearer, more ringing sound than pottery and are much more fragile. Ordinary pottery is made from clays that make it heavier than porcelain and capable of standing a more severe blow or drop. Care must be exercised in granting the extension of breakage coverage to porcelains. Breakage coverage can be granted safely only when the property is set in well-protected display cases. Much glassware is similar to porcelain in its fragility and is underwritten in a similar manner.

Special burglary protection, the presence or absence of fire protection, and the stability of the building in which the property is located are all factors to be taken into account in underwriting a fine arts collection.

GOLFER'S EQUIPMENT

The golfer's equipment coverage under the personal articles floater applies to golf clubs, golf clothing, and golf equipment (except watches and jewelry). It also covers other clothing of the insured while it is contained in a locker in a club house or other building used in connection with the game of golf. The intent is not to provide a general personal effects floater but rather to cover losses which are related to the insured's golf playing. The coverage is against "all risks of loss of or damage to the insured property," subject to the exclusions of the personal articles floater.

Golf balls are covered only against loss by fire or burglary. There must be visible evidence of forcible entry on the building, room, or locker, if a burglary claim is to be paid. Property held for sale is not covered.

The rate is $2.50 per $100 of coverage, and the minimum premium is $15 irrespective of term.

There is no requirement for scheduling the insured items, but this can be done. If the insured has an expensive set of clubs, it may be desirable to schedule them. There is no coinsurance, and there is a likelihood of an inadequate amount of insurance unless expensive items are specifically listed. The description of property covered is broad enough to include a motor driven golf cart. These may cost upwards of $1,000, and many underwriters feel that they should be specifically listed in order to make certain that sufficient premium is secured to compensate for the exposure.

MUSICAL INSTRUMENTS

Musical instruments may be insured under a personal articles floater or under a broad form or a restricted form of policy. The coverage of the broad form musical instruments policy is the same as that which is provided under the personal articles floater. The comments which follow regarding the broad form policy apply equally to musical instruments coverage under the personal articles floater. However, there is no provision under the personal articles floater for the restricted or limited coverage.

Musical instruments are comparable in value and damageability to cameras and fine arts. The owner of an expensive instrument needs protection against damage from all the numerous hazards that can ruin the instrument. Most musicians carry their instruments with them to take lessons and to play in concerts, and there is a need for insurance that covers the property while it is in transit as well as when it is located at the owner's residence.

Broad Form Coverage. The property that may be covered under a musical instruments floater includes musical instruments and articles of equipment pertaining thereto. Auxiliary equipment may be covered, and the rules of the inland marine rating bureaus provide that sheet music also may be covered. Instrument cases, reeds, strings, music stands, special lights, and amplifying equipment may be insured if they are used in connection with the musical instruments. Property of others in the custody or control of the insured is covered.

It is intended that all articles be scheduled on the policy and that an amount of insurance or an agreed valuation be shown for each article. It is permissible under rating bureau rules to include a blanket item aggregating not more than 10 percent of the total amount insured on scheduled items. The rules of the Inland Marine

Insurance Bureau provide for permission to increase the blanket item to more than 10 percent if the facts are submitted to the Bureau and the circumstances justify a higher percentage.

There is no territorial limitation, which has the effect of providing worldwide coverage.

There are only three exclusions, plus an agreement or representation which has the effect of an exclusion. There is a war damage exclusion and a nuclear exclusion similar to those appearing in other personal inland marine policies. Another exclusion applies to loss or damage caused by wear and tear, gradual deterioration, insects, vermin, or inherent vice. It is felt that the insured can avoid losses from these causes by taking proper care of his instruments.

A condition which amounts to an exclusion provides that the "insured represents and agrees that none of the instruments insured hereunder will be played for remuneration during the term of this policy," unless permitted by endorsement, with the payment of an additional premium. This provision of the broad form is not quite as strong as the comparable provision of the limited form which says that the policy shall become void if the insured plays for remuneration any instrument insured under the policy.

A professional musician is defined in the rating bureau rules as "a person who receives any remuneration for playing a musical instrument insured during the term of the policy." This definition ties in the insured instrument with the playing for remuneration. The insured might be a professional musician in the popular sense of the term, but this would not affect the coverage of the policy so long as he did not play for remuneration any instrument insured under the policy. On the other hand, the coverage is not intended to be effective on any instrument played by the insured for remuneration during the policy term.

The exclusion concerning instruments played for remuneration is deleted from policies covering bands, orchestras, chamber music ensembles and similar groups, and property of boards of education or municipalities, and from policies covering individuals when the policies are written at the rates applicable to professionals.

There is provision for automatic coverage on newly acquired equipment. This is limited to 25 percent of the amount of insurance, or $10,000, whichever is less. The insured is required to report the new acquisition within thirty days and to pay additional premium.

Classification of Musical Instrument Owners. The owners of musical instruments are divided into several groups for underwriting and rating purposes. Individual owners are classed separately from groups, such as bands and orchestras. The individual owners are then divided between nonprofessionals and professionals, and the groups are divided between dance bands and other bands or orchestras.

There is no definition of dance bands. There are no policy provisions relating to dance bands, and it is a matter of underwriting whether a band shall be classified as a dance band or not. Usually there is little difficulty, because dance bands engage in that form of playing on a regular basis.

The bureau manuals do include a definition of orchestras and bands in order to assist the underwriters in making a distinction between individual policyholders and such groups. An orchestra, band, or similar group is "construed to be any formally organized group of musicians who perform as a musical unit before the public at regular or frequent intervals." Thus, a group that rehearses for a year in order to give an annual concert would come within the definition because of its "regular" performance each year. So also would a group that performs frequently but on an irregular basis. A further explanation of the rule states that it is not permissible to rate as a single group any combination of individuals, or combination of bands or orchestras, because they are members of or controlled by booking agents, unions, associations, sales organizations, professional music schools, or similar arrangements.

It is permissible to insure the privately owned instruments of bona fide members in the same policy as the instruments of the organization itself.

Rates for Musical Instruments. The rates for insurance on instruments of individual nonprofessional musicians are somewhat less than the rates for individual jewelry policies. The rates for individually owned professional instruments are much higher than those of nonprofessional musicians. Instruments of bands, orchestras, chamber music ensembles, and bands of schools, boards of education, and municipalities take rates higher than those for individual nonprofessional musicians, but lower than the rates for professional musicians.

Organs of a mobile nature are insurable at the same rates as other musical instruments. Organs not of a mobile nature (such as permanently installed church, hotel, club or residential organs) take the highest coinsurance fire and extended coverage contents rates, plus a nominal loading to cover the other hazards insured against. Policies covering such nonmobile organs have an additional exclusion applying to mechanical or electrical breakdown, failure, or loss from a servicing operation, unless fire or explosion ensues, and then only covering the loss from the ensuing fire or explosion.

Dance bands and orchestras pay the highest rates because of the circumstances under which such organizations must work. There are large numbers of people circulating about a dance hall, or ballroom, and they have access to the orchestra stage during intermissions when the orchestra members may be away from their instruments. The situation is entirely different from that at a symphony concert where the orchestra plays on a stage removed from the audience. Dance bands and orchestras play before the public much more frequently than other types of musical ensembles. The dance band is likely to have several engagements a week, whereas another band or orchestra will rehearse many times to present a few public performances.

Usually it is to the advantage of a professional musician to have his instrument insured with the other instruments of the group. When the value of his instruments does not exceed $500, the individual may pay at the rate of about $4.50 if he is a professional. The group rates are less than these amounts, and the individual would get the advantage of the average rate paid by the group. It is only in the case of a small dance band that the individual rates are lower than the professional group rates. The lower rates for groups of instruments are justified by the savings in expense in writing policies. It is a much simpler job to write a single policy on a hundred instruments than to write a hundred policies. However, when high values are to be insured, the lowest rate obtainable is on the property of an individual musician. The saving to the individual by insuring under the group policy is possible only when the value of the individual's instruments is low and the aggregate value of the group's instruments is high.

The minimum premium is $15 irrespective of term for both the broad form and the limited form.

Coverage Under the Limited Form Musical Instruments Floater. The limited form of the musical instruments floater insures against loss or damage caused by fire, lightning, cyclone, tornado, flood, theft, and accident to conveyances. This is a much more limited coverage than is provided in the broad form. The most important differences are the lack of protection against losses due to mysterious disappearance, breakage of instruments, explosion, and theft from unattended vehicles. There is an exclusion that excludes any loss or damage to the property insured while it is left unattended in or on any automobile unless it is in the custody of a common carrier.

In addition to the unattended vehicle exclusion just described, there are only three other exclusions. A war damage exclusion is used which is identical to the similar exclusion in the broad form. The exclusion relating to instruments played for remuneration is stronger than the similar condition in the broad form. There is the usual nuclear exclusion.

Territorial limits are worldwide, the same as in the broad form.

The rates for the limited form are 10 percent less than the rates for the broad form.

Underwriting of Musical Instruments Policies. Many underwriters prefer to insure the individual musician who has a valuable instrument that he plays as a hobby. The value of the instrument plus the owner's interest in it as a hobby means that the instrument will be well cared for. Such an instrument is subjected to comparatively little outside exposure because the owner takes it out only to take lessons or to play in some amateur group.

Collectors of rare instruments have a deep interest in their property. If the fire hazard where the instruments are kept is satisfactory, such collectors are desirable policyholders. If the fire rate is higher than the musical instruments rate, it may be advisable to insure rare instruments under a fine arts form because the rates for fine arts coverage are based upon the fire rate at the location where the property usually is kept. The musical instruments rate is based on the assumption that the property will be subject primarily to a transit hazard and will not be stored at a fixed location.

Underwriters are cautious in their acceptance of insurance on property of professional musicians and particularly in connection with instruments used by dance bands and orchestras. This type of playing may result in a considerably more frequent exposure to theft or breakage.

School bands are likely to show a good experience if the supervision and control of the band are strict. Many school band leaders insist upon the members' being present at rehearsals and require that a serious attempt be made to develop a worthwhile organization. The members of such a group are forced to take their music seriously, and they will learn to handle their instruments carefully. A school band composed of happy-go-lucky participants who wander in and out of rehearsals at will is likely to have members who treat their instruments carelessly.

SILVERWARE

Silverware, silver-plated ware, goldware, gold-plated ware, and pewterware may be insured under the personal articles floater. This type of property is similar to jewelry in that it is made of precious metals, but the exposure to loss from the insurance standpoint is much less than the exposure to jewelry. The burglar or robber usually can dispose of jewelry much more easily than he can dispose of silverware and related property. The fact that jewelry is worn away from home makes it subject to loss, whereas silverware generally is used at home.

The coverage of silverware is that of the personal articles floater without any special exclusions. The only provision specially applicable to silverware is that this does not include pens, pencils, flasks, smoking implements or accessories, or articles of personal adornment. Such articles if made of precious metals may be insured as jewelry.

Silverware may be insured on a scheduled basis or on a blanket basis. It is preferable to schedule more valuable pieces or sets. Antique silverware would be more properly insured under the fine arts coverage.

The rate is very low, being about 20 cents per $100 of insurance. The minimum premium is $15 irrespective of term.

Occasionally an insured will lend his silverware to a club for some special function. Persons whose business or social status requires that they have frequent parties of large size may have a considerable exposure to loss. These hazards are not contemplated by the very low rate for this coverage. There is no coinsurance provision in the policy, but it is intended that the property be insured for its full value.

STAMP AND COIN COLLECTIONS

Millions of people collect stamps and coins, and such property owned by a collector may be worth many thousands of dollars. There is probably no other hobby, except perhaps the collection of gems, in which the values of the collection are represented by such small and delicate objects as stamps. It is characteristic of stamp collectors to be extremely proud of their collections and to take excellent care to prevent loss or damage. If this were not the case, it would be impossible to insure such fragile articles without sustaining frequent and expensive losses.

Postage stamps are collected in greater numbers than any other type, but there are many collectors of revenue stamps and other types of stamps issued by governmental authorities for tax or other purposes. Collectors may specialize in stamped envelopes, in blocks of stamps, in the stamps of one country, or in covers. A "cover" is an envelope with a stamp on it that has been canceled by the Post Office in the mailing process.

Many collectors make a specialty of "first-day covers." These are envelopes that bear stamps of a particular issue and have been mailed on the first day that the particular stamp was issued by the Post Office. Frequently the Post Office or some civic body at the point of first-day issue will put a special notation on all envelopes mailed at the place and on the day of issue. This is known as a "cachet," and envelopes bearing such notations are much in demand by collectors of covers.

The United States Post Office Department encourages the collection of stamps and of first-day covers by issuing a large number of commemorative stamps. These are issued first at a place or places related to the event commemorated. On the following day the stamps are placed on sale at all other Post Offices throughout the country. The postmark on the first-day cover identifies the date on which it was sent.

Insurance for Private Collections. Rates, rules, and forms for private stamp and coin collection floaters are filed by the inland marine rating bureaus. The property that may be insured under such a policy is described as:

> Postage stamps including due, envelope, official, revenue, match and medicine stamps, covers, locals, reprints, essays, proofs and other philatelic property owned by or in custody or control of the insured, including the books, pages and/or mountings therefor.
>
> Rare and current coins, medals, paper money, bank notes, tokens of money and other numismatic property owned by or in custody or control of the insured, including coin albums, containers, frames, cards and display cabinets in use with such collection.

The description of philatelic property is sufficiently broad to include any property that may be associated with stamp collecting. For example, many people have collections of Christmas seals. These are not postage stamps, but they are used extensively on letters and have come to be associated with stamps of other kinds. A collection of Christmas seals could be insured as philatelic property.

The coverage is written by means of the personal articles floater attached to the scheduled property floater policy. The coverage is of the "all risks" type, subject to the exclusions of the personal articles floater which have been described and also subject to special provisions and exclusions which apply to stamp and coin collections.

Property may be insured on either a blanket or a scheduled basis. Bulky schedules may be kept on file with the insurance company or at some other designated place after examination by a representative of the insurance company. It is not intended that each individual stamp be listed and described. The general practice is to describe the stamps by groups or classes, with an amount assigned to each group or class, and to list specifically only the more valuable stamps.

The rules do not include provision for automatic coverage on new acquisitions. It is intended that the description in the policy shall be sufficiently broad to cover ordinary acquisitions of the collector in his efforts to complete the various sections of his albums and that he will report immediately any highly valuable acquisitions.

The coverage of the policy is worldwide.

Exclusions in the Stamp Collection Form. As in all the "all risks" policies, the actual coverage for stamp and coin collections is set out by the exclusions.

The first exclusion is a variation of the wear and tear clause. It excludes loss or damage resulting from "fading, creasing, denting, scratching, tearing, thinning, transfer of colors, inherent defect, dampness, extremes of temperature, gradual depreciation, or damage sustained from handling or while being actually worked upon and resulting therefrom." The rules do not provide for any modification of this exclusion. It is felt that all the perils and changes listed in this exclusion are uninsurable because they are the result of either the inherent nature of stamps or carelessness on the part of the insured.

Mysterious disappearance losses might be frequent and troublesome if there were no restrictions on this coverage. Stamps are so small that they are easily lost in the leaves of books or thrown away in trash. The form excludes coverage for mysterious disappearance of individual stamps, coins, or other individual articles unless specifically scheduled with a definite amount set opposite their description, or if not specifically scheduled, unless they are mounted in a volume and the page to which they are attached is also lost. Any article of high value should be scheduled with an amount of insurance applicable to it. Under these circumstances the mysterious disappearance of a stamp or coin would be covered. It is also considered acceptable practice to provide mysterious disappearance coverage for an entire page of an album.

The intent of the exclusion is to avoid loss for stamps that are carelessly mislaid or thrown away. The insured probably would be more careful with a valuable stamp and would not be so likely to lose it in trash or by throwing it away accidentally. The loss of an entire sheet from an album is unlikely unless someone stole it. Mysterious disappearance that really is a theft loss is intended to be covered.

Loss or damage to property in the custody of transportation

companies is excluded. Shipments by mail are excluded from coverage unless sent by registered mail.

Theft from an unattended automobile is excluded except while in the custody of the Post Office when shipped as registered mail. This exclusion may be deleted for the payment of a substantial additional premium. This exclusion differs from those used in other inland marine forms in that it excludes loss from any unattended automobile and does not limit the exclusion to those that are not locked. The deletion of the exclusion gives full unattended automobile coverage and does not limit the coverage to locked automobiles. Because stamps and their albums usually are small in size and can be carried conveniently, there is little reason for the collector to leave his albums in an automobile. A request for deletion of this exclusion may indicate that the stamps or coins are carried about frequently and that there is a considerable transit hazard.

There is an exclusion of loss or damage to any property which is described but which is not a part of a stamp, money, or numismatic collection. This is intended to exclude any loss of money or stamps that are not part of a collection.

There could be an application to a stamp or coin collection of that portion of the war damage exclusion of the personal articles floater that refers to seizure or destruction under quarantine or customs regulation, confiscation by order of any government or public authority, or risks of contraband or illegal transportation or trade. A collector who trades with foreign correspondents might sustain such a loss.

Valuation of Lost or Damaged Stamps. The form includes special provisions for the determination of value in case of loss. The valuation section is divided into four parts, the first of which reads as follows:

> In case of loss of or damage to property scheduled herein and representing any one stamp, coin or other individual article insured, this company shall pay or make good to the insured such loss or damage up to but not exceeding the amount(s) set opposite the item(s) involved.

The basic policy to which the form is attached contains an actual cash value clause. The valuation clause quoted here provides for payment up to the amounts set opposite the items involved but does not specify that the amounts are the agreed values of the items. Ordinarily the insurance company would pay the amount scheduled for the loss of any individual item when the item is scheduled on the policy or in a list referred to in the policy.

The valuation clause also provides that the company "shall pay or make good" the items involved. This is intended to give the company the privilege of replacing lost or damaged articles. It is a desirable privilege because the company sometimes can make replacement more advantageously than the insured can. Usually an insured would be pleased by this type of settlement because it would re-establish his collection in the same condition it was in before the loss.

The second part of the valuation section also refers to scheduled items, but instead of mentioning individual items it refers to scheduled pairs, strips, blocks, series, sheets, or the like. Many times a block or other group of stamps is worth considerably more as a unit than the total value of all individual items would amount to separately. This is particularly true when the block of stamps is from the margin of the sheet and contains the plate number that appears on all sheets of stamps issued by the United States. For example, a typical stamp about ten years old with a face value of 3 cents may be worth 8 cents. However, a block of four stamps from the margin with the plate number attached may be worth 55 cents.

The valuation clause pertaining to such groups that are scheduled reads as follows:

> In case of loss of or damage to property specifically described in the above schedule as pairs, strips, blocks, series, sheets, covers, frames, cards or the like, this company shall pay in the event of total loss of such an item up to but not exceeding the amount set opposite the item involved and in the event of partial loss not more than the cash market value of the whole set, less the cash market value of the remainder at the time of loss, it being however understood and agreed that in the event of the property being insured for less than the cash market value, the liability of this company shall not exceed the proportion that the amount insured bears to the cash market value.

In case of total loss of a set, the settlement under the clause just quoted is to be made in the same way as provided in the preceding clause, and payment is to be up to but not exceeding the amount scheduled.

In case of partial loss, the amount payable is to be the difference between the cash market value of the entire set and the cash market value of the portion remaining. The effect is similar to that of the pair and set clause in the basic inland marine policy to which the form is attached, but with special application to stamps and coins. These clauses are a recognition that the value of the set may be greater than the total values of the individual parts.

The final phrase of the clause is intended to encourage the

insured to carry insurance equal to the value of such sets. If such sets are underinsured, the insurance company will pay only a part of any partial loss, the amount to be paid being in the proportion that the amount of insurance bears to the cash market value.

The third part of the valuation section limits recovery on nonscheduled items to the actual cash market value at the time of loss less depreciation. It also provides that the company shall not be liable for more than $1,000 on unscheduled numismatic property and not exceeding $250 on any one stamp, coin, or other individual article or any one pair, strip, block, series, sheet, cover, frame, card, or the like. These limitations are intended to encourage the insured to schedule his more valuable items and also to limit the company's liability for unscheduled property.

The final part of the valuation section is a full coinsurance clause applying to unscheduled property, which provides that the company "shall not be liable for a greater proportion of any loss on property not specifically scheduled herein, than the total sum insured on such unscheduled property bears to the actual cash market value thereof at the time such loss shall happen."

A policy that is written properly to protect the insured's collection shows a schedule of all philatelic property worth more than $250 per stamp or set and includes a blanket item for the smaller units in an amount sufficient to cover the full market value.

Rates. The rates for the extremely broad coverage of the stamp and coin collection floater coverage are comparable to the rates for jewelry. The rates for coins are higher than for stamps. This rate level for coins reflects a higher loss ratio for this type of property. It appears to be more susceptible to robbery and theft losses.

A credit of 10 percent of the premium may be allowed if the policy contains an agreement by the insured to keep at least 75 percent of the insured property in a fireproof safe or vault with combination lock when not in use or on exhibition.

The minimum premium is $15 irrespective of term.

Special Exhibitions and Societies. The rules, rates, and forms which are filed for private stamp and coin collections do not apply to special exhibitions held under the auspices of and insured in the names of societies and organizations. Policies may be written to cover such exhibitions according to the needs of the sponsoring organizations. Such policies cover any possible loss on the part of the organization. It is not considered proper to issue policies in the name of an organization to cover individuals under certificate.

Underwriting of Stamp Collections. The best stamp collection policyholders are those serious stamp collectors who maintain complete records of their collections. In addition to the schedules attached to their policies, they maintain records of the stamps included in any miscellaneous items. Without such complete records, the adjustment of losses is extremely difficult.

Collectors trade and sell stamps, and it is questionable how much trading and selling by a collector would make him a dealer. It is difficult to draw a fine line between the hobbyist and dealer, but ordinarily the hobbyist is interested primarily in improving his collection rather than in trading for profit.

Many collectors receive stamps on approval from other collectors or dealers so that they can examine them prior to purchase. The blanket coverage of the stamp and coin collection floater extends to such property if it is at the risk of the insured while in his custody or while in transit. Collectors who deal in foreign stamps may expose the insurance company to a considerably greater risk than collectors who deal only in domestic stamps.

Underwriting of Coin Collections. The description of the property insured is broad enough to include commemorative coins, private gold coins of the sort issued by private companies where there was no government currency available, tokens issued by merchants when currency was scarce, tax tokens issued by states for use in payment of sales taxes, and paper currency of all kinds issued by existing and former governments.

The underwriting of coin collections follows the same principles as the underwriting of stamp collections. The persons who collect such property are likely to take extremely good care of it, and usually they are willing to provide a complete catalog of their permanent items. It is desirable to have a catalog at some other place than where the collection itself is if the property is not scheduled in detail on the policy. Coins are not so easily destroyed by fire as stamps, but the value of coins depends largely upon their condition. Smoke might tarnish them so that their value would be reduced considerably. Collections of modern United States coins and currency may be subject to greater pilferage hazard than stamps because the money can be spent.

Loss experience has been worse from the more valuable coin collections because of burglaries and robberies. The elimination of silver from United States coins seemed to increase the general interest in coin collections. It also appears that some people established coin collections as a hedge against inflation in the economy of the country. This increased interest in coin collecting made it easier for criminals to profit by theft of coin collections. This has prompted underwriters to inquire regarding the protection that an insured provides for his collection, and also to inquire about the amount of transit exposure.

QUESTIONS

1. Explain why you consider that it has been possible for insurance company to issue extremely broad coverage policies on such valuable articles as furs, jewelry, and cameras.
2. Why are rates for insurance on personal cameras uniform throughout most of the United States with little variation from state to state?
3. Why has it not been considered feasible to apply manual rates and rules to television cameras, coin-operated cameras, and property of photographic dealers and manufacturers?
4. Compare the exposure to loss of cameras used by professional photographers with those used by amateurs.
5. What information does an underwriter need regarding a fur coat that is to be insured?
6. What do you consider to be the most important threat of loss to a fur coat?
7. Explain the purpose of the "pairs and sets" clause which appears in the personal jewelry coverage.
8. Outline the information which you would request from an agent in connection with the underwriting of personal jewelry.
9. Distinguish between the coverage which applies to jewelry and that which applies to fine arts.
10. Define the meanings of the word "carat" as used in connection with diamonds and "karat" as applied to gold.
11. Distinguish between the Wedding Presents Floater and the wedding and engagement ring insurance under a jewelry coverage.
12. What are fine arts?
13. Why is it considered proper to insure fine arts under an inland marine policy even though they may never be subject to a transit hazard?
14. Why is there a special "pairs and sets" clause which applies to fine arts under the Personal Articles Floater?
15. Explain why a blanket policy might be issued to cover the property of a fine arts dealer but all items are required to be scheduled for a private collection.
16. Explain why the broad coverage of the fine arts insurance may often be provided at rates lower than the fire and extended coverage rates.

17. Under what circumstances are windows considered to be fine arts?
18. Discuss the relative desirability from the company underwriting standpoint of insuring guns and golfers' equipment.
19. Explain the reasons for higher rates on musical instruments that are played by professional musicians than for instruments played only for amateur purposes.
20. Discuss the desirability of school bands from an insurance underwriting standpoint.
21. What is the difference between jewelry and silverware from the insurance standpoint?
22. Describe the exclusions in the stamp and coin collection coverage that are designed specifically for this type of property.
23. Compare the exposures to loss of stamp collections and coin collections.

21

The Personal Property Floater

The personal property floater was developed in the late 1920s and early 1930s when an increasing use of the automobile brought a need for insurance coverage away from the domicile of the insured. Fire insurance was extended to cover up to 10 percent of the policy amount on property away from the insured's home, and the use of the extended coverage endorsement added coverage for additional perils. The fire and extended coverage policy continued to be deficient for the traveler because the principal chances of loss to property were from theft and the perils of transportation. It has been calculated that the traveler would have to buy at least five insurance policies to give himself reasonably complete protection under the old mono-line concept of insurance. These would be a fire and extended coverage policy, a residence theft and burglary policy, a water damage policy, an earthquake policy, and a personal effects policy. He might also have a need for special policies for cameras, jewelry, fine arts, or furs. All of these policies remained deficient because the insured would have no coverage for the unusual loss that was not mentioned in any of his policies. Inland marine underwriters reasoned that an "all risks" type of coverage in the marine tradition was a proper answer.

The personal property floater continues to be important for several reasons. It is the only policy generally written which provides a broad, "all risks" type of coverage for the person who wants insurance on the contents of his home independently of another policy. It is substantially broader in its coverage than the "tenant's" form of the Homeowners policy. It is the basis for the Comprehensive Form 5 of the Homeowners policies. Long-established practices in the interpretation and underwriting of the personal property floater are the basis for handling the "all risks" coverage under this form of Homeowners policy.

Questions which have been determined for the personal property floater and which now affect the newer broad coverages include: What is personal property? What is a family of the same household? What is property that is owned, used, or worn by an insured? What are the premises of the residence of the insured? The breadth of coverage in the personal property floater makes it really a multiple line policy. Its history as an inland marine policy was the result of a willingness on the part of marine underwriters to provide what their insureds needed.

The origin of the personal property floater is obscure. It was established by 1933 when the first Nation-Wide Definition was adopted by the National Association of Insurance Commissioners. It was accorded the dubious recognition of being prohibited by that Definition. However, by the time the 1953 Nation-wide Marine Definition was adopted the personal property floater had become thoroughly entrenched as an inland marine policy and it was included in the 1953 Definition.

BASIC POLICY CONDITIONS OF THE PERSONAL PROPERTY FLOATER

The basic policy for the personal property floater is the scheduled property floater policy, which is the same as used for the other personal inland marine coverages. The effect of these conditions as part of an insurance policy has already been discussed. The personal property floater form and its provisions and limitations are discussed here.

Property Covered. The personal property floater covers:

> Personal property owned, used or worn by the person in whose name this policy is issued and members of the insured's family of the same household, while in all situations, except as hereinafter provided.

The words "personal property" are not defined in the form. In the absence of such a definition, it is necessary to depend upon legal definitions of personal property to find out just what property is covered. Unfortunately, this is not a simple problem. Two general types of property are recognized by the laws, real and personal. Real property, which is also known as "real estate" or "realty," consists of the land and objects attached to the land. There may be some question about just where the line is to be drawn in connection with property that may become part of the realty when attached to the land or attached to a structure that is attached to the land.

Personal property, roughly, is any property that is not real property. Personal property may be divided into three groups.

The first consists of movable objects not in any way connected with or attached to the land. Included in this group is such obviously personal property as clothing, jewelry, furniture, sports equipment, money, and all the many items that may be included in the term "household furnishings."

Objects that have been attached to the land but have been removed therefrom by a person who has the right to make such removal become personal property. Examples are lumber, flowers, farm crops, and the products of mines. These objects remain a part of the real property as long as they are attached to the land. The owner of the land has the right to remove them and sell them as personal property.

A tenant has certain rights of removal, either by custom or by contract with the owner of the land. For example, if a farmer rents a farm for the purpose of operating it as a farm, there is the implication that any crops he raises are his to remove and sell. The person who rents a house and lot in the city may raise vegetables or flowers, and the owner does not question the tenant's right to remove and use the vegetables and flowers. On the other hand, the owner of the land might question the right of the tenant to remove a tree without his permission. Once the object has been removed by a person having the right to make the removal, the object ceases to be real property and is personal property.

A second type of personal property is the evidence of ownership or interest in the property. Examples are stocks and bonds, notes, and other evidences of debt. The deed to a piece of land is personal property, although the land itself is real property.

A third type of personal property consists of objects that are attached to the land but that because of some special conditions retain their identify as personal property. A building that sits on leased land may remain personal property by agreement between the owner of the land and the owner of the building. A written lease making provision for the building's remaining the property of the tenant would establish the fact that the building is the personal property of the tenant. It is customary, for example, for persons who own summer homes or fishing lodges to lease ground and set their own buildings on the land, with a specific provision in the lease allowing the tenant to retain ownership of the building and giving him permission to remove the building at will.

The personal property floater does not contain any exclusion of loss or damage to "buildings." It is entirely possible when a building retains its identity as personal property that an insurance company would be obligated to pay for loss or damage to it under the personal property floater if the loss were not excluded by any other provision of the policy. Inland marine underwriters prefer to put a special exclusion referring to buildings in any policy covering the property of a person who is known to have a building on leased land.

Fixtures also qualify as property that is attached to the land but that may retain its identity as personal property. Many problems arise in connection with fixtures under the personal property floater. There does not seem to be any clear-cut rule about when a fixture is personal property and when it becomes a part of the realty. A strict view would hold that anything attached to the land (or to a building that is itself attached to the land) would therefore become a part of the real estate. A more liberal view has held that objects that have been installed by a tenant and that can be removed without defacing the building are personal property.

Insurance companies have received claims under the personal property floater for damage to shrubbery that has been planted about a residence. The prevailing opinion seems to be that growing plants and trees are part of the real estate as long as they are attached to the ground and are not personal property.

Understandings and customs of the neighborhood have much to do with the determination of what can be removed when a tenant leaves the premises. In some sections of the country, the window shades are provided by the landlord and are looked upon as part of the real estate, whereas in other sections they are put in by the tenant and are removed when he leaves. The same thing is true of refrigerators, stoves, and floor coverings.

Some of these facilities which are provided by the landlord but are not attached to the building may be personal property, but are the property of the landlord. The fact that they may be covered by the landlord's building insurance policy does not convert them into real property. Such objects would be covered under the personal property floater only if the tenant is responsible for them.

The coverage does extend to certain kinds of real property. Improvements, alterations and additions made by the insured to buildings occupied as residences, but not owned by him, are covered. Such improvements are a part of the realty, but the policy is extended to cover them for a tenant. This extension of coverage for a tenant is limited to 10 percent of the amount of insurance, and covers only for fire and the extended coverage hazards.

This extension does not apply to premises owned and occupied by the insured. There are claims presented by owner-occupants for damage to fixtures when the damage is not covered by other insurance policies. If a dwelling owner had a loss from a leaking roof or from rain blown in through an open window, it would be to his advantage to have as much of the building equipment considered personal property as the insurance company would allow under the personal property floater. The legal definitions of real and personal property might have to be relied upon to distinguish between the two and to draw a line where the insurance on personal property would cease to cover.

Persons Whose Property is Covered. There have been problems with the phrase referring to "members of the insured's family of the same household." The word "family" frequently is interpreted to imply a blood relationship, but the definitions of the word are many and varied. A synonym for "family" is the word "household," and under its meaning all the persons living under the same roof (including servants and boarders) could be considered members of the same family. Apparently it was the intent of the framers of the personal property floater to mean relationship by flood or by marriage, because the rules of the inland marine rating bureaus contain a provision that "It shall not be permissible to issue a policy naming as the insured persons not related residing together."

Many of the questions that have arisen in connection with the wording "family of the same household" have to do with children away at school, persons in military service, and married children who may not have an establishment of their own. It seems to be generally recognized by inland marine underwriters that children who are away at school but who intend to return to the family establishment for vacations or when their studies are finished remain a part of the family of the same household.

There has been no unanimity of opinion regarding persons in military service. Two decisions that seem to be on the point are in disagreement, although the one on a personal property floater rules that the person was a member of the family of the same household.[1] Certain property of the insured's son, who was away from home in military service, was stolen from his quarters at camp. The son was nineteen years of age, and it was his apparent intention to return home and to school after his term of military service was over. The Supreme Court of Arkansas held that there had been no change in the domicile or residence of the son by his entering the Army, and they interpreted the word "household" to mean the same as domicile, residence, or place of abode. Therefore, it was held that the son was still a member of the insured's family of the same household.

An automobile liability case involving the words "a member of his [insured's] household" was decided in an opposite way by the Supreme Court of California.[2] The circumstances were somewhat different in that the son was married, although he and his wife were living with the insured before going into the service. The case involved an automobile owned by the son, which the insured was driving at the time of the accident. The insured had an automobile of his own, and he had purchased a liability insurance policy to cover it. The policy also protected the insured for his liability as a result of driving any other private automobile except an automobile owned in full or in part by "a member of his household." The court held that the son was not a member of the insured's household, stating, "We are rather inclined to believe that the term 'member of the household,' in view of the rules of law hereinbefore set forth, should be construed to refer to a person who at the time of the accident is actually dwelling under the same roof with the insured. . . ."

In this case the decision of the court was against the company, since there would have been no coverage under the policy if the son had been found to be a member of the insured's household. In the Arkansas case the decision also was against the company, inasmuch as there was coverage only if the son were held to be a member of the father's household. In view of the uncertainty concerning the exact meaning of the phrase "members of the insured's family of the same household," it appears possible that a court will decide any questionable case against the insurance company.

For practical purposes, the underwriter might apply a test involving the two following points:

1. Are the persons related? If so, this would make them eligible to be considered members of the same family. Relations by marriage could be considered as related.

[1]Central Mfrs. Mutual Ins. Co. v. Friedman, 209 S.W. (2d) 102 (Ark. 1948).

[2]Island v. Fireman's Fund Indemnity Co., 172 P. (2d) 520 (Cal. App. 1946), affd. 184 P. (2d) 153 (1947).

2. Are they living under the same roof as part of the same housekeeping unit? If they are living in the home for an indefinite period and are not merely casual visitors, this would seem to qualify them as members of the household.

It is not intended that servants, visitors, boarders, or persons who have established a home elsewhere be included.

Coverage for Borrowed or Rented Property. The personal property covered by the policy is that which is "owned, used or worn" by the insured and his family. This extends the coverage beyond the property belonging to the insured and his family to any property they may use or wear. The effect is the same as the phrase "owned or used by an insured" which appears in the Homeowners policies.

An insurance company also may be liable, under a personal property floater, for damage to property belonging to a hotel in a room occupied by the insured, on the ground that the furnishings are used by the insured. Hotels have billed their patrons for damage done to furnishings as a result of fires in hotel rooms.

This problem may be serious in connection with an insured who rents a furnished apartment. The insurance company would be liable for any loss to the furnishings of the apartment, but the insured probably would purchase only enough insurance to cover the value of his own property. There would be an exposure to the insurance company far greater than would be contemplated by the premium paid for the policy.

Extensions of Coverage to Property of Others. The coverage is extended by specific provisions in the form to certain other property in addition to personal property owned, used, or worn by the insured and his family. The insured may elect to have the coverage extended to the personal property of others while on the premises of his residences. Since this extension is made "at the sole option of the insured," other persons cannot make claim directly on the insurance company; the claim must be made through the insured and at his direction.

The insured has the option of extending the coverage to the personal property of others only when such property is "on the premises of the residences of the insured." There is no definition of "premises" in the form, and courts have held variously as to whether the premises extend beyond the building itself. Two Texas cases illustrate the opposite views that have been taken, depending upon the circumstances. Both involved suits on fire insurance policies. A part of one opinion reads:[3]

> The word "premises" has been construed to mean the building, and does not prevent the insured from storing gasoline on his own lot outside of the building.

An opposite opinion contains the following:[4]

> The term "premises" has attached to it various meanings, owing to the connection in which it is used but, generally speaking, the term includes not only buildings, but the lot or land upon which the same are situated.

The apparent intention of the framers of the personal property floater may be indicated by the fact that later in the form the words "residences of the insured" are used. This seems to indicate that "premises of the residences" is intended to be more inclusive than "residences." It is likely that a court would take a liberal view and would interpret "premises of the residences" to include the land surrounding the residence as well as the residence building itself.

It should be noted that the word "residences" is plural. Coverage can be extended to more than one residence of the insured. A loss occurring at a secondary residence could be covered as well as one occurring at the main residence.

The coverage also may be extended at the sole option of the insured to the "personal property of servants while they are actually engaged in the service of the insured and while in the physical custody of such servants outside such residences." (Personal property of servants on the premises of residences of the insured may be covered under the previously discussed clause, inasmuch as servants would be included in the category of "others.") This further extension applies to property of servants who are outside residences.

Questions arise as to what is meant by the words "actually engaged in the service of the insured." It appears that the intent was to allow coverage to a servant's property only while the servant is performing an act for and at the direction of the insured. Coverage does not seem to be intended when the servant is engaged in handling his own personal affairs.

Coverage may be extended to the property of a servant outside the residences of the insured only while the property is in the physical custody of the servant. The intent seems clear that there is to be no coverage if the property is in the hands of someone else at

3Fireman's Fund Ins. Co. v. Shearman, 50 S.W. 598, 599 (Tex. Civ. App. 1899).

4Merchants' & Mfgrs.' Lloyd's Ins. Exchange v. Southern Trading Co., 205 S.W. 352, 358 (Tex. Civ. App. 1918).

the time of the loss. Presumably if a loss occurred to property of one servant while in the hands of another servant who was engaged in the service of the insured, the loss could be covered if the insured so elected. The reference in the clause is to "servants" (plural); it specifies, not that the property must be in the custody of the servant who owns it, but merely that it must be in the physical custody of "such servants."

It is permissible to restrict the policy so that it excludes property owned, used, or worn by any named person. This is an important permission. There may be a member of a family whose property the company does not wish to insure. The hazard in connection with the property of a particular person may be high, whereas the rest of the family may be perfectly satisfactory.

Extension of Coverage to Other than Personal Property. A further extension of the coverage to other than personal property of the insured is provided by the clause reading:

> The company will also pay the actual loss of or damage (except by fire) to property of the insured not specifically excluded by this policy caused by theft or attempt thereat.

The intent of this extension is to provide coverage for damage that may be done by thieves or burglars to residence buildings owned by the insured. It does clearly provide this coverage, and any damage done by burglars to the insured's residence would be covered. The reference to property "specifically excluded by this policy" is intended to avoid liability on the part of the insurance company for loss to vehicles, animals, business property, and other types of property excluded in the form. The coverage would apply to any building owned by the insured except one that might be considered as "pertaining to a business, profession or occupation" of the insured. (See discussion of exclusion of business property later in this chapter.) The coverage would apply to secondary residences as well as to the main residence. The theft of shrubbery, trees, or contents of a vegetable garden, for example, would be covered by this extension.

This paragraph also extends coverage to the interior of the residences of the insured for any damage done by vandalism or malicious mischief. There is no limitation on the number of residences, nor is it specified that coverage is limited to residences occupied by the insured. The intent probably is that "residences of the insured" means structures occupied by the insured for residence purposes, but the wording is not specifically to this effect. Nothing would seem to prevent an insured from collecting from the company for a loss by vandalism to residences rented to other people. There is no reference in this clause to property specifically excluded. The exclusion of property pertaining to a business, profession, or occupation of the insured does not seem to apply to vandalism.

The popularity of the condominium type of apartment house, and the tendency for people to install improvements in apartments and dwellings which they are renting, made it desirable to include coverage for improvements and alterations. The company will also pay for loss of or damage to improvements, alterations or additions made by the insured to buildings occupied as residences by but not owned by the insured, or to premises occupied by the insured in condominiums, caused by fire, lightning, windstorm, hail, explosion, riot, smoke, or damage by vehicles or aircraft. Liability of the company for such damage is limited to 10 percent of the blanket coverage on personal property.

The final paragraph of this section does two things. It provides, first, that any loss payment under this section shall not reduce the amount of coverage under the blanket coverage on unscheduled personal property, and it also provides that the company's combined liability for loss under this extension of coverage and the blanket coverage shall not exceed the amount of insurance on unscheduled personal property. That is, this section extends the coverage of the policy to certain property of people other than the insured and to certain kinds of real property, but it does not increase the amount of insurance.

LIMITATIONS ON PROPERTY COVERED

The paragraph entitled "Amounts of Insurance" sets out the limitations on different groups of property. The first subparagraph places an amount of insurance on unscheduled personal property, and the second subparagraph places an amount on "personal jewelry, watches, furs, fine arts and other property as per schedules attached hereto."

This distinction between scheduled and unscheduled property is one of the basic principles of the personal property floater. The coverage on unscheduled property is intended to replace the many other policies the householder formerly had to buy in order to have complete insurance protection for his personal property. It is intended to insure his furniture, clothing, books, tableware, rugs, linens, and the other miscellaneous articles with which a house is furnished and which the insured and his family use.

The insurance on scheduled property is intended to cover the more valuable articles, such as those insurable under the personal articles floater.

Inland marine underwriters believe that it is not feasible to provide blanket insurance coverage without qualification on such valuable property as jewelry, watches, and furs. The principal danger of loss to these valuable articles is from theft. A burglar or robber seldom gets all the property of a person whose dwelling he enters or whom he holds up on the street.

A person who owns much jewelry wears only a portion of it at one time. If he could get a blanket insurance coverage, he might be willing to take a chance on a partial loss and buy insurance for only a portion of his total value. This would work out satisfactorily if everybody bought a policy in the same proportion to his total value, but this is not the case. The more valuables a man has, the less likely is he to have a total loss. Thus a man who owns \$10,000 worth of jewelry might feel that he would need at least 50 percent insurance to value in order to be taking a reasonable chance, whereas the man who owns \$500,000 worth of jewelry might feel that a policy for \$100,000 (20 percent of his value) would be all right for him.

Inland marine underwriters feel that the only equitable way to insure high-value articles is to have them scheduled on the policy and to have each one insured specifically for its full value. Then there can be no discrimination in favor of the man who considers that his property is sufficiently well distributed that he can take a chance on partial insurance to value.

The scheduled portion of the personal property floater assembles into this policy all the individual coverages available to inland marine policyholders for their personal belongings. Jewelry, furs, fine arts, professional property, and stamp collections are insurable under the personal property floater under the same rates, rules, and conditions as if separate policies were issued, except that the individual minimum premiums do not apply. Other property may be scheduled if the rating bureau rules provide for individual scheduling of such property, but the rates and coverage will be those of the blanket portion of the policy.

Limitation on Unscheduled Jewelry, Watches, and Furs. The limitation on unscheduled jewelry, watches, and furs reads:

> As respects any one loss of unscheduled jewelry, watches and furs, the company shall not be liable for more than \$250 unless the loss is covered under Item (c) Paragraph 3, in which event the company's liability for such loss is limited to the amount stated therein.

The \$250 limitation on loss of unscheduled jewelry, watches, and furs has been in the personal property floater for many years. Underwriters feel that the $250 is sufficient to cover miscellaneous small items that might be lost, but that all items worth more than $250 should be scheduled.

This limitation of coverage on unscheduled jewelry, watches, and furs to $250 caused a competitive problem. The coverage on these items under the personal property floater is less than the amount of coverage under fire and extended coverage policies and residence theft policies. This problem is met by optional extensions of coverage. The personal property floater form has an item where additional fire and lightning coverage may be added. Endorsements are provided under which coverage may be added for loss by wind, hail, smoke, explosion, riot, aircraft, vehicle, vandalism, malicious mischief, and collapse of building, and by burglary and hold-up. Additional premiums are charged for these optional extensions of coverage to these unscheduled articles. The use of these endorsements can make the coverage of the personal property floater the equivalent of the fire and extended coverage and the residence theft policy, but it is still necessary to schedule such articles if the "all risks" type of coverage is desired.

Secondary Residence Limitation. Another limitation provides that the insurance company shall not be liable for more than 10 percent of the amount of coverage on unscheduled personal property ordinarily situated throughout the year at residences other than the principal residence of the insured. This is intended to limit the coverage at secondary residences, such as summer homes, where the hazard may be much higher than at the principal residence. The fire hazard at summer homes is likely to be high because frequently they are located in country districts where there is no fire protection, and the burglary hazard may be severe because of long periods of unoccupancy.

The limitation applies to property "ordinarily situated throughout the year" at secondary residences. Property that the insured or his family move out to the summer home temporarily for their stay is not subject to the limitation but is covered fully, even though it is lost while at the summer home.

The amount of coverage on property situated throughout the year at secondary residences may be increased by endorsement beyond the 10 percent. In such as case, the rate is adjusted according to the fire rate at the secondary location.

Money and Securities Limitation. A third limitation on the property covered applies to money and securities. This subparagraph reads:

> As respects any one loss of money including numismatic property, the company shall not be liable for more than $100. As respects any one loss of notes, securities, stamps including philatelic property, accounts, bills, deeds, evidences of debt, letters of credit, passports, documents and railroad and other tickets, the company shall not be liable for more than $500.

This limitation on money coverage may be extended to a total of $500 for the payment of an additional premium. The limitation on securities and similar documents may be extended to a total of $1,000 for the payment of an additional premium. These extensions of the limitations do not increase the amount of insurance on unscheduled property but merely extend the restriction as far as the specific type of property involved is concerned.

It is the intent of this coverage for money and documents to protect against burglary, robbery, and the loss of such property from a risk that is covered by the policy. It is not the intent to cover loss from the acceptance of counterfeit money, from forgery, or from loss by a confidence trick. The policy does not guarantee that the insured will get full value for his money when he trades with others. The loss from the destruction or loss of documents normally would be the cost of replacing the documents. A bond usually is required when stock certificates are replaced. The loss in this case would be the charge for the bond, not the value of the stock which is represented by the certificates.

COVERAGE OF THE PERSONAL PROPERTY FLOATER

Territorial Limits. The short phrase "while in all situations," which appears near the end of the first paragraph in the form, provides worldwide coverage for the insured property. There are no territorial restrictions.

It is customary for the insured's address to be inserted in the policy but this does not restrict the coverage to the location named. The only restriction in regard to location is that already discussed, which applies to property at a residence other than the principal residence of the insured. The address given in the policy is not declared to be the principal residence.

Perils Insured Against by the Personal Property Floater. The perils insured against by the personal property floater are "all risks of loss of or damage to property covered except as hereinafter provided." The actual coverage is determined by the limitations, the exclusions, and the amounts of insurance in the personal property floater form.

Exclusions. The exclusions in the personal property floater determine the actual coverage of the policy. These exclusions are grouped into ten paragraphs.

The first exclusion provides that the policy does not insure "animals." The insurance companies usually follow the dictionary definition, which is to the effect that all members of the animal kingdom (as differentiated from plants) are animals. Under this interpretation, birds and fish are not considered to be covered.

The second exclusion refers to:

> Automobiles, motorcycles, aircraft, boats or other conveyances (except bicycles, tricycles, baby carriages, invalid chairs and similar conveniences), or their equipment or furnishings except when removed therefrom and actually on the premises of residences of the insured.

Automobiles and other conveyances usually are insured under separate policies designed to fit their peculiarities. The exclusion in the personal property floater is necessary to prevent overlapping and conflicting insurance. The exception of bicycles "and similar conveniences" was added to clarify the intent.

There have been some questions concerning motorscooters and motor-driven bicycles. The dictionary definitions of "motorcycle" are broad enough to include any two-wheeled vehicle driven by a motor, and the motor vehicle laws of most states classify them as motorcycles. Motor-driven golf carts are conveyances and appear to be excluded. They are not similar to bicycles and baby carriages because they are motor-driven.

Equipment and furnishings of conveyances are covered when they are removed from the conveyances and are on the premises of residences of the insured. Equipment and furnishings of conveyances do not have to be within a building to be covered, but merely on the residence premises. An outboard motor, for example, that had been detached from the boat and was resting on a pier owned by the insured and adjoining his residence could be considered "on his premises."

It is permissible to extend the personal property floater to cover boats (excluding inboard powerboats) and outboard motors for loss by fire, lightning, and theft to an amount not exceeding $500 on any one boat and its equipment, furnishings, or outboard motor. An additional rate is charged.

The third exclusion refers to "property of any government or any subdivision thereof." This is necessary because a government official may be responsible personally for a large amount of government property. This may be used or worn by him and thus would be covered by the personal property floater if there were no exclusion pertaining to it. Obviously the insured is not going to carry sufficient insurance to cover such government-owned property. In the absence of an exclusion referring to government property, the insurance company would be insuring property for which it receives no premium.

Business property is the subject of the fourth exclusion, which reads:

> Unscheduled property pertaining to a business, profession or occupation of the persons whose property is insured hereunder, excepting professional books, instruments and other professional equipment owned by the insured while actually within the residences of the insured.

This exception of property within the residences of the insured means that if a doctor or lawyer had his office in his residence, his professional books and equipment located within the residence would be covered. A question might arise with a professional man who owns an apartment house and has his office on the first floor and his living quarters on an upper floor. The question is whether the insured's residence is limited to his living quarters or consists of the entire building. An underwriter can provide specifically for such a situation whenever he becomes aware of it before writing a policy and can either include or exclude the professional property. Another question for which there is no satisfactory answer is whether trade equipment such as carpenter's tools would be considered professional equipment.

The framers of the personal property floater felt that the extremely broad coverage of the policy could not be provided for articles that are broken easily by carelessness on the part of the insured. The fifth exclusion is designed to eliminate these breakage claims and reads that the policy does not insure:

> Against breakage of eye glasses, glassware, statuary, marbles, bric-a-brac, porcelains and similar fragile articles (jewelry, watches, bronzes, cameras and photographic lenses excepted), unless occasioned by theft or attempt thereat, vandalism or malicious mischief, or by fire, lightning, windstorm, earthquake, explosion, falling aircraft, rioters, strikers, collapse of building, accident to conveyance or other similar casualty, nor unless likewise occasioned, against

marring or scratching of any property not specifically scheduled herein.

Difficulty is experienced in connection with the term "similar fragile articles." The insurance companies usually depend upon the legal principle known as *ejusdem generis,* which means "of the same kind." The application of the principle to the phrase "similar fragile articles" requires not only that the other articles be fragile but also that they be similar to those just enumerated. For example, the word "porcelain" refers to a particular type of pottery, but a piece of pottery that is not porcelain in a strict sense might be considered a similar fragile article because of its close similarity. On the other hand, it might be argued that a fragile article made of wood is not excluded if it is not similar to eyeglasses, glassware, statuary, marbles, bric-a-brac, or porcelains.

The sixth exclusion pertains to loss due to "mechanical breakdown." This refers to the breakage of parts in a machine, such as a refrigerator or sewing machine. It is interesting to note that consequential loss resulting from a mechanical breakdown is not excluded. In some cases freezer units have broken down and food has spoiled as a result. The breakage in the freezer mechanism is not covered by the policy, but there is no exclusion applying to the loss of food that was a consequence.

The seventh exclusion is a corollary to the mechanical breakdown provision and applies to loss or damage "to electrical apparatus caused by electricity other than lightning unless fire ensues and then only for loss or damage by such ensuing fire." This is similar to the electrical damage clause discussed for other types of inland marine coverages and has a similar application.

Exclusions of loss due to wear and tear and loss due to deterioration, insect, vermin, and inherent vice may be grouped together and considered to be an eighth exclusion. These are similar to comparable provisions in other "all risks" policies, and the application is similar.

The ninth exclusion applies to:

> Loss or damage caused by dampness of atmosphere or extremes of temperature unless such loss or damage is directly caused by rain, snow, sleet, hail, bursting of pipes or apparatus.

This excludes loss due to the damp atmosphere that is natural around lakes and seashore areas, but it is not intended to exclude a loss resulting from moisture escaping from a broken steampipe. The exclusion also refers to a subsequent flood and water damage exclusion, which will be discussed later.

A tenth exclusion relates to damage "to property (jewelry,

watches and furs excepted) occasioned by or actually resulting from any work thereon in the course of any refinishing, renovating or repairing process." It is felt by the underwriters that the insurance companies cannot accept the responsibility for the work of repairmen, but that the insured should investigate the reliability of the people to whom he entrusts his property and should hold them responsible. An exception is made in the case of jewelry, watches, and furs in order that the coverage may be comparable to that provided under specific policies.

The eleventh exclusion concerns loss to property on exhibition at fairgrounds or on the premises of any national or international exposition unless the premises are described specifically in the policy. The reasons for this exclusion have been discussed in connection with fine arts and similar property.

The exclusion relating to war damage and loss from confiscation by governmental authority is the same as found in other inland marine policies. Its effect has already been discussed.

The nuclear damage exclusion also is the usual wording found in other inland marine policies.

A rather lengthy exclusion applies to flood, surface water, tidal wave, water that backs up through sewers or drains, and underground water that seeps in through walls or floors. The exclusion does not apply to an ensuing fire or explosion loss if fire or explosion ensues. It does not apply to loss arising from theft. This flood and water damage exclusion was placed in the personal property floater following the occurrence of large water damage losses from heavy rains and overflow of bodies of water during the 1950s. These losses proved to be so catastrophic that underwriters felt that the flood hazard was no longer insurable.

There is also an exclusion of loss caused by animals or birds owned or kept by an insured or by a residence employee of the insured, unless loss by fire, explosion, or smoke ensues, and then the company shall be liable only for the ensuing loss. This exclusion is considered necessary in order to avoid losses from careless habits of pets which might be kept by the insured or his employees.

DECLARATIONS OF THE INSURED

The Inland Marine Insurance Bureau form provides a space for filling in a statement of the values declared by the insured. These are broken down by groups of property such as would be owned by a typical dwelling resident. This declaration of values is made on the application the insured is supposed to fill out when he applies for a personal property floater policy. The insertion of these values in the form has no effect on the liability of the company under the form used in most of the country. The declarations are put in the form in order to call to the insured's attention any inadequacy in the amount of insurance.

OTHER INSURANCE

It is the intention of the underwriters that the personal property floater shall replace all other policies the insured might have to cover his household goods, clothing, and similar personal property. The Inland Marine Insurance Bureau form prohibits other insurance on the property covered by the policy (unless specific permission for such other insurance is endorsed on the policy), except that other insurance is permitted on property of others on the premises of the insured, the property of servants, residences and property not personal in nature that are covered against theft and vandalism, unscheduled jewelry, watches, and furs, money and documents, equipment of vehicles, and business or professional property.

If there is other insurance that would attach on such property and would have applied to the loss had the personal property floater not been purchased, the personal property floater applies as excess insurance on that property and pays only after the other insurance has been exhausted.

Personal property floaters are sold to many people who have other policies covering their personal property. It is intended that the personal property floater shall replace all other policies, but it would work a hardship on the insured if he were forced to cancel his other policies on a short-rate basis in order to secure a personal property floater. Accordingly, the personal property floater rules provide for existing specific insurance and permit a credit in calculating the premium.

The endorsement used to give permission for the other policies lists each policy specifically, giving the type of policy, the amount of coverage, the effective and expiration dates, and the amount of unearned premium credit allowed.

The endorsement further provides that the personal property floater shall be excess insurance above such existing specific insurance but that in case the amount of a loss should exceed the total of the specific insurance, the personal property floater shall pay the difference between the amount paid by the specific insurance and what would have been payable under the personal property floater had no specific insurance existed.

REINSTATEMENT OF LOSSES

Practices in connection with the blanket portion of the personal property floater follow those of the fire insurance field. Loss payment does not reduce the amount of the insurance under the blanket item. Practices differ in respect to scheduled items. It is generally considered that the insurance is no longer in effect when a scheduled item is lost. This is reasonable because the insured item is no longer in the insured's possession to be insured. The loss clause of the basic scheduled property floater policy to which the personal property floater form is attached reads:

> Any loss hereunder shall not reduce the amount of this policy, except in the event of payment of claim for total loss of an item specifically scheduled hereon. If claim is paid for total loss of one or more scheduled items, the unearned premium applicable to such items will be refunded to the insured or applied to the premium due on item(s) replacing those on which the claim was paid.

DEDUCTIBLE POLICIES

A large proportion of personal property floaters are made subject to a deductible clause on all losses except those from fire, lightning, windstorm, civil commotion, hail, explosion, riot, riot attending a strike, smoke, damage by vehicles or aircraft, burglary, or holdup. (In states where the windstorm rate is added specifically as part of the personal property floater rate calculation and where the rate used contemplates a deductible windstorm coverage, the deductible also applies to the windstorm coverage under the personal property floater.)

The deductible clause serves two purposes. First, it eliminates the handling of many small losses and thus reduces the claim expenses of the insurance company. Second, it tends to make the insured more careful.

The saving to the insurance company under a deductible policy is especially high in connection with an "all risks" policy. The coverage is so broad that there are numerous small claims. The savings from the elimination of these losses are passed on to the insured in the form of lower rates.

The deductible does not apply to scheduled items. Full coverage is provided for scheduled items so that the personal property floater is comparable to specific policies on such property.

Substantial rate credits are given for the use of a deductible clause.

RATES

The rating system for the personal property floater is based upon a mixture of fire and casualty insurance rating theory. The basic rate is the fire insurance rate for the property as promulgated by the fire insurance rating bureau having jurisdiction in the place where the residence is located. To this basic fire rate is added a loading to pay for the other coverages included in the policy. (In certain states where the windstorm hazard is considered to be high, the extended coverage rate is added.) The rate of the loading varies according to the size of the policy. For example, in one territory the loading for the first $5,000 of coverage is $1.55 per $100 per year; for the next $5,000, 85 cents; for the next $10,000, 35 cents; and for all in excess of $20,000, 13 cents.

The full fire insurance rate is used regardless of the amount of the policy. This is because a total fire loss is a possibility in almost any residence, and there is much the same chance of a total fire loss in a $50,000 home as in a $10,000 home.

In connection with losses from other causes, there is not the same chance of a total loss under the larger policies. For example, in an apartment or small dwelling, a leaking water pipe or bathroom fixture might result in water damage to most or all of the insured's property. In a large house, the chances of such damage to all the property are remote; it is likely that such an occurrence would damage a relatively small part of the insured's property. This is held to justify a reduction in the rate of the loading for the larger policy amount.

A credit is given in the rate when a deductible clause is attached to a policy. For example, the credit for the $50 deductible is 40 percent of the premium for the blanket portion of the policy. The credit for the deductible clause applies to the entire premium for the blanket portion even though the deductible does not apply to losses from a specified list of perils. The rating system would be more consistent if the credit for the deductible clause were applicable only to the portion of the rate that covers the losses to which the deductible applies.

The credit applies only to the portion of the premium that pays for the unscheduled portion of the policy, because the deductible does not apply to scheduled items.

MINIMUM PREMIUMS

The rules for issuing many types of insurance coverages set up minimum premiums. A company will not issue a policy for a smaller premium than the minimum even though the rate and the amount of insurance are such that a smaller premium would be produced by the application of the rate to the amount of insurance.

This minimum premium is justified because it costs an insurance company several dollars to issue a policy. The cost varies between companies, depending upon their efficiency of operation. The minimum premium covers the cost of the printed documents that make up the policy, the time of the personnel who do the clerical and underwriting work, and the many miscellaneous costs entailed in the operation of an insurance company. The minimum premium is intended to cover these minimum expenses plus an amount of premium for the coverage provided by the policy.

The minimum premiums for the personal property floater are much higher than would be justified merely by the cost of issuing the policy. The lowest minimum premium is $30, and the full coverage policy cannot be written for less than $60 for one year.

These relatively high minimum premiums are necessary because of the broad coverage, which produces numerous small claims. The majority of persons who buy fire insurance policies never make a claim against their insurance companies because they do not have damaging fires. There are several thousand fire insurance policies for each one that results in a claim. In constrast, claims are made under a relatively large number of personal property floaters. Regardless of the amount of insurance under a personal property floater, the insured is likely to have some loss of personal belongings during the policy term. The minimum premium for the personal property floater is considered justified by the frequency of losses, which in turn are a result of the broad coverage provided by the policy.

FUTURE OF THE PERSONAL PROPERTY FLOATER

The initial effect of the Homeowners policies on the personal property floater was a drastic reduction in the amount of personal property floaters that were written. This effect leveled off after a few years. The premium remains substantially less than it was before the introduction of the Homeowners policies, but there still is a need for the personal property floater, judging from public acceptance. It provides the broadest coverage available to the tenant occupant of an apartment or dwelling, being considerably broader than the tenant's form of Homeowners policy. Loss experience has tended to improve somewhat with the smaller volume and more stable premium amounts. It appears that many people will continue to want the very best coverage that they can secure for their possessions.

QUESTIONS

1. Name the insurance policies an insured had to purchase in order to get reasonably complete protection on his personal property before the personal property floater was developed.
2. Why did the Nation-Wide Definition prohibit the writing of the personal property floater?
3. What is personal property?
4. What is meant by the phrase "members of the insured's family of the same household"?
5. What property is covered by the personal property floater in addition to property belonging to the insured?
6. Under what circumstances does the personal property floater cover real property?
7. Why do inland marine underwriters consider it important to have valuable articles specifically scheduled on the personal property floater?
8. What are the important limitations on the coverage under the personal property floater?
9. Discuss the extent to which the exclusions determine the coverage of the personal property floater.
10. Under what circumstances is the personal property floater written to include permission for other insurance?
11. Discuss the advantages to the insured and to the insurance company in having a deductible clause on a personal property floater.
12. Why is the rate less for large amounts of insurance than for small amounts under a personal property floater?
13. Why is a higher minimum premium justified for the personal property floater than for a fire insurance policy?
14. What are some of the steps taken by underwriters to improve the loss ratio for the personal property floater?
15. Compare the coverage of the personal property floater with that of the Homeowners tenants' form. Considering the differences in cost where you live, which would you buy?

22

Package Policies and Marine Coverages

Insurance in the United States over a period of 150 years developed according to separate lines of coverage. Insurance against loss of property was written principally as a fire insurance and later as fire plus extended coverage insurance. Protection against loss from theft and other crimes developed as a casualty coverage. Theft insurance was written by companies that were occupied principally in the writing of liability insurance.

These traditional lines of coverage began to break down following World War II. During the 1950s the package insurance policies were developed so that a dwelling owner and businessman could secure most of their insurance in packages of insurance. These changes in the methods of providing insurance coverage have an important effect upon the writing of insurance policies, but they do not change the exposures of the insured to loss. The hazards to property which existed previously are still present, and have even increased to a considerable extent because of new industrial and social conditions.

OCEAN MARINE INSURANCE AND PACKAGE POLICIES

The ocean marine policy is really a multiple line policy of insurance. For hundreds of years these policies have covered a wide range of risks including property loss from most of the hazards which threaten maritime ventures. The exclusions in the broad ocean marine policies have been few in number. The coverage of the running down clause is a property damage liability coverage, and that of the protection and indemnity clause is a bodily injury and property damage liability coverage.

Multiple line insurance and package policies in the United States have not had as much effect upon ocean marine insurance as upon other types of insurance. The ocean marine exposures to loss are substantially different from exposures on land. The average householder in the United States does not have an important ocean marine exposure, if indeed he has any at all. His personal effects can be covered on a worldwide basis if he does desire a broad coverage policy. This is included in his inland marine insurance or in the broad forms of the Homeowners policy coverage. The overseas exposure to personal effects is so incidental as far as the average householder is concerned that it need not be considered as a portion of ocean marine insurance.

A large proportion of the businessmen in the United States do not have any regular ocean marine exposures to loss. The businessman who has an occasional ocean marine exposure can secure a special policy to cover whatever risk may develop in connection with some specific business transaction. It has not become customary to include ocean marine coverage in the package insurance policies that are written for commercial operations.

The businessman who does have a regular ocean marine exposure still finds it advantageous to have ocean marine insurance written separately from any package insurance policy that he may have. The conditions of exposure to loss and the practices of covering these exposures by insurance are so different that it is still customary for the ocean marine coverages to be written under marine policies rather than as a part of the package policies. Therefore, it may be concluded that ocean marine insurance is not affected greatly by the development of the package policies in the United States.

EFFECT OF THE PACKAGES UPON INLAND MARINE EXPERIENCE

The development of the package policies in the United States has had a substantial effect upon the inland marine business. The result has been a considerable shifting of the inland marine coverages from specific inland marine policies to the package policies. It has not meant the elimination of the inland marine coverage but rather a change in the method by which the coverage is provided.

Exposure to property loss in domestic transportation may be divided roughly into two divisions. A large number of policyholders, including householders, have an incidental exposure to transit losses. This is also true of many businessmen, such as retail merchants whose supplies are sent to them at the risk of the supplier. It has become the practice to include insurance for incidental transit exposure in the Homeowners policies and in the coverage for businessmen such as the Special Multi-Peril Policy Program.

There are many businessmen whose operations include considerably more than an incidental transit exposure to loss. Most of the commercial package insurance policies have provisions for adding transit coverage to meet the exposures of the insured. These specific provisions for covering transit exposures in most cases are not labeled as inland marine coverage, but they are inland transit coverages. The methods of handling this transit exposure to loss are essentially the same as writing an inland marine transit policy. Thus inland marine insurance is being incorporated into the package policies. It is included incidentally and in a blanket manner for those policies where the transit risk exposure is substantial. This chapter on the package policies will identify the inland marine coverages that are present in many of the package insurance policies. This identification is desirable and will be helpful to the underwriter in his evaluation of exposure under the package policies.

HOMEOWNERS POLICIES

The Homeowners policies provide in a single policy the coverages that most householders need to cover loss of real and personal property and loss from liability in connection with home and personal activities. The property loss coverage which is provided by the Homeowners policies is primarily against loss to the dwelling structure and to personal property at the dwelling location. Four of the Homeowners policies provide a specified perils type of coverage against loss of personal property. There is an extension of this coverage to property away from the dwelling of the insured in the amount of 10 percent of the coverage on personal property but not less than $1,000. This coverage away from the residence of the insured is essentially a transit coverage. However, there is no specific provision for loss of property due to transit exposures. The coverage of property away from the residence premises is only against the perils named in the policy. These perils do include theft, with some limitations, and also damage from aircraft and vehicles. This is not an "all risks" type of insurance but covers only against loss from the perils specified in the policy, whether the property is away from the residence premises or on the residence premises.

It has been suggested by some underwriters that a policyholder should buy an "all risks" type of transit insurance policy such as a personal effects policy in order to secure complete off-premises and transit coverage for his personal belongings.

The Form 5 Homeowners policy is essentially the personal property floater which has been added to an "all risks" type of coverage on the dwelling structure. The considerable attention which has been paid to the personal property floater in this text is based upon the need of the underwriter to understand that policy in order to understand the Form 5 Homeowners policy.

The conclusion is that the Homeowners policies include a nominal transit coverage for a portion of the coverage applying to personal property. The Form 5 Homeowners policy is clearly a combination of the personal property floater with the other coverages of the Homeowners policies. Therefore, the underwriting of Homeowners policies must include an evaluation of the transit and off-premises exposures to the same degree and in the same manner that such evaluation would be made for specific inland marine policies which provide that type and breadth of coverage.

There is no rating factor specifically included in the Homeowners rating for the incidental coverage of transit exposure in the Homeowners policies. All of the Homeowners policies, including Form 5, are now rated by the rating bureaus on the basis of the total experience of the various Homeowners policy forms. Therefore, any transit or inland marine exposures are included in the total rating of the Homeowners policies. The Homeowners underwriter no longer has any problem of considering specific inland marine rate against inland marine exposure as far as the blanket inland marine coverages of the Homeowners policies are concerned.

SCHEDULED COVERAGES

The Homeowners policies all include provision for the scheduling of articles which are sufficiently valuable or otherwise sufficiently exposed to loss to justify scheduling and specific insurance. Included in the Homeowners forms is an endorsement which is the same in its effect as the personal articles floater. Personal jewelry, personal furs, fine arts, cameras, muscial instruments, silverware, golfer's equipment, stamps and coins, may all be scheduled for specific insurance coverage in the Homeowners policies. The rules provide that the rates which are to be used for these scheduled articles are the inland marine rates which are on file for the company. Therefore, the Homeowners policies include scheduled articles coverages which are identical with the scheduled articles coverages of the inland marine personal articles floater. The underwriting and rating problems in connection with these types of property have all been covered in this text in connection with the personal articles floater. There are no differences in underwriting and rating when such properties are insured under the Homeowners policies instead of being insured under a specific inland marine policy.

COMMERCIAL INSURANCE PACKAGES

There are many forms of package policies for commercial and industrial operations. These have been developed by individual insurance companies or groups of insurance companies in addition to the ones which are filed by the rating bureaus.

MANUFACTURER'S OUTPUT POLICY

One of the earliest of the multiple line policies which provided a broad coverage in transit was the Manufacturer's Output policy. This does not include any liability coverage but is a property loss policy. It was designed originally for the manufacturer who ships his products to dealers on consignment or under some other arrangement where the exact location of the property at any specific time might be difficult to determine. Continuous coverage is provided from the time the property leaves the factory until it is sold and becomes the property of a purchaser.

The Manufacturer's Output policy covers all personal property owned by the insured, the interest of the insured in improvements and betterments to buildings which are not owned by him, the interest of the insured in the legal liability for property of others in the actual or constructive custody of the insured, personal property which has been sold by the insured to others but which the insured has agreed prior to loss to insure for the account of the purchaser during course of delivery, property of others in the custody of the insured which prior to loss the insured has agreed to insure, and property of others sold by the insured under an installment sales agreement where the insured's responsibility continues until installation is accepted by the purchaser. These obviously include a substantial amount of coverage during transit. The transit coverage applies to the insured's property while it is being shipped from one point to another and also includes coverage on property which the insured has sold to others but which is still at the insured's risk. The insurance against transit losses is an inland marine coverage even though it is incorporated in the very broad Manufacturer's Output policy.

The calculation of the rates for the Manufacturer's Output policy is largely on a judgment basis. This is essential because the transit exposure varies widely from one manufacturing and distributing operation to another. The calculation of the rate is essentially the same as that for an annual transit policy which would be used as an inland marine coverage. Here again, the transit insurance coverage of the Manufacturer's Output policy is an inland marine coverage and is handled in almost all respects in the same way that an inland marine transit policy would be handled.

COMMERCIAL PACKAGE POLICIES

The rating bureaus have filed a set of policies which are called Special Multi-Peril policies. These include various policies for retail merchants, schools and other institutions, apartment houses, manufacturing operations and many other types of commercial properties. Individual companies have similar policies which vary in some degree from the bureau filings, but all are attempts to put into a single policy as much of the coverage as possible that the insured may need.

The more limited of the Special Multi-Peril policies include virtually no transit coverage. A minor or very small percentage of off-premises coverage is included merely for the purpose of covering items of property which may be away from the insured's premises for repair or servicing. The amount of the extension in these more limited policies is an off-premises coverage of 2 percent of the amount of insurance at a described location but not to exceed $5,000. This can hardly be considered as an inland marine coverage because in some of the forms, at least, it is specifically provided that this does not include transit coverage. It is merely a minor coverage for certain types of property which may be away from the premises temporarily for a specific purpose.

There are other Special Multi-Peril policy contracts which do provide more or less transit insurance. A typical contract of this kind divides the insurance on property in an actual or technical state of transportation between (1) property in transit on vehicles owned, operated, or leased by the insured; (2) property in the custody of salesmen away from the insured's premises; and (3) property in the custody of carriers for hire. Limits of liability are provided in the form for each of the situations named.

TRANSIT PROBLEMS WITH PACKAGE POLICIES

The package insurance policies are developed to cover primarily at the location of the insured's operations. This is a reasonable approach because the operating location normally is the one which has the greatest exposure to loss and the one where coverage provisions and restrictions must be effective. The result is that some package policies are deficient in their coverage of the transit exposure. The advantage of a separate inland marine policy to cover the transit exposure is the specific attention which the underwriter gives to the transit coverages and exposures when developing a policy specifically for this coverage. It is important that the underwriter in using one of the package policies such as the Special Multi-Peril policy should examine the transit exposure and coordinate it with the transit coverage of the package policy. There are several areas where there may be problems. Some examples will serve to point out the type of special attention that is necessary.

The commercial property form of the Special Multi-Peril policy has a listing of several types of property that are not covered by the policy. This includes property sold by the insured under some form of conditional sale or installment payment plan, property shipped by mail after it passes into the custody of the Post Office department, and property while waterborne except ferry operations incidental to other modes of transportation. It is possible that the insured's operations include property that would be in a state of transportation under one or more of these situations. The inland marine underwriter in developing a transit policy to fit the needs of the insured would take these factors into consideration to make sure that all property being shipped at the risk of the insured would be covered under all situations. The package policy underwriter must be equally alert to covering any unusual transit exposures of the insured that might involve property in these situations.

The Special Multi-Peril policies also include exclusions of theft losses under certain conditions. A typical exclusion applies to property that is stolen from a motor vehicle unless the property is taken from a fully enclosed and locked car.

Most of the package policies also have an exclusion of loss from earth movement, and from flood and surface waters. This exclusion is similar to that appearing in inland marine policies which cover property at fixed locations. However, it is not customary to exclude flood losses under purely transit policies. The Special Multi-Peril policies usually provide that these exclusions of flood and earth movement loss shall not apply to property in due course of transit or to loss arising from theft. It is desirable to examine the insured's operations to see whether property away from the premises of the insured would always be in due course of transit within the meaning of the package policy exclusion.

Many of the package policies include deductible provisions designed primarily to affect coverage at the locations where the insured is doing business. The deductible provisions should be examined by the package underwriter to see that they also fit the situation in connection with property in transit.

These are but a few of the examples which show the need for specific consideration of the transit exposure by the underwriter who is handling package policies.

The basic principle in the package policies is the combination of coverages from individual policies into a single policy or group of policies. The effect of packaging has been primarily that of combination rather than the broadening of coverage. In some areas there has been some broadening of coverages which are available to the public in that coverage has become available where frequency of loss is low but where there may be a high severity problem. The combining of coverage for such perils into packages permits the insurance company to charge a lower premium as compared to the cost of issuing many individual policies for low frequency but high severity perils.

A high degree of homogeneity among properties or operations is necessary for the development of satisfactory packages of insurance. The inland marine approach for transit exposures permits a more careful examination of the individual risk of loss as compared to the averaging and blanketing of coverage.

RATE MAKING AND FILING

It has been explained that the rates and coverages for transit coverage under inland marine policies are at the discretion of the insurance company. There is no requirement that rates be filed for those unusual types of inland marine risks which do not lend themselves to manual rates or rating plans. This permits a freedom on the part of the company underwriter under the inland marine procedure to develop coverages and rates according to his judgment of the risks involved.

It has been ruled by some insurance departments that package insurance policies and rates for them must be filed in their entirety even though some portions of these packages would not require such filing if they were written separately. This is an undesirable development as far as flexibility of coverage and rate are concerned in a state where the entire package and the rate for it become subject to the filing requirements.

It appears from developments up to this time that marine principles will continue to be applicable to the transit portion of package policy risks. The transit exposure continues and in fact is growing because of the increased amount of worldwide shipping. The increasing speed of transportation permits manufacturing and warehousing concerns to establish their distribution points at greater distances from points of sale or use. This means an increased proportion of transit exposure and a shorter period of time within warehouses and other distribution points. It is only when the transit exposure is nominal that it can be blanketed with the location coverages, both as to coverage and rate. The transit exposure must be specifically considered in any case where it is an important part of the total exposure. Marine principles will continue to be applied in the coverage and rating of the transit exposure wherever it is necessary for this to be taken into account specifically in the writing of a policy, regardless of whether it is a specific transportation policy or whether the transit coverage is part of a package policy.

QUESTIONS

1. Why is the ocean marine insurance policy a multiple line policy from the standpoint of the way in which insurance developed in the United States?
2. What has been the effect of multiple line developments on ocean marine insurance?

3. In what respect are the package insurance policies an outgrowth of marine insurance?
4. Compare the off-premises and transit coverages of the Homeowners policies with those of the personal property floater.
5. Discuss the underwriting and rating of the coverages for scheduled articles under the Homeowners policies and under inland marine policies.
6. Compare the Manufacturer's Output policy with the dealers' policies that are written as inland marine coverages. Is there any essential difference, and if there is, describe it.
7. Describe the methods used to provide transit insurance coverage under the Special Multi-peril policies.
8. Discuss the advantages and disadvantages of providing transit coverage as a part of the package policy and as a separate coverage under a marine policy.
9. In what respect do marine policies covering transit exposures differ from the typical package policy in regard to flood, wavewash, and landslide hazards?
10. Do you consider that the growing popularity of package insurance has resulted in a broadening of the coverages? What additional perils, if any, may now be covered by insurance which were not considered insurable prior to the packaging of insurance?

23

Reinsurance of Marine Risks

Marine insurance, both ocean marine and inland marine, involves the coverage of losses that far exceed the capacity of a single insurer or even of a single group of insurers. The maximum amount to which a large insurer would commit itself might be in the vicinity of $200,000. Smaller insurance companies may limit their own liabilities to $5,000 or $10,000 per loss. Reinsurance is a method used to spread liabilities for loss among many insurers.

NEED FOR REINSURANCE OF MARINE RISKS

Ocean marine losses within recent years have included the loss of the oil tanker the Torrey Canyon off the coast of England with a hull valuation of $16 million and the Andrea Dorea in the Atlantic Ocean with a hull loss of $16 million. The largest potential losses in the inland marine field are from bridge insurance. The Delaware River and Bay Authority sought coverage of $98 million for its twin bridges over the Delaware River near Wilmington. The Verrazano Narrows Bridge across New York Bay cost $325 million to build. A jumbo jet airplane which carries hundreds of passengers, costs in the vicinity of $25 million.

One method of spreading the risk of loss among several insurance companies is for each company to write a policy for the amount which it is willing to assume. The result may be a multitude of policies on one property. This is cumbersone, but it is still used in many cases. It is customary in Lloyd's of London for each underwriter to indicate on a slip above his signature how much he will assume for the particular risk.

Another method of securing sufficient insurance capacity to cover large amounts at risk is known as reinsurance. The originating insurance company in which the policy is written for the policyholder passes on a part of its liability to other insurance companies.

Reinsurance is the same in principle as other insurance. When an insurer assumes a risk for a policyholder, it acquires an insurable interest in the subject of the insurance because of the chances of financial loss. If the potential loss is greater than management feels it should assume for a single loss, insurance is bought from another insurer to cover a part of the possible liability. This passing on to another insurer a part or all of the liability which has been assumed under an insurance policy is called *reinsurance.*

The need for reinsurance is universal among insurers. Even though a large insurer may have enough assets and surplus to pay a large loss, such a payment in one year may distort its operations more than is considered desirable. Wide fluctuations in operating results would not allow an insurer to provide a consistent service to its agents and policyholders. Thus an insurer needs reinsurance in order to protect it from catastrophe losses which are larger than its financial position would justify, and also to stabilize its operations.

FUNCTIONS OF REINSURANCE

The four basic functions of reinsurance are: (1) to provide capacity for lines of insurance larger than the insurer can write by itself; (2) to protect against large losses from catastrophes; (3) to stabilize operations so that good and bad experiences are spread over several years, and (4) to give relief from the demands of large unearned premium reserves when business is growing at a rapid rate, or the company wishes to reduce the unearned premium reserve.

Reinsuring Large Single Risks to Increase Capacity. A problem of management is to determine the maximum amount to which the company can be committed for a single loss. This is called the company's *net line* or *net retention.* In writing insurance against loss of property, such as in writing fire insurance, the agent may write several policies in different companies, thus spreading any loss. No further spread is needed if the size of each policy is within the individual capacity of the company. This is not feasible in any case where the rate varies according to the size of the policy, for example, with many inland marine lines.

Reinsurance enables one insurer to issue a single policy in a total amount many times that which it can retain for its own account. The company's "capacity" is increased as far as its relationship to agents and policyholders is concerned. The trend toward the packaging of insurance into fewer policies has increased the need for a company to have a large capacity. Agents tend to represent fewer companies than was formerly the case, and they like to write as few policies as possible for the risks to be covered.

The spread of loss from a very large loss may reach to remote points. The reinsurance on a large exposure to loss may spread to almost all of the insurance organizations in the world that are willing to assume some of the liability. Under such circumstances the possibilities of extremely large losses mean that each insurer must keep its liability within its net retention because most other organizations are also assuming some of the risk.

Reinsuring Catastrophe Exposures. An insurer can restrict its exposure to loss from a single property or occurrence by keeping the amount of its liability within its net retention. It is more difficult for a company to control the amount of loss it might suffer in case of a conflagration, a widespread windstorm, or other catastrophic loss. Catastrophe reinsurance provides an insurer with a contract under which the reinsurer agrees to reimburse the reinsured company up to a specified limit for a catastrophe loss which exceeds the amount agreed upon. "Catastrophe," in property reinsurance terminology, generally refers to an occurrence which involves more than one property or location. Management must set what might be called a "catastrophe net line." A review of the amounts of insurance written in a certain area may indicate the existence of a potential catastrophe loss of, for example, one million dollars. Management may decide that the company's financial position is such that it should not be exposed to a catastrophe loss of more than $100,000. The company then would buy a reinsurance coverage of $900,000 to reimburse it for the amount of any loss above $100,000 up to the estimated one million dollar catastrophe potential. If a loss exceeding one million dollars should occur, then the reinsured company would have to stand that part of the loss also. A company may buy a second or even a third catastrophe reinsurance contract to cover above the first. Ordinarily, the larger the amount of retention, or the larger the amount of underlying reinsurance, the lower is the cost of each succeeding reinsurance contract.

Stabilization of Company Operations. Another important use of reinsurance is to stabilize an insurer's underwriting results. Management wishes to avoid wide fluctuations in the loss experience from year to year. Reinsurance in order to secure additional capacity, and catastrophe reinsurance, as just described, tend to level off the company experience. Under each type of such reinsurance the larger losses which may occur during a year are likely to be spread among reinsurers. In addition, companies may buy reinsurance to reduce the fluctuations from good and bad loss experience in different years where these fluctuations do not result from catastrophes.

Several methods are used to reduce the effects of a bad experience in a given year. One method is to arrange for reinsurance to cover any single large loss. While underwriting aims at keeping the loss from any single risk within the intended net retention, circumstances may arise under which an unexpectedly large individual loss may occur.

Another possibility is an arrangement under which the reinsurer pays a portion of any excess in loss ratio in a given year. The company may wish to stabilize its loss ratio at not more than 70 percent, for example, in which case the reinsurer would reimburse the company for the excess of losses above 70 percent, up to an agreed limit. In such a case the company probably would agree to pay back the excess to the reinsurer in future years. The reinsurance rate or premium may be adjusted upward or downward each year in accordance with the experience. This has the effect of financing the large losses of the company over an agreed period, avoiding wide fluctuations in earnings.

This stabilization of a company's operations in effect costs the company a financing fee. The net result of the reinsurance over a period of years is an increase in the company's total operating expenses, but this is considered worthwhile in order to avoid great fluctuations in earnings. It also lessens the likelihood that an insurer would become financially embarrassed because of a very bad experience in any one year.

Unearned Premium Reserve Financing. A large proportion of the premium received for term policies must be set up as a liability in an unearned premium reserve. If an insurer is growing rapidly and is writing a large amount of business for three-year terms, the reserves which must be set up may seriously deplete the surplus. It is an important problem to a company expanding into new territories and into new fields of business. By reinsuring a portion of its liability, the insurer can reduce the net amount of its unearned premium reserve. This is done by taking credit in its unearned premium reserve (subtracting from its gross unearned premium reserve) the proportion of unearned premium reserve on the portion of its business reinsured in companies licensed to transact reinsurance in its state. (A company is not prohibited from buying reinsurance in an unlicensed company, but it cannot take credit in its unearned premium reserve for unauthorized reinsurance.)

TYPES OF REINSURANCE

Reinsurance may be on either a pro rata or an excess of loss basis. When reinsurance is on a pro rata basis, the reinsurer agrees to pay an agreed portion of all losses which are subject to the reinsurance contract. The reinsurer participates in all such losses, no matter how small.

Under a reinsurance contract which is on an excess of loss basis, the reinsurer agrees to pay all or a specified part of each loss that exceeds an agreed amount.

All reinsurance contracts are either pro rata or excess of loss or a combination of the two. There are many variations of these principles, and many different forms of reinsurance, but all of them are based upon the pro rata and excess of loss principles.

Facultative. The word *facultative* indicates a voluntary or optional placing of reinsurance. For example, two insurers may place reinsurance with each other on specific policies if one or the other of them writes a policy for a larger amount than it wishes to retain. With this type of reinsurance, there is no agreement on the part of either company to place a certain amount of all their business with the other company, and there is no agreement on the part of the accepting company to take any or all of the business so offered. The company that writes the original insurance makes the decisions as to whether it will offer the reinsurance, and the accepting company is entirely free to accept or reject the reinsurance.

In some cases an insurer that is offered insurance on a large property will consult with other insurers to determine whether facultative reinsurance can be placed before writing the insurance for the policyholder. Much facultative reinsurance is exchanged on an informal basis between companies that do a regular insurance business. Facultative reinsurance also is accepted by many professional reinsurance companies.

The facultative reinsurance may be on either a pro rata or an excess basis. If pro rata, the portion of the premium passed on to the reinsurer is in proportion to the liability which is passed on, subject to an agreed discount for such expenses of the originating company as broker's commission, agent's commission, and taxes. If on an excess basis, the premium is agreed to between the reinsurer and the reinsured company, either specifically for the one risk, or perhaps under a general agreement covering such cessions of reinsurance.

Treaty Reinsurance. A reinsurance treaty is a contract between two insurers relating to reinsurance. It contains agreements between the insurer and reinsurer for acceptance of reinsurance on a regular basis, as contrasted with a facultative arrangement under which individual contracts applying to specific policies would apply. An important reason for such a treaty is to overcome the main disadvantage of facultative reinsurance, which is that the reinsurer can reject the reinsurance on any policy offered. This uncertainty of facultative reinsurance leads insurers to seek obligatory contract arrangements under which the reinsurer agrees automatically to accept all business offered that complies with conditions as specified in the contract.

Almost any number of variations may be agreed to between insurers in a reinsurance treaty. Reinsurance may be on a pro rata or an excess of loss basis, or a combination of both. The reinsured company may agree to report specific policies to the reinsurer. This may be done by means of individual reports for each policy, or it may be done by combining reports onto a bordereau. *Bordereau* is a term meaning a listing of data regarding a number of policies in abbreviated form on a large sheet of paper. Premiums, return premiums, losses, and other information usually are required by the reinsurer. Many reinsurance treaties provide that the reinsured company (also called the *ceding company*) will report totals of premiums and losses periodically as desired by the reinsurer. The reinsurer generally has the privilege of examining the reinsured company's books to check the accuracy of the reports, but this right is seldom exercised.

An insurer might have several treaties, and may have separate reinsurance contracts for marine and other lines. A common arrangement is for a company to have a so-called "first treaty" intended to include reinsurance on the company's normal operations The reinsurer picks up all business that exceeds the reinsured company's net retention and carries its share of these larger risks up to the amount specified. Such a treaty might provide that the reinsured company would retain for its own account all risks not exceeding an amount for example, of $5,000, and the reinsurer would cover any amount above $5,000 up to a maximum of perhaps $50,000. This would give the reinsured company an automatic capacity of $50,000 on any one risk. This may be in effect a combination of pro rata and excess of loss reinsurance. The reinsurer covers in excess of $5,000 in this example, but it may cover on a pro rata basis when it does not participate. Many variations are possible.

Quota-share Reinsurance. A *quota-share* reinsurance is an arrangement under which the reinsurer participates for a portion of all the business of the reinsured company on the basis of an agreed percentage. Quota-share contracts also may be arranged so that the reinsurer will participate in an agreed percentage in all the business of a certain type written by the reinsured company. The reinsurer participates in the premium in proportion to its liability, after deduction of a discount to cover the expenses of the reinsured company in writing the business. This type of reinsurance may be used to help a new company get started, or it may be used in the operation of a fleet of insurance companies in which a portion of the business written by each company in the fleet automatically is reinsured in other companies of the fleet. Quota-share reinsurance is frequently used for financing the unearned premium reserve.

Pro Rata Reinsurance. Another type of reinsurance contract provides for the reinsurer to share in the reinsured company's business according to size of line or some other agreed condition. A company that wishes to participate in marine insurance but does not have its own marine underwriting facilities may accept an agreed portion of another company's marine business.

Excess of Loss Reinsurance. This type of reinsurance differs from quota-share and pro rata reinsurance in that the reinsured company pays the full amount of any loss up to an agreed amount, and the reinsurer pays all or an agreed portion of the excess of any loss above an amount specified. There is no proportionate sharing of premiums and losses as is the case with quota-share or pro rata reinsurance.

Excess of loss reinsurance is not related to any one particular policy written by the reinsured company but applies either to all business of the reinsured company or to a specified class of business.

Excess of loss reinsurance has the advantage that it is completely automatic in its operation, it involves a minimum of detail, and the reinsured company does not have to set up records or make any reports relating to individual policies. This should offer a large saving in clerical work on the part of both the reinsured company and the reinsurer.

A possible disadvantage to excess of loss reinsurance is that little or no credit is available for the unearned premium reserve. It is akin to catastrophe reinsurance. Under quota-share or pro rata reinsurance, a portion of the liability for a specific policy is ceded to the reinsurer, and credit may be taken for an appropriate portion of the unearned premium reserve.

Catastrophe Reinsurance. Reinsurance against loss from a catastrophe is similar to an excess of loss type of coverage, but the amount of loss retained by the reinsured company is set at a much higher figure that would be reached only in case of a catastrophe as defined in the contract. It is specifically designed to protect the reinsured company against loss from a conflagration, a widespread or severe windstorm, an earthquake, or a similar catastrophe. Catastrophe reinsurance usually is arranged specifically for each line or lines of insurance. It is written in contracts separate from the other types of reinsurance, which are considered to be working contracts.

Catastrophe reinsurance contracts may be written to cover specified perils, or types of insurance. Coverage may also be limited as to time and territory. A company that has extensive liability in boats or yachts in a particular harbor or marina may secure catastrophe reinsurance to protect it from a wind or conflagration loss at that point. A contract might include coverage against loss by fire and windstorm, or there may be separate contracts for these coverages. Any other peril may be included, or the contract may be on a general basis covering the company against any catastrophe that might cause a loss under the policies it is writing. Windstorm catastrophe reinsurance usually specifies that all losses occurring within a certain number of hours in the same area are considered the result of a single windstorm. There may be two or three separate windstorms in different parts of the country, but if they occur within a specified length of time (frequently 72 hours), all of the losses occurring within that time are considered to have resulted form the same catastrophe. Fire catastrophe coverage, on the other hand, relates to individual conflagrations, and the provision relating to occurrences within a specified number of hours does not apply.

Excess of Loss Ratio Reinsurance. Another variation of reinsurance is one under which a company reinsures the amount by which its losses exceed a certain percentage of its premium income. This is figured on the basis of the ratio of losses to premiums. The loss ratio used for such purposes usually is high, and the percentage is set at a figure beyond which the company could not long continue to operate. A loss ratio for this purpose might be 70 or 80 percent. The purpose of the excess of loss ratio reinsurance is to alleviate the results of a disastrous experience for a particular year.

Pool or Syndicate Reinsurance. A special facility for reinsurance is the company pool or syndicate. These are voluntary combinations of insurers which agree to exchange reinsurance with each other for some special purpose, and usually under an automatic arrangement.

Each member of the pool agrees with all the others to cede to them and to accept a certain proportion of the liability on each property insured by pool members, subject to agreed limits of liability. These pools may reinsure the policy as written by the company originating the business, or members of the pool may write separate policies covering their portions of the liability. In some cases there are combination policies on which appear the names of all members of the pool (although this often is referred to as coinsurance rather than reinsurance). There are many syndicates or pools such as the Furriers' Customers Syndicate, the Jewelers' Block Syndicate, the Registered Mail Syndicate, the Oil Insurance Association, the Improved Risk Mutuals, and others. The American Hull Insurance Syndicate, for example, was reported to have covered half of the $16.5 million loss on hull and machinery of the Torrey Canyon, which was previously mentioned.

Other Variations. Many other variations of reinsurance are used to meet particular needs of insurance companies. The principle of each reinsurance contract is to protect the reinsured company from an unusual or unexpected loss that would be greater than it should stand in its normal operations. The reinsurer seeks to protect itself from careless underwriting on the part of the reinsured company, and generally adjusts its charges according to the experience of the reinsured company. All of these various reinsurance plans are modifications or combinations of the reinsurance types which are described above.

SETTING INSURED COMPANY'S RETENTION

In determining the amount of liability that it will retain, an insurance company management has several factors to consider. Statutory limitations must be taken into account. Management must consider the type of insurance written, the size and financial condition of the company, the average and maximum amounts of insurance written, and any other conditions that would affect the probable size of losses to which the company would be exposed.

Statutory Limitations. State insurance laws generally contain a provision limiting the amount to which an insurer may expose itself without reinsurance. A typical provision is that a company shall not expose itself to a loss on any one risk or hazard to an amount exceeding 10 percent of its surplus (amount of admitted assets in excess of liabilities). Thus if a company has a surplus of $1,000,000 assets above liabilities, it is not permitted to carry more than $100,000 insurance on a single risk or hazard unless it reinsures the excess in licensed reinsurance companies. In actual practice insurers seldom expose themselves to the extent of the statutory limit.

The insurance laws recognize the value of reinsurance by the provision that the amount of reinsurance carried in an approved reinsurer shall be deducted from the amount of liability in determining the company's statutory limit.

Much reinsurance is placed in reinsurers that are not licensed by the states. This is particularly true of the reinsurance placed with alien reinsurers such as the members of Lloyd's of London. When an insurer places reinsurance on a large specific risk, the reinsurance may have to be placed in a licensed reinsurer so that the statutory limit of liability will not be exceeded.

Frequency and severity of losses are factors to be considered in setting an insurer's net retention. Usually it is expensive to have a reinsurer participate in a large proportion of the reinsured company's losses. The basic purpose of reinsurance is to reimburse the reinsured company for those unusual losses which may distort normal operations. A company studies the frequency and severity to see at what amount the frequency drops off. If the reinsurance attaches at approximately the amount at which frequency of losses becomes less, then the company will be paying its normal losses directly without any cost for reinsurance, and it will be recovering from the reinsurer the larger losses which are less frequent.

Financial Considerations in Setting Net Lines. Most insurers set their net lines at conservative figures well under the statutory limitations, and low enough so that if several losses are experienced within a short time, the financial position of the companies will not be impaired. Other factors considered are the premium volume and the degree of fluctuation in loss ratios. An insurance company that is doing a large amount of business with a relatively constant loss ratio from year to year usually sets a somewhat higher net line because more premiums would be available quickly to replace funds that might be depleted by a large loss.

An insurer's net line may vary from one type of insurance to another. Marine insurance is the subject of special net lines or other provisions in some reinsurance contracts. This may be the result of catastrophe potentials in the kind of marine business the company is writing or may be because the company is new at underwriting marine business.

REINSURANCE AND THE POLICYHOLDER

The reinsurance contract generally is solely between the reinsured company and the reinsurer. In such a case the policyholder of the reinsured company has no claim against the reinsurer. Any benefits that may occur under a reinsurance contract are for the general benefit of all the creditors of the reinsured company.[1] This is true even though the reinsurance was bought because of the special problems of a particular policyholder's risk. This principle is challenged from time to time, and it is possible that some court will rule in a specific case that the reinsurance will be used for the benefit of a particular insured.

Under special circumstances a reinsurance contract might provide for special benefits to a named policyholder of the reinsured company. This is not a common arrangement, but in such a case the policyholder would become a named beneficiary under the contract, and the contract would appear to inure to his special benefit rather than to the general benefit of all creditors.

Reinsurance is beneficial to the policyholders because it makes

[1]Insurance Company of the State of Pa. v. Park and Pollard Co., 129 N.E. (N.Y. 1920); and Vial v. Norwich Union Fire Insurance Society, 100 N.E. 929 (Ill. 1913).

the reinsured company more stable and less likely to get into financial difficulties. Reinsurance further benefits the policyholders by enabling them to secure large amounts of insurance under a smaller number of policies.

Some of the state insurance laws provide for protection of the policyholder's interest in the reinsurance even though his interest is general and not specific. The fact that the reinsurer is obligated to pay the reinsured company only what the reinsured company pays out means that if an insolvent reinsured company's losses are reduced to whatever it can pay, the reinsurer's obligation would be reduced in the same proportion. Insurance laws of some states provide that credit cannot be taken in connection with the statutory limitation of risk for unearned premium reserve if the reinsurance obligation would be reduced because of insolvency of the reinsured company. Most insurance contracts between United States insurance companies now provide that the reinsurer's liability shall not be reduced because of the insolvency of the reinsured company.

If an insurer ceases to operate, arrangements usually are made to reinsure all of its outstanding business in some other insurer. This is helpful to the policyholders because it permits their insurance to run to expiration and saves them the trouble of replacing their insurance in mid-term. The unearned premium reserve is available to pay the assuming company for this outstanding business.

TYPES OF REINSURERS

Exchange of Reinsurance. Much reinsurance is exchanged between insurers that do a general insurance business with the public. Large insurers add to their profits by doing a reinsurance business with smaller companies. Many companies exchange reinsurance on a reciprocal basis with other companies of similar size. This is advantageous to both companies because it helps to spread the liability of each company.

Professional Reinsurance Companies. There are many insurance companies in the United States whose principal business is the writing of reinsurance. Some of them do a small amount of direct insurance business with the public, but many of them write only reinsurance for other insurers. These companies are subject to regulation by the state insurance departments in much the same way as are companies selling insurance to the public. These reinsurance companies generally use any or all of the reinsurance methods described above, depending upon their facilities and the needs of their clients.

They often reinsure their business with still other reinsurers, thus further spreading the risk.

Pools and Syndicates. The pool or syndicate method of operation described previously in this chapter is mentioned here to give a complete picture of the types of reinsurers. While the members of such groups usually are companies selling insurance to the public, there is nothing to prevent a reinsurance company from belonging to such a group.

Lloyd's of London. One of the most important markets for reinsurance is the London market—principally Lloyd's of London. A large proportion of all the reinsurance on high-value risks is reinsured at least in part with members of Lloyd's of London. This reinsurance market is perhaps the largest of any single group in the world. The operations of Lloyd's members in the United States are largely in the reinsurance and marine fields. The professional reinsurance companies in the United States in turn place much reinsurance under catastrophe contracts and on individual large lines with members of Lloyd's of London.[2]

The members of Lloyd's of London cannot be licensed in most of the states in the United States, and their direct reinsurance facilities therefore cannot relieve the companies of their unearned premium reserve problem. Much of the reinsurance placed with Lloyd's of London is on a catastrophe basis, an excess of loss basis, or through other reinsurance companies that are licensed in the United States.

Other Reinsurance Markets. In addition to Lloyd's of London, other alien insurance companies, such as those in the Swiss or German reinsurance market, participate extensively in American reinsurance. Such participation results in a spreading of reinsurance practically throughout the world. This is desirable because it lessens the impact of any single loss on any one insurance market.

REINSURANCE RATES

Rates for reinsurance are based upon experience and judgment. If two companies reinsure each other on a sharing basis with approximately the same class of business, they expect to receive a propor-

2The reinsuring of reinsurance which has been accepted from another insurer is called retrocession.

tionate share of the premium for the risks that are reinsured. The reinsured company is allowed as a discount a percentage of the premium ceded to pay the agents' commissions and other expenses of writing the business.

Excess of loss, catastrophe, and other types of reinsurance contracts that are not a pro rata sharing of the risk require premiums based upon a percentage of the reinsured company's premiums. Reinsurance underwriters base this upon the proportions which they previously have found to be adequate to cover losses experienced for similar amounts of reinsurance, and upon the hazards of the types of risk covered and the chances of a large loss. A catastrophe reinsurance contract might be less expensive for a company operating in rural areas than it would be for a company operating principally in large cities where conflagrations are more likely.

The rates for many reinsurance contracts tend to become experience rates. Reinsured companies are likely to keep their reinsurance in the same markets for many years. The rates are likely to be adjusted upward or downward, depending upon the amounts which the reinsurers are called upon to pay from year to year. Even though a contract may not have an automatic adjustment clause applying to the rates, the rates usually are adjusted from time to time as the experience changes. Reinsurance tends to become a method of financing large losses over a period of years. The exceptions to this are the catastrophe losses so large that they must be spread over the entire industry because they cannot be charged to the experience of individual companies.

REINSURANCE PRACTICES

The normal arrangement for reinsurance covering specific policies is for the reinsurer to follow the obligations of the reinsured company. If the reinsured company is liable for the loss, the reinsurer cannot question its obligation to reimburse the reinsured company. Reinsurance of specific policies usually runs until the expiration of the policies even though the reinsurance contract expires before the policies expire.

Reinsurance may be passed along in diminishing shares from one reinsurer to another. This is called *retrocession.* This is in the interest of insurance companies and of the public because it further spreads the risk and liability among additional reinsurers. As has been pointed out, many of the professional reinsurers in the United States retrocede a portion of their liability to alien reinsurers.

A requirement under some reinsurance contracts is that the reinsured company keep what is known as a guarantee line. The reinsured company may agree under such a contract not to reinsure its liability below a certain point.

Reinsurance Brokers. A large proportion of the reinsurance business is handled through brokers. The reinsurance broker is especially qualified to examine the needs of an insurer and to match them with the facilities available. This is particularly true in placing reinsurance with Lloyd's of London. Lloyd's members operate individually or in groups, and placements must be made with Lloyd's members through Lloyd's brokers in London. These London brokers know the reinsurance markets; they know the likes and dislikes of the various Lloyd's members and their syndicates and are in a position to guide the reinsurance business toward the most advantageous market. Reinsurance brokers in the United States wishing to use the facilities of Lloyd's deal through brokers in London. The combination results in an advantageous handling of reinsurance contracts for the reinsured company.

Reinsurance brokers are also often used by companies to secure domestic reinsurance. The reinsurance broker has the experience to advise a company concerning the most advantageous placement of business, whether to place it in the domestic market, in the foreign market, or whether to use a combination of the two.

Reinsurer and Reinsured. The general practice with reinsurance is for the liability of the reinsurer to follow that of the reinsured company. Under some reinsurance contracts the reinsurer has the right to intervene in the settlement of a loss if the loss exceeds a specified amount, or if other specified conditions occur. Even in such cases, the reinsurer is likely to let the reinsured company take the lead with the settlement. The liability of the reinsurer is dependent upon the liability of the reinsured company. If the reinsured company were not liable for the loss but made a gratuitous payment for reasons of its own, the reinsurer would not necessarily be obligated to make payment. However, the reinsurer probably would make payment if the loss were paid for good reasons. The reinsurer is also not liable for more than the amount of the policy reinsured.

The utmost good faith must exist between the reinsured company and the reinsurer. Because reinsurance is a cooperative arrangement that helps to stabilize the operations of an insurance company, it works best when relations continue over a period of years between reinsured company and reinsurer. The profits of good years can build up a fund with the reinsurers that will smooth over the reinsurance claims from excessive losses of the bad years.

MARINE REINSURANCE PROBLEMS

Reinsurance on marine lines differs in several respects from the reinsuring of other property coverages, such as fire and windstorm. The problem of capacity for extremely large lines may be serious. This is complicated by the fact that many marine lines have what might be termed a dual loss expectancy. There are the normal losses contemplated in the everyday operations of the insured and in addition there are the possible catastrophe losses. An example is the possible experience with motor truck cargo operation. In the course of a year an insured who is carrying loads worth a maximum of $25,000 may have many losses of a few hundred dollars each and an occasional loss approaching $25,000. These can be averaged over a period of four or five years when the trucker handles a large amount of business, and an adequate rate can be calculated for the loss expectancy. The problem of reinsurance is not serious because the reinsurer can calculate what his chances of loss may be on whatever limits the originating company may desire.

The large truck line frequently includes another and more disturbing factor. The insured may operate a large terminal and may desire insurance to protect him against liability for loss of cargo in a terminal fire or other catastrophe. It may be that the value in the terminal will be in the millions of dollars in an accumulation over a week-end or holiday. The underwriter must arrange for reinsurance to cover a possible total loss in a terminal fire.

Reinsurance of oceangoing vessels must take into account the possibility of collision between two ships that are insured under the same policy or in the same company.

Some inland marine policies insure property that is subject primarily to catastrophe hazards. Examples are registered mail, furriers' customers, and jewelers' block. The loss frequency is low, and the rates are extremely low, considering the tremendous limits required to cover the values involved. Nonnegotiable securities that are shipped by registered mail or express may be insured for 1½ cents per $1,000 of value or for a premium of $15 for a million-dollar limit of liability.

It is necessary that the reinsurance be spread as widely as possible so that the entire experience in the field may be available to the reinsurers. A single company could not afford to write the insurance on registered mail, for example, because a catastrophe would wipe out all the premium it could expect to receive in a hundred years. When the entire experience of all insurance companies is combined through the medium of reinsurance, the rates can reflect the true experience of the business.

QUESTIONS

1. Describe some of the large exposures to loss which insurance companies may face under marine policies.
2. How does reinsurance ease the mechanics of covering large values?
3. What are the four basic functions of reinsurance?
4. What is meant by an insurer's net line? Explain how reinsurance is related to an insurer's capacity.
5. What is meant by a catastrophe loss in reinsurance?
6. Explain how reinsurance can stabilize an insurer's operations.
7. Explain the effect of different types of reinsurance upon the unearned premium reserve.
8. Distinguish between catastrophe reinsurance and excess of loss reinsurance.
9. What is a reinsurance treaty?
10. What factors must be taken into account in determining how much liability an insurer should retain and what reinsurance it needs?
11. Of what benefit is reinsurance to the policyholder?
12. Explain how reinsurance is handled by the method of a pool or syndicate of insurers.
13. Discuss the effect of statutory limitations on the amount to which an insurer may expose itself with reinsurance.
14. Distinguish between the different types of reinsurers operating in the United States.
15. How are the rates for reinsurance established?
16. Discuss the effect upon the reinsurance rate that an insurer must pay if it sustains heavy reinsured losses during a year.
17. Discuss the complications that may result in reinsurance arrangements because of the dual loss expectancy under some marine policies. Outline such possibilities from terminal fires under motor truck cargo policies in addition to the over-the-road exposures, or from collisions of two ships of the same fleet that are covered under one policy.

24

Adjustment of Marine Losses

The adjustment of property insurance losses follows the same basic principles for all kinds of insurance. The adjuster must determine (1) that a loss has occurred, (2) that the policyholder has a financial interest in the property that is the subject of the loss, (3) that the policy covers the property and the peril which caused the loss, (4) how much the loss is, and (5) the application of any limiting clauses that may be in the policy and that may affect the amount payable by the insurance company. Variations of practice and such additional problems as the possible liability of common carrier insureds may be involved with some losses. This chapter will consider the problems that affect marine losses in general with particular attention to the handling of inland marine claims. Attention will also be given to the differences from general loss adjustment work as practiced in ocean marine losses.

INLAND MARINE LOSS ADJUSTMENTS

The adjusting of inland marine losses is more complicated in several ways than the adjustment of other property loss claims. The adjuster of a fire or extended coverage claim can tell at a glance that a loss has occurred, because a fire, windstorm, or explosion leaves plenty of evidence that there is damage. The insured who has had a fire loss usually is known where the property is located, and his reputation can be checked with neighbors or business associates. Ownership, title, interest, and values of property at a fixed location can be determined from known sources. The work of proving the interest of the insured and the value of the property damaged by fire may be a considerable task, but the procedure follows a well-established routine.

In contrast, when an inland marine claim is presented, it may not be evident immediately that a loss has occurred. The insured may report that valuable jewelry has been lost or stolen, and the first task of the adjuster is to make certain (1) that the insured actually had the property that is claimed to be lost, and (2) that it is gone and not merely mislaid.

Inland marine insurance basically is the insuring of property in the course of transportation, and a loss may occur a long distance from where the insured's reputation, ownership, and interest can be checked. Inland marine insurance frequently ceases to cover when the property no longer is in a state of transportation, and the inland marine adjuster must determine whether the property is covered by the policy at the time of the loss. This chapter is not intended as a general treatise on the adjustment of property losses, but points out the many ways in which the handling of marine claims differs from the adjusting of other types of property damage losses.

DETERMINING WHETHER A LOSS HAS OCCURRED

The investigation first must determine that the property did exist and that its loss or damage took place. If there is no tangible evidence that there was such property, the adjuster should inquire from the insured and from other persons regarding the exact nature of the property, when it was last seen, and the likely causes of disappearance. Vague answers may indicate that an investigation should be made of the circumstances of the loss.

An example will illustrate the necessity for careful inquiry. An insurance company received a report of the disappearance of a fur coat that was insured under a personal fur policy. The insured could not give much information except that the coat has disappeared, apparently from the home. The company decided to pay the claim, inasmuch as the reputation of the insured was unquestioned and there was no evidence of dishonesty.

About a year and a half later, the insured called up and told the insurance company that the coat had been located. A furrier had telephoned and asked when the insured intended to call for her coat, which had been in storage a year and a half. It developed that the insured had told her maid to send the coat to storage and had forgotten about it. The adjuster had taken the word of the insured that the maid was thoroughly reliable (as in fact she was) and had not made any inquiry of the maid herself. Had he questioned the maid, undoubtedly he would have located the coat and determined that no loss had occurred.

The adjuster next must determine whether the loss has occurred under circumstances covered by the policy. In the case of clothing and personal effects, the coverage usually applies to all situations, but in the case of property insured under transit policies, the coverage ceases at some point. The policy must be examined to see when the coverage ceases, and then the actual circumstances of the shipment must be determined. Transportation policies frequently cease to cover upon delivery to the consignee. It may be necessary to examine the records of the transportation company to see whether delivery had been made before the loss occurred.

An example of a careful investigation is one that was made of a loss under a legal liability policy on household furniture being transported by a furniture warehouseman. The policy covered the legal liability of the warehouseman while the goods were being hauled in his trucks and also during the presence of the property in his warehouse incidental to transportation for a period of not more than 30 days.

The warehouse burned down and there were dozens of claims under the policy. The adjuster examined each claim to determine (1) whether the property had been in the warehouse more than 30 days, and (2) whether the goods were in the warehouse temporarily pending their being moved on to another location or had been placed there in storage.

One load of goods that had been in the warehouse less than 30 days was to be shipped to another city and was being held for the convenience of the warehouseman while he located another load to go in the same direction. There was no doubt that this load was in the course of transportation and its presence in the warehouse was incidental to transportation.

Another load had been placed in the warehouse on the instructions of the owner, who had said that he expected to be traveling for several months before he located a place to live and would send word to the warehouseman when he wanted the goods. It was decided that this load of goods was in storage and that its presence in the warehouse was not incidental to transportation.

The warehouse to warehouse clause of an ocean marine insurance policy may cease to cover after 60 days from the time of discharge overside of the goods from the overseas vessel at the final point of discharge. The adjuster of a loss to such goods would have to determine when the goods were unloaded from the vessel to see if they were still covered by the ocean marine policy.

The loss must be the result of a peril insured against by the policy. An example of a question concerning the perils insured against arose under a transit policy covering several record playing machines, or "juke boxes." The policy insured against loss from fire, lightning, windstorm, theft, and collision or overturn of transporting conveyance. An automobile in which one of the machines was being transported was caught in a low spot during a heavy rain, and the water rose over the machine. There was no damage from wind, the vehicle did not overturn or collide with anything, and the only damage was from the water. It was concluded that the policy did not cover the loss because it did not mention flood or water damage as a peril insured against.

Ownership or interest has to be checked, and usually the adjuster can locate documents that will prove interest and title. Difficulty may be encountered in connection with shipments when the loss occurs at about the time title passes from the shipper to the consignee. In one case, some merchandise was to be shipped F.O.B. the shipper's factory, and the goods had been placed on the factory shipping platform for pickup by the carrier. Apparently the goods were stolen during or about the time the pickup was to be made. The shipper claimed that the title had passed to the consignee when the goods were placed on the platform. The consignee and his insurer argued that the title never had passed, since the carrier was able to prove that the goods had not been turned over to him. The shipper finally agreed and there was no court determination of the question, but the settlement seems reasonable.

A loss under a legal liability policy, such as a motor truck cargo policy, is investigated to make certain that the insured is liable for the loss. There may be interline agreements between truck lines that would affect the liability of the insured. Occasionally there is a loss for which the insured is not liable (such as a loss caused by an "act of God"). When the policy insures against loss due to the liability of the insured as a bailee (not a bailees' customers policy), the adjuster examines the possible liability of the insured carefully, because a bailee ordinarily is liable only if it can be proved that he was negligent in connection with the loss.

The liability of a carrier by sea may be completely different from the liability of a common carrier on land. The Harter Act, which was passed by Congress in 1893, exempted a carrier by sea from responsibility for damage or loss due to errors in navigation. Thus a cargo owner could not proceed against the carrier for losses resulting from a negligent collision. However, the cargo owner could proceed against the operator of the other vessel in a collision if both vessels were at fault. This is cited as an example of the important differences between the handling of cargo losses from land transportation and from sea transportation.

Occasionally an adjuster suspects that a claim is fictitious or that a part of the story is being held back in order to support the claim. The adjuster usually considers it unwise to reveal his suspicions to the insured, but it may be advisable to withhold settlement temporarily while a thorough investigation is made. All the witnesses are queried, and it may be desirable to question the insured and witnesses under oath. People who are willing to lie for the sake of collecting from an insurance company, or to help a friend or employer collect may be afraid to lie under oath.

SUBROGATION

Perhaps the greatest difference between marine loss adjustments and those in connection with other property insurance policies is that a large proportion of marine claims offer chances of recovery through subrogation. Property in transit frequently is in the custody of a carrier or a bailee who has some degree of responsibility for the safe delivery of the property.

The adjuster must know the liability of common carriers for the safe delivery of property and how to protect the interests of the insured and the insurance company. Delaying tactics on the part of a common carrier in handling a claim may be carried out in the hope that the claimant will fail to file a claim or suit until after the time limit has passed.

One of the first tasks of an adjuster is to make certain that a written notice of claim has been filed against a common carrier that may have been responsible for a loss. The claim must be followed up and suit filed within the time limit if the company and insured decide to pursue the claim in court. Negotiations for settlement by the carrier cannot be depended upon as a waiver of the time limits for filing claim or suit.

The liability of a bailee is not so extensive as that of a common carrier, but the adjuster must pursue any possible liability to its limit when there is a possibility that a bailee has been negligent in handling the insured's property.

If the insured has collected his loss from a bailee or other third party, he may not collect it again from the insurance company. Many policies have a clause which provides specifically that the insured cannot collect under the policy if he has collected from others.

The application of the subrogation right in an ocean marine case may be different under American law than under English law. It is generally held under American law that the insurance company and the insured will share in any subrogation recovery in the proportion of their respective losses. The insurance company would get the complete recovery only if the insured had been fully reimbursed for his loss. Under English law the insurance company would receive the entire recovery up to the amount that it had paid to the insured.

It is an interesting point also that when two vessels of the same ownership collide there can be no subrogation recovery. An owner could not subrogate against himself. The underwriters can acquire only such rights as the insured may have. No additional right can accrue to the underwriters under subrogation. This, of course, is not peculiar to ocean marine insurance but is the case with all subrogation.

"No Benefit to Bailee" Clause. Common carriers for many years have attempted to secure the benefit of any insurance that the shipper or consignee may have. A provision of the uniform straight bill of lading that is intended to accomplish this reads as follows:

> Any carrier or party liable on account of loss of or damage to any of said property shall have the full benefit of any insurance that may have been effected upon or on account of said property, so far as this shall not avoid the policies or contracts of insurance.

Insurance companies have countered this effort of carriers by inserting in their transit policies a "no benefit to bailee" clause, which reads:

> This insurance shall in no wise inure directly or indirectly to the benefit of any carrier or other bailee.

This clause refers to bailees as well as carriers because a carrier may become a bailee under some circumstances, such as when goods remain on the premises of the carrier beyond the time for which the carrier is responsible for them. The provision of the bill of lading referring to insurance seldom is found in other bailee contracts.

The provisions of the bill of lading and of the "no benefit to bailee" clause are in direct conflict. The bill of lading provision means that if the insured collects the amount of his loss from an insurance company, the carrier does not have to pay the claim. The insurance policy, on the contrary, provides that if the carrier is relieved from his obligation by the existence of the insurance, the insurance company pays nothing. The adjuster secures copies of all such contracts before suggesting payment under the insurance policies. Payment of the loss in the face of such a bill of lading provision might stop any recovery from the carrier by the insurance company under its rights of subrogation.

The United States Carriage of Goods by Sea Act provides that "A benefit of insurance in favor of the carrier, or similar clause, shall be deemed to be a clause relieving the carrier from liability," and as such it is declared to be null and void and of no effect. However, there may be circumstances under which the carrier would have custody of goods but for which the Carriage of Goods by Sea Act would not apply. Then the carrier's benefit of insurance clause might be effective. It is considered good practice to put a "no benefit to bailee" clause in ocean marine insurance policies.

The "no benefit to bailee" clause generally has been held effective in preserving the right of the insurance company to pay a loss to the insured and then collect from the carrier. However, this is not universally true. When there is doubt, it is considered good practice for the insurance company to lend the insured the amount of loss rather than to pay it outright.

Use of a Loan Receipt. A loan receipt generally is used when there is such a conflict between the insurance policy conditions and the carrier or bailee contract. In this situation, the proper procedure is for the insurance company to lend the amount of the loss to the insured, under the condition that the loan will be repaid only if the loss is recovered from the carrier or bailee.

Suit then is entered against the carrier or bailee in the name of the insured. If he recovers the loss from the carrier or bailee, he repays the loan to the insurance company. If he does not recover, he is under no obligation to repay the insurance company. This seems like an involved way of handling the conflict, but it has been held by the courts that such a loan is not payment of the insurance such as to give the carrier the benefit of the insurance.[1]

It is important that the adjuster secure a written loan receipt. It might be possible to prove that the payment was intended only as a loan even in the absence of a formal receipt, but it is much safer to

[1] Luckenbach v. McCahan Sugar Ref. Co., 248 U.S. 139, 63 L. ed. 170 (1918).

have all the conditions in writing so that the bailee or carrier cannot contend that the insurance payment was a payment of the loss rather than a loan.

Collection of Baggage Losses. The adjuster may have occasion to adjust losses under personal property policies when the losses have occurred to baggage in the hands of common carriers. The liability of a common carrier for the safe transportation of baggage is almost absolute and is comparable to other common carrier liability. When baggage has been delivered to a carrier, the owner has no further responsibility for it until it is delivered back to him. The contractual relationship between the owner and the carrier may limit the recovery, but ordinarily a common carrier cannot entirely relieve itself of liability.

In order to present a valid claim against a common carrier for loss of baggage, it is necessary for the adjuster to determine that the property falls within the definition of baggage that appears in the tariffs filed by the carrier. This definition usually includes clothing and other belongings a traveler would be likely to carry. The samples carried by a salesman are not considered baggage unless the tariff so states.

There may be statements on baggage receipts that purport to limit the liability of the carrier. These are not always valid as contracts between the passenger and the carrier. These statements may prove to be in the nature of a notice to the passenger and not a contract. Occasionally such notice is proved to be invalid by circumstances connected with the shipment.

The tariffs filed by common carriers usually specify limits of liability for baggage shipments. The passenger is assumed to have had notice of these limitations even though he has not seen them, because the filings are public information and are available to anyone.

Subrogation Against Landlords or Other Negligent Parties. During the past few years there have been an increasing number of cases in which courts have held a person or corporation liable for property damage resulting from fire or bad plumbing, or some other act of neglect. The spread of fire from a building where flammable materials were stored in violation of a state statute was held to be the result of negligence.[2] A landlord has been held responsible for loss due to the freezing of plumbing when he did not

[2]Newburgh Transfer and Storage Co. v. Pure Oil Co., 259 App. Div. 910, 20 N.Y.S. (2d) 141 (1940).

supply sufficient heat over a week-end to prevent freezing.[3] It is important that the insurance company be notified at once if there are possibilities of subrogation, so that the proper investigations can be made and counsel can be retained if advisable.

Impairment of Subrogation Right. Inland marine policies may contain a clause that is intended to invalidate the policy if the insured has entered into any agreement with a carrier or bailee that would remove or limit the insured's right of recovery against the carrier or bailee. Examples of agreements that come within the intent of such a clause are the settling of a loss without the consent of the insurance company and the acceptance of a contract or bill of lading that limits the amount of recovery. The uniform express receipt limits recovery to $50 per shipment or 50 cents per pound for shipments of more than 100 pounds. The acceptance of this receipt impairs the insured's right of recovery and consequently impairs the insurance company's right of recovery under subrogation. Under a strict interpretation of such a clause, the acceptance of the uniform express receipt would avoid the policy.

A more recently developed clause for inland marine policies is one that gives permission for the insured to accept the ordinary bills of lading or carriers' receipts but is intended to invalidate the coverage if the insured enters into any special agreement that would impair the right of recovery against a third party.

RECOVERY AND SALVAGE

Inland marine claims differ from fire and other property loss claims in that the property frequently is not destroyed but is lost or stolen. There may be a substantial chance of recovery. Adjusters find it advantageous to maintain contacts with police departments and particularly with the pawnshop details of city police forces. Many jewelry losses are reduced by recovery from pawnshops. The obvious place for a small-time thief to dispose of his loot is through a pawnshop, although a well-organized gang is likely to have arrangements whereby jewelry can be changed in appearance before it is passed into the trade or into a pawnshop through a "fence."

Detailed descriptions of all articles are secured, and the police are advised of the loss at once. Many times recovery efforts have been thwarted because the insured could not identify the articles.

[3]Par-X Uniform Serv. Corp. v. Emigrant Industrial Savings Bank, 268 App. Div. 699, 53 N.Y.S. (2d) 16 (1945).

Salvage operations are important in any loss involving damaged property. Many jewels, and particularly diamonds, are resistant to fire and are likely to be merely charred on the outside. If a substantial amount of jewelry is involved in a fire loss, it often is worthwhile to sift the ashes to recover the jewels. Frequently jewels can be recut and a considerable reduction made in the loss.

Immediate action is necessary following a motor truck collision or overturn if the cargo is partially damaged. A guard should be posted and the merchandise removed to a safe location. Passers-by and neighbors often feel that the contents of a wrecked truck are their legitimate prey unless there is a representative of the owner at hand. In his first contact with the insured, the adjuster takes care to point out the insured's obligation under the "sue and labor" clause to assist in salvage operations. Many policyholders do not understand this requirement and they may try to offer abandonment to the insurance company.

The salvage of foodstuffs may involve conferences with health authorities. It is understandable that a health officer may condemn a load of canned goods or oranges if he sees it as a complete mess with half the load smashed to bits. It is essential to get the undamaged portions of the load out of the wreck where they can be examined, without the authorities' having to paw through a mess of obviously unfit merchandise. Rapid handling and the immediate use of local refrigeration services help to convince authorities that the adjuster and owner are working to protect the health of the community and that no attempt is being made to salvage food that is unfit for human consumption.

Losses in fur storage warehouses, laundries, and other places where clothing is damaged call for immediate salvage operations to get the clothing cleaned and dried as rapidly as possible. After stains and mildew have accumulated, as they will within a few hours, it may be impossible to clean the clothing sufficiently to have it accepted by the owners.

The principles of recovery and salvage of damaged property which have just been described apply equally to property which is covered under ocean marine insurance. Damage to cargo on shipboard is likely to involve large quantities of merchandise. A common method of disposing of such property is by auction. The insured or the consignee may be willing to accept the damaged property and to recondition it. This is advantageous to everybody if the firm has facilities for immediate processing.

Ocean marine insurance also involves what is known as "marine salvage." This is the saving of ships and cargoes from the perils of the seas. Marine salvage is a highly specialized business. It is important to the ocean marine underwriter because it substantially reduces ocean marine insurance losses. It is mentioned here in order to distinguish this type of operation from the reconditioning of merchandise, which is also known as salvage.

DETERMINATION OF LOSS AND SOUND VALUE

An inland marine policy may or may not include specific provisions setting out the method for ascertaining the value and loss. The scheduled property floater policy, which frequently is used as a basic inland marine policy, contains an actual cash value clause. In the absence of any modifying clause in the form attached to the policy, the adjuster follows usual practices, such as are common in fire loss adjustments, in order to determine the value and the loss.

Policies on fine arts, antiques, and perhaps other personal property scheduled on a policy may have an agreed value that is to be paid in case of loss. Ordinarily these amounts are paid without question unless the adjuster has reason to believe that there is evidence of fraud. Fraud is a rare occurrence, but its possibility cannot be ignored.

Inland marine policies covering commercial property, and particularly property in transit, are likely to contain a clause setting forth the method of determining the value. This may be the invoice value at the time and place of shipment, the invoice value at the time and place of delivery, or the invoice value plus certain freight or carriage charges. Since there is no uniformity, the adjuster examines the pertinent clause and applies it according to the circumstances of the loss.

The determination of value and loss under an ocean marine policy is likely to follow different procedures from those used with an inland marine loss. Ocean marine policies in many cases state a valuation in the policy. The underwriter and the insured are bound by this statement of value, unless there is a gross overstatement of value which was made with fraudulent intent. Partial losses (particular average) often are adjusted on the basis of the percentage of damage to the property. A method which is frequently used is to determine the value of the property before loss and the value of the property in its damaged condition. These are based upon the actual market value of the property. Then the percentage is applied to the amount of insurance on the property. The insured receives payment for the full amount of his damage if he has enough insurance to cover the full value before the damage occurred. The insured will have to stand his proportion of the loss if he does not have enough insurance to cover the full value. He can secure more than his actual loss if he has more insurance than the actual value of the property. This is different from the results in inland marine insurance. It is customary for inland marine practices to follow those of fire insurance, under which the recovery is limited to the actual cash value of the property. The only situation where an inland marine policyholder might recover more than his actual loss would be where a valued policy has been issued for more than the actual value of the property.

COINSURANCE

There is seldom a coinsurance clause on policies covering household goods and personal effects, but such clauses are used frequently on policies covering commercial property. Many motor truck cargo policies contain clauses which provide that the company shall not be liable for a greater proportion of any loss than the amount of insurance bears to the value of the goods on the truck at the time of the loss. This is equivalent to a 100 percent coinsurance clause.

There may be a difference over whether the coinsurance applies to the value of the cargo or to the insured's liability. A contract carrier may limit his liability by contract and the coinsurance may apply to that amount rather than to the total value. There is no uniformity in the practices of the inland marine insurance companies; the adjuster handles losses under each clause as he finds it.

Ocean marine policies seldom use the word "coinsurance," but adjustment practices have the effect of a 100 percent coinsurance clause. The insured is considered to be a coinsurer to the extent of any underinsurance in relation to the value of the property.

OTHER INSURANCE

The problem of other insurance is one of the most troublesome of all adjustment problems in connection with inland marine losses. This arises because the property that is the subject of insurance is likely to be in the custody of someone other than the owner. The owner may have his insurance to protect himself from loss, and a bailee or carrier may have insurance to protect him from loss due to his legal liability. Occasionally there is more than one bailee involved in a loss because the original bailee may have found it necessary to send the goods to another bailee for some special process. Frequently an owner, a bailee, and a carrier are involved in a loss, each with his own insurance.

Inland marine underwriters often insert clauses in policies that are intended to avoid the coverage if there is any other insurance covering the insured's interest. This follows the principle that an insurance company has the right to know about all insurance covering the interest of the insured, because overinsurance may tempt the insured to bring about a loss.

It has been held that there is no other insurance within the meaning of such a clause if the policies cover different interests.[4] The owner of property had insurance to protect himself against loss of the merchandise, and a bailee had insurance to protect himself against loss due to his legal liability for damage while the property was in his custody. The insurance on the property for the protection of the owner had been set up as a defense by the insurer of the bailee. The court held that the policies covered different interests and there was no other insurance within the meaning of the policies.

Another type of "other insurance" clause is intended to make a policy excess over all other policies that may cover interests in the property. The situation arises when there are several policies covering interests in the same property and all the policies have clauses stating that each policy is excess insurance over all other policies involving the property.

Some policy has to be considered primary insurance; otherwise it would be useless to carry insurance on property that may be in the custody of others. A general rule has come to be applied that specific insurance is primary and pays ahead of any blanket or floating insurance.[5] For example, a person might have a policy that specifically described and insures a diamond ring. The ring might be in the custody of a jeweler who has an insurance policy to protect the property of his customers while such property is in his possession. If a loss occurs under circumstances that absolve the jeweler as a bailee from responsibility for the loss, the question would arise which insurance policy covers the loss. The company whose policy describes the ring specifically would pay, since it covers the value of that particular piece of property, whereas the jeweler's policy provides blanket coverage on any property that might be in his possession.

Occasionally there are several policies all of which are floating or blanket and none of which describe the property specifically. In a New York case the Appellate Division, First Department, placed the payment of the loss on the policy it considered to be "more specific" than the other policies; that is, the policy that came the closest to

[4]Oakley v. Firemen's Insurance Co., 70 N.Y.S. (2d) 458 (1947).

[5]Fairchild v. Liverpool and London Fire and Life Ins. Co., 51 N.Y. 65 (1872).

describing the property and the circumstances of the loss. This decision, however, was reversed by the Court of Appeals of New York, which laid down the rule that when all of several policies are intended to be excess policies and there is no primary policy, they all should be compelled to contribute. The Court of Appeals further commented that such a rule would lead to prompt payment of a loss and elimination of litigation.[6]

The payment of a loss under a specific policy issued to an insured is a separate matter from the possible collection of the loss from a bailee if he is responsible for the loss. Even though a bailee's insurance is less specific, it still may be necessary for the bailee to pay the loss if it can be proved that the bailee was negligent and the bailee's policy insures him against loss due to his legal liability. This, however, is subsequent to the original determination of which policy is primary coverage and which is other insurance.

Double Insurance. The existence of more than one insurance policy covering the same interest on the same property is called "double insurance" in the ocean marine field. Under American practice, if there are several policies which bear different effective dates, the policy with the earliest date is considered primary insurance and that company is liable for the entire loss, up to the amount of the policy. All policies share on a pro rata basis if they have the same effective dates.

Under English practice the insured may collect in full from any of the companies regardless of the effective dates of the policies. However, the company which pays the loss can then turn to the other companies for their pro rata share of the loss. The effect is that the companies contribute to the loss on a pro rata basis regardless of the effective dates of their policies.

Double insurance is unusual in ocean marine insurance. The practice is for one party to arrange for all insurance in connection with a transaction involving cargo. It is only where there is some confusion about the placing of insurance that double insurance is likely to occur. The existence of double insurance is also unlikely on ships. Underwriters usually want to know about all of the insurance that there is on a particular ship in order to avoid any overinsurance and possible moral hazard.

OCEAN AND INLAND MARINE LOSS ADJUSTMENTS

This discussion of marine loss adjustments has been directed primarily to the handling of inland marine losses but with attention to

[6]Davis Yarn Co. v. Brooklyn Yarn Dye Co., 293 N.Y. 236, 56 N.E. (2d) 564 (1944).

the more important differences with ocean marine losses. Ocean marine loss adjustment is more specialized than most other kinds of insurance adjusting. It is necessary for the ocean marine adjuster to know maritime law and practices. He must know when it is to the advantage of the insurer to accept abandonment; he must know the terms of the oceanmarine insurance policy and the meaning of the terms. The four kinds of losses on a broad basis are total loss or constructive total loss, total loss of part of a shipment, particular average (partial loss), and general average. Each of these may affect in one way or another losses to hull, cargo, or freight. Liability and workmen's compensation claims may also be involved under ocean marine policies.

General average claims especially require the services of specialists. Each interest which is involved in a general average claim must be evaluated. There may be hundreds or even thousands of interests when the ship is one carrying many shipments of general merchandise. Each of those interests is obligated to pay its proportion of the general average sacrifice. It often takes months or even years to work out all of the detail for such a case. One of the first tasks is to make certain that each interest will pay its share when it is determined. A shipment of cargo will not be released to the consignee until this payment is assured. Ocean marine insurance policies almost always cover general average charges. This insurance is accepted by the general average adjuster as satisfactory evidence that the charges will be paid when the allocation is determined. There may be cases where the shipment is not insured, or for some other reason does not have insurance that will pay the general average charges. It is necessary for the owner or the consignee in such cases to put up the money or a bond to guarantee that the charges will be paid.

There are many documents that must be completed when there is a loss at sea. The master of the vessel must certify to the circumstances of the accident. The operator of the vessel wants to make as good a case for himself as he can in order to avoid liability for damage to cargo. All of the persons who have knowledge of the circumstances may be called upon for statements. The insurance policies, bills of lading, invoice, or other evidence of value must be produced for each shipment in order to prove the loss and valuation.

The adjuster for cargo losses must determine whether there is any claim against the ship, or perhaps against another ship if the loss is the result of collision. The situation is similar to the handling of claims on land that claims must be presented to the carrier within a specified time.

The adjustment of ocean marine losses is affected by the maritime practices of the country where the ship is registered, the location of the accident, the country where the claims are pursued, and by many other features of alien and American law and practice. It is for this reason that no detailed attempt is made here to describe all of the ramifications of ocean marine loss handling. There are volumes of material which are available to the student who wants to inquire further into these questions.

"AGREEMENTS OF GUIDING PRINCIPLES"

The problem of adjusting insurance losses involving conflicting "other insurance" clauses came to public attention in connection with laundry fires. Fire insurance policies covering household furniture had been extended so that 10 percent of the coverage could be applied to property off the premises named in the policy. Insurance companies that had issued bailees' customers policies to laundries and were presented with claims for fire losses contended that the fire insurance policies of the owner were more specific coverage than the bailees' customers policies. They advised their laundry insureds to tell their customers to put in claims with their fire insurance companies under the 10 percent extension of the household fire policy.

There also had been several cases involving mercantile or commercial policyholders in which conflicting clauses had had to be interpreted by the courts because there was no satisfactory way that the insurance companies could agree about which company was liable for the loss. Sometimes policyholders were left to wait for their payments while the insurance companies wrangled over the liability.

Executives of leading insurance companies decided that many of the disputes could be settled in advance if the companies were to agree on certain principles to be followed when there was overlapping coverage between two or more insurance policies. After many conferences between all sections of the insurance industry, there were developed several intercompany agreements known as the "agreements of guiding principles."

There are three such intercompany agreements that may affect the settlement of inland marine claims. There is an Inland-Inland agreement, which applies when there are two or more inland marine policies covering property affected by the loss. A Fire-Inland Marine agreement is applicable when there are fire and inland marine policies applying to the claim. The third agreement relates to overlapping coverage between casualty and inland marine policies and is known as the National Bureau and IMUA agreement. This refers to the National Bureau of Casualty Underwriters (now the Insurance Rating

Board) and the Inland Marine Underwriters Association. These agreement have been signed by most of the leading insurance companies, both stock and mutual.

These agreements are effective only when they have been signed by both of the companies involved in a claim. If one or both companies involved have not signed the agreement that would apply to a loss, the agreement has no effect and the liabilities of the companies must be settled in the same way that all such claims were settled before the agreements were drawn up. The claim would have to be settled by negotiation and, failing that, by resort to the courts.

It is important that insurance company departments that handle loss matters, and the adjusters, maintain complete and up-to-date lists of these signatory companies so that they can determine immediately whether an "other insurance" problem is to be handled in accordance with the applicable "agreement of guiding principles" or whether they must resort to general practices outside the agreements.

The Inland-Inland agreement is based on the principle, first, that a carrier or bailee is responsible for property in his custody; and second, that specific insurance shall be considered primary insurance before any floater coverage. Therefore, any insurance issued to a carrier or bailee covers to its limit of liability before a policy issued to the bailor is expected to contribute to the loss payment. A policy specifically describing the property covers to its limit before a policy that provides floater coverage—or that covers in general terms—is expected to contribute, except when the floater policy is issued to a carrier or bailee.

The Fire-Inland Marine agreement follows the same principles as the Inland-Inland agreement concerning specific insurance and bailees' insurance, and adds a third idea—that a policy specifying location is primary insurance ahead of insurance that is of a floating nature.

The Fire-Inland Marine agreement largely resolved the trouble that had been experienced in connection with Laundry fire losses. Under the agreement a bailees' customers policy is considered the primary insurance and covers first, up to its limit, before the 10 percent extension of the bailor's household fire insurance policy is called upon to contribute. If the bailees' customers policy is exhausted before the loss is paid in full, the household fire policies of the bailors would be called upon to contribute up to the limit of their off-premises coverage.

It may happen that some customers of a laundry have household fire insurance policies or their equivalent and others do not. In such cases the bailees' customers policy is made to apply first to the property of those bailors who have no insurance of their own. Next, the bailees' customers policy applies to the property of the bailors who have insurance of their own. Finally, the fire coverage of the bailors comes in to pay the remainder of their losses if the bailees' customers policy has been exhausted before all claims have been paid.

The National Bureau and IMUA (casualty-inland marine) agreement consists of two principles only. The first principle applies to problems involving the casualty policy known as a "residence and outside theft" policy and the inland marine forms known as the personal effects floater and tourist baggage forms. The methods of determining which is primary insurance follow those already described for the other two agreements.

The second principle sets out the method of apportioning a loss between the two policies when both cover the property. Briefly, this provides that the limits of liability of the policies shall be added together and the loss apportioned according to the amount of liability under each policy.

All the agreements provide that they shall not affect the right of action accruing under subrogation against a bailee except as such action might be in conflict with the purpose of the agreement. Neither do the agreements rewrite policies or make liability where none exists, nor do they increase the extent of the liability to the policyholder under the policies as written. The purpose of the agreements is to disregard the "other insurance" clauses in the policies and to apply the policies on an equitable and reciprocal basis, depending on the nature of the liability assumed by each underwriter.

REPORTING AND PROOF OF LOSS

Inland marine insurance policies contain certain requirements the insured must meet in case there is a loss under the policy. The provision of the scheduled property floater policy (which is the basic policy used for many inland marine coverages) is typical and reads:

> The insured shall as soon as practicable report in writing to the company or its agent every loss, damage or occurrence which may give rise to a claim under this policy and shall also file with the company or its agent within 90 days from date of discovery of such loss, damage or occurrence, a detailed sworn proof of loss.

The words "as soon as practicable" are used in place of the word "immediate," which formerly was used generally. In practice the clause means that notice must be given within a reasonable time. Delays of as long as 60 days have been held as not unreasonable when the court felt that there was adequate reason why the insured could not have reported the loss any sooner.[7] An insurance policy may require written notice of loss. An oral notice is not sufficient when a written notice is specified.

The clause requires that the insured give notice of every loss, damage, or occurrence which "may give rise to a claim." The insured may not wait until he is certain that a claim will be presented. He must report as soon as practicable after he becomes aware that there has been an occurrence which might give rise to a claim.[8]

The requirement for immediate notice of loss is reasonable because the insurance company deserves the opportunity to investigate the loss and also should have an opportunity to attempt salvage and to prevent further loss, if that is possible. Unnecessary delay on the part of the insured in reporting the loss may hamper the company sufficiently to increase the loss.

The insured also is required to file with the insurance company a sworn statement in proof of his loss. It is not the responsibility of the company to establish the amount of loss or damage. This is a responsibility of the insured. Most insurance companies supply forms that the insured may fill out with the pertinent information, but the policy terms do not require the use of any particular form.

The time limit for the filing of proofs of loss varies in different policies; time limits frequently used in inland marine policies are 30, 60, and 90 days. There is a long list of conflicting court decisions on the validity of the time limit for the filing of proofs of loss. In order to be safe, the insured should be certain to file the proofs of loss within the time limit provided in the policy, even if there is reason to believe that the company will not enforce the provision.

The policy also contains a provision regarding payment of loss by the insurance company. In the scheduled property floater policy it is provided that

> All adjusted claims shall be paid or made good to the insured within sixty (60) days after presentation and acceptance of satisfactory proof of interest and loss at the office of this company. No loss shall be paid or made good if the insured has collected the same from others.

Although the term may vary, a 30-day payment provision is found in many inland marine policies. This time interval is given to

[7] Will & Baumer Co. v. Rochester German Ins. Co., 140 App. Div. 691, 125 N.Y.S. 606 (1910).

[8] Travelers' Ins. Co. v. Myers, 62 Oh. St. 529, 57 N.E. 458 (1900).

the company in order that it may investigate and check the claim. Since the contract does not require payment before the time specified, a suit against the company would not be effective until after the time interval had expired without payment by the company.

The registered mail policy provides for payment within seven days after receipt of proofs of loss and interest. This short period is a recognition that any delay in paying for lost securities may cause a substantial additional loss in income from the securities.

Most policies require that any suit under the policy must be commenced within 12 months after the occurrence of a loss. However, this provision is modified in those states that permit a longer interval. In a few states the interval permitted by law within which suit may be filed is as long as five years.

DOCUMENTS OTHER THAN NOTICE AND PROOF OF LOSS

In the adjustment of most inland marine claims, the adjuster works closely with the insured and helps in the preparation of the proof of loss. There are several documents that may be necessary for the proper presentation of the claim and that may not be considered strictly a part of the formal proof of loss. This is true especially when the policy covers the legal liability of the insured for loss or damage to the property of others. It is necessary to present proof of the liability of the insured as well as proof of the amount of the loss. In the case of a policy covering property belonging to the insured but in the custody of others, the adjuster must secure proof of what happened to the property and must include all the documents so that the company can proceed against the carrier or bailee who was responsible for the loss.

The motor truck cargo claim is a good example of the type of claim in which the policy covers the legal liability of the insured. The adjuster must secure (1) copies of the receipt or bill of lading issued by the trucker, including the description of the property; (2) an affidavit by the consignee that he did not receive the goods (unless the loss is such that the insured knows that there was loss or damage, as in the case of a collision or fire); (3) copies of invoices or other documents to prove the value; and (4) a copy of the owner's claim on the trucker.

When the loss involves property in the custody of a carrier or bailee, the adjuster secures copies of the bills of lading or receipts, the letter making claim on the carrier or bailee, affidavits or other evidence that the goods shipped were those described in the invoices, and statements from all parties who may have knowledge of the circumstances of the loss.

WAIVER AND ESTOPPEL

Either party to a contract may waive provisions that are in his favor. The inland marine insurance policy contains a clause relating specifically to waiver of policy provisions. This usually provides that no officer, agent, or other representative of the company may waive any provision of the policy unless the waiver is in writing and is attached to the policy. When the company intends to waive some provision and the waiver is endorsed on the policy, there is no question regarding the fact that the provision is waived as stated in the written endorsement.

In spite of the clause in the policy stating that no waiver shall be effective unless it is in writing and attached to the policy, in many cases courts have held that the acts of the insurance company have acted as a waiver of certain requirements affecting the insured. For example, the requirement that the insured must file a proof of loss within a specified time has been held to have been waived by a denial of liability on the part of the insurance company.[9] When it is held that the company has waived a requirement, the company is estopped (prohibited) from setting up the requirement as a bar to recovery under the policy. That is, if the company has waived the requirement for filing a proof of loss, the fact that none was filed cannot be used by the company as a defense against recovery.

It is important for the adjuster and the agent to follow carefully all the policy requirements after a loss has occurred, especially if there is any reason to believe that the company may have reason to deny liability. Sometimes it is desirable to secure a nonwaiver agreement. This is an agreement between the insured and the company that neither party waives any of its rights under the policy by acts in connection with a loss. This agreement permits the company to make its investigation without waiving the requirements to which the insured normally is subject. It permits the insured to proceed with salvage and other activities without waiving any of his rights against the company.

[9]Cooper v. Ins. Co. of the State of Penna., 96 Wis. 362, 71 N.W. 606 (1897).

QUESTIONS

1. Describe briefly some of the ways in which adjustment of marine insurance losses can be more complicated than adjustment of other property insurance losses.
2. What steps should an adjuster take to determine whether a loss has occurred under the terms of a marine policy?
3. What are the obligations of an adjuster in connection with a loss that occurred while the property was in the custody of a common carrier?
4. Explain the difference between the liability of a common carrier on land for damage to cargo from a collision and the liability of a carrier by sea from a collision between two ships.
5. What is the purpose of a loan receipt in connection with loss of property in the custody of a bailee or common carrier?
6. What impairments of subrogation rights might an adjuster find in his investigation of a loss under a marine policy?
7. Describe the difference between English law and American law in respect to subrogation recoveries under an ocean marine policy.
8. Why are salvage operations important in marine loss adjustments?
9. Distinguish between salvage as it applies to reduction of loss to damaged property and marine salvage.
10. Outline the procedures that are followed in handling a general average loss.
11. What circumstances brought about the signing of the "agreements of guiding principles" for adjustment of losses?
12. What principles are followed in the "agreements of guiding principles" in the adjustment of losses under policies having conflicting "other insurance" clauses?
13. What are the obligations of the insured in case of loss?
14. List the documents that an adjuster usually presents to the insurance company in connection with the settlement of a claim involving common carrier liability.

25

Governmental Regulation of Marine Insurance

The insurance business is subject to a substantial degree of regulation by governmental bodies. The operations of insurers are subject primarily to regulation by state officials. Some of the more important purposes of state regulation are the following:

1. Supervision of financial operations to avoid, as far as possible, insolvency of insurance companies;
2. Collection of revenue for state governments;
3. Protection of the policyholders from unfair and discriminatory practices;
4. Supervision of rates to see (1) that the rates are not too high for the public, (2) that they are not so low that they threaten company solvency, and (3) that the rates are not unfairly discriminatory as between policyholders;
5. Supervision of policy coverages so that the policyholders will get a reasonable protection for the premium paid.

All of the insurance business, including marine insurance, is subject to the first three of these regulatory purposes. Ocean marine insurance is exempt from rate regulation and the supervision of policy coverages in all states. Ocean marine underwriters have complete freedom to use whatever rates they consider proper for the circumstances and the risks involved. Ocean marine insurance operates in an international market that is free of restrictions as far as rates and coverages are concerned. American insurers must have the same freedom as the insurers of other nations if they are to operate in this field. Therefore, most of the comments in this chapter relating to governmental regulation apply to inland marine insurance.

The inland marine operations of the insurance companies have been subject to less regulation of rates and coverages than many other parts of the insurance business. Whereas the rates and forms of coverage for fire, automobile, and workmen's compensation insurance have been subject to approval by many state insurance departments since the early 1900s the rates and forms for inland marine coverages were quoted individually by the companies until about 1930.

From 1930 until about 1945, a portion of the inland marine business was operated on an individual company quotation basis, but a considerable portion of the business came to be regulated to a degree by company-operated bureaus. There was comparatively little state regulation of inland marine rates or coverages.

There were two principal reasons why the companies were allowed a free hand in the making of inland marine rates.

The first reason was that property insured under inland marine policies was primarily property in transit, and the hazards to the property varied greatly from one shipment to another. Rates were quoted by each underwriter according to his judgment of the hazards involved and his company's loss experience with similar properties on comparable journeys. There were thousands of towns and cities between which the property might be in transit, and different common carriers exercised varying degrees of care in the handling of goods in their custody. It was seldom that any two policies covered property under identical or closely similar circumstances.

A second reason for the comparative freedom from regulation of inland marine rates was the fact that inland marine insurance was a relatively minor line of insurance. It was overshadowed by other types of coverage that produced far more premium income. Inland marine rates were not a problem for a majority of the people who purchased insurance, and the state insurance departments paid more attention to problems concerning lines of insurance that affected more policyholders.

The 1933 Nation-Wide Definition was an early form of regulation. It set up certain boundaries within which marine underwriters could operate. The Nation-Wide Definition was a combination of state and industry regulation. Much of the policing under the Definition was done by the Joint Committee on Interpretation and Complaint, which was composed of company organizations, but the Definition also had the approval of the insurance departments of many states as well as the approval of the National Association of Insurance Commissioners.

One of the circumstances that resulted in the establishing of the 1933 Nation-Wide Definition was the fact that properties occasionally were being insured under marine policies at rates less than the fire insurance rates, even though the coverage under the marine policies included fire insurance. A few states acted under their fire rate regulatory powers and issued orders intended to prevent an insurance company's issuing a policy that provided fire coverage at a rate less than the fire insurance rate. These actions on the part of a few states constituted rate regulatory action in connection with marine rates, but they were only scattered instances. Within the limitations set up in the 1933 Nation-Wide Definition, inland marine underwriters remained almost entirely free to set up such coverages and rates as they felt justified by the hazards to the property insured.

It is worthy of note in this connection that neither Definition made any distinction between ocean marine and inland marine insurance. It was not until the new rate regulatory laws were enacted in the 1940s that inland marine rates were made partially subject to rate filing requirements and ocean marine rates were clearly separated from inland marine rates in this respect.

A distinction should be made between the effect of the 1933 Nation-Wide Definition and that of the 1953 Nation-wide Marine Definition. As indicated by its full title, the 1933 Definition was also an interpretation of the insuring powers of marine and transportation underwriters. It was intended as a limitation on the insuring powers of marine underwriters. The 1953 Definition by its own terms is merely a classification document and does not limit any company's underwriting powers. The Committee on Interpretation of the 1953 Definition merely has authority to determine whether a particular situation falls within the Definition, whereas the Joint Committee on Interpretation and Complaint for the 1933 Definition had authority also to assess fines against companies that violated the terms of that Definition. This change in status was considered necessary because state insurance laws had been broadened to permit multiple line underwriting. The insuring powers of companies are now determined by the state laws and the qualifications of the companies. The 1953

Definition merely supplements the laws in determining what is to be classified as marine and inland marine insurance.

INDUSTRY REGULATION

The first widespread regulation of inland marine rates and forms was the industry regulation that followed the setting up of the Inland Marine Underwriters Association on January 1, 1931. A majority of the stock fire insurance companies that were writing inland marine insurance became members of the I.M.U.A., and the Association was instrumental in stabilizing the rates for many inland marine lines. The Mutual Marine Conference was established in 1936 to perform similar functions for mutual fire companies.

The character of inland marine business had been changing during the 1920s and there was a need for standardization of the rates for many of the newer coverages. Inland marine insurance originally was used to cover many different properties in varying situations, principally in connection with property in transit.

There arose several types of inland marine coverage under which the insured properties were similar and the situations in which they were insured were more nearly uniform. For example, business in the insuring of fur coats and jewelry was rapidly increasing. It began to appear that the hazards to one fur coat were much the same as those to another. Neither was there much observable difference between the hazards to which different collections of personal jewelry were subject. It came to be recognized that such variations in hazards as there might be were not sufficient to justify the expense of having an underwriter calculate a special rate for every fur coat or for every piece of jewelry that was to be insured.

Manual or class rates were set up by the Inland Marine Underwriters Association and by the Mutual Marine Conference to cover personal jewelry and fur policies and other types of inland marine insurance that underwriters agreed could be treated in class groups.

There were several advantages to the setting up of these class or manual rates. There was a saving of expense, because underwriters and agents were able to quote rates without reference to the insurance company main office or to any special rating formula.

It became possible for the first time for insurance companies to determine whether the general rate level was correct for these classes. Statistics had not been of any significance previously because of the variation in rates for similar properties and hazards. Underwriters decided that other groups of properties for which class rating is not feasible could be rated according to schedules.

It has not been feasible to set up class rates for coverages such as furriers' customers, jewelers' block, railroad rolling stock, garment contractors, and dealers policies because of (1) the difference in the construction of the buildings in which the property may be located, (2) the difference in the hazards of cities and towns, and (3) the various loss prevention devices that might be installed. It has been possible, however, to prepare schedules that take all these factors into account and to allow debits and credits in a manner similar to the methods used in the rating of buildings for fire insurance. The rating schedules were prepared for several types of property.

This industry regulation of inland marine insurance resulted in a three-part division of inland marine classes.

The first were those classes of coverage for which there were class or manual rates. The member companies of the Inland Marine Underwriters Association and the Mutual Marine Conference were provided with manuals in which the rates and rules were set out. The manual-rated classes were largely the personal lines of inland marine insurance, such as the personal property floater, the personal fur and jewelry floater, and policies for coverage of stamp collections, fine arts, and personal effects.

The second group consisted of those coverages for which schedules had been developed and on which the Association or Conference office provided rate-making service to its members. The schedule-rated classes consist principally of jewelers' block, furriers' customers, furriers' block, garment contractors, bridges, and railroad rolling stock coverages.

The manual- and schedule-rated classes comprise about one-half the total inland marine premiums.

The other half of the inland marine business is rated by the individual company inland marine underwriters. These are the property insured while in the course of transportation and the many odd properties and circumstances that do not fall into any uniform group.

INSURANCE NOT CONSIDERED TO BE COMMERCE

References have been made herein to state regulation of insurance rates and other phases of the insurance business. Up to this point no reference has been made to the federal government. For many years it had been assumed that the business of insurance was not commerce and consequently that the federal government had no regulatory jurisdiction, because any such power would stem from federal authority over interstate commerce. This assumption was based on a decision of the Supreme Court of the United States handed down many years ago.[1] This decision had upheld the right of the state of Virginia to regulate insurance. Subsequent decisions of the Supreme Court of the United States had followed the idea that the right to regulate insurance lay within the province of the state governments.[2]

Since the federal government did not exercise any control over the business of insurance, there was no attempt to apply the antitrust laws to insurance practices. The insurance companies were considered free to set up rating bureaus, which were combinations of companies for the purpose of setting prices (the making of rates). The federal antitrust laws are based on the principle that any agreement to set prices (even though the agreement may be between only two people) is a combination in restraint of trade.

Other Federal laws prohibit unfair trade practices and the making of price differentials solely on the basis of volume of business. If the selling of a large quantity of goods to one person or company results in economies, it is permissible to pass those economies on to the purchaser in the form of reduced prices, but it is not permissible to favor a large purchaser with lower prices solely because of the volume of his business.

None of these restrictions was believed to apply to insurance, and there were many practices in this field that were not permissible in other forms of business.

THE S.E.U.A. DECISION

Officials of the federal government were aware of the fact that there were insurance practices which the antitrust laws prohibited in interstate commerce. There were officials who believed that insurance was commerce, and they felt that the antitrust laws should be applied to the insurance business. After a long investigation, criminal prosecution was brought by the United States against the South-Eastern Underwriters Association, its officers and member companies. It was alleged in the indictment that there was a conspiracy to fix prices and monopolize commerce in violation of the Sherman Antitrust Act.

The defense for the South-Eastern Underwriters Association contended that the federal courts did not have jurisdiction, and they depended on the former decisions of the Supreme Court. The question of federal jurisdiction was taken to the Supreme Court of the

1Paul v. Virginia, 8 Wall. 168, 19 L. ed. 357 (1868).

2Hooper v. California, 155 U.S. 648, 39 L. ed. 297 (1895); New York Life Ins. Co. v. Deer Lodge County, 231 U.S. 495, 58 L. ed. 332 (1913).

United States. On June 5, 1944, the Supreme Court handed down a decision that had the effect of reversing completely the position of the insurance companies in their interstate operations.[3] For the first time, insurance companies were faced with the problem of having to comply with the same restrictions as other business in respect to combinations in restraint of trade, unfair trade practices, and discrimination in price setting.

The insurance industry was in a dilemma. The antitrust laws were not designed to regulate insurance companies. If these laws were to be so applied, it was hard to see how rating bureaus could continue to exist, because they are price-fixing organizations. On the other hand, it was hard to see how property and casualty insurance companies could operate without the benefit of rating bureaus. No one company has a sufficient spread of business to set its own rates. A free and open competition for business would be almost certain to result in insolvency for many companies, yet the financial stability of all insurance companies is a primary objective of governmental regulation.

It is true that some insurance companies operate without belonging to rating bureaus. However, these companies generally depend upon the rates promulgated by the rating bureaus. The so-called "independent" rates of these companies are mostly variations from the bureau rates, and are based upon the statistics and promulgations of the bureaus.

The general thought in the insurance business was that the state governments had done a good job of regulating insurance. Insurance officials, generally, felt it would be desirable to continue state regulation rather than to have the federal government supplant state control. Another Supreme Court decision appeared to offer a means of accomplishing the retention of state control of the insurance business. The Supreme Court had held the states can regulate interstate commerce in respects in which Congress had not acted.[4] Therefore, plans were formulated to pass rating laws in states that did not already have statutes regulating combinations of companies for the purpose of setting rates.

It was clear that time would be needed to secure the passage of legislation in all states. The problem was laid before Congress, and it was explained that a continuation of state control appeared desirable but a moratorium in the application of the antitrust laws would be advisable if the necessary measures were to be passed by the states.

[3]United States v. South-Eastern Underwriters Association, *et al.*, 322 U.S. 533, 80 L. ed. 1440 (1944).

[4]Parker v. Brown, 317 U.S. 341, 87 L. ed. 315 (1943).

The Seventy-ninth Congress passed an act known as Public Law 15, which gave the insurance industry and the states until January 1, 1948 to make the necessary arrangements.

This later was extended to June 30, 1948, upon which date the insurance industry came under the full effect of the federal antitrust laws except as their operation was modified by the application of state laws.

Public Law 15 not only granted the moratorium from federal authority until June 30, 1948, but also set out the authority of the federal government in those areas in which the states do not act. The labor laws that apply to interstate commerce in general are applicable also to insurance companies and to the insurance business. The minimum wage standards and other labor acts that have been passed by Congress all are applicable to the insurance business. The antitrust laws are effective except in those areas in which state governments have passed legislation and the federal government has not passed conflicting legislation. Several states have passed laws that regulate certain monopolistic practices in the insurance business, and these laws are effective in all respects as long as they do not conflict with any applicable federal law.

The authority of the federal government to regulate insurance is clear. If at any time in the future Congress should decide to pass laws regulating the insurance business, those laws would become effective and would supersede any state laws in conflict with them. State officials have been conscious of the fact that the federal government has authority over the insurance business even though this authority is not being exercised to a large extent at the present time. It is considered necessary for the states to maintain an effective control over the insurance business and to prevent the development of any practices that would be injurious to the public if federal control of the insurance business is to be avoided. In an era of increasing concentration of power in the federal government, insurance company officials and state officials both have been conscious of the threat of federal control.

During the moratorium, representatives of all branches of the insurance industry and the state regulatory officials conferred many times, and there were submitted to the legislatures of the various states what were known as the "Commissioners-All-Industry" bills for the regulation of insurance. These bills provided for state regulation of rates and that rates would have to be filed with and approved by the insurance commissioner before they could be used. They were known as "prior approval" laws. These laws proved to be acceptable to most of the insurance business for several years. However, the insurance commissioners of some states became increasingly reluctant to approve rate increases in spite of a deteriorating loss experience. There developed a strong demand for repeal of the "prior approval" laws and the enactment of more liberal legislation that would permit rating bureaus and insurance companies to increase rates when experience justified an increase.

THE "COMMISSIONERS-ALL-INDUSTRY" PATTERN OF STATE REGULATION

The pattern of state regulation set up in the "Commissioners-All-Industry" bills is that by which inland marine underwriters must meet the problems of rate regulation. One of the problems recognized by the framers of the legislation was the difficulty of making a statutory definition of inland marine insurance. There are so many variations in the types of property and the circumstances under which it can be insured under an inland marine policy that the wording used in many state laws reads:

> Inland marine insurance shall be deemed to include insurance now or hereafter defined by statute, or by interpretation thereof, or if not so defined or interpreted, by ruling of the commissioner of insurance hereinafter referred to as the commissioner, or as established by general custom of the business, as inland marine insurance.

This statement permits the setting up of definitions or interpretations by the regulatory official when there is no satisfactory statutory definition to fit a particular situation. This is considered preferable to a rigid definition that would be binding on the industry regardless of later developments. It gives authority to the insurance commissioner to adopt as a state regulation such a document as the Nation-wide Marine Definition.

The sections of the "Commissioners-All-Industry" bill that concern the rating of inland marine business recognize several needs of the inland marine underwriter.

It is recognized that the companies need to act in concert in the establishing of rates for classes of business that include many properties of a uniform nature. The classes of business are designated as those "which by general custom of the business are rated according to manual or class rates."

The rate regulatory laws provide for the licensing of rating bureaus, which are required to file with many insurance departments all the manual and class rates to be used by their member and subscriber companies. Thus the companies had the way cleared for them to combine for the fixing of prices (rates) without being in violation of the federal antitrust laws. They can collect statistics and perform such other functions as are necessary to determine whether the rates are adequate and fair and do not unfairly discriminate between policyholders with approximately the same hazard.[5]

Rate regulatory laws of the states have become a mixture. Many states continue to require the filing of rates and the approval of the insurance commissioner before they can be used. Other states provide that rates must be filed with the commissioner, but the rates may be used immediately and may continue to be used unless the commissioner takes action to have them disapproved. This is known roughly as a "file and use" law. There are also states in which rates are not required to be filed. The commissioner in most of these states does have the authority to investigate and to take action against the further use of rates which he considers to be wrong in some respect. The rating bureaus operate for inland marine insurance in accordance with the applicable law in each state.

There are two rating bureaus that operate countrywide for inland marine coverages. They are the Inland Marine Insurance Bureau (which is controlled by stock companies) and the Transportation Insurance Rating Bureau (which is controlled by mutual companies). The rates and forms which are filed or promulgated by the two bureaus are the same in most respects.

The property insured under an inland marine policy usually is in course of transit between two points or of a floating nature and may be moved to any part of the country or perhaps to any part of the world. The fur coat insured in Chicago may be lost in New York, and the jewelry insured in Philadelphia may be lost on a trip between Seattle and Portland. It is impossible to say whether such a loss should be charged to the state in which the policy was written or to the state in which the loss occurred. The very nature of the inland marine insurance business makes it national in character. The rate regulatory laws of most states recognize this situation in connection with inland marine insurance by requiring regulatory officials to give consideration to "the past and prospective loss experience . . . both within and without this state . . ." and "to past and prospective expenses both countrywide and those specially applicable to this state. . . ."

In addition to the floating nature of most property insured under an inland marine policy, there is a further reason why local loss experience cannot be given full credibility in the making of inland marine rates. There are fifty or more classes of inland marine insurance,

[5]In the case of North Little Rock Transportation Co., Inc. v. Casualty Reciprocal Exchange, *et al.*, 181 F. (2d) 174 (1950), a federal court upheld an all-industry type rate regulatory law as providing the type of regulation contemplated by Public Law 15.

and the largest amount of premium in any one class, nationwide, is about $90 million. Spreading this amount of premium over the fifty states means that there is too little premium in any one state to use as the sole basis for determining adequacy and fairness of rates. Other classes of inland marine insurance have smaller volumes of premium, and some of them are so small that even the nationwide figures must be examined over a period of many years in order to judge their fairness and adequacy.

Such classes of inland marine business as registered mail, furriers' customers, and jewelers' block present catastrophe hazards of large proportions, and the nationwide premiums for a period of several years may be necessary to offset the results of one or two losses. Present inland marine premium volume is not sufficient to relate the experience of many such classes of insurance to state or local areas.

The rate regulatory laws also recognize that there is need for rating service by the bureaus on some properties that may be rated according to filed schedules or according to the judgment of underwriters who have rated similar properties. Furriers' customers, jewelers' block, garment contractors, and dealers' type coverages may be rated according to filed schedules that measure the hazards present in those types of properties. Bridges and tunnels are rated according to the judgment of seasoned underwriters, because each bridge or tunnel is an entirely different project from any other bridge or tunnel. It has not been practical to prepare a rigid schedule for these divergent types of property. All such specifically quoted rates are filed with most state insurance departments when they are calculated by a rating bureau.

It became extremely important to the future of the inland marine business to see to it that rate regulatory laws were drawn in such a way as to recognize that many inland marine coverages cannot be rated according to any schedule or class rate. Those coverages, which according to the custom of the business are not rated by manual or class rates or by schedules, are to be rated individually by each company. That is, there is no collective action in connection with rates on that portion of the inland marine business for which rates, by long-established custom, are quoted by the individual company.

The rate regulatory laws recognize the need for rating by company underwriters for many inland marine risks. Exempted from the rate filing requirements are those risks which by general custom of the business are not rated according to manual rates or rating plans. There is no definition of what constitutes rating "according to manual rates or rating plans," but by usage this has come to mean those risks for which the rating bureaus make rate filings. This portion of the inland marine business frequently is referred to as the "unregulated portion" of the business. This is not an accurate reference. All inland marine business and rates are subject to the provisions of the rate regulatory and other insurance laws, except that these risks are not subject to the rate filing requirements. The accurate reference is to "that portion of the inland marine business which is not subject to the rate filing requirements."

THE PLACE OF JUDGMENT IN MAKING INSURANCE RATES

It has been contended that judgment should be eliminated in the calculation of insurance rates and that all rates should be made according to rigid schedules or class rates. A fallacy in this argument is that no one can determine whether the schedules are exactly correct in every particular.

Even though a schedule is made up with the greatest of care, the weight attached to each factor of the schedule is established according to the judgment of some person or group of persons. It is not possible to determine statistically whether each factor is given the correct weight, because the detailed statistical system for securing such information would be too costly for the insurance business to support. Past experience does not accurately forecast future happenings, but is merely an indication of the trend. In addition there is the ever-present threat of a catastrophe that might throw out of line all the computations based on past experience. Judgment necessarily remains a factor in inland marine insurance rating, and it is a large factor in all classes when the premium volume is small or when the losses are few but likely to be catastrophic when they do occur.

Judgment calculation of inland marine rates is directly comparable to the judgment calculation of ocean marine rates. There is a wide variation of exposure to loss in the transportation of property. No two carriers are alike in their operations and no two routes or trips are the same. The underwriter's judgment is seasoned by experience and by the information that he has accumulated from the experience of others. The validity of judgment rate making is indicated by the fact that loss ratios for judgment-rated inland marine lines are very close on the average to those from the rates that are made by the rating bureaus.

INLAND MARINE RATING BUREAUS NOT MANDATORY

The rate regulatory laws do not require that an insurance company be a member or subscriber to an inland marine rating bureau. Companies that desire to operate independently may do so, and they may file their rates directly with the state insurance departments. In fact, in the states where rates must be filed it is the company's obligation to make the filing. It is permissible for a company to use the rating bureau as a matter of convenience or economy.

Thus a company may make its own filings or it may avail itself of the convenience of joining or subscribing to a rating bureau and having the bureau make the filings. Most of the insurance companies that write inland marine insurance are members of or subscribe to either the Inland Marine Insurance Bureau or the Transportation Insurance Rating Bureau. The task of making filings with many insurance departments assumes large proportions, and most companies find that any small advantage to be gained by independent filing is outweighed by the convenience and economy of having the bureaus make the rates and the filings where required.

DEVIATIONS FROM FILED RATES

Many of the rating laws provide that a member or a subscriber company of a rating bureau may deviate from the filed rates of the bureau if it secures the approval of the insurance department. A company may find that its method of operation is such that its expense ratio or its loss ratio is less than that of the average of all companies. Insurance company expenses and loss ratios vary from company to company, depending upon the efficiency of management, the types of business written, the territory in which its agents are located, and other factors. The rates of the rating bureaus must be set so that all companies have an opportunity to operate at a fair profit. This means that the rates must be an average of what all the company experiences would require.

An insurance company that can operate at a lower cost than the average (including losses or expenses, or both) may wish to allow a part of the saving to benefit its policyholders in the form of reduced rates. This may be achieved by means of a downward deviation from the rates filed by the rating bureau. The usual procedure is for the company to file with the state insurance department a request for permission to deviate. A copy of the request is sent to the rating bureau of which the company is a member or subscriber.

The rating bureau has an opportunity to object if it regards the deviations as undesirable, in which case the insurance department may hold a hearing so that all interested parties may be heard. The rating bureau and the insurance company may waive the right to a hearing if they do not wish to be heard. The insurance department then decides upon the basis of all the facts presented whether to give the company permission to deviate from the bureau rates.

The rate regulatory laws vary in their provisions which apply to companies that do elect to join a rating bureau. The states that do not require the filing of rates generally permit a bureau member or subscriber to deviate from the bureau rates. The bureau rates in such states are essentially guide rates.

AUDITING OF INLAND MARINE DAILY REPORTS

For many years it has been customary in many states for the insurance companies to send all their fire insurance daily reports through an audit bureau, where they are checked for accuracy of rate and policy conditions. This has been done with automobile policies in some states. Some insurance companies believe it is more efficient to have a central checking office than to have each company do its own checking. A central checking office also serves to prevent the deliberate use of incorrect rates, although this does not appear to be the major reason for operating such checking offices.

It has not been customary to have inland marine daily reports checked by any central checking office. A large proportion of inland marine business is written at rates established by company offices or the inland marine departments of the individual companies. The checking of these policies would serve no purpose because they are written by specially trained personnel in the same office where the rate is calculated. There is believed to be much less chance of error than with fire insurance policies, which are mostly written by agents and branch offices.

THE PLACE OF STATISTICS IN THE MAKING OF INLAND MARINE RATES

The ultimate measure of whether rates are adequate and yet not excessive is the ratio of losses incurred to the premiums earned by the insurance companies for the coverage granted in the policies. It is easy for the underwriter to look at the premiums earned in a past year and to compare them with the incurred losses to determine whether the year's operations were profitable. It is not so easy to project those results into the future to determine what changes should be made in order to adjust future rates to the desired levels of adequacy and fairness.

A major difficulty in applying loss statistics to rate making is the fact that inland marine insurance is made up of 50 or more different types of insurance coverage. The year's results may have been profitable in one class and extremely unprofitable in another. It is necessary to separate the losses and premiums into the major groups that go to make up inland marine insurance. This is done by means of a coding system, under which the various types of inland marine insurance are assigned numbers. The premium for each policy and the amount of each loss are coded according to the number designated for the type of business.

Insurance companies use electronic data processing equipment for the computation of experience results. The code number, the amount of premium or loss, and other desirable information regarding each policy and loss are punched on a specially prepared card or are put on electronic tape. The machine computes the total premiums and losses for each of the classes which have been set up in the coding system. Each company then reports to a central organization its total experience as segregated by classes. The rating bureau then takes the company figures and combines them into totals for the insurance business. This combined experience is used by the rating bureaus in their consideration of whether rates should be increased or decreased. The experience reports are also filed with the state insurance departments for their guidance in determining whether inland marine rates are proper.

The basic experience as it comes from the companies shows the premiums written and the losses paid during the calendar year. The ratio of losses paid to premiums written is not a good indication of profit or loss. The better figure is the ratio of the premiums that were earned during the year in relation to the losses that were incurred during the year. Many insurance policies in effect for the company were written during previous years, and many policies which were written during the year will extend their coverage into future years. The true income of the company for profit or loss purposes is the premium which was earned for that portion of each policy that was in effect during that year. The outlay of the company that helps to measure profit or loss is the total of losses that were incurred during the year. The customary method of calculating the earned premiums and incurred losses is by applying an appropriate formula to the premiums written and the losses paid during the year. This sounds complicated, but it is not difficult when a company uses modern electronic data processing equipment.

A difficulty in relating loss experience to rates is that the experience of any one year is inconclusive. There may be a series of large losses that makes the loss experience look bad, or a year may be exceptionally good because there happened to be no large losses. It is felt by many inland marine underwriters that a minimum period of five years must be used in order to determine whether the rates for any type of insurance are adequate or fair. In times when loss ratios are changing, the five-year experience may be inadequate, because the trend may be changing in the middle of the period being studied.

Another difficulty that is particularly troublesome in inland marine classified loss experience is the fact that the premium volume in many classes is extremely small in relation to the possible losses. For example, a few years ago a single fur storage warehouse loss amounted to more than $3.5 million, yet the annual premium volume in this class amounted to only about $4 million.

The loss experience for the registered mail class in many years appears to be extremely favorable, yet the annual premium volume is only about $2 million. The amount at risk subject to a single loss frequently amounts to many millions of dollars. It may take ten or twenty years' experience to get a true indication of the profit or loss in a small premium class.

The multiplicity of rating factors makes it impossible to apply loss statistics to each of them. For example, the experience on the personal property floater was unsatisfactory for many years, but a dozen or more factors are used in rating a personal property floater. Any attempt to break down the loss experience to show the effect of each individual rate factor would result in a classification system with thousands of divisions. The divisions would be so small that the results in any one of them would be entirely inconclusive.

The question arises as to the use that can be made of the statistics collected from the companies and consolidated by the rating bureaus. The total loss experience in the inland marine business does tell the companies and the rate regulatory officials whether the general rate level in the inland marine business is excessive, adequate, or inadequate.

When the general rate level appears to be satisfactory, a further inquiry may be made by examining individual classes to see if they appear to be out of line with the general experience. If the general experience is not satisfactory, an examination of the breakdown by classes may indicate where the excessive or inadequate rates are located. For example, a distinctly unsatisfactory loss experience in connection with the personal property floater showed up in the classified loss experience. The experience in different states did not show any uniform pattern, but the total personal property floater experience over a period of years showed an upward trend and was consistently at an unprofitable level. It was evident that some upward adjustment of rate was necessary.

The rating bureaus were faced with the problem of determining what changes to make. A further examination of individual claims indicated that the bulk of personal property floater losses come from a multitude of small claims and that a smaller proportion come from large losses.

The rating bureaus proposed to the state insurance departments that increases be made in the rates for the first $5,000 of coverage and in the minimum premiums. It is true that the actual increases were based on the judgment of the underwriters, but the judgment was based upon the available figures and upon the long experience of the inland marine underwriters in handling this type of coverage.

The insurance companies emphasized deductible policies in their sales. This was an example of a situation where a rate increase by itself was not the entire answer to a high loss ratio. Underwriting practices and rate levels are complementary factors in achieving a satisfactory experience.

Statistics may be used as a guide in the adjustment of rate levels, and sometimes these figures may indicate the actual changes that should be made. In most cases the statistics are used only as a guide to the general rate level, and the actual changes are based largely upon judgment.

Standardization has proven helpful when there is sufficient uniformity within a class to justify a standard system of rates. It is easier for the insurance agent to sell a policy when he can quote a rate from a manual than when he has to write to an insurance company office for a quotation. It is easier for the state regulatory officials and the insurance companies to check the adequacy of rate levels when the rates are standardized.

QUESTIONS

1. What are the purposes of governmental regulation of the insurance business?
2. Why are ocean marine insurance rates exempt from rate filing requirements in all states?
3. Discuss the reasons why some forms of inland marine insurance are subject to rate filing requirements in many states whereas other inland marine lines are exempt from the rate filing requirements.

4. Compare the procedures which are used by an ocean marine underwriter in establishing a rate and those followed by an inland marine underwriter in setting the rate for a non-filed line such as motor truck cargo insurance.
5. Discuss the circumstances that brought about some industry regulation of inland marine rates and forms in the 1930s.
6. Upon what basis had the state governments established the right to regulate the insurance business?
7. Discuss the effect upon the insurance business of the S.E.U.A. decision.
8. What needs of the inland marine underwriter are recognized in the "Commissioners-All-Industry" pattern of state regulation?
9. Why is the nationwide experience considered to be necessary in determining the fairness and adequacy of inland marine rates?
10. Why is it not considered possible to eliminate judgment as a factor in the computation of inland marine rates?
11. What are some of the difficulties encountered in trying to determine the fairness and adequacy of inland marine rates by statistical reports?
12. Compare the purpose of the 1933 Nation-Wide Definition as a regulatory document with the effect of the 1953 Nation-wide Marine Definition.
13. Discuss the prevalence of independent rate filings and deviations from bureau filings in the inland marine field in your state, and tell why you think they are good or bad for the insurance business and the public.

Index

D

E

N

R

S

T

U